THE BLACK JEWS

WE THE BLACK JEWS

Volumes I & II

By
Yosef A. A.
ben-Jochannan

Dr Yosef A A ben-Jochannan 10/28/01 C.E.

We The Black Jews

Published 1993 by
Black Classic Press

Published with the permission of the author. Cover art by Tony Browder, rendered from the original cover design by Yosef ben-Jochannan.

Library of Congress Catalog Card Number 92-81884

ISBN 0-933121-40-7

Printed by BCP Digital Printing, ***a division of Black Classic Press***

Founded in 1978, Black Classic Press specializes in bringing to light obscure and significant works by and about people of African descent. If our books are not available in your area, ask your local bookseller to order them. Our current list of titles can be obtained by writing:

Black Classic Press
c/o List
P.O. Box 13414
Baltimore, MD 21203

A Young Press With Some Very Old Ideas

Visit us on the world wide web at www.blackclassic.com

We The Black Jews

Foreword to the Black Classic Press Edition

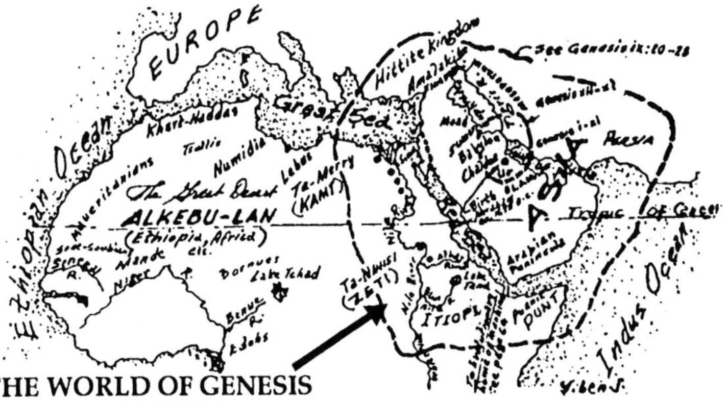

THE WORLD OF GENESIS
ca. 1675 BCF

THE WORLD OF EXODUS
ca. 1298 - 1232 BCE

The two dates cited above, 1675 B.C.F.-1232 B.C.E., are primarily related to the major dramas of Judaeo, Christian, and/or Islamic theosophy. Yet, these dates are much more recent than the "original belief and practice" of the Nile Valley High Culture (civilization). The revelation of this fact often causes religious zealots of Judaism to holler, "anti-Semitism," and to place the word, "Black," before the expression whenever an African American is involved. Usually, the charge of anti-Semitism has brought fear to the minds of Africans in Africa, and those in the so-called diaspora. But this charge does not bring fear to most of us who are labeled irresponsible Negro (Black/colored/African American, etc.). And this response always results in the paranoic charge of Black/Negro anti-Semitism from European American Jews (white/caucasoid/semitic, etc.) in the United (racist) States of America. These charges, even against African American (Black/Africoid-hamitic, etc.) Jews, compelled me to write this new foreword to ***We The Black Jews: Witness To The "White Jewish Race" Myth,*** particularly because this myth has a solitary purpose: "keeping the nigger" who refuses to be controlled "in his or her place"—as a slave.

For as long as I can recall, white Jews in America have vehemently denied the existence of any legitimate African (Black/colored/Afro, etc.) Jews, recognizing only fellow Caucasian (caucasoid/semitic) Euro-Jews from any place. Furthermore, white Jews have only conditionally accepted the Black Jews of North Africa and Southwest Asia. Thus, the so-called entry of Ethiopian/African (or Black/Falasha, etc.) Jews into Israel under the nefarious terms, "Exodus" and "Moses," fooled no one who is familiar with the history of the white Jews in Israel and West Asia. From 1947 C.E., white Jews, officially through Israel's Knesset (parliament), consistently denied "The Right of Return" to Black Jews (so-called "Falashas"). Of course, white Jews from anywhere, everywhere on the planet earth, particularly from the former Soviet Union, were freely admitted.

To add injury to insult, even the disgusting requirement that all Ethiopian (African/Black) Jews must be recircumcised (by European/white Jews) in order to be accepted as Jews upon entering Israel is racist. To require all adult males of the Falasha community to have their "penis pricked," symbolically or not, was and still is Jewish racism and religious bigotry. Such racist beliefs are no different than those inflicted upon European Jews by their fellow Caucasian Europeans, Christians, Muslims(Moslem) and atheists, etc., which eventually led to Europe's holocaust.

On the other hand, not a solitary African (Black) woman, man, or child of any religion was involved in any aspect of the genocide, holocaust and/or enslavement of Jews in Europe at any period. The opposite is true for European, Euro-English and Euro-American Jews who were committed to genocide, holocausts, and/or enslavement of countless Africans—Black Jews included. (See Joseph J. William's ***Hebrewisms of West Africa.)***

If "Jehovah (Ywh/God, etc.) is Truth," then it is about time that African (Falasha/Black, etc.) Jews tell the "truth" about the racism and/or religious bigotry they (like myself) suffered from European (white/caucasoid/semitic, etc.) Jews, until the need for their physical presence as "buffer bait" was more than overbearing, thus, "Operation Exodus/Moses!"

Now that the African American (not the "responsible Negro/Afro/colored") community is aware of the fact that there are millions of Jews who are other than white in color, and also of different facial (physical) characteristics than the so-called Caucasian, it has become extremely necessary that the history of the Jews of both ancient and contemporary times be stated in a manner that includes African and Asian Jews.

It must be noted that Judaism's most important "revealer of God's (Jehovah's) truth" was, in fact, an African (or Egyptian) named "Moshe/Moses." And most of what Moses knew about "Jehovah" was in reality what he learned from his fellow Africans of the Craft of Amun-Ra ("Mysteries System") in Egypt, centered in the Grand Temple (Lodge) at Wa'set (called "Thebes" by the Greek conquerors from ca. 332 B.C.E., and "Luxor" by the Arab conquerors, ca. 638-640 C.E. or ca. 18-20 A.H. See ***Second Book of Moses).***

All of the sacred teachings originated within the minds of Black (African) men of the Nile (Blue/White) Valley and areas of the Great Lakes (Mwanza, Tanganyika, Malawi, etc.). The "Golden Calf" was, in fact, Goddess Het-Heru (Hathor/Hator, etc.). Khnum, instead of Jehovah, was the first "creator of man and woman-God." Amenhotep IV (or Akhen-Aten), rather than Moses, first proclaimed the "one and only true God Aten." These and so many more of the sacred teachings which Moses learned from the priest-scribes of the Craft of Amun-Ra ("Mysteries System") were recorded before the I Dynasty, ca. 4100 B.C.E at Sakhara, on a great reserve of papyri. The best known of the sacred teachings is the ***Papyrus of Ami*** and ***Book of Coming Forth by Day and Night*** (or ***Book of the Dead,*** as translated into English by Sir Ernest A. Wallis

Budge from the original Mdu Ntr (Medu Netcher) in 1895 C.E./A.D.).

The main tragedy of all this is that most of us cannot deal with "truth" other than that forced upon us by our past and present physical and mental slave masters and mistresses of Judaism, Christianity, and Islam, those whose God we serve.

How will all of the above, and more to follow in the main text of these combined two volumes, affect the current "curriculum of exclusion" and pending "curriculum of inclusion" in terms of prayer in the schools, etc.? Will we be able to call any of these proven contradictions a lie, plagiarism, paraphrased information, stolen legacy, allegory, mythology, mere belief, pagan, heathen, devilishness, etc.? Shall we particularly discredit those in the "sacred writings"of the former slave masters from Arabia (Asia), Europe, Euro-England, and Euro-America (north, central, and south), who are still in control of our minds by virtue of their descendants, who now preach about their own "chosen people" status to a "holy land," here or there?

Judaism, Hebraism or whatever else anyone elects to call the practice of the current theosophy in the ***Holy Torah*** or ***Five Books of Moses*** (and ***Old Testament*** of the Judaeo-Christians), must be ready to face the 21st century C.E., totally updated, minus the overthrows of Jewish racism and religious bigotry. Such practices were inherited from the racists and religious bigots who wrote their sixth century C.E. European version of the ***Babylonian Talmud***, upon which all of the "anti-African (Black/Negro/colored/Afro, etc.) propaganda" seems to be based. In other words, the so-called "curse of Ham by his father Noah" was passed down for Canaan and all of his descendants to follow for eternity. Worse yet, the sign of the curse is the color Black! And all of this was sanctioned by God Jehovah!

Thus, I, a former believing Gadite and son of a so-called "Falassa" (lately "Falasha") from Gonda Province, Ethiopia (Cush/Kush) East Africa—one who must equally carry the so-called curse for my so-called negroid characteristics which allegedly make me a "Shankala" (native/African with Black skin, broad nose, thick lips, woolly hair, etc.) like those of Manen, the late

Emperor Haile Selassie's Empress—now repeat this so-called "curse":

> Now, I cannot beget the fourth son whose children I would have ordered to serve you and your brothers! Therefore, it must be Canaan, your first born, whom they enslave. And since you have disabled me. . . doing ugly things in Blackness of night, Canaan's children shall be born ugly and Black! Moreover, because you twisted your head around to see my nakedness, your grandchildren's hair shall be twisted into kinks, and their eyes red; again because your lips jested at my misfortune, theirs shall swell; and because you neglected my nakedness, they shall go naked, and *their male members shall be shamefully elongated! Men of this race are called Negroes, their forefather Canaan commanded them to love theft and fornication, to be banded together in hatred of their masters and never to tell the truth.*

In view of the above quote, I, as a former practicing African (Ethiopian/Black or so-called "Falasha," etc.) Jew ask: WHY HAVE WE CHANGED FROM RA AND OSIRIS TO YWH/JEHOVAH AND/OR AL'LAH?

I have answered my question by assuring you that this volume contains only historical facts about African (Ethiopian/Falasha/Black) Jews. It is definitely not an endorsement of the theosophical teachings of Judaism (Hebraism, etc.). Since Judaism is the first step from the Nile Valley Africans' theosophical (spiritual) base of the so-called "Three Revealed Religions—Judaism, Judaeo-Christianity, and Judaeo-Christianity-Islam," it is only rational to assume that they too must fall in line. For after all is said and done, there were and are "heaven" and "creation" concepts thousands of years before that of Judaism (God Ywh/Yvh/Jehovah), Christianity (God /Joshua Cristo /Joshua the Anointed /Jesus the Christ) and Islam/Mohammedism (God /Al'lah).

VOLUME - I

WE THE BLACK JEWS:

WITNESS TO THE "WHITE JEWISH RACE" MYTH

by

Yosef Ben-Jochannan

VOLUME ONE CONTENT:

[Volume One continued]

VOLUME TWO CONTENT:

VOLUME ONE ILLUSTRATIONS:

[Volume One Illustrations continued]

1. "I need no certification for my own Jewishness from any Jew from Europe any-more-so than I needed from my fellow Beta Israel Rabbis or Priests in Ethiopia, East Africa." See the document about Rabbi Wentworth Matthew I have presented on p. lxxxxii in this Volume. I placed it here solely for effect, as directly following is the Chapter on "The Fallacy Of A White Jew" that is more Kosher/Pure than all other colors of Jews there are.

[Volume One Illustrations continued]

[Volume One Illustrations continued]

[Volume One Illustrations continued]

[Volume One Illustrations continued]

Title

VOLUME TWO ILLUSTRATIONS:

Title

[Volume Two Illustrations continued]

በሀገራችን ፡ ልዩ ፡ ልዩ ፡ የቤት ፡ ሥራ፡አቅድ፡ሲኖር፡የጉራጌ፡ክፍለ፡ሀገር፡የቤት፡አሠራር ፡ ይህን፡፬ደኛ፡ ነው፡

A Guraghe-type Tukul [1]

Special CREDIT FOR ILLUSTRATIONS... on the following page.

1. Tukul or Rural House; never a "HUT." This is a rural Synagogue of a poor farming community of the Gondar area of Northwestern Ethiopia, East Africa.

SPECIAL CREDITS FOR ILLUSTRATIONS:

Very special citations must be extended for the adoption [with amendments and/or alterations] and use of all illustrations... [pictures, graphs, maps, documents, etc.] not made by or originally belonging to your author - which are not footnoted in the text. The books, periodicals, magazines and other documents they are extracted from are listed in the BIBLIOGRAPHIES at the rear of this Volume. I shall only mention the author and title of each here. Thus, maps on page 42 from R. L. HESS' "Ethiopia: The Modernization of Autocracy. Ethiopic Syllabaries on pages 59 and 60 from D. Buxton's "The Abyssinians;" monolithic rock-hewn churches on pages 69 and 78 from S. Pankhurst's "Ethiopia;" map on page 75 from D. Buxton's "The Abyssinians;" sites and ruins on pages 79 - 81 from S. Pankhurst's "Ethiopia;" market scenes on page 123 from J. Doresse's "Ethiopia;" Yemenite and Cochin Jews pictures on page 176 from S. Deutch's "Jewish Current Events;" two top pictures on pages 203 and 205 D. Buxton's "The Abyssinians;" religious scenes on page 231 from D. Buxton's "The Abyssinians;" maps on pages 243, 244 and 262 from J.D. Fage's "An Atlas of African History;" maps on pages 250 and 259 from A Boyd and P van Rensburg's "An Atlas of African Affairs;" picture on page 295 from the cover of H.M. Brotz's "The Black Jews of Harlem;" original candid shots of Ethiopians in Ethiopia on pages xlvi and 325 by a foremer student - Robert Johnson, Jr. - at Cornell University's "Africana Studies and Research Center," Ithaca, New York, during a field trip in Ethiopia in 1972 C.E. on a graduate fellowship; the youngster's picture on page 406 - nine month old "Kamamu" [the son of Mr. and Mrs. Abubakan of Detroit, Michigan] was graciously given to me by his parents, who are themselves teachers in the field of general education and the arts. "Kamamu," presently, is eight years and months old.

Any oversight in not listing a particular ILLUSTRATION will be properly credited upon oral or written communication. Pictures, graphs, documents of other types, etc., which I have shown in my previous publications are repeated herein only if they are of major importance to the subject, and to document what may have otherwise been labeled "...controversial issue..."

The extensive visual documentation is due to the so-called "CONTROVERSIAL NATURE" of the entire content of the subject title of this volume - WE THE BLACK JEWS! - for it is a common fact that the subject content will [as it has always in the past] ignite all sorts of denial that there is such an animal as a "BLACK JEW." Thus resorting to the age-old adage that "ONE PICTURE IS WORTH A MILLION WORDS," I am certain that this too will not be sufficient to convince those who have "...ALREADY MADE UP THEIR [my] MINDS, AND DO NOT NEED TO BE CONVINCED BY THE FACTS..." they are seeing in front of their eyes. The dozens of ILLUSTRATIONS I have used in this volume are primarily for such readers who must be shown visual documentary proof along with chronological data and historical references; all of which they might equally choose to ignore!

DEDICATION

This aspect of the history and heritage of the "Black Jews" is dedicated to all oppressed African People whose religion differ from those who controlthe power of life and death over most of us. Out of this it is hoped that a better understanding between African People will prevail in spite of our religious differences. Remember; Religion Is Nothing More, or Less, Than A Belief. And That Any One Of Them Is As Godly As Another.

Yosef A. A. ben-Jochannan
6083 N.Y., 5744 H.C.
1983 C.E., 1361 A.H.

AUTHOR'S SPECIAL NOTE:

This two volumes project represents an undertaking that began originally as a pamphlet sometime in 1934 C.E./A.D. in a colony of the United States of America - known as the U.S. Virgin Islands, particularly the largest one - ST. CROIX, and another one presently called the "COMMONWEALTH OF PUERTO RICO"- where it was finally completed and published as NOSOTROS HEBREOS NEGRO [in English: WE THE BLACK JEWS]. The first translation from the original Spanish into English was in 1950 C.E./A.D.

After the original publication of no more than FIVE-HUNDRED mimeograph copies, it took over TWENTY YEARS [1938 - 1971/1972 C.E.] to dispose with all of them. To be exact, the thousands of brothers and sisters who read my BLACK MAN OF THE NILE and AFRICAN ORIGIN OF THE MAJOR "WESTERN RELIGIONS" in 1969 and/or 1970 C.E./A.D. respectively began demanding that I republish NOSOTROS HEBREOS NEGRO in the English language. I resisted very strongly, solely because it meant taking time away from other very urgent projects on NILE VALLEY HIGH-CULTURES of which I had given myself deadlines to complete. It also meant a translating feat from Spanish to English, but most of all - to mentally return to "RELIGIOUS PRINCIPLES" which I would have preferred to remain dormant as they were in my mind. There were many frustrations to overcome in reissuing NOSOTROS HEBREOS NEGRO in any language.

Another aspect of gravest concern was the editing of certain personal information about people who are now deceased. To reveal certain deeds about them at this late date would not have been in good faith on my part. But most of all, there were certain facts that involved my own parents' personal "RELIGIOUS BIGOTRY" that came from their inheritance from their "JUDAEO EXPERIENCES" which I had to reexamine and conclude if they were worth including in this New and Enlarged Edition. TIME and CHANGE dictated differently.

I finally succumbed and began retranslating the 1950 C.E./A.D. original ENGLISH TRANSLATION of this project to the point where the manuscript was completed in 1974 C.E. on schedule. There were in fact TWO VOLUMES instead of the original ONE in 1950 C.E., as I had included for the very first time a separate VOLUME on the "African [Black] HEBREW ISRAELITES [Jews]" of the Caribbean Islands, South, Central and North America - particularly the extensively wide range of divisions in the United States of America. This later VOLUME caused some problems to arise in my mind, many of which I am still not clear - thus I have not dealt with them in certain instances, and only partially in others. I have only touched on this area believing that the "AFRICAN/BLACK ISRAELITES" must do their own writings on their own origin, development, connection, etc. with the world-wide "BETA ISRAEL/FALASHAS," and also their own attitude towards "WHITE/SEMITIC/CAUCASIAN" European and European-American "JEWS" everywhere - including the "STATE OF ISRAEL" or "PALESTINE," etc. I am a strong believer that the best person to present a people's HERITAGE, CULTURE, HISTORY, STRUGGLE, etc., with all "AUTHORITY," must be their own respected sons and daughters.[1]

The second VOLUME of this project is nevertheless a study and conclusion of my views as I experienced the locally developed "HEBREW-ISRAELITE MOVEMENT." However let me say without hesitation that:

> NO ONE HAS ANY MONOPOLY ON HOW JUDAISM/HEBREWISM IS TO BE PRACTICED OTHER THAN FOR HIS OR HER OWN SELF AND/OR THOSE WHO ARE WILLING TO FOLLOW SUIT. YWH COMMISSIONED NONE TODAY.

This equally holds true for the "HEBREW-ISRAELITE COMMUNITY" in the State of Israel and/or Palestine today. Who is protesting the racism and religious bigotry against them in Israel today! ?

Quite a lot of revisions to the 1938, 1950 and 1974 C.E./A.D. completed manuscript had to be made in 1982 and 1983 C.E./A.D. All of them were due to deaths, overthrows of political figures, outdated information, and other matters, etc. dealt with in this project. But most of all, I had to remove PEOPLE'S NAMES, those who were quite uncomfortable with the possibility of being labeled "ANTI-SEMITE" because certain facts herein will not set well with a number of European and European-American [WHITE/SEMITIC/CAUCASIAN] Jews, especially those who adhere to a religiously bigoted form of "ZIONISM" and "RACISM" in terms of their WHITE-SEMITIC JEWISH RACE myth. I could not exclude any one of these two issues from this project. Neither could I water-down their effectiveness. Nor could I fail to say that "ISRAEL" and/or the native "ISRAELI" were/are "WRONG" or "RIGHT" whenever, or wherever, I found either to be the case. This holds true for any group of "JEWS" anywhere.

Your author only hope that this project, VOLUME I and II, will bring about definite clarification on the issue of the so-called "LOST TRIBE OF JEWS OF ETHIOPIA" or so-called "FALASHAS OF ETHIOPIA," etc. Your COMMENTS and QUESTIONS are solicited. Write the publishers of this project in order to reach me - Yosef A. A. ben-Jochannan, 1361 A.H., 1983 C.E./A.D., 5744 H.C., or 6683 N.Y.[2]

MAN'S MIND ["CIVILIZATION/GOD," ETC.]! ?:

Amen, 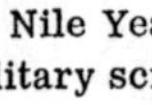 **Ra** 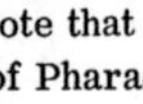

In a vignette from the Papyrus of Nekht,[3] shown on the following page, the deceased NEKHT and his WIFE are in a praying position as they stand between the lake and residence in the garden while giving praise to God of Resurrection ASAR [, or **Osiris**], Goddess MAAT

1. I have refused to assist in writing the history of many Israelite groups for this reason.
2. A.H. or After the Hejira; C.E. or Common [Christian] Era; H.C. or Hebrew Calendar; and N.Y. or Nile Year. Note that A.D. is the same Calendar schedule as C.E.
3. A military scribe of Pharaonic Egypt about ca. 1450 B.C.E.[Presently in the British Museum].

[ ] standing behind him. On the top of the frieze we note the text of a HYMN TO GOD RA [ ]. Let us examine both the overall frieze and the Hymn below.

NEKHT AND HIS WIFE HONOURING GOD ASAR/OSIRIS

RA, symbolisms of whom appear on the following page, "...created Himself God above all other Gods..." including MENU [ ] - God of the Primeval Waters we see lifting the Atet Boat of the SUN unto HEAVEN as the SOLAR DISK is rolled into the sky by God KHEPRA [ ]. Goddess ISIS [Ast,] and Her sister NEPHTHYS [Nebthet,], on either side of the Atet Boat, watch "THE CREATION/TWAT" and beyond. The TWAT/KINGDOM OF GOD OSIRIS is shown surrounded by God OSIRIS' body. We also see in the Atet Boat God of the Earth GEB, God of Scribes THOTH - also known as "A," God HET, God HU, and God SA or SAA.

Beyond Heaven God RA, the offspring of God TEMU - who before God RA "...came from the Primeval Waters MENU/NU..." and is the "...Father of the Gods..." the same as God YWH/JEHOVAH of the Hebrews or Jews is to God JESUS - the Christ/Anointed - of the Christians...,heard His Father say:

"I CAME INTO EXISTENCE [being] FROM MENU."[1]

The "HEAVEN" or "ABYDOS [ ]" where the Temple of Pharaoh SETI I still stands in its dedication to God OSIRIS, and "HELL" or "AMENTA [ ]," are of the most ancient and contemporary AFRICANS of the banks of the GREAT LAKES of East Africa/Alkebu-lan and the NILE [Blue and White] VALLEY - from ZIMBABWE [formerly the Capital of Monomotapa][2] at the south of the Equatorial Line all the way north to EGYPT [formerly Ta-Merry, Kampt,etc.] They are the forerunners of JEWISH, CHRISTIAN and MOSLEM/MUSLIM allegories. Thus like the

1. From the "Book Of The Coming Forth By Day And Night" as translated by your author.
2. One of the oldest nations of the East Coast of Alkebu-lan/"Africa" that existed up to and beyond the arrival of the very first European so-called "explorers" with Bartolome Dias in ca. 1486 C.E./A.D. which has been clearly outlined in my Black Man Of The Nile And His Family, 1981 Edition, pp. 65 - 70, etc.

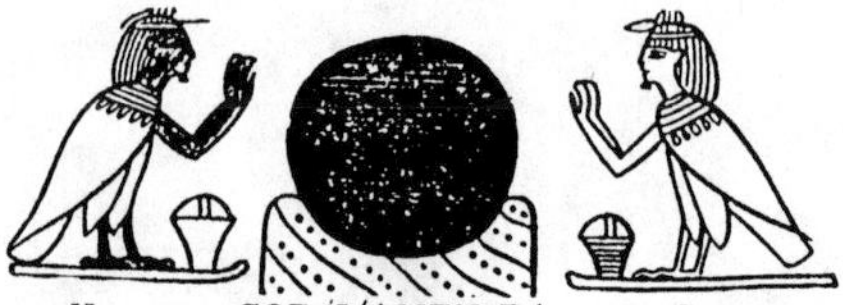

The ancient Egyptian code of morals, as may be seen from chap. cxxv., was the grandest and most comprehensive of those now known to have existed amongst any nation.

The " Recension," no doubt, was drawn up by the priests of On or Heliopolis (Moses was one of them), and it contains the views held by the priests of the colleges of that very ancient city

The souls of Osiris and Rā meeting to embrace each other in Busiris.
(From the Papyrus of Ani.)

God Of The Nome
Of On
["Heliopolis"]

All of the above comments with respect to the Gods and Goddesses, also the comments on Horus, were extracted from Dr. Albert Churchward's book, SIGNS AND SYMBOLS OF PRIMORDIAL MAN, pp. 421 , 422 and 423. One should not forget to examine the Judaeo-Christian-Islamic "Holy Works" for another look at their origin in the above. For we have seen that AMEN is still carried in them, the God of the Africans of Egypt which the Jews and Christians claimed to be : "SO BE IT." But, AMEN - RA was the God that Moses knew before YAWEH or JEHOVAH. AMEN - RA preceded all of the so-called "Western religions" - Judaism, Christianity, and Islam." Before the creation of ADAM AND EVE, THE GARDEN OF EDEN, even before JEHOVAH and the TRINITY. All of this can be found in the BOOK OF THE COMING FORTH BY DAY.

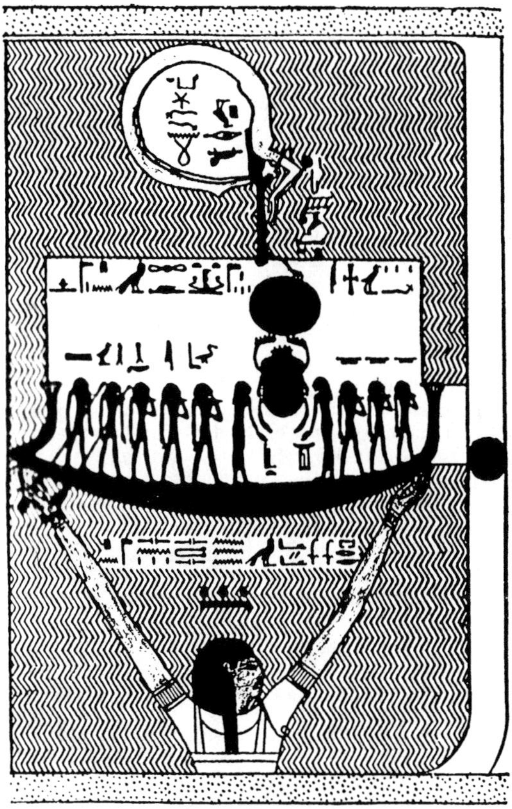

"THE CREATION"

Hebrew "SHEOL" and Greek "HADES" or "GEHENNA."Certainly not like the monstrous "HELL" in The Authorized King James Standard Version of the New Testament's BOOK OF JAMES, Chapter III, Verse 6, etc. The "HELL FIRE" and "BOTTOMLESS PIT" allegories of the Christians and Moslems/Muslims are from the distorted and perverted minds of little men and women who would like to have everyone, like themselves, live in constant mental pain and fear of their own Deity/God JESUS and/or AL'LAH they have presented to the entire world as the all-time torturer.

The monster APEP [𓊪𓊪𓆙, or Apophis],[1] who allegedly tries to stop God RA from rising by causing THUNDER, STORMS, HURRICANES, LIGHTENING, etc., became God SATAN

1. See the "Book Of Overthrowing Apep" in the writings of the ancient Africans of the Nile Valley: Egyptians, Nubians, Meröwites, Ethiopians, Puanits, et al. Is it not religious bigotry that made Christian and Moslem missionaries suppress the above "Creation Story."

or LUCIFER of the Christian Religion as He is in al-Islam. This is the same "EVIL" or "BAD GOD" shown equally "overthrown" in the BOOK OF KNOWING HOW TO LOVE RA AND OVERTHROW APEP, the basis of the story adopted for the "OVERTHROW" of the "EVIL/BAD" God SATAN/LUCIFER when God YWH/JEHOVAH banished Him. This is the same SATAN/LUCIFER implied equally in European and European-American-style "LILY WHITE/SEMITIC/CAUCASIAN JUDAISM," etc.

Note that God NEBERTCHER [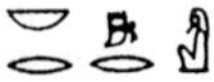, "Lord to the limit"] is the "GOD ABOVE ALL OTHER GODS" who said the following before HE was imitated by God JEHOVAH, JESUS "the Christ" and/or AL'LAH, et al:

> There was no heaven, no earth, no serpents or reptiles; all of these I produced out of the primeval mass of water of Menu. I spoke a word that controlled my mind, thus set the foundations that became the basis of all that I created from that time forward. I was with myself - neither Shu or Tefnut did I create yet. I, alone, set the basis in my mind the creation of all other things that they later made, also of which they caused to be materialized through birth. I, with my own shadow [*khaibit,* 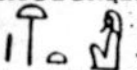][1] produced my offspring God Shu [light, heat and atmosphere] and Goddess Tefnut [moisture and humidity]. From one God I became three Gods [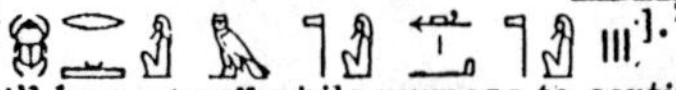].[2]

There will be no worthwhile purpose to continue quoting from the sayings of God NEBERTCHER here, as the main point of concern is to show that the ancient Africans along the Nile [Blue and White] River Valley - from PUANIT to TA-MERRY - created and developed the concept of the very first...

"ONE, AND ONLY, TRUE GOD"[3]..."I AM,"...

etc., etc., etc., ad infinitum, thousands of years before the thought of "monotheism" was adopted and passed on to their fellow Africans of Egypt/Ta-Merry and other Nile Valley and Great Lakes region; even further south of Puanit to beyond Zimbabwe[4] at the end of Monomotapa. At this juncture we have to remember that the African GODS and GODDESSES I have thus far mentioned existed within the literature of African People for thousands of years before the birth of the very first Hebrew or Israelite/Jew named AVRM/ABRAHAM [אברם] in ca. 1775 B.C.E. or 1986 H.C., when said Africans were already in their XIIIth Dynastic Period, much less before the birth of MOSHE/MOSES [an African claimed by the Hebrews/Israelites or Jews] in ca. 1346 B.C.E. or 3333 H.C. - this time the same period of the Africans XVIIIth Dynastic Period. More so, it was

1. Also written "Khaibit." Hieroglyphic words are written phonetically, thus many variations.
2. As translated from Hieroglyph to English by your author.
3. See p. xv of Volume I of this project.
4. The ancient Capitol of the nation of Monomotapa Europeans met in southern Africa?Alkebu-lan.

before the publication of the first Hebrew/Israelite HOLY TORAH, which is euphormistically renamed "FIVE BOOKS OF MOSES" and "OLD TESTAMENT" [by Christians], yet it was only written in ca. 700 B.C.E. or 3061 H.C. by scribes at the Sanhedrin that completed it in ca. 500 B.C.E. or 3261 H.C. at which time the Africans of the entire Nile Valley were already in their XXVIth Dynastic Period.[1] AFRICANS, otherwise known as "ETHIOPIANS," were ruling from as far south as PUANIT/PUNT all the way down north to TA-MERRY/EGYPT shown on the Nile Valley and Great Lakes region map on page xliii following. Remember that the "WORLD" of the Hebrew Scribes minds was nothing more than what appears next.

THE WORLD OF GENESIS
ca. 1675 BCE

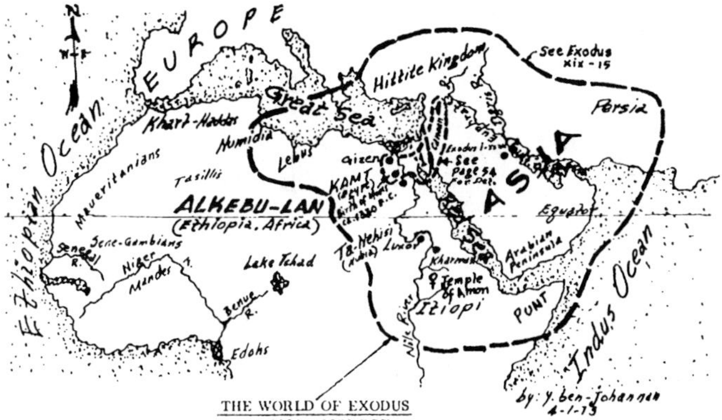

THE WORLD OF EXODUS
ca. 1298 - 1232 BCE

In this context, let us not forget that these "SCRIBES" were the same ones who also invented the "ROUTE OF THE EXODUS" we see on the following page and described in the so-called SECOND BOOK OF MOSES/EXODUS in the Holy Torah or "Old Testament."

---

1. See List Of Dynasties on pp. xxii-xxiii of this Volume, etc. p. xxiii and xxxvi for highlights.

Remember that God RA [𓂋𓂝𓇳𓀭] provides for us in the Present World, whereas God ASAR [𓁹𓊨𓀭, or 𓊨𓁹, *i.e.* **Osiris**] takes care of us in the After World [beyond physical death].[1] Our ancient African ancestors were so clear on this point that they left us the following description of our deceased ancestors in the Next/Nether World.[2]

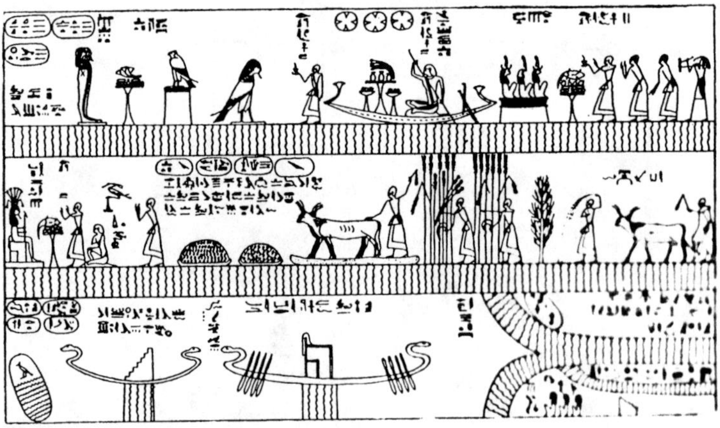

This is the teaching, up to this very day, of and by Africans who still follow "...the Most Holy/Sacred Words of the One And Only True God Ra...," and/or whatever other "ONE" he or she selects to follow spiritually and/or religiously in the Mysteries System with its underground Headquarters still in Ta-Merry/Egypt in spite of the Moslem Government attempts to destroy it.

1. The top frieze shows the paying honour to the Gods with respect to Sekhet-hetep paddling his boat; the center frieze showing the deceased planting and harvesting while adoring the God of the Nile Valley; and the bottom frieze shows the boats of the mysteries of God Ra moving themselves.

I beg to end this prefertory note with the following from the "LAST JUDGMENT" concept Hebrews, Israelites or Jews, Christians and Moslems or Muslims have copied and distorted from the PAPYRUS OF KHATI [ca. 1250 B.C.E., XXth Dynasty], which deals with KHATI telling his son the following:

> Understand that the Tahatchat [ ],[1] who will exact Judgment on all evil doers, and will not show any forgiveness in judging the wrong doers, at the time when they are doing their assigned task. It is awful for the man who knows his wrongful dealings to be charged with them. Be sure in your mind that the length of time past will not cause you to be forgiven, as in their consider ation and entire lifetime is equal only to about one single hour. They wait upon the death of a man before they start his trial, his life's history is then presented before him. In the Nether/Next

The weighing of the heart of the scribe Ani in the Judgment Hall of Osiris. (From the Papyrus of Ani.)

> World time is forever, the man who ignores this is foolish. Anyone who is free of wrongdoings in the Nether World will live there as a God, and as the other Lords Forever he too will be free to move about from any place to another.

Lastly, we see an illustration of the "SOUL" and the "BODY" as two distinctly different entities in the following frieze on page xxiii depicting God OSIRIS KHENTI AMENTI [, or] - the Great God and Lord over Abydos - stretched out on His death bed with His "SPIRIT SOUL" [shown as a hawk] in a kind of suspended flight in mid-air over Him. Certainly there should be no reason for you not to be seeing that the so-called HOLY TORAH, NEW TESTAMENT and/or HOLY QUR'AN are just plagiarized versions of basic and most fundamental aspects of the NILE VALLEY AFRICANS teachings that originated in the GRAND LODGE of Wa'at [called "Luxor" today by Arab colonialists, before this "Thebes" by Greek colonialists, et al]!

1. Also known as "Assessors" or "Chiefs," who conduct all of the interrogations in the Nether or Next World. They are considered "Scribes of God Osiris" in the Nether/Next World."
2. See my "The Black Man's Religion: Extracts And Comments From The Holy Black Bible," etc.

MAN BROUGHT BACK FROM DEATH TO LIFE
ALL BEFORE THE BIRTH OF "JESUS THE CHRIST/ANOINTED"! ?
Surely: Not With The Same "CLAY" God Khnum Used On His Potter's Wheel!
RELIGION'S BEGINNING!
PHALLICISM, or PORNOGRAPHY!
THE SERPENT, or PENIS!
[Second Frieze Below]
All Of This In The Africans' Mysteries System Life

Anubis, under the direction of Thoth, reconstituting the body of Osiris with the help of the Frog-goddess Heqet. Nephthys sits at the head of the bier and Isis at the foot.

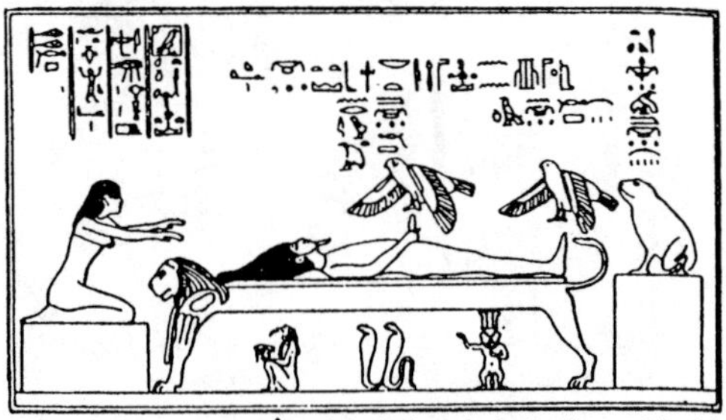

Osiris begetting Horus by Isis,[1] who is in the form of a hawk; the second hawk is Nephthys. At the head of the bier sits Hathor and at the foot the Frog-goddess Heqet.

[Extracted from E.A.W. Budge, OSIRIS: THE EGYPTIAN RELIGION OF RESURRECTION, University Books, Hyde Park, New York, 1961, p. 260]. Could this be the original source of ADAM'S "SERPENT" that "TEMPTED EVE" of the "GARDEN OF EDEN" in the FIRST BOOK/GENESIS of the FIVE BOOKS OF MOSES/OLD TESTAMENT? What about the "SERPENT" under the "PENIS" above or around the "FORBIDDEN FRUIT TREE" in the so-called "GARDEN OF EDEN"?

1. Although the primary reason for this project is the origin, etc. of the so-called "Falashas" and other related matters, we cannot overlook the fact that here is more evidence of the so-called "... Immaculate Conception" of Mary and "Virgin Birth" of Jesus the Christ of the New Testament.

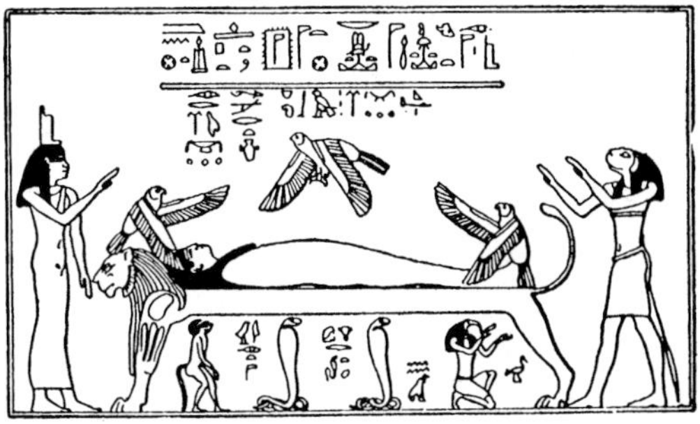

In the scene above we see the mummy of God Osiris Khenti Amenti, the Great God and Lord of Abydos, stretched-out on his death bed while His Spirit-Soul in the image of a Hawk tarry over Him. Isis or Ast [His widow], Heqet [, appearing as a Frog] and God Thoth [, **Tehuti,** or Tchehuti] reciting special prayers to cause God Osiris' [**Asar,** , or] resurrection from the dead and freedom of His Heart-Soul. Goddess Isis and Her sister Nephthys [**Nebthet,**] are equally shown as Hawks at both ends of the death sofa-bed.

The previous pages are presented to my reading audience in order that you will realize neither BLACK AFRICAN or WHITE EUROPEAN HEBREWS/JEWS have any justification in using the racist and bigoted religious term "THE CHOSEN PEOPLE OF GOD." For are we to believe that all of the "ONE AND ONLY TRUE GOD" that preceded the birth of Judaism, Christianity and Islam by thousands of years did not consider everyone they "CREATED" or "MADE" before the birth of the first HEBREW, CHRISTIAN, and/or MOSLEM," even "ADAM" and "EVE" in the allegorical folklore of the book of GENESIS [or First Book Of Moses], Chapter I, Verses 1 - 5 and GENESIS, Chapter II, Verses 1 - 10 below, as equally "CHOSEN," etc. ?

1 [The Story of Creation] In the beginning God created the heavens and the earth;[2] the earth was waste and void; darkness covered the abyss, and the spirit of God was stirring above the waters.
3 God said, "Let there be light," and there was light. God saw that the light was good.[4] God separated the light from the darkness, calling the light Day and the darkness Night.[5] And there was evening and morning, the first day.

On the other hand, we also find the following in the BOOK OF THE COMING FORTH BY DAY AND BY NIGHT [English translation by Sir E.A.W. Budge, Egyptian Book of the Dead, p. 174]:

[Khnemu was] - the father in the beginning," ; "the Maker of "things which are. Creator of things which shall be. Source "of the lands, Father of fathers, Mother of mothers," ; "Father of the fathers of the gods and goddesses, lord of "things created in himself, maker of heaven, and earth, and

" the Tuat, and water, and the mountains," 

 ; " supporter of the sky upon its four pillars, raised up of the same in the firmament (?) "

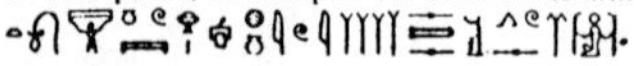

A Black Bible that will restore the following extract from the PYRAMID TEXT OF PHARAOH PEPI I to its First Book. Here we have "... THE OLDEST OF THE GODS... Tem"... letting everyone know that HE existed when...

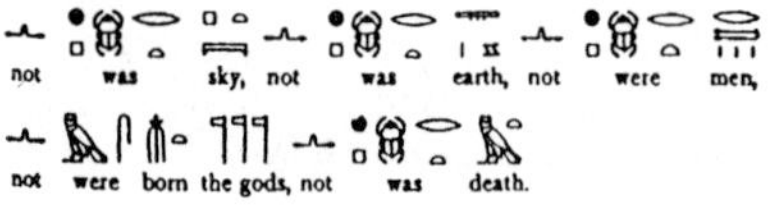
not was sky, not was earth, not were men,
not were born the gods, not was death.

The above was in reference to the "OLDEST GOD... THE DIVINE GOD." His name is written in Hieroglyph as follows:

Tem, or Àtmu

God – TEM – was said to be the 'ONLY'...

"divine god," the "self-created," the "maker of the gods," the "creator of men," "who stretched out the heavens," "who illumineth the Tuat with his Eyes" (*i.e.*, the sun and moon).

And He was even more POWERFUL than Jehovah, Jesus Christ and/or Al'lah. TEM even "CREATED HIMSELF;" and for His own survival He made...

"THE GREAT MASS OF CELESTIAL WATERS... OF Nu .

The common cry of "ANTI-SEMITISM" cannot deter or stop the evidence presented in this project thus far. This does not mean no one will ever try to holler loudest in the use of this ploy, even though the preponderance of evidence proves the origin of "JUDAISM, CHRISTIANITY and ISLAM" in Africa/Alkebu-lan by Africans, and for Africans; call them "EGYPTIANS" or "SEMITES" and "HAMITES" if you prefer! But just remember that as long as there are countless AFRICAN artifacts, written documents, etc. indigenous to the Nile Valley and Great Lakes region, evidence will always show that the presently despised so-called "BLACK AFRICANS" [that include "Hebrews" or "Jews" of all shades of "black"] gave to all human beings of so-called WESTERN CIVILIZATION the major theosophical concepts of man's mind; a –

"DEITY/GOD/NETER [, , or].

This, I hope, will convince Jews, Christians, Moslems and others who believe that they, alone, have the first "...ONE AND ONLY TRUE GOD...," and that their own "...RELIGIOUS BELIEF" is nothing more or less than second-hand dogmas. I suggest that they read the following from "THE KASSIDAH" by Haji Abu el-Yezdi, as translated from the Classical Arabic writing into the English language by Sir Richard Burton of Great Britain sometime during the 19th Century, C.E.:

"All faith is false, all faith is true,

Truth is the shattered mirrors strewn
In myriad bits; while each believes
his little bit the whole to own."

Yes, for millions, it is still God RA [] or AMEN-RA [] of Ta-Merry/Egypt and the rest of the Nile Valley and Great Lakes region who is and will always be -

"THE ONE, AND ONLY, TRUE GOD/I AM."

The following pages, from xxvi through 1, might appear to be somewhat repetitious of all that have been written from page xiii through page xxv. However upon careful examination you will note that there are many basic factors not covered in the former which are in the latter. Plus a bit of redundancy will be more than educational, it is indelible on your memory. Let this be the order for our children and children's-children, those born and yet unborn to come and be aware of the academic gimmickry being used to usurp the theosophical and philosophical concepts and teachings of the ancient Nile Valley Africans as the following:

The New York Times

MONDAY, OCTOBER 11, 1982

Ancient Papyrus a Riddle No More

By CHARLES AUSTIN

A Yeshiva University professor has cracked a 2,000-year-old linguistic puzzle and discovered portions of Jewish psalms addressed to Egyptian gods in a previously untranslatable Egyptian manuscript.

The scholar, Dr. Richard C. Steiner of the university's Bernard Revel Graduate School, said the discovery might provide the earliest concrete evidence that the psalms were used for worship outside of Jerusalem, as well as a rare and early example of an ancient religion borrowing another's rituals.

Dr. Steiner, a linguist, also said the translation would be of immense help in understanding how Aramaic, a Semitic language with some parallels to ancient Hebrew that was the lingua franca of the ancient Near East for centuries, was spoken.

He and Dr. Charles F. Nims, professor emeritus at the University of Chicago's Oriental Institute, will report on their analysis of the so-called "mystery papyrus" in a forthcoming issue of the Journal of the American Oriental Society.

Discovered in 19th Century

The manuscript, 422 lines of text believed to date from the second century B.C., was discovered sometime in the 19th century in Thebes, Egypt. It is now housed at the Pierpont Morgan Library, Madison Avenue and 36th Street.

The papyrus, which is written in a symplified version of Egyptian script known as demotic, has long been a linguistic mystery because even scholars familiar with the Egyptian script did not recognize that it was being used to transcribe spoken Aramaic.

The solution to this ancient puzzle began in the summer of 1981, when Dr. Steiner, who was working on another linguistic problem in Aramaic, was shown photographs of the mysterious papyrus by Dr. Nims.

After studying the manuscript, Dr. Steiner concluded that the papyrus's scribe had not known Aramaic and thus had written the manuscript phonetically and perhaps from dictation, without knowing the meaning of what he had taken down. The resulting errors in spelling and punctuation made the text look like "pure gibberish," Dr. Steiner said, even to scholars of Aramaic.

Found Words From Prayers

In the process, he recognized words commonly found in Jewish prayers. Starting with those words, he worked on other portions of the manuscript.

"Several phrases I translated reminded me of the Jewish liturgy," he said, "but it wasn't until I stared at the text for an entire summer that it dawned on me that the portion of the Jewish liturgy that most resembled the prayer was Psalm 20." He found a nearly exact parallel to a part of the psalm that reads: "May the Lord answer you in time of trouble. May the name of the God of Jacob keep you out of harm's reach."

Another verse of the psalm, which also has a nearly exact parallel in the papyrus, reads, "May He grant you your heart's desire, and may He fulfill your every plan," In the Aramaic manuscript, however, the name of the Egyptian falcon-god Horus is inserted into the text. There are other mentions of Egyptian gods in the manuscript as well, the professor added.

"We can't be sure who paganized the psalm text," Dr. Steiner said. It could be that Horus worshipers simply appropriated a prayer used by the Jewish community in Egypt. Or syncretistic Jews, those who blended their religion with that of their neighbors, might have altered

Continued on Page B4

Who proved that this was used by indigenous Egyptians of the Worship of any Egyptian God? Couldn't it belong to a Jew rather than an Egyptian of the same period? Y. ben-J.

Yeshiva University

Part of Egyptian manuscript containing portions of Jewish psalms.

Note capitalization of "God" for the Jewish and Christian Deity; but always lower case "god" for God Horus or any other African/Egyptian God. Is this not part of the religious bigotry that drove Steiner to believe as he does in this matter? Certainly if he read more about "Gods" he would see! Y. ben-J.

Ancient Mystery Is Solved

Continued From Page B1

the prayers by inserting the name of the Egyptian god.

Although crossover in religious practices was common in ancient times, much of the evidence of this sort of mixing has been from much later manuscripts.

In translating the manuscript, Dr. Steiner also discovered that the psalm had been transformed from a blessing spoken by the priest into a communal prayer. Noting that little is known of the worship of Jews outside Judea, Dr. Steiner said the manuscript might be the earliest evidence of the liturgical use of the psalms by scattered Jewish communities.

Dr. Steiner and Dr. Nims believe that the prayer may have come from the Jewish community in Edfu, about 60 miles southeast of Thebes, the ancient city now known as Luxor. Edfu was a leading center for worshipers of the falcon god, and a temple to Horus stands there.

Asked about Dr. Steiner's conclusions, two other scholars, who have not yet seen the manuscript, said textual evidence of the liturgical use of psalms outside Jerusalem would be an important discovery.

"One could guess that the psalms might have been used by Jews in worship elsewhere," said Dr. Horace Hummel, professor of Old Testament at Concordia Theological Seminary in St. Louis. But, he said, textual evidence such as this "would be very rare indeed."

And Dr. Robert Bornemann of the Gettysburg Theological Seminary in Pennsylvania said the substitution of the Egyptian god Horus for the God of the Jews would be a significant discovery as well.

The translation, which Dr. Steiner is still completing, is now considered by linguists to be an invaluable tool for learning how Aramaic was spoken, especially since this is the longest manuscript of its kind. As such, Dr. Steiner expects the translation to overturn several established theories about the ancient Aramaic and Hebrew phonetics.

"We may have here the closest thing to a tape recording of how the language was actually spoken," Dr. Steiner said. Interest in Aramaic has greatly increased in the past generation, as scholars seeking more authentic translations of the Scriptures search for the Aramaic roots of biblical texts.

Dr. Richard Steiner, an associate professor at the Bernard Revel Graduate School, and considered by his school "...one of the leading Semitic language scholars and phonologists in the world...," must have also figured-out another "mystery papyrus" of equal value and the same origin that reverts to the ancient Africans of Egypt to be given to the very much later Haribu/Israelites and later "Jews" that received their first insight into theosophy and philosophy from the age-old "Mysteries System" at the Grand Lodge of Wa'at [later "Thebes" by the Greeks, and "Luxor" by the current Arab invader-colonialists]. I am sure Yeshiva University will equally aid him; thus·

THE COMPARATIVE WORKS[1]

ISRAEL (Asia-Minor) PROVERBS XXII. 17-XXIII. 14; The "teachings of King Solomon" of Israel	EGYPT (North-Africa) THE TEACHINGS OF AMEN-EM-OPF Pharoah of Egypt
1. Incline thine ear, and hear my words, And apply thine heart to apprehend; For it is pleasant if thou keep them in thy belly, That thy may be fixed like a peg upon thy lips.	1a. Give thine ear, and hear what I say, And apply thine heart to apprehend; It is good for thee to place them in thine heart, Let them rest in the casket of thy belly. That they may act as a peg upon thy tongue.
2. Have I not written for thee thirty sayings Of counsels and knowledge! That thou mayest make known truth to him that speaketh.	2a. Consider these thirty chapters; They delight, they instruct. Knowledge how to answer him that speaketh, And how to carry back a report to one that sent him.

1. See Y. ben-Jochannan's "Black Man Of The Nile And His Family," New York, 1931 Rev. Ed.

3. Rob not the poor for he is poor, Neither oppress the lowly in the gate.	3a. Beware of robbing the poor, And of oppressing the afflicted.
4. Associate not with a passionate man, Nor go with a wrathful man, Lest thou learn his ways And get a snare to thy soul.	4a. Associate not with a passionate man, Nor approach him for conversations; Leap not to cleave to such a one, That the terror carry thee not away
5. A man who is skillful in his business Shall stand before Kings.	5a. A scribe who is skillful in his business Findeth himself worthy to be a courtier.

The above comparisons are but a choice few of the selected sayings of the entire so-called "PROVERBS OF KING SOLOMON" of Israel, which have been earmarked for cross reference. However the entire PSALMS ["Songs of Solomon"], and all of the HOLY TORAH generally, are full of direct copies of works written WORD-FOR-WORD as their African [Egyptian, Nubian, Ethiopian, Meröite, etc.] sayings and teachings. This should not be supprising to anyone, since Moses and most of the earliest Haribus [Hebrews or Israelites later on] in GENESIS and EXODUS were all Africans. They were all born in Ta-Merry, Ethiopia [the Falashas], and Ta-Nehisi [Nubia]. Even the theory of "MONOTEISM," the belief of "ONE GOD" above all others, was taught in Ta-Nehisi [Nubia], Ta-Merry [Egypt], and Itiopi [Ethiopia] before the birth of Moses by the Pharaoh Akhenaten [Amen-hotep IV], c. 1370-1352 B.C.E. Moses did not live until the reign of Pharaoh Rameses I, c. 1340-1320 B.C.E. or Seti I, c. 1318-1298 B.C.E. For it was during the period of the reign of Pharaoh Rameses II, c. 1298-1232 B.C.E., at which time Moses was allegedly more than "NINETY [90] YEARS OLD," that one is to hear of Moses receiving the so-called "TEN COMMANDMENTS" from the Haribu God - "JEHOVAH, ON MOUNT SINAI."

These literal translations are extracted from very much older versions and less complex conservative texts than the presently revised versions of the Hebrew Holy Torah [Christian Old Testament]. Prófessor W.O.E. Oesterley had been given the greatest amount of credit by leading scholars in this field, with respect to his first-hand research and revelations on this particular point in literature, which influenced other noted historians and theologians to equally observe and examine the mythology of certain alleged "HEBREW ORIGINS." Besides the works of Professor Oesterley, the following specialized bibliography on the "COMPARATIVE WORKS"[1] [Solomon and Amen-em-eope] should be of particular benefit to the researcher and student who desire to delve deeper into this area of biblical history and mythology:

Griffith, THE WORLD'S BEST LITERATURE, 1897
Esman, DIE LITERATUR der AGYPTER, 1897
Griffith, Ranke [in: Gressman], Sange, DAR WEISBEITSBUCH des AMEN-EN-EOPE, 1925. [English translation: "Amen-em-eope Teachings"]
Blackman's Essay in "THE PSALMISTS," [edited by D.C. Simpson], 1926
ben-Jochannan, Y. AFRICAN ORIGIN OF THE MAJOR "WESTERN RELIGIONS," 1971
Hooke, S.H. [ed.], MYTH AND RITUAL, 1933
Blackman's English Translation of Die LITERATUR der AGYPTER, 1923
Cook, S.A. THE RELIGION OF ANCIENT PALESTINE IN THE LIGHT OF ARCHAEOLOGY, 1930
Buchler, DIE TOBIADEN und die ONIADEN, 1899
Cowley, JEWISH DOCUMENTS OF THE TIME OF EZRE, 1919
"ARAMAIC PAPRI OF THE FIFTH CENTURY B.C., 1923
Peet, EGYPT AND THE OLD TESTAMENT, 1922
Osterly and Robinson, A SHORT HISTORY OF ISRAEL, 1934

1. There are thousands more Dr. Steiner could have read to change his conclusion if he wanted.

Jack, J.W. THE DATE OF THE EXODUS, 1925
Breasted, J.H. ANCIENT RECORDS OF EGYPT: THE HISTORICAL DOCUMENTS, 1905
-------- THE DAWN OF CONCIENCE, 1934
Smith, H.W. MAN AND HIS GODS, 1953
Frazier, Sir J. THE GOLDEN BOUGH, [13 vols.], 1922
Wallis Budge, Sir E.A. THE BOOK OF THE DEAD, 1895
------------ OSIRIS, 1920

The current trend of making everything of ancient African origin either done by the ancient Hebrews/Jews, Greeks, Romans, and even "men from outer space," is mad. But can we take this aspect of so-called "ACADEMIC RESEARCH" and "WESTERN SCHOLARSHIP" as we have too often done in the past? Are we to follow the same line of distorting our own African/Black HISTORY and HERITAGE while keeping in step with our European and European-American so-called "AUTHORITY ON AFRICA" and "AFRICAN PEOPLE"? We must begin our rejection by first ignoring those who continue to call us "BLACK AFRICANS, PYGMIES, BANTUS, FOREST PEOPLE, SAVANNAH PEOPLE, AFRICANS SOUTH OF THE SAHARA, HAMITES, NILOTS, THE NATIVES," and all of the other derogative nomenclatures we have so far allowed others to call us. This we must equally do in the United States of America with those who insist on calling us "NEGROES, COLOREDS, INNER-CITY PEOPLE, GHETTOITES, UNDERDEVELOPED, CULTURALLY DEPRIVED, UNDERPRIVILEGED," etc., etc., etc., ad infinitum. In order to do this we must first avoid ourselves being in the position of those of us in the 1983 C.E./A.D. Chicago, Illinois MAYORALITY ELECTIONS when the loser warned the "RESPONSIBLE NEGROES" about being cut off from further FINANCIAL AID TO THE NEGROES. In otherwords, we will have to pay for what we get, remembering at all times to be...

"AWARE OF" WHO IS "BEARING GIFTS;"

...and for what purpose.

The game of the "LIBERAL WHITE JEWS," no less so than the "LIBERAL WHITE CHRISTIANS," et al., must be cited for just what it really is. We must remember that the so-called "WHITE/SEMITE" and/or "WHITE JEW" in the United States of America is equally the same in culture, race and belief as the WHITE CHRISTIAN, MOSLEM, BUDDHIST, ATHEIST, CAPITALIST, COMMUNIST, SOCIALIST, etc. when the issue boils down to "BLACK vs. WHITE" any time, any place and any reason. We, the so-called "BLACK JEWS" especially, must constantly be aware that our struggle everywhere is that of being "AFRICAN/BLACK" first, and probably "RELIGIOUS" next. There is no exception, as even in the European and European-American [WHITE/CAUCASIAN/SEMITIC, etc.] dominated STATE OF ISRAEL or "PALESTINE" we are no better off than our fellow AFRICAN/BLACK PEOPLE in anyother European and European-American stronghold. If in fact you cannot visualize this now, you must by the end of this two volumes project dealing with WE THE BLACK JEWS: WITNESS TO THE "WHITE JEWISH RACE" MYTH.

RELIGION:

"Religion Is The Deification Of Culture."

The above conclusion has been mine ever since I recognized that in each religion's major teachings I ever examined. The SCRIBES, THEOSOPHERS, PHILOSOPHERS, PROPHETS and PROPHETESSES, SAINTS, GODS and GODDESSES, even FIRST TWO PEOPLE, et al., were and are of the local culture or civilization of the religion involved. Thus it is that God PTAH is or was an Egyptian; God YWH/JEHOVAH is an Israelite; God JESUS [the anointed] is an Nazarene; and God AL'LAH is an Arabian, etc. ad infinitum. I found that this observation is the KEY to the enslavement of too many of us African minds as we become entraped with the various forms of our conquerors' religions. The worst of these experiences being the PROSYTELISING RELIGIONS - thus Judaeo-Christianity and Judaeo-Christian-Islam. The base of these two being Talmudic Judaism, which copied the theosophical and philosophical works of the Nile Valley Africans, from the first Haribu or Hebrew AVRM ABRAHAM to the contemporary followers of him even in the modern state called "ISRAEL" and or "PALESTINE" today. "ISRAEL" by European and European-American Jews, and "PALESTINE" by Asian and Asian-American Moslems, joined by others sympathetic to the cause of the "PALESTINIANS" fighting against the State of Israel. For the Africans it is still the ancient name - "CANAAN" of the "CANAANITES/AFRICANS" that were exterminated to the very last one in one of the earliest acts of GENOCIDE in man's history. Yes!, here was the very first recorded "HOLOCAUST" in so-called religious history. And I am told that the so-called "CANAANITES" were the "BLACK DESCENDANTS" of the so-called "CURSE" that came upon us as a direct result of "NOAH'S" act against his youngest son - HAM. I am sure you have already dealt with this allegorical story in your own "BIBLE," and as researched by Robert Graves and Raphael Patai in their most profound work - HEBREW MYTHS: THE STORY OF GENESIS - - I am citing throughout these two volumes - as on page 2.

Thothmes III, XVIIIth Dynasty, dancing before Goddess Hathor

The plagiarisms by the HEBREW SCRIBES started with the CONVERSION OF AVRM TO ABRAHAM in his own WORSHIP OF GODDESS HATHOR [Hether,] -the so-called "GOLDEN CALF" - in 1775 or 1695 B.C.E., and finally his "CIRCUMCISION" about the same time - an ancient African custom that began thousands of years before at the southern waters of Africa's GREAT LAKES on the Equatorial Line and below. On the following page we see an African of Egypt being "CIRCUMCISED" about ca. 2500 B.C.E. - 750 years before Abraham's birth in Chaldea. This was common

AN ANCIENT NILE VALLEY "CIRCUMCISION" IN EFFECT THOUSANDS OF YEARS BEFORE ABRAHAM'S BIRTH

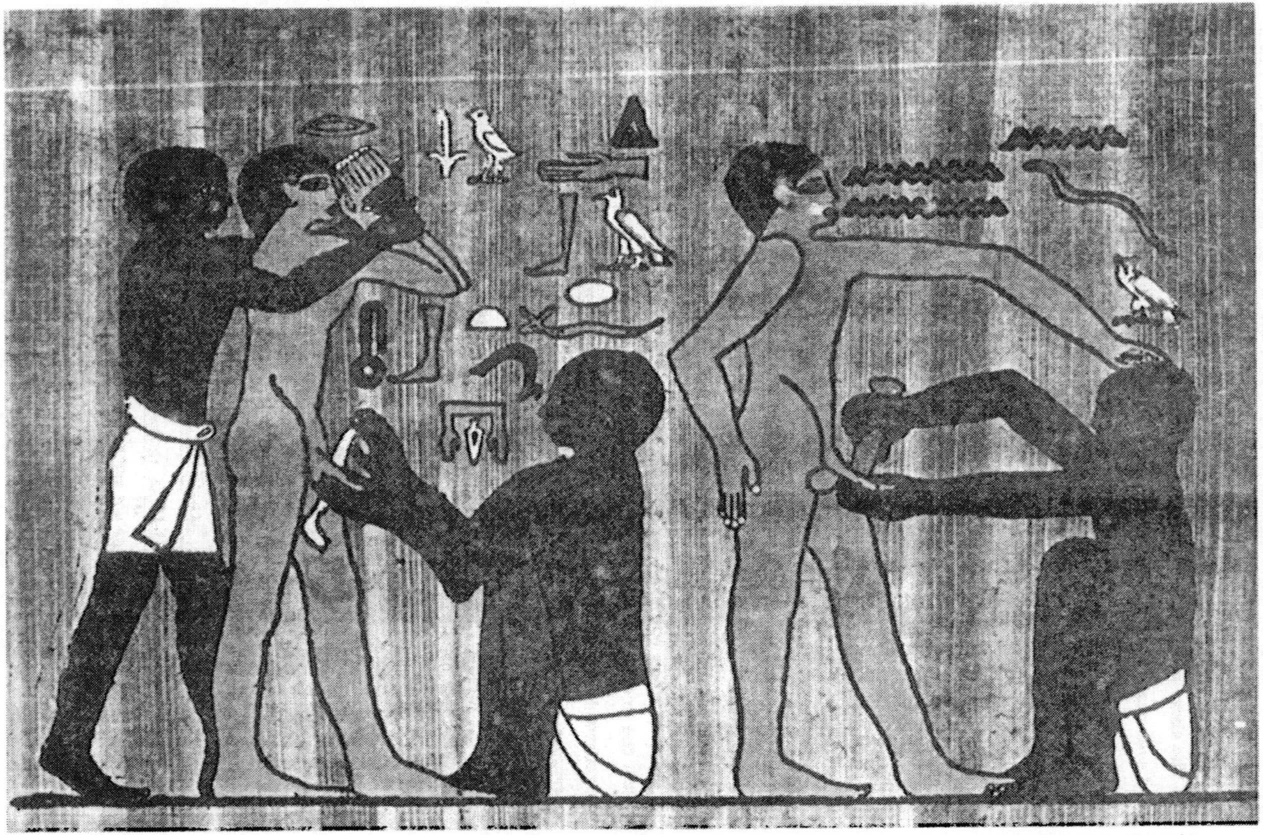

See reference to "circumcision" on page 344 of Volume II for the Jewish copy; Abraham's "circumcision" in Genesis
[From the Sphinx Papyrus Exhibition, Ghizeh]

throughout all of the High-Cultures of the Nile Valley and Great Lakes region, as even in the TWA and HUTU High-Cultures there are still numerous "CIRCUMCISION AND FERTILITY RITES AND RITUALS" shown in rock drawings that date back to centuries before Egypt's First Dynasty with Pharaoh Narmer or Aha in ca. 4100 B.C.E. I am using the creator of the "Dynastic System" chronological dating procedure - High Priest MANETHO of Sybenetos - because he differed with no one, as all others followed his DYNASTIC THEORIES before they decided to create their own in contradiction to him - as we see on pages xxii - xxiii following.

The chronological data for the first existence of God JEHOVAH started 80 years after the birth of Abraham in ca. 1775 B.C.E., of God JESUS [the Christ or Anointed] with Pantaeus and Boetius in ca. 1983 years ago, and God AL'LAH with Mohamet ibn-Abdullah in ca. 18 A.H./622 C.E. or 1,361 years ago. Yet about 2,325 years before Abraham, 4,000± years before Pantaeus and Boetius, and 4,722 years before Mohamet ibn-Abdullah, Africans along the Nile Valley and Great Lakes regions were already worshiping God PTAH and Goddess HATHOR.[1] More than this, these Africans had already reduced much of their THEOSOPHICAL and PHILOSOPHICAL concepts and practices into published literature such as we find in their BOOK OF THE COMING FORTH BY DAY AND NIGHT, PAPYRUS OF HUNEFER,[2] PYRAMID TEXT,[3] COFFIN TEXT,[4] etc. ad infinitum.

I wonder if we should even relate to the Egyptians in terms of Abraham/Avrm and Sarah or Sara's [Hadassah]entry and sojourn in Egypt [ca. 1675 - ? B.C.E., Genesis viii : 10], as the indigenous Africans/Egyptians were not ruling the Delta Region they settled before this period [XIIIth Dynasty, ca. 1675 B.C.E.] when they arrived in Egypt. The rulers of the Nile Valley were at this time Asians called "HYKSOS" or "SHEPHERD KINGS" of Beduina. The following chart on page xxxii gives the time in chronological order of the so-called "First Intermediate Period" - all of which refer to the origin established by High-Priest Manetho of Sybenetos, Egypt.

The sneaky attempt by most Judaeo, Judaeo-Christian and Judaeo-Christian-Islamic writers to make their readers believe that "...

THE EGYPTIAN PHARAOHS ENSLAVED THE ISRAELITES/JEWS,

..." when in fact the Egyptians/Africans were themselves at that period ENSLAVED at the hands of the earliest HARIBU/HEBREWS [misnomered "Jews"] and their fellow Asians from around the nation of Chaldea [today's "Iraq"] - the HYKSOS, compelled this reassesement of my own relationship to JUDAISM or HEBREWISM and/or PAN-AFRICANSM. I had to ask myself the major ques-

---

1. Symbolized by a "golden calf" or a "woman with the sun disc on her head between the Crown of the North and South," and a "woman with cow's ears," etc. The ancient Hebrews refused to pay her the honour of addressing her "Goddess Hathor" in their so-called "Sacred Scriptures."
2. Presently renamed "Egyptian Book Of The Dead and Papyrus Of Ani" as translated by E.A.W. Budge in 1885 C.E./A.D.
3. Ibid. There are special works dedicated solely to this text in English translations.
4. Ibid.

DATES OF EGYPTIAN DYNASTIES BY EUROPEAN "AUTHORITIES IN EGYPTOLOGY" COMPARED TO MANETHO'S ORIGINAL WORKS

Period or DYNASTY	Manetho (280 B.C) DATE	Champollion-Figeac (?A D) DATE	Lepsius (1858AD) DATE	Brugsh (1877AD) DATE	Mariette (?AD) DATE
	First Book				
I	9K, 253Y	5,867*	3,892*	4,400*	5,004*
II	9K, 302Y	5,615	3,639	4,133	4,751
III	9K, 214Y	5,318	3,338	3,966	4,449
IV	8K, 284Y	5,121	3,124	3,733	4,235
V	9K, 248Y	4,673	2,840	3,566	3,951
VI	6K, 203Y	4,225	2,744	3,300	3,703
VII	70K, 0Y, 70D	4,222	2,592	3,100	3,500
VIII	27K, 146Y	4,147	2,522	?	3,500
IX	19K, 409Y	4,047	2,674**	?	3,358
X	10K, 185Y	3,947	2,565**	?	3,249
XI	192K, 2300Y, 70D	3,762	2,423	?	3,064
XII	7K, 160Y	3,703	2,380	?	2,851
XIII	?	3,417	2,136	2,235	?
XIV	76K, 184Y	3,004	2,167	?	2,398
XV	?	2,520	2,101	?	2,214
XVI	32K, 518Y	2,270	1,842	?	?
XVII	86K, 151Y	2,082	1,684	?	?
XVIII	16K, 263Y	1,822	1,581	1,700	1,703
	Second Book				
XIX	7K, 209Y	1,473	1,443	1,400	1,462
XX	12K, 135Y	1,279	1,269	1,200	1,288
XXI	7K, 130Y	1,101	1,091	1,100	1,110
XXII	9K, 126Y	971	961	966	980
XXIII	4K, 28Y	851	787	766	810
XXIV	1K, 6Y	762	729	733	721
XXV	3K, 40Y	718	716	700	715
XXVI	9K, 150Y, 6M	674	685	666	665
XXVII	8K, 124Y, 4M	524	525	527	527
XXVIII	1K, 6Y	404	525	?	406
XXIX	4K, 20Y, 4M	398	399	399	399
XXX	3K, 38Y	377	378	378	378
	Third Book				
XXXI***	??????????	399	340	340	340

DIVISIONS OF THE 4,100 B. C. E. NILE YEAR CALENDAR USED BY THE INDIGENOUS AFRICAN HIGH-PRIESTS FOR THEIR CALCULATIONS OF THE PERIODS OF THEIR HISTORY

Akhet, season of inundation.	*Peret*, springtime, appearance of crops.	[illegible]
1. Thoth. **or** *tepy* January I	5. Tybi. May I	9. Pa[illegible] September I
2. Paophi. February II	6. Mechir. June II	10. Payni October II
3. Hathor. March III	7. Phamenoth. July III	11. Epiphi. November III
4. Choiak. April IIII	8. Pharmouthi. August IIII	12. Mesore December IIII

12 Months, 365 1/4 Days, 3 Seasons of 4 Months each: AKHET (Season of Inundation), PERET (Springtime), and SHENU (Summer),

CHRONOLOGICAL CLASSIFICATIONS & DATES OF EGYPTIAN, NUBIAN, MERÖEAN, THEBAN and ITIOPIAN HIGH-CULTURES

[With special reference to Jewish history][1]

	ERA	DESCRIPTION	DATE B.C.E.
		Lower Palaeolithic Period........................ Middle Palaeolithic [Old Stone] Period............	250,000 - ? 100,000 - ?
	Prehistoric Era	Neolithic [New Stone] Period:.................... Tasian Period:....................................... Badarian Period:..................................... Predynastic Period:................................	6000- ? ? ? 6000-3200
	Old Kingdom	Archaic Period: Ist & IInd Dynasty...... Great Pyramid Age: IIIrd - VIth Dynasties................. VIIth-Xth Dynasties..................	3200-2780 (4400-4266)* 2780-2270 (4266-3100) 2270-2100 (3100-2533)
The first foreigners and colonizers in Egypt	Middle Kingdom	XIth-XIVth Dynasties..................	2100-1675 (2520-2500)
		Birth of Abraham, Ywh, Adam and Eve, Avrm in Egypt	
	Hyksos Era	Hyksos invaders from Asia in Africa: XVth-XVIIth Dynasties................	 1675-1600 (2500-2333)
The period the <u>Exodus</u> supposedly took place from Africa to Asia	New Kingdom	Theban Period: XVIIIth-XXth Dynasties................	 1600-1090 (1700-1333)
		The death of Joseph, birth of Mōses, Flight of Israelites	
		Tanite & Bubasite Period: XXIst-XXIIIrd Dynasties................	 1090-718 (1133-733)
		Solomon and Makeda/Sheba and Menelek I of Ethiopia	
Israel saved by Ethiopians before its conquest by Assyrians	Itiopian Era	Kushite & Saite Period: XXIVth-XXVIth Dynasties................	 718-527 (733-666)
		Beginning and publishing of Torah/Old Testament	
	Late Kingdom	Old Persian & Mendesian Period: XXVIIth-XXXIst Dynasties................ Persian invaders from Asia in Africa.	 527-332 (666-336)
		Persians bring Greeks in mass into Egypt for education	
Greek fifth-columnists began infiltration of Egypt, beginning of Greek conquest	Ptolemaic Era	Macedonian-Greeks Period: XXXIInd Dynasty?...................... Macedonian-Greeks from Europe in Africa.	 332-47-30 (332-30)
	Greco-Roman Era	Roman Colonial Period: XXXIIIrd Dynasty (so-called)?........	 47 or 30 B.C.E. - 324 C.E.
The Horus story renewed for Jesus "the Christ" from Temple of Seti I, Abydos		**Jesus' birth, beginning and publishing of New Testament**	
	Byzantine & Coptic Era	Greco-Roman-African Period: XXXIVth Dynasty (so-called)?.................... Institutionalized Religion & Wars in Egypt.	 324- 640 C.E.
The arrival of the ancestors of the foreigners from Asia [Arabia] who still rule Egypt	Arab Jihad Muslims	Islamic Period: Arabs from Asia in Africa..........................	 640-1798
	French Imperialism	French Imperial Period: Frenchmen from Europe in Africa....................	 1798-1882
	British Imperialism	British Imperial Period: British subjects from Britain in Africa..............	 1882-1952
	European Imperialism Ended	Arab, Arab-European Period: Britain returned Egypt to Arab invaders descendants.. Farouk et al control of Arab-African population	 1952-1958

*Bracketed dates given to show comparisons by European and European-American "AUTHORITIES ON EGYPT" and AFRICA generally.

1. Assuming that one could rely on the authenticity of the biblical stories of the Jews, the added information on the left side of the chronological data would clearly show that the Israelites were in cohoot in Egypt, N.E. Africa along with the Hyksos - the origin of their knowledge.

tion: WHICH TAKES PRIORITY!, MY "JUDAISM" or "MY PAN-AFRICANISM"? In so doing the following observations were made by closely examining JUDAISM [Talmudic or Rabbinical] as against NILE VALLEY and GREAT LAKES REGION SPIRITUALITY. To my astonishment, at first, I found that the creating fathers of "JUDAISM" were for the most part plagiarists at best, and very plain co-opters at the least, as they copied and distorted countless SPIRITUAL TEACHINGS of their African/Egyptian hosts and hostesses that gave them HAVEN and HEAVEN when they were about to suffer extinction in the Eastern Desert from which they had to run into Egypt.

In the FIRST BOOK OF MOSES or GENESIS, Chapter I and II for example, the Hebrew scribes would like us to believe that the following came from their own THEOSOPHICAL investigation into the COSMOS and conclusion:

Section of an early Christian concept of the Creation Of Eve out of Adam, and the Serpent Of Eden. [From a sarcophagus in the Lateran Museum, Rome, Italy].

Adam and Eve picking the Forbidden Fruit [From a painting on the ceiling of the Cisteen Chapel, Rome]

On the other hand we find the source of the above in the following taken from the writings of the ancient HEBREWS/HARIBU or JEWS' hosts and hostesses - the AFRICANS OF EGYPT and other Nile Valley High-Cultures, etc. The "EGYPTIANS" being the ones most written of.

GOD KHNEMU [𓎸𓅓𓀭 the great "builder," 𓎸𓅓𓀭, of the universe] FASHIONING MAN ON HIS POTTER'S WHEEL. [From the Temple Of Esna]

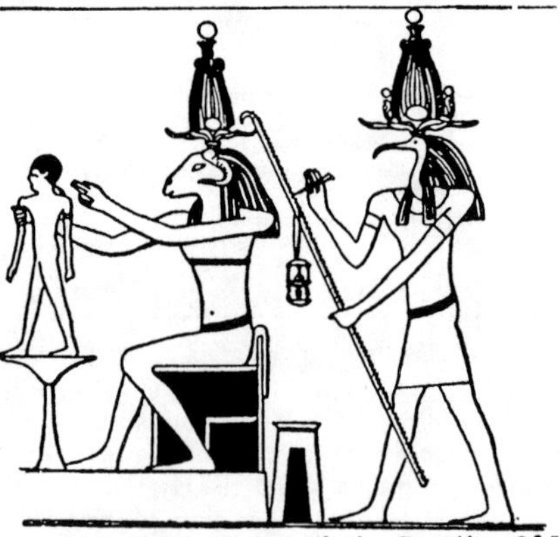

Scribe Thoth Taking Notes Of The Creation Of Man

CHNUM - the God Of Creation - fashions the First People on His Potter's Wheel.
(Egyptian conception of The Creation from a bas-relief depicting the birth of Pharaoh Amenhotep - father of Akhenaten - at Luxor or Thebes, Egypt)

The above, God KHNUM/CHNUM [**Khnemu,** 𓎸𓅭𓅱𓀭], was honoured with an anusual temple to His name at a place now named "ESNA" by the current descendeants of the Arab-Moslem invader-conquerors of EGYPT -which they call "MIZRAIR/MZR;" thus the TEMPLE OF GOD KHNUM. Most of the friezes that showed "God Khnum at work making human beings out of the clay of the earth on His Potter's Wheel" on this temple's walls have been faded almost into oblivion because of it having been submerged for centuries under the moving sand of the Egyptian Desert [Eastern Sahara] before it was excavated at the ending of the last century - 1800 - 1900 C.E./A.D., etc.; many, of course, were lifted off by European thieves calling themselves such names as EGYPTOLOGIST and ARCHAEOLOGIST, etc.

The critical personalities upon which JUDAISM/HEBREWISM must stand or fall, Avrm/Abraham, Joseph, Moses, et al., are equally shown not to have had any training in, and/or experience with, THEOSOPHY and PHILOSOPHY before their arrival at or birth in Ta-Merry/Egypt which they later did rename MIZRAIN, etc. in ca. 1675 B.C.E. - the XIIIth Dynasty or later. Thus the following with regards to the Hebrews' super-star - MOSHE/MOSES, who was himself allegedly...

INSTRUCTED IN ALL THE WISDOM OF THE EGYPTIANS...

according to Acts, Chapter VII, Verse 22, "in the Court of Pharaoh,"[1] etc. Whether Jewish and/or Judaeo-Christian scribes of the past, as contemporary writers, they can not extricate MOSES from his own EGYPTIAN/AFRICAN BIRTH and HERITAGE. Yet MOSES is never mentioned by any of them as just another "EGYPTIAN" or "AFRICAN;" but as a "HEBREW, JEW," etc. as if being a "JEW" at that time had anything whatsoever to do with nationhood or race, etc. This too, of course, comes from the notorious so-called inheritance of the racist "JEWISH MOTHER"[2] syndrome. And equally, because said "JEWISH MOTHER" has been chronologically carried back to the so-called "GREAT DELUGE" or "FLOOD,"[3] and before even this to the first two people -

1. Why is the pharaoh's name usually left out; but not the name of the Jewish personality?
2. This makes Judaism a "race" or a "religion"? One's religion does not come from birth.
3. See R. Graves and R. Patai's "Hebrew Myths: The Story Of Genesis," pp. 120 - 122, etc.

"ADAM" and "EVE" in the so-called "GARDEN OF EDEN" - ever created by the Hebrew/Jewish "ONE AND ONLY TRUE GOD OF THIS ENTIRE UNIVERSE - YWH/JEHOVAH" according to the First Book Of Moses/Genesis I. Here we see one of the earliest forms of what later became known as "RACISM" in so-called "Western Civilization" [a combination of Judaism, Christianity, "Greek Philosophy," Democracy, etc.] If this is not the foundation of the "DEIFICATION OF JEWISH CULTURE;" do tell me what it should be called!

In the case of JOSEPH, of whom there is equally no Egyptian records proving his existence any place in all of EGYPT to validate the HEBREW/JEWISH FOLKLORE or sacred writings as per Genesis xxi: 5, xxv : 26, xxxvii : 2, xli : 46, xlv : 6; he supposedly arrived 200 years following ABRAHAM [ca. 1675 - 1475 B.C.E. ?] They were HYKSOS [ca. 1675 - 1600 B.C.E. or 2500 - 2333 B.C.E., the XIVth - XVIIth Dynasty according to different chronologists] - from Aa-peh-Set to Abeh...-en-xepe Apepa? Note that certain sources maintain it is from the XVth to the XVIIth Dynasty or ca. 1675 - 1555 B.C.E. as shown on the following chart...

CHIEF-KINGS OF THE FIRST NON-AFRICAN INVADERS - THE HYKSOS OF ASIA PERIOD
(1675-1555: XVth - XVIIth Dynasties)
Aa-peh-Set to Aah-mes-se-pa-ari

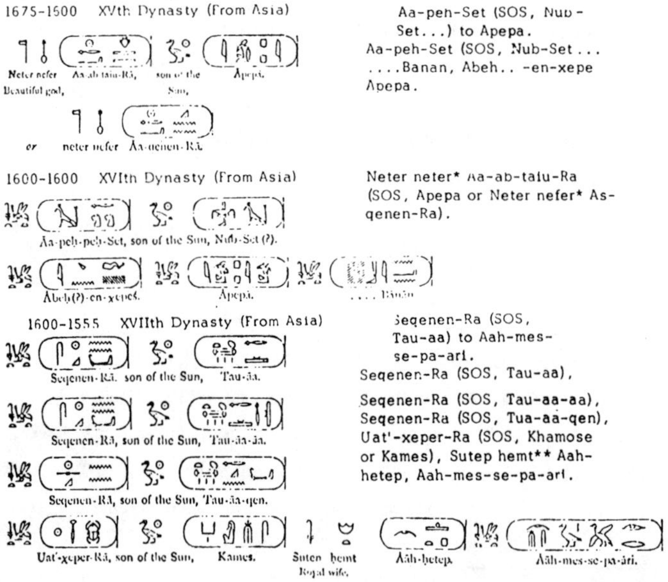

...which JOSEPH must have been totally influenced by with respect to the AFRICAN/EGYPTIAN CULTURE his fellow co-conspirators and slavers seized. And so it is that one must be very careful when the Hyksos are called "EGYPTIANS [Africans]" and "PHARAOHS;" as legitimately they were neither. They were ASIANS from around the Oxus River somewhere near CHALDEA - to-day's Iraq. These people only ruled over the Delta Region, the rest of EGYPT remained under the control of the indigenous AFRICANS OF EGYPT, otherwise known as "EGYPTIANS," etc. Thus it is that we find in Exodus I : 8 that there ...

> "BECAME A PHARAOH/KING [, PER-Ā, *i.e.* the "Great House"] WHO
> DID NOT KNOW JOSEPH [Egyptian **Zaphnath-paaneah**, Hebrew צָפְנַת פַּעְנֵחַ]...

anymore so than any other Haribu/Hebrew or "Jew" in the service of the foreign colonialists - the Hyksos or Shepherd Kings from Beduina, Asia. Even if JOSEPH, did in fact, became...

> AN EMPLOYEE IN THE EMPLOY OF POTIPHER [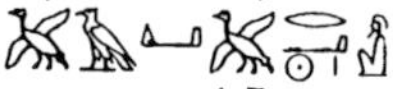
> PA-TI-PA-RA, Hebrew פּוֹטִי פֶרַע, PÔTI-PHĔRA' priest of On (Egyptian , ANU)];

...according to Genesis xli : 45, it was not as "an official" of an "Egyptian Government" anymore so than the Germans who served in the Nazi's Occupational Government during World War II in colonized France under Adolf Hitler's Storm Troopers, et al., became "Frenchmen" in a "French Government." This fact of the Hebrews/Jews being equally slavemasters and colonizers of the Africans of Egypt [Egyptians] is carefully suppressed even by so-called "Negro Theologians" of the Judaeo-Christian theological and philosophical persuasions, which equally holds true for "African/Israelite Jews."

The Hyksos, who had no citadel even close to the type of High-Culture they met in Egypt, adopted all that was Egypt they did not destroy or otherwise tried to destroy. Thus the Africans/Egyptians refusal to follow Joseph's alleged "AUTHORITY" [Genesis xxxix : 6] was due to his trying to change customs which the Hyksos dared not disturb in fear of not being able to correct if anything went wrong. The same holds true with Joseph having to present himself as "...a member of the [so-called] Egyptian Priesthood..." when he was forced to "...shave his head and dress in the garments of the station of his office" [Genesis xli : 14]...." No doubt the myth that...

"THE HYKSOS INTRODUCED THE HORSE INTO EGYPT"[1]

...is equally ludicrous, as the Africans from Puanit/Punt [today's Somalia, Kenya, Northern Tanzania and Uganda- most of which are directly below the Equatorial Line of Africa] are shown arriving in Egypt in chariots drawn by "wing steeds" [very fast horses] to pay tribute to Queen-Pharaoh Hatshepsut - the cousin of Queen Ati and King Parihu of Puanit/Punt in ca. 1555 B.C.E. Are we to believe, equally, that the Hyksos "INTRODUCED THE HORSE" to the Puanites/Puntites, Ethiopians, Meröwites/Meröites, Nubians, and other Nile Valley Africans with whom there is no record of any contact whatsoever? Let us look at the common picture of the frieze of the Queen and King of Punt that appeared the walls of the Temple of Queen-Pharaoh Hatshepsut, which is presently in the EGYPTIAN MUSEUM, Cairo, Egypt, Northeast Africa and shown on page xix.

1. See pp. 168 - 177 of my "Black Man Of The Nile And His Family, New York, 1981 [Enlarged Ed.]

Look At This African Queen Before The Queen Of Puanit/Punt
WHAT IS THE RACIAL DIFFERENCE BETWEEN THE QUEEN OF PUANIT/

QUEEN OF TA-NEHISI/ZETI/NUBIA/SUDAN/etc.
[from Lepsius, published in Lenormant's HISTORY OF EGYPT, date unknown; taken from Egypt without permission from the African People of the Nile]

PUANIT, ETHIOPIA, SUDAN [above] AND EGYPT - HATSHEPSUT - BESIDES THE SEMITIC- HAMITIC RACISM AND RELIGIOUS BIGOTRY OF "WESTERN SCHOLARSHIP" IN THE BIBLE AS ELSEWHERE? DID THE ANCIENTS MAKE SUCH DIFFERENCES? RACE!

Queen Ati [shown with the steatopygous] of Punt The King and Queen of Puanit/Punt[1]

From a bas-relief in the temple of Hâtshepsut at Dêr al-Bahari (now in the Egyptian Museum, Cairo).

EGYPTIANS/NUBIANS/ETHIOPIANS/PUANITS!

BRINGING TRIBUTE TO TUTANKHAMUN

(THEBES, TOMB OF HUY)

The myth we have just dealt with does not have as much impact as the myth about...

"THE JEWS [Israelites] BUILT THE PYRAMIDS OF EGYPT,"

...when, in fact, all of the pyramids throughout Egypt were completed before the birth of the first Hebrew/Jew Israelite, etc. - Avrm/Abraham - in Asia sometime during Egypt's XIIIth Dynasty, ca. 1775 B.C.E., or 2086 H.C. The last of the "GREAT PYRAMIDS" was built during the IVth Dynasty - ca. 2420 - 2270 B.C.E. or 1340 - 2420 H.C., the first being the STEP PYRAMID OF SAKHARA/SAQQARA in the IIIrd Dynasty - ca. 2780 - 2680 B.C.E. The "GREAT" and "SMALL PYRAMIDS" and their "PHARAOHS" are the following:

LIST OF THE GREAT AND SMALL PYRAMIDS OF EGYPT

[Note that everyone of the above was built before the birth of Avrm/Abraham - the first of the Haribu/Hebrews or Jews. None was built during the Ist and IInd Dynasty of Egypt, NA]

Date BCE	Period	Monarch
2780-2680	IIIrd Dynasty (From Memphis, the SOUTH)*	T'at'ai to Humi. T'at'ai, Neb-ka, Ser or Djoser, Nefer-ka-Ra (Son of the Sun,** Set'es), Serteta, Ahtes, Neb-ka-Ra, Humi.

1. Racism caused the removal of this frieze from its original location on Queen Hatshepsut's Tomb

Reconstruction of funerary buildings by Jean-Philippe Lauer, Paris, France. Main PYRAMID dimensions: L=431'0" x W= 344'0" x H=200'0". Height of exterior wall enclosure, 33'0".

*The first of the GREAT PYRAMIDS was built during this dynastic period of Djoser[1]

RUINS OF THE TEMPLE OF THE STEP PYRAMID OF SAKHARA

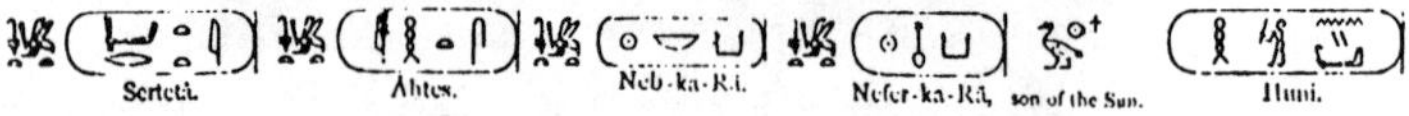

PHARAOH	LOCATION and TITLE	
Ser/Djoser	Sakhara/Saqqara:	The Step Pyramid
Sekhem-khet	" "	Unfinished Step Pyramid
Kah-ba	Zawiet el Aryan:	Layer Pyramid
Neb-ka	" " "	Unfinished Pyramid
Humi/Hu	Meydum	" "

THREE UNIDENTIFIED ROYAL PYRAMIDS

Unknown	Seila
"	Zawiet el Amwat
"	el Kola

Date BCE	Period	Monarch
2680-2565	IVth Dynasty (From Memphis, the SOUTH). Continuation of the Great Pyramid Age.	Seneteru to I-em-hetep. Seneferu, Khufu (Xufu), Khafra, (Xa-f-Ra), Men-kau-Ra, Tet-f-Ra, Shepeses-ka-f-Ra, Sebek-ka-Ra, I-em-hetep.

1. The "world's first multi-genius," Imhotep, architect, builder, physician, etc. built this one.

ERA OF THE "GREAT PYRAMIDS OF GIZEH/GIZA" IV DYNASTY

"GREAT PYRAMIDS OF GHIZEH"

(Akhet Khufu, Horizon of Pharaoh Khufu)

.. 1420 - 1535 N.Y. or ca. 2680 - 2565 B.C.E.

(A view from the South)

Left: Pyramid of Khufu ("Cheops"), 147m high; Center: Pyramid of Khafra (Chephren), 143m high; Right: Men-kau-Ra ("Mycerinus"), 66.40m high. The three (3) small Pyramids in the foreground are of Queens of the IVth Dynasty - c. ? - 2258 B.C.E. [Encyclopedia of Egyptian Civilization, p. 195].

PHARAOH	LOCATION and TITLE
Sneferu	Dashur: South Stone Pyramid
"	" : North Stone Pyramid
Khufu [called "Cheops"]	Ghizeh/Giza: Great Pyramid [largest]
Rededef	Abu Rawwash
Khafra [called "Chephren"]	Ghizeh/Giza: Great Pyramid [2nd largest]
Men-kau-Ra [called "Mycerinius"]	" " : Great Pyramid [3rd largest]

Date BCE	Period	Monarch
2565-2420	Vth Dynasty (From Elephantine, the SOUTH). Continuation of the Great Pyramid Age.	Usr-ka-f to Unas. Usr-ka-f, Sah-u-Ra, Nefer-ka-ari-Ra (SOS, Kahaa), Nefer-f-Ra (SOS, Shepses-ka-Ra), Nefer-xa-Ra (SOS, Heru-a-ka-u), Usr-en-Ra (SOS, An), Men-kau-Heru, Tet-ka-Ra (SOS, Assa), Unas.

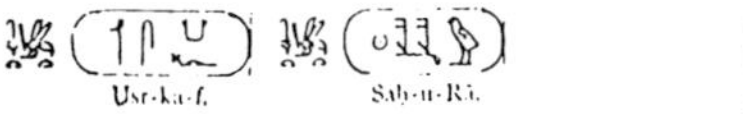

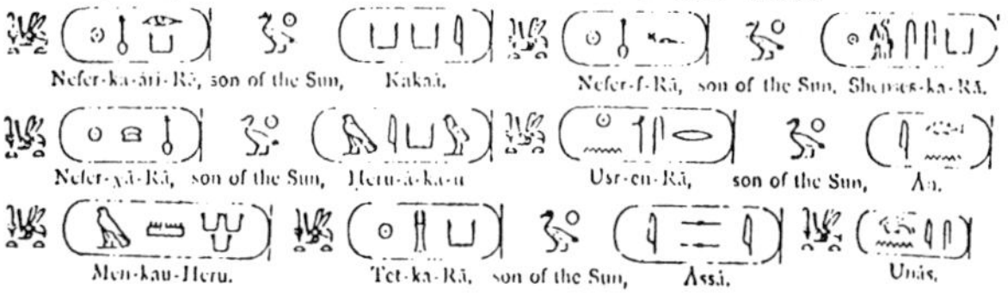

PHARAOH	LOCATION and TITLE
Weserkaf	Sakhara/Saqqara
Sahure	Abusir
Neferirkare	"
Neferefre	"
Neuserre	"
Isesi	Between Sakhara and Sakhara South

[Vth Dynasty continued]

PHARAOH	LOCATION and TITLE
Wenis	Sakhara/Saqqara

2420-2270 VIth Dynasty (From Memphis, the SOUTH). Continuation of the Great Pyramid Age.

Teta to Men-ka-Ra.
Teta (Teta-mer-en-Ptah or Teta the Beloved of Ptah), Usr-ka-Ra (SOS, Ati), Meri-Ra (SOS, Pepi I), Mer-en-Ra (SOS, Heru-em-sa-f), Nefer-ka-Ra (SOS, Pepi II), Ra-mer-en-se, Neter-ka-Ra (SOS, Netaqerti).

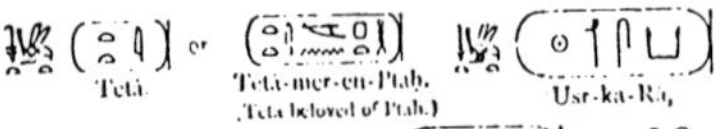

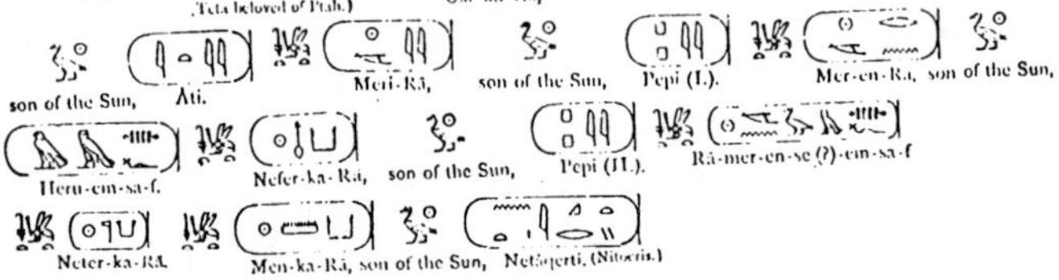

2270-2100 VIIth - Xth Dynasties. Beginning of the INTERMEDIATE PERIOD. (From Memphis, the SOUTH) - VIIth-VIIIth. (From Heracleopolis, the NORTH) - IXth-

Neter-ka to Nefer-ka-ari-Ra.
Nefer-ka, Nefer-seh..., Ab (Aba), Nefer-kau-Ra, Xaroi, Nefer-ka-Ra, Nefer-ka-Ra-Nebi, Tet-ka-Ra-maa, Nefer-ka-Ra-Xentu, Senefer-Ra,

PHARAOH	LOCATION and TITLE
Teti/Tete	Sakhara/Saqqara
Pepi I	Between Sakhara and Sakhara South
Merenre	" " " " "
Wenis	Sakhara/Saqqara

[Last Of The "Major Pyramids Pharaohs"]

Not one [1] solitary "brick" is in a single "pyramid" above; inspite of the "Book Of Exodus", etc.

The following "LESSER PYRAMIDS" were built in many different styles and with all sorts of masonry material combinations. Until you reach the XIIIth Dynasty, when the first Haribu, Hebrew, Israelite or "Jew" - AVRM or ABRAHAM - entered Ta-Merry/Egypt, ca. 1675 B.C.E. or 1586 H.C., there could not have been any Hebrew/Haribu/Israelite or "Jewish" envolvement at any level in the building of a solitary PYRAMID whatever. The "LESSER PYRAMIDS" and their "PHARAOHS" follow below [none for the VIIth Dynasty]:

PHARAOH		LOCATION and TITLE
	VIIIth DYNASTY [2270 - 2244 B.C.E.]	
Iby		Sakhara/Saqqara
	IXth - Xth DYNASTY [2244 - 2052 B.C.E.]	
Khui		Dara: Middle Egypt
	XIth DYNASTY [2052 - 2000 B.C.E.]	
Nebhepetre-Mentuhotep		Deir el-Bahri

PHARAOH	XIIth DYNASTY [2000 - 1785 B.C.E.]	LOCATION and TITLE
Amenemhat		el Lisht
Senusert I		" "
Amenemhat II		Dahshur
Senusert II		el Lahum
Amenemhat III		Hawara
Amenemhat III		Dahshur
	XIIIth DYNASTY [1785 - 1675 B.C.E.]	
Khendjer I		Between Sakhara South and Dahshur
[Unknown]		South of the site of Khendjer's
"		Mazghuna: North Pyramid
"		North Pyramid

[Last of the known Pyramids of Egypt]

I used the most common dating scheme by "Westerners" for the sake of my reading public convenience. By so doing you will be able to cross-reference other works that much easier. However, note that ca. 3200 B.C.E./B.C. is the same Ist Dynasty as ca. 4100 B.C.E./B.C. Thus when using Dynastic Periods as per High-Priest Manetho [Creator of the Dynastic Period System of Egypt] ca. 4100 B.C.E./B.C. is correct as against 3200 or 3100 B.C.E./B.C. By the standard established by most European and European-American "academicians" the latter two are used, as they give closer possibilities to an earlier European contact with Africa:Greece-Egypt.

I have added the following page, a map of THE NILE VALLEYS AND GREAT LAKES REGION, specially for you to be able to understand the total scope of the origin of the Africans/Egyptians who built all of the LESSER and GREAT Pyramids along the Nile River. For in ancient times there were PYRAMIDS in other parts of this area, some still existing in Ta-Nehisi/Zeti/Nubia/es-Sud or Sudan. They said:

> WE CAME FROM THE BEGINNING OF THE NILE WHERE GOD HAPI DWELLS, AT THE FOOTHILLS OF THE MOUNTAIN OF THE MOON.[Rwenzuri in Uganda and Kilimanjaro between Kenya and Tanganyika/Tanzania are both called "Mountain of the Moon" in their respective country].

Continuing where we left off with respect to "Joseph in Egypt," etc. If his death coincided with the final expulsion of the Hyksos from Egypt by Pharaoh Ahmes/Ahmose I, ca. 1580 B.C.E. or the XVIIIth Dynasty as some "scholars" noted, then Moses/Moshe must have been born under the reign of this Pharaoh instead of Pharaoh Haremheb.[1] Note that from Pharaoh Haremheb mounting the Egyptian Throne in ca. 1340 B.C.E. to the assumption of the same Throne by Pharaoh Ahmose/Ahmes I in ca. 1580 B.C.E. amounts to 240 years difference. This will change

1. Note there is no record of these happenings during this period anywhere with respect to "Jews."

ALKEBU-LAN'S AND ASIA'S WORLD OF THE CREATION OF MAN BEFORE ADAM

[Note that Europe was not yet in history]

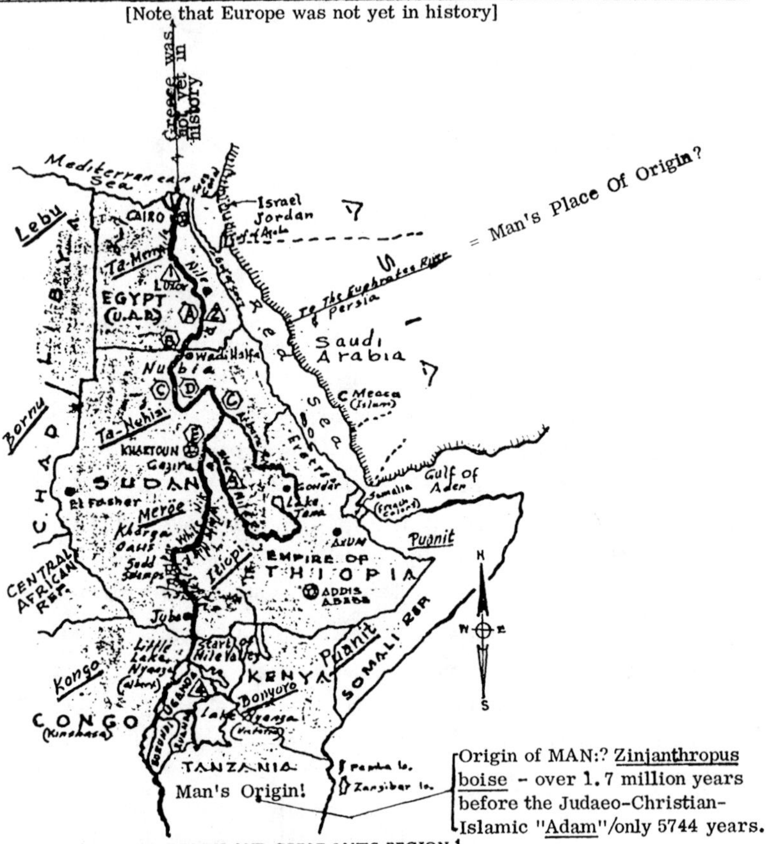

THE NILE VALLEYS AND GREAT LAKES REGION [1]

ca. 4100 BCE – 1975 C.E. [A.D.]

KEY

Cataracts: A, B, and C
Dams: 1 Asiut 2 Aswan 3 Sennar
4 Nyanza (Owens) Falls
[4,100 + statute miles, south to north)

by: Yosef ben-Jochannan 1983 C.E.

---

1. Further south at Zimbabwe, originally the ancient Capital City of the Empire of Monomotapa, there are still hieroglyphic writings on the walls of the ruins equivalent to others along the entire route north of Puanit, Axhum, Ta-Nehisi, Ta-Seti, Meröwe and Ta-Merry, etc.; even Lebus, Numidia, Khart-Haddas, etc. at the Northwest, etc. Is it not strange that the original Jewish scribes mentioned all of these African nations in their Book Of Genesis except Monomotapa?

the so-called "EXODUS" and/or "PASS OVER" from ca. 1236 B.C.E. under the reign of Pharaoh RAMESES II in ca. 1298 - 1232 B.C.E., or the XIXth Dynasty, back to ca. 1147 B.C.E.; this is providing "...the Hebrews slaved under the Egyptian Pharaohs for Four Hundred and Forty-three years..." as propagandized by rabbis, ministers, priests, imams, et al., orally from their pulpits and in constant writings. Of course the "EXODUS" forced upon African people by European and European-American Christians, Jews, Moslems, et al., is never dealt with as a "holocaust"!

Another method of back-checking the above is the breakdown of the period of the so-called "EXODUS" to the final construction of KING SOLOMON'S TEMPLE in Jerusalem sometime in ca. 966 B.C.E. used by most Jewish, Judaeo-Christian and Judaeo-Christian-Islamic religious "scholars," et al. They give the following chronological data to substantiate their myth:

HEBREW PERIODS: FROM THE EXODUS TO SOLOMON'S TEMPLE

40 years - The Hebrews/Isrealites wandering in the Sinai Desert
40 years - The period of rule by Othniel [Jud. 2 : 3]
80 years - The period of Ehud [Jud. 3 : 30]
40 years - The period of Deborah [Jud. 5 : 31]
40 years - The period of Gideon [Jud. 7 : 28]
40 years - The period of Samson [Jud. 16 : 31]
40 years - The period of Eli [I Sam. 4 : 18]
40 years - The period of David [I Kings 2 : 2]
40 years - The period of Solomon [I Kings 6 : 1]
400 years - Total from the Exodus to the completion of King Solomon's Temple in Jerusalem, Palestine/Israel, West Asia.

AFRICAN/EGYPTIAN RULERS OF EGYPT AND THE EQUAL CHRONOLOGY OF HEBREW/ISRAELITE ["Jewish"] PERSONALITIES OF THE FIVE BOOKS OF MOSES/OLD TESTAMENT CITED IN THE TEXT

Name of Personality	H.C.* Date	B.C.E.	Equiv. Dynasty	Pharaoh
Adam [Gen. 5 : 3]	1 - 130	3760 - 2830	Ist	Teta
Eve [Gen. 1 : ?]	1 - ?	3760 - ?	Ist	Teta
Noah [Gen. 5 : 28]	1056 - 1406	2704 - 2354	IIIrd	Serteta
Shem/Sem [Gen. 5 : 32]	1556 - ?	2204 - ?	IIIrd	Neb-ka-Ra
Japhet [Gen. 5 : 32]	1556 - ?	2204 - ?	IIIrd	Neb-ka-Ra
Ham/Cham [Gen. 5 : 32]	1556 - ?	2204 - ?	IIIrd	Neb-ka-Ra
Canaan [Gen. 10 : 6]	1406 -?	2354 - ?	IIIrd	Humi
Abraham/Avrm [Gen. 1:26]	2005 - 2180	1755 - 1580	XIIIth	Apepa
Joseph [Gen. 10 : 26]	2014 - 2124	1746 - 1636	XIVth	Ahmose
Moshe/Moses [Ex. 1 : 1 - 10]	2124 - 2564	1316 - 1196	XIXth	Rameses IInd
David [I Kings 2 : 46]	2100 - 2750	1010 - 970	XXIst	Her'heru
Solomon [I Kings 1 : 30]	2750 - 2830	970 - 930	XXIst	Painet'em Ist

* H.C. - Haribu/Hebrew Calendar. B.C/B.C.E. - Before The Common/Christian

Era.....Note the usage of N.Y. - Nile Year For Africans Of Egypt. [Data shown above relates to the time-periods established by High-Priest Manetho of Symbenetos, Egypt/Ta-Merry/Mizrain, etc. as shown on page xxxiii also the Nile Year Calendar shown on page xxxii of this volume. Note that the Year of these periods was 365 1/4 Days long; at least 1/4 Day longer than the current Calendar Year, etc.]

CHRONOLOGY OF THE "GODS" MENTIONED IN THE TEXT, ETC.

Name of God-Head	Religion	Nile Year	Hebrew Year	Christian Year	Moslem Year
Ptah/Ra/Osiris	Mysteries	1900 N.Y.	340 B.H.C.	4100 B.C.E.	4722 B.H.
Ywh/Jehovah	Judaism	2240 N.Y	1 H.C.	3760 B.C.E.	4382 B.H.
Jesus[the Christ]	Christianity	N.Y.	3760 H.C.	1 C.E.	622 B.H.
Al'lah	Islam	6621 N.Y.	4382 H.C.	622 C.E.	1 A.H.

Reversing our track= ca. 966 B.C.E. + 400 years = ca. 1366 B.C.E., at which time the "Pharaoh of all-Egypt" was Rameses I - the grandfather of Pharaoh Rameses II [1298 - 1232 B.C.E., XIXth Dynasty] and father of Pharaoh Seti I [1318 - 1298 B.C.E., XIXth Dynasty]. Taking these figures as being "authentic," we must add "433 years the Hebrews" allegedly "slaved for the Egyptians" [Africans of Egypt] = ca. 1366 B.C.E. + 433 = ca. 1799 B.C.E. - the reign of a pharaoh during the XIIIth Dynasty - ca. 1785 - ± 1675 B.C.E. This is very close to the reign of the African Pharaoh Xu-taaiu-Ra of Wa'at ["Thebes" by the Greeks, "Luxor" by the current Arab Moslem colonizers] or Pharaoh Semen-Ka-Ra, the last dynasty before the Hyksos overthrow of the indigenous African/Pharaonic Rule until the Africans/Egyptians destruction of the foreigner Hyksos' XVIIth Dynasty and their expulsion from Lower Egypt, Northeast Africa/Alkebu-lan.

It is suggested that my most basic work, BLACK MAN OF THE NILE AND HIS FAMILY, 1981 Revised and Enlarged Edition, pages 170 - 199, be consulted for the chronological dates used above in conjunction with other sources of reference. Page 204 must be equally consulted with regards to the Chronological Periods from "ADAM" [Genesis V : 3] to "SOLOMON" [1 Kings I : 30].

All throughout ancient Israel's/Palestine's very short history the constantly moving contact between African and Hebrews or "Jews" have been both hostile and hospitable. Even the Africans as far south as Ethiopia had to come to the aid of the Hebrew/"Jewish" nation [Isaiah xviii - xx]; the classic citation being the romance between King Solomon and Makeda or Queen of Ethiopia and Empress of Sheba [ca. 972? B.C.E. - at which time Pharaoh Suten-hemt Mat-ka-Ra, XXth Dynasty - ca. 1085 - 950 B.C.E., was ruling in Egypt [Kebra Hegaste];[1] and Moses' marriage to the daughter of the High-Priest of Ethiopia [Numbers xii : 1] was a gem, as modern European scholars have tried to make Ethiopia - the land of Kush - somewhere between Arabia, Egypt and

1. Ethiopia "History [or Chronicles of the Kings]." An overall annual record of each monarch that ever sat on the Throne of the Ethiopian Kingdom and Empire - from Ori to Haile Selassie I [last of Ethiopia's Monarchs].

and Nubia/Sudan, solely for the main purpose of lily white racism and the so-called "Semitic-Hamitic" syndrome mankind suffers from the sons of Noah's allegory [Genesis ix : 20 - 28]. His, Moses/Moshe, alleged...

"ADOPTION BY PHARAOH'S DAUGHTER"...

[Exodus ii : 10] justifies his education in Egyptian/African culture as an African/Egyptian boy and man [Acts vii : 22]. Moses' education in the African/Egyptian "Mysteries System"[1] became the most fundamental belief system of the following Hebrews/"Jews" of Africa, and of those who left for the "Land of Canaan" [Exodus viii : 17] - later called "Palestine" or "Judaea" and "Israel." Later yet of those who fled into Europe, England and the so-called "New World" [of the "Americas" - North, Central and South] following the "Destruction of the Second Temple of Jerusalem" by the Romans in ca. 37 B.C.E. From Joseph to Moses was the beginning of the introduction of the lowly "IGNOBLE PEOPLE" - HYKSOS and "HARIBU/HEBREWS" - into "civilized living"/High-Culture in Egypt, Nubia Sudan, Meroe/Meröwe, Ethiopia, Puanit/Punt, and all other lands along the entire Nile Valley and Great Lakes region of Africa/Alkebu-lan [or whatever other names by which this continent have been known throughout ancient history], and Ghana at Africa's West Coast. This is an origin of "Jews" among West Africans like the Yorubas and Peuls, et al.[2]

The domination of the areas around and about "Palestine" by the Africans/Egyptians under the reign of Pharaoh Neku/Necho I during the XXVIth Dynasty [2 Kings xxiii : 29] before it was captured by the Assyrians, who were encouraged by JOSIAH - the Assyrians' "Jewish puppet" and "Uncle Tom", was welcomed by HEZEKIAH [Isaiah xviii - xx]. The Hebrews vassalization even caused Pharaoh Tirhakah [an Ethiopian by birth] to be soundly defeated by King Sennacherib, and the Assyrians to continue their control of Judah/Judea in ca. 714 B.C.E. It was following this experience that Pharaoh Necho I counterattacked and overturned JEHOAHAZ whom he took to Egypt as a captive of war after he appointed JEHOIAKIM to succeed him. This lead to the eventual destruction of JERUSALEM and overthrow of JEHOIAKIM in ca. 653 B.C.E. or 3108 H.C. at the BATTLE OF CARCHEMISH. NEBUCHADREZZAR then burned Jerusalem to the ground and took its people into captivity in Babylon/Babylonia. Certainly Africans always aided their "HEBREW/JEWISH" proteges! Thus whatever "MONIES" latter-day "JEWS" spend on contemporary AFRICANS are only defered payments long overdue.[3]

The impact of the Nile Valley Africans, EGYPTIANS included, upon the ISRAELITES that began when they were in TA-MERRY/EGYPT, etc. included the more than ill-conceived...

"ONE AND ONLY TRUE GOD OF THE WORLD"

...concept taught by Pharaoh AMEN-HOTEP IV - who called himself "AKHENATEN," and others

1. G.G.M. James, Stolen Legacy, New York, 1954.
2. J.J.Williams, Hebrewism In West Africa: From The Nile To The Niger With The Jews, N.Y.
3. It is correctly written: "He who pays the fiddler calls the tune."

before him. This was before the birth of his fellow African/Egyptian named "MOSES/MOSHE in ca. 1346 B.C.E. Until this period the HEBREWS/ISRAELITES/"JEWS" only reference to any form of a deity was as...

"THE GOD OF OUR [the Hbrews/Israelites] FOREFATHERS"...

[Exodus iii : 3]..., since they had not yet adopted YWH/JEHOVAH [in Egyptian Hieroglyph it is  ; in Hebrew יהוה or יה; in Greek  ; and in Latin  - who in fact replaced "El Shaddai [Exodus vi : 3] - a tribal deity without any form of a HOLY/SACRED SCRIPTURE before one was introduced in Moses' name following the latter's alleged "education in the Mysteries System" from which he learnt everything he knew up to his walk on Mount Horeb in the Sinai Peninsula during ca. 1196 B.C.E. - the XIXth Dynasty, assuming that this story of Moses has validity. Thus A. Wiedemann in his most noted book, RELIGION OF ANCIENT EGYPTIANS, page 12, stated this position best when he wrote the following:

> "From the Hyksos period onwards the origin of all forms of religion was sought in sun-worship; nearly all the principal deities were thenseforth amalgamated with the sun-god."

Sir Godfrey Higgins said much the same thing in his own masterful work - ANACALYPSIS, Volume I, pages 62 - 63, as follows:

> 4. The fact that Abraham worshiped several Gods, who were, in reality, the same as those of the Persians, namely, the creator, preserver, and the destroyer, has been long asserted, and the assertion has been very unpalatable both to Jews and many Christians; and to obviate or disguise what they could not account for, they have had recourse, in numerous instances, to the mistranslation of the original, as will presently be shewn.
>
> The following texts will clearly prove this assertion. The Rev. Dr. Shuckford pointed out the fact long ago; so that this is nothing new.
>
> In the second book of Genesis the creation is described not to have been made by Aleim, or the Aleim, but by a God of a double name—יהוה אלהים *Ieue Aleim*; which the priests have translated LORD *God*. By using the word LORD, their object evidently is to conceal from their readers several difficulties which arise afterward respecting the names of God and this word, and which shew clearly that the books of the Pentateuch are the writings of different persons.
>
> Dr. Shuckford has observed, that in Genesis xii. 7, 8, Abraham did not call upon the name of the LORD as we improperly translate it; but invoked God in the name of the Lord (i. e. Ieue) whom he worshiped, and who appeared to him; and that this was the same God to whom Jacob prayed when he vowed that the Lord should be his God. Again, in Gen. xxviii. 21, 22, והיה יהוה לי לאלהים erit Dominus mihi in Deum; and he called the place בית אלהים *(Bit alcim)*, Domus Dei. Again, Shuckford says, that in Gen. xxvi. 25, Isaac invoked God as Abraham did in the name of this Lord, יהוה Ieue or Jehovah. On this he observes, "It is very evident that Abraham "and his descendants worshiped not only the true and living God, but they invoked him in the "name of the Lord, and they worshiped the Lord in whose name they invoked, so that two per-"sons were the object of their worship, God and this Lord: and the Scripture has distinguished "these two persons from one another by this circumstance, that *God no man hath seen at any* "*time nor can see*, but the Lord whom Abraham and his descendants worshiped was the person "who appeared to them."
>
> In the above I need not remind my reader that he must insert the name of *Ieue* or *Jehovah* for the name of Lord.
>
> Chapter xxi. verse 33, is wrong translated: when properly rendered it represents Abraham to have invoked *(in the name of Jehovah)* the everlasting God. That is, to have invoked the everlasting God, or to have prayed to him in the name of Jehovah—precisely as the Christians do at this day, who invoke God in the name of Jesus—who invoke the first person of the Trinity in the name of the second.
>
> The words of this text are, ויקרא-שם בשם יהוה אל עולם et *invocavit ihi in nomine* IEUE *Deum æternum*.
>
> The foregoing observations of Dr. Shuckford's are confirmed by the following texts:

Gen. xxxi. 42, "Except the God of my father, the God of Abraham, and the fear of Isaac," &c.

Gen. xxxi. 53, "The Gods of Abraham, and the Gods of Nahor, the Gods of their father, judge betwixt us, אלהי אביהם. Dii patris eorum, that is, the Gods of Terah, the great-grandfather of both Jacob and Laban. It appears that they went back to the time when there could be no dispute about their Gods. They sought for Gods that should be received by them both, and these were the Gods of Terah. Laban was an idolater, (or at least of a different sect or religion—Rachel stole his Gods,) Jacob was not; and in consequence of the difference in their religion, there was a difficulty in finding an oath that should be binding on both.

In Gen. xxxv. 1, it is said, *And* (אלהים *Aleim*) *God said unto Jacob, Arise, go up to Bethel, and dwell there; and make there an altar unto God* (לאל Lal) *that appeared unto thee, when thou fleddest from the face of Esau thy brother.* If two Gods at least, or a plurality in the Godhead, had not been acknowledged by the author of Genesis, the words would have been, *and make there an altar unto me, that*, &c.; or, *unto me, because I appeared*, &c.

Genesis xlix. 25, מאל אביך ויעזרך ואת שדי ויברכך, a Deo tui patris et adjuvabit te; et omnipotente benedicet tibi. By the God (Al) of thy father *also* he will help thee, and the Saddai (Sdi) *also* shall bless thee with blessings, &c.

It is worthy of observation, that there is a marked distinction between the *Al* of his father who will help him, and the *Saddi* who will bless him. Here are two evidently clear and distinct Gods, and neither of them the destroyer or the evil principle.

Even by the God (אל *Al*) *of thy father, who shall help thee: and by the Almighty,* שדי *omnipotente, who shall bless thee with blessings of heaven above, blessings of the deep that lieth under, blessings of the breasts and of the womb.* The *Sdi* or *Saddi* are here very remarkable; they seem to have been peculiarly Gods of the blessings of this world.

Deut. vi. 4, יהוה אלהינו יהוה אחד. This, Mr. Hales has correctly observed, ought to be rendered Jehovah our Gods is one Jehovah.

The doctrine of a plurality, shewn above in the Pentateuch, is confirmed in the later books of the Jews.

Isaiah xlviii. 16, ועתה אדני יהוה שלחני ורוחו. Et nunc Adonai Ieue misit me et spiritus ejus: And now the Lord (Adonai) Jehovah, hath sent me and his spirit.

Certainly I recommend that my own audience read both volumes of Anacalypsis. This is in spite of its shortcomings with respect to India being the original source of Egyptian and other Nile Valley theosophy, etc. according to Higgins. For at times Higgins left his religious field to become an "historian" European-style. And partly due to the absense of data available today almost everyone which was not known to have existed by researchers of his time-period in the 1800 to 1850 C.E./A.D., and even later for most.

Having read some of the highlights about the African origins of "JUDAISM" - the parent of "CHRISTENDOM" otherwise called "CHRISTIANITY" still, and grandparent of "ISLAM" - we can surely enter into the issue of WHITE/CAUCASIAN/SEMITIC JEWISH ANTI-AFRICANISM/BLACKISM in the State of Israel/"Palestine" and elsewhere, even against AFRICAN/ETHIOPIAN [Black; never "Negro" or "Colored," etc.] JEWS - whose correct nomenclature is "BETA ISRAEL" or "CHILDREN OF THE HOUSE OF ISRAEL." Of course we will hear from those white RELIGIOUS BIGOTS and RACISTS who constantly rehash the same stereotype academic myth that...

"THE ANCIENT EGYPTIANS WERE WHITE-CAUCASIAN SEMITES,"

...already like the Europeans along the border of southern Europe and the Mediterranean Sea. If not this, that:

"THE ANCIENT EGYPTIANS WERE DARK-SKINNED CAUCASIANS" and/or "HAMITES, NILOTS, CAUCASOIDS," ETC.

Since WHITE, CAUCASIAN, SEMITIC, HAMITIC, INDO-EUROPEAN-ARYAN, etc. define "EUROPEAN CHRISTIANS, JEWS, GENTILES, ATHEISTS, MORMONS, MOSLEMS," etc., one has to realize that "EUROPEAN AND EUROPEAN-AMERICAN JEWS" are no less and no more WHITE RACISTS and/or RELIGIOUS BIGOTS than EUROPEAN AND EUROPEAN-AMERICAN CHRISTIANS, MOSLEMS, ATHEISTS, et al. This holds true in ENGLAND, SOUTH AMERICA, CENTRAL AMERICA, SOUTH AFRICA, AUSTRALIA, and wherever else EUROPEAN/WHITE PEOPLE have control of the economy directly - COLONIALISM - or indirectly - NEO-COLONIALISM. This, however, is also a STATE OF MIND; as one can be COLONIZED MENTALLY without even being aware, RELIGION being the easiest form of this.

From page xiii to page 1.... I have attempted to recreate the historical background that made this documentary necessary today, which has changed very little from the original single volume - NOSOTROS HEBREOS NEGRO - I published in 1938 C.E./A.D. in San Juan, Puerto Rico, the so-called "Commonwealth of Puerto Rico," etc. Thus the myth that...

> "WHITE JEWS HAVE ALWAYS BEEN THE BEST FRIENDS OF THE NEGRO [COLORED] PEOPLE IN THE U.S.A."[1]

...is no less true today than the statement that:

> "NO WHITE JEWS WERE EVER SLAVEMASTERS OF THE NEGRO [COLORED] PEOPLE ANYWHERE IN THE WORLD,"

etc. yesterday. Yet all of this is perpetuated by so-called "Responsible Negroes/Coloreds" who pride themselves in organizations which have historically been dominated by so-called "Liberal [White-Semitic-Caucasian] JEWS and CHRISTIANS," even their creation like the NATIONAL ASSOCIATION FOR THE ADVANCEMENT OF COLORED PEOPLE [NAACP, originally the "Niagara Movement"], NATIONAL URBAN LEAGUE [NUL], and a host of others of like ilk. Thus it is again that this type of historical analysis will enrage the so-called "RESPONSIBLE NEGROES/COLOREDS" as it equally will their European and European-American "WHITE LIBERAL" mental slavemasters and slave mistresses for over the past one hundred and eighteen [118] years from the so-called "...END OF SLAVERY IN 1865 C.E./A.D. TO THE PRESENT IN 1983 C.E./A.D...." The truth is that most of these tried and true "RESPONSIBLE NEGROES/COLOREDS"[1] have been made to believe that "AFRICANS/BLACK PEOPLE" cannot equally be "JEWS" unless they came by the route of "CONVERSION"/"HALACHA" EUROPEAN/WHITE-STYLE "JEWS," etc. This type of mental masturbation continues even into the minds of the so-called "IRRESPONSIBLE NEGROES/COLOREDS" who are mentally controled from the pulpits, classrooms, radio stations, periodicals, etc., etc., etc., almost ad infinitum, and other institutions of the "RESPONSIBLES" controled by others' money.

Why will the CHAINS of this form of SLAVERY be fractured, and more so broken? Because "...nothing last forever...;" not even the role of an "UNCLE TOM" or "AUNT TOMISINA"

---

1. See R.B. Moore's "The Name Negro, Its Origin And Evil Use," New York, 1961.

1 = "l" = 50 of FM

can violate this in contemporary times. There comes that time when any man or woman desire to live and act as a human being regardless of the price to be paid. In your author's case, I had to complete what I originally started back there in 1938 C.E./A.D. in San Juan, Puerto Rico, letting the world know that WE:THE BLACK JEWS were not going to sit idly by while even THEY: THE WHITE JEWS continue the myth that "JUDAISM/HEBREWISM IS WHITE [CAUCASIAN/SEMITIC/ INDO-EUROPEAN]." I hope that this work will bring the end to the above that much closer, at least put a terrible rupture, in this MENTAL and PHYSICAL SLAVE CHAIN African/Black People constantly suffer as a result of the EUROPEANIZATION/WHITENING OF JUDAISM and CHRISTIANITY from their teachings in Africa along the Nile Valley and Great Lakes region. For one day "HIS-STORY" will prove, as it always does, that...

"THE FIRST SHALL BE THE LAST, AND THE LAST SHALL BE THE FIRST;"

which I sometimes find doubt in spite of the source. Probably you have already recognized that I read this in somebody's "HOLY BIBLE" - Jewish, Christian and/or Moslem, etc.! But how do you, personally, fit into all of this?; and what is to follow from here on in? Will you read these two volumes and then sit the future out? Will you check the data and become active in your own future? Will you say: "HE IS JUST CRAZY"?, as you may have said so many times before when you failed to do your share to stop "WHITE JEWISH ANTI-BLACKISM" in the past?

WHAT DO THEY CALL THESE BELOW!?

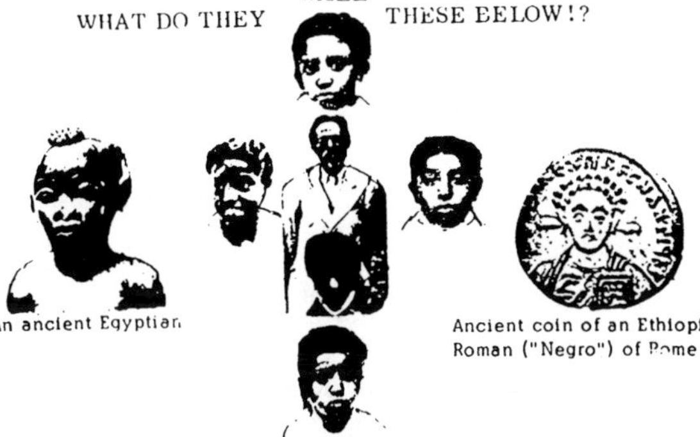

An ancient Egyptian

Ancient coin of an Ethiopian-Roman ("Negro") of Rome

Rabbi Abraham and Falasa ("Jewish") students of Gondar, Ethiopia, East Africa

The above should have prepared us for the following chapter - A PRE-CLIMAX CONCLUSION. This type of presentation will be unusual, but this is the very reason why this work is being done. I am not following the standard course of HIS-STORY for MY-STORY, which will certainly exclude equally HIS-FORMAT, etc. We must establish for our selves, no one else, our own value system. AMEN..RA!

A PRE-CLIMAX CONCLUSION:

What is "A Pre-Climax Conclusion" might be your first question arising from the Chapter of this safari. Well!, it is nothing more than an explanation of a subject to which I have already anticipated the outcome although much of the materials may indicate the need for further studies before I concluded; thus the following:

The fact that His Imperial Majesty, HAILE SELASSIE I, was still reigning monarch of the Empire and Kingdom of Ethiopia, East Africa during the original draft of this manuscript and subsequent completed data of these two volumes in 1954 C.E./A.D., the REVISED EDITION in 1974 C.E./A.D., and even the much later REVISED AND ENLARGED EDITION of the near final manuscript of this latest REVISION in 1983 C.E./A.D., you will understand why certain portions will still appear as if he was Head of the Government of the Empire of Ethiopia even today. Nothing could be further from the truth, as Emperor SELASSIE I was overthrown by his own Armed Forces on 13 SEPTEMBER, 1974 C.E./A.D., which was followed by a very short period of "...HOUSE ARREST..." until his death in Addis Ababa, Ethiopia, 1975 C.E./A.D., of natural cause incidental to old age and a broken spirit caused by his overthrow.

Your author has decided to leave any personal and/or political reaction to and about this one-time very honoured "WORLD LEADER" who fell from grace within his own homeland, and among even members of his own biological family, out of the general project. However, because of the major role he had in modern history at certain instances reference will have to appear in both of these volumes. I will keep to properly documented facts with respect to him, the same as I have always done with others of like or less political stature.

The past Government of the Kingdom and Empire of Ethiopia, East Africa under the rule of His Imperial Highness Emperor Haile Selassie I was no more and no less friendly to the BETA ISRAEL [so-called "Falassa" or "Falasha"] than is the present PEOPLE'S GOVERNMENT of Ethiopia under the rule of Colonel MARIAN MINGHESTU, et al, of the DERGE.[1] The same holds true for the past GOVERNMENT OF ISRAEL under the late Prime Minister DAVID ben-GURION and GOLDA MEIR, along with the current ex-Prime Minister ITZAK RABIN, and also the current Prime Minister MANACHEN BEGIN.[2] The vast majority of European and European-American [WHITE] Jews could care even less about the future of the BETA ISRAEL/"FALASHA" as never once has there been any outcry about the "PERSECUTION OF JEWS [Semites] IN ETHIOPIA" and/or any clamour for their immigration to Israel under "...THE RIGHT OF RETURN..." applied to almost every single WHITE JEW that declared such an interest. Worst of all is the fact

1. The ruling military committee or "junta" that rules Ethiopia under chairman Colonel Minghestu.
2. Not one of these "Prime Minister" was from Asia or Africa like the vast majority of the people.

that the same "Responsible Negroes/Coloreds" who demonstrated before the United Nations Organization's Headquarters Buildings on Sunday, 22 May, 1983 C.E./A.D., as countless times before, protesting "...AGAINST THE OPPRESSION OF JEWS IN SOVIET RUSSIA..." with their "Liberal White Anti-Communist Jews, Christians, Moslems," et al.; not one solitary member of said "... ANTI-COMMUNISTS..." having ever raised a smothering voice in public "PROTEST" against "... WHITE [Caucasian, Caucasian, Indo-European, etc.] JEWISH/SEMITIC RACISM" and/or "RELIGIOUS BIGOTRY..." directed against the "FALASHAS/BLACK JEWS OF ETHIOPIA" and other "AFRICAN/BLACK/ETHIOPIAN JEWS" not of European and European-American -WHITE - creation or "HALACHA" - like the "Sammy Davis" varieties.

Those of us who understand the role of the EUROPEAN/WHITE JEWS in the racist illegitimate so-called "GOVERNMENT OF THE REPUBLIC OF SOUTH AFRICA," along with the official support it enjoys from the racist posture of the present GOVERNMENT OF THE REPUBLIC OF ISRAEL - with regards to African/Black People ["JEWS" included] enslaved in this Hitlerite regine, know too very well that:

> WE MUST FIND OUR OWN SPIRITUAL SALVATION OTHER THAN IN THE STATE OF ISRAEL AND FROM EUROPEAN AND EUROPEAN-AMERICAN JEWS THEREIN.

We know that:

> WE MUST HAVE A DEITY, OR DEITIES, OF OUR OWN AFRICAN/BLACK/ETHIOPIAN MAKING,

which is no less so than European/White Israelis' "DIETY" and/or "DIETIES" created for their own "WHITE RACIST VERSION" of the so-called "HOLY TORAH" or "FIVE BOOKS OF MOSES/ OLD TESTAMENT [of the Christians] and other so-called "GOD INSPIRED SACRED/HOLY WRITINGS," etc. For acts of NAZISM and/or FASCISM seem to be Godly when committed against AFRICAN/BLACK/ETHIOPIAN people by EUROPEAN/WHITE/AMERICAN people as in South Africa, even when said European and European-American [WHITE] people are comprised of former "VICTIMS OF NAZI CONCENTRATION CAMPS" and/or FASCIST ATROCITIES under European and European-American RACISTS and RELIGIOUS BIGOTS in Europe, Great Britain and the so-called "Americas," etc. Too many Europeans and European-Americans have carefully forgotten that NOT ONE SOLITARY AFRICAN/BLACK/ETHIOPIAN HELPED HITLER WITH THE HOLOCAUST and/or MUSSOLINI WITH HIS TORTURES against ANY of the eleven or twelve million Jews, Christians, Moslems, Communists, Atheists, et al., EXTERMINATED anywhere. I wish I could say the reverse for the opposite situation by changing positions with all concern.

"Never Again;" yes!; but not only for what took place by EUROPEAN WHITES against EUROPEAN WHITES for Hitler and Mussolini, et al. This is equally due to the "HOLOCAUSTS" [plural] Africans/Blacks/Ethiopians experienced under such as Cecil John Rhodes, Dr. Jaimeson, Harry Opphenheimer, Captain [later "Lord"] Frederick Lugard, Queen Victoria of England, King Leopold II of the Belgians, Prime Minister Disraeli, the Vanderbilts and Rockefellers, et al., of the United States of America, and the countless others - some of whom descendants are still selling the blood and sweat of the African people in the DIAMOND CENTER of New York City, New York that secures most of all of its DIAMONDS from the NAZIS and FASCISTS of the so-called Republic of South Africa where thousands upon thousands of JEWS, CHRISTIANS, ATHEISTS, et al., acquies in the ENSLAVEMENT and GENERAL EXPLOITATION of African labour. Yes!, NEVER AGAIN with the more than THIRTY to FIFTY MILLION AFRICANS EXTERMINATED in South Africa alone, much the equal amount in the so-called "CONGO FREE STATE" without even adding to any of these the MULTI-MILLIONS ACROSS THE ATLANTIC OCEAN in the so-called "TRIANGULAR TRADE." Yes!; NEVER AGAIN as we remember that they were CHRISTIANS, JEWS, MOSLEMS, et al., as the GRANDEES provided the monies for the SLAVE TRADING OF AFRICANS who are now being blamed for their own victimization by so-called "HIS STORIANS/HISTORIANS" of emotionless qualities called "SCHOLARSHIP," etc.

This project, VOLUME I and VOLUME II, is for all Africans/Blacks/Ethiopians of every RELIGIOUS EXPERIENCE whatever - including JEWS, CHRISTIANS, MOSLEMS, et al., who believe that they alone have the "ONLY TRUE GOD," and those who WORSHIP GODS and GODDESSES strange to the ears and eyes of those who cannot recognize what you will find on the following page - liv. For there is nothing within these pages that is not equally JEWISH, CHRISTIAN and/or MOSLEM, etc. in origin especially whenever the so-called "BLACK-WHITE CONFRONTATION arises. The quicker African/Black/Ethiopian People, no need in fact to mention "BLACK AFRICANS," since there is no other kind anywhere on this Planet EARTH, understand this basic fact as I have shown in the case of the "BLACK JEWS-WHITE JEWS," the better-off all of us will be.

As I wind down this rather sharp "PRE-CLIMAX CONCLUSION," which was meant to be nothing else but "LIKE IT IS," I am more than proud to know that for the very first time to my knowledge someone other than a EUROPEAN or EUROPEAN-AMERICAN will be telling to our own people what we know and feel about ourselves and from our vantage point. Here there is no one other than an African/Black/Ethiopian MAN deciding what we find to be the TRUTH from an AFRICAN PERSPECTIVE. Here we do not care what the opposite side feels should have been said to appease it. Here is the MY STORY/HISTORY of my people - BETA ISRAEL/"FALASHA" or "ETHIOPIAN JEWS" as told by at least one of us. And yes!; it is not the standard way that has raped us for more centuries than we would like to admit. I only wish my mother and father were alive to see that someone of us have the nerve to finally TELL IT LIKE IT WAS and IS without wondering how

THE ANCIENT NILE VALLEY AFRICANS AND THEIR BELIEF IN GOD[S] AND GODDESS[ES] THOUSANDS OF YEARS BEFORE THE CREATION OF YWH, JESUS, AND AL'LAH. Who Is "I AM"?

GODS and GODDESSES of THE BOOK OF THE COMING FORTH BY DAY of Ta-Merry

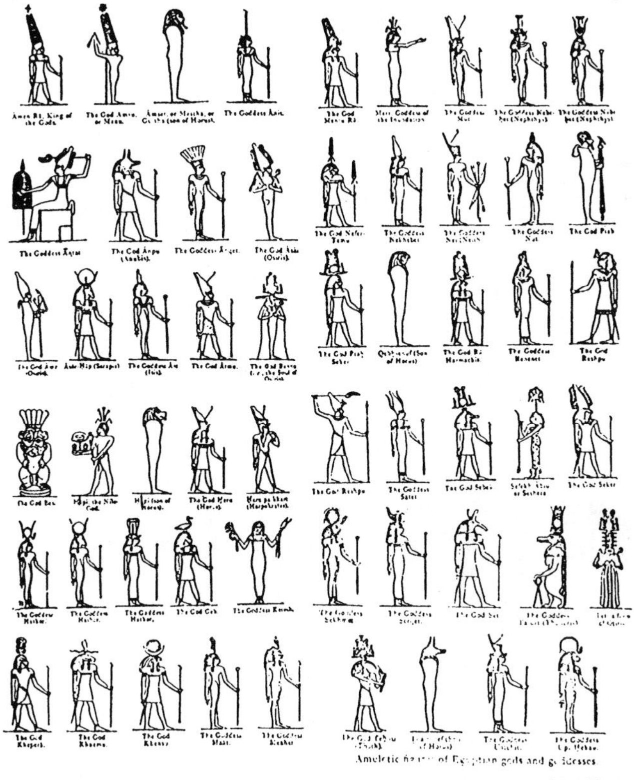

THESE SHALL SUFFICE, BUT OTHERS ARE AVAILABLE

those who have lied about us for so long feel. AMEN, RA, HATHOR, ISIS.......PTAH, et al.

THE AUTHOR/SON OF A BETA ISRAEL

YOSEF ALFREDO ANTONIO ben-JOCHANNAN/JOHANNES[1]
[Photo by Graham A. Stroude, May, 1983]

Who Is So Sacred/Holy That He/She Is Beyond Constructive Criticism?

1. Johannes is the proper spelling in the National Language of Ethiopia - "Amharic;" whereas ben-"Jochannan" is from one of the many languages of Northwest Ethiopia called "Agu/Agaw," etc. Of course there is the Hebrew compliment of "Jochanan," and/or other so-called "Semitic" and also Ethiopic Scripts of the general Red Sea area lands and peoples, etc. In the long run it is what meaning I place on my name; that is: THE LION TAMER - from a most beautiful mother/ancestor.

PRELUDE:

If any justification for all of what I have written in this project, particularly in Volume [Sect.] Two, would be necessary, nothing better than the following article below by Edward B. Fiske could have been much more appropriate at this time. Yet the answer to this dilemma is quite as obvious in the three pages of individual pictures and collages I have shown following this article. Let us examine the entire article first; thus:

NEW YORK TIMES, THURSDAY, FEBRUARY 4, 1971

Ethiopia's Black Jews Are Building in the Wilderness [1]

By EDWARD B. FISKE
Special to The New York Times

AMBOBER, Ethiopia, Jan. 14—Five thousand acres of wilderness in the malaria-infested lowlands of northwestern Ethiopia are becoming something of a 20th-century promised land for 25,000 black Falasha Jews.

The Falashas, whose primitive form of Judaism survived more than 2,000 years in isolation from other Jews, live here in Ambober and other nearby villages where they earn meager livings as sharecroppers, potters and metal workers.

The living patterns of centuries are now threatened by changing economic conditions and a steady loss of young people into urban areas.

As a result, the community has launched a resettlement project 100 miles to the northwest, in the town of Abderafi. Seventy young men have begun farming on new lands obtained with the help of Government officials. Leaders hope that they will become the vanguard of a major population shift that could take decades to complete.

Threat to Traditions

"We must act to keep our young people in the community," said Yona Bogale, the unofficial leader and spokesman for the community. "The survival of our traditions is in danger."

The term Falasha, by which they are usually known, means "stranger" or "immigrant" in the ancient Ethiopian language, Geez. They refer to themselves as Beta Israel, or House of Israel.

The Falashas believe that they, like other Ethiopians, are descendants of King Solomon and the Queen of Sheba.

Others say their ancestors found their way into Ethiopia

The New York Times Feb. 4, 1971
The area of the Falashas is near Gondar (cross).

after the destruction of the First or Second Temples, or even at the time of the Exodus. Still another theory is that they are descendants of an indigenous population converted to Judaism by immigrants from southern Arabia.

Whatever their origin, the Falashas have the black skins of their fellow Ethiopians and speak Amharic, the national language. They also follow local customs such as removing their shoes before entering a place of worship.

Based on Biblical Sources

Their religion, however, is a primitive brand of Judaism that is all their own. It is based almost entirely on Biblical sources, and until they were "discovered" by Europeans in the 19th century they had never heard of the Talmud, the Mishnah, the feasts of Purim and Hanukkah or other elements of the post-Biblical rabbinic tradition.

"Our fathers were surprised to learn that there were other Jews," said Asnakew Sendeke, a 28-year-old Israeli-trained teacher here. "They thought that we were the only ones."

The Falashas consequently call their religious leaders "priests" in the tradition of the Torah and strictly follow the Mosaic laws regarding diet, festivals, circumcision and ritual purification. Their only conspicuous concession to rabbinic Judaism was the abandonment about 50 years ago of animal sacrifice.

The visitor to Ambober is struck by the extent to which their style of life has been almost as immutable as their religious traditions. There are few manufactured items to be seen, and the land is still turned by wooden plows. Transportation is by donkey or foot, usually barefoot.

The village is a bumpy one-hour ride by Land-Rover from Gondar. There are approximately 300 families, almost all of which live in mud huts called tukuls, which are about 15 feet in diameter and covered with straw or tin roofs. Inside are stones set on the dirt floor for cooking and slightly raised beds fashioned of bamboo and sprinkled with straw. The only source of light and ventilation is the door.

In accord with the book of Leviticus, Chapters 12 and 19, women who are menstruating or have given birth must be isolated and undergo ritual purification. On a recent afternoon one of the special huts devoted to this was occupied by a 23-year-old woman named Aragu, who had a son in late December and must remain there 40 days.

---

1. "The wilderness" of Ethiopia is a whole lot more than no where in all of Israel/Palestine, where "the right of return" is racistly denied "Ethiopia's Black Jews" and other Africans.

One-Room Synagogue

During the day the men and older children work in the fields growing teff, wheat, peas and other crops and tending the animals. The women, who cut their hair short and like the men wear toga-like garments of undyed cotton, can be seen taking care of the infants or squatting in their doorways making pottery.

Slightly above the main section of the village is a rectangular one-room synagogue with a Star of David on the roof and a dirt floor covered with mats. Decorative fabrics are hung over parts of the walls, and in one corner is a wooden cabinet containing the Ark.

Nearby are two long, low buildings, one old and one new, that house the village's six-grade school. The classrooms contain crude wooden writing benches, blackboards and cards on the wall with Hebrew letters and other educational aides.

Mr. Asnakew said that there were 154 children in the elementary school but that only 12 attended the secondary school in Gondar. The secondary-school students leave at the beginning of the week carrying their own kosher food and return in time for the sabbath on Friday.

The Falashas receive some support from Jewish philanthropic agencies abroad, mainly for teachers' salaries. That is not sufficient to significantly improve their subsistence level of living, and now the community is facing even more problems than before.

Modern agricultural techniques make it possible for farmers to operate with fewer people, and the Christian landlords, who receive from one-quarter to one-half of all the Falashas grow, are beginning to try to reclaim the land for their own use.

The number of Falashas in the area has already dropped from an estimated 250,000 at the beginning of the century to the present level of about one-tenth of this, and significant numbers of young people are drifting away from the immediate community in search of jobs.

Their cultural survival is also threatened by a group of European missionaries who for decades have been successfully making the Falashas a special target.

Mr. Yona, who was one of four Falashas sent to Europe and Israel to be educated during the 1920's, conceived of the resettlement plan as a way of changing the status of his fellow black Jews from virtual serfs to landowners and of providing incentive to young people to stay within the community.

The Falashas applied to the Government for the right to settle in a new area being opened up near Sudanese border. It has remained undeveloped largely because the climate is hot and humid and malaria is a constant threat.

Two years ago 40 young men began farming in the frontier area, but their crops were burned by Sudanese troops who heard they were Israelis. This year the community took over three new plots of land farther away from the border on the Anquareb River, and 70 men from various villages set out to clear and work it.

Ambiguous Relationship

Thus far the Falashas, who regard themselves as part of world Jewry, have had a somewhat ambiguous relationship to Israel.

The state has welcomed students, and many young Falashas express eagerness to visit Israel and possibly even to emigrate. On the other hand, Mr. Asnakew reported that some Falashas have encountered difficulties because of their color or the inability to match their training with the demands of the modern Israeli economy.

The rabbinical establishment in Israel is also suspicious about the lack of documentation on their origin and less than enthusiastic about their shunning of post-Biblical traditions.

For these reasons many young Falashas are concluding that their future looks brighter in Abderafi than in Jerusalem. "The rabbis discriminate against us, so our people come back," the teacher said. "They say that we're not true Jews."

Author's Note: Emperor Haile Selassie's Government was overthrown in 1974 C.E. Being one of the African rulers tied to the North Atlantic Treaty Organization economically and militarily, his acts of religious bigotry and economic suppression were tolerated by the same lot of White Jews who are presently claiming "...genocide against Ethiopia's Black Jews by Ethiopia's Communist Government...," etc.; all of this only from 1974 C.E. to the present.

Yosef A.A. ben-Jochannan

Certainly the "...Ambiguous Relationship..." the above article speaks of does not now, has not in the past, and apparently will not in the future, come from the so-called "FALASHAS" in Africa, the Americas and/or the Caribbean Islands. The average "...fellow black Jews from virtual serfs to landowners..." with Ethiopian Christians and Moslems have not experienced any better treatment from their so-called "...fellow Jews in the State of Israel..." upon their arrival, nor have since. The RACISTS and RELIGIOUS BIGOTS we Jews have been speaking about when we call others ANTI-SEMITE[1] are surely in our midst. They are called in this article "...The rabbinical establishment in Israel...;" those who are "...also suspicious about the lack of documentation of their " [Falashas] "origin...," but not the "ORIGIN" of any European WHITE Jew.

1. This term is constantly used to suppress all unfavorable comments about any Jewish act.

POINT OUT THE JEWS AMONG THE AFRICANS[1]
YES! FIVE ARE HERE

Maybe you would like to match them with the African-American Jews of the Harlems of the United States of America, called "Negro Jews."

1. Just imagine: most "Western academicians" consider each a "member of a separate race." The irony is that not one is a "Negro;" only "Nilots, Semites, Dark-skinned Caucasians," etc.

ALL OF THEM ARE "SEMITES" AND "HAMITES;" NOT ONE "NEGRO"

Left: Haile Selassie Ist's oldest daughter. Right: Selassie as a little boy.

Center: One of Haile Selassie's late daughters.

Left: An Ethiopian of the Galla People - a "Hamite."

Right: An Egyptian of Arabic and African parentage.

All on this line are of Egyptian origin.

NILE VALLEYS AFRICANS; NOT ONE A "NEGRO"

KEY

1. Ta-Nehisi (Nubia)
2. Ta-Merry (Egypt)
3. Itiopi (Ethiopia)
4. Ta-Nehisi (Meroe)
5. Ta-Merry (Kimit)
6. Ta-Nehisi (Nubia)
7. Bunyoro (Uganda)
8. Puanit (Kenya, etc)

What is the racial difference between the late Princess Tsahi [eldest daughter of Haile Selassie Ist shown at top left and her father[at age six shown on top right] to all of the others above? May-be "Western academicians" can point out the "NEGRO" in some and the "SEMITES" in others! See Yosef ben-Jochannan's BLACK MAN OF THE NILE AND HIS FAMILY, page 183 [1981 Edition].

THESE TWO EXISTED BEFORE JEHOVAH [Ywh or Ywah] MADE MAN AND WOMAN

Ptah, an Egyptian creator-god [from statue in the Manchester Museum]

The strangest chain of events in Egyptian religious history is topped by the XXVIth Dynasty's divine emblem of the figure of one of the Gods named " YWH, YAHWA, YAWHE . . ."etc. written in Hieroglyph  The first FOUR [4] letters mean "DIVINITY"; the last is a picture of the God himself. Note that this Egyptian God was adopted by the Haribu [Hebrews, colloquially " Jews "] in their own mythology about the " CREATION OF THE WORLD." YWH was the name of a very minor God; equally AMON, who later became the "AMEN" at the end of most Jewish and Christian prayers and hymns. "Modern Theologians " have claimed that the word "AMEN" means ". . . SO BE IT," thereby ignoring the "AMEN-RE" and "AMEN-RA" the Haribu African, Moses, also worshipped in the lodges of the Mysteries System of Egypt.

RECONSTRUCTION OF FOSSIL-MAN [1]

Full figure attempt
by
Maurice Wilson.

---

1. Zinjanthropus boise, the reconstructed fossil-man, existed 1,750,000 years before "Adam and Eve in the Garden of Eden." Ptah and Zinjanthropus boise were created in Africa. Strange! ?

This work is arranged in a manner whereby the reader will not be distracted by ever having to search for footnotes. Whenever notes become necessary, most will appear in the text itself.[1]

The basic material content of the text is taken from the written and oral traditional history of the Agaw [Beta Israel or so-called "Falasha, Falassa," etc.], and from first-hand knowledge of the mores, dogmas and other customs practised by my people - another group of so-called "African People." Other peoples' works, particularly those from Europe and European-America, are shown with their sources directly connected thereto.

I feel that it would be unnecessary to write of documents already summarized by other known authors, since the purpose of this work is to help fill in the gaps left by European and European-American Jewish and Christian "missionaries" and "writers" on the history of my people; also to correct to some degree the inaccuracies which I have found in such works.

Sources on the communities are from my first-hand knowledge of my people, due to my being a son of a Falasha, also from the Pentateuch - otherwise known as the Sacred Torah [Old Testament, Holy Scriptures, Orit, etc.], and Falasha works in the language of Gheeze [Geeze, etc., one of the past national languages of the Kingdom and Empire of Ethiopia]. Certain portions of this work also stem from the Agu and Old Coptic writings of the Falasha communities. Agu and Old Coptic are ancient languages of Ethiopia, the former even predated the origin of the Hebrew ["Israelite"] people and religion sometime during ca. 1775 and 1675 B.C.E., which of course was thousands of years before the "first European civilization" [Greece] came into existence; a language that is presently used by very few Ethiopians. Geeze [Gheeze], on the other hand, is solely used by the Ethiopian Orthodox [formerly Coptic] Christian Church for liturgies today.

Illustrations are hand-designed to bring out details that photography would have failed to expose. Pictures of the African-American Hebrews [Ethiopian Jews] of Harlem, New York City, New York were made by photography because of the simplicity of details and the familiarity with the type of photographic materials herein used by European-American Hebrew Jewish Communities. Collages are composed of many photographs; most of them new, a few from my other published and/or unpublished works.

Special acknowledgement must be given to Mr. Marcellus Portilla for many of the illustrations [ink drawings] we created together in order to bring a visual picture of certain hand-painted Falasha pottery, life-style, etc. Miss Effie Mathis of Tuskegee, Alabama, who was a student at the time I translated the primary draft of this work from the original Spanish Edition as I equally lectured at Columbia University Teachers College, and where she also studied, for her reading and criticism of the manuscript. Acknowledgement also goes to Rev. C.V. Howell for his major

1. Notes of this nature are only added information which have distracted the reader if they appeared in the main text.

efforts in urging me to undertake this task, and for his suggestions as to what type of information the "Christian community" would like to know about my people - the so-called "Falashas." Particular acknowledgement is due the "Pro-Falasha Students Committee" I headed during the 1950's for its unselfish aid in advising me on all matters and in making this publication possible when I considered the undertaking too strenuous because of my regular work with the United Nations Economic, Scientific and Cultural Organization [U.N.E.S.C.O.] and my Visiting Lectureship at Teachers College. To Miss Mildred Bann for typing the original handwritten translations with all of the editing and corrections there were. It must be noted that the original work was translated into English as early as January 1950, and typed in June 1953. The people and organizations referred to above were all connected in the above manner stated during said periods.

My appreciation is gratefully expressed to all who allowed me to quote from their own works, and to those who have allowed me to take pictures or make other illustrations of their activities and groups. In this respect I am most grateful to the late Rabbi Wentworth Matthew, leader of the African-American Ethiopian Hebrew Congregation of Commandment Keepers in Harlem, New York City, New York; Rabbi Marshall and Rabbi Ford of Brooklyn, New York City, New York; and of course the wise old "sage" Rabbi E. Eleazer from the Falasha Community of Ambober, Ethiopia, East Africa who has equally passed on to glory.

For further readings about the "sacred writings and teachings" of the Falashas I recommend the works of Dr. Jacques Faitlovitch, much of which is available in the Hertzl Institute Library at 59 - 60th Street and Park Avenue, New York City, New York; and Professor Wolf Leslau, "FALASHA ANTHOLOGY," Yale University Press, New Haven, Connecticut, 1951. The latter's recommendation applies solely to the "sacred writings" given therein, and nothing else, as I am in total disagreement with most of what he wrote with regards to the origin and history of my own people - the "Beta Israel, Kylas" and "Agaw" [so-called "Falashas,"etc.] For example, on page xliii of the "INTRODUCTION" of Leslau's book he too repeated the unfounded theory most of his fellow European and European-American Jews that associate "WHITENESS" with Judaism always write about the Falashas and/or Kylas:

"THE FALASHAS WERE CONVERTED TO JUDAISM."

Other sources recommended are Louis Rittenberg [Edited], THE UNIVERSAL JEWISH ENCYCLOPEDIA, published by The Universal Jewish Encyclopedia, Inc., New York City, New York; Dr. Jacques Faitlovitch's NOTES D'UN VOYAGE CHEZ LES FALACHAS; Ephraim ben-Malachai's MY PEOPLE THE JEWS [a very small pamphlet], London, 1918; Princess Asfa Yilma's HAILE SELASSIE EMPEROR OF ETHIOPIA, 1935 [with "foreword" by the Minister Extraordinary of Ethiopia, Honourable Warqneh Martin]; and the PRO-FALASHA COMMITTEE

OF AMERICA REPORTS, New York City, New York, 1937 - 1941, same of which may still be housed in the Jewish Theological Seminary at 122nd Street and Broadway, New York City, New York, or at The American Pro-Falasha Committee, 507 Fifth Avenue, New York, N.Y. 10017].[1]

The arrangement of this volume is intentional, since I wanted to accomplish the same result as in 1953 when I first decided to translate NOSOTROS HEBREOS NEGRO to WE THE BLACK JEWS as I have done in Volume One. However, you will also observe in Volume Two the transformation from a "ZIONIST" perspective to a "PAN-AFRICAN" involvement was achieved. And that I have been able to see beyond the narrow path of my JUDAIC religious background to the much broader international scope of my PAN-AFRICANIST ideology. Like all of the other people of Africa [BLACK PEOPLE], I had to go through a period of RETRO and INTROSPECTION about where I must rest my future: -with White-Semitic-Caucasian European-American, etc. "Zionism" that excludes me because of my "THICK LIPS, BROAD NOSE, WOOLLY HAIR, BURNT SKIN," etc., or with "Pan-Africanism" that opened its outstretched arms of my mother Alkebu-lan - whom the Greeks and Romans renamed "AFRICA," or "AFRIKA" [see page 24 for various other names].

Volume Two of this project gives the total perspective of a former "BLACK JEW" who found it intolerable and impossible to continue being a hypocrite by going to worship a God - YWH, ADONI, JEHOVAH, etc. - with fellow coreligionists who would have been that much better off had I not shown my "BLACK SKIN" and so-called "NEGROID CHARACTERISTICS" within the walls of their SYNAGOGUE [House of Worship]. However, this rejection on my part does not bind any other African Jew to my position; neither does it make any other person's participation good or bad because he or she remains under the guide of ZIONISM and the belief in a "PROMISED LAND" somewhere in Asia, rather than in "Mother Alkebu-lan." For this reason I am explaining in the text what my people have done, their customs and traditions in biblical and secular JUDAISM, and their response to European and European-American "TALMUDIC [Rabbinical] JUDAISM" as against our own African and African-American TORAHDIC JUDAISM and/or "WAY OF LIFE," etc.

I do hope that the reader will be able to make the distinction between the reporting I am doing in Volume One and the analytical criticism in Volume Two. In Volume One I am reporting without making any analysis of RIGHT and/or WRONG. The issue in the areas of Volume Two's analysis relative to the history and heritage of the African-American people in the Americas and the Caribbean Islands reflects a few similar problems as those of Black Jews in Mother Alkebu-lan/Africa. Thus it is that you can read an anthropological report of another group of African People without the usual "TRIBE, PRIMITIVE, NATIVE, HEATHEN, UNCIVILIZED, CONVERT," etc. semantical diatribe common in the writings of all European and European-American "academicians." This

1. This group probably change address to other quarters before the end of this manuscript. Dr. Moshe Finklestein of the Jewish Theological Seminary was its President. He's retired.

type of racism and/or religious bigotry is, never the less, American as "Ice Cream and Pie."

Your author has agreed to write this presentation on the Falashas after repeated requests from Jews and Gentiles alike. These people so requesting have heard of the Falashas through reading books written by Western authors who have paid very short visits to Ethiopia and came backto write about the entire history of my people. Among my previously mentioned friends it was decided that at least one Falasha now living in the "Western World," and specifically America, must write about his [or her] people in Ethiopia and the "Western Countries." After giving many lectures about my people I agreed to undertake this task. I had rejected it on previous occasions because of my involvement in the fight to free My Mother "AFRICA" from White colonialism. The latter task was directed through United Nations' channels with which I was also connected. It is but one of the many ways of gaining our independence. However I had to agree, for there are very few Falashas here to whom this group of people could turn. A "Committee" was formed to gather and suggest points which most African-American and European peoples of all religions and every walk of life would like to know about us. The "Committee" was disbanded when it became obvious that funds would not be available for the publication of this work.

This work, the original Spanish Edition, was the introduction to the much more expanded works I have presented in my many volumes which I have written and published. In this Edition I presented all of the existing Falasha religious writings and historical data in their English translation. This task, you will understand, took a lot of time; yet we, the Falasha Committee, worked at the fastest speed possible. All of us that were connected with this latter project were professionals in many fields of endeavour to which we contributed the greater portion of our time daily.

At the many places where it has been my good fortune to give lectures I have been consistently asked to suggest materials written in the English language about the Falashas. Questions such as the following are always placed to me, thus:

> "Why don't the Falashas in the United States of America present articles about themselves in American Jewish periodicals? What about that book by Professor Wolf Leslau called FALASHA ANTHOLOGY, etc. ? Why don't your people let other Jews know that you are alive and that you have a history like your other brothers and sisters of the Hebrew Faith who came to America from Europe? Why doesn't Rabbi Matthew of the Black Community in Harlem write about his community? Why isn't there a movement to organize a community synagogue where all Jews can meet together regardless of color, thereby closing the gap that exist between our two groups?"

Other questions like the above could go on and on forever and ever without exhaustion. Yet, this work was the preview of the answer before my much more expanded works were completed and published, of course in its original shorter edition, and without Volume Two, etc.

The late Reverend Clarence Howell of "Community Church Center" at 40 East 35th Street, New York City, New York offered free his facilities to my service. Only expenses paid by him were to be reinbursed by me for the production of the book. His organization - "Reconciliation Trips, Inc." - of the above address assisted me also. Here at the Howell's organization was where I began correcting the many untruths that were passed on about my people in Ethiopia, East Africa, the Caribbean Islands and the Americas, all of which I had already done when I wrote the original edition of NOSOTROS HEBREOS NEGRO [We The Black Jews]; but all of which it had become necessary once again to do with specific interest on the African-American [BLACK] Jews in Harlem, New York City, New York and throughout the United States of America.

I decided that this work had to meet the price range of the poor student and general reading public. Therefore, we had to use "short-cut" methods of producing this work in its final stage as a book. It was also planned in a manner whereby I would not be forced to cut the amount of information I wanted to produce. And you can readily notice that it is very extensive, not costly. Any such cut would have been harmful to the factual presentation of this work. I could not take such chances of hurting the history of the cultural development of my people, thereby falling into the path of giving misleading information as European and European-American missionaries and other writers have done for over two hundred [200] years to date.

The Joint Committee For The Publication Of We The Black Jews, which I had established in 1953 C.E., felt that I should deal...

> "with matters which might be considered non-kosher in the realm of certain critics of the authenticity of the Falashas as Jews"....

This they believed, as they could observe that I was going to meet head-on resistance whenever I begin to show any disagreement with other writers of the past and present European, and surely European-American, origin on the subject of the "BLACK JEWS" [Falashas, Falassa, Kylas]. It was also felt that:

> "There could be no better way to help in the elimination of the fallacies about the Black Jews than by calling the shots as I know them, and let the axe fall wherever it may."

Then we would be prepared to meet any self-appointed authority on our people's history. The committee further agreed that I...

> "should not use quotations from any source which we could not verify to be true upon our own investigation and research, irrespective of the reputation of the author"....

This latter condition made it very hard on your author, because it meant that I had to keep writing back home to Ethiopia for all of the information I did not know first-hand which was of major importance to the full text of the general work at hand. My people at home made this task extremely easy by giving each and every letter prompt attention, and by even adding more information on each point than I had requested. The documents I requested were of historical data that were not available in the best of libraries any place in the United States of America at that time, some being unavailable to the present time. They included such items as the "KEBRA NEGASTE [Ethiopian Chronicles]" and the "SACRED WRITINGS OF THE AGAW [Falashas] COMMUNITIES." Other information than these sources are generally based upon my personal knowledge, and that of other Falashas living or studying in the United States of America, South America and the so-called "West Indies"[Caribbean Islands]in general.

We, from here meaning the Ad Hoc Committee of the Joint Committee For The Publication Of We The Black Jews, came to another conclusion that:

> "the book must be written in a manner which can be easily read and understood by children of public school level."

We wanted to reach the minds of everyone interested, also those who by chance come in contact with this work.

We had agreed that"...

> no praising, or decrying, of people should be resorted to...;"

and that I should "...

> have a work on as high a plateau that one could possibly produce; only with observations of the facts as they are known to be, and you experienced them. . . ."

Mr. Israel ben-Addi of Harlem's African-American ["BLACK"] Hebrew Community was called upon to make contacts for the presentation of the history of his group. His cooperation cannot be overrated when we say that this work could not have been possible without the aid that he has given me in presenting the chapters on the Ethiopian-American Hebrew Communities and the African-American Hebrews; particularly where comparisons became necessary.

The "Joint Committtee" wishes to join me in thanking you for your interest in reading this account of my people and yours - the "AGAW" or "AGU" [the so-called Falashas], all of whom are better known as BETA ISRAEL or CHILDREN [OF THE HOUSE] OF ISRAEL. This was the manner in which the "Introduction" ended when the first draft was written in January, 1953.

POST SCRIPT:

There are many points stressed in this project of which I am in total discord as they are presently practiced by my people in their communities in Africa, the United States of America, the Caribbean Islands and the Americas generally. But I shall not take issue with them in Volume One of this project, as it is my express purpose to bring you a report of the WAY OF LIFE of

ALL OF THESE ARE "SEMITES" AS THE CAUCASIAN "JEWS"

Peasant Prisoners on the Tomb of Pharaoh Horemneb[1]

!!! "THICK LIPS, BROAD NOSES, WOOLLY HAIR AND BURNT SKIN"[2]

Pharaoh Djoser, IIIrd Dynasty, c.2780 - 2680. The STEP PYRAMID OF SAKHARA. First of the COLOSSAL PYRAMIDS.

Pharaoh AMONEMHAT III XIIth Dynasty (Cairo Museum)

GREAT SPHINX OF GHIZEH

Right: A "TYPICAL" African of the type commonly found all along the Nile Valley (Blue and White) to the present day, 1972).

Left: Pharaoh Neb-Maat-Ra, mighty ruler and builder of the the 17th Pyramid.

---

1. Do not fail to note the myth that "the AFRICANS [so-called"Negroes"] were only SLAVES in Egypt" ignores that Egypt was an African country ruled by Africans until foreign invasions from Asia and Europe.
2. See Herodotus' "The Histories [Euterpe]," Greece, 450 B.C.E., on the Egyptians, et al.

WHAT MAKES ONE A "NEGRO" AND THE OTHER A "SEMITE, HAMITE, NILOT" ETC.?
THICK LIPS, BROAD NOSE, WOOLLY HAIR AND ALL SEMITES

Egyptian Women Making Perfume

"Semitic prisoners" [slaves] " of war pleading for mercy to Pharaoh Haremheb

SUTHERN/NILE VALLEY BEAUTIES OF AFRICA

NOT ONE OF THESE IS A "NEGRO" OF ANY TYPE WHATSOEVER. WHY NOT? EXPLAIN!

my people, and not a CRITICAL ANALYSIS of them here.

However, I wish to state that there is quite a strong force working at the present time to develop a better relationship between Falashas and other Ethiopians, and also to bridge the gap of distrust created by "Westerners" -most of whom are not Jews, who assumed to write as the sole "AUTHORITY" on the Falasha communities both in "Africa" and the "Americas."

I hope that persons now planning to visit our communities in Ethiopia and anywhere else in the world would remember that any talk of "CONVERSION" to my people would be met by the greatest of hostility possible; this even holds true for "CONVERSION" to Talmudic [Rabbinical] Judaism, and more so European and European-American Christianity or Arabian [Asian] Mohammedanism [Islam]. I do know that matters will be mutual if this latter point is heeded and said desire is left at home before visiting the Falasha communities. But I do think that an elaboration on the above reasons is necessary here; thus the following paragraph:

We were not trying to change the position of not permitting Gentiles to visit our homes. Yet it could be modified to have some provisions made whereby Gentiles may stay in the Falasha communities after Sundown [Sun-Fall or Sun-Set]. But, it must be noted that Gentiles do not necessarily mean Christians only, as all other non-Jews must leave a Falasha community in Ethiopia by Sundown.

The rule stated in the last paragraph above is due to the "LAWS ON CLEANLINESS" and many other functions of which the Christians and other Gentiles will have to undergo if they were to remain in a Falasha home or community after Sundown; such as "RITUAL BATHS," etc. It is no doubt that such a demand would be offensive to many. This disadvantage would work in a very difficult manner to all concerned in such a situation. Again, I remind you that:

I AM YOUR REPORTER IN THIS WORK; NOT YOUR ANALYST OF CONCLUSIONS ABOUT THE RIGHT AND WRONG OF FALASHA THEOSOPHY.

You will have to decide what better way was there to begin this "safari" than with this Introduction into "THE FALLACY OF A JEWISH RACE, SEMITIC RACE" and/or "HAMITIC RACE" as shown on the following page with regards to the Falasha Elder and Maiden, both of whom are no different than the Harlem Jews shown on pages 295 through 310 of Volume Two. Thus we can see the first step in this ironic RACIST MYTH in the following article extracted from the noted LONDON JEWISH CHRONICLE of April 1973,[1] which brings into fruition what your author has maintained from the beginning when I wrote the original Spanish Edition of this very much larger expanded work in 1934 - 1936 C.E. But the declarations in the 8th paragraph with reference to the "...RUSSIAN JEWS..." and the FALASHAS regarding "...THE LAW OF THE RETURN...,"

1. Here is added proof of "Zionist Racism" the Arabs could have cited at the United Nations Org.

WHAT IS "SEMITIC" or "HAMITIC FEATURES?"
WHAT IS THE "SEMITIC COLOR?"

TYPICAL FALASHA faces. The [illegible] above, who is the wea[illegible] of Ambober, has almost pure Semitic features, while the [illegible] at right shows Hamitic fea[illegible]

WHAT IS IT ABOVE THAT IS NOT IN THE JEWS OF HARLEM?

THE FALASHAS are a Judaic tribe living in the highlands of Ethiopia whose origins date back to Biblical times. They faithfully keep the precepts of the Torah but know nothing of later Rabbinic laws. Above, a kohen in the village of Ambober reads the Torah at a Sabbath service. At right is the door to the local synagogue decorated in Hebrew and Geez, an ancient Semitic language now used only for prayer by both the Falashas and the Ethiopian Christians. At far right is a general view of Ambober showing the synagogue in the background, several tekels, round thatched huts in which most Falashas live, and the "modern" home of a teacher trained in Israel. Ambober also boasts of piped water, bottom left, installed by an Israeli a few years ago.

IS IT NOT TRUE THAT "SEMITIC" and/or "HAMITIC" REFER
TO LANGUAGE DESIGNATIONS!;
NEVER "RACE"?

the 11th paragraph about "...THE FALASHAS AS JEWS OR WHO HAVE REGARDED THESE PRIMITIVE PEOPLE AS AN UNDESIRABLE ELEMENT IN THE COUNTRY...," the 13th paragraph that "...THE ETHIOPIANS - CHRISTIANS AND JEWS ALIKE - CLAIM DESCENT FROM THOSE JEWS...," etc., and the 14th paragraph that "...THERE IS NOTHING IN JEWISH LITERATURE TO SUBSTANTIATE THIS THEORY...," do nothing more than show the Falashas inside and outside of Ethiopia that "RACISM" is as much a part of Israel's WHITE JEWS basic socio-political-religious fabric against BLACK JEWS as it is among WHITE JEWS in the United States of America against BLACK JEWS in the HARLEMS of the so-called "Western World." Yet, at least there was "Chief Rabbi Ovadia Yosef" in Israel, and only an ordinary Rabbi Block [see page 303 of Volume Two when he was a student Rabbi] in the United States of America. However, more than all of this, whether "...FROM THE TRIBE OF DAN...," or from any of the other "TRIBES", the FALASHAS and/or anyother type of "BLACK JEWS" do not have to prove **OUR** heritage as "JEWS" to anyone more so than European and European-American [white] JEWS have to prove their so-called "JEWISHNESS" to us. And the fact that "...ELDAD HA-DANI..." was "...THE FIRST" [White Jew] "TO WRITE ABOUT THE FALASHAS UP TO THE 17th CENTURY C.E...." has absolutely nothing to do with the "ORIGN" and/or so-called "DISCOVERY" of the Falashas. But, when will the European and European-American [WHITE] Jews realize that our "JUDAISM" is not a so-called "SEMITIC RACE" controlled by themselves; and that time is on the side of the rejected BLACK JEWS - Yemenites, Falashas, Cochins, Arabians, North Africans; and yes, those of the Americas and the Caribbean Islands? The following article does not mention the "COCHIN JEWS" of India;[1] but did the Sephardi Chief Rabbi of Israel equally had to declare that those below "...ARE JEWS..." in any ruling? Unfortunately, Rabbi Yosef lost his post during the 1983 Rabbinical Elec- tions for Chief Rabbi of Israel for Sephardi Jews. He was defeated by an Iraqi Rabbi Mordecai Eliahu.

1. The general body of Asian Jews are treated with the same type of "benign neglect" like African American/Blacks in the United States of America and Jews of Ethiopia, etc.

LONDON JEWISH CHRONICLE, April 1973

Chief Rabbi Yossef[1] officially recognises Falashas as Jews

From a Special Correspondent

Rabbi Ovadia Yossef, the Sephardi Chief Rabbi of Israel, has given a rabbinical ruling that the Falashas of Ethiopia are Jews and has accepted their claim that they are the descendants of the Tribe of Dan. Rabbi Yossef has also accepted the presidency of a public council on behalf of the Falashas, of whom there are some 26,000 in Ethiopia, calling themselves Beta Israel.

In a letter dated February 9, 1973, Rabbi Yossef wrote to Mr **Ovadia Hazi, who speaks on behalf of some of the Jews of Ethiopia in Israel, informing him of his ruling.**

After quoting a number of eminent religious authorities who had earlier ruled that the Falashas were Jews, including the late Rabbi Avraham Kook, Ashkenazi Chief Rabbi of Palestine, and the late Rabbi Itzhak Herzog, Ashkenazi Chief Rabbi of Israel, Rabbi Yossef continued.

"I have therefore come to the conclusion that the Falashas are descendants of the Tribes of Israel who went southwards to Ethiopia, and there is no doubt that the above Sages, who established that they [the Falashas] are of the Tribe of Dan, investigated and inquired and reached this conclusion on the basis of the most reliable witnesses and evidence.

"I, too, a young man of the Tribes of Israel, have investigated and inquired well into their matters after the leaders of the Falashas had applied to me with the request to be joined to our people, the House of Israel, in the Spirit of the Torah and the halacha, the Written Law and the **Oral Law,** without any restriction, **and** to perform all the mitzvot of the holy Torah according to the instructions of our Sages . . . and I have decided that—in my humble opinion—the Falashas are Jews, whom it is our duty to redeem **from assimilation, to hasten their immigration into Israel, to educate them in the spirit of our holy Torah and to make them partners in the building of our sacred** land. . . .

"I am certain that Government **institutions and** the Jewish Agency, as well **as organisations** in Israel and the **diaspora,** will help us to the best of their ability in this holy task that you, sir, have taken upon yourself. This task is the mitzva of redeeming the souls of our people . . . for everyone who saves one soul in Israel, it is as though he had saved the whole world. . . ."

Chief Rabbi Yossef

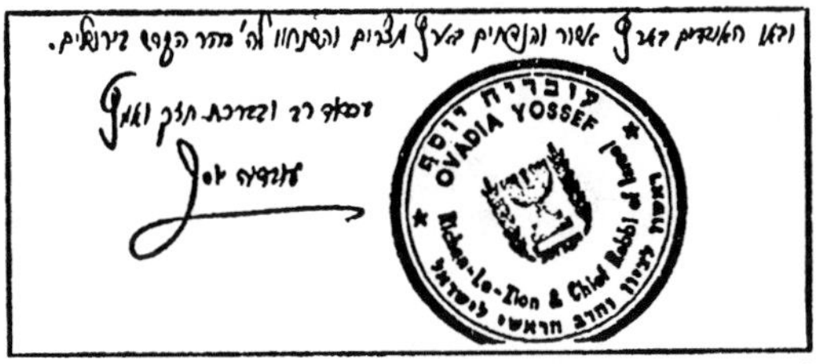

The last lines of Rabbi Yossef's letter to a Falasha spokesman in Israel, with his signature and official stamp

A correspondent writes:

There can be no doubt that this letter from the Sephardi Chief Rabbi of Israel, representing the largest religious community in the country, is of historic importance.

While it will no doubt bring great comfort to the Falasha community in Ethiopia, together with those few who have already settled in Israel, it may create something of an embarrassment for the Israeli authorities.

If Chief Rabbi Yossef declares that the Falashas are Jews who should be brought speedily to Israel, they must surely be entitled to invoke the Law of the Return to facilitate this. If Russian Jews are able to come, they will ask, why should they may not also be admitted.

This may raise an awkward diplomatic problem with Ethiopia, with which Israel has strong and friendly ties. It is known that Emperor Haile Selassie is opposed to a mass emigration of Falashas and, up to the present, the Israeli Government has been careful not to encourage it for fear of damaging relations between the two countries.

If a clamour should now arise for a mass movement of the 26,000 or more Ethiopian Jews, the Israeli Government will have to negotiate their emigration with the Ethiopian authorities while attempting to maintain their present excellent relations.

In Israel itself, the Sephardi Chief Rabbi's declaration may be

---

1. He fought racism and religious bigotry against "Black Jews" by Israel's "White Zionists" and others elsewhere. Maybe it caused his defeat as "Sephardi Chief Rabbi of Israel"!

looked upon askance by certain sections of the population who have either refused to recognise the Falashas as Jews or who have regarded these primitive people as an undesirable element in the country.

On the other hand, the acute shortage of labour will encourage others, particularly employers, to welcome them as an economic asset.

The tradition that the Falashas are descended from the Tribe of Dan may stem from the possibility that members of the tribe, which had maritime connections, were among the crews of King Solomon's Red Sea trading vessels and some could have reached Ethiopia and settled there.

Moreover, the Ethiopians — Christians and Jews alike—claim descent from those Jews who accompanied the legendary Menelik, the son of King Solomon and the Queen of Sheba when he returned from Israel to Ethiopia bearing, according to the legend, the Ark of the Covenant.

However, there is nothing in Jewish literature to substantiate this theory. The origins of the Falashas' claim to be descendants of the Tribe of Dan can be traced back only as far as the ninth century C.E., in the writings of the Jewish traveller, Eldad Ha-Dani.

He caused a stir with his purported revelations about tho lost Ten Tribes, which were partly based on the existence of a Jewish kingdom in Ethiopia, which preserved its independence until the beginning of the 17th century C.E.

The HUMILIATING TRAGEDY of a proud people - the AGAW or FALASHAS - is demonstrated in the preceding article. But it is more than surpassed in the following article. Thus, let us examine further the type of characterization and distortion of the reserved history of the "BLACK JEWS," whether they are from Ethiopia, India, Yemen or New York City's Harlem. For at this juncture we are to read from page 3 of the JEWISH CURRENT EVENTS, February 16 - 28, 1974, Vol. 15 - Number 10 [published at 430 Kesler Avenue, Elmont, N.Y. 11003, and edited by Mr. Samuel Deutsch] the extract I have shown on page xxxii and page xxxiii dealing with Jewish racism.

I have underscored some of the highlights which must have offended each and every BLACK JEW who read this article, as you will notice such comments that drew the following responses: Which, or whose, "...WORLD KNEW LITTLE ABOUT THEM" [Falashas]? Yemenites, Cochins, Sudanese, Kenyans, Arabs, Zarians, etc. knew of and about the so-called "FALASHAS" for centuries. The fact that Europeans and European-Americans did not know about US changes nothing about OUR existence as "AFRICANS" of Ethiopia - first; and as "HEBREWS" or "JEWS" -second. Next, what does the Editor mean by we were "...DISCOVERED... ?" Who discovered us? We were never in history LOST, a fact which I am constantly saying to the rumor mongers who proverbially put out this type of propaganda on the Falashas. "ETHIOPIA IS THE OLDEST KINGDOM..." not only "...IN AFRICA..." today, but in the entire world. And, there are many hundreds more than a "FEW FALASHAS" who "OWN THEIR OWN FARMS... " Tell us about those owned by the Kyla and others in communal communities of the Ethiopian Highlands?

The most nauseating aspect of the following article is in the fact that we are told : "ALREADY 250 FALASHAS ARE IN THE COUNTRY" [Israel]. "THEY NOW ARE RECOGNIZED AS FULL JEWS, BUT MUST GO THROUGH THE PROCESS OF CONVERTING AND RE-ACCEPTING JUDAISM." But who decided that the Jews with the most ancient traditions to date must conform to their own version of "JUDAISM" Rabbinical Talmudic-style? The article will tell us more; but it will not identify the "KOSHER JEW MAKERS." Let us read Deutsch's editorial on Ethiopia's Jews:

1. "The origin of European and European-American Jews are to be proved" by whom?

WHOSE "WORLD KNEW LITTLE ABOUT THEM" [FALASHAS/BLACKS]?

JEWISH CURRENT EVENTS 3

CONCERN IS FELT FOR ETHIOPIA'S BLACK JEWS;[1] 25 THOUSAND REMAIN AFTER MANY CENTURIES

ETHIOPIA:—Concern is being felt for the future of Ethiopia's 25 thousand remaining *Falashas.*

The Falashas live mainly in mud huts. Most of them are farmers. They rent the farms on which they work.

The Falashas are black Jews. They were discovered about 100 years ago. Till then the world knew little about them. At one time they numbered 70 thousand.

Ethiopia is the oldest kingdom in Africa. Its capital is Addis Ababa.

The Falashas share the crops with the owners. They live a very poor life. Few own their own farms.

SELASSIE

Now, the farm owners need the land. The government, therefore, plans to relocate nearly 1½ thousand Falasha families to other parts of the country.

It is feared they thus would mix with the rest of the population and gradually give up their Jewish practices.

Israeli leaders are considering ways to help them settle in Israel. Already 250 Falashas are in the country. They now are recognized as full Jews, but must go through the process of converting and re-accepting Judaism.

Ethiopia's King

Ethiopia's king, Haile Selassie, has many titles. One is *King of Kings and Conquering Lion of Judah.*

The country's emblem shows a lion wearing a gold crown. The lion and crown also are Jewish symbols Both can often be seen on Torah mantles or on ark covers where the Torahs are kept.

A "FALASHA" SYNAGOGUE IN ETHIOPIA

Ethiopia's king believes his ancestors were the Queen of Sheba and King Solomon of Bible days.

On the outskirts of Ethiopia's ancient capital is the tomb of the Queen of Sheba. Selassie is the country's 225th king, the longest succession of kings in history.

A FALASHA TORAH

The country's language is called *Amharic.* It is a branch of the same language family as Hebrew. It is called a Semitic language.

The "Falashas"

The Falashas, or black Jews, live mostly in separate small villages. Their synagogues often are small huts. The Torahs are in an ancient language called *"gheez."*

A few scholars believe the Falashas settled in Ethiopia when the first Temple was destroyed about 2½ thousand years ago.

A "FALASHA" WARRIOR

Within Ethiopia, some believe, they are the remnants of the 10 lost tribes of Israel.

They brought with them many religious practices and have observed them ever

---

1. Why!, because Israel needs "Black Jewish Bodies" to replace "White Deserters" to the U.S.A.

Interrupting once more; the late Emperor's symbols were used in Africa before "Adam and Eve."

sinc.

The Falashas practice a few dietary laws, the Sab-bath, and observe all Jewish holidays except Chanuka and Purim.

Their Observances

The Falashas observe only the Bible laws. They don't accept the laws found in the Talmud or other religious books. Their observance of the Sabbath is very strict.

Their religious leader is called the *"Kohain"* (high priest).

Falashas are known to be good fighters and warriors. They excel in the army. Most of them are tall and they are good marksmen.

Cleanliness

They keep themselves very clean and take daily baths in running water. Visitors to their villages must first bathe in running water, as they do.

Some Falasha synagogues have an opening on top so that the worshipers may see the sky. Outdoor services often are held in market places where Falasha men come to sell their wares.

Falashas don't have last names. Many believe the word Falasha means "stranger." They were thus called when they first settled there.

Helped By Israel

Israel has helped Ethiopia over the years. Israeli ambulances were donated for use in poor Ethiopian villages. Selassie greeted the Israeli ambulance team of doctors personally when they delivered the gifts.

Israel also has helped Ethiopia establish a meat packing plant which now is one of the country's largest employers.

Israeli doctors, too, have served in Ethiopian hospitals and have helped train staff. They also have set up an ambulance system for the country.

Ethiopia often issues stamps showing lions, the nation's symbol for courage. Some also contain 6-pointed stars, similar to the 6-pointed Jewish Star of David.

Ethiopia recently turned against Israel and has sided with the Arabs in the present oil conflict.—*S.D.*

FALASHA PUPIL IN ISRAEL

KING SELASSIE GREETS ISRAELI AMBULANCE TEAM

After reading the above, it is obvious that a few more questions and observations become that much more necessary at this time. But it is the last observation which really is the most nauseating. Who is the AUTHORITY Ywh commissioned to separate "JEWS" on the basis of so-called "ETHNIC PEOPLE, SEMITIC RACE, HAMITIC RACE" and the likes? Is it not true that the "AUTHORITY" comes from the power of those in control of GUN POWDER, THE STATE and RELIGIOUS PROPAGANDA? Black Jews, even in their/our own "PROMISED LAND" - Israel, equally are not wanted because of their/our "BLACK COLOR" and "AFRICAN RACE," etc.

At this point there needs to be no more underscoring. The last observation is more than enough to explain the SEMITIC and/or WHITE RACISM in Israel that controls the destiny of all of the BLACK JEWS - Cochin, Yemenite, Falasha, etc. But why don't the WHITE RUSSIAN JEWS shown below from page 1 of the same publication and editor on November 16 - 30, 1973, Vol. 15, Number 4 have"... TO GO THROUGH THE PROCESS OF CONVERTING AND RE-ACCEPTING JUDAISM..." like the BLACK [African] JEWS? The answer: Plain and simple WHITE RACISM by those European and European-American Jews that control Israel. Their fellow WHITE JEWS are exempt, although they may not know the first fact about the Hebrew Religion or Culture.

RUSSIAN JEWISH FAMILY IN NEW HOME IN ISRAEL

THE ABOVE "JEWS" DO NOT GO THROUGH THE PROCESS OF CONVERTING AND RE-ACCEPTING JUDAISM; THOSE AT THE BOTTOM MUST. WHY?[1]

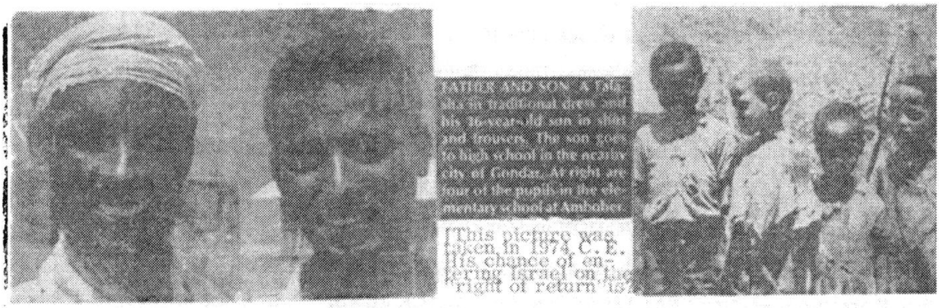

FATHER AND SON. A Falasha in traditional dress and his 16-year-old son in shirt and trousers. The son goes to high school in the nearby city of Gondar. At right are four of the pupils in the elementary school at Ambober.

[This picture was taken in 1974 C.E. His chance of entering Israel on the "right of return" is?

Like the references to the above, the propaganda that Ethiopia "... TURNED AGAINST [white] ISRAEL... " is equally as ridiculous to suggest some sort of a conspiracy on the part of the total Ethiopian people and their government because of Arab oil. But the fact is that Ethiopia has much more than enough of her own oil. The action of Ethiopia in breaking off diplomatic relations, etc. with Israel is this African nation's RIGHT, which is bound to her obligations to defend all other

1. What makes White Jewish Racist Acts against Black Jews less offensive than Nazi Racism against White Jews of Germany and the rest of Europe, etc. Are White Jews free to be "racist"?

African nations and people as a sister member of the Organization Of African Unity [O.A.U.] - which Secretariat [Headquarters] is located in Addis Ababa [Ethiopia's Capital City]. Egypt, Algeria, Tunisia, Sudan, etc. are also sister member nations in Africa, and equally of the O.A.U. And all of them have charged Israel with "OPEN AGGRESION UPON AFRICAN SOIL...," etc. The question is not one of MORALITY or RELIGION, or even of "RACE" and "ETHNIC ORIGIN;" it is strictly and squarely INTERNATIONAL POLITICS and ANTI-COLONIALISM. Ethiopia's interest is not tied to Israel's political future and/or decisions made by her Kneset [Israel's Parliament], irrespective of the Emperor's relationship to the historical and biblical King Solomon of Israel and the Empress of Sheba-Queen Makeda of Ethiopia. As such Ethiopia must make, and take, actions beneficial to herself first and foremost; the same being equally true as Israel does for herself, and as all other independent nations do for themselves. Selassie was deposed in 1974.

There should be none so INSENSITIVE to the justification for this work, particularly after reading these two articles. Equally, one should understand why your author took the final step of leaving the fold of a religious and/or cultural group dominated by RACISTS whose concepts are decided solely upon ETHNIC GROUNDS. Thus who is, or is not, a so-called "FULL JEW," etc.?

Is it not a TRAVESTY OF HUMAN DECENCY and DIGNITY that one so-called "ETHNIC GROUP" must be humiliated by another in the name of RELIGION and GOD in order to qualify for a few crumbs from the SEDER TABLE? Who did YWH commission to be the CHIEF FULL KOSHER JEW MAKER? And, WHEN? What is the requirement for a KOSHER JEW MAKER? Who is to say that the PROUD and RESPECTED AGAW [Falasha or Kyla] PRIEST on the following page should not be allowed to sit on the BOARD OF FULL KOSHER JEW MAKERS with respect to Jews entering Israel from the Soviet Union [Russia] and other parts of Europe and the Americas? What is it about him, and even the Honourable Rabbi Hailu Moshe Paris[1] - who appears in the following article, that make them LESS THAN RABBIS from Europe and the Americas? Is it not their "BLACK SKIN?" Is it not their "WOOLLY HAIR?" Is it not their "THICK LIPS"? It certainly cannot be their DEVOTION and/or COMMITMENT to Judaism! For who amongst the "WHITE JEWS," rabbis included, can show greater love for their RELIGION and/or CULTURE than these two so-called "FALASHAS" and/or "BLACK JEWS?" This is the basis upon which Twentieth Century C.E. "TALMUDIC [Rabbinical] JUDAISM" expects loyalty from BLACK JEWS and respect from the greater BLACK COMMUNITIES all over the world, all of whom will receive the "ANTI-SEMITE" label if they protest such as the above and preceding acts of RACISM.[2] But,

1. Rabbi Paris was once the "Acting Secretary" of Alkebu-lan Foundation, Inc., which owned Alkebu-lan Books Associates - the Publisher of these two volume, and others, by this author.
2. Selassie's Government differed none to the present Minghestu Government of Ethiopia, East Africa in terms of diplomatic relations for many years because of this and other reasons.

FALASHA KAHAIN [Priest] OF AMBOBER READING THE SACRED TORAH

Too Black To Be A Kosher Jew; And Too "Jewish" To Give Up Judaism!

like the present Kahain of Ambober, Ethiopia Rabbi Paris is no different than the indigenous [BLACK] African - AKHENATEN [shown on page xxxviii] - who taught "MONOTHEISM" before the birth of his fellow Black/African - MOSES - that was born in Goshen, EGYPT, North Africa.

JEWISH CHRONICLE March 2 1973 7

A black 'rabbi' in New York jungle[1]

From RICHARD YAFFE—New York

Hailu Moshe Paris, who was born in Ethiopia but speaks the soft English of the West Indian couple who adopted him as an infant, is in a quandary, the same quandary, in fact that ten years ago gave his group of Black Jews the keys to Mount Horeb Synagogue in the Bronx—a changing, deteriorating neighbourhood in which his congregants are afraid to live.

Young Israel, the Orthodox congregational organisation which worshipped in Mount Horeb for many years, turned over the mortgage to a group of Black Jews, Mr Paris among them, when the neighbourhood became Negro. The congregants had a place to go to —a still-white neighbourhood or to the suburbs.

Mount Horeb is no longer in a changing neighbourhood. The South Bronx, in fact, is not really a neighbourhood any longer. It is a jungle, a vast slum with the highest crime and drug rate in New York City.

Mr Paris' congregants are afraid to go out at night, even to a Holyday service, so their unordained rabbi tries to squeeze both the evening and morning services into one long service just before sunset, so that his people can get home before it is dark.

"I don't think there's much of a future here, as far as the Jewish community is concerned," Mr Paris told me. "Maybe as individuals some can assimilate into a White congregation which will take a Black or two. But I don't see any future for our movement as a whole here. It's a lot of energy going down the drain."

Some of his congregants are thinking of going to the West Indies, whence they came a generation ago. Groups will visit the various islands first—Jamaica, Barbados, Curaçao and others—and see if they can still find whether some of the old roots are still there.

Although born in Ethiopia, Mr Paris is not a Falasha. "My parents were indigenous to Ethiopia," Mr Paris said. "They were from the Amhara and Gallia tribes. The Amhara were the ruling class."

They were Copts, but probably in touch with the Falashas and when they died during the Italian invasion in the 1930s Falashas in Addis Ababa got in touch with a group of Black Jews from America, who adopted Hailu and brought him here when the group returned.

The group stemmed from a Negro[2] congregation in Harlem called "The Commandment Keepers of the Living God," but was better known as the "Royal Order of Ethiopian Hebrews," led by Rabbi Wentworth A. Matthew, who claims to be a Falasha, but was probably born in Lagos and brought up in the West Indies. At one time, it is believed, he was a Baptist preacher.

Mr Paris went through the twice-a-week Hebrew school of the "Commandment Keepers" and continued with his Hebrew in a public high school, DeWitt Clinton.

After graduation he and several of his fellow-Black Jews applied to Yeshiva University (Orthodox) high school, and he and a number of others were admitted.

Still others went to the Jewish Theological Seminary of America (Conservative) and some went to

---

1. The use of the term "JUNGLE" is quite selective. But is it surprising that the "White" Jewish author selected it to describe an African-American [BLACK] community that include BLACK Jews?

2. There is no "Negro Congregation of Jews" anywhere. The Portuguese colonialists created their "Negroes" and country - "Negroland." See R. Moore's The Name Negro, Its Origin And Evil Use.

Hailu Moshe Paris in his pulpit at the Mount Horeb Synagogue [1]

Israel and stayed. "We started really to become in a true sense more Jewish," he said.

He earned his bachelor's degree in Hebrew literature and a master's certificate in the science of education. He would have wanted to go on to the Rabbi Isaac Elchanan Rabbinical Seminary of the Hebrew University, but could not get in.

So Mr Paris, whom everyone calls "Rabbi," has no *semicha* (ordination), although he performs all rabbinical duties except those that require a document, such as marriage. Then he gets an ordained rabbi to officiate and he acts as an assistant, and signs the marriage contract as a witness. [2]

He earns his living as an instructor at a leading private school, Horace Mann, where his American Black Jewishness serves him well. He teaches American history, Jewish studies and Negro history.

Mount Horeb is a one-storey building which bears the marks of the great army of graffiti artists of New York.

"We have about sixty families," he said. "We had more, but some of our people have gone to the West Indies. We have a mixed group—some from North Africa, some from the West Indies, some from the second generation of Rabbi Matthew's congregation."

How traditional is his congregation? "It's traditional. I have brought it the Orthodox spirit. We all keep kosher and most of our service is in Hebrew. We stick to the *nusach* (ritual), with some modifications, like the Reform movement might make. Men and women sit separately, but we have no physical separation, although on some holy-days we put up a curtain between the men and women."

Saturday morning services are sparse, but on the holy-days "we have some 200 to 250 people coming in. All of them once lived in Harlem. Now they live in Queens and come even from New Jersey."

What about the young people and the problem of marriage, I asked. Do they meet and marry other Black Jews?

"No, unless they go to Israel," he replied. "That's why a lot of people are leaving and that's why I'm going to go to Israel."

---

1. Mount Horeb Synagogue has since moved to Laurelton, Queens, New York City, New York , another part of this City where White Christians, Jews, Moslems, Atheists, et al., began moving out as the first African/Black family began moving in. What was "all White" is now nearly "all Black."
2. Why does Rabbi Paris, or any other African/Falasha Rabbi, has to constantly seek approval of European/White Kosher Rabbinical so-called "AUTHORITY" to function as any type of a "RABBI"? Where in the "Sacred/Holy Torah" is it mentioned that only European/White Jewish "RABBIS" are allowed or in charge of making all KOSHER/FULL RABBIS? The HASSIDIC, SEPHARDIC, ASHKENAZI, etc. make their own KOSHER/FULL RABBIS; why not the ETHIOPIAN-AMERICANS too!

THE FATHER OF MONOTHEISM [1]
AND FAMILY

[From grandfather Amenhotep III - ca. 1405 - 1370 B.C.E. to grandaughter and her husband Pharaoh Tutankhanon - ca. 1348 - 1349 B.C.E. a total of fifty-six [56] years of the religious principle known today as "Monotheism"][2]

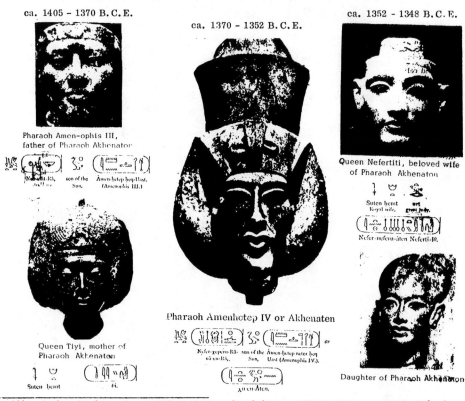

ca. 1405 - 1370 B.C.E.

Pharaoh Amen-ophis III, father of Pharaoh Akhenaton

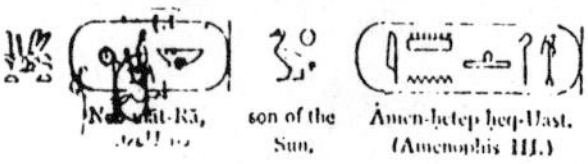

Queen Tiyi, mother of Pharaoh Akhenaton

ca. 1370 - 1352 B.C.E.

Pharaoh Amenhotep IV or Akhenaten

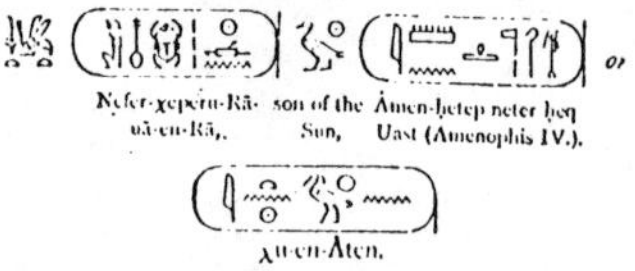

ca. 1352 - 1348 B.C.E.

Queen Nefertiti, beloved wife of Pharaoh Akhenaton

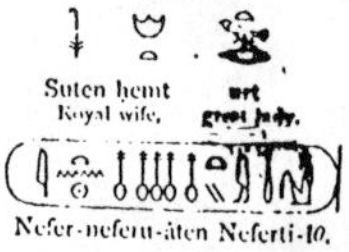

Daughter of Pharaoh Akhenaton

---

1. Akhenaten's reign began in ca. 1370 B.C.E. and ended in ca. 1352 B.C.E., a period of about eighteen [18] years. This was during the XVIIIth Dynasty ca. 1555 - 1340 B.C.E. Akhenaten died more than thirty-six [36] years before the birth of Moses in ca. 1316 B.C.E. during the XIXth Dynasty ca. 1340 - 1232 B.C.E. He preached about a GOD ABOVE ALL OTHER GODS and ONE GOD before Moses was born in Ta-Merry [Egypt], Northeast Alkebu-lan ["Africa"]. Moses also adopted the "Ten Commandments" from the "Negative Confessions" [see pages xl and 157] Moses equally coopted much of the teachings in the "Book Of The Dead" and "Papyrus of Ani" [see transl. by Sir E.A. Walis Budge, London, 1895 C.E.]
2. See Y. ben-Jochannan's Black Man Of The Nile And His Family, pp. liii - 23 , 1981,Rev. Ed.

THE TEN COMMANDMENTS AND THEIR "AFRICAN" ORIGIN

Exodus 20 : 1 - 17

[Found In The Hebrew "Five Books Of Moses"]

The ten commandments

20 AND God spake all these words, saying,
2 I *am* the LORD thy God, which have
brought thee out of the land of Egypt, out of the house
of bondage.
3 Thou shalt have no other gods before me.
4 Thou shalt not make unto thee any graven image,
or any likeness *of any thing* that *is* in heaven above,
or that *is* in the earth beneath, or that *is* in the water
under the earth:
5 Thou shalt not bow down thyself to them, nor
serve them: for I the LORD thy God *am* a jealous God,
visiting the iniquity of the fathers upon the children
unto the third and fourth *generation* of them that
hate me;
6 And shewing mercy unto thousands of them that
love me, and keep my commandments.
7 Thou shalt not take the name of the LORD thy
God in vain; for the LORD will not hold him guiltless
that taketh his name in vain.
8 Remember the sabbath day, to keep it holy.
9 Six days shalt thou labour, and do all thy work:
10 But the seventh day *is* the sabbath of the LORD
thy God: *in it* thou shalt not do any work, thou, nor
thy son, nor thy daughter, thy manservant, nor thy
maidservant, nor thy cattle, nor thy stranger that *is*
within thy gates:
11 For *in* six days the LORD made heaven and earth,
the sea, and all that in them *is*, and rested the seventh
day: wherefore the LORD blessed the sabbath day, and
hallowed it.
12 ¶ Honour thy father and thy mother: that thy
days may be long upon the land which the LORD thy
God giveth thee.
13 Thou shalt not kill.
14 Thou shalt not commit adultery.
15 Thou shalt not steal.
16 Thou shalt not bear false witness against thy
neighbour.
17 Thou shalt not covet thy neighbour's house,
thou shalt not covet thy neighbour's wife, nor his
manservant, nor his maidservant, nor his ox, nor his
ass, nor any thing that *is* thy neighbour's.

29 OF 42 NEGATIVE CONFESSIONS THAT GAVE BIRTH TO THE TEN COMMANDMENTS[1]

[South wall of the Tomb of Pharaoh Rameses III and VI in the Valley of Kings, Wa'at [Thebes of Luxor], Egypt][2]

[1] I have not done iniquity.
[2] I have not committed robbery with violence.
[3] I have not done violence to no man.
[4] I have not committed theft.
[5] I have not slain man or woman.
[6] I have not made light the bushel.
[7] I have not acted deceitfully.
[8] I have not purloined the things which belonged to the God.
[9] I have not uttered falsehood.
[10] I have not carried away food.
[11] I have not uttered evil words.
[12] I have not attacked man.
[13] I have not killed the beasts which are the property of the Gods.
[14] I have not eaten my heart . . . i.e., done anything to my regret.
[15] I have not laid waste ploughed land.
[16] I have not pried into matters.
[17] I have not set my mouth against any man.
[18] I have not given way to anger concerning myself without cause.
[19] I have not defiled the wife of a man.
[20] I have not committed transgression against any party.
[21] I have not violated sacred times and seasons.
[22] I have not struck fear into any man.
[23] I have not been a man of anger.
[24] I have not made myself deaf to words of right and truth.
[25] I have not stirred up strife.
[26] I have not made no man weep.
[27] I have not committed acts of impurity or sodomy.
[28] I have not eaten my heart.
[29] I have not abused no man.

---

1. See Y. ben-Jochannan's THE BLACK MAN'S RELIGION, Vol. II, p. 46; Homer W. Smith's MAN AND HIS GODS, Boston, 1964; Y. ben-Jochannan's BLACK MAN OF THE NILE AND HIS FAMILY, New York, 1981; and p. 135 of Volume One for further detailed facts on this aspect of "African Origins of Judaism."
2. The original name for what the Greeks called "Thebes," and Arabs "Luxor." This was used by everyone connected with ancient Egypt before the arrival of the first foreigners - Hyksos, et al.

INTRODUCTION:

As a founding member of Alkebu-lan Foundation, Inc. I take special enjoyment in writing a short introduction to this work. As the author puts out his first efforts to set the record straight began in 1953 with the Joint Committee For the Publication of We the Black Jews; it has now taken twenty long years to bring this book up to date. The readers of this work are in for the most enlightened interpretation of Ethiopian Jewish history. First of all, one can not deal with this question unless we look into all the histories of the past. A knowledge of Africa in general is needed; throughout the book Dr. ben-Jochannan continues to show the relationship of the Holy Bible with that of ancient Egyptian writings. Furthermore, he delved into the ancient manuscripts of Ethiopia: Kebra Negast [Glory of the Ethiopian Kings] and Sacred Writings of the Agaw People. What I believe this will do for the reader is give him a broader understanding of that which we call "Jewish History and its African Relationship." Dr. ben-Jochannan shows that the culture, religion, customs, theosophy and tradition of the people we call "Falashas" [Ethiopia's Black Jews] and the "Agaw People" along with the Coptic Amhara Tribe of Ethiopia are all related to the ancient Israelite Tribe of Dan. If one is to be true to the discipline of anthropology you can not really make a sharp difference between a Falasha and an Ethiopian Coptic [Orthodox] Christian of Northeastern Ethiopia. As you will notice on page lxxiii of this Volume, Chief Rabbi Yossef officially recognizes the Falashas as Jews. The good rabbi of Iraqi background has traced the Falashas through the books of the Talmud and came to the position that Jewish History justifies calling them True Jews. We in the Western World want to know, if this is so; why then must they "convert" under Rabbinical Laws of Israel. The question is asked: Do the Russian Jews who have been in Russia for fifteen hundred years also "convert" when they come to Israel? As far as I know only some of them who have parents that are half-Jews. Otherwise, most Russian Jews come to Israel without anyone interrogating them about their "Jewishness" as done to "Falashas."

Dr. ben-Jochannan brings out in the open the real reason why Rabbinical Authorities seem not able to accept Rabbi Yossef's decision on the Falashas. It really boils down to; why are the Falashas BLACK like most of the people in the "Afro-Asian World?" Is it not true that Ancient Israel was also of the same people found in that part of the world? He quotes from Dr. Karl Kautsky who said:

> "...the Jews were a mixed race from the start, they in course of their migrations have come into contact with a great succession of new races and their blood has become more and more mixed...."

All this and more made Dr. Kautsky's book "ARE THE JEWS A RACE" very controversial. In the picture on "Panel Of Jewish Scholars Translating The Bible " one of the "Scholars" by the name Bernard Bamberger wrote a book - "PROSELYTISM IN THE TALMUDIC PERIOD," which records in Jewish History the conversions of many Romans and their citizens in the first centuries of that period. Could the rabbis speak of RACIAL PURITY among Jews! ;I think not. If one should look into Biblical History it certainly does not exist. I hope when the Falashas, who will contest the "CONVERSION CEREMONY" in Israel by taking the case to the Supreme Court of Israel, will have a copy of this document to substantiate their historical claim.

Dr. ben-Jochannan has not only delved into the past of the BLACK JEW but also his present. He documents in this work the spiritual, physical and religious connection between the JEWS OF AFRICA and AMERICA. Little has been said of BLACK JEWS of the West Indies who have been there ever since Christopher Colombus, living and marrying with the JEWS of the "Middle East" of Sephardic Heritage. If one was to travel to Jamaica, St. Astasia and St. Thomas you would see the descendants of these early JEWS living as their forebearers.

In the closing lines of this "Introduction" I want to tell a little of the story of the HARLEM BLACK JEWS who left this country to search for their brothers in Ethiopia. Rabbi Ford, one of the early leaders of the Black Jews, took his congregation to Ethiopia. There they met Dr. Tamrat Emmanuel who was later to open a Hebrew School in Addis Ababa in 1945. He met this group of Black Jews in 1931 and shared much of the rich culture of the Falashas at the time, as Dr. Yosef ben-Jochannan has shown in this Volume THE [FALASHA] COMMUNITIES DURING THE ITALIAN FACISTS OCCUPATION OF ETHIOPIA IN WORLD WAR II, Chapter 8. The Falashas had lost much as the rest of their Ethiopian brothers during the Facists attack on Ethiopia. During this time Rabbi Ford kept in contact with the Black Jews in Harlem. As it was recorded at that time in the AFRO-AMERICAN of February 8, 1936, Rabbi Matthew had become the official representative of the Black Jews in America through the AUTHORITY given by the group in Ethiopia under Rabbi Ford. Rabbi Matthew said in this article:

> "My mission here is to develop the Hebrew language among my people.... The Colored man was the original Jew....It is my duty to induce him to accept his real religion anew. The Colored man was a great man as long as he could hold on to his true religion. When he lost it, he developed an inferiority complex and became the slave of the White man."

I..., like the author..., am an Ethiopian by birth. I was taken to America by American parents who came with Rabbi Ford. I grew up in the community of the Black Jews and know how the problem that has existed in America for SEVENTY [70] YEARS; the full acceptance of Black Jews in the Jewish Community. In 1952 Rabbi Matthew's credentials were not accepted by the New York Board of Rabbis.[1] In 1962 some of us started HAZAAD HARISHON in order to see if the Jewish

1. He had degree from Germany, and studied in a Yeshiva there - where he completed training as a Rabbi. How many White Rabbis have less credentials as Rabbis in the United States of America?

Community was ready; however, that also was not accepted. Meanwhile, Rabbi Matthew had opened many temples in New York City. Rabbi Marshall opened a temple in New York also. Rabbi Moses, recently deceased, was Head Rabbi of my temple in the Bronx. Most of the Congregations maintain a more "EASTERN SERVICE" and will relate to the brothers in Israel by supporting their claim to the "Holy Land."

The purpose of this book is to examine certain facts in World History that show the existence of Black Jews. Furthermore, Dr. ben-Jochannan deals with the reaction of the White Jewish Community in America as well as Israel. Our full reaction to this World Community will be made in the "HOLY LAND" at the proper time. While this is the FIRST BLACK INTERPRETATION of African Jewish History, we hope that others will be encouraged to complete this scholarship to the enlightenment of JEW and Non-JEW alike.

Rabbi Hailu Moshe Paris
Mount Horeb Congregation
Bronx, New York, N.Y.
5734 or 1974 C.E.[1]

THE ROYAL "HOST" OF THE FALASHAS AND A VISITING DIGNITARY

ግርማዊ ፡ ቀዳማዊ ፡ ኃይለ ፡ ሥላሴ ፡ ለክቡር ፡ ፕሬዚዶንት ፡
ሴኩቱሬ ፡ የንግሥት ፡ ሳባን ፡ ኒሻን ፡ ሲሸልሙ ።

President Toure was awarded the Collar of the order of Queen of Sheba

by His Imperial Majesty Haile Selassie Ist [see MENEN, June 1962]. He too persecuted "Falashas."[2]

1. Rabbi Paris granted permission to use above "Introduction" in the current Edition of 1983 BCE.
2. On Friday, 13th September, 1974 Selassie was overthrown by the Ethiopian Army and Navy.

JUST IMAGINE; NOT A SINGLE ONE IS A "NEGRO!" WHO IS?

Two Ethiopian Armies At War, 19th Century C.E. [Musee de l'Homine]

HERODOTUS [ca. 502-432 BCE] REVIVED!

"Semitic prisoners" [slaves] " of war pleading for mercy to Pharaoh Haremheb who, allegedly, was "one of the true Negrc pharaohs ofEgypt," Note the same... "thick lips, broad nose, woolly [kinky] hair... " Herodotus and others wrote of with reference to the"...Colchians, Ethiopians and Egyptians."[From a bas-relief of the Tomb of Horemheb at Memphis, Ta-Merry, Northeast Alkebu-lan].

---

1. One needs to ask: Who is the original Semite? Were the Semites originally Asians, Africans or Europeans? How did they loose their "Negroid Characteristics" we see in these pictures? When was the first one "created" and/or "born?" Is the term "Semite" linguistic, ethnic or racist? Before the 1920's C.E. it was always considered to be "linguistic." Who changed it?

GLOSSARY:[1]

Amharic [äm-här-ic]. . .The present national language of Ethiopia. A "Semitic" Language.

Ethiopia [e-thi-opia] . . .The land of the Sacred Torah, Christian and Moslem scriptures - "Cush."

Addis Ababa [ad-dis ah-ba-ba] Capital City of Ethiopia.

Gentiles [gen-tiles]. . . .All Ethiopian religions other than Judaism practiced by the Falashas.

Fäläshä [fa-la-sha]. . . .An Amharan language - Amheric - word of Gheeze origin.

Betä Isräel [beh-ta is-ra-el] Correct name of the so-called Falashas or Agaw people.

Käylä [ky-ee-la]. . . . . . .One of the groups that make up the Agaw [Falashas] people.

Gheeze [gee-ez]. . . . . . .Ancient national language, currently used for religious worship only.

Kähäin [ka-hen]. . . . . . . Falasha Priest

Tellek [tal-lek]. . . . . . . .Tellek Kähäin or Chief Priest of the Falashas.

Däbtärä [dab-ta-ra]. . . Divorced Priest who must surrender his right to officiate at services.

Mäokse [mah-ok-see]. . Falasha Monk. A Priest of very high religious dedication.

Yänessehä äbät [ya-nes-seha ab-at] Falasha Confessor that receives dying confessions.

Arde,'et [ar-de-et]. . . .Book of the Disciples which is read over an infant in the House of Child-bed.

Toräh [to-rah] . . . . .Hebrew Sacred [Holy] Bible, Pentateuch, Five Books of Moses, etc.

Orit [oh-rit] . . . . .Falasha word for Torah.

Sälot [sal-oot]. . . . . .Prayers used in the Falasha Synagogue.

Qwerbän [qu-er-ban]. . .Name for the Animal Sacrifice in memory of Abraham's son.

Mäswäeet [ma-swa-e'eet] Food offerings of Falasha women to Priests on days of Sacrifice.

Awd [ard]. . . . . .Area where the Sacrificial Lamb [or Ox] is slaughtered.

Amolye [a-mol-ye] . . . .The sack of salt held over the Sacrificial Animal/ Leviticus 2 : 13.

Qeddestä qeddosän [qed-des-ta qed-dus-an] Holy of Holies. Section reserved for the Falasha Monks, Priests and Deacons alone in the Synagogue; also, where the Sacred Scrolls [Books] and Sacred Implements are kept.

Mägid [ma-gid] . . . . Falasha Synagogue or House of Worship [never "Temple" outside Israel.

Qitä [qui-ta] . . . . .The Unleven Bread baked on a stone in the open air from the heat of the Sun and eaten on Passover - Pesach.

Gezrät [gez-rat]. . . . . . .Circumcision of all Falasha males at age Eight [8] Days old.

Celqä [cel-ka]. . . . . .The drink for breaking the Passover Fast.

Sämbät Säläm [sam-bat sa-lam] Greeting for the Sabbath equivalent to "Shabbath Shalom."

Ensäsläye [en-saas-la-ye] The evening of the surrender of the bride to her husband on the day of the Marriage Ceremony for her to be able to mate and surrender the proof of her virgin status if it was her first marriage.

Yämärgäm gogo [yamar-gam go-go] House Of The Woman In Blood, where the Falasha woman go to pass her menstrual period.

Yäräs gogo [yar-as go-go] House Of The Woman In Child Bed, where the Falasha woman goes to deliver her child during the late stage of her pregnancy.

Zäze [za-zee] . . . . .Root extract for giving scent of sweetness to the ritual bath used by the woman leaving the House Of Blood and House Of Child Bed; also used in making perfume for Falasha women, and cologne for Falasha men.

Oryäres [or-yaa-rees] Name of the Sun.

Aräft [ar-aft] . . . . Place of repose or Cemetary.

Fec [fek]. . . . . To be divorced; a divorcee.

Tälmud [tal-mud]. . . . . .A standardized VERSION of the Sacred Torah made by European rabbis to suit their own interpretation of what the literal language of the Torah is saying; this is contrary to the literalist Falashas.

Uryäs [ori-as]. . . . . The Sun in the Heavens.

Simhat Torah [sim-hat tor-ah] Midrash, Prayer Book, for the Feast Days.

---

1. Some of these words may have completely different meaning in other areas, and amongst other peoples of Ethiopiá. Others only specially trained "Learned Men" can translate at present.

[Glossary continued]

Bĕrnăēl [ber-nä-el] Hell, as a place for the sinful during life, after death in which one remain; but not the Christians' place of "fire and brimstone" where there is a "Devil" that supervises the burning of people forever. This was from the influence of Falashas returning from experiences in Christianity.

Diyāblos [di-äb-los] Satan the Devil or Master of Sin and Evil. This is also adopted in form from the above Falashas experiences. Note the commonality with the Spanish-Moorish word "diablo" and English -Christian word "devil."

NOT A SINGLE ONE OF THE FOLLOWING IS A "NEGRO." WHY? BECAUSE THEY ARE IN ETHIOPIA. THEY ARE MOSLEMS, JEWS, CHRISTIANS, ETC. IN THE U.S.A. THEY ARE ALL "NEGROES"?!

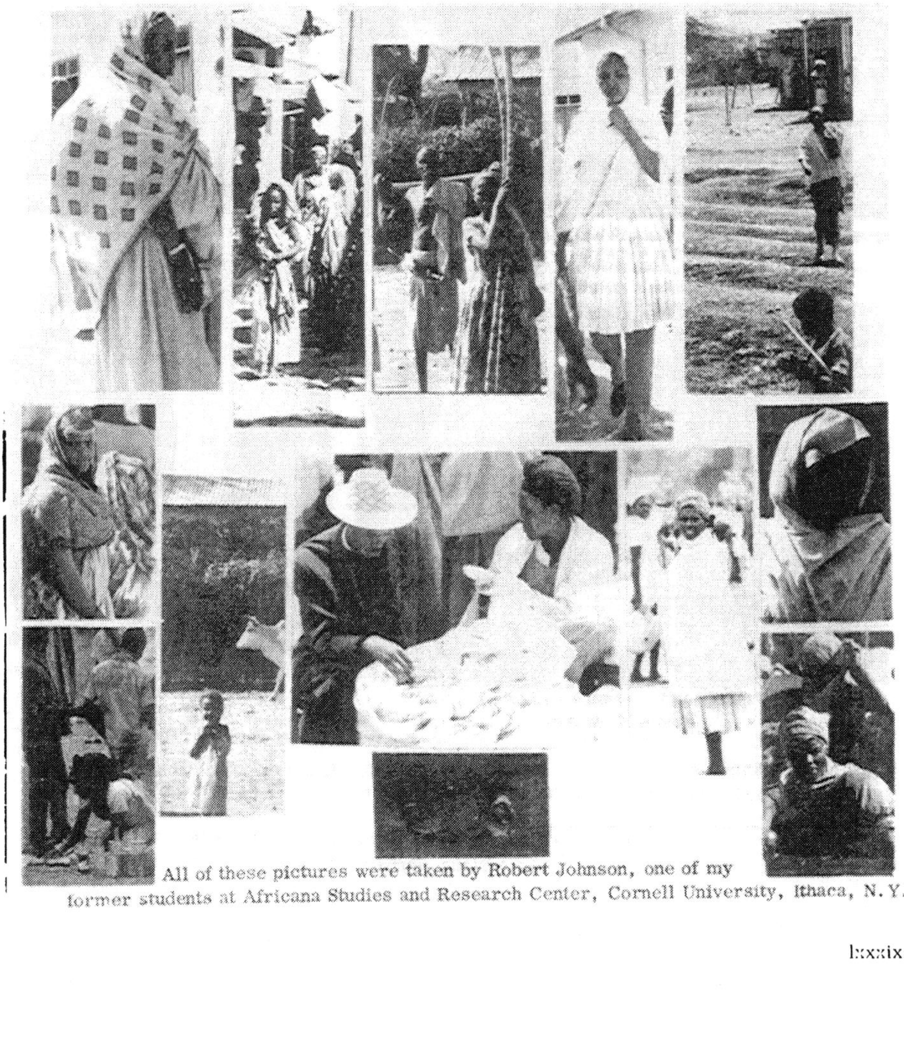

All of these pictures were taken by Robert Johnson, one of my former students at Africana Studies and Research Center, Cornell University, Ithaca, N.Y.

EVERYONE ON THIS PAGE IS A "SEMITE" OR "HAMITE" EXCEPT ONLY TWO? CORRECT YOU ARE; ONLY THE PRESIDENT OF GUINEA AND HIS FIRST LADY!

ግርማዊ ፡ ንጉሠ ፡ ነገሥት ፡ ክቡር ፡ ፕሬዚዳንት ፡ ሴኩቱሬና ፡ ባለቤታቸው ፡ማዳም ፡ ሴኩቱሬ
ከሊሻን ፡ ሺልማት፡ ስነሥርዓትበኋላ ፡ እንደተቀመጡ፡

His Imperial Majesty seen withPresident Toure and Madame Toure after exchanging decorations at Asmara Palace

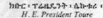

ክቡር ፡ ፕሬዚዳንት ፡ ሴኩቱሬ ፡

H. E. President Toure

በፕላኒንግ ፡ ቦርድ ፡ ወይዛዝርት ፡ ጸሐፊዎች ፡

Stenographers at work

ሁለት ፡ ፓፑዋንስ ፡ አዲስ ፡ አበባን ፡ በጐበኙ ፡ ጊዜ ፡ ከጋዜጠኞች ፡
ጋር ፡ ተገናኝተው ፡ ሲወያዩ ፡

The Capital was visited recently by two Papuans who met the Press. Their slogan was "Papualand for Papuans"[1]

THEY ARE "NEGROES"??? Pictures extracted from "Ethiopia's Leading Illustrated Magazine" MENEN, June 1962. Note that the name is similar to the name of the Emperor's late Empress.

---

1. The late Hon. M.M. Garvey [1887-1940 C.E.] reminded us that "Africa Is For The Africans, Those At Home, And Those Abroad." The African-Papuans are saying the same in their case.

MAP OF ETHIOPIA AND HER NILE VALLEY NEIGHBOURS
[with biblical, pre-biblical, colonial and 20th Century C.E. names and boundaries]

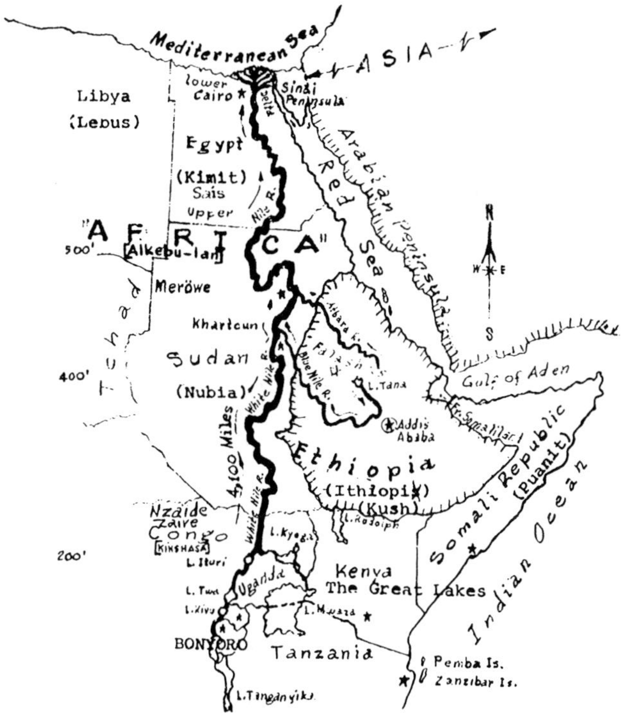

0 ±

THE NILE VALLEYS
By: Y. ben-Jochannan, 1983 CE

This map shows the areas of Alkebu-lan (Africa) which Europeans and European-Americans for the last two-hundred (200) years have been trying to claim as the original home of the "CAUCASIANS" and "SEMITES"; a theory which is in total disagreement of their former claim of the so-called "GARDEN OF EDEN" around the Tigris and Euphrates rivers and their valleys. Note the location of the major nations of the Nile and Great Lakes where "CAUCASIANS NEGROES, SEMITES, HAMITES," etc., allegedly were created independently of each other; thus the RACIST and RELIGIOUS BIGOTRY of today's "CAUCASIAN RACE" and "GOD'S CHOSEN-PEOPLE" myth.

Note the common relationship between Punt, Ethiopia, Nubia, Merõwe and Egypt with respect to Israel [Palestine]. Note full length of the Nile - from Uganda in Central East Africa to Egypt at the coast of North Africa.

ETHIOPIAN HEBREW CONGREGATION, INC.
BETH - HA - TEFILAH
HEADQUARTERS

1 WEST 123rd STREET
NEW YORK, N. Y. 10027
Telephone: 212-534-1058

P.O. BOX 235
MAILING ADDRESS

May 14, 1983

FOUNDER:
LATE RABBI W. A. MATTHEW

PRESIDENT:
RABBI CHAIM WHITE

TREASURER:
MRS. EVELYN SHELLMAN

FINANCIAL SECRETARY:
MR. DAVID LEE

RECORDING SECRETARY:
MRS. KITURAH RILEY

HONORARY TREASURER:
MRS. LOUISE BURRELL

Shalom, Shalom

We of the Ethiopian Hebrew Congregation, Inc., are again honored to request your presence as an honored guest speaker at our Rabbi Wentworth A. Matthew's Day program in honor of our late founder. This day was so designated by our former Boro President, Percy Sutton in June, 1976.

Rabbi Matthew was born in Ghana. He studied at the Haden Theological Seminary and graduated from the School of Dr. Jake Weinberg and Reibstein. He studied the Hebrew language and won a scholorship to attend the University of Berlin in Germany. There for two and a half years, he studied Anthropology and Sociology. He spoke seven different languages. After graduating, he returned to the United States and organized the Commandment Keepers Congregation; he then began his work educating the Black race to return to the original law.

In 1926, Dr. Jake Faithlovitch and Dr. J. Chrombach granted another scholorship to Rabbi Matthew for the Hebrew Union Theological Seminary. After graduating in 1929, he returned to New York City. In 1930, he organized the Commandment Keepers Congregation, Inc., and Hebrew School, from which many Rabbis and Elders were ordained.

The program will be held on Sunday, June 26, 1983 at the Ethiopian Hebrew Congregation, Inc., Beth - Ha - Tefilah, Headquarters, located at 1 West 123rd Street, New York City, from 2:00 P.M. until 8:00 P.M.

Please let us know by June 12, 1983 if you will be able to attend. We are looking forward to your participation.

Shalom, Shalom

PRESIDENT RABBI CHAIM WHITE [1]

Mrs. Kiturah Riley

Recording Secretary: Mrs. K. Riley

KR:sjh

1. This letter was received by your author with a sense of awe I could not believe. This was/is an honour I could believe would have been mine only if my ego was getting away with my mind. How could I believe that I would have gotten this opportunity so many amongst us African/Ethiopian/Hebrews/Beta Israel would have gladly paid enormous sums of monies to do? I feel so happy to be so honoured; I can do nothing else but make the honour befitting of me.

THE FALLACY OF A "JEWISH" [Semitic] "RACE:" Chapter I.

This examination, which is nothing more than a historical recording of facts, should assist my readers in formulating a better or much more comprehensive understanding of the influences and reactions which this chapter bears. Thus you have a basis upon which you can start to understand the effects of the fallacy of racial Judaism, and some of the reasons why many Jews also became "ANTI-SEMITIC, ANTI-JEWISH" and/or "ANTI-ZIONIST, etc.[1]

In many rabbinical writings severe color prejudice is found, especially among some of the early ones who in abundance reaffirmed each other's position by claiming that:

"The Black man [or black skin] is the result of a CURSE on Ham by Noah."

The symbols of this so-called "CURSE" certain rabbis have maintained are the following:

"A black skin, misshapen lips and twisted woolly hair with separated roots."

But some of the same rabbis were so color-prejudiced that they even arrived with the theories propounded by their own Sacred [Holy] Torah [or Christian Old Testament]. For example, a version of the Sacred Torah states that the "CURSE" was placed on Canaan, Ham's son. But some of the rabbis contradicted the biblical scholars and offered their own myth; that:

"THE CURSE WAS PLACED DIRECTLY ON HAM."

Rabbi Huja stated that:

"Ham came forth from the Ark black-skinned."[2]

Of course, he meant to show that Ham had a WHITE or LIGHT skin before he entered the Ark; and that he had undergone a rapid change of pigment discoloration in only one hundred and ninety [190] days while he was in the Ark. These rabbis and their descendants 'owed that Ham had been guilty of sodomy, or having illicit intercourse with his own wife.

The French anthropologist, Topinard, concluded that the rabbis of the First Century C.E. were the first to expound the spread of RACE and COLOR differences as we know them today. He noted that such was unknown in the periods of far-off antiquity, and at least in the "West." He further went on by correctly citing that Aristotle [the so-called "father of natural history"] and Hippocrates [the so-called "Father of Medicine"] did not mention "RACE" in any of their works, even though both studied anatomy and the known differences of the human family [including the Black man and other peoples of dark pigmentation] while they were students in Egypt and Nubia,[3]

1. These two terms have been used much too frequently to suppress any form of Jewish criticism.
2. L. Ginsberg's LEGENDS OF THE JEWS. See Index, Vol. 7 for Ham, Hamite, Ethiopia, Ethiopian, Egyptian and Cain [1938]; and S. Raporport's TALES AND MAXIMS FROM THE MIDRASH, pp. 233-4, p. 167 [1907].

3. De la notion de race en anthropolgie. Revue d'Anthrop 2nd Ser. Vol. 2, p. 589, Paris 1879.

Northeast Alkebu-lan [Africa].

Topinard, whom I have quoted previously, said that:

> "In the first century when Christianity was beginning to seat itself in Rome the doctrine of a separate creation of whites and blacks was defended by the Babylonian rabbis, and later by Emperor Julian. In 1415 A.D. when one council was debating whether the Ethiopian was descended from Adam and the theory he wasn't was making progress, St. Augustine in his CITY OF GOD intervened and declared that no true Christian would doubt that all men, of no matter what form, color, or height were of the same protoplasmic origin." [1]

Of course those rabbis holding the theory that -

> "The Ethiopians were not created by God, or descended from Adam,"

were no less than hypocrites, since they were professing belief in the following from the First Book Of Moses [or Genesis], Chapter I, Verses 26 - 27 of the FIVE BOOKS OF MOSES [Torah]:

> 26 And God said, Let us make man in our image, after our likeness: and let them have dominion over the fish of the sea, and over the fowl of the air, and over the cattle, and over all the earth, and over every creeping thing that creepeth upon the earth.
> 27 So God created man in his own image, in the image of God created he him; male and female created he them.
> 28 And God blessed them, and God said unto them, Be fruitful, and multiply, and replenish the earth, and subdue it: and have dominion over the fish of the sea, and over the fowl of the air, and over every living thing that moveth upon the earth.

But how could they, or any other professed believer in Judaism or Christianity, conclude as they did with regards to the Ethiopians? Because of the same reasons their Talmudist descendants of Sixth Century C.E./A.D. Europe wrote the following:

> Now I cannot beget the fourth son whose children I would have ordered to serve you and your brothers! Therefore it must be Canaan, your first born, whom they enslave. And since you have disabled me...doing ugly things in blackness of night, Canaan's children shall be born ugly and black! Moreover, because you twisted your head around to see my nakedness, your grandchildren's hair shall be twisted into kinks, and their eyes red; again because your lips jested at my misfortune, theirs shall swell; and because you neglected my nakedness, they shall go naked, and their male members shall be shamefully elongated! Men of this race are called Negroes, their forefather Canaan commanded them to love theft and fornication, to be banded together in hatred of their masters and never to tell the truth. [2]

---

1. Op. cit. p.1, footnote. Augustine was himself an African [black]; see his "CONFESSIONS," etc.
2. Y. ben-Jochannan's BLACK MAN OF THE NILE AND HIS FAMILY, p. 13, 1972 Edition, and also repeated on p. 25 of the latest Revised and Enlarged 1981 Edition for extended comments.
3. The best analysis is in R. Graves and R. Patai's HEBREW MYTHS: The Story Of Genesis, p 120.

Let us examine a little closer why the White Jews at both periods were developing color prejudice; and why they stated that the "curse on Ham" was identifiable by a "black skin." Next only to the so-called "Aryan Indo-European Christians," the "European-American" and "European Jews" have been much more "COLOR CONSCIOUS" than anyother people of ancient history. They have been using "WHITE" and "BLACK" to depict some sort of "CURSE" upon each other.[1] Therefore, it is no doubt that since we were enslaved by our fellow Nubians, Ethiopians and Egyptians of other religions we placed "CURSES" on them. Thus it is we described other Nubians, Meroites and Egyptians by the ridiculous nomenclature "NEGRO" from past legends our European brethren wrote. But we became much more furious in our denounciation of dark-skinned or black-skinned peoples, even though we ourselves were originally "BLACK" and/or "DARK-SKINNED" in Palestine, and suffered invasions twice at the hands of the Egyptians, Nubians and Ethiopians in whose homeland we once also lived for almost four hundred years [ca. 1675 or 1678 B.C.E. to 1236 B.C.E.] One such invasion was by the Ethiopians and Egyptians under the rule of Pharaoh Shishak [biblical Sheshonk according to the Sacred Torah] who conquered Palestine and raided the Temple of King Solomon, taking along with him a great number of fellow Jews as captives ["slaves"] into Egypt, Nubia and Ethiopia [see II Chronicles, Chapter 12]. This was followed by King Zerah [another Ethiopian ruler] "...with a host of a thousand and three chariots" according to II Chronicles, Chapter 14. Strange it is that we are to believe that the Black [so-called "Negro, Colored," etc.] Ethiopians that conquered the so-called "Semitic White Caucasian," etc. Palestinian JEWS left them spotlessly pure white; if such they were! Of course that is providing "SEMITIC" and "CAUCASIAN" are synonymous [see map of Ethiopian Empire on page 46].

We "JEWS" could not argue with good conscience at that time [era] successfully on the issue of "COLOR" and/or "RACE " when we left Ethiopia, Nubia and Egypt; for we were ourselves of "dark of color," and most of us "Burnt [BLACK] of Skin." Many rabbis [teachers] and other so-called "scholars" or "scribes" in those times even mentioned that we were "BLACK;" and that the passage in the Sacred [Holy] Torah or Pentateuch [Old Testament] which states"...black but comely..." in the Song Of Songs or Song Of Solomon really meant:

"I WAS BLACK IN EGYPT, BUT COMELY IN EGYPT."[2]

With the extreme amount of amalgamation between the Ethiopian Hebrews and other religious groups, and the Egyptian Hebrews and other religious groups, also the Nubian Hebrews[3] and

---

1. R. Graves and R. Patai, HEBREW MYTHS, p. 121; Y. ben-Jochannan, BLACK MAN OF THE NILE AND HIS FAMILY, p. 13 [see p. 25 of the 1981 Revised and Enlarged Edition].
2. Freedman and Simon MIDRASH BABBA. SONG OF SONGS, p. 51 [1939]; GENESIS, Vol. 2, p. 293.
3. There were Jews, who looked like any other African along the length and breadth of Africa.

other religious groups, neither group could have produced anything else but an amalgamation of people if none existed before. Remember that the Egyptians, Nubians, Meröites and Ethiopians in all of the records of those ancient times were described as having what Herodotus reported:

"THICK LIPS, BROAD NOSES, WOOLLY HAIR AND BURNT OF SKIN."

Therefore, the only difference between all of us was religion; but in no sense whatsoever was it "COLOR" and/or "RACE." And the argument about Miriam's objection to Moses marrying his Ethiopian wife was based upon the rejection of a so-called "HAMITE" in the equally so-called "SEMITIC RACE" is nothing less than asinine as any fool could reach. Those who still harbour such arguments cannot protest against Adolph Hitler's analysis as regards to "Jews" not being a part of the so-called "ARYAN RACE," since both arguments are based upon likely myths. In this regards the ancient writer Strabo said the following:

"Many of my time considered Jews as an African people."

Some of Adolph Hitler's prize members of the "Aryan Master Race" like Ludvig von Beethoven,[1] and of course Germany's "Celestial Saint" Maurice,[2] both of whom are shown on the following page, were of African origin. Of course there are so many of us who will not for the first minute believe a single word, not even the picture of what is being revealed here. But we - "JEWS" - will still believe that our ancestors placed a "CURSE" on a white brother and turned him into a "BLACK" man, who eventually became the ancestor of the so-called "NEGROES." Yet we were ourselves at least "DARK-SKINNED," and at best "BLACK-SKINNED." Those of us who came to this realization by virtue of research had to answer our racist Jews at this stage. But our own mixing with "FAIR-SKINNED" and/or "WHITE-SKINNED" Europeans came after we left Egypt,[3] Nubia and Ethiopia in North and East Alkebu-lan. All of this only after we were forced to flee into the land of the so-called "Caucasian" following the destruction of the last temple by the Romans sometime during the First Century B.C.E. But the so-called "PURE WHITE SEMITES" that resulted from our amalgamation in Europe can now state that "BLACK PEOPLE," including "BLACK JEWS," are the result of the so-called "...CURSE ON HAM...." It is more than funny that the accepted VERSION of the Five Books Of Moses [Pentateuch, Old Testament, etc.] by most "Jewish [Hebrew] Scholars," the so-called "MESORETIC TEXT," has no mention whatsoever of the first word with regards to "HAM'S" or "CANAAN'S" color of skin and/or race.[4] For one cannot find a single chapter, verse or word where it is still shown in said TEXT that the so-

---

1. Springer B. Die Blutmischung als Grundesetz des Lebens; NATIONALISM AND CULTURE, p. 319 [1937]; J.A. Rogers, SEX AND RACE, Vol. I, p. 7.
2. J.A. Rogers, 100 AMAZING FACTS ABOUT THE NEGRO WITH COMPLETE PROOF, p. i.
3. See reference to "Moses marriage to the daughter of the High Priest of Ethiopia/Kush" in the Holy Torah/Old Testament, etc.
4. See blatant racist story in R. Graves and R. Patai's, HEBREW MYTHS, pp. 120 - 122, etc.

AFRICAN-EUROPEANS [Blacks] OF HITLER'S "MASTER RACE"[1]

Ludwig van Beethoven, at the age of 44. Drawn from life by Letronne; engraved by Hofel

Saint Maurice of Aragon, Celestial Saint of Germany.

"BLACK/NIGGER" MEN OF THE "MASTER RACE"! ?

His mother was a Moor — His mother was a Moor

1. See Joel A. Rogers' SEX AND RACE; NATURE KNOWS NO COLOR LINE, WORLD'S GREAT MEN OF COLOR; AFRICA'S GIFT TO AMERICA; SUPERMAN TO MAN; etc., etc., etc. For ancient "BLACK" Europeans see Frank H. Snowden's BLACKS IN ANTIQUITY: A GRECO-ROMAN EXPERIENCE; and Y. ben-Jochannan's BLACK MAN OF THE NILE AND HIS FAMILY, p. 99, etc.

called "CURSE" had anything whatsoever to do with the "COLOR" of anyone. It merely states:

"A CURSE PLACED ON CANAAN."

Neither is this said in the Book Of Genesis [First Book Of Moses], Chapter 10, Verse 25 where the story of Noah cursing his own grandchildren-to-be is shown. Yet the racist VERSION I have shown on page 2 of this Volume prevails unabated as the "most holy inspired words of God."

The matter of "BLACK SKIN," and now "NEGRO" or "COLORED SKIN," before the latest revised KING JAMES VERSION OF THE [Christian] HOLY BIBLE, is indisputably willful and malicious in its distortions that were edited into the teachings of the HEBREW BIBLE for the purpose of also bringing into the Christian Community the racist teachings of the old rabbis who propagandized what you have read on page 2; all of which was [and still is] to throw scorn and disgrace upon the indigenous African people and their descendants scattered all around the world due to the effects of colonialism, imperialism, and most of all SLAVERY. But the strangest part about this aspect of the history and heritage of mankind is that all of us -"Sun Worshipers," Jews, Christians, Moslems, and all others, have suffered one time or another from the same type of character assassination.

How could the European rabbis of the past, and so many of the European-American communities of the present, maintain that:

"THE ETHIOPIAN, NUBIAN AND EGYPTIAN JEWS" WERE DESCENDED FROM HAM,"

who was declared to be condemned by God - YWH - because of this racist proclamation by Noah:

"A SLAVE OF SLAVES SHALL HE BE ?"

But it was the same "slave of slaves" that was controlling all of the "ISRAELITES" when we were in Egypt, Nubia, Meröe and Itiopi; the same people who also taught us out of the first books written many thousands of years before our first "AFRICAN BROTHER" named Moses gave us his version of the teachings of other "AFRICANS" from the Grand Lodge of Wa'at and other subordinate Lodges - wisdom known at the time as the "MYSTERIES." Those of us who were allegedly descended from the so-called "...SONS OF SHEM...," and supposedly "...RECEIVED OUR BLESSINGS FROM NOAH...," were then unfortunately the "...SLAVES OF SLAVES..." for the CANAANITES [Egyptians, Nubians, Meröites and Ethiopians] that received the "CURSE" from the same "NOAH" because they were the "...DESCENDANTS OF HAM/Noah's Son;"God's Words."

Another aspect in this type of biblical teachings of the mythology and allegory is the fact that the so-called "CURSE" was placed upon the "CANAANITES," according to the Masoretic Text [a version of the "Holy Bible"]. But the "CANAANITES dwelled in the land" that later became Palestine and/or Israel, all of which is distinctly located in Asia; not Europe. Therefore, they were "CURSED" [Black] ASIANS, and more closely connected with the "WHITES" to the north of them, the source of their lighter skin. But the so-called "SHEMITES " who were living in Alkebu-lan ["Africa" or "Afrika"] - Egypt, Nubia, Meröe and Ethiopia - from ca. 1675 B.C.E. [during the XIVth Dynasty] among another "CURSED" group of "BLACKS" - the noted "HAMITES"- got their darker color in Africa. Is it not true that this entire allegorical myth is a bare-faced lie? For, is it not written in the Sacred [Holy] Torah that:

"GOD GAVE THE LAND OF THE CANAANITES TO HIS CHOSEN PEOPLE - ISRAEL?"

If so, as it is written, why then "CURSE" on "GOD'S CHOSEN PEOPLE" of Canaan? Or is it that "God's inspired holy scribes" were equally a team of liars? Should it not be that modern European and European-American translators were/are equally racist liars?

As we look at the racist interpretations of the Hebrew and Christian "...Holy Scriptures written by God's Inspired Holy Scribes..." further, we find another type of nonsense; this time the same type of vicious propaganda, but directed against the opposite parties to the above. Thus certain BLACKS in the course of seeking revenge over the myth of "HAM'S CURSE" have countered with the following:

"The White man originated from an albino ape, who was the ancestor of the Whites." [1]

Many more, in reaction to the European-Americans [Whites] epiteth, said that:

"The white skin was caused by leprosy; it comes from their ancestor Gehazi, who was the servant of Elisha. He placed his curse upon Gehazi for having solicited money from Noaman."

Of course they always quote II KINGS, Chapter 5, Verse 21 as one of their sources of documentation. Since the "Holy Scriptures" of any religion can be translated and interpreted to suit any occasion, one should find no uneasiness understanding these equally warped versions. This author thus believes that these reactions are topped by the following quotation the late ethnologist Joel A. Rogers cited in one of his noted works - NATURE KNOWS NO COLOR LINE. He wrote:

"Some Negro preachers and expounders of the Bible have even proved that white people will not go to heaven because Jesus placed a curse on their hair. As authority they quote the parable of the sheep and the goats [Matthew, 25:32], where Christ said that when he comes again in all his glory he shall separate the sheep from the goats, place the sheep on his right hand and say to them; Come ye blessed of My Father, inherit the kingdom prepared for you from the foundation of the world.[2] Now there is this dis-

1. See "Foreword" in J.A. Rogers, NATURE KNOWS NO COLOR LINE, New York, 1952, Vol. I, p. etc.
2. The "Holy Bible" is subject to thousands of interpretation of any Chapter, Verse and/or Line, etc. This is only one of thousands. One man's "Sacred/Holy Scriptures" is another's pagan beliefs.

tinction: The goats have straight hair like whites; the sheep, wool, like Negroes."[1] From this quotation we see very little of the consistency among these "Negro" racists and their white racist teachers; for they too have forgotten that many African-Americans try very hard in European-America to straighten their hair to the straightness of that of the "goat" or "white man." How uniformly the theory of RACIAL SUPERIORITY falls asunder by the acts of its own proponents!

"Cain turned black [according to the rabbis] through a curse placed upon him by God." The European-American version of a Christianized Black Man states:

> "Cain turned white and gave origin to the whites, when God shouted at him in the Garden of Eden after he had killed Abel; and because of his fright he turned white."[2]

The following is from the words of another White man - Parkyn, a traveler who once toured Ethiopia, East Alkebu-lan/"Africa":

> "The Ethiopians claimed I had cat's eyes and monkey's hair, and I lost my skin."[3]

I think that a work by Leo Frobenius[3] should help some of us "racists" to clean our system from racial prejudice, regardless of whom we are prejudiced against, if we are to be able to forestall another series of persecution directed against us - solely on the basis that we pray differently to our persecutors. But we must be willing to heed our own teachings, not one of which we do not; even to the point of calling African people "NEGRO" and "NEGRESS" following our own fellow White Jews protest against being called "JEW " and "JEWESS," etc., etc., etc.

I wish to go further and show you how silly the issue of "RACE" affects us. The late Asfa Yilma, who claimed to have been "an Ethiopian Princess" from some connection which she could not justify, and who was white blonde in skin color, but also wished to ignore her background of BLACK so-called "NEGRO" origin, thus found it necessary to rant in her racist work - HAILE SELASSIE, Appleton, Century, New York, 1936, page 23 about her own aberration; thus a . . .

> "third race whose hair is woolly and thick. There are no Negroes in Abyssinia except as slaves."

Now as an Ethiopian or African, I could say that this woman either was too racially prejudiced or too ignorant of the facts when she maintained such on the basis of features and/or anatomical appearance of the people of Ethiopia - which she called "Abyssinia." Obviously she must not have seen the face of Empress Menen - the late wife of Emperor Haile Selassie Ist - as shown on

---

1. W. Reade, SAVAGE AFRICA, p. 24, New York, 1864
2. M. Parkyn, LIFE IN ABYSSSINIA [in: London Quarterly Review, Vol. 1, pp. 178 - 79; Vol. 3, 1854 -55, p. 495.
3. Leo Froebenius, AFRICAN GENESIS ALSO PREHISTORIC ROCK PICTURES IN EUROPE AND AFRICA, Berlin, 1874 [date in doubt, not mentioned on the title page or elsewhere].

page 53 of Chapter III in this Volume. For it was no accident that the vast majority of the entire population of Ethiopia ["Cush, Abyssinia," etc.] - just north of the Equator in East "Africa" - are:

"BLACK WITH WOOLLY THICK HAIR."

All of these features were equally visible in the face of Haile Selassie Ist and his Royal Family, down to the ebbs of the Ethiopian "Upper" and "Lower" classes and castes. This is also obvious in the picture of the "Royal Couple" shown on page 53, Chapter III of this Volume. Some of us in Ethiopia and other parts of the entire continent of Alkebu-lan ["Africa"] look even more so fitting her classification than many of the people of other lands whom Asfa Yilma prefered to call "Negroes." Was she afraid or ashamed of her African "BLACK," or as it is otherwise called - "NEGROID ANCESTRY"? If so, she certainly had a very bad mental problem; for there has never been in man's civilization a history and heritage greater than that of the people - sons and daughters - of "Mother Alkebu-lan" [Africa], all of whom were/are "BLACK" - past and present.

H.G. Spearing wrote that:

> "The Chaldeans were negroid; the discovery was very disconcerting to literary historians and philologists for that race was proved to be...not a branch of the civilizing Aryans, nor of the gifted Semites but a Negroid people affinities with Mongols." [1]

Whereas Chaldea, the seat of Sumerian civilization from whence Abraham originated, is today considered to be "WHITE ARYAN." Abraham came from "UR," a city in Chaldees [Chaldea], according to the Pentateuch [or Sacred Torah, Old Testament, etc.].

Strabo in ca. 30 B.C.E. wrote that:

> "The people of Western Judea are partly from Egyptian ancestry." [He continued]. "Although the inhabitants are mixed up thus the most prevalent of the accredited reports in regard to the temple of Jerusalem represents the ancestors of the present Judeans, as they are called, Egyptians." [2]

S. Rapoport wrote that:

> "When the Jews returned from Babylon their wives had become brown almost during the years of captivity and a large number divorced their wives. The divorced women probably married black men which would to some extent account for the existence of black Jews." [3]

From T. Waitz we have the following:

> "An interesting gradation of all shades down to the black is exhibited by the Jews."

Napoleon's Ambassador's [to Portugal] wife, Dutchess D'ambrantes, said of the Jews of Portugal.[4]

---

1. H.G. Spearing, THE CHILDHOOD OF ART, New York, 1912, p. 255.
2. H.L. Jones [transl.], GEOGRAPHY, XVI, 2, 34 [Vol. 7, p. 281.
3. S. Rapoport, TALES and MAXIMS FROM THE MIDRASH, p. 71, New York, 1907.
4. These Jews were totally mixed with the Moors; Spinoza being the most noted of all of them. Most Spanish and Portuguese writers of early Iberian history maintained that "in those days one could not distinguish Jews from Mulattos with 100 percent accuracy," etc.

"The Jews, the Negro, and the Portuguese could be seen in a single person." [1]

What state of error on "RACE" most people are in! For example; Barbot wrote in his volume:

> "The German Jews, as for example those of Prague, are as white as most of their German countrymen." [2]

John Bigelow said that:

> "The Jews expelled from Portugal by King John II settled in the West Indies, specifically in Jamaica in 1850, children were negroid." [3]

Count Adam Gurowski [Poland] said of his visit in the United States of America in 1857 C.E.:

> "Numbers of Jews have the greatest resemblance to the American mulattoes. Sallow complexion, thick lips, crisped black hair. Of all the Jewish population scattered over the globe one-fourth dwells in Poland. I am, therefore, well acquainted with their features. On my arrival in this country, I took every light-colored mulatto for a Jew." [4]

Certainly we cannot disagree with any of the above commentators on what they experienced with respect to the so-called "RACIAL AFFINITIES" of the Jews in the United States of America and Europe. The following pictures of Black Jews on pages 11-15 add to their support and documentation. Those on pages 299, 301, 303, 308, 310, etc. equally add to the Jewish dilemma."

In this struggle for RACE, COLOR and RELIGIOUS purity we Hebrews [Israelites or Jews] have been caught. To keep our ties to the least economic resistence which goes hand in hand with being a member of the so-called "WHITE RACE," Hebrews who profess to be of the same "WHITE RACE" must reject all other Hebrews [Jews] of very dark or black complexion [pigment], this being equally true for all others who are unable to meet the designation of a member of the "GREAT WHITE RACE." This rejection is done for the sole purpose of proving to European and European-American Gentiles that although they are "JEWS," they are still of the so-called "GREAT WHITE RACE." But when the issue of the Jews being a "RACE" arises in certain quarters, and it is advantageous for most of them to claim that they are of a distinctly different "RACIAL GROUP" to the "GREAT WHITE RACE," these same Jews claim that they are the... "CHOSEN PEOPLE" of the "SEMITIC RACE." This latter classification has been the basis upon which your writer and others of his geographic and pigment groups found ourselves rejected by our brother and sister Jews of WHITE SKIN. They give the following reason for their overt action; thus:

> "The Falashas are converts to the Hebrew Faith; but they are not of our race."

---

1. I. Waitz, INTRODUCTION TO ANTHROPOLOGY, New York, 1863, pp. 47 - 8. See other pages.
2. MEMOIRES, Vol. 5., Chap. 26, New York, 1865, 12 Vols. There is a single Edited Edition.
3. DESCRIPTION OF GUINEA, New York, London, 1746, p. 9. A colonialist appraisal of Africa.
4. JAMAICA IN 1850, London, 1851, pp. 15 - 22. Written from a British colonialist point of view.
5. AMERICA and EUROPE, London , New York, 1857, pp. 177 - 78.

36 YEARS IN ISRAEL [ca. 5727 or 1947 C.E. - ca. 5743 or 1983 C.E.]; WHO KNOWS?

BLACK JEWS OF ISRAEL

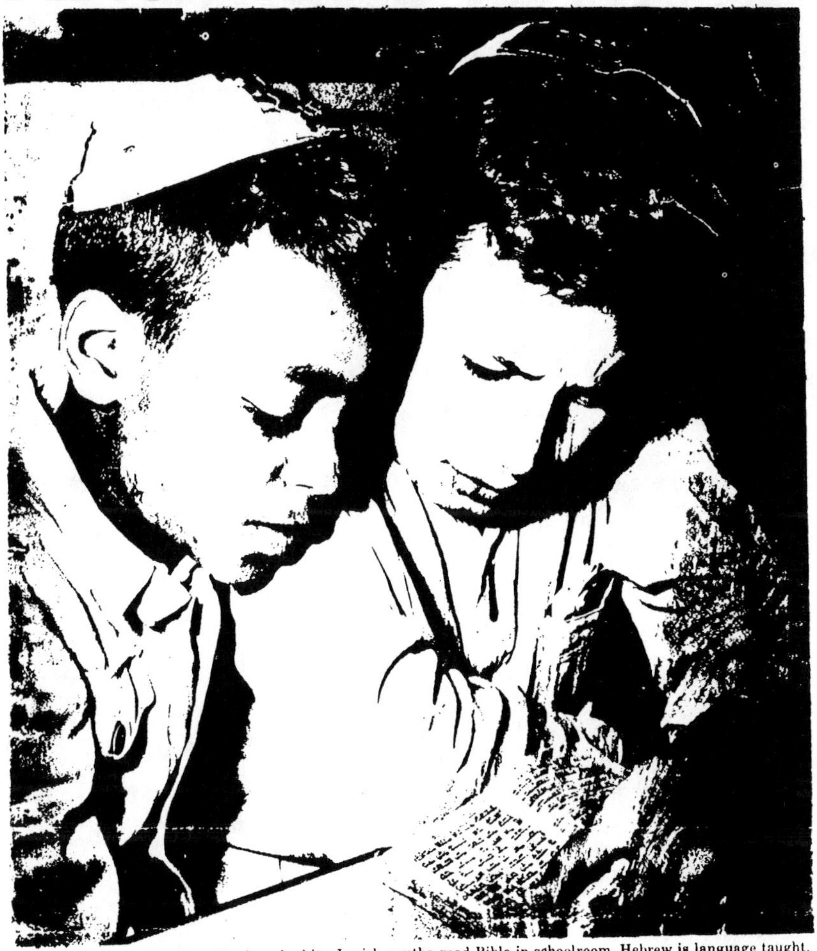

Studying together, black and white Jewish youths read Bible in schoolroom. Hebrew is language taught.

New nation makes swift progress solving race problem

WHEN ISRAEL became a nation ten years ago, the new republic had many headaches and one of the most aggravating was its race problem. Among the Jews

BLACKS OF THE "SEMITIC RACE;" BUT NOT IF YOU ARE FROM THE U.S.A.
WHAT MAKES THE DIFFERENCE: HAIR. LIPS, NOSE???

Weaving is learned by youth in a factory room.

In wedding ceremony, Jewish girl from India

skin so dark that they immediately became known as "black Jews."

Like colored peoples elsewhere, the black Jews became the object of color discrimination. Unskilled workers, they were forced to take the most menial jobs in Israel, working as porters and bootblacks. They lived in the worst slums in Tel Aviv and for a while there was even an attempt to keep them out of trade unions. But the principles of the Israel republic, which called for bringing all Jews back to their homeland on an equal basis, were finally made dominant and today a decade after Israel was born, color prejudice is fast becoming unknown.

Intermarriage is now common in Israel and is in fact encouraged as a means of merging all Jews into one nation with one language. Coming from Arab countries where they adopted local customs, some of these black Jews used to give their girls away in marriage when they were 11 or 12. But now by an act of the Knesseth, the Israel congress, the legal minimum age for girl to marry is set at 17 and the black Jews obey the law.

The black Jews of Israel have demonstrated their ability to adapt to a "westernized" standard of living. They are shrewd[1] and ambitious as well as gentle and accommodating.

1. Black Jews are no more "...shrewd..." than White Jews; all kinds of people are "shrewd." Today We - "Black Jews" - make up the majority of Israel's population, but have lest power of control than any group of "White Jews" within the country. Why? White Racism?! God's People! ?

BLACK SHADES OF THE SO-CALLED "SEMITIC RACE"

How Much Better-Off Are They Than The "U.S.A.'s Negroes" Now?

marries Yemenite groom. Yemenites from Arab countries predominate.

Bridegroom is blessed by rabbi who puts hands on his head as Jacob did to his grandchildren as narrated in the Bible. Black Jews range in color from deepest black to dark brown and mulatto. Features vary from Negroid to Oriental.[1]

---

1. The touch-up letters are due to the damaged original. No changes made to any word. What is an "Oriental feature" and/or "Negroid feature," etc. ? From Abraham to Moses and the creators of Israel/Palestine were all Asians and Africans; not one solitary "European" envolved.

MEMBERS OF THE "SEMITIC [Jewish] RACE;" ARE THEY NOT? THEY COME FROM EUROPEAN-AMERICA, AFRICA AND EUROPE. BUT ONLY THE "WHITE" ONE IS A SO-CALLED "TRUE JEW?"

At prayer. Members of the choir, wearing prayer shawls, await signal. Other [Negro] Jewish communities are set up in Philadelphia, Brooklyn, Pittsburgh, Chicago and Youngstown, Ohio.

Alphabet lessons. Children of the Commandment Keepers Congregation are taught Hebrew.[1]

Hebrew is official language of Israel and youngsters learn language at school. Here dark-skinned Jewish youth gets instruction in writing on the blackboard.

---

1. Of all the "Black Jews" shown on pages 11 - 16 only those on the top row of this page are called "NEGROES" and/or "COLORED JEWS." The "Black Jew" at the bottom is from Ethiopia, Mother Alkebu-lan [Africa or Afrika]; thus a "Nilo-Hamite, Nilo-Semite, Hamo-Shemite, Dark-skinned Caucasian, Lost Jew, Falasha/Falassa, Beta Israel, Jew of the Tribe of Dan," etc.

MEMBERS OF THE ISRAELI BLACK JEWS
The range from Jet Black to Snow White, etc.

?ARE THEY TOO NOT TRUE JEWS?
WHO IS ONE?

Assistant rabbi recites benediction at wedding under Jewish Star of David

The DOUBLE PYRAMID DOG STAR or TUAT We Saw While We Were In Ta-Merry [Mizrain or Egypt], From ca. 1675 B.C.E. to ca. 1236 B.C.E., We Have Since Renamed And Claimed As Our Own "STAR OF DAVID" Everywhere We Are Since ca. 1600 C.E.[1]

---

1. See Y. ben-Jochannan's BLACK MAN OF THE NILE AND HIS FAMILY, pages 340 - 372. The Dog Star or "Mogen Dovid" is in fact two up-side-down pyramids: △ ▽ ✡ .... There is no historical basis back to biblical King David of Israel to justify its usage.

Life on a sunny Israeli kibbutz includes much field labor with hand tools.

Donkeys carrying local produce are frequent passengers on ferries like this one across the Nile River.

Let us look at this racial fallacy from a different viewpoint to see how destructive this type of discrimination can get. We - BLACK [darker skin] JEWS - who came freely to the United States of America can easily notice the separation between Eastern and Western European and European-American WHITE JEWS. The Jews with their PAYES from Eastern European Orthodox Communities are looked at with shame because of their old customs the earlier immigrants from Western Europe have already discarded. The Westerners, having taken Christian traditions and materialism from capitalist industry as being part and parcel synonymous with their form of Talmudic [Rabbinical] Judaism now, even find it necessary to reject this branch of their fellow European Jews, much less their fellow Jews [BLACK] from Africa, the Caribbean Islands, the United States of America and all other parts of the Americas. On many occasions your author had to make peace between these two European and European-American groups. Thus it is not at all astonishing to me that later on I would have had to disassociate myself with both as a matter of principle over the issue of a ..."Semitic [or Jewish] White Race..." from Adam and Eve.

In the above gathering I overheard Jews from Germany and Austria make slurring remarks about their Eastern European fellow Jews' ignorance and backwardness. The Eastern group also countering with the fact that the Western group"...

> aided and abetted Adolph Hitler and his Nazis regime before they too were persecuted after he had no more Orthodox to send to the Gas Chambers...."

They further stated that:

> "The German and Austrian Jews were disbanding their Jewish Faith by starting a somewhat quasi-Christian Religion under the pretext of being a Reform Judaic Movement."

These charges and countercharges got so heated on one occasion that physical violence occurred on the very floor of a synagogue. However, in this latter incident between Eastern and Western European and European-American "Jewry" there is a "COMMON BOND" theory. This is for the means of protection in the event of there being another attempt at Jewish persecution from Gentile communities in the United States of America, and once again in Europe. There is no such closing of the ranks when the persecution is directed against Ethiopian, African-American and/or African-Caribbean Jewish communities. For how could there be any closing of the ranks between Black and White Hebrews in this latter case, when in fact they will be on separate sides? The White Jews with the White Gentiles, and the Black Jews with the Black Gentiles; for African Jews in the United States of America are not recognized by the greater body of White Jews as being "authentic Jews." The arguments put forward to justify this myth and racist propaganda are too many to try and list here. And the fact that the African [BLACK] Jews of worth do not care one way or the other if White Jews recognize them is another reason they will not be detailed.

The racial issue we have dealt with came to a head with the unwritten covenant tactics employed by some fellow Jews in their manner of selecting persons to reside in their neighborhoods. This condition was tested by the accounts given below.

A few of us on a Select Committee in Harlem, New York City, New York had the following experiences: The New York Herald Tribune [before it became defunct] advertised a few "apartments in the Jackson Heights section of Queens, New York City, New York stating that they were "...available for immediate occupancy." We made phone calls to the three owners advertising. Upon telephoning, all three assured us that we could"...have the apartment ..." because we were "...the first to inquire." Following these answers, we arrived at the home of the first man. As we entered we took note of the "Star Of David" on the apartment's window and felt somewhat relaxed because this Hebrew brother needed an apartment desperately, and here was another Hebrew brother who would help another out of his condition of desperation. But as we asked about the apartment, he looked at us and said:

> "The person taking this apartment has to know Hebrew because very few of the people in this building speak English."

I then spoke to my European-American Jewish brother in Hebrew,[1] only to discover that he only knew a few quotations from his prayer books. He followed with an answer we would have never expected. He stated:

> "This is a white Jewish community; you people could not seriously be expected to feel comfortable here, even though you call yourselves Hebrews."

The next place we visited we were told by a couple:

> "As white people we are no different than the Christians when it comes to admitting Negroes in our neighborhood. Why don't the colored people, call yourselves Jews or Christians, build your own neighborhoods to live in."

We tried other areas in Manhattan, Brooklyn, Staten Island and The Bronx; all with the same results in most details to the above. The last person I spoke to stated

> "I have an apartment across the street where my wife and I live. I would let you, my friend, have it."

I guess this man really meant just that, and was willing to turn over the key of the apartment to me, when a wench that identified herself as "..a self-respecting white woman..." appeared and overheard our conversation and demanded of the landlord that he "...better not rent to any colored in my brother's building." She immediately made an about-face and left the premises in haste, only to return very shortly thereafter with at least fifteen[15] irate fellow white women who joined her in open protest about our being there for the purpose which we were. One of these "God-fearing" women was overheard saying:

1. The original for this word was "HARIBU." This is the English translation; not "JEW," etc.

"You allow the first one of them in your neighborhood, and down goes the moral standards of your children and the destruction of your property."

We thanked the gentleman and told him we were not willing to have him become a martyr for any cause on our part. We thanked him for his human understanding, and for his courage; for he had insisted:

"You are going to have the apartment if it is the last thing I do in this life."

The tenants, who were led by the one woman that overheard the original conversation, had the gall to ask the landlord:

"Didn't you hear the Rabbi's lecture last week that we Jews, white people, must stick together, or we will die together as we did in Hitler's Germany?"

The landlord's reply was quite significant; he said:

"My Rabbi told me; all people should live like people, and stick together."

There you have the opposition, which is the rare exception of the general rule in this type of cases relative to Black Jews and White Jews and their living pattern of exclusiveness based upon "RACE" and/or "COLOR;" even "RELIGION" - according to "SECT"[Orthodox, Reform, etc.]

Looking back into the history of the invasion of Ethiopia by the Italian Fascist Armies of Dictator [Il Duce] Benito Mussolini, King Victor Emmanuel II and Pope Pius XIth of Italy we found that our brother and sister European and European-American [WHITE] Jews responded the same way in which the parties above did; this being so even though the Falashas were persecuted jointly by the Fascists and Nazis before their brothers and sisters in Europe under the tortures of Adolph Hitler, et al. But when the Ethiopian [BLACK] Jews asked for aid against the acts of persecution and genocide inflicted upon them by the Fascists and Nazis the European-American LILY WHITE Jewish communities did not respond one-ninetieth [1/90 th] the manner in which they responded to the cries of the Jews in Germany.[1] There were only a few, or shall we say a mere handful, which amounted to one specific group giving any direct or indirect aid to the Falashas in Ethiopia. This group is none other than the presently almost defunct "Pro-Falasha Committee Of America" - a mere handful of European-American [WHITE] Jews, with the exclusion of the African-American [BLACK] Jews, living in the New York City, New York area. This group was but a drop in the bucket in numbers when one considers its strength and compares it against the general community of Jews in the entire United States of America, the Caribbean Islands and other areas of the American continents - North, Central and South. However, it was not very long after 1935 C.E. when my fellow African [BLACK] Jews were being persecuted to the point of total genocide by the Italian Fascist Armies and civilian personnel that Adolph Hitler and his Nazis started their attacks against our brother and sister European [WHITE] Jews, beginning in

1. There were "mass rallies" and "presidential appeals" to Pres. F.D. Roosevelt for White Jews in Europe, but not one solitary rally or appeal on behalf of a solitary Black Jew in Ethiopia.

1936 C.E. Of course, then there was an all-out protesting force of every Jewish organization: WHITE, BLACK, BROWN, YELLOW, RED, and whatever other types of Jews there were over the entire world; and no less those in the United States of America. They made their own government, and other governments of the entire world, recognize their contributions to its development. Then they demanded reprisals against the entire German people and nation. Here you can observe the difference in pressure applied for the BLACK JEWS of Ethiopia and equally for the BROWN JEWS from Yemen during the periods when their contributions to "JEWISH LIFE" were believed to have been unimportant. Until their loss became evident to the modern political State of [Eretz] Israel there was never a time when the "JEWS OF THE WESTERN WORLD" rallied in mass to the cause of the Yemenite Jews while they were being persecuted by the Yemeni Arabs. The reaction amongst American [WHITE] Jews was not there as it was in the case of European [WHITE] Jews. Yet the so-called "ANTI-SEMITIC ATTACKS" were the same as directed against African [BLACK] and Asian [BROWN] Jews; no less so than they were in Hitler's Nazi Germany of the 1930's C.E.

The reason, or shall I say one of the many reasons, given for our - BLACK JEWS - rejection by the greater body of our - WHITE JEWS - of the "Western World" was [or is] that the so-called:

"FALASHAS ARE NOT ETHNICALLY JEWS; BUT INSTEAD CONVERTED TO THE HEBREW RELIGION CENTURIES AGO BY PASSING JEWISH TRADERS."

We [at home and abroad] challenge the issue here; that the so-called:

'PURE LILY WHITE SEMITIC CAUCASIAN RACIAL [Kosher White] JEWS,'

the religious protectors of the HEBREW [Jewish] FAITH, who have maintained that:

'FALASHAS WERE ALLOWED INTO THE JEWISH FAITH, BUT NOT IN THE LILY WHITE SEMITIC CAUCASIAN INDO-EUROPEAN RACE,'

need to examine closer the fact that one of the last authors to have written that BLACK JEWS ARE NOT ETHNICALLY JEWS is one Professor Wolf Leslau of Brandeis University. His notorious book, FALASHA ANTHOLOGY [published by Yale University Press, 1951], is academically classic, so far as "Western academia" goes with respect to Africans. Thus he too went along with other designated so-called "AUTHORITIES" on the history on anything African; his conclusion reflecting this: "FALASHAS WERE CONVERTED TO JUDAISM." The amazing thing about this is that Leslau, like all others before him from European-America and Europe, shows that there isn't any actual proof of when and where our conversion to Judaism occurred other than by hearsay evidence reported by past European [Jewish and Christian] travelers to Ethiopia. Yet he still found it necessary to adopt the same conclusion of those professors and travelers who believed that:

"THE FALASHAS WERE CONVERTED TO JUDAISM BY YEMENITE JEWS."

But he equally rejected those who reported that:

"THE FALASHAS WERE CONVERTED TO JUDAISM BY JEWS FROM ELEPHANTINE." He further indicated that the reason for his conclusion was based upon the Yemenites having much more contact with the Ethiopians than with the Egyptians in past history. Even on this point history refuses to validate the able professor's claim. For it is written on the pages of African history that:

> "On several occasions Ethiopia, Nubia, Meröe and Egypt were combined under one dynasty by several pharaohs from each of these countries during different dynastic periods...,"[1] etc., etc., etc.

It is further shown in this great history and heritage of Africa that Ethiopia's major connection with Yemen in this manner was during the period when Empress Makeda's [also known as the "Queen of Sheba"] armies captured Yemen and imposed Ethiopian colonialism on the Yemenites. There were only two [2] other times in history when Ethiopians again crossed their national borders of the Kingdom of Ethiopia and entered into the land and Kingdom of Yemen.

For Professor Leslau to have reached the conclusion that the Falashas are not ethnically Jews, he must have produced for public scrutiny at least one of his own "ETHNIC [Racial] JEWS" from any part of the European and European-American communities where they still [allegedly] exist. But he must have started with the theory that there are such persons of "ETHNIC JEWISH ORIGIN" dating back to the allegorical and mythical "ADAM AND EVE IN THE GARDEN OF EDEN" to validate his classification. Yet if his theory is correct, then WE - Black Jews - should withdraw from the main body of JEWS and form our own system of Torahdic Judaism. But we cannot do this, for we must first search the evidence to show causes why we should be subjected to take such action on the basis of propaganda by those who set up themselves as the Kosher Jew Examiners. And after searching the records of the history of the Hebrew peoples all over the known world, particularly those of lighter pigment, we are unable to find one good reason why we should withdraw as a group from the greater body of our brother and sister Jews who appreciate us as we are, along with the major contributions we have made to the overall culture and religious way of life in Judaism; this being no restriction upon the individual Jew who may desire to leave the fold of world-wide Judaism; not to be confused with "World Zionism."

The white so-called "Christian Missionary" Isaac Stern, who came on a "conversion mission to the Black Jews of Ethiopia" in the latter part of the 19th Century and the turn of the 20th Century C.E., had already reached the same conclusion long before Professor Leslau and others before and after him. But Stern's conclusion was made in order that it could have become a convincing weapon to be used in the "CONVERSION" of the Falsahas to what he called "CHRISTIANITY." He, like all other so-called "Christian Missionaries," reminded us - FALASHAS - that:

You people are not wanted by the white-skinned Jews of your own religion.

---

1. See the "Kebra Negaste" [Chronicle of the Kings], which also deals with Ethiopia's Armies that saved Israel from the Assyrians in ca. 714 B.C.E., etc.

They have refused to accept that you are members of the Semitic Race.

To this the Falashas replied:

> Christianity cannot disclaim Judaism; therefore we will not leave Judaism for Christianity through the escape route of conversion. Judaism has never been the basis of the origin of any race or ethnic group except among whites in the United States of America and Europe and their master race policies.

Once when the Agaw [Black Jews, Falashas, Beta Israel, etc.] communities in Ethiopia, East Africa [Alkebu-lan, Ethiopia, Ortegyia, etc.] were only known to European and European-American [WHITE] Jews as the -

COMMUNITY OF THE LOST TRIBES;[1]

there was no rejection of us as "JEWS," and no theory about our "CONVERSION" to anything. On this we could ask no better authority than the late honourable Professor Dr. Jacques Faitlovitch, who came to our communities in Ethiopia more than three [3] most eventful generations back and lived amongst us as a brother, who proved himself worthy of being a member. It is therefore quite funny that we note this brother Jew of WHITE hue did not equally reach the conclusion of other European and European-American [WHITE] Jews and Christians who came for a quick curiousity trip to see the "natives" for their next volume to be published about the "...heathens of darkest Africa...," etc., etc., etc. One has to bear in mind that Professor Faitlovitch spent over twenty-five [25] years with the Agaw communities and could not conclude that in any part of biblical and post-biblical history we -

" WERE CONVERTED BY JEWISH TRAVELERS FROM."

anywhere whatsoever; the same being equally true for European Jews to their African-Asian base.

Who was Professor Dr. Jacques Faitlovitch? He came to the Agaw [Beta Israel, Black Jews] Community of Begermder Province of Northwestern Ethiopia, East Alkebu-lan ["Africa" - shown on the following maps on pages 42 - 44] quite by good fortune. He was sent to Yemen "...to make a study of the Yemenite Hebrew communities...," etc. across the Red Sea on the continent of Asia by a Rabbinical Board located in Holland, Europe. While in Yemen on said mission he was advised by Yemenite Jews of -

" THE MOST ANCIENT TRADITIONAL HEBREWS LIVING AT
A PLACE CALLED GONDAR, AND CALLED FALASHAS."

He thereupon made immediate contact with his home office in Europe, and was given permission to continue and look into the truthfulness of his information. He came, he saw, and he agreed; but he refused to return to Europe. By this time when he had sent messages of the fact that...

"THERE ARE HEBREW TRIBES STILL EXISTING IN ETHIOPIA, EAST AFRICA,"

---

1. Even the "American Indians" were once labeled "The Lost Tribes Of Judah" by certain Jewish groups in the United States of America in order to have original status as the indigenous people.

etc., Western [WHITE] Jews went wild with the news about the discovery of the century:

"A LOST TRIBE OF JEWS FOUND IN ETHIOPIA."[1]

We did not have to correct the fact that no contact with "Western Jews" had for centuries made both groups believe that the other did not exist. Neither were we aware of the fact that there were any other Jews in the entire world beside those in Yemen [Yemenites] and India [Cochims], and ourselves [Agau]. The first two groups were known because a few of our brothers and sisters had mothers who were of said origin. And upon Professor Faitlovitch's arrival in our community, we taught was one of -

"A LOST TRIBE OF JEWS FROM SOMEWHERE ELSE,"

just as he believed we were "lost." But the surprise and superficiality contrived in the minds of all concerned, and the elation that ensued, quickly subsided when it was made very clear to the "Western Jewish communities" that:

"THE LOST TRIBE OF ETHIOPIAN JEWS" THEY DISCOVERED

were in fact no different in their BLACK color, WOOLLY hair, THICK lips and other general PHYSICAL characteristics than the so-called "NEGRO AMERICAN CHRISTIANS" within their own midst in the United States of America, other parts of the American continents, Great Britain, the Caribbean Islands and elsewhere throughout the world where African [BLACK] people reside.

The fact that the "LOST TRIBE" turned out to be nothing more than the so-called "NEGRO" community in the United States of America, so far as physical characteristics are concerned, had to have had its repercussion on the so-called "SEMITIC CAUCASIAN JEWS" living side by side [so to speak] with "NEGRO CHRISTIANS," all of whom were for centuries made to believe that the "JEWS ARE A RACE." But the rejection on the basis of the AGAW [Falashas] not being part of said racial myth was met by the following from Giordano Bruno early as 1591 C.E.:

> "No intelligent person could believe that Negroes and Jews had a common origin. At that time, the Jews, descendants of Shem, were believed by some to be the ancestors of European whites. But once again the Christian Church had acted in the manner it professed, and put it foot down."

It is to be noted that Bruno was "...burnt alive..." for the above statement [and others of fact] which the political and religious so-called "authorities" feared and labeled "heresies." If he was alive today, and dared to utter the same statement, he would not have been "burnt alive," and certainly would not have been called an anti-Semite. Probably he would not have been sent to the place of the so-called "...everlasting hell fire...!"

1. The myth of the "Lost Tribes" continues unabated by European-American Jews until this day in 1983 C.E./A.D. Racism against African people equally continues unabated.

MAP Of AFRICA.

1688 C.E.

AFRICA, by the Ancients, was called *Olympia*, *Hesperia*, *Oceania*, *Corysbe*, *Ammonis*, *Ortygia*, and *Æthiopia*. By the *Greeks* and *Romans*, *Lybia* and *Africa*. By the *Æthiopians* and *Moors*, *Alkebu-lan*.

Note: European colonialists from the 15th through 19th century C.E. refused to accept their ignorance about Africa's interior and produced the type of maps as the above; with waterways, mountains, nations and peoples where in fact none existed, or where one should have been the other or others were placed.

Note: If ever most of the Europeans, European-Americans and African-Americans who have any occasion to think, speak or write about Africa and Africa's sons and daughters [BLACK PEOPLE] they should first stop for a second or more and remember that Africa is more than THREE [3] TIMES LARGER than the United States of America. Most Americans think, speak and write about Africa and her indigenous people therein as if this continent had only one nation - ITSELF. The scaled map at the right is shown in this graphical image to prevent the reader from making this type of error.

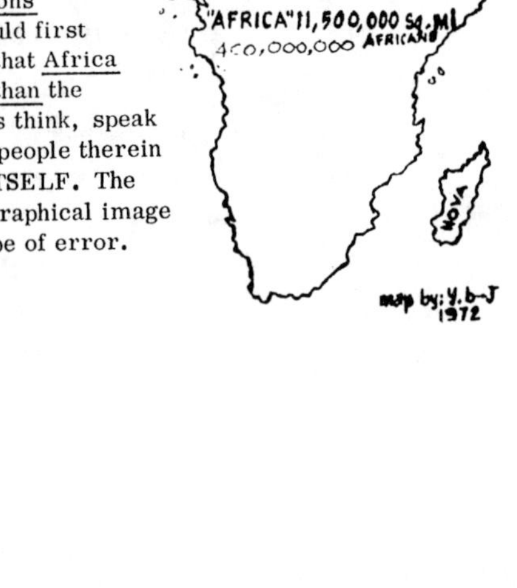

The following text of this chapter relates to the present contemporary aspects of rabbinical RACISM and RELIGIOUS BIGOTRY that made "BLACK" the color of scorn because of the so-called

"SIGN OF THE MARK OF SIN PLACED UPON HAM."

Thus, it may become necessary for the reader to once in a while consult this "Introduction" when you are engaged in deep thoughts about the validity and contents of the evidence in this entire PROJECT - Volume I and Volume II.

Your author submitted a much more recent updating of the facts of what "Hebrews [Israelites, Jews" and/or whatever else one calls the followers of the religion dedicated to the worship or the One and Only True God, YWH, Jehovah, Adoni, etc.] look like in the pictures shown on pages 11 through 15 of this chapter. If they have not changed one's confusion about the so-called "WHITE SEMITIC CAUCASIAN JEWISH RACE" and/or "CHOSEN PEOPLE," nothing else will. These pictures are representative visual facts of the "JEWS" who comprise the vast majority of the present inhabitants of the State of Israel; this being in spite of the fact that in said declared "democracy" it is the European and European-American ["WHITE"] minority that dominates the nation's economic and religious policies locally and internationally. This you should understand when comment upon this subject is brought in the public light with regards to the current confrontation between BLACKS and WHITES in the United States of America over ISRAEL'S INVOLVEMENT WITH AFRICAN NATIONS, PARTICULARLY WITH EGYPT AND UGANDA. For within this area the term [or word]. "BLACK" will be purposefully compared to the term and/or word "NEGROID" to cause confusion with respect to the "BLACK JEWS" of Israel, equally with the so-called "ARABS," both of whom appear on the following page side by side. This is not to say that all "NEGROES" and/or "ARABS" look like the following collage. What it does indicate however, is that the semantics governing both terms depend strictly upon the individual using them; but most of all the interest involved. On the following page, equally as pages 11 through 15 that preceded this page, the images shown are the same as the "CHOSEN PEOPLE" that were told in Israel:

"BLACK BREAD IS FOR BLACK JEWS, WHITE BREAD FOR WHITE JEWS."[1]

Few European and European-American Jews, Christians, Atheists, etc. have come to us with love for all which the late Professor Dr. Jacques Faitlovitch displayed.[2] Therefore, it is only natural that praises and credit must be given where due; to the Doctor, and the Pro-Falasha Committee of America, Inc. for accepting his works and trying to make them known to the en-

1. See The New York Times, 31 March, 1952, and p. 273 of this Volume for further details and references. This issue helps to prove the racist nature of "Zionism;" but who dared to bring this fact before the United Nations Organization when Israel was being judged for racism?
2. He, personally, displayed no sense of "racism" and "religious bigotry" like the general White Jewish Communities.

ALL OF THEM ARE CALLED "ARABS;" AND THEY ARE ALL AFRICANS.
LOOK FOR THEM IN ISRAEL

COULD MOST OF THESE BE FOUND IN HARLEM!

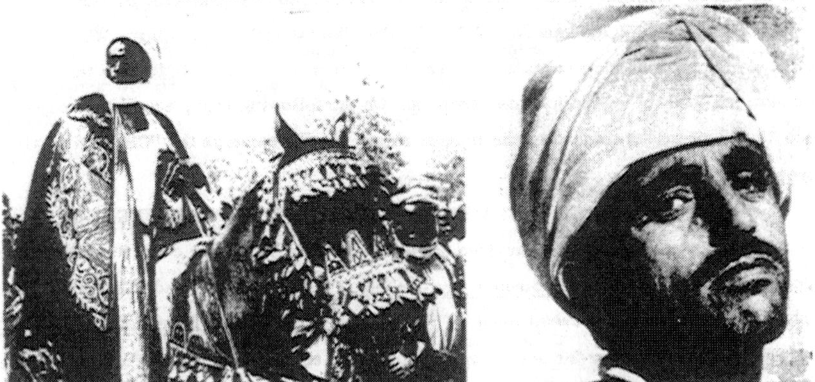

A Birthplace of Cultures

tire world community of Jews. President Emeritus Dr. Moshe Finklestein of the Jewish Theological Seminary, located at 122nd Street and Broadway, Manhattan, New York City, New York and others connected to this institution in the 1930's are to be equally congratulated for calling the major Jewish communities in the United States of America to "...render aid to tne beleaguered Falasha communities in Ethiopia..." when we were down, and almost out, after the Italian Fascist armies invaded and occupied most of the Kingdom of Ethiopia in 1935 C.E., followed by their systematic slaughtering of our people. The Falashas also extended their love and warmth to those very few White Jews who are not mentioned here, but who made their personal contributions towards their fellow human beings of Ethiopia, and the so-called "BLACK JEWS" in particular.

Our historical data is open to all investigators for investigation. Our history and heritage state exactly how and when we arrived in the land of Ethiopia [Cush, Habassha, Abyssinia, etc.] from other High-Cultures in the North - Ta-Nehisi [Zeti or Nubia], Meröe and Ta-Merry [Sais, Kimit, Nak, Mizrain, Egypt, etc.], and equally from Palestine in two different periods. This does not evade the fact that originally the Falashas, like all of the indigenous people of the Nile River [BLUE and WHITE] valleys High-Cultures, originated around the areas of the Great Lakes of Central Alkebu-lan [Africa]; the same area where modern European and European-American ethnologists, archaeologists, egyptologists, palaeontologists and other scientists have maintained. All of mankind had OUR evolutionary beginning. But the return to ETHIOPIA by the Falashas took place in the following manner: 1 Before Moshe [Moses] began his march or retreat from Ta-Merry [Egypt as mentioned in the Sacred Torah]; 2 Before the destruction of the very First Temple in Jerusalem; 3 With Prince Menelik Ist, son of King Solomon of the Kingdom of Israel and his Queen Makeda of Axum [Empress of Sheba, etc.], upon his return from his father. All of this trip is recorded in past Falasha biblical history, equally that of Israel. The last two of these three [3] stories refer to the...

> "Birth of a son born to the Queen to the South, at the land of Cush in the City of Axum,[1] and to King Solomon of the Kingdom of Israel/Palestine"....

Can anyone reject this part of biblical history and still call himself [or herself] a "Hebrew" and/or "Jew?" Obviously European and European-American [WHITE] Jews have no problem doing just this; even after making the terms "SEMITE" and "HAMITE" names of "RACES" for the sake of differentiating the indigenous Africans of Ethiopia from those of other parts of the entire continent of Alkebu-lan ["Africa, Afrika," etc.] and the Americas - the Caribbean Islands also.

It is also important to note that the biblical history spoke of a "...marriage..." between Abraham and a "...Cushite woman...,"equally as it did "...Moses to a Cushite Woman." And

1. Axum/Akhsum was her Kingdom, Sheba a Kingdom in her Empire. She was Empress of Sheba.

it is equally written in biblical history about all Jews:

> "And the father of Abraham's second wife was the Chief Priest and King of one of the Hebrew Tribes living in the Land of Cush/Ethiopia."

Among Falashas the group of Hebrews to whom the biblical story refer is the "Tribe Of Ephraim." The majority of the Agaw and/or Kylas [Falashas or Beta Israel], historically-speaking, descended from this "Tribe." Some have claimed that it is the "Tribe Of Dan" and/or "Gad."

Due to the difficulties "Western" writers encounter in trying to interpret the languages of Agu, Gheeze and Amharic [see pages 58 - 62] they have made countless, very serious, errors in translating the "ETHIOPIAN CHRONICLES" [also known as the "KEBRA NEGASTE" in Amheric] and other writings with reference to the voyages of Queen Makeda and her only child - Menelik Ist - to King Solomon. This problem adds to the distortions and belief that the Falashas now have to correct at all times in the presence of European and European-American writers who feel that they know more about us than we know about ourselves.

Falashas' written and oral traditions about the birth and voyage of Menelik I/Abna Kakin are in many documents. These works are available to all visitors to our communities who must know how to respect their hosts and hostesses; this being very much abused by "Westerners," particularly those calling themselves "Christian Missionary." They will have to read the Agu, Amheric or Gheeze language; for no one in the communities has taken the task to translate any of them into the English language, this being a major error on the part of those of us Falashas in the "Western World" [the Americas and the Caribbean Islands].

We must turn to look for those persons who have not converted to the Hebrew [Jewish] Religion and are of the so-called "JEWISH RACE" through lineal descent. They must be able to trace their "RACE" back to its place of originality. They must also present at least one of their members who can trace his or her ancestry back to Palestine generation by generation for a few thousand years - ca. 3760 B.C.E. - 1947 C.E., a period of 5707 years. If this is possible for any Jewish family to trace their generations back to their original ancestors in Palestine and Egypt or Nubia, then this theory of the so-called "JEWISH RACE" must be given validity; if not, it falls asunder.

Are we to assume that Jews in so-called "BLACK AFRICA" living in the land of Ta-Merry [Egypt] under the yoke of slavery imposed upon them by the various pharaohs [Kings or Heads of the Great House] did not have any social and physical intercourse with the indigenous population there? It is very important to note that Egypt's population at that period in history - from about 1630 to 1234 B.C.E. [the XVth through XIXth dynasties], a period of a little more than four hundred [400] years, was not constituted like the present amalgamation of African-

Asian-European peoples. It was basically of predominant indigenous African people who came from the southern inland areas all the way up to Central East Alkebu-lan's [Africa's] Great Lakes regions; this the ancient Egyptians, Nubians and Meröites made very clear in their references to their origin in the papyri they left their indigenous African descendants whom the European and European-American SLAVERS colonized and committed genocide upon. All of this control their artifacts and documents, thousands upon thousands which still adorn the halls of European and European-American public and private museums, schools, churches, synagogues and other collections to this very day. It was not the predominantly Arabian population that controls EGYPT today; no more so than it was the present Europeans and European-Americans that control the State of Israel today. The ancestors of today's Arabians arrived there in the middle of the Seventh [7th] Century C.E. [or 18 A.H.]. The European Jews arrived in Palestine during the latter part of the Eighteenth [18th] Century C.E. and the turn of the Nineteenth [19th] Century C.E. I have not overlooked the arrival of the Asian - Hyksos - in Africa during ca. 1675 B.C.E.; the Asian Persians in ca. 525 B.C.E.; the European Macedonians [and also Greeks] in 332 B.C.E.; the European Romans in ca. 47 B.C.E.; the European Byzantines at the turn of the so-called "Christian Era" [C.E. or A.D.] following the birth of the Christians' God-head - Jesus Christ [Joshua the anointed] and death; and of course the English, French and others who followed the Asian Arabs of ca. 640 C.E. [18 A.H.] and Asian-European Turks of 1200 C.E.

Must we assume further that the Jews living in Spain [Iberia] during the rule of the Africans from the Mauritania Empire's Kingdom of Morocco, otherwise called "MOORS," from ca. 711 C.E. through 1485 C.E. in some areas - a period of seven hundred and seventy-four [ca. 774] years, did not cohabit freely with their BLACK masters and BROWN masters that later came from other parts of the Moorish Empire - the Arabs?[1] And that from said cohabitation not a single "BLACK CHILD" was born to any of these so-called "SEMITIC WOMEN" of the "JEWISH RACE?" Remember, carefully, that the vast majority of the original Moors that invaded and conquered Spain and Southern France were indigenous Africans who had adopted the Mohammadan [Islamic] Religion, and not people from Arabia as we are sometimes led into believing for the purpose of maintaining the Great White Race mythology of purity. History has very distinctly shown us that:

> "The Moors were not interested in converting the peoples they met in Spain as much as they were interested in the labor forces of the area; the establishment of trade routes for economic control of the Mediterranean Sea; and the development of an independent school system for their religion."[2]

---

1. Even the recognition that the vast majority of Moors in Spain/Iberia were Africans is being racistly suppressed by "Western Academicians" who were/are Christians, Jews, Moslems, Atheists, et al.
2. M. Delacorte, Los Africanos Moros y Arabes, Madrid, 1740.

It is shown that all peoples within the Moorish rule of Spain shared in said Moslem society, depending upon his or her social standing. And that the Moors mixed freely with all therein, allowing no room for segregation of groups because of nationality, race, color and sex. Why? Because discriminating upon these grounds was contrary to their African Culture and Mores.

Joel A. Rogers wrote about the above in all of his works mentioned in the preface of this book [which many other writers have done in similar research with proof beyond hearsay] that:

> "...the children of these Hebrew intermarriages with Moslems took to the religious leanings of either parents. Some followed the Hebrew faith and others followed Islam or Mohammedanism" [see Introduction of this chapter].

Is it not true that we [Jews] captured nations in the past and forced "conversion" upon those who we did not wipe out completely; such as the Moabites, Zebusites, Parazites, Hittites and Amorites?[1] WE also refer to our ancestors [whom WE boast of daily] whenever "WE" have to hear or read good things about them. But do they allow us to say with any degree of certainty:

> 'I DID NOT ARRIVE AT BEING A HEBREW BY ANY OF THE METHODS INDICATED ABOVE?' [or], ' I AM NOT DESCENDED FROM SUCH PARENTAGE OF EITHER CONDITION MENTIONED ABOVE?' I AM A PURE WHITE

On this latter point Falashas have proudly stated in very loud voices:

> We descended from such parentage and all of the wandering Tribes of the Hebrew Nation of the past, equally those whose slavemasters sired them.

This includes the latter two cases mentioned above with respect to Spain and the Moors [Africans, and also Asians]. We can say all of this, since we do not have any proof that we are of any kind of "PURE RACE" [as the term goes, and for whatever it is worth].

Does color of skin or facial appearance show the difference of "CONVERSION" or not? How! Is the color called "WHITE" the criteria for being considered "AN ORIGINAL JEW?" Or, does the facial characteristic called "CAUCASIAN" separate the "CONVERT" from the so-called only "ORIGINAL JEW?" We will have to investigate these latter points further.

There are many Jews of "CAUCASIAN APPEARANCE" who have children with "WOOLLY HAIR, THICK LIPS" and "DARK [burnt] SKIN." But this physical appearance is equally classified as "NEGRO" and/or "NEGROID" in the United States of America. You and I know WHITE JEWS [Semites] who are sometimes taken for "NEGROES," or are sometimes called "NEGROES," which results in their desperate effort to prove that they are not. Daily we also meet hundreds of people who are called "NEGROES," but they meet the above description of "WHITE" and/or "CAUCASIAN" more so than many who are designated "WHITE" [review "Introduction" to this chapter] - the so-called "Coloreds passing as Whites/Caucasians," etc. all over the U.S.A.

We must now look at the other side of this picture, for it is not all one-sided. There is quite

1. These acts of genocide in the Biblical Holocaust are still being taught as having been directed by God Jehovah/Ywh; but not those supposedly committed against the "Hebrews/Jews," et al!

a few light-skin [WHITE] brothers and sisters of the Hebrew Religion who do not reject the darkest [BLACK] Jews. On this latter point I wish to quote you a few cases. These cases do not represent the only ones of the kind that could be shown here; neither do they represent the very best situation which could exist; just as those above do not represent the worst. Never the less, the fact is that on a whole Black Jews are not openly welcome by the greater White Jewish community as equals in "JUDAISM" - Talmudic and/or Torahdic.

I have selected these two following units - "HILLEL" - of B'nai B'rith and the "INTERCOLLEGIATE ZIONIST FEDERATION OF AMERICA" of the Uptown Branch of the College of the City of New York, New York City, New York and Columbia University as examples. These two groups are/were campus organizations of Jewish students. Their attitude about the darkest skin Jews were in some cases completely the reverse of what you have been reading above. In these two organizations Falashas found luke-warm, but not heated, friendship and love. Some of us were shown understanding by a few individuals, and given personal guidance which was not available to all. Here you found not only Jews who were given a place of "luke-warm" welcome, but also Gentiles who stopped by for an occasional conference. Amongst these students were their adult leaders, a few of whom were themselves rejected by some other groups who felt that their method of practicing JUDAISM is the one and only correct [godly] method. Among these leaders I found a few I could very safely call somewhat of a personal friend, such as Rabbi [Chaplin] A. Zuckerman- the spiritual leader of the HILLEL FOUNDATION of B'nai B'rith at City College. This Rabbi saw to it each year that the late Rabbi Wentworth Matthew of the Harlem African-American or Ethiopian Hebrew Congregation and Community, then located at West 128th Street and Lenox Avenue, New York City, New York, could address the above group under his directorship, in order that his [Rabbi Zuckerman's] students were informed about their BLACK brother and sister Hebrews of the Harlem Community and others throughout the Americas, the Caribbean Islands, West and East Alkebu-lan [Africa], as elsewhere.[1]

Rabbi Zuckerman made it a custom to encourage Africa and America - based "Falashas" to visit his group, and accepted all of us as Jewish equals, also to participate in Hillel's activities in his center. The students of the Intercollegiate Zionist Federation of America [I.Z.F.A.], now defunct[2] also admitted us to their organization on the same basis as did Hillel. This group was based at Columbia University, and met frequently in Earl Hall, West 116th Street and Broadway, New York City, New York, under the leadership of Columbia's "Jewish Chaplain" Rabbi Hoffman.

He had discussion groups on the various "Hebrew Communities of the World" which were not of Europe and North America; but there were also other periods for the latter two groups.

1. See pp. 293 - 387 of Volume Two of this project for further details on these Israelites, etc.
2. This group did not exist on many campuses throughout New York City's Metropolitan Area.

All groups of Jews were discussed there as just "JEWS;" not as 'special kinds.' We were not required to have been "Orthodox, Reform, Reconstructionist, Conservative," or of anyother type or form of JUDAIC leanings - including "JEWISH SCIENCE" and the modern "JEWS FOR JESUS," etc.

From the above evidence and experience many of us black-[darker]-skinned Jews concluded, somewhat reservingly, that:

"Hillel of CCNY Uptown Division and IZFA of Columbia University are living Judaism."

We found that in the past these two organizations' students and their leaders had thrown the "Ethnic Jewish Race" mythological theory out of their windows, where it justly belong. Your writer and all other people of black [dark] skin, whether Jews or Gentiles, never had to complain of being mistreated or insulted as we had in too many other places of White Gentile and Jewish gatherings. Unfortunately, the leadership of Rabbi Hoffman and Zuckerman was unique.

The Park Avenue Synagogue congregation, located at 78th Street, under the leadership of the late Rabbi Dr. Milton Steinberg and Rabbi Simon Novack was another Jewish Community that was somewhat typical of the above college groups, where one of black skin or complexion was never made to feel rejected. Of course there were a few places which could have been pointed out in this light; but they were/are in the minority as against those groups holding to their "PURE WHITE ETHNIC" [Semite] "JEWISH PEOPLE" and/or "WHITE JEWISH RACE" myth.[1]

I will consider the older Hebrew groups and see if it is true that the last groups mentioned above are not the exception to the general rule of the "White American Hebrew Communities." In these older groups, Jews of an African-American background and black color were/are always greeted in the following manner:

> "GLAD YOU CAME TO VISIT US. WE HEARD OF NEGRO JEWS IN HARLEM. WHEN DID YOU PEOPLE CONVERT TO JUDAISM? WHY ARE THE NEGROES IN HARLEM AND OTHER PLACES CONVERTING TO JUDAISM," etc., etc., etc.

The matter of the so-called "NEGRO JEWS" designation demands immediate correction. There is no such individual as a "NEGRO," much less "NEGRO JEW." Amongst people of African descent in the Caribbean Islands, Spanish, Portuguese or Dutch-speaking America, and all other parts of the world except in the United States of America and some other English-speaking colonies, this term - "NEGRO" - is not used with respect to a human being unless with the 'contempt' its original creators [the Portuguese in the 17th Century C.E.] meant for it to have. "NEGRO" is rejected by all of the dark-skinned peoples of the world who are conscious of their ilustoious heritage. "Black Jews, African-American Jews, African-American Israelites" and/or "Falashas" are all acceptable to various groups of Jews of African background, both at home and abroad; but never "NEGRO JEWS" and/or "COLORED JEWS," etc. BETA ISRAEL is correct.

---

1. In the United States of America the myth of a "White Jewish Race" is accepted almost everywhere; even among the so-called "Repectable Negroes/Coloreds," et al., of the "Harlems," etc.

The term - "NEGRO"[1] - has no history pertaining to black or dark-skinned peoples; therefore it cannot be representative of people of African heritage. If we should go through the White and/or light-skinned population of the United States of America and ask each person what he or she is, we will receive answers such as the following:

"I AM GERMAN-AMERICAN, FRENCH-AMERICAN, DUTCH-AMERICAN,"

etc., etc., etc. You must have gathered that the above names or designations can be referred back to definite geographical and geo-political areas of the continent of Europe. You can also trace the history of the peoples mentioned above to land and culture. But where is the land, culture and history of the so-called "NEGRO-AMERICAN?" And where is the national entity of the

... "NEGRO" and/or "NEGROLAND"...

other than that the Portuguese created for "West Africa" during the 17th Century C.E. on the following map on page 34?[1] Did it begin at Jamestown, Virginia in the year 1619 or 1620 C.E. in the "English colonial American" period when the Dutch boat brought the first boat-load of Africans from Barbados- British West Indies? I am certain that it did not come from those free Africans; neither did it come from the Africans who came to America with the French colonialist settlers in Louisiana before 1619 C.E.; nor with Cristobal Colon and his Captain of the Santa Maria - Pietro Olonzo Niño; not even with Cortez's Chief Confidant - Estevanico - to Azteca [once Nueva Españia or New Spain, also Mexico today].

When you say "AFRICAN-AMERICAN" you can associate this name with two continents by the representation of the FIRST and LAST words. Thus "AFRICAN" from Africa, and "AMERICAN" from America. This carries a history which no other history of any nation or continent can overshadow. "AFRICAN" also carries the history of the cradle of what is now called "WESTERN CIVILIZATION." Remember that the word "AFRICAN" implies that one came from Egypt, Timbuctoo, Carthage, Ghana, Ethiopia, Nubia, Punt and many other nations of ancient glory, all of which has never departed from "MOTHER [Africa] ALKEBU-LAN," even though they many have disappeared from your own school books, or they may have taken a trip to Europe with your European-American "academicians" and became a part of European and European-American history. In certain cases it maybe correct to have them in European history also; but they were developed in Africa, and as such they are African, for the land from which they stemmed is still in "AFRICA" or "ALKEBU-LAN." "GREEK PHILOSOPHY" and the foundation of "MONOTHEISM" are of this same type of "carry-over" when African people, nations and cultures became European, English, Australian and European-American, etc., ad infinitum.[2]

You may have wondered why your author has remained on the subject of "The Fallacy of

1. See Richard B. Moore, The Name Negro: Its Origin And Evil Use, New York, 1961.
2. See George G.M. James, Stolen Legacy, New York, 1954.

The Mythical "LAND OF THE NEGRO" and/or "NEGROLAND" White Style

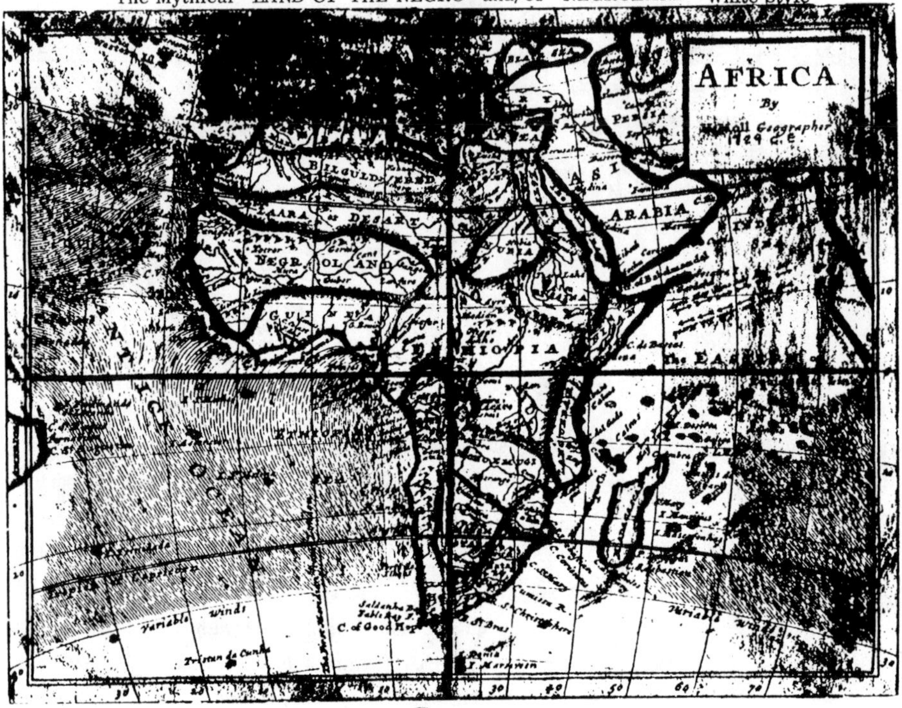

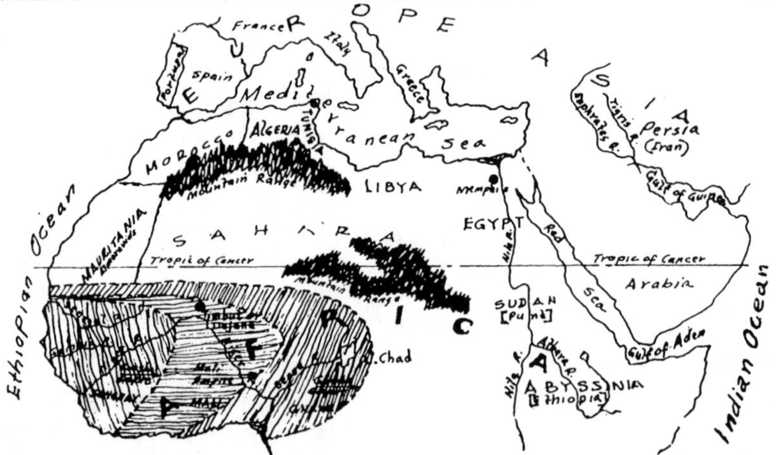

[Top] "Negroland" as per European colonialists. [Bottom] The empires of Ghana, Mali and Songnay occupied the area from ca. 100 B.C.E. - 1591 C.E. Strange is it not?

Racial Jews" so long, because your primary purpose for reading this work was to learn about the Jews of Africa and their culture. The answer to this type of reasoning should have been obvious to you by now, because this "FALLACY" has bearing on the "BLACK-WHITE" turmoils in the entire world today. If you have grasped the answer, I shall try to assist you in reaching some more of the conclusions through the following facts.

In these times of growing "NATIONALISM" throughout the world, and by the colonial peoples freeing themselves from the political, economic and cultural yokes forced upon them by Western European and European-American imperialist nations from the sixteenth [16th] Century C.E. to the present twentieth [20th] Century C.E. it has, therefore, become very important and necessary for everyone of us to know and understand these people in revolution more than we ever had before. There is, also, an urgent need for all of us to develop an open-mindedness to prepare for the history of these people which WE will be soon forced to read voluntarily or involuntarily.

The colonial peoples, mostly non-White and non-Judaeo-Christian, hold a great deal of power over the so-called "...highest standard of living in the world..." in the palm of their hands. We will find that most of the Black Jews are amongst them. We will also find that our attitude against one segment of them will affect the attitude of all of them towards all of US. We will find that the racial fallacy White Jews may hold against BLACK JEWS will affect the reaction which your so-called "highest standard of living" will suffer. Take what is happening in Alkebu-lan and Asia today against "COLONIALISM" and "NEO-COLONIALISM" as an example of what I am saying to you; no gasoline, no heating oil, no soap, and no whatever else? In Kenya for example, the policy of "WHITE RACIAL SUPERIORITY" has already backfired; and now when "...the shoe is on the other foot..." those who sponsored "White RACIAL Superiority" are crying murder, cannibalism, heathenism, uncivilized savages, etc., etc., etc. But no one cried "MURDER" when the Africans were first butchered, and are still being butchered. No one ran to start a war in "WHITE RACIST NAZIS" South Africa to protect the indigenous Africans from the extermination tactics of the program of APARTHEID developed by the late Dr. Malan and his "Calvinist" oriented neo-Nazis party comprised of White Christians and White Jews alike.[1] Yet if the shoes turn on the other feet there in South Africa, as they have done in Kenya, you are bound to hear the "WESTERN NATIONS" calling for, and carrying out, military reprisals against the African [BLACK] People within their own continental "PROMISED LAND" - Alkebu-lan/"Africa."

In the midst of these African People remain strong traces of what is called "JUDAIC" and/or "HEBRAIC TRADITIONS." Some of these customs you once thought to be "LOST." Your "HERIT-

1. There are no "Mass Rallies" in the Garment Center of New York City protesting Falasha suppression in Israel today, nor in the past - Independence Day in 1947 C.E. to the present 1983 C.E.

AGE," you will find, is the "HERITAGE" of many of these now rejected African [BLACK] People which you too dislike. Some of these revelations you will reject, but others you will rush to embrace. Some of them you will disclaim and say they could not have been in your past history, because you feel too racially involved to acknowledge that your forefathers once lived amongst these same people and received their first basic education and culture you now look at with total disdain. Another reason is that you may have found that you descended from these people, millions of whom you can still find in Nigeria, Egypt, Nzaide [Zaire, Congo, etc.], Sudan, Ethiopia and other parts of Alkebu-lan [Africa] and Asia where there are such very strong traces of the "Hebrew Religion" and "Culture," and which you will not be able to disassociate yourself. It is the fact that most of your biblical ancestors were former residents and indigenous people of these areas. If you reject this, you will have to admit that we - "JEWS" - were not the originators of any specific culture, and that others had developed along similar lines in a similar type society long before we did. But is it not true that our Hebrew foreparents got their "religious foundation" and "Ten Commandments" from the Africans of Egypt, Nubia, Meröe, Punt, Ethiopia and Great Lakes region of Central Alkebu-lan, even as they did from the indigenous brown-skinned Asians around the Tigris and Euphrates rivers of Asia?

On the latter point above I suggest that you should read the following books: C.K. Meek, A SUDANESE KINGDOM, Humanities Press, New York and S.B. Glough, THE RISE AND FALL OF CIVILIZATION, McGraw Hill Company, New York. To climax these two great works read Joel A. Rogers, SUPERMAN TO MAN; WORLD'S GREAT MEN OF COLOR, Vol. I and II; also NATURE KNOWS NO COLOR LINE, New York [and others published by Joel A. Rogers[1] himself in Harlem, New York City, New York]. Added to these is the noted work by Karl Kautsky, ARE THE JEWS A RACE, New York, 1918. All of these books should help you to better understand and respect yourself and the peoples of dark pigment, which you may now reject. You may reconsider your position after you have read these works; and you may take a different outlook on human beings than you now have. I also suggest that you will have to read other recordings on history along with the above, since most of them deal with AFRICA and AFRICANS predominantly; but in this case these are the ones which you must have. In otherwords, WE must read independently thinking non-European oriented African scholars and other writers works to understand the "FREE AFRICANS" and their "MIND." Previously held "CHRISTIAN MISSIONARY" propaganda equally topples when its colonialist and neo-colonialist support leaves with the colonizers.

It cannot be stressed enough that the FALLACY OF A "PURE WHITE ETHNIC GROUP" and/or "RACE" should be erradicated from the mind of thinking individuals in a world where everyone is becoming so close to each others. So close that a person can have lunch in China and dinner

1. His death took away one of the foremost "African Authority" on African palaeontology to date.

in California within almost a few hours of the same day.

To see the Falashas connection with the above, and all that is said about colonialism, etc., etc., etc., it will be necessary to take a peep into the ancient and biblical history of Egypt, Nubia, Punt, Ethiopia and Israel. You may find a copy of this aspect of comparative African-Asian history under the dust in the public libraries, or maybe your own college library, but definitely within the pages of the volumes I have written - all of which is listed on page iii at the front of this work titled "OTHER WORKS BY THE AUTHOR, AND WITH CO-AUTHORS," etc.

What is presently coming out of the so-called "Republic of South Africa" about the great history of these Africans now being trampled by the "...FOR PURE LILY-WHITES ONLY..." government should also help in showing why you should try to understand the need for this chapter of my work. Further notice of all of the hardships your own country has in taking a definite stand against the "RACIAL THEORIES" of itself and other nations within the United Nations Organization should make you understand the reason for this chapter. For there is no easy road to PEACE and UNDERSTANDING, no "LAW AND ORDER" to an angry man; and no "GOD" is as "godly" as the other person's "GOD," etc., etc., etc., almost ad infinitum.

Look at the damages of destruction the hatred of peoples' color, geographic origin and religious conviction have caused. You too, I suppose, can recall to memory Benito Mussolini's Italy and Adolph Hitler's Germany of the "Axis Powers." Can you find and associate any conduct in this entire WORK with the practise of "GENOCIDE" by these last two societies named other than in Germany and Italy before, and including the Second World's War? If not, it is due to the fact that you are now part and parcel of the "OPPRESSOR" instead of the "OPPRESSED;" strange!, is it not?

It is a surprise you receive when you meet people from far-off lands and your inquiries are met with the following:

"WE HAVE BEEN DOING JUST WHAT YOU ARE DOING FOR CENTURIES."

The latter quotation happens frequently, for too many citizens of the United States of America [USA] believe that the WORLD begins and ends in their own backyard or some place in Europe. And that everyone in the entire WORLD depends upon them for everything their now need, and everything they have ever needed, also everything they will ever need. Just go down stairs or across the street to your car. Take up your telephone and make a call. Where did the materials in the telephone, gasoline, etc. came from? Are YOU, all of US, equally dependent too!

Would it surprise you to know that there were Africans [not slaves] with Cristobal Colon[1] [Christopher Columbus] upon his arrival in the so-called "NEW WORLD?" Are you surprise to

1. The Captain of the Santa Maria, Pietro Alonzo Nino, was the Admiral-In-Charge of the Fleet of seven [7] ships of Colon's Expedition.

know that the Captain of the Niña [Columbus' lead or Flagship] was an African [BLACK] Moor by the name of Pietro Olonzo Niño? Have you ever heard of "Little Jon" the African explorer who traveled with Vasco da Gama? Well, if you are not surprise to hear of these Africans in your own history, along with Akhenaten [Amenhotep or Amenorphis IVth]-the Pharaoh who dealt with "MONOTHEISM" over ninety [90] years before the birth of the biblical Moses of the BOOK OF EXODUS, I am very happy. For you will find that it is the racial theories of prejudice which have kept these facts from most of the history books in your schools and public libraries, and of which yourself may be guilty of. This is mostly caused by those who taught us to reject people because of their COLOR, RELIGION, GEOGRAPHIC ORIGIN and a host of other delusions.

I close this chapter with these words which were often spoken by the late Reverend Clarence V. Howell of the Reconciliation Trips, Inc., an organization that was based in the basement of Community Church Center, 45 East 35th Street, New York City, New York:

> "Do not beat them with the butts of guns and the waving of money, instead, defeat them at the game of fair play and respect for all mankind, recognizing each man's merits. Then, and only then, shall we have no need to fear Isms, Schisms and/or Frisms."

Is it not the writings of our ancestors such as Aha, Ori, Imhotep, Akhenaten, Moses, Abraham, Isaac, Jacob and others WE find in the Holy and Most Sacred Torah [Bible] - the BOOK OF GENESIS? Or, were our biblical ancestors lying when they recorded the following:

> "And God created man from the dust of the earth in his own image?"

Were they also telling another lie when they stated further in the same source of information:

> "And God made man, and from his rib he made woman, and from them all of mankind originated?"

If the above be true, then from where does all of these "RACES" we are speaking of came? Yes, including the so-called "SEMITIC RACE" and "HAMITIC RACE?" The following quotations from the Sacred Torah are very much indicative of the type of COLOR and RACISM the so-called Sacred Scriptures indulge in:

I AM BLACK BUT BEAUTIFUL................Songs of Solomon 1 : 5.

LOOK NOT UPON ME BECAUSE I AM BLACK....Songs of Solomon 1 : 16.

MY SKIN IS BLACK...........................Job 30 : 30.

FOR I AM LIKE A BATTLE IN SMOKE..........Psalms 119 : 83.

In the reverse of the above, where the color "BLACK" is maligned, it is the color "WHITE" that suffers the malignment in the following extract from Numbers 12 : 1 - 16:

12 AND Miriam and Aaron spake against Moses because of the {Ethiopian / Cushite} woman whom he had married: for he had married an Ethiopian woman.
2 And they said, Hath the LORD indeed spoken only by Moses? hath he not spoken also by us? And the LORD heard *it*.
3 (Now the man Moses *was* very meek, above all the men which *were* upon the face of the earth.)
4 And the LORD spake suddenly unto Moses, and

Interrupting somewhat, ...remember that MOSES was an African/Egyptian - except only religion.

unto Aaron, and unto Miriam, Come out ye three unto the {tabernacle of the congregation. / tent of meeting.} And they three came out.

5 And the LORD came down in the pillar of the cloud, and stood *in* the door of the tabernacle, and called Aaron and Miriam: and they both came forth.

6 And he said, Hear now my words: If there be a prophet among you, *I* the LORD will make myself known unto him in a vision, *and* will speak unto him in a dream.

7 My servant Moses *is* not so, who *is* faithful in all mine house.

8 With him will I speak mouth to mouth, {even / clearly, / apparently,} and not in dark speeches; and the similitude of the LORD shall he behold: wherefore then were ye not afraid to speak against my servant Moses?

9 And the anger of the LORD was kindled against them; and he departed.

Miriam's leprosy is healed though God commands her to be shut out of the host

10 And the cloud departed from off the tabernacle; and, behold, Miriam *became* leprous, *white* as snow: and Aaron looked upon Miriam, and, behold, *she was* leprous.

11 And Aaron said unto Moses, Alas, my lord, I beseech thee, lay not the sin upon us, wherein we have done foolishly, and wherein we have sinned.

12 Let her not be as one dead, of whom the flesh is half consumed when he cometh out of his mother's womb.

13 And Moses cried unto the LORD, saying, Heal her now, O God, I beseech thee.

14 ¶ And the LORD said unto Moses, If her father had but spit in her face, should she not be ashamed seven days? let her be shut out from the camp seven days, and after that let her be received in *again*.

15 And Miriam was shut out from the camp seven days: and the people journeyed not till Miriam was brought in *again*.

Certainly we will not forget that all of this took place in Africa among dark-skinned/Black Jews.

In the above there is ample proof that "MIRIAM" could not have been "WHITE" and/or so-called "SEMITIC" [if this is a color and race]. If she was, God could not turn her "WHITE WITH LEPROCY." I suggest that pages 36 and 37 of Vol. II of my three volumes work - THE BLACK MAN'S RELIGION, Alkebu-lan Books Associates, New York, 1974 for further elaboration on this aspect of biblical racism in the "Holy Scriptures" [Holy Torah, Old Testament, etc.]

TRIBES OF ISRAEL FROM WHOM THE FALASHAS ORIGINATED

	Tribe	Leader	Son of		Tribe	Leader	Son of
1.	Reuben	Shammua	Zaccur	7.	Zebulun	Goddiel	Sodi
2.	Simeon	Shaphat	Hori	8.	Manasseh [Joseph]	Gaddi	Susi
3.	Judah	Caleb	Jephunneh	9.	Dan	Ammiel	Gemalli
4.	Isaacher	Igal	Joseph	10.	Asher	Sethur	Michael
5.	Ephraim	Oshea	Nun	11.	Napthali	Nahbi	Vophsi
6.	Benjamin	Palti	Raphu	12.	Gad	Geuel	Machi

[Ephraim and Gad are your author's tribes. Most of us are from Dan]

The original pamphlet that formed the basis of this expanded volume was written in the Spanish language under the title - NOSOTROS HEBREOS NEGRO [We The Black Jews]. It was completed in 1934 and published in 1937-38 C.E. I was more than pleased to have been able to translate the original into English in 1953 C.E. However, you will notice that I have since made a change from my Judaeo-African Zionist stand to a strict Pan-Africanist stand, thus dropping every aspect of my former tie with worldwide "Zionism."[1] The reason for this was, and still is, very obvious. The two positions are inconsistent and incompatable with each others. The following extract revisits upon Pan-Africanists the justification of our action to be free of religious

1. Falashas feel no loyalty to this form "White/Semitic Zionism" that ignored them/us for generations until it needed our bodies to use against the "Palestinian Arabs," et al.

acts that implicate us in foreign ties to nations whose interests conflict with that of African anti-colonialism and imperialism. The African and/or African-American HISTORIAN must be free of advocating any particular RELIGION if he/she is to be able to deal fairly with other African People whose RELIGION differ to his/hers. It is quite unfortunate that most of us cannot separate our HISTORY and HERITAGE from our own PERSONAL RELIGIOUS obligation. This author refuses to be a party to projecting my PERSONAL RELIGIOUS BELIEF to be synonymous with PAN-AFRICAN NATIONALISM. Due to this position the following makes for interesting historical politics today.

Amin-Israel Feud Recalls Fascinating Bit of History

By STANLEY MEISLER
Special to The Press
From Los Angeles Times

NAIROBI — In his new and sudden feud with Israel, President Idi Amin of Uganda has invoked the memory of a little-known event in both African and Jewish history.

While ousting all Israeli military and civilian advisers last week, Amin issued a statement in which he said that in 1946 "British imperialism had a plan to settle large numbers of Jews in Uganda."

If this had happened, the statement went on, a conflict like that in the Middle East "would have been with us here in Uganda and in the whole of Africa."

Gen. Amin, who is not a very educated man, failed to get either the date or the country correct, but his statement still recalled a fascinating bit of history—the British offer to the Zionists in 1903 of a piece of East Africa as the Jewish homeland.

The offer was made by Joseph Chamberlain, the British colonial secretary and father of Neville Chamberlain, the future prime minister, in August 1903. The offer stirred great controversy among the Zionists.

* * *

THE LAND that Chamberlain had in mind was in the British East Africa protectorate, which later became Kenya. But in those days the Uganda Protectorate was far better known than the East Africa Protectorate. Jews and the British public, who knew very little about Africa, lumped the two protectorates together and assumed that Chamberlain had offered part of Uganda to the Zionists. The mistake has been repeated often since then, even in history books. It is not surprising that Gen. Amin did it as well.

The British proposed a "Jewish colony of settlement" under British rule. It would have a Jewish official as chief of local administration and local autonomy. At first the British did not name a specific site, but they later proposed almost 5,000 square miles on the Uasin Gishu Plateau in the highlands of Western Kenya.

It is not clear exactly why Chamberlain made the offer. But Dr. Robert G. Weisbord of the University of Rhode Island, who has written the only book on the subject, has suggested a few possible motives.

Weisbord believes that Chamberlain was worried that [illegible] and massacres of Jews in Eastern Europe would send a flood of Jewish immigrants to Britain. Chamberlain hoped to head this off by settling many in East Africa. Chamberlain, according to Weisbord also wanted more white immigration to East Africa to develop the economy and justify the enormous funds that had been spent on building the railways there.

The position of General Amin had to be that of every Pan-Africanist, his argument having not suffered none whatsoever if the country in question was KENYA instead of UGANDA. European Jews and Christians who sat down to discuss the annexation of any part of AFRICA for the purpose of added colonialist settler-groups, like those mentioned above, were acting as enemies of the African People; this being equally true for those who aided the invasion of Uganda and overthrow of Amin.

The suggestion of a PROMISED LAND in Africa for European Jews, if carried out, would have resulted in much more of an "ANTI-SEMITIC" fervor among non-Jewish Africans than in the past over the issue of Israeli militarypersonnel in Africa's Sinai Peninsula. Yet this so-called "ANTI-SEMITIC" feelings which the Africans supposedly hold for the European Jews that control Israel has nothing to do with religion. Most Africans view European and European-[WHITE]-American Jews in Israel in the same light they view European and European-American Christians as colonialists and imperialists. If the Jews that control Israel should suddenly become Moslems in the morning and still maintain military personnel as invaders in the Sinai Peninsula the Pan-Africanist position towards Israel would still be the same. The action of the Africans in the case of Arab colonial control in Zanzibar during the latter part of 1963 and the first half of 1964 C.E. supports my argument. And what happened? The Africans overthrew the Moslem Arabs in a most bloody revolution. Yet, practically all of the Africans who fought against the Arabs were themselves Moslem. It is unfortunate that in the United States of America African-Americans are unable to make this type of critical selection and analysis between their role as an African People and that of being Christians, Moslems and/or Jews, etc.

Probably one day in the not to distant future African-Americans would understand that they are not being discriminated against because of their particular religious affiliation, but instead mainly for their BLACK COLOR, WOOLLY HAIR, THICK LIPS and other facial characteristics; this being a fact whether one is identified as a "CIVIL RIGHTER, INTEGRATIONIST, BLACK NATIONALIST" and/or "SEPARATIST," etc., etc., etc., ad infinitum.

The fact that it is always a matter of treating Judaism and Jewishness with being WHITE and/or SEMITIC, is the same fact that those who are BLACK and/or SEMITIC will always fight back. Until such time that WHITE JEWS are willing to accept the fact that they are JEWS who are not WHITE, and have as much right as they have in claiming a heritage that goes back to the biblical characters in the Sacred Torah, there will always be a need for clarity between just who is right or wrong in the so-called BLACK-WHITE CONFRONTATION between all who identify by either of these two words - "BLACK" or "WHITE."

In examining the history and heritage of the so-called "FALASHA" of Ethiopia, East Africa one has to remember that as an African People they [we] freely relate to the entire Pan-Africanist struggle in Africa today. Also, that they are not to be considered part of the "WORLD ZIONIST" struggle above their "PAN-AFRICANIST" position.[1] The issue of a religious race cannot be extended to the Falashas, nor to any African person, on the basis as it is seen from an African-American or European-Amerioan perspective. The Falashas must be heard; and will decide.

1. Unfortunately, Falashas have been brainwashed against any form of "African Nationalism" by "White Zionists" who enforce their own form of European/White Nationalism as "Judaism," etc.

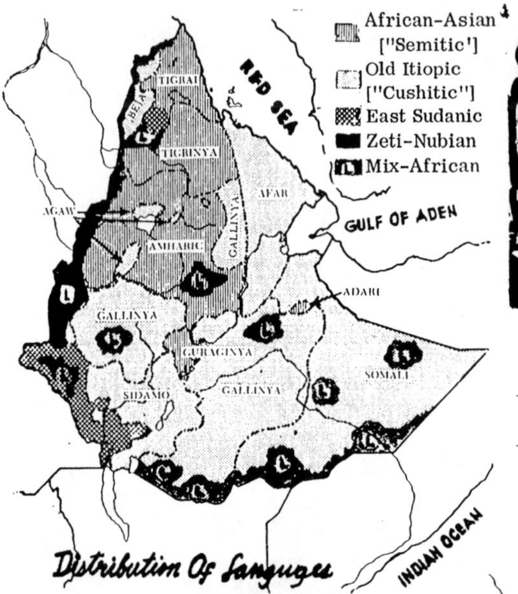

AMHARANS

ALKEBU-LAN
[Ethiopia, Ortygia, etc.]

ETHIOPIA

TIGRENO

DANAKILS

GALLA

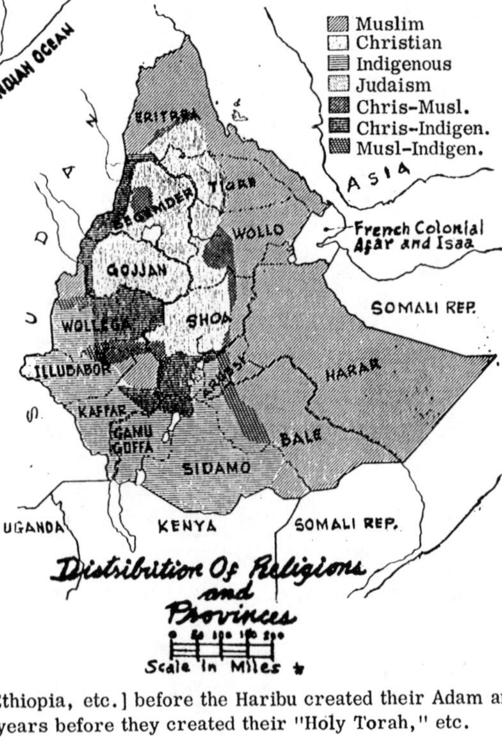

1. They existed in Africa [Egypt, Nubia, Ethiopia, etc.] before the Haribu created their Adam and Eve folklore, and many more hundreds of years before they created their "Holy Torah," etc.

PROVINCES AND MAJOR CITIES OF ETHIOPIA, EAST AFRICA

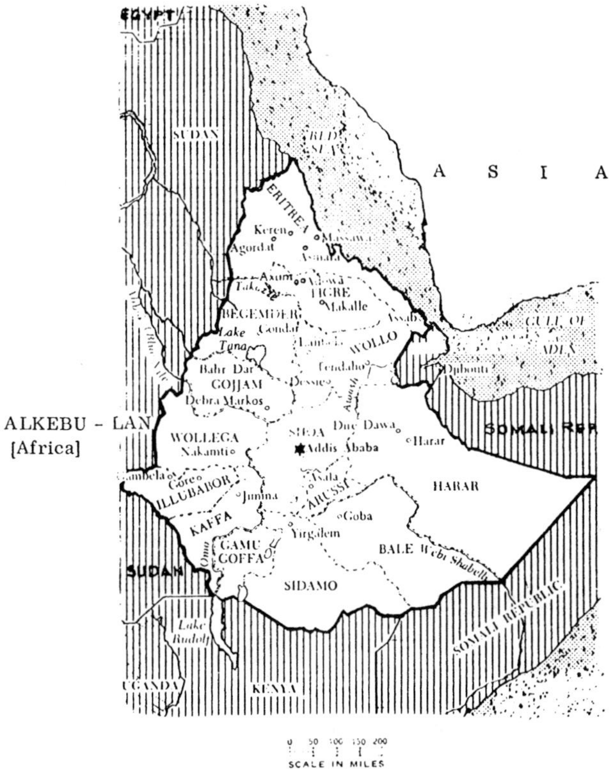

KEY

Neighbour State [Nation] — Ocean and/or Sea

River — River/Border — Border

o Major City ★ Capital City

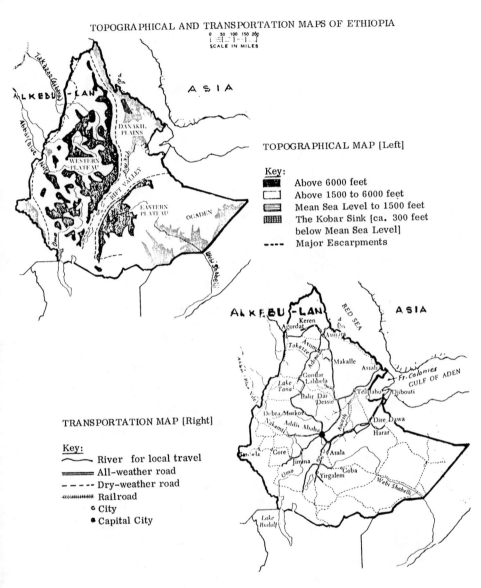

TOPOGRAPHICAL AND TRANSPORTATION MAPS OF ETHIOPIA

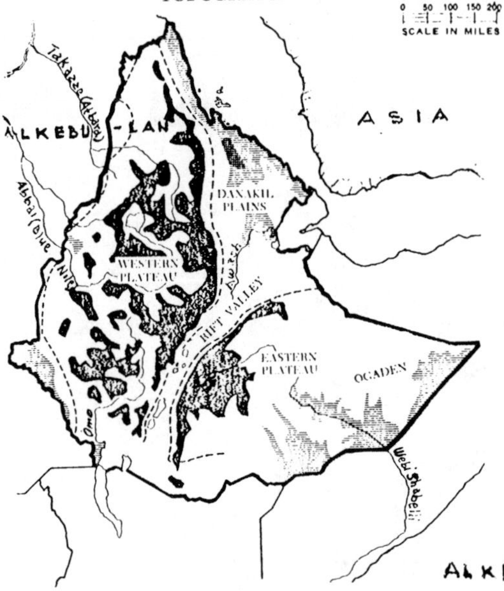

TOPOGRAPHICAL MAP [Left]

Key:
- Above 6000 feet
- Above 1500 to 6000 feet
- Mean Sea Level to 1500 feet
- The Kobar Sink [ca. 300 feet below Mean Sea Level]
- ---- Major Escarpments

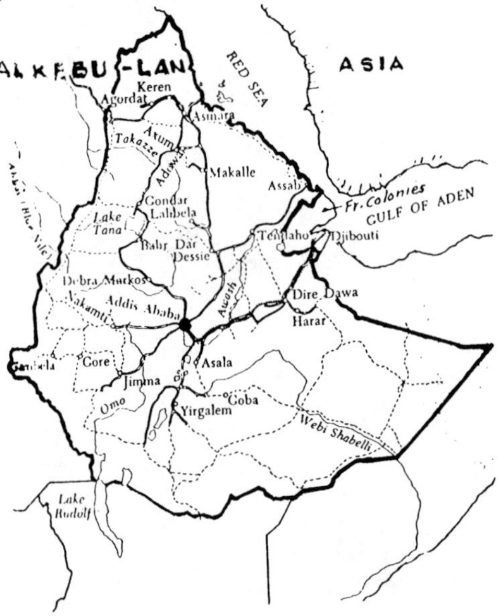

TRANSPORTATION MAP [Right]

Key:
- River for local travel
- All-weather road
- ---- Dry-weather road
- Railroad
- City
- Capital City

1. The British colonial name - "Lake Rudolph - has been replaced with the original indigenous African name - Lake Turkhana, equally "Lake Victoria" - back to Mwanza Nyanza.

Beta Israel, by "Westerners"[1] nomenclature - "Falasha," will not abandoned Ethiopia for Israel.

One of the most ancient, if in fact not the most, existing organized governmental society of history today is the Kingdom and Empire of Axum- which has become known as "Itiopi," and which the Hebrews[or Israelites]called "Cush" [Kush], also today's "Ethiopia." The Arabs and Turks called it "Habeshstan" and "Abyssinia" respectively. This land is the present home of the so-called "FALASHAS" [Agaw, Kylas, Beta Israel, Ethiopian Jews and Black Jews] and their offshoots that wandered off to other lands in the Americas, Caribbean Islands and elsewhere, all of whom we are about to examine further historically. This land, Ethiopia , historically, is even older than Nubia, Babylon, Sumeria, Egypt, Israel and many other nations of ancient days, most of which are not in existence today. Ta-Merry or Kamt, which we will call "Egypt" henceforth, is the same nation of the indigenous "woolly hair and burnt skin" Africans from whence the pre-biblical and biblical "pharaohs" and other African leaders originated. It is not of the present "Egyptian" population of the descendants of Arab invaders of the Seventh [7th] Century C.E.[or 18 A.H.] who came there with their "JIHADS" [Holy Wars] imposing Islam upon the indigenous African people, just as the Europeans were to do a few centuries later when they imposed "European-style Christianity" with their so-called "Christian Crusades" -SIX- to be exact. These two facts are very necessary to point out because they are keys in the history of both Egypt and Ethiopia and all of the Africans whom this aspect of Alkebu-lan's [Africa's] history applies. It is also important to make the distinction, because Egypt and Ethiopia combined represents the "CRADLE" of present and past European and European-American - so-called "WESTERN CIVILIZATION." It is also the Egypt of Africans now down-trodden by European, European-American and Arabian "CIVILIZATIONS" and their "NEO-COLONIALISTS." You will notice that these two countries - "ETHIOPIA" and "EGYPT" - up until the Eight [8th] Century B.C.E. were at different periods in history united as "ONE NATION," particularly during the pre-Asian and pre-European "DYNASTIES" that were imposed upon their indigenous African People..."Ethiopians" and/or "Egyptians." They extended as far east into India, and as far north into Greece, Turkey and all around Colchis, Assyria and Israel, etc. [see maps on page 46].

Though this brief historical, sociological and religious background of the home of the so-called "FALASHAS" will not be sufficient to cover the history of Ethiopia, or even scratch its surface, lest that of Egypt, Nubia, Meröe and Punt combined, it is basically necessary for the reader to understand that there was always a commonality between all of these High-Cultures and their indigenous African populations. Thus, I have selected only those portions I thought to be of greatest importance to the introduction of your very short SAFARI [visit or journey] with

1. They had forgotten Christianity, not "Christendom," originated in Alexandria, Egypt, Africa.

THE ETHIOPIAN EMPIRE
750–650 BCE

The conquest of Egypt by the Ethioprans in 750 B.C.E. during the reign of Pharaoh Sheshonk or Oroskon III was not the first time Ethiopians ruled Egypt.

Pharaoh Psamthik I of the XXVIth Dy nasty forced the Ethiopians out of Egypt in 650 B.C.E. after they were already withdrawing to the SOUTH, this due to the Israelites failing to fight the Assyrians as agreed in their treaty with the Ethiopians. King Essarhadden drove them from Assyria and restored the Temple of Bel-Merodach at Babylon as Assyria's second capital.

The ETHIOPIAN EMPIRE
850 BCE

The Ethiopians captured all of Arabia and Persia in 850 B.C.E., and up to india.

all of US - Falashas, Black Jews, Black Israelites, Kylas, Beta Israel, etc. - in our original indigenous homeland-Ethiopia, East Alkebu-lan [Africa or Afrika, etc.]. This I hope will make you understand that much more the origin of the same group of people who have extended their living quarters to the Americas and the Caribbean Islands.

"Ethiopia" is known as "LAND OF THE NEGUS NEGUSI" [Land of the King of Kings], and was always spoken of in this manner by the ancient Greeks and Romans of upper-class status and education. The current national boundaries of Ethiopia geo-politically, as shown on the following map on page 48, indicate a landmass surrounded by the Republic of Sudan at the northwest and south, the Republic of Kenya at the south, the Republic of Somalia at the south and southeast, the very tiny nations of Afar and Isaa [formerly called "French Somaliland"] at the east, and the Red Sea at the east and northeast. Ethiopia's geographic location historically is enhanced by the fact that the BLUE NILE begins at the equally historical LAKE TANA in the so-called "ETHIOPIAN HIGHLANDS." Because it is on the top of a few not too irregular plateaus, with mean elevation no less than four thousand [4,000] feet above sea level. Lake Tana sheds her majestic waters down the valley of the Blue Nile along the same path that the various High-Cultures [CIVILIZATIONS] that began in Ethiopia took in order to reach Ta-Nehisi [Nubia, Zeti, etc.], Meröe and Ta-Merry [Kamt, Egypt, etc.] before crossing into Asia, and finally Europe among the Greeks and Romans who passed them on to other Europeans later. The few plateaus are inhabited by human life as high up as six thousand [6,000] and more feet above mean sea level in some sections. And this general area of East Alkebu-lan presents a most interesting topography, particularly for aerial photography, and more so for land travel. The small lakes also present a picturesque pattern, blending in with the largest and ever famous Lake Tana that dominates them in worldwide importance and historical significance. ADOWA, the site of the Italian armies defeat in 1896 C.E. by Emperor Menelik IInd and his "lion killers," also plays a most significant role in the beauty of Ethiopia's terrain. A map of Ethiopia and its surrounding territories during the defeat of the Italians at the BATTLE OF ADOWA is shown on the following page 48; and on page 50 we have the comparison of the area before European colonialism at about 1619 C.E. Do observe that this map of "AFRICAE nova descriptio" [Africa with a new description] indicates the ignorance of the Europeans about "AFRICA" up to that late period.[1]

The temperature of Ethiopia climbs as high as 102 degrees F.H. above zero [0] during August in the Capital, Addis Ababa to a low 60 to 55 degrees F.H. above in the nights. These are the extremes of the range of the temperature limit. However, it can be safely said that Ethiopia's climatical changes are much more comfortable than that of the State of California and equally

1. The errors imposed on this map are no different than those showing "Negroland" in West Africa.

LEGEND

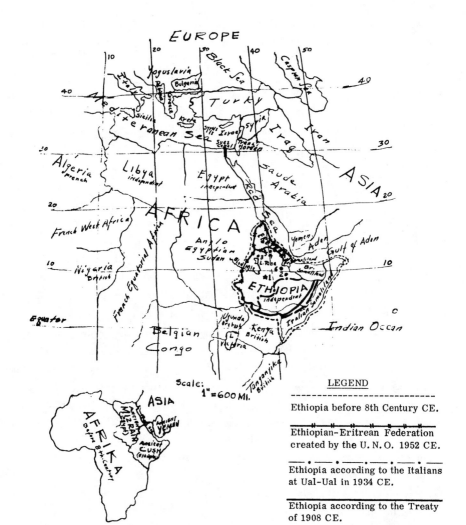

Ethiopia before 8th Century CE.

Ethiopian-Eritrean Federation created by the U. N. O. 1952 CE.

Ethiopia according to the Italians at Ual-Ual in 1934 CE.

Ethiopia according to the Treaty of 1908 CE.

Ethiopia as drawn on a map by the Emperor Menelik IInd after his defeat of the Italians in 1896 CE.

ETHIOPIA

[350,000 Square Miles]

Before and after the Arab and European invasions of the 8th and 19th Century CE.

1. Addis Ababa [Capital] 2. Harar 3. Gondar 4. Adowa 5. Aksum [Holy City]
6. Dire Dowa 12 Provinces 6,000 Mi. of Railroad 5,300 Mi. of modern highway
23,000,000 population Major religion - Orthodox [Coptic] Christian, Moslem, Hebrew, etc.

GONDAR

HOME OF THE "FALASHAS"

[the greatest concentration]

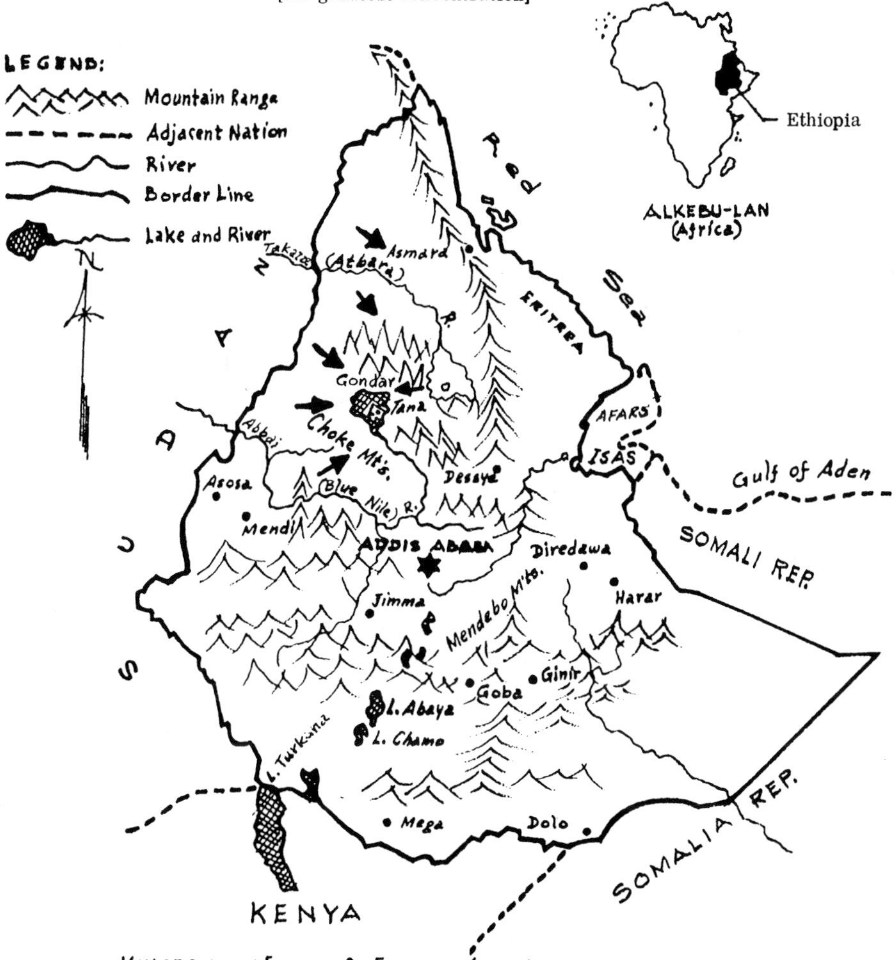

KINGDOM and EMPIRE OF ETIOPIA (Itiopi) - ca. 5000 BCE - 1974 CE.

Area: 398,500 Square Miles (population 24,000,000). Capital: Addis Ababa (900,000).

The National Flag: Three Horizontal Stripes Of GREEN, YELLOW and RED, With A Crowned Lion

Languages: Amheric, Galigna, Tigregna, Somali, Agau, Gheeze, English, etc.

1. There is no more colonialist "Lake Rudolph;" it is still 'Lake Turkhana' from ancient times.

ALKEBU-LAN/"AFRICA" [etc.] BEFORE THE 1886 C.E. COLONIAL PARTITION

[From France's Invasion Of Cueta, To The Berlin Conference: 1830-1886 C.E.]

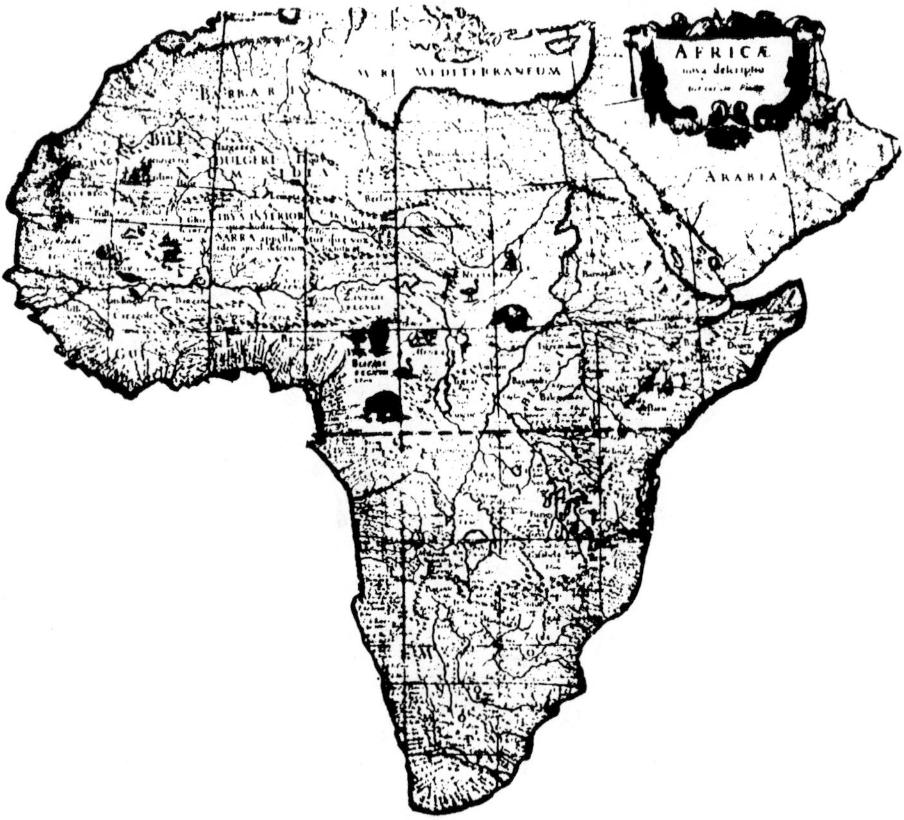

MAP OF AFRICA - 1619 A.D.[1]

1. Note that up to this period the use of the word "NEGROLAND" had not affected this map; and that it was not accepted by all of the map makers of Europe. You will also note that the Europeans had rivers, mountains, lakes, etc. all over "Africa" where none existed. The same equally holds true for "jungles" and states where there were no such things. These aspects of misinformation are still the basis for much of our anti-African racism to date. This type of "RACISM" also applies equally to the so-called "FALASHAS" everywhere we are living. The basic textbooks, out of which "Westerners" learn of Africa, are founded on these lies.

Florida in the United States of America, North America all year around. Being a tropical country, and with a physical location of at least 4,100 feet above mean seal level on a few plateaus of the "Ethiopian Highlands," the rainfall season does play an important role in the temperature and general characteristics of the climatical picture, but not sufficient so as to cause alarm due to few disastrous floods or swamps ever developing. This condition is due to the Blue Nile emptying its greater portion of intake waters from rivers at higher terrain into the White Nile at the juncture where both converge at a place in Sudan about the Capital City - Khartoum. Other bodies of water like the Atbara River drain the land likewise. The mildness of the rainfall still causes Ethiopia to be unable at times to keep up with the unusual irrigation problems facing some of her indigenous people; thus droughts and resultant famines are not exactly too infrequent in certain areas of the country. This problem was increased by the invasion of Africa by Europeans and Asians during the Nineteenth Century C.E./A.D. and the Seventh Century C.E. respectively. As Ethiopia also had to rebuild herself as a result of the destruction brought down upon her by the cannon and gun fire of the Europeans and the swords of the Asians, all of which reduced Ethiopia's institutions of every kind to mere shambles of their former selves.

Since Ethiopia had no outlet to the Red Sea from the latter part of the Nineteenth [19th] Century C.E. due to the imposition of imperialism and colonialism by French, Italian and British imperialists and colonialists [backed by European-American military and financial aid it was impossible to develop an efficient system of irrigation with the meager funds in her treasury; particularly when one considers how much the monarchist class and the officials of the National Religion [originally the Coptic Church, presently the Orthodox Church] pocketed for themselves. This was aggravated by the fact that the European powers purposefully locked Ethiopia into a land trap, thus controlled all of her exports and imports. Added to all of this was the fact that the Blue Nile presented a most difficult problem for Ethiopian and foreign engineers trying to harness its water for projects where hydroelectric power was needed. Of course European and European-American type industrial power installations can be constructed to harness this source of energy; but agriculture is Ethiopia's most important priority,[1] since she will not be able to become the type of industrial power so many of her leaders dreamt of. But Ethiopians, as so many other Africans, were too willing to ape the "Western" countries rush to industrialization at the cost of allowing agriculture to retrogress; thus creating all forms of famine in the land.

The population of Ethiopia is about twenty [20] to twenty-three [23] million people of many different cultural and religious backgrounds. A very small percentage is interrelated to Eastern

1. The leaders of Ethiopia's Revolutionary Government under Colonel Minghestu Marian started to change this too.

[or Asian] foreparents. But the overwhelming majority of the population's origin is indigenous to East, North, South and Southeast Alkebu-lan cultures. Various "Western European" colonial influences of the Twentieth Century C.E. in Ethiopia's population can be traced to the small, but economically and socio-politically powerful, European grouping which adds to the general so-called "RACIAL" and/or "ETHNIC" composition of present day Ethiopia's people. The make-up of the peoples facial characteristics and physiological body characteristics are as follows: On the northern border are the so-called "Bedouins," who resemble Eastern Europeans in facial characteristics; not color. The "Gallas" are generally huskily built, tall, and with very bright receding eyes. The "Amharans" comprise a very slight majority, about forty [40] to forty-eight [48] percent of the total population. The "Tigrenos" will be described with the Amharans, due to their very common resemblance, but generally with lighter black skin tone. The latter two groups generally have small body type, thin lips, small nose and woolly hair. The vast majority of Ethiopians are generally average size like all of the other populations of Alkebu-lan [Africa]. European and European-American academicians of all kinds, also visitors, always seem to find it necessary to generally describe Ethiopians as being "PROUD IN APPEARANCE." The next group is the "Agaw" [so-called Falashas, Black Jews, Ethiopian Jews, Beta Israel, etc.], about whom this work is basically dealing with. The "FALASHAS" do not vary in resemblance to the other groups mentioned above, except for the foreigners from Europe and European-America. But they are most dissimilar to the Amharans, Gallas, Tigrenos, etc. in their religious and/or cultural characteristics, needless to mention their political ideas. The roles this latter condition force upon the Falashas will be magnified above the other inhabitants of Ethiopia; but it must be borne in mind that all other people of Ethiopia herein mentioned above, and those not mentioned, are as great in Ethiopia's heritage and history as the Falashas, or maybe more so.

It must now be stated that the Amharan socio-political culture is the dominant one throughout all of Ethiopia. Therefore, it should be a bit difficult to understand why they are not the majority. Their language - "AMHERIC" - is the "OFFICIAL LANGUAGE" of the nation of Ethiopia. However, the general culture of the nation is one mixed with all of the indigenous groups mentioned before. You will also note on the following page - 53 - that Emperor Haile Selassie Ist represented what is generally called the "AMHARAN TYPE" by "Western" anthropologists and paleontologists. And yet the same page shows two members of the former "ROYAL FAMILY" that were made up of the several physical characteristics represented by all of the people of the total population. For example, the deposed Emperor's late wife,[1] Empress Manen, facially resembled the vast majority group commonly called "Gallas."[2] Another picture of the Emperor in full regalias of his Office

1. Deposed Emperor Haile Selassie I died of natural cause incident to old age, and of broken spirit.
2. Generally considered typical of the original Africans of Akhsum/Axum/Ethipia, East Africa.

THE LATE EMPEROR HAILE SELASSIE Ist[1] AND EMPRESS MANEN IN FULL ROYAL REGALIA

Emperor Haile Selassie
in
Ceremonial Regalias

Wearing the Crown of Emperor Melenik I, Son of King Solomon of Israel and Empress Makeda (Queen of Sheba) of Cush (Ethiopia)

(Amharan Features)

Empress Manen
Wife of Emperor Haile Selassie
in Ceremonial Regalias

Wearing the Crown of Empress Makeda (Queen of Sheba) Mother of Emperor Menelik I of Cush (Ethiopia).

(Gallas Features)

1. See footnote on p. 55 of this Volume for details on Emperor Haile Selassie's overthrow. These pictures were taken at the height of his power. Note the stereotyped "Negroid Features" of Manen.

is shown on page 55 following. You will notice that the PROFILE of the Emperor on page 53 is as much "CAUCASIAN" as many other indigenous Africans found all over the continent of Alkebu-lan [Africa].[1] This should cause more reexamination of the question of "RACE". It is very sad that the "RACE" myth was a factor for many years that separated Ethiopians; all due to Europeans coming into Ethiopia and making some of the population feel that they were of a "SEPARATE RACE" to all of the others, and as such they were "SUPERIOR" - a - la Semitica.

The precedent of an "EMPEROR" was established by Emperor Ebna Hakin, who changes his name to "Menelik Ist." Historically he was "...the son of King Solomon of Israel and Queen [or Empress] Makeda of Axum [later Ethiopia] and Sheba." Menelik also prohibited the practice of the "OFFICIAL STATE RELIGION," which was at that time "SUN" and "FIRE WORSHIP;" and which he changed to "HEBREWISM" or "JUDAISM" to please his father. For centuries the Hebrew Religion dominated this nation, only to be changed after the invasion of Ethiopia by the Christian tyrants from Egypt and Nubia during the early part of the Second [2nd] Century of the so-called "Christian Era" [C.E. or A.D.] Thus from this period the "OFFICIAL RELIGION OF ETHIOPIA" became the "COPTIC CHRISTIAN RELIGION," with intermittent periods when Judaism and Islam took hold of the nation. This explanation will no doubt confuse you without further clarification. It is clarified by the previous laws of the land, which provided that "...the Emperor of the Empire of Ethiopia's ancestors must have been lineally of the throne of Judea, and must be a member of the Coptic [presently Orthodox] Christian Church of Ethiopia...." Until the overthrow of Selassie it was the Amharan Christians that comprised the rulers of Ethiopia's government and people, a condition that existed from about ca. 180 C.E. Of course this does assure that a member of the Royal Family who follows the Hebrew [Jewish] Religion is excluded from the throne by virtue of the fact that he is "Jewish." This fact compels all members of the Royal Family to become Christian before any can be installed as King and/or Emperor of Ethiopia. Yet Ethiopians are aware of the fact that all through the history and heritage of Ethiopia the Agaw [Falashas or Kylas] had periods when they ruled Ethiopia, and which time the Emperor had to be of the Hebrew Religion. This tradition came during the reign of Emperor Menelik Ist [Ebna Hakin]- son of King Solomon of the Kingdom of Israel and Queen Makeda of the Kingdom of Axum [Ethiopia or Cush] and Empress of Sheba. All of this can be found in Ethiopia's KEBRA NEGASTE [Book of the Chronicles of the Kings, or History of the Kings], and it ended in September 1974 C.E.

The Emperor supposedly ruled by "DIVINE POWER, PROVIDENCE AND GRACE," just as all other emperors, empresses, kings and queens of the past - like Haile Selassie. You, by this period in time, should be able to understand why the Kingdom and Empire of Ethiopia must have

1. There are countless more Africans with thin lips and narrow nose than the stereotyped so-called "negroids" we read of as "Bantus, Savannah People, Africans South of the Sahara," etc.

HE DEPOSED EMPEROR LIDJ YASU IN 1924 C.E. AND WAS ILLEGALLY CORONATED IN 1928

Favourite Portait

Haile Selassie, Emperor of Ethiopia
Former Tafari Makonnen, Son of the late
Ras (Governor) of Gondar, Ethiopia.

C.E/A.D. HE WAS OVERTHROWN BY THE ARMY ON THE 13th OF SEPTEMBER 1974-C.E. AND "PLACED UNDER HOUSE ARREST." HIS SON CROWN PRINCE ASA WORSEN, WAS APPOINTED "EMPEROR" [CEREMONIAL] THE SAME DAY. THIS HAS BEEN DONE UNOFFICIALLY. THE EMPEROR ONCE CLAIMED TO HAVE BEEN A "SEMITE RACIALLY," BUT IT DID NOT HELP.

an OFFICIAL RELIGION." If you did not grasp the reason, then let us reexamine it together. For the Emperor to be deemed "...ruling by Divine Grace... " there must be some kind of religious connection with his rule, and this connection was through the "Official Church." As a result you once found the "CHURCH" and "EMPEROR" as one unit;[1] for one will fall without the other. This principle of selection started in ancient Itiopi upon the return of Crown Prince Ebna Hakin [Menelik Ist] from a visit with his father - King Solomon of Israel. The KEBRA NEGASTE [Ethiopian Chronicles] gives this account of Hakin's voyages to and from his father in Israel:

> When Menelik was only twelve years of age his mother - Her Imperial Highness Queen Makeda of Itiopi and Empress of Sheba, etc., etc., etc.- sent him to visit his father - His Majesty King Solomon of the Kingdom of Judea [Israel]-as it was agreed between the King and Queen. Prince Menelik remained for seven [7] years in the Kingdom of Judea with his father. Upon the time for return to his mother, he was given the Ark of the Covenant to take with him to Itiopi. He was told by his father, that he had to reestablish the Kingdom of Itiopi in the name of the God - Ywh - of Israel and Itiopi.

Upon Menelik's return to Itiopi [Cush] his mother Makeda/Queen of Ethiopia and Empress of Sheba

> ...was on her throne in Aksum. She relinquished her rule to her son as agreed, and as the King wished and suggested; thus Menelik Ist was proclaimed 'Lion of Judea, King of Kings, Emperor of Itiopi and Sheba,' etc., etc., etc. Now Emperor, Menelik Ist proclaimed his Decree that 'henceforth the Kingdom and Empire of Itiopi [Ethiopia or Cush] must have one Official Religion, this being the Religion of the Worship of the God - Ywh, the God of Israel and of Judea. He installed himself with the title "Negus Negusi, Lion of Judea, and Divine Ruler,".'[2] etc., etc., etc.

Since this historical fact the Throne and Government of Ethiopia have gone through many changes until they reached their present form, the same being true for the Emperor's "rule by divine power and grace." And Itiopi had been a family affair ever since the rule of Queen Makeda and her son Emperor Menelik[Ebna Hakin] Ist up to the symbolic ruler- His Imperial Majesty Asa Worsen [son of deposed Emperor Haile Selassie Ist - a cousin of the late Emperor Lidj Yasu whom Selassie murdered in the early 1920's- the rightful heir to the throne left him by his grandfather Emperor Menelik IInd][3] There were times when one member of the Royal Family would dethrone another before Selassie did the same to Lidj Yasu; the last time before this being his poisoning of Empress Zaditu during the early 1920's.[4] Somehow these palace intrigues did little to change

1. Church and State in Ethiopia were always a single unity until the 1974 C.E. "People's Revolution" that succeeded in overthrowing the Emperor and the Abuna or Head of the National Church.
2. A direct word by word translation from Gheeze and Amheric to English is impossible.
3. See Y. ben-Jochannan's BLACK MAN OF THE NILE AND HIS FAMILY, p. 288.
4. Note that the overthrow of Emperor Haile Selassie in September, 1974 C.E. caused his own son, Crown Prince Asa Worsen, to replace him. He had deserted his father's cause on a previous attempt made to overthrow him. Worsen plays no part in the present Government today.

the family line of Itiopi. They always remained the ruling power, once up to the present son of dethroned Emperor Haile Selassie Ist. Yet this family's rule was interrupted early as the period when the "Ethiopian-Nubian-Merowite-Egyptian" dynastics flourished. But for some unknown reason the original family always returned victorious with the help of the Ethiopian people. The last time this happened was the return of Emperor Haile Selassie Ist in 1942 C.E. following his overthrow [after he fled his country and left his people to suffer under the heals of the Fascists and Nazis] by Il Duce Benito Mussolini, King Victor Emmanuel IInd and Pope Pius XIIth of the Roman Catholic Church in Rome. For further details relating to the period when Ethiopia, Nubia, Meröe and Egypt shared common dynastic reigns see the chronologies in BLACK MAN OF THE NILE, pages 136 - 164. It will be more than worthwhile that you also read the entire Chapter in which the chronologies equally appear in BLACK MAN OF THE NILE AND HIS FAMILY, pages 131 - 164. There is equally a 1981 C.E./A.D. Enlarged Edition of this work, page 175, etc.

Going back to the once dominant cultural group- "Amharans" - we find that their center of influence was also established in the Province [state] of Amhara. Amhara, geographically speaking, is located around the central area of Ethiopia. This former seat of "Amharan Culture" still sets the basis upon which the government functions from its power-base in Addis Ababa - Capital City of Ethiopia. It is this "culture" from whence the present National Federal Language, AMHARIC," comes; as it is named for its people - "AMHARANS." It is one of the so-called "SEMITIC" and/or "HAMITIC" languages. Of course this language is a mixed composite of a few other languages of much more ancient origin than the first so-called "SEMITE" - the Hebrews mythological character named "SHEM" or "SEM" [the first son of Noah, Noe or Noa], all of which can be found in the story of NOAH AND THE FLOOD in the Pentateuch [or Sacred Holy Torah, also called the "Old Testament" by the Christians. See the Book Of Genesis or First Book Of Moses]. The names of some of the languages that contributed to Amheric are: "Agu, Geeze [or Gheeze] and the "Old Coptic."The first one is the oldest of the three. It was the very first language of Akhsun [Axum, Cush, or the original Itiopi that became Ethiopia]. Amheric has about eighty-five [85] distinct "characters." These "characters" make up the alphabet and other foundations of the entire grammar of the Amharic language. However, it must be understood that all of the characters in the language are not always used as individual letters. Some represent complete words, prefixes, suffixes, syllables, etc., while others serve as phrases and phonics. The following on pages 58 - 63 are examples of Amheric writings. Page 58 was extracted from LIGHT AND PEACE, the late Emperor Selassie's personal newspaper of 1929 C.E. This old form bears a closer similarity to OLD COPTIC and GHEEZE than any of the other languages of the Nile Valley which helped give birth to it. "Western educators" have insisted that there is very much more

EXAMPLE OF AN AFRICAN LANGUAGE OTHER THAN HIEROGLYPHIC AND DEMOTIC SCRIPTS, ETHIOPIA'S "AMHERIC" or "AMHARIC" [review "distribution of languages" on page 42 of this volume][1]

3ANNEE N° 50

JEUDI 4 DECEMBRE 1929

ብርሃንና ሰላም

LUMIERE et PAIX

Sa Majeste le Roi Teferi Makonnen, profondement désireux de voir regner dans son pays la lumière et la paix, a voulu que ce journal soit intitulé" Lumière et Paix"

Hebdomadaire paraissant tous les Jeudis

Diréction et Rédaction
Addis Abeba (Ethiopie)

Abonnement
Ethiopie: Un an 5 Thalers
Etranger: Un an 7 Thalers
le numero 2 piastres

[Extract from the front page of former Emperor Haile Selassie's newspaper, LIGHT AND PEACE, published in 1929 C.E. Note that the CHARACTERS preceded that of Hebrew]

1. Strange! Most Europeans and European-Americans still maintain that "...the natives [meaning Africans] never developed a language of their own before the arrival of the Christian Missionaries from Europe and America." This language base preceded Europe's first civilization - Greece.

THE ETHIOPIC SYLLABARY

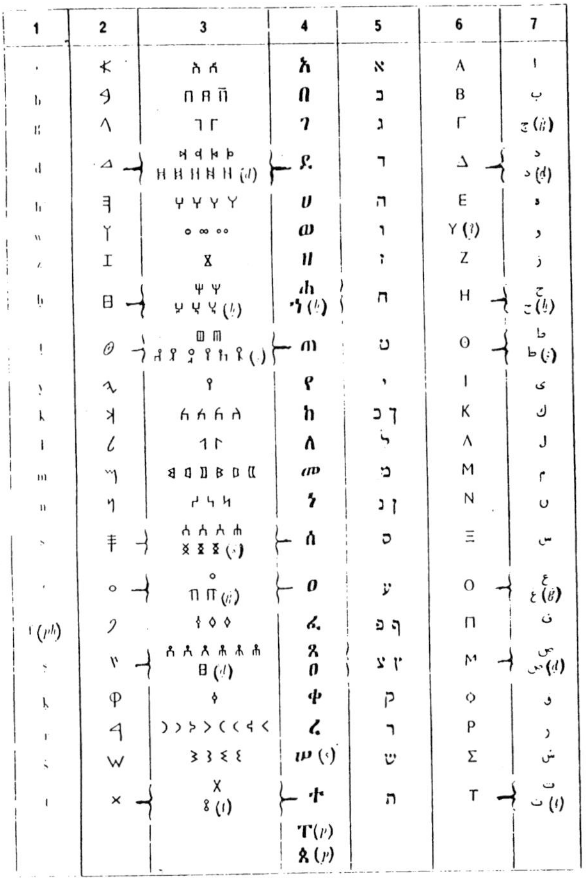

KEY

1. Phonetic origin
2. Phoenician
3. Southern-Arabian
4. Itiopic [Ethiopic], Agau, etc.
5. Hebrew [aramaic]
6. Old Greek
7. Old Arabic

Note that I have not used the term "SEMITIC" for either of the above alphabetical symbols; this being, because the term is a misnomer that originated in the "Noah and the Ark" biblical allegory. The same equally holds true for "HAMITIC," as they have no proper place in African heritage.

THE ETHIOPIC SYLLABARY

1		2		3		4		5		6		7	
ሀ	hä	ሁ	hu	ሂ	hi	ሃ	hā	ሄ	hē	ህ	h, *or* hi	ሆ	ho
ለ	la	ሉ	lu	ሊ	li	ላ	lā	ሌ	lē	ል	l, *or* li	ሎ	lo
ሐ	hä	ሑ	hu	ሒ	hi	ሓ	hā	ሔ	hē	ሕ	h, *or* hi	ሖ	ho
መ	ma	ሙ	mu	ሚ	mi	ማ	mā	ሜ	mē	ም	m, *or* mi	ሞ	mo
ሠ	sa	ሡ	su	ሢ	si	ሣ	sā	ሤ	sē	ሥ	s, *or* si	ሦ	so
ረ	ra	ሩ	ru	ሪ	ri	ራ	rā	ሬ	rē	ር	r, *or* ri	ሮ	ro
ሰ	sa	ሱ	su	ሲ	si	ሳ	sā	ሴ	sē	ስ	s, *or* si	ሶ	so
ሸ	sha	ሹ	shu	ሺ	shi	ሻ	shā	ሼ	shē	ሽ	sh, *or* shi	ሾ	sho
ቀ	*ka*	ቁ	*ku*	ቂ	*ki*	ቃ	*kā*	ቄ	*kē*	ቅ	*k*, *or* *ki*	ቆ	*ko*
በ	ba	ቡ	bu	ቢ	bi	ባ	bā	ቤ	bē	ብ	b, *or* bi	ቦ	bo
ተ	ta	ቱ	tu	ቲ	ti	ታ	tā	ቴ	tē	ት	t, *or* ti	ቶ	to
ቸ	cha	ቹ	chu	ቺ	chi	ቻ	chā	ቼ	chē	ች	ch, *or* chi	ቾ	cho
ኀ	ha	ኁ	hu	ኂ	hi	ኃ	hā	ኄ	hē	ኅ	h, *or* hi	ኆ	ho
ነ	na	ኑ	nu	ኒ	ni	ና	nā	ኔ	nē	ን	n, *or* ni	ኖ	no
ኘ	ña	ኙ	ñu	ኚ	ñi	ኛ	ñā	ኜ	ñē	ኝ	ñ, *or* ñi	ኞ	ño
አ	ä	ኡ	u	ኢ	i	ኣ	ā	ኤ	ē	እ	i	ኦ	o
ከ	ka	ኩ	ku	ኪ	ki	ካ	kā	ኬ	kē	ክ	k, *or* ki	ኮ	ko
ኸ	kha	ኹ	khu	ኺ	khi	ኻ	khā	ኼ	khē	ኽ	kh, *or* khi	ኾ	kho
ወ	wa	ዉ	wu	ዊ	wi	ዋ	wā	ዌ	wē	ው	w, *or* wi	ዎ	wo
ዐ	ä	ዑ	u	ዒ	i	ዓ	ā	ዔ	ē	ዕ	i	ዖ	o
ዘ	za	ዙ	zu	ዚ	zi	ዛ	zā	ዜ	zē	ዝ	z, *or* zi	ዞ	zo
ዠ	zha	ዡ	zhu	ዢ	zhi	ዣ	zhā	ዤ	zhē	ዥ	zh, *or* zhi	ዦ	zho
የ	ya	ዩ	yu	ዪ	yi	ያ	yā	ዬ	yē	ይ	y, *or* yi	ዮ	yo
ደ	da	ዱ	du	ዲ	di	ዳ	dā	ዴ	dē	ድ	d, *or* di	ዶ	do
ጀ	ja	ጁ	ju	ጂ	ji	ጃ	jā	ጄ	jē	ጅ	j, *or* ji	ጆ	jo
ገ	ga	ጉ	gu	ጊ	gi	ጋ	gā	ጌ	gē	ግ	g, *or* gi	ጎ	go
ጠ	*ta*	ጡ	*tu*	ጢ	*ti*	ጣ	*tā*	ጤ	*tē*	ጥ	*t*, *or* *ti*	ጦ	*to*
ጨ	*cha*	ጩ	*chu*	ጪ	*chi*	ጫ	*chā*	ጬ	*chē*	ጭ	*ch*, *or* *chi*	ጮ	*cho*
ጰ	*pa*	ጱ	*pu*	ጲ	*pi*	ጳ	*pā*	ጴ	*pē*	ጵ	*p*, *or* *pi*	ጶ	*po*
ጸ	*tsa*	ጹ	*tsu*	ጺ	*tsi*	ጻ	*tsā*	ጼ	*tsē*	ጽ	*ts*, *or* *tsi*	ጾ	*tso*
ፀ	*tsa*	ፁ	*tsu*	ፂ	*tsi*	ፃ	*tsā*	ፄ	*tsē*	ፅ	*ts*, *or* *tsi*	ፆ	*tso*
ፈ	fa	ፉ	fu	ፊ	fi	ፋ	fā	ፌ	fē	ፍ	f, *or* fi	ፎ	fo
ፐ	pa	ፑ	pu	ፒ	pi	ፓ	pā	ፔ	pē	ፕ	p, *or* pi	ፖ	po

KEY

Consonants

k = explosive k
ñ as in Spanish; French or Italian gn
kh = ch in *loch*; German ch
zh = s in *leisure*: French j

Vowels [using Italian base]:

1st form neutral as in French 'le'
2nd ,, long u
3rd ,, long i
4th ,, long a

There is no attempt being done to give a course here in Amharic, only a few examples relative to qualities of the language are given. There are many books written in English with regards to learning this rather difficult language. However, here is another part of the evidence which shows "Western Academicians" as liars when they say that "the Africans never invented any language."

1

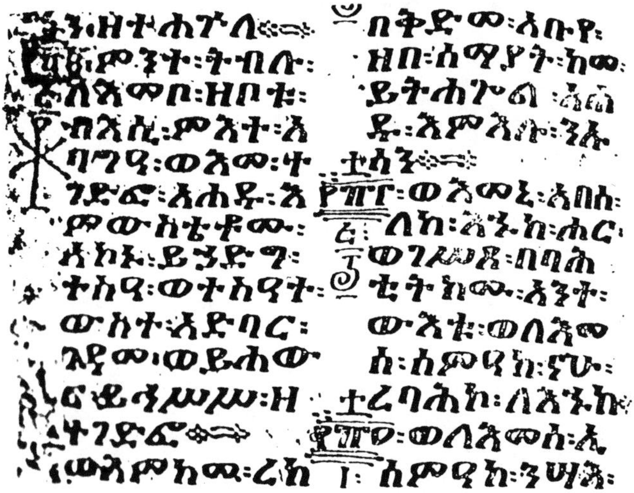

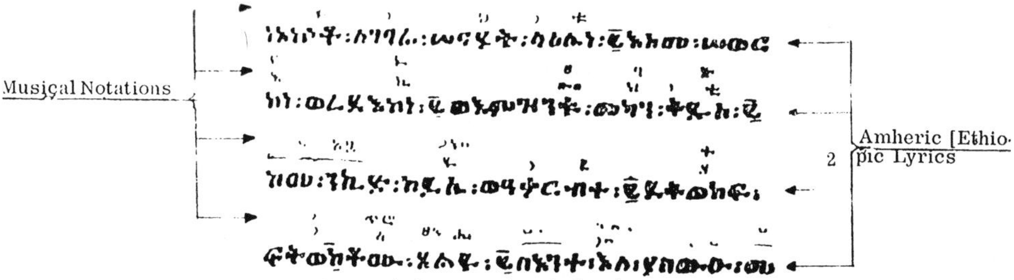

2

Example of Ethiopian musical notation from a breviary

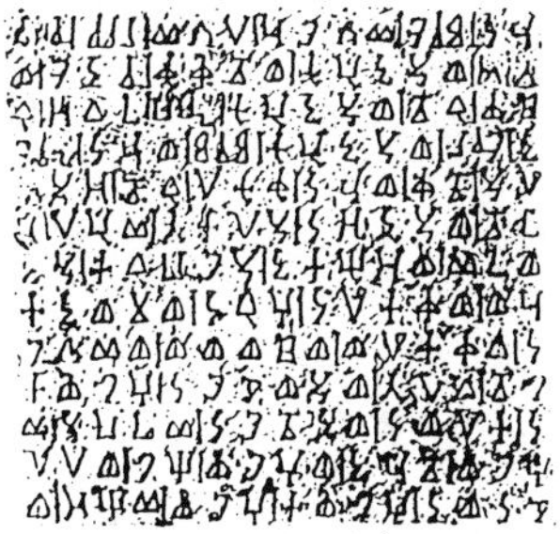

3

4

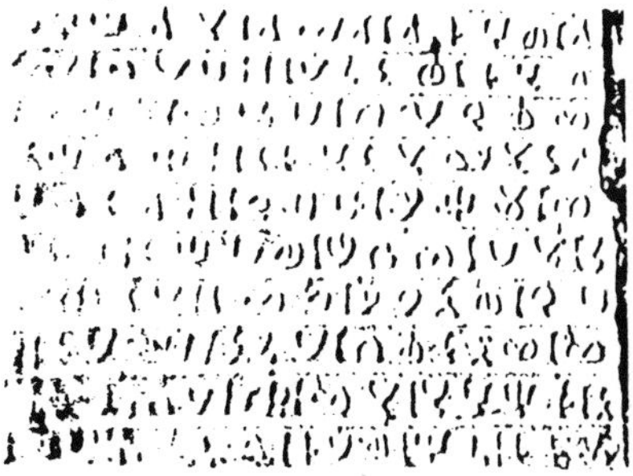

1. Extract from a page [note two columns] of the "Lake Hayq Gospels" in the National Library, Addis Ababa; 2. Amheric words; 3. Itiopic inscription of King Ezana [see Deutsche Aksum Expedition]; 4. Grave stone inscription, Ham, Eritrea [dated back to the Eight Century C.E. or A.D.] in Old Itiopic.

AFRICAN, ASIAN, "AMERICAN, EUROPEAN SCRIPTS[1]

Specimen of Coptic writing.

ግርማዊ፡ቀዳማዊ፡ኃይለ፡ሥላሴ፡ክቡር፡ሚስተር፡አርተ
ር፡ኤል፡ሪቻርድር፡ላደረጉት፡ንግግር፡መልስ፡ሲሰጡ።

His Imperial Majesty called H. M. S. ETHIOPIA a sign of the continuing friendship between the governments of Ethiopia and the United States

Specimen of Amheric writing.

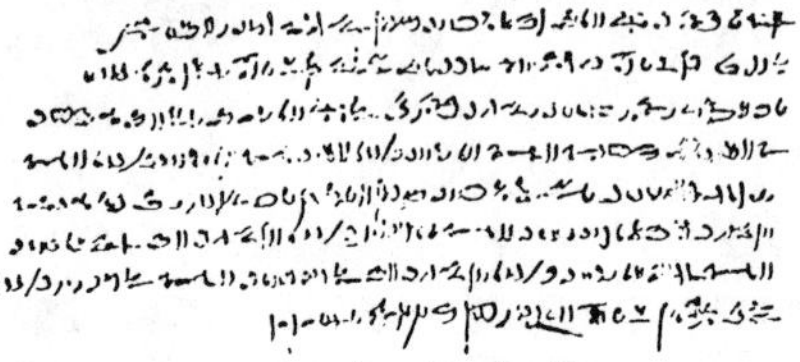

Specimen of Demotic writing.

IRELAND AND GREAT BRITAIN
MAYAS CENTAMERS MEXICAN
EGYPTIAN
IRELAND AND GREAT BRITAIN
MAYAS CENTAMER & MEXICO.
EGYPTIAN

1. Where is the European indigenous language as old as that of Ethiopia and Egypt; Europe's oldest is Greek or Etruscan, either having no origin before 1500 - 2000 B.C.E. - if this much!

ALKEBU-LAN/"AFRICA" SPEAKS AND WRITES
NILE VALLEY "AFRICA" SCRIPTS

SOME SAMPLES OF WRITING IN EGYPT DURING SEVERAL PERIODS [1]

ALPHABETIC SIGNS.
HIEROGLYPHS

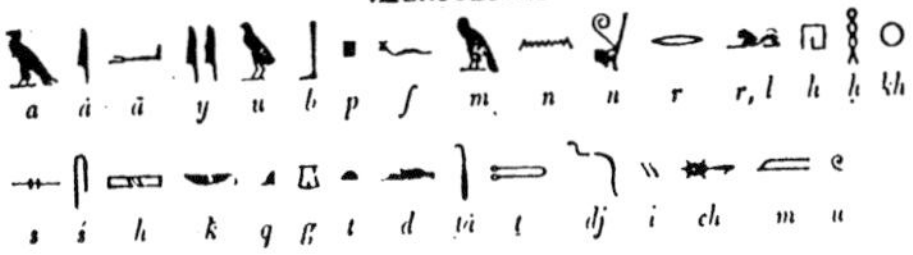

SYLLABIC SIGNS

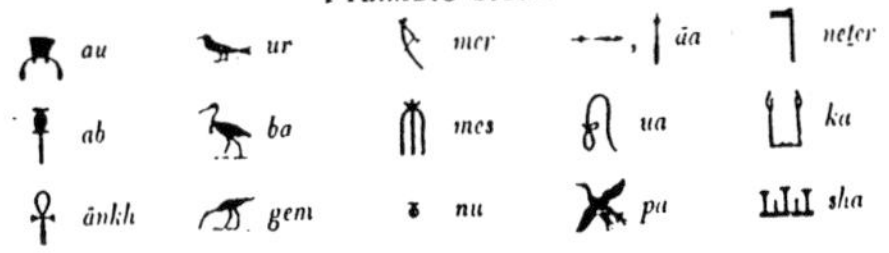

Maāt-ka-Rā. Ḥat-shepsut-chnem-Ámen (Hatshepsut).

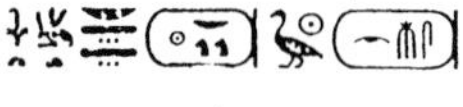

Neb-peḥti-Rā, Àāḥ-mes I (Amasis).

Religious scene and writing (Ist Dynasty).

Royal names (3rd set from the top) were placed in catouches. Try to decipher the names in the catouches from the above alphabet, etc.

1. Note that Nubia, Merowe, and other High-Cultures along the Nile River Valley equally used similar writings and languages; and even the same language as Egypt during certain periods. There are similar hieroglyphic scripts shown on the Zimbabwe Ruins of Zimbabwe [formerly renamed "Southern Rhodesia" in honour of Africa's worst colonialist murderer - Cecil John Rhodes - who caused to be exterminated more than 50,000,000 Africans. Zimbabwe was the ancient Capital City of the Monomotapa Empire, South Alkebu-lan [see p. 66 of this Volume].

difficulty in learning Amharic even when living in Ethiopia for extended periods of time, all contrary to the common belief that "AFRICA HAS NO NATIVE LANGUAGE." But the rules of the GRAMMAR are such that even English is not simpler to learn, even less so for other Latin-based languages of Europe. Ethiopian students find very little problem in learning English, French, Italian, Portuguese, etc. from their base in Amheric. Of course the fact that they are in common usage of Italian, French and English is not being overlooked, as there is no doubt that the progress generally shown in these areas of Latin-based languages by Ethiopian students proved that their everyday contact with Europeans of said languages background is the major factor. This does not belittle the fact that the technique of teaching foreign languages in Ethiopian schools is not of the highest. What it does say, is that the Africans highly sophisticated language - AMHERIC - is on a higher plain than that of the three most common Latin-based languages; and that Europeans do not show as much desire to learn any African language as do Africans to learn theirs, because of the same arrogance their "Christian Missionaries" displayed.

Ethiopia's school systems are government controlled. This is true whether they are privately owned and financed or government owned and financed. Most of the non-government owned schools were by foreign missionaries of the Christian Religion - both Roman Catholic and Protestant.[1] Of course there are many Moslem schools, all of which belong to local groups. The original language used in these schools is "AMHERIC" - the "NATIONAL LANGUAGE." The language of the privately owned schools - such as Arabic, English, Italian, French, etc. - are secondary requirements, but very important indeed for the student who plans to study abroad in Europe or the United States of America and Great Britain. Thus, the next language of major importance in the Ethiopian school system was English. All of the students in science oriented courses had to study in English in preference to any other foreign language, as most of the science textbooks are written in English. Your answer is also in the fact that the medical profession demanded that all of the students in medicine read Latin. Another factor is that most of the medical students and allied fields were studying medicine in English-speaking countries. A limited group studied in Eastern European countries. However, the paramount reason as to why Russian is not the language preferred at this stage in international politics is due to prior socio-political ties and spheres of influence between Great Britain, the United States of America and Ethiopia, augmented also by the style of the British and Ethiopian systems of "Divine Rule" by a monarch; plus the fact of their having common monetary systems. Supporting these latter points is the fact that stories of Ethiopian subjects [citizens] are still studying other major subjects in English-speaking countries such as Canada and the United States of America. These students would find a great disadvantage upon entering these foreign schools if they were not pre-

1. They gave aid and comfort to Selassie and the Abuna of Ethiopia's former Official Religion.

pared in the language of their study. Another important point in this issue of the importance of the English language is England's former stake in the colonization of Africa and the effects of her former colonial borders with Ethiopia through her own former member colonies - such as Kenya, Sudan, British Somaliland, Uganda, etc., "neo-colonialism" being ever prevalent.

French and Italian are the other foreign languages of major importance in most of Ethiopia's school system. They follow English in importance in order of their listing above. Their importance is also due to the stature of their colonial influence at various periods of European domination of the African people in their own continent - Alkebu-lan ["Africa"].

Religious groups are the Orthodox Christians [formerly Coptics], Moslems, Hebrews [or "Jews"] and many others of faiths and beliefs practiced in Alkebu-lan. These religions follow in importance of the order which they are listed due to their size of membership and socio-political impact on the present national economic system. The Orthodox ["Coptic"] Christian Church was the Official Religion of Ethiopia. This Christian group is "the oldest of all existing Christian order [Church] in the world today" according to records of "Christian Church History." It predated the "Christian Church Of Rome and Greece" by at least one hundred [100] years. Thus Coptic Christian Religious History states that "Saint Peter left Israel and entered into Egypt. Here, first he converted followers of the indigenous population of Egypt, namely Sun Worshipers."[1] These Egyptian converts thereafter formed the Christian House Of Worship for the express purpose of worshiping God - YWH - through JESUS "the Christ" - their leader. The Chief or Head Priest of all Ethiopian and Egyptian Coptics was seated in Egypt. The change in 1956 C.E. came about by the Emperor of Ethiopia, Haile Selassie Ist, who decreed that: "The Abuna [Archbishop or Head] of the Church of Ethiopia must reside in Ethiopia." His reason for this action was based upon the fact that there are very few "COPTS" [Coptics] in Egypt today, the vast majority now residing in Ethiopia. He also noted that the influence of the new religious order - MOHAMMEDISM and/or ISLAM - in Egypt had overpowered whatever remaining influence the Spiritual Leader - ABUNA[2] - of the Holy Coptic Church may have had. That the indigenous African population of modern Egypt had decreased to a very low percentage by comparison to that of the Arab population; and that there was no forseeable upgrowth of the COPTIC CHURCH there. He further cited that the present trend was mainly of complete conversion to Mohammedanism by the indigenous African population of Egypt. Also, that the indigenous African Copts were so rapidly decreasing in numbers as the years passed by, in a very few years there wouldnot be a minute hand full remaining faithful to the Coptic Faith. Based upon these points, and others, the Emperor decreed that:
"The Head of the Coptic Christian Church Of Ethiopia must be the existing Head of the Order in

1. The Emperor and Abuna, in public, always presented a united front on matters of religion.
2. Equivalent of the Pope in Rome with regards to his dictatorial control over Roman Catholics.

Ethiopia." This decree was carried forward [as was to be expected] and the seat of leadership of the Coptic Christian Church of Ethiopia changed from Egypt to Ethiopia; thus the change of name to "The Ethiopian Orthodox Christian Church."

The Mohammedans [Moslems] are the followers of the Prophet Mohamet ibn-Abdullah. They need no special introduction. They are similar to the Coptic Christians in at least one respect. They too accept that "Jesus [the Anointed]" was sent by God - AL'LAH - to save mankind from our SINS. However, they differ as to his being the "MESSIAH" and/or "GOD." The Moslems believe that he was second in importance only to "PROPHET" Mohamet ibn Abdullah. They claimed that:

> "Mohamet [Mohammad] followed Jesus with later and greater understanding of the fulfilment of the Laws of God, which Moses also failed to carry out."

Westerners should be as familiar with this religion as your writer, therefore I shall not continue further with details as I did with the Copts. Details were given on the Coptic Religion because it is not familiar to the ears of "Westerners," who believe that:

> The only true Christians are Europeans, European-Americans and the former "heathens" they have converted almost everywhere.

They seem to forget that the "Christian Religion" and "Christian Church" began in Alkebu-lan [Africa] at a place still called "EGYPT;" and that it traveled South before North.

Other groups are the Roman Catholic Christians and Protestant Christians - such as the Baptists, Presbyterians and Methodists. There are other smaller groups also represented in Ethiopia. The latter groupings need no special intruduction, as you may know much more about them than I do. Of course there are many varieties of solely indigenous Ethiopian origin scattered about

The last, and most important, group to be mentioned for this work is the "BETA ISRAEL." This group is called by various other names depending upon who is speaking, and where. Anything from "FALASHAS, BLACK JEWS, ETHIOPIAN JEWS, NEGRO JEWS, COLORED JEWS," etc. to "NIGGER JEWS," and a host of other "JEWS," are names given to these people.[1] I shall deal with this group more than anyother. I will also refer to them in many instances by saying "WE." "WE," because I am a member of this group, even though I am not practicing our religion, nor the culture. But it is about this group that you will read from now on exclusively. They are the main characters in your educational SAFARI [journery or trip] with me. The correct [true] name of this group is "AGAW, KYLAS" and/or "BETA [Bet] ISRAEL" [House of Israel, and also Children of the House of Israel]; anyother name is a misnomer. You will notice that I will use the nomenclature "FALASHA" [singular] or "FALASHAS" [plural] consistently; the sole reason being that most "Westerners" know "US" by this name. I will use this name at various instances to include "AFRICAN-AMERICAN [Black] JEWS" in the America [the Caribbean Islands included].

1. They are my people as much as other Africans of countless other religions throughout Africa.

YES: THEY [Egyptians] CAME FROM THE BEGINNING OF THE NILE

COMPARATIVE EASTERN AFRICAN ARCHITECTURE AND ARTISTRY AT THEIR BEST; YES.[1]

ST. GEORGE. MONOLITHIC CHURCH AT LALIBELA, ETHIOPIA, EAST AFRICA

Elevation [Isometric drawings by Lino B. Barriviera] Section

The construction of the above church is typical of the great architects who lived in Ethiopia and other Nile Valley nations before they were murdered by the invading Christian and Moslem armies of the conquerors that entered parts of Ethiopia. These "Wonders of the World" were overlooked by "Western Academicians" for centuries solely due to their own "white racism" and "religious bigotry", etc.

1. The genius of Nile Valley Africans engineering and architecture is amply applied above.; true!

THE GREAT SOUTHERN TEMPLE OF THE NILE "MYSTERIES SYSTEM"[1]

Zimbabwe/Built in Stone

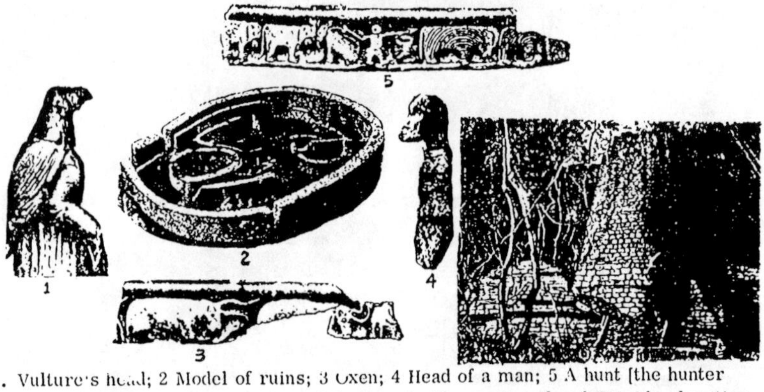

1. Vulture's head; 2 Model of ruins; 3 Oxen; 4 Head of a man; 5 A hunt [the hunter is shown as suffering from steatopygia]. Top: Inside courtyard and Outside elevation.

From J.C. deGraft-Johnson, AFRICAN GLORY, London, 1954, page 52, etc.

Note the majesty of the architectural beauty and astetic richness of the Africans of Monomotapa, Alkebu-lan. The engineering achievment demonstrated in this structure has never been surpassed in any of ancient Ta-Merry, Ta-Nehisi, Itiopi, Numidia, Khart-Haddas or Puanit, etc.

1. No. 5 shows a typical form of hieroglyphic writing as anything we will see in Egypt, Nubia, Ethiopia, etc. along the Nile Valley's sacred shrines. This is the genius that was Africa's people.

COMPARATIVE NORTHERN AND WESTERN AFRICAN ARCHITECTURE AND ARTISTRY AT BEST

Reconstruction of funerary buildings by Jean-Philippe Lauer, Paris, France. Main PYRAMID dimensions: L=431'0" x W= 344'0" x H=200'0". Height of exterior wall enclosure, 33'0".

[Ta-Merry/Egypt, Northeast Africa]

Southern Elevation of the Step Pyramid of Sakhara (Saqqara)

Tombut's/Timbuctoo's

GREAT MOSQUE AND 500 YEARS + OLD TOMB OF THE ASKIA KINGS/EMPERORS

Tombut, Mali/Melle, West Africa

FROM THE SOUTH [PUANIT] TO THE NORTH [KAMT]
COMPARATIVE AFRICAN ENGINEERING AND ARTISTRY AT ITS BEST ANYWHERE

ONE OF THE "GREAT STELAE" OF AXUM, ETHIOPIA, "AFRICA" Erected in ca. 850 B.C.E. [See page 206 of Yosef A. A. ben-Jochannan's BLACK MAN OF THE NILE AND HIS FAMILY, New York, 1981 Revised and Enlarged Edition. There are very much older Ethiopian stelae and other sites of a Sacred/Holy nature in this end of the Nile Valley than in the north. "We came from South."]

But in either case you will be able to distinguish which group I am refering to.

I shall elaborate somewhat on the term [or name] "FALASHA" that you may be much better informed about the full weight of its meaning in the installments ahead in this work. The term and/or word "FALASHA" derives its meaning and stigma from the OLD ETHIOPIC language. It means: "TO MIGRATE" or "AN IMMIGRANT," and also "STRANGER." This word has been corrupted over the centuries until finally it reached its present stage. The correct spelling was in ancient times "F-A-L-A-S-S-A," and pronounced "FA-LAS-SA" or "FA-LAS-SHA." There are numerous other spellings and pronounciations of this word, even among fellow Ethiopians in the Motherland - Ethiopia/Kush or Cush/Axum or Akhsum/Itiopi, etc., Northeast Alkebu-lan/"Africa," etc.

Before we actually get underway with our reexamination of the history and heritage of one of the world's oldest Hebrew People and Communities we must continue a little further into the major geography and culture of the country where the original body settled, and where the majority still resides - ETHIOPIA, Northeast Alkebu-lan/"Africa."

By this time you may have received the impression that the Kingdom and Empire of Ethiopia had an "OFFICIAL RELIGION;" and that the Head of State was one of its leaders. That there was RELIGIOUS PERSECUTION in full force against those who were not disciples of said "Official Religion." If you have so gathered, I wish not to dispell or remove this information from your mind this moment. This I assure you as a former member of the smallest religious group represented in Ethiopia, which absolutely had no connection with the "OFFICIAL RELIGION"[1] other than origin. For in Ethiopia "RELIGIOUS INTOLERANCE" has been one of the worst scourges to date. Ethiopia once was in the forefront of the other so-called "CHRISTIAN NATIONS" in their continuous official persecution of all who did/do not accept the "MESSIAH - Jesus the Christ - as God. This nation presently shows numerous visible scars due to past RELIGIOUS PERSECUTION. It is not to be forgotten that Ethiopia suffered some of the bloodiest "RELIGIOUS WARS" of genocide during the invasions by the so-called "CHRISTIAN ARMIES" and "CHRISTIAN MISSIONARIES" from Nubia and Egypt in the First Century and Second Century of the Christian Era [100 to 200 A.D., and even later]. Ethiopia also had to overcome persecutions when the so-called "MOSLEM ARMIES" and "MOSLEM MISSIONARIES" carrying "THE WORDS OF AL'LAH" swooped down upon their helpless victims of their "JIHADS" [Holy Wars] from the same areas before the "CHRISTIANS" aped them.[2] But it is very pleasant to know that today some of the scars are now being successfully wiped away; and sometimes even forgotten by the younger generation who know about them personally, and by their history books. The turn over of government does not mean there would be no more "RELIGIOUS DISCRIMINATION" by certain members of the DERGE [ruling body of Ethiopia].

1. There is no more "Official Church" and "Religion" connected to the Nation of Ethiopia
2. See Y. ben-Jochannan, African Origins Of The Major "Western Religions," New York, 1970.

Let us look at some of the LAWS against religious persecution Ethiopia had, neither of which was ever in effect against the privileged class - the monarchists, et al.

1. No person shall be permitted to use slurs against the religion of another person.
2. No one can deny public service to another because of his or her religion and/or God.
3. No one shall be permitted to slur any religion because it is not of Ethiopian origin and development.

You may say that these laws were once in the statute books and not practiced, and you will be most correct. But government officials claimed total adherance "... by law enforcement officers responsible for such violations of Human Rights." The offenses covered by these laws were "... punishable by imprisonment..." upon the finding of guilt; never by fines alone. Many were allegedly punished in the past. But since religious discrimination was A WAY OF LIFE in Ethiopia in recent years there have been too many of these cases. Hopefully these claims will become realities now.

Apart from former Emperor Haile Selassie Ist role in government and politics there was a type of legislative rule by Ethiopia's two [2] CHAMBER OF DEPUTIES [equivalent to the United States of America's "House of Representatives" and "Senate" or Great Britain's two bodies: House of Commons and House of Lords]. There was also an "EMPEROR'S COUNCIL OF MINISTERS" [equivalent to the United States of America's President's "Cabinet of Secretaries"], whose departments or ministries were guided by MINISTERS instead of SECRETARIES. Both representative bodies were accountable to the Emperor; and to no one else. Members of the Upper House [Senate] were appointed directly by the Emperor himself. Members of the Lower House [House of Representatives] were elected by the people of the Thirteen[13] Provinces [equivalent of States] of the nation in popular electoral processes. The Emperor was proclaimed a "DIVINE RULER" - by tradition. He had the "...power to veto any and all legislations passed by any of the two houses..." Whenever there was any disagreement over any legislation and it was not settled by either of the two houses the Emperor acted as the "MEDIATOR" between them. If they still could not come to any agreement the Emperor made the final decision on his own, and it became "LAW." The powerful Upper House and Lower House had nothing to do with the appointments of "GOVERNORS, DIPLOMATS" or any of the MINISTERS of the government. It will be correct to say that there were very little domestic or foreign legislative powers controlled by either of the two houses to change the course or structure of the government. However, you must realize that it was not until 1952 C.E. that former Emperor Haile Selassie Ist "DECREED" through his so-called "POWER OF DIVINE GRACE" the right of the Ethiopian People to representation by direct election of their representatives.

You must bear in mind that while this type of representation was not exactly what the Ethiopians intend to stop at, they do not necessarily want to follow the United States of America's example of what it calls "DEMOCRACY," as they have their own ideas about what is "DEMOCRACY." Ethiopians, by their own expressions in voting patterns of the past, believe that:

> Democracy does not essentially mean a republican form of government, or a two party system, as it is in the United States of America today.

They have also expressed that:

> Democracy does not necessarily mean capitalism, or socialism, but instead a system whereby the majority of the people affected by an economic structure control the means of the profit from their labor - production.

At least this is the position of most of the young Ethiopians one meets on the streets of the United States of America, Europe and Africa. No doubt there are others who feel differently. But, I can safely say that even though Ethiopia's "DEMOCRATIC" objectivity to please Ethiopians was too slow in changing to suit the needs of the vast majority of the youth, it was even slower for the armed forces. Most effective of all who demanded changes that Ethiopia needed were those young people that identify with the growing "PAN-AFRICANIST MOVEMENT" Selassie had claimed to equally endorse, but unfortunately did not express with regards to the matter of much more direct representation by the Ethiopian People in their own government domestically and internationally. This type of African involvement was being forced upon the Emperor as a historical event, which of course stems from the "anti-colonial" and "anti-imperial" stand of the young revolutionist college students inside and outside of Ethiopia on the mainland - ALKEBU-LAN [Africa].

The land of Ethiopia, in spite of a Twentieth Century Emperor who was still living in the Tenth Century, is enhanced by its Capital City - "ADDIS ABABA. It has a total population of about over five hundred thousand [500,000] to six hundred thousand [600,000] resident subjects or citizens. Of this total figure more than seven thousand [7,000] to ten thousand [10,000] are of European birth and/or origin. Addis Ababa[1] is the geographical location of the former IMPERIAL SEAT, CENTER OF ALL GOVERNMENTAL AGENCIES, FOREIGN EMBASSIES and CONSULATES; but most of all the seat of the "ETHIOPIAN ORTHODOX [Coptic] CHRISTIAN CHURCH"- once the power behind the throne of Ethiopia in the person of the "ABUNA" [equivalent of the Pope of the Roman Catholic Church in Rome, Italy]. Day and night life is comparable to that of "Western cities" its size and population. Bus service is the main method of public transportation, but there is also a goodly number of private taxi cabs. International air services to points in Asia, the British Isles and Europe are frequent; also domestic flights by the Ethiopian Airlines System that also flies internationally. The nation's art treasures are almost inexhaustable; paintings and carvings like the following on page 74 are in public view by the thousands everywhere, all of them

1. See geographic location on the map on p. 75 of this Volume for the City of Addis Ababa, etc.

[courtesy of the Ethiopian Airlines]

overshadowed by Ethiopia's carved-out cathedrals in the mountains and ground. The single railroad system with its main spur from Addis Ababa to Djibuti, which was originally controlled by the French, Italian and English colonialist governments until after World War II, will take you to points where much of the art treasures can be seen, equally the ruins of the great structures from pre-Christian and early Christian periods as shown on pages 43 - 44 and 74 - 81, etc.

The climatic conditions of Ethiopia caused the output of bumper wheat, coffee [generally labeled the first and best in the whole wide world] and other grains that overshadow the export of wool and other animal byproducts. The chief imports are in the areas of farm machinery and tools for industrial development. These equipments are of very grave importance to the "industrial revolution" presently underway in this country as it is in most of the other formerly agricultural colonies controlled by European, European-American and Asian colonialists and imperialists throughout Alkebu-lan from France's invasion of Cueta in 1830 C. E. - "The Partition."[2]

Medical facilities are lagging behind the time and need of the population. However, there has been a steadfast [somewhat slow at times] growth in this field; but the trend is to catch up with the medical needs of the people. There are three [3] major ultra-modern hospitals in Ethiopia that are comparable to community facilities of nations way in excess of the size of populations they serve, even by the standards established by the American Medical Association for the United States of America. There is also a network of "Health Stations" and "Health Centers" scattered all over the Thirteen Provinces. These were established during the reign of Emperor Selassie.

Sanitation control is also gaining momentum under the auspecies of the Ministry of Health. The medical programs and other long range sanitation development schemes, like the hundreds of students on scholarship from the government studying "Public Health Administration" and "Medical Science" outside and inside Ethiopia, are gaining their objective. Needless to say that

1. See Sir Edward Hertslett, The Map Of Africa By Treaty, London, 1888, 3 Vols. for details.

ARCHAEOLOGICAL and TOPOGRAPHICAL MAP OF ETHIOPIA, EAST AFRICA
Showing Roads and Sites

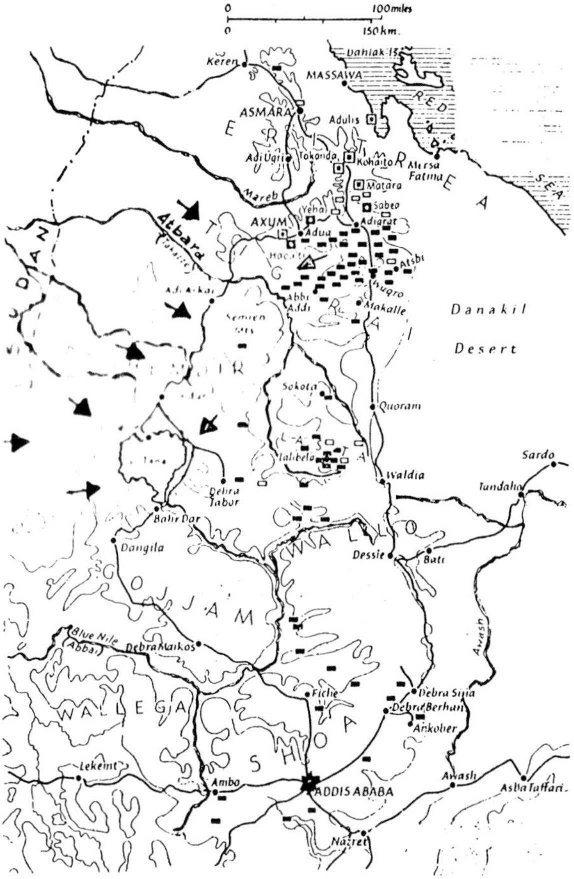

KEY[1]

Areas above 6,600 feet   Main roads and cities [towns]   Capital City

Pre-Ahksum [Axum] site   Post Ahksum [Axum] site   Built-up church [ruins, new]

Monolithic rock-hewn churches [one or more per symbol] Border line ---- Water

FALASHA CONCENTRATIONS

1. In some cases a single symbol could represent quite a few artifacts or structures; this is due to the scale of the map. Note that the elevations and outline of contours are approximate.

Addis Ababa, the capital of Ethiopia.

The seventeenth-century castle of Emperor Fasiladas at Gondor.

ASPECTS OF THE "SOUTHERN ORIGIN" OF THE EGYPTIANS

ARCHAEOLOGICAL FINDS OF PRE-CHRISTIAN ETHIOPIA BY NILE VALLEY [Black] AFRICANS[1] EVEN BEFORE "ADAM AND EVE"

An ancient Ethiopian [Itiopic] language inscription on a fallen column from the ruins of the TEMPLE OF YEHA, dating back to ca. 700 B.C.E. This piece was dug up in 1955 C.E. [or A.D.]. It is Hieroglyph, otherwise called "Itiopic Script" by "... Western Academicians", et al, ... and much more alphabetical of the same period than Meröe, Nubia, Egypt, etc.

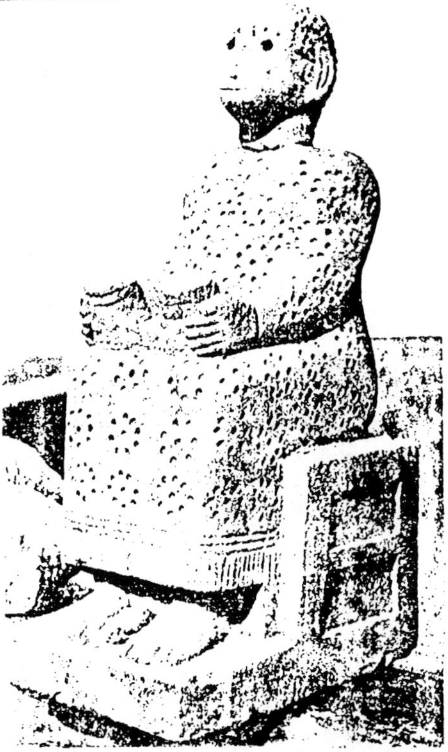

An effigy of an ancient Ethiopian of the period during ca. 800 B.C.E., at Azbi-Dera,[2] Northern Ethiopia. Due to racism and religious bigotry in "Western Academia" this nation's heritage became the foundation of Egypt's High-Culture that is purposely suppressed daily.

---

1. Both of the artifacts above are shown by Jean Dorsse in his book "ETHIOPE." Note that these ruins are of the same type found in Punt/Puanit [Somalia], Meröe and Nubia [Sudan], Kamt [Egypt] and Zimbabwe [Monomotapa, colonial "Southern Rhodesia"]. During the period when they were placed in their original position the Ethiopian Empire stretched all the way to the so-called "Near East" and "Far East" [Eastern Greece to Western India].

There are many of these ancient statues all over Ethiopia; some even older than anything of its kind in all of Egypt and Sudan.

2. Remember that Ethiopia predated Egypt by thousands of years in World History. Read Joseph E. Harris, Ed.2 Vol. work of W. L. Hansberry's "Pillars In Ethiopian History." Howard University Press, Washington, D.C., 1972

NORTHEAST "AFRICAN" ARCHAEOLOGICAL SITES [1]

Rock-cut church near Wogro, Tigre, hewn out of a bed of red sandstone

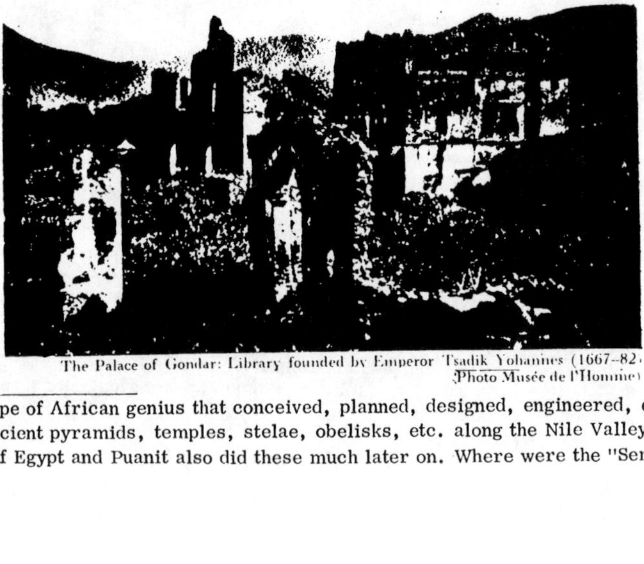

The Palace of Gondar: Library founded by Emperor Tsadik Yohannes (1667–82) (Photo Musée de l'Homme)

1. The same type of African genius that conceived, planned, designed, engineered, erected and managed the ancient pyramids, temples, stelae, obelisks, etc. along the Nile Valley and Great Lakes region of Egypt and Puanit also did these much later on. Where were the "Semites"?

BY AFRICAN ENGINEERING/ARCHITECTURAL GENIUS! SEMITES?
ARCHAEOLOGICAL SITE OF 17th CENTURY, C.E. ETHIOPIA, AFRICA

A Man From "Outer Space"!

TWO 16th - 18th CENTURY C.E. [A.D.] CASTLES OF GONDAR,[1]ETHIOPIA.
INSERT OF ETHIOPIAN ORTHODOX PRIEST

1.This is the area of Gondar, Ethiopia where the vast majority of the FALASHAS live. It was the original stronghold of FALASHA CULTURE. It was here that Queen YUDITH ruled Ethiopia during the 9th Century C.E. and led the Falashas to victory over the Christian and Moslem conquerors that persecuted them earlier. For centuries Gondar was the CENTER OF ETHIOPIAN HIGH-CULTURE. It became Ethiopia's third Capital city after AKHSUM [AXUM]. Haile Selassie Ist changed this and made Addis Ababa the Capital during the 1920's after he had illegally seized the Government from the legitimate Head of State, Emperor Lidj Yasu, in 1924 C.E. with the aid of the late Abuna Johannes.

THESE TWO ESCAPED THE EUROPEAN COLONIALIST PLUNDERERS' HANDS

[Scores Have Been Stolen And Carried Off To Rome, Paris, London, New York City, And Numerous Other Capitals Of The So-called "Western World." Even Vatican Thieves Have Taken Scores For The Popes Of The "Holy See"]

Left: An Egyptian Obelisk of On/Heliopolis.
Right: An Ethiopian Monolith, typical of many.

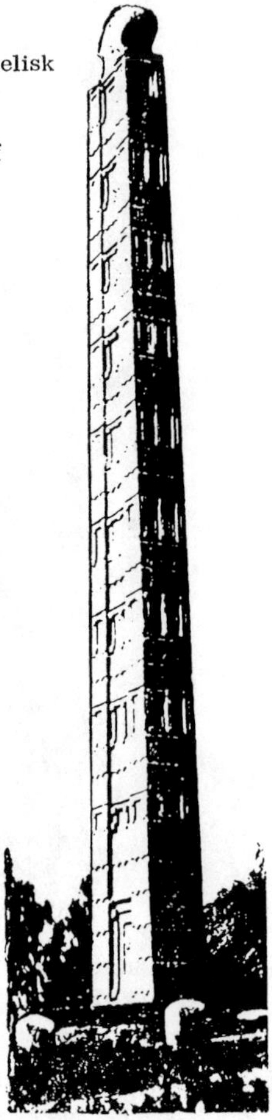

On was renamed "Heliopolis" by the Macedonian-Greek conquerors of Egypt in ca. 332 B.C.E.

---

1. Like everything else, European, European-Australian and European-American so-called "Academicians" have changed the indigenous names of people, places and things in their colonies. They equally gave all kinds of names to the "OBELISKS" above, and even those they stole - shown on pp. 234 - 235 of Yosef ben-Jochannan, Black Man Of The Nile And His Family, New York, 1981 Ed.

BY AFRICAN TECHNOLOGICAL GENIUS!
[No Semites From "Outer-Space" Did It!]
ARCHAEOLOGICAL SITE

THE "GREAT CASTLE"
Of Emperor Fassilades
17th CENTURY, C.E. GONDAR, ETHIOPIA

1. The African GENIUS shown in this, and all of the other Castles, etc. were conceived and built centuries before the arrival of the "Western Europeans" as visitors to East Alkebu-lan [Africa]. Note that the "African Architecture" does not reflect any Asian influence from either Arabs or Persians; a common myth always used by so-called "Western [European and European-American] " Africanist Historians, "etc.

there are overwhelming shortcomings in these programs. But when one considers that it was not so long ago that the children of the poor in Ethiopia were allowed these previleges, it is almost impossible to understand the extra slow rate of change in both the field of MEDICINE and SANITATION in the former Government of the late Emperor Haile Selassie Ist.

Water and electric power supplies and sources seem to be the fastest growing need in the development for modern Ethiopia's industrial and agricultural needs. Electrical power is of the gravest to the industrialization of the country, as without it there can be no energy necessary for the movement of the machines, even tractors, to do the work demanded for basic production for local consumption, muchless for foreign export to other indigenous African countries, Europe, Asia and the Americas. Yet there is an astonishingly small amount of hydroelectric plants, other minor power plants and electrical substations added to the topographical scenery that once fed the needs of the very rich "FEUDAL LANDLORDS" in the many years following the end of World War II, and since the second to last attempts at dethroning Emperor Haile Selassie in 1969 C.E./A.D.

The petroleum [oil] deposits of Ethiopia have been systematically exploited since the late 1960's at least, some of its revenues having been used to underwrite the educational programs in medicine and sanitation mentioned above. Many of the industries related to this product have been developed from the excess capital funds produced by this industry, all of which came from the combination between the government and private [foreign and local] investors for capital gain. Of course the majority of the investors were from the United States of America. Thus some of the industries related directly to petroleum have been built by the "United Nations Technical Assistance Program" under the domination of the so-called "Free World Bank" and other independent sources. The Soviet Union, for example, contributed to the building of two [2] of the three [3] major hospital facilities I mentioned before, equally roads and other service-related projects in return for natural resources of mineral ore and wool.[2] The United States of America contributed through its "Point Four Plan," which is not in operation in Ethiopia for the past two decades plus. There were private individual investors in oil; but it was the giant corporation like Sinclair Oil Company, Inc. of the United States of America, and others like it, that dominated Ethiopia's Oil Industry, and more so established most of Ethiopia's long-range plans that depended upon a lot of the revenues accrued from the Oil Industry. Of course the Government had a sort of "PROFIT-SHARING" arrangement with the private investors. And of course such so-called AGREEMENTS were closely guarded secrets of which the general Ethiopian population was never privilege to know, only the Emperor and his monarchist class and colleagues. But all of such foreign enterprises had to have local technicians and professionals. They also had to be

1. Most of the monies generated from the Oil Industry wound up in the monarchists' bank accounts.
2. The competition between the U.S.A. and U.S.S.R. for "Sphere of Influence" was vicious.

involved in training programs to provide the necessary personnel that would eventually start to efficiently operate the industry involved. The entire "UNSKILLED" and "SEMI-SKILLED" labor force had to come from the general local communities around the installations involved. All of the private companies had to be capable of carrying on construction and development projects other than their main center of interest, or they had secure this service from others as a part of their contract with the Ethiopian Government. Their contracts generally embodied conditions for "ROAD BUILDING, SCHOOL CONSTRUCTION" and "CASH PAYMENTS" from profits to the treasury of the Ethiopian Government - the late Emperor and his monarchist chronies, et al.

Ethiopia, like all other African nations, has all kinds of major problems of which the military government has since undertaken in this ancient High-Culture [reputedly the oldest in the entire wide world community of nations] with all of its complex cultures, religions, "ethnic" groupings, etc. Be ever mindful that there existed a very strong anti-government political undercurrent formenting since the former Emperor - His Imperial Majesty Haile Selassie Ist - began his reign following his overthrow of the legitimate Government and Emperor LIDJ YASU, sometime about the end of 1923 C.E. There was even a deeper - seated dissatisfaction with the method used by the Emperor to gain control of the Ethiopian Throne, which is commonly rumored to have been by the brutality of a 10th Century-type despot with the help of Great Britain, France and Italy from their colonial lands on the borders of Ethiopia, all of which Lidj Yasu's grandfather H.I.M. Emperor Menelik IInd warned Ethiopians of[1] before his death in about 1906 C.E. These facts were underlying caused for the many attempts to assassinate the former Emperor Haile Selassie Ist; one as late as 1968 C.E.; the latest was in 1974 C.E. Added to these were many minor insurrections that resulted from within the Emperor's own " PALACE GUARD" and "OFFICIAL FAMILY" within the past ten years. There had been times when the RASES [Governors] of certain provinces [States] tried to break away from the control of the Central Government in Addis Ababa and formed organized reprisal units, only to have further appeasements by the Emperor to protect his own continued reign along with the Abuna. The highlight of the February 1974 C.E. revolt of the Royal Ethiopian Navy and Army, allegedly "...for higher wages...," sharpened the bitter class struggle between the extremely poor Ethiopian People and the extraordinarily wealthy and most visible monarchist class of the ultra-bestial landlords, feudal priests, and their Christian Church. These two bodies [church and government] were determined to maintain the most stagnant type of "FEUDAL SYSTEM" forever and ever; all with the help of the local armed forces and foreign colonial nations that supported Ethiopia's Monarchists against the interest of the Ethiopian People. The United States of America's military base at Asmara was the worst example of the foreign intrigues which

1. Selassie wilfully ignored the warning and instead cohered with enemies of Ethiopia and himself. He was duped into believing that the "West" accepted him other than as an African/Black Man.

the late Emperor Menelik IInd warned the Ethiopian People against, fought against when he defeated the Italians at the Battle for Adowa in 1896 C.E., and which his grandson Emperor Lidj Yasu [see page 65] was against. The following maps on pages 243, 244, 248, etc. tell the story.

The conditions about which we have just read were partly caused by the fact that Ethiopia was land-locked by the imperialist colonies owned by England, France and Italy. Thus, her inability to reach the only natural body of water - the RED SEA - she used all through her history until the European and British imperialists imposed their control on the African people of East Alkebu-lan ["Africa" or "Afrika"]. The fact that Ethiopia was denied a SEA PORT from the middle 1800's C.E. up to the 1940's C.E. when she regained her natural rights to the so-called "INTERNATIONALIZED SEA PORT OF JIBUTI" highlighted the new problem of the need for rebuilding a merchant fleet of ships for international commerce. This former colonial imposition by the European colonizing powers had equally caused Ethiopia to be without a naval fleet for over seventy-five [75] years. But Ethiopia's refederation with her people that were colonized by the Italians in the former Italian colony of "ERITREA" during 1952 C.E. has compelled her to build a new navy to protect her East Coast on the Red Sea. Yet Ethiopia must also cope with the unique problem which the United Nations Organization forced upon her as a result of the "FEDERATION" with Eritrea against the desire of the vast majority of the Eritrean People,[1] who had a written "CONSTITUTION, UPPER and LOWER LEGISLATIVE" assemblies with much broader local representation than that of the Empire of Ethiopia to which they were reunited. But these two foundations had equally caused disruption amongst the Ethiopian population, as the average Ethiopian became jealous of their reunited brothers and sisters hard-won freedom in legislative representation which was unheard of in their own government in Addis Ababa. This envy had brought about added turmoil and extreme pressure upon the monarchists and religious feudalists that ruled over Ethiopia to meet the new situation, which they had carefully ignored to the extent that constant socio-political uprisings and civil insurrections amongst Ethiopian youths, had become common place. Vitally needed social reforms for the improvement of the "STANDARD OF LIVING" of the vast majority of the common people of Ethiopia in the sense of PENSIONS FOR THE AGED and SOCIAL SECURITY for the unemployed were added to the problems that confronted the monarchists exploiters of each and every facet of the Government of Ethiopia and the Orthodox Christian Church that affects the mind of the vast majority of Ethiopia's population - particularly the aged. But of course there are many other problems confronting the Government of Ethiopia which cannot be enumerated here because of the complexities in treating the subject of the "ETHIOPIAN GOVERNMENT IN TURMOIL" fairly in so short a chapter as this all of which the current military leaders who now control the destiny of the Ethiopian People must solve with haste; not only in due course.

1. They forgot that they were originally Ethiopians before colonization by Italy in ca. 1881 C.E.

VICTIMS OF EUROPEAN-AFRICAN IMPERIALISM REVERBERATING TO-DAY FROM THE GRAVESIDE PAST

Above: THE LATE EMPRESS ZADITU,[1] DAUGHTER OF EMPEROR MENELIK IInd
[ca. 1887 - 1927-29 C.E.]

Below:THE LATE EMPEROR LIDJ YASU,[2] GRANDSON AND ONLY LEGAL HEIR OF
[ca. 1904 - 1924 C.E. ? ?]
EMPEROR MENELIK IInd APPOINTED

1. Poisoned by Ras Tafari Makonnen and officials of the Coptic Church. Tafari Makonnen seized the throne as Emperor Haile Selaasie Ist with help of England, Italy and France. The U.S.A. assisted
2. Sadistically murdered by Selassie,et al,after being jailed in a dungeon and held in chains until he died of torture. Abuna Johannes of the Coptic Church assisted in Yasu's murder.

Ethiopia must produce some results, and very fast indeed, in her so-called "DEMOCRATIC" activities, as the eyes of all of the indigenous people of Alkebu-lan are upon her. This is also augmented by the former colonial sister nations surrounding Ethiopia, all of whom are fighting to break the imperialist yoke that once enslaved them totally - including Ethiopia from ca. 1935 to 1942 C.E. The needed leadership which Ethiopia should have been able to give her very much younger sister nations still has not materialize. But if Ethiopia cannot raise herself to this position, and very fast indeed, she can only expect to stand the risk of losing her friends all over the continent of ALKEBU-LAN/AFRICA in the Africans struggle against "COLONIALISM" and "NEO-COLONIALISM." It will be more than disastrous that the nation in which the ORGANIZATION OF AFRICAN UNITY [O.A.U.] is housed should be the object of the scorn of the general population of the indigenous African people and their fellow African people abroad. However, it must be borne in mind that any criticism of Ethiopia resting on the monarchist feudal lords must be based upon actual knowledge of the existing and past historical condition and heritage of this most ancient of all nations of the entire world community. Yet to base criticism upon NEW and/or OLD sentiments and prejudices will only help to worsen an already exhaustabated decadency rather than relieve a single condition on behalf of the more than twenty-three million [23,000,000] Africans that make up the population of Ethiopia. The best criticism can only be made by those who have interested themselves in the PEOPLE and HISTORY of Ethiopia's PAST and PRESENT; those who can best understand Ethiopia's GROWTH and/or DEGENERATION. This author strongly suggests that a trip to Ethiopia and her surrounding sister nations, including the nations of "AFAR" and "ISAS" - formerly colonized by France, for the purpose of gaining your own first-hand over-all appreciation of the situation existing within Ethiopia's borders. Your author cannot pass sufficient detailed conclusions on this subject due to the lack of space in this work to lend itself to a fair analytical "African" enterpretation, evaluation and presentation of my points of differences and/or agreements with the Ethiopian monarchists and their government before they were deposed.

Certainly Italy's King Victor Emmanuel IInd, Dictator Benito Mussolini, Pope Pius XIth and the Fascist militarists have opened the eyes of every Ethiopian on the street, and in every walk of life, as to the meaning of "PAN-AFRICANISM" above "NATIONALISM." The former makes the Ethiopian people, as all of the other indigenous people of "Africa," conscious of the fact that they were "...SOLD DOWN THE RIVER..." by the so-called "Western Powers"...including the United States of America under the leadership of the late President Franklin Delano Roosevelt in the war with Italy that began on October 5th, 1935 C.E., an outgrowth of the 1934 C.E. WAL-WAL incident in which Italy tried to seize Ethiopia's artisian wells in this region.[1]

1. See Sir Edward Hertslett, The Map Of Africa By Treaty, London, 1906, Vol. 3 of 3, p. 86, etc.

Thus there is no doubt that there are many Ethiopians who were, and still are, willing to break away from the "Western Nations;" those who can go back in time to that "WHITE DAY OF INFAMY" when the Italian Facists unleashed... "THE WORLD'S FIRST ACTS OF GENOCIDE"... that initiated the beginning of WORLD WAR II on October 5th, 1935 C.E. This was the period when the "NAZI-FASCIST AXIS" imperialist conspirators strafed the Africans of Ethiopia with POISON GAS, which was allegedly "...OUTLAWED BY THE " [so-called] "CIVILIZED NATIONS OF THE WORLD...;" all of whom were the sponsors of the imperialist "...LEAGUE OF NATIONS...."[1] Ethiopia could not move from her dominant hold on the "coat strings" of "Western Nations." Why? Because of her former system of "DIVINE RULE" through the monarchy and the Orthodox [formerly Coptic] Christian Church. The deposed Emperor Selassie Ist could not turn to any other direction; for government ruled by an emperor, empress, king or queen is rejected almost everywhere today. Yet the conditions in the so-called "Republic of South Africa" played a most significant role in Ethiopia's clinging to the West's coat tail; as it has always been the desire of the Union's White Supremist Settlers to "annex" all of the African territories around the Great Lakes up to the border of Ethiopia. This fact was never forgotten by the Ethiopian People, as well as other African Nationalists and Pan-Africanists at home and abroad who equally suffered the same type of colonialist expansion by the Italians in 1935 C.E. with the aid of all of the so-called "Western Democracies" - the United States of America included.[2] This may be far-fetched!

I must mention that you need much more materials on the subject before a full picture of this most ancient of all nations can be observed; for you are involved with a period of more than ten thousand [10,000] years of recorded history. If you should make further research in the annals of history you will soon discover that the Ethiopian nation is one of the foundations of so-called "WESTERN CIVILIZATION, GREEK PHILOSOPHY, JUDAISM, CHRISTIANITY, neo-JUDAEO-CHRISTIANITY" and "ISLAM;"[3] all of which she now lags behind in the Twentieth [20th] Century C.E. Thus, you will feel somewhat hurt by the treatment Ethiopia has received from her offsprings in the "West." Looking at the values which have become so basically essential to the "Western forms of government," we discover that all of their origin also dates back to this Nile Valley LAND presently called "ETHIOPIA." Therefore, we are forced to look with shame at ourselves as Africans for the periods of destruction this LAND has suffered at the hands of the European, European-American and Asian imperialists and colonizers; and of course by the local feudalist

1. The foundation of the current United Nations Organization [U.N.O.]
2. See Sir Richard Hertslett, THE MAP OF AFRICA BY TREATY, London, 1900, 3 Vols., with regards to the U.S.A., Gr. Britain and the 13 other colonialist nations of Europe at the Berlin and Brussels conferences of 1884 - 85 C.E., where "AFRICA" was "PARTITIONED" by all of them.
3. See Y. ben-Jochannan, Black Man Of The Nile And His Family, New York, 1981.

landlords led by the Abuna of the Orthodox Christian Church and Emperor Haile Selassie Ist. Most of us - AFRICANS, AFRICAN-AMERICANS and AFRICAN-CARIBBEANS - have forgotten that agriculture, surveying, civil engineering, architecture, embalming, medicine, pharmacology, natural science and most of the other sciences and disciplines we now consider to be of "WESTERN ORIGIN AND CULTURE" [civilization] have their roots in the Nile Valley and Great Lakes nations of Alkebu-lan [Africa] such as Ethiopia, Puanit, Meröe, Nubia, Egypt, etc. as shown on the various maps already displayed in this Volume. All of these "African" nations are of High-Cultures [civilizations] of hundreds and thousands of years gone before the nations called Greece and Rome - Europe's oldest civilizations of no antiquity whatever before ca. 1000 B.C.E. Yes!, Ethiopia, Puanit, Nubia, Meröe and Egypt existed as indigenous African High-Cultures before the first Haribu [Hebrew, Israelite or Jew] named "ABRAHAM" was born in the City of Ur, Chaldea in Western Asia on the banks of the Tigris and Eurphrates rivers. Ethiopia, as all of the others, had already helped to "CIVILIZED" the world of antiquity before the arrival of the European conquerors in the early 4th Century B.C.E. and the Asians in the 17th Century B.C.E., much less speaking of the arrival of the European "Christian Crusaders" in the 19th Century C.E. and the Arab Jihadists in the 7th Century C.E. [or the First Century After The Hejira = A.H.].[1]

Before we end this Chapter I must welcome you into the doors of the cultural, religious and socio-political life of the AGAW or KYLAS [Falashas, Beta Israel, Black Jews, etc.] of Ethiopia, the Americas and the Caribbean Islands. But in so doing let me also welcome you in the name of my people, and maybe yours, in the manner customary among Hebrew-speaking People all over the world: "SHALOM, SHALOM, SHALOM" [Peace, Peace, Peace and/or Welcome, Welcome, Welcome] from the depth of our souls: "DENESTLING" - in Ethiopia's National Language.

Now that you have been welcomed into the midst of the BLACK JEWS, and African People in general, I cannot help but remind you that the AGAW and/or KYLAS are no different to any of the "NEGROES" and "NEGROIDS" one hear so much of lately, particularly the "NEGRO[?] JEWS OF HARLEM." Certainly we are no different than those who originated from the WOMBS of the millions of BLACK MOTHERS like the following "SABLE VENUS FROM ANGOLA, WEST AFRICA" taken from Joel A. Rogers, 100 AMAZING FACTS ABOUT THE NEGRO WITH COMPLETE PROOF, shown on page 89. Is it not strange that in the year 1818 C.E. the rejected "BLACKS" of the late 1900's were still producing "BLACK FEMININITY" like those we are about to read of in the many Ethiopian Hebrew Communties, African-American Hebrew Communities and African-Caribbean Hebrew Communities? Even as "NEGROES" and/or "CANAANITES" the Falashas are as much ignored and/or maligned like the "SABLE VENUS'" ancestors and descendants by the same People.

1. The wars that brought about the Arab Moslems enslavement of hundreds of millions of African people from ca. 639 C.E. or 18 A.H. to the present 1983 C.E., 1361 A.H. under Islam's disgrace.

"SLAVE"!, OR "GODDESS" LIKE HER SISTERS "HATHOR AND NUT?
BASED UPON THE SEMITES WE SEE IN THIS VOLUME; MAYBE SHE WAS ALSO ONE!

The Voyage of the Sable Venus[1] from Angola, West Africa, to the West Indies, escorted by a White Neptune and a nimbus of white Cupids. Painted by T. Stothard in 1818. Fanciers of fair black femininity from Boston, Mass., to Buenos Aires used to await the slave-ships for the arrival of these black Venuses.

(See "Poetic Expressions on the Black Woman by White Western Writers" in "Sex and Race," Vol. II, pp. 217-220, (1942).

1. And this period the "BLACK WOMAN" was still the "PRIDE OF WHITE MEN" who were engaged in conquest and slavery throughout Africa, the "Americas" and the "West Indies." Even European Kings and European-American Presidents passionately awaited her arrival! Ask President Thomas Jefferson about his own "SABLE VENUS" - Sally Hemmings - the mother of four of his children;all four of which he kept as "SLAVES" until the day he died "a God-fearing man, Freedom Fighter,!" and a "Founding Father of American Democracy," etc. "Be it resolved that all men are created"?!

A HISTORICAL BACKGROUND OF THE "FALASHAS," THEIR BIBLICAL ORIGINS AND HERITAGE: Chapter III, Part One.

Like European and European-American Jews all over the world the Falashas have contributed to the cultural, social and spiritual development of all of the countries in which they lived, and still live. Falasha history and heritage in Ethiopia, East Africa revert back to the days of the Ethiopian Pharaohs that ruled Puanit, Nubia, Meröe, Egypt, Israel, Assyria, Persia, Median, etc. during various periods before, during and after the biblical era when this land was called by the name "CUSH." Of course that period predated the coming of so-called "JEWISH" [White] MERCHANT TRAVELERS INTO ETHIOPIA" - such as "ELDAD HADANI" and "BENJAMIN OF TUDELA," and even the mythological "PORTUGUESE CHRISTIAN MISSIONARY PRESBYTR [or Prestor] JOHN,"[1] by thousands of years. We - "FALASHAS" - revert back in our history and recall to memory the times when WE were members of the entire "CUSHITE [Ethiopian] NATION." During that period everyone wanted to be associated with the so-called "JEWISH TRIBES" of Cush, some of whom came down to Cush even before the "PASSOVER" began in approximately 1236 B.C.E., which was during the reign of Pharaoh Rameses IInd - ca. 1298 - 1232 B.C.E. But, it is no doubt our own historical teachings emphatically state that the vast majority of the "TRIBES" that made up the "FALASHAS" left Palestine [Israel] because they had refused to accept the rule of the existing king. Until this very day FALASHAS follow the economics of "COMMUNAL LIVING," and believe that - "RULE BY POLITICAL POWER IS EVIL." And amongst the Falashas are also members of the other "TRIBES" that comprise all of the so-called "HEBREWS" or "HARIBU" [Jewish, etc.] PEOPLE;" namely:

JUDAH, ISSACHAR, ZEBULUM, REUBEN, SIMEON, MENASSEH, BENJAMIN, DAN, ASHER, NAPTHALI, GAD and EPHRAIM [see page 39 for "Chronology"].

The last two named, "GAD" and "EPHRAIM," are those from whence the vast majority of the old "AGAW" and/or "KYLAS" [Falashas, Beta Israel, Black Jews, etc.] came during ancient times, even before Moses fled his native EGYPT, Northeast Alkebu-lan [Africa] and his fellow Africans that worshipped their own God - AMEN-RA. A few historians claimed "DAN" and "EPHRAIM."

The separation of the "TRIBES" brought on all kinds of wild speculation by European and European-American [WHITE] Jews that:

"THE FALASHAS OF ETHIOPIA ARE THE LOST TRIBES."

This, of course, could not be substantiated, as FALASHAS were never in history "LOST" anywhere they lived. WE were not looking towards returning to ISRAEL, or going to EUROPE, to live under European Jews tutelege. WE found a home in -

THE LAND TO THE SOUTHWEST [Cush] WHERE ALL SPICES AND

1. This man and his story represent the lowest aspect of Ethiopian history and culture; myths and lies of a type never to be overcome so long as European "scholarship" remains "racist" as it is.

HONEY ARE TO BE FOUND IN ABUNDANCE EVERYWHERE;[1] WHERE COMMON MEN SIT ON GOLDEN CHAIRS AND THE CRAFTSMEN MAKE LOOMS FOR THEIR QUEEN WHILE THEIR WOMEN GLOW IN JEWELS."[2]

The above is a quotation from Professor Nidge Bibase Solomon's book in which he gave an account of how Ethiopia was described by the ancient people of Colchis, Assyria, Nubia, Israel, Egypt and Meröe, Even the Greeks that came into civilization much later on spoke of Aetiopicus as the origin of Greece's Gods Zeus and Apollo adopted from the Ethiopians.[3] But people are only "LOST" when they are looking for some place to go and cannot find their own way. The FALASHAS have always known where they were/are, and will make their own plan for immigrating in the future.

Let us take a look at the ancient history and cultural heritage of the Falashas reign and leadership in Ethiopia [Cush]. We refer you to the KEBRA NEGASTE or ETHIOPIAN CHRONICLES [History of Ethiopia], which is written in one of the Ethiopian languages known as GHEEZE. It is an almost day to day account of the history of Ethiopia, and kept by the Official Library of the Government of the Kingdom and Empire of Ethiopia during the reign of each and every King and/or Emperor since Menelik Ist. The section of the Kebra Negaste that takes us from "THE GREAT ZAGUE" in 1269 C.E. back to the establishment of the nation of "UNIFIED CUSH" [Ethiopia] by His Imperial Majesty Ebna Hakin Ist [the son of King Solomon of the Kingdom of Israel and Queen Makeda of the Kingdom of Axum, Empress of Ethiopia, Sheba, etc., etc., etc. in about 900 B.C.E.] is dealing with the beginning of Falasha rule and power in Ethiopia. But the Falashas Hebrew origin in Ethiopia even go further back than the return of Ebna Hakin [who was also given the name "MENELIK"] from his visit with his father in Israel. We recall that our most ancient biblical Hebrew history informed everyone that:

WHEN MOSES WAS FLEEING MIZRAIN [Egypt] HE TRAVELED SOUTH INTO THE LAND OF CUSH [Ethiopia] WITH THE ISRAELITE CHILDREN. THERE HE MARRIED THE DAUGHTER OF THE HIGH PRIEST..., etc.

For the above quotation we only need to examine NUMBERS XII: 1-15 and Chapter I, pages 38 - 39 of this Volume. Note that it is also recorded that:

ABRAHAM MARRIED A CUSHITE WOMAN WHO WAS THE DAUGHTER OF THE CHIEF OF THE HEBREW TRIBES IN CUSH - LAND OF THE CUSHITE.

As for King Solomon, we know that he had wives by the dozens "...FROM LANDS NEAR AND FAR...," plus his extra concubines; the greatest of all of his WOMEN being the "Queen of Ethiopia and Empress of Sheba" - who was the ruler of Cush with her seat of rule in the Kingdom of

1. Ethiopia was at the time of the ancient Judaeo-Christian biblical figures very prosperous.
2. See Falashas teaching about their origin in Ethiopia; and Nidge Bibase Solomon, THE BETA ISRAEL, Sudan, 1874. Note that the Sacred Torah speaks in equal terms about Ethiopia [Cush].
3. "Zeus," Homer said in the Odyssey, "came from Ethiopia;" and so did "Apollo."

Akhsum [Axum]. For proof of this we do have an account of Ebna Hakin's trip to King Solomon in Chapter I, which deals with the establishment of AKHSUM as modern Ethiopia's first capital city hundreds of years before the second capital - GONDAR, and the present one - ADDIS ABABA.

Ebna Hakin's voyage is in detail as recorded in the "KEBRA NEGASTE" [The Ethiopian Chronicles] and TRADITIONAL TEACHINGS, a part of which follows below:

> Upon the request of King Solomon of the Kingdom of Palestine [or Israel] to Makeda, Queen of Ethiopia and Empress of Sheba, that she should send him back the child she was to deliver for him when he reached his maturity of age twelve [12], he gave her a ring. This token was to be returned with their child in order that the King would have been able to recognize the offspring as his own true heir, and not an imposter. This time came, and the young Ebna Hakin [later renamed "Menelik"] was sent to his father with Ambassador Ethibar, who was the most trusted member of Queen Makeda's entire Empire.
> Upon arrival in Palestine the young Prince was received by his father and all in the Kingdom of Israel. The wise King Solomon kept him for many months, in the hopes that the Queen would have followed in pursuit of her son; instead she repeatedly sent other representatives with offerings of precious stones and jewelry, myrrhs, gold, animals, etc. to the King, bading her son's return. The Queen pleaded for her son's return, because she needed him to take over her Kingdom and Empire due to her very poor health. Finally Prince Ebna Hakin was returned by his father, who loaded-down his caravan with precious presents for his mother. He also gave the young Prince the ARK OF THE COVENANT to Cush [Ethiopia]. Ethibar or Aethibar, the Ambassador of Her Imperial Majesty's Government, was placed in charge of the Prince's return, as he had been when he was sent to his father. The news of the Prince's pending return spread joy in all of the Kingdom of Ethiopia, particularly in the Queen, who knew that she would also"... receive words of great wisdom from the King..." After a six months journey the caravan arrived in Cush to the welcome of festivities unlike anyother before, all of which was ordered by Queen Makeda for her son - Ebna Hakin. Announcing the change of the Young Prince's name from Ebna Hakin to "MEMELIK," the Queen proclaimed him: "KING OF CUSH, Emperor of SHEBA AND LION OF ALL JUDAH" [the last part of his title was in honour of his father]. He was crowned before all: "HIS IMPERIAL MAJESTY MENELIK Ist, EMPEROR OF ALL CUSH AND LION OF ALL JUDAH. "Emperor Menelik Ist immediately decreed the "HEBREW RELIGION" to be "... THE OFFICIAL RELIGION OF CUSH...."[2] He ordered all of the "HEBREW SCRIBES" to form the "OFFICE OF SPIRITUAL WORSHIP OF THE CROWN OF CUSH."

The above historical recordings and teachings go on to much greater lengths; but this work alone cannot afford to continue Emperor Menelik's rule, much of which is also shown in Volume Two of this project.

After the "... glorious reign of Emperor Menelik Ist, which lasted for more than twenty-one years...," many other "HEBREW DYNASTIES" followed in the history of Ethiopia. Those were truly

1. See Joel A. Rogers, World's Great Men Of Color, Vol. I - II, New York, 1949.
2. In fact, the religion of Cush was the same as all other nations of the Nile [Blue and White] Valley.

the days and years when MIZRAIN [Egypt], NUBIA [Sudan], PUNT [Somalia] and CUSH [Ethiopia] were also the MAIN CENTERS OF WORLD CULTURE for Europe and Asia- including Palestine at the gateway to the East. They were often referred to as "Nile Valley High Cultures" [or civilizations].

Then came the reign of the Egyptian Coptic Christians to crush the so-called "HEATHENS" as they called us This invasion from Egypt was caused by the Egyptians need for revenging the capture of Egypt by their fellow indigenous Africans from Ethiopia on previous occasions. The arrival of the Coptics, along with the local Ethiopians that joined them, was supposedly to put to an end any practice of the HEBREW RELIGION and HEBREW CULTURE in Ethiopia. The Coptics [or Copts] issued all kinds of decrees for "VOLUNTARY" and/or "FORCED" conversion into the "NEW FAITH" - the earliest name of what is today called "CHRISTIANITY." We, the FALASHAS and/or KYLAS, were at that time in our history very strong militarily, and fully established as a centralized government with a moving economy. The Coptics attacked, never the less, with their full force and overwhelmed ours thereby causing us to surrender in a few short years of combat. Most in our ranks fell victim to the path of least resistance. And from this point on you will find the beginning and development of the "CHRISTIAN RELIGION" in Ethiopia. This was partly due to "CONVERSION" by thousands of Falashas to the "NEW FAITH" from Egypt, whose followers were now committing all forms of GENOCIDE against our people: Christendom had come to stay until the present time. With it came the bigotry of another "ONLY TRUE GOD."

As late as the Thirteenth [13th] Century C.E. the Falashas had certain areas of land in Ethiopia which we were still controlling independently of the Central Government. At the end of the Thirteenth [13th] and the beginning of the Fourteenth [14th] Century C.E. came the reign and rule of King and Emperor Anda Seyon. He took away the last vestige of POWER we had left that was free of the Coptics domination. With this complete loss of power a goodly number of the AGAW [Falashas and Kylas] or BETA ISRAEL went by the way of "CONVERSION" to the New Faith, which had become the sole "NATIONAL RELIGION OF ETHIOPIA." Those Falashas who remained Hebrew were always able to RECONVERT some of their members who were not very determined in their desire to surrender their own HEBREW RELIGION for the ease of the economic comfort of not being persecuted by the zealots of the "NEW RELIGION - CHRISTIANITY." By this latter method we were able to regain some strength against the rulers and their "NEW RELIGION" which had become too overbearing for many who had originally accepted it.

In the Fifteenth [15th] Century C.E. another king named Gatz Yaqob, who was also a Coptic Christian, started to persecute us with the intent of wiping away all semblance of the HEBREW

1. The white racist Jews are demanding that "Falashas in Israel must reconvert." The Jews with the oldest traditions in Judaism "must reconvert." Why? Racism or Religious Bigotry!

[Jewish] RELIGION because we were again holding powerful influence in the fields of art, law and science. This type of oppression was successfully passed through; but then came the reign of Muhammad Gragan, who was known as "THE MIGHTY LEFT-HANDED RULER." His correct name was "AHMAD ibn IBRAHIM." This indigenous Ethiopian Moslem leader, who was of Falasha grandparents, and his armies invaded the northern borders of Ethiopia where we were in control and dethroned King Lebna Dengel in 1536 C.E. "The Mighty Left-Handed" ruled very well for a time, and was "quite liberal in his treaties for us to live together with our differences in faiths." But like others before him, "The Mighty Left-Handed" resorted to rule by "strong-arm" methods. He began confiscating our wealth; then he tried forcing "CONVERSION" to Mohammedism upon us. He was making a good job of it until he tried to interfere with the Coptics lower down in Central Ethiopia. That caused the battle to expand, and the Coptic Christians felt obliged to call upon the Portuguese for assistance. This aid came promptly for "The Mighty Left-handed" had become a menace to all East African nations, including the Portuguese enclaves these Europeans were preparing for their colonialist expansion drives that followed later in the Nineteenth [19th] Century C.E. Protection of the "ENCLAVES" and the Christian Missionaries' positions was responsible for the Portuguese giving aid to the Coptic Christians.[1] The Portuguese also thought that it was a great opportunity to defend themselves against the British expansion towards East Africa; for the British had also become a threat to the Portuguese plans. The Portuguese helped Ethiopia in order to help themselves, even though it was known that Ethiopia was on the list of the Portuguese, British, French and Italian plans for eventual conquest of Alkebu-lan [Africa].

After the arrival of the Portuguese colonialists the Moslem Asians, and some Africans, were driven from Northern Ethiopia, thereby causing some semblance of peace in that section of the country with the prospect of a better future as time passed by. However there came another tyrant in the person of King Serge Dengal Melek Segael who ruled from 1563 to 1597 C.E. and was historically known as "THE GREAT AND POWERFUL RULER OF ETHIOPIA." About him much is written in the KEBRA NEGASTE [Ethiopian Chronicles].[2] He instituted a campaign to crush the last semblance of any sign of the Flashas regaining power or influence in Ethiopia's civil government. We fought very hard against him under the leadership of Chief Rada'i, who had led us before to many victories over the Moslems and Christians. But like all other men, the day came for the defeat of our "...GREAT CHIEF RADA'I...." He had fought to the last of the breath he had in his own body. Men, women and children of the Agau People died with him in his armies. The Maidens who were not killed on the battle field against King Segael and his forces committed mass suicides rather than become prisoners. They had formed lines and marched to the top of

1. The rule of the Christian Missionaries as forerunners of the colonialist was long before set.
2. Too many historians cannot understand Egyptology because of their ignorance of Ethiopia.

a precipice where they hurled themselves over the cliff as they shouted with a sense of relief that they were maintaining their honour:

"YWH HELP US; YWH HELP US; YWH HELP US; YAAWAAH."

This request was said just before each one leaped to her death. Here you have seen the deep value placed upon the "PHYSICAL VIRGINITY" among the Falasha women; and particularly their desire not to have contact with other men than their own Hebrew communicants. It will play a much more dominant role as you read other chapters to follow. Some "Western" writers wrote that:

"THE FALASHA WOMEN SHOUTED YWH HELP ME."

This could not be true; but this is what happens when one translates from one language to another without having full command of either or both. The direct English translation word by word would be correct; but such an interpretation does not take into account that the Falashas use "WE" even when speaking of a single person, including ones self. This is typical of the manner in which the Falashas live COMMUNALLY. In reality any Falasha would call on "YWH" to "HELP" more than himself or herself, even when the individual alone may be in distress. Our "DABTARA" [Learned Men] teach that:

"THE MAIDENS SHOUTED; YWH HELP US; YWH HELP US, '

etc., etc., etc. We can understand why this error was made by the "Western" writers, as the languages - AGU, AMHERIC and GHEESE [Gheeze or Geeze] - are very difficult to interpret and translate into English; and very few "Westerners" can do this competently in their very short whirlwind visits to Ethiopia. Of course this does not stop any of them; we have felt the results.

We passed through some turbulent years after the death of Chief Rada'i. But the Falashas came back fighting under the leadership of Chief Kalef, who was the brother of Chief Rada'i. We regained full strength under his stewardship, and remained so until the appearance of "...the greatest Chief of the Falasha People, Gedeon...." He reigned during the late Seventeenth [17th] Century C.E., and was able to negotiate with other Ethiopian Kings and Chieftains; as he made many treaties and alliances with them for "PEACE." Said alliances and treaties were made with Chiefs that were fighting against King Susneyos, who was ruler of the greater portion of the Kingdom and Empire of Ethiopia [Cush or Kush, etc.]. We joined them in their battles against King Susneyos as allies under a most bitter struggle. The struggle on our part came to an end following the death of our "....Illustrious Chief Gedeon...." on the battle field. This was equally the "end of the rope" of the Agaw People as an influential force in Ethiopia's history-making. We were only to contribute indirectly to Ethiopia's cultural development from then on. After Chief Gedeon's death the Falashas were driven out of the Semyen Territory by King Susneyos; and many

1. Falashas are basically communal people, but do not surrender very easily to anyone.
2. "King" was a title not acceptable to Falashas of the past and present; it was/is 'political."

of our people were forced to accept "CHRISTIANITY and CHRISTENDOM" in one form or another in every place we entered, solely for the sake of mere survival. Those of us who did not meet with such vile unfortunatecy, were able to fight and flee to the hills, were to become the forces that regrouped into what was to be the foundation for the present descendants located throughout the nation of Ethiopia, the Caribbean Islands, "the Americas" and elsewhere today. Again hundreds upon hundreds fled into other surrounding nations to escape the new wave of persecution and genocide that raised their ugly heads once more.

Many writers, such as the so-called "Christian Missionaries" Isaac Stern and Jan Jeaneaux, totally distorted their reports to show that:

"THE FALASHAS, IN MASS, ADOPTED CHRISTIANITY."

This was far from the whole truth; for the Falashas that "converted" to any form of Christendom did so solely to please the rulers; but inwardly they still practiced "JUDAISM," and in their homes asked "YWH's [God] FORGIVENESS FOR HAVING TO PRETEND WE ARE CHRISTIANS" to stay alive. They worshiped their own God - "YWH" - in their homes; and they considered the "NEW RELIGION" foreign to their thinking, and still do up to the present time, and with the same future outlook. This was typical of many other AFRICAN NATIONALS who were subjected to the Christian and Moslem colonization and missionizing a-la European and Asian styles.

Falashas gradually returned to the lower lands of Ethiopia and scattered all over the Empire. The majority remained in Western and Northwestern Ethiopia. Even today you will find most of the Falashas living around and about the ever famous Lake Tana, which is about 6,000 feet above mean sea level. Falashas reside in large numbers around Tigre, Asmara, and throughout much of Begemder Province. There is also a large amount of Falashas living apart from the general Ethiopian communities. These present the most ancient of Hebrew religious customs and traditions. For their protection they have avoided wholescale social contact with other Ethiopians who are not of the Hebrew [Jewish] Religion and Culture; all of this because of constant persecution.

The third grouping of Falashas are those living with the general population of Ethiopians in the major cities, such as the late Professor Tamrat Emmanuel, Atta [Mr] Nidge Bibase Solomon and Atta Taddese Yakob.[1] These three individuals were the best known Falashas outside of the communities that are exclusively controlled by the Falashas. The first - Professor Emmanuel - served as "Cultural Attache" for the Ethiopian Embassy in Paris, France after World War II. The second - Mr. Solomon - was one of Ethiopia's "greatest historians" of all times, who had to live in exile in the Sudan because of Emperor Haile Selassie's vindictiveness. The third - Mr. Yaqob - was the Chief of Customs of Ethiopia." There were, and still are, many other Falashas

1. Presently in jail for his activities in leading Falashas to Isreal and back to Ethiopia because of racism and religious bigotry encountered in Israel against all non-white, especially black, Jews.

in high government positions in Ethiopia - including the Foreign Office; operating not as Falashas.

Falashas living in the Americas and the Caribbean Islands are another grouping separated from the general body of the communities in Ethiopia. The late Rabbi - Wentworth Matthew, Solomon Marshall and Eli ben-Eleazer, all of whom resided in the United States of America, were African, African-American and African-Caribbean Falashas who worked in the field of education about the general body of Falashas the world-over right in your midst. Their contacts with the "motherland - Ethiopia, East Africa," and with Falasha philosophy, customs and traditions. were constantly renewed periodically. The same is true for Ethiopian-born Rabbi Hailu Paris, probably the best known Falasha Rabbi in the United States of America today; at least the best known among European-American [WHITE] Jews. Rabbi Paris is also a well known lecturer on his fellow Falashas' history, culture and religion before European-American Jewish audiences all over the United States of America, particularly in synagogues and temples.

Writers of European and European-American origin consistently juggled the figures of the Falashas presently living in Ethiopia from a high 200,000 to a low 10,000. Our figures are much different, and to the best of My Own Knowledge, there is a minimum of 60,000 known Falashas in communities, and many thousands more scattered here and there throughout all of the 13 Provinces of Ethiopia. The saddest aspect of this controversy is that more than 1,500,000 lived in Ethiopia before the Fascist armies of Italy invaded and occupied Ethiopia in 1935 C.E./A.D. and committed all forms of GENOCIDE upon the Falasha communities. In the Gentile communities the atrocities were somewhat less severe; the Falashas not being Christians made our victimization that much worse. For there was a weird accomodation between Italian and Ethiopian Christians.

Except for clothing and perfumes Falashas use they are not distinguishable from others of the general Ethiopian population. Falashas are often mistaken for Moslems, Voodooists, Christians, etc. by foreign visitors traveling through Ethiopia because of the fact that there is no special physical differences between them and others; the same being equally true between White Jews and White Christians in the United States of America and elsewhere. The vast majority of Falashas living in the Gentile [Christian, Moslem, etc.] areas, particularly in the larger cities, do not convert to the Gentile Religions even when there is no Hebrew Synagogue to attend. But most of the Falashas living under these conditions generally find each others home to come together for the purpose of Hebrew prayer sessions. Some of them even take part in activities headed by Orthodox [Coptic] Christians, whenever such activities are not in conflict with their own religious beliefs. Falashas in these cities are generally very liberal socio-politically, and find no extreme hardship getting along with the general Christian, Moslem, etc. Gentile popu-

---

1. The current take-over by the Ethiopian Armed Forces may have invalidate this statement. This is true because of the loyal role of so many Falasahas to "Zionism;" the same "Zionism" that continually snubs them.

lation. Of course this is not necessarily true everywhere in Ethiopia; nor with everyone.

The distinguishing features for identifying a Falasha from a communal community who is visiting in the city differ for male and female. The male generally use an OIL, the female a PERFUME, neither of which is available in the Gentilė communities. Although these scents are not offensive, they nevertheless present a unique aroma which makes the user stands out in public. I have already describe the type of clothing both males and females use in the Falasha communities, which except for color and other small details are no different to the general clothing and styles of the general population of fellow Ethiopians of other faiths. One of the distinguishing traits is in the fact that Falasha women wear their dress at least five [5] inches above their ankles and up to their throat, thereby covering their entire body. Unlike others, they never wear "Western style" dresses. And except for very special occasions Falashas don't wear hats; but turbans.

Up in the mountain regions outside the City of Gondar where the vast majority of the AGAW reside there is another group of US commonly known by the name "KYLA."[1] The Kyla have a very significant religious community, which is even much more rigid in its traditional taboos on the most ancient forms of JUDAISM than other Falashas. Visitors consider the term "KYLA" to be simply the same as the term "FALASHA." But, its background and origin is strictly from the SHANU SCRIPT. "FALASHA" is surely from OLD COPTIC or ETHIOPIC SCRIPT and GHEEZE - with a little influence from Ethiopia's oldest language - AGU - known to date.

The Kyla never permit Gentile visitors of any denomination or religion to come close to their homes; only brother and sister Falashas who are equally a part of the Agaw Communities. They, like the Falashas, do not eat any food produced from outside of their communities. The Kyla in their own communities will not permit food to be brought into their communities by fellow Falashas living in Gentile communities; because they know that we, so living, must come in constant contact with Gentiles - who in their standards are "UNCLEAN." And they/we do not permit their children to study any other book than the SACRED SCROLL [Torah or Bible]. They believe that:

"ALL THINGS USED BY MEN WHICH ARE NOT NATURAL ARE EVIL,
AND NOT OF GOD,"

including the books of every religion other than the Sacred Torah [Pentateuch or Five Books of Moses - which the Christians call "Old Testament"].

The Kyla religious and cultural festivities are much more colorful than other Falashas, and generally last for much longer periods. They are generally taller than the average Falasha of the Communal Communities. They will never permit any social contact with Falashas who ever lived

---

1. They are at the core of the movement to remain in Ethiopia; not move to Israel like Yakob's group. Note that Yakob and his followers had to return to Ethiopia from Israel because of racism.

in any Gentile community. They will turn their face, rather than look at a Falasha who has ever "CONVERTED" to another religion or faith. This should be particularly interesting to European and European-American Orthodox Jews who treat such persons as being dead, and resort to saying "PRAYERS FOR THE DEAD - KADDISH"-as they bury them into oblivion. These brother and sister Agaw[1] are so careful about the Sabbath that they will not even... "RUN ON THE SABBATH" ...in fear that God - YWH - will consider such an act:

"WORKING, AND BREAKING THE SACRED COVENANT OF SABBATH."

The Kyla. more so than the Falashas, are knowledgable of the Aramaic Language, but very little Hebrew, if any. They are believed to have predated the Falashas into Ethiopia in the ancient days before Ethiopia was known to the world as the replacement of the names: "ITIOPI" and "CUSH." They are very good weavers, and the best silversmiths and goldsmiths I have ever seen in my entire life anywhere in the world, considering that I have done so much extensive traveling globally.

It is very essential that you remember your author is not attempting to suit your ideas about what he has written so far, and in the following pages. However, it is certain that you have already read much of what you believe is "WRONG" and/or "RIGHT;" and as such you would like to'tell him off.' Your conclusion in this regard, so far as your author is concern, does not matter beyond the facts presented to you. The author does not intend to point out GOOD, BAD or INDIFFERENCE in his historical reporting on his people that will follow, whether it be the Agaw [Falashas or Kylas] or the African-American [BLACK] Jews in the Americas and Caribbean Islands. This reminder is necessary at all times throughout this volume, unless otherwise stated. In Volume Two of this study the author will make analysis of certain FACTS and their many CONCLUSIONS. But said FACTS and CONCLUSIONS will be treated and related to the existing "BLACK - WHITE JEWISH CONFRONTATION" that brought about the so-called "WHITE JEWISH BACKLASH" and "NEGRO [black] ANTI-SEMITISM" that permeates almost all of the relationships between European-American [White] Jews and all African-American [Black] People, irrespective of religious affiliation, if they dare to carry the label - "MILITANT."[2] Yet everyone active in anything socio-political is in fact a so-called - "MILITANT." But "MILITANCY" against White Gentile WRONGS perpetuated by White Jews is acceptable; but not "MILITANCY" against White Gentiles and White Jews injustice perpetuated upon Black Jews, Black Christians, Black Moslems, etc. WHY? Because there is still the "Great White Father" mentality existing amongst all White groups; the major concern of which is the continued belief that BLACK PEOPLE, irrespective of religious belief or GOD worshiped, must be told what we CAN and CAN NOT do. The sad part

1. "Agaw" is singular or plural. There are special prefixes to change to male or female gender.
2. A state of mind in which one comes in order to defend nis or her integrity as a human being.

of this theory is that it CAN ONLY OPERATE when the advocate has his or her victim in irons physically and/or mentally. This is not the case with any of the BLACK JEWS any place throughout the world at any era in OUR history; not even in Eretz Israel!

Right: A "TYPICAL" African of the type commonly found all along the Nile Valley (Blue and White) to the present day.
Left: Pharaoh Neb-Maat-Ra, mighty ruler and builder of the the 17th Pyramid.

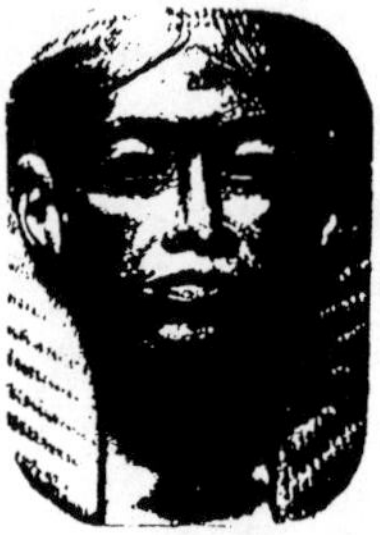

Is it not strange that only the figure at the lower right is a so-called "NEGRO?" Also, that all of the others are "SEMITES" and/or "CAUCASIANS?" Yet, the two figures at the bottom are on the handle of Pharoah Tut-ankh-Amon's walking cane that allegedly indicates a so-called "Negro" and a so-called "Semite" slave. The person in the middle, Haile Selassie Ist late daughter, is also considered a "SEMITE" and/or "HAMITE;" never a "NEGRO." Strange? But academical. Review page 51 etc. of Y. ben-Jochannan, Cultural Genocide In The Black And African Studies Curriculum, New York, 1972.

FALASHA ELECTORAL SYSTEM: Chapter III, Part Two.

There is a distinct difference between the methods of the "ELECTORAL PROCESS" in most Falasha communities and all of the Gentile Communities in Ethiopia. A method was in the Ethiopian Government's election of DEPUTIES,[1] which you noted - under the subject heading: PRESENT HOME OF THE FALASHAS," Chapter II of this Volume. The following should cause you to notice the differences in methods of the election processes used in various communities within the same country - ETHIOPIA, East Alkebu-lan [Africa]. You will also observe these differences without hardship due the extremity in opposite direction between the two systems.

The center of the election of officers in a Falasha community is the "COUNCIL OF ELDERS." This COUNCIL is composed of the older men of the community. Women are never permitted to serve as "ELDERS," and will never be in this society. The entrance age requirement of the members of the COUNCIL is at a minimum of fifty [50] years of age [2 score and 10] to a forced retirement of about seventy [70] years of age [3 score and 10]. The reason behind this age limit is expressed in the following manner:

> "A man at three score and ten will start to decline in his broad outlook on life due to the physical and mental handicaps which he must undergo at such an age." [This is not always tied to senility "Western style"].

The same holds true for a woman at that same age who was serving on the COUNCIL OF WOMEN. The high age of entry into the COUNCIL is also based upon the "WISDOM OF THE AGED" theory. It suggests that:

> "The aged has superior experiences, thus greater wisdom of life to that of the young; so that they must guide." [Quite the reverse in the "West"].

Many believe that the"...

> first-hand knowledge of conditions of the past will make one better prepared to give guidance for the future benefits of the community...."

Yet, it is equally emphasized that:

> "A man of too many years [past seventy] mind ages like his body deteriorates."

The next influential group in the Electoral System is the "COUNCIL OF THE PRIESTHOOD." This COUNCIL is the guide to the Council of Elders theosophically, religiously and/or philosophically. All of the members of the Priesthood are eligible to become members of their Council. There is no age limit in the Council of the Priesthood, because by the time a Priest [Kahen] gets to the age of seventy [3 score and 10] he would have become a member of the LEARNED MONKS, whose task it is to "...

> live a life of complete meditation with his God - YWH - and separation from the rest of the community...."

1. Note drastic change from "feudal capitalism" to "African socialism" - 1974 C.E. to present.

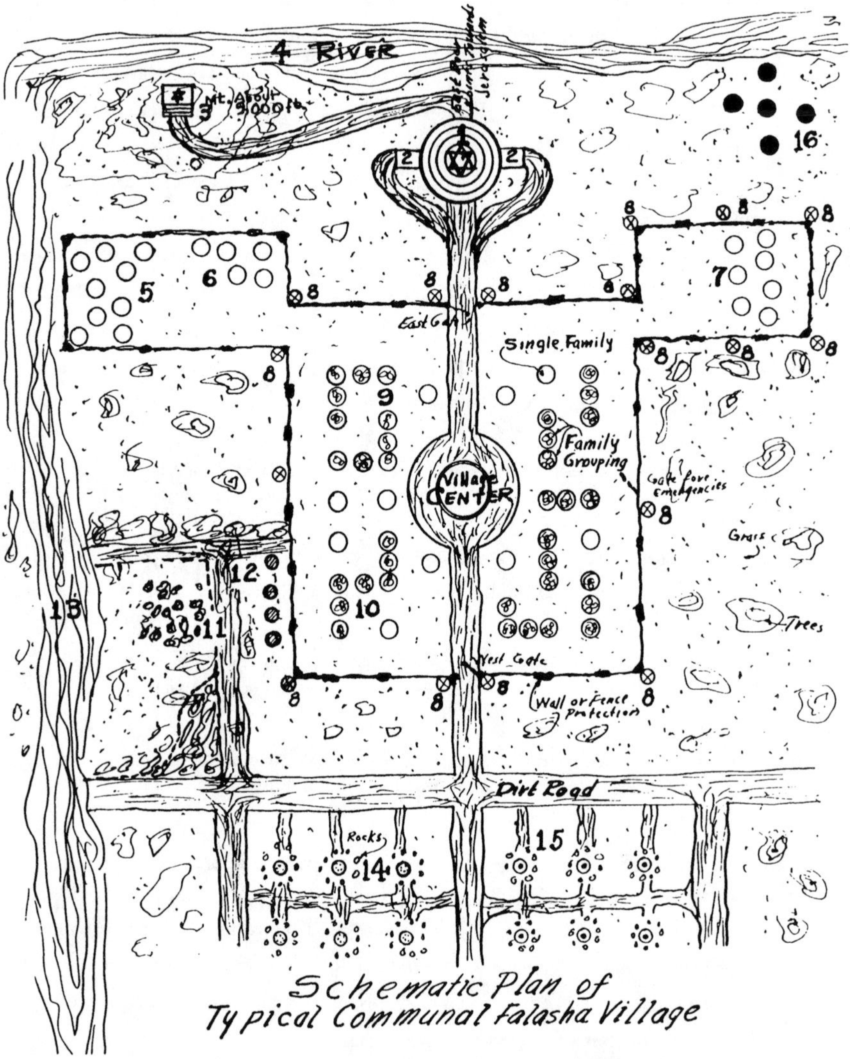

Schematic Plan of Typical Communal Falasha Village

1. SYNAGOGUE
2. SECTION FOR WOMEN
3. SACRIFICIAL ALTAR
4. RIVER OF SACRIFICE
5. PRIESTHOOD
6. MONKS
7. SISTERHOOD
8, GUARD HOUSES
9. SINGLE FAMILY
10. FAMILY CENTER
11. BURIAL GROUND
12. ATTENDANTS HOUSES
13. CLEANSING RIVER
14. HOUSE OF WOMAN IN CHILD-BED
15. HOUSE OF MALEDICTION
16. HOUSE OF CLEANLINESS, FOR RETURNING FALASHAS

The "GENERAL [male] COMMUNITY" is the first in order of government, though it is the last in order in the selection of the candidates. This is better understood by the following : When the votes are casted by all groups the General Community will have a majority of more than seventy percent [70 $^0/_0$] of the total. One must remember that Falasha communities are established upon a "THEOCRATIC" foundation. Thus, Falashas are not interested in a "Western [type] Democracy" and/or "Constitutional [form of] Republic," etc. ; because of this the above occurs.

As we are now becoming that much more involved it is necessary to remind you that the Falasha System is in no way similar to any electoral system of the so-called "Western World." Therefore you should try to forget your own system at this time in order that you may not become confused in trying to evaluate between the two while you are reading this work. If you follow my suggestion on this latter point you will be better able to understand the full impact of the Falasha Electoral System for governing under a Theocracy.

When a new CHIEF [Head of the Community; never King] is to be elected from the people the Council of Elders meets and proclaims the opening of the office and receiving of new candidates. The Council of Priesthood is then called upon to give prayers and blessings for help in the wise election of a candidate. Soon after the prayers and blessings are given the Council of the Elders goes to the people of the communities and ask them to make their suggestions for a candidate that they would like to hold the office. The Council goes to each person individually or in group. The women are first asked for their wise opinion as mothers of the communities; but they are not allowed to vote. The men are asked for their opinion as "PROTECTORS OF THE MOTHERS AND DAUGHTERS" of the communities. The youths of less than twelve [12] years of age are asked if they have any opinion,as they are to become inheritors of the communities. The Council of Elders is the last to make their selection as a group for the candidate they believe to be the best. The Council of the Priesthood cannot make any suggestion for a candidate because of the religious position which they hold. Many Falashas would not vote against the Priests' choice in fear that the Priests must know best, even when they feel different about the candidate.

After all the candidates are recruited their names are turned over to the Council of the Priesthood.[1] This Council must look into the candidates background for seven [7] generations passed.

The examination of the candidates covers the following:

> [1] The religious upbringing of the candidates; [2] Investigation for records of any adulterous act ever committed by any of the candidates lineal ancestors [their grandparents back seven generations]; [3] To see if any of their parents at least seven generations back had any communicable dicease; [4] If there was any conversion to a Gentile religion in their parental line for at least seven generations back; [5] The quality and status of their formal and informal educa-

1. Not to be confused with the "Priests" in the Gentile Religions anywhere in structure or function. This group of men are not go-between with their God; they are spiritual leaders only.

tion;[1] [6] Their knowledge of the Sacred Torah and Levitical Laws; [7] Their knowledge of the entire affairs of the communities in which they live.

The result of each of the above seven [7] points must turn out to be in the favor of the candidates. It is not allowed that they should receive any liberalism, nor excused from anything that appears to be unfavorable to them under any consideration whatever, as their records must be spotlessly clean-cut and uncompromising. All of the candidates who meet all of the qualifications would be notified to this effect, also the Council of Elders.

At a special date set aside all of the qualified candidates are gathered together and the ELECTION declared open. The candidates must each pick a Sheep-Skin Ballot from a bag. Among the skins are three specially marked. The three candidates who drew the three marked skins are the official candidates left in the running for the office. The unsuccessful candidates must vote and elect one of the three successful candidates of the temporary selected ballot skins. Because the election is not by secret ballot, each candidate knows who voted for whom. The candidates receiving the most votes and the second most votes will be considered the OFFICIAL TEMPORARY CANDIDATES for the office. The last balloting elects one of these two candidates; but the unelected one equally cast his vote for one of the remaining two. The candidate with the most votes out of the two becomes the ELECTED OFFICIAL OF THE OFFICE or ELDER-[Chief]-ELECT of all of the Communal Communities of the Falashas; not the Kyla.

After the candidate's election the Council of Elders is notified of the results. They in turn notify the Council of the Priesthood, who in turn notifies the GENERAL COMMUNITY of the wise election. The unelected [defeated] candidates gather around in the presence of the "ELECTED" and listen to the High Priest proclaim before the General Community:

THE CANDIDATE-ELECT WAS ELECTED BY MEN, ALL OF WHOM ARE EQUAL TO HIMSELF IN HONOUR.

The Chief Priest calls each of them by his name, and ask each one:

WAS THE ELECTION A FAIR AND JUST ONE? DID THE CANDIDATE-ELECT MAKE ANY SPECIAL BARGAIN WITH ANYONE OF YOU FOR ANY FAVOR?

If they answer "NO;" then the INSTALLATION CEREMONY for the Chief Elder is declared ready to begin. Note that the term "KING" is never used in the Falasha System of Government, as they are strictly THEOCRATIC in ideology.

On the "DAY OF THE INSTALLATION OF THE CANDIDATE-ELECT" he is carefully warned:

"You must use your office in the spirit of all of the Hebrew Leaders before you. You are responsible to all of your ancestors in the Hereafter for a just and compassionate reign. You must protect your people at all times, just as our ancient Chief Gedeon and Rada'i had done. You must give your life, rather than allow

---

1. Not in the "Western" sense - the so-called 3 R's, but instead general knowledge of the community where everyone of the Falashas live.

your people to fall into the hands of the Christian and Moslem missionaries who have always brought havoc upon us in their efforts to convert us. Under all conditions, even at the point of the loss of your own life, you must guard the Sacred Torah from the hands of the unclean. The only Laws you must lead by are those of the Ten Commandments, which were given to your forefather Moses on the Mount of Sinai while we were in Egypt. You must serve our women and children, and respect them; at the same instance not allowing any woman to make you rule for the benefit of her personal love."

The Candidate-Elect is then carried off to the Synagogue where the High [Chief] Priest, Subordinate Priests, Monks and Sisters [who remain outside of the building with the other women] offer prayers to YWH for him, and for his wise leadership.[1] For a leadership of understanding which may be followed by men everywhere due to the good example he will show.

The SACRED [Holy] TORAH and another special scroll with the TEN COMMANDMENTS alone are handed to the Candidate-Elect while his hands are in an outstretched position. He must proclaim, thusly:

"I have received the Sacred Scriptures and Holy Laws; they are the same teachings of YWH which my forefathers received. I have acknowledge them to be the only authority in leading my people - Israel.[2] And if I should break any one of these Laws and Commandments set forth therein I will, as I must, voluntarily relinquish my authority to lead my people - Israel."

The TEN COMMANDMENTS are recited by the Candidate-Elect from memory. He is given the "ELECTION BLESSINGS" from the High Priest and the "INSTALLATION PROCESSION" begins.

The INSTALLATION PROCESSION follows a path towards the center of the community. There the Candidate-Elect will remain until the marchers [male only] arrive at the center where he is awaiting. The High Priest turns to the people of the entire communities whom the new Head of the Agaw will lead, and proclaims the Candidate-Elect:

"OUR PERMANENT CHIEF ELDER-ELECT OF ISRAEL."

He introduces the new Head of the Agaw as:

CHIEF [calling his name] OF THE BETA ISRAEL [Children of the House of Israel or House of Israel], SERVANT OF GOD.

The new CHIEF follows in reciting the Ten Commandments[3] - the "LAWS OF HIS OFFICE" - from his memory. He also reads various "COVENANTS" from the "SACRED TORAH;" and then proclaims to his followers:

"My memory of the Laws handed down by my forefathers are the same as those recorded in our original Sacred and Most Holy Torah. These are the Laws upon

1. Falasha's education is still tied to their/our Sacred or Holy Torah and local traditions of Cush.
2. Note that I had to use words and phrases in English to convey certain actions and ideas which may not mean the same literally in the Agu language when translated word by word. "Israel," as mentioned here means "The People, People, The Hebrew People," etc.; not state or country, etc.
3. Unfortunately the Falashas, Kyla, et al., have no idea of the Laws originally taught in Egypt.

which I will lead my people - Israel, and for which I will give my life to protect, and also for my people - Israel. I will respect all of the Civil Laws of the Government of Ethiopia which do not conflict with my faith. And, I will collect all of the worldly goods belonging to the Goverrment of Ethiopia" [taxes, or any other objects not of a religious nature, etc.]

The "Chief" offers a prayer to God - YWH - for his own guidance. He asks the people - Israel:

"Help me to be a just leader as was the illustrious Chief Gedeon."[1]

The mother of the new Chief is proclaimed by him: "CHIEF MOTHER," if she is alive. If she is deceased the "OLDEST WOMAN" of the communities would be designated as the "CHIEF MOTHER-SELECT." She [his natural mother,or select] becomes the "ETERNAL SYMBOL OF THE SOURCE OF THE COMMUNITIES," as he leads in her honour; and because "...it is from the Chief Mother's womb [symbolically] the Beta Isra'el originated...," etc.,etc., etc.

The Chief Mother has a meaning which refers back to the HONOUR OF THE VIRTUOUS DAUGHTERS who committed mass suicides to uphold the integrity of the communities and their virginity, rather than submit themselves to the Christian and Moslem invading armies. She also represents the "HONOUR" and "RESPECT" to all of the other "MOTHERS" of the communities. This is that they may know the men realize we could not exist, nor be of any use, without them, although we control every aspect of community living. This "HONOUR" helps, because there is no direct way for a woman leading the communities; but women are not to be disrespected or misrepresented. The Chief Mother's indirect leadership is based directly through the Chief Elder, who also represents women as equally as he does with regards to men. It is written:

"Her place is ahead of all men on the road to the Hereafter. She gains her place through the pains she suffered in bearing Israel in the Holy of Most Holies of her Womb. Our Chief Mother is the symbol of our respect for our women."

I ask you to pause for a little while before reading the other installments of this detailed socio-historical and socio-anthropological work about my people - the AGAW [Black Jews, etc.] Now look at your own "ELECTORAL SYSTEM." See if you can find any similarity between your own "SYSTEM" and that of the so-called "FALASHAS' SYSTEM OF ELECTION." Consider if there exists any "DEMOCRACY" in that of the Falashas and your own.[2] Since the Kyla are a part of the Agaw People, and it is mostly in their communities that the system outlined is most common, you must treat your response with respect to all of the Agaw People in all of the Communal Communities throughout Ethiopia. For example; you pick out the Falasha from the Kyla on the following page, and from the other BLACK HEBREWS, also from the "NEGRO JEWS" if you can recognize them. Probably not a single one is a HEBREW, HARIBU, JEW, SEMITE,..., etc.

1. Historically considered the wisest and bravest of the Beta Israel/Kyla of all times.
2. Assuming that you believe "democracy" is a reality in your own country; the U.S.A. included.

NOT ONE OF THESE IS A "NEGRO" OF ANY TYPE WHATSOEVER, WHY NOT?

Only Alexander Pushkin at the bottom left is not a Jew on this page. According to THE NATIONAL GEOGRAPHIC MAGAZINE, August, 1928 the top three left to right are : SEMITIC, HAMITIC and NILOTIC. The center shows two Falashas: Isazah Adomic [16] and his fellow Falasha in Israel with two European-Israelis [Jews]. Surprise? Your author at bottom right.

PRESENT RELIGIOUS PRACTICES AND CUSTOMS.
FOUNDATIONS, LAWS, ETC.: Chapter IV, Part One.

The "SACRED [Holy] TORAH" is the philosophical basis for all of the Falasha Communities, and of all of life's meanings. It is their "CONSTITUTION" from whence all reasoning derives, and upon which the "LAWS OF COMMUNAL ADMINISTRATION" among the Falashas are based. They do not legislate any "WRITTEN LAWS;" for they base all acts which are not regulated by the "SACRED TORAH" upon aged-old CUSTOMS and TRADITIONS. These practices are developed through voluntary acceptance of CUSTOMS, DOGMAS and MORES, rather than by legislations developed by modern politicians who are for the most part lawyers.

The "CHIEF PRIEST" or "HIGH PRIEST" [Tellek Kahain] is the religious head of everyone of the Falasha and Kyla "COMMUNITIES," the only person who ranks above the "CHIEF ELDER-ELECT." Once in ancient history the Chief Priest was also the Chief of all functions of the Communities; but this authority has been gradually shared by the office of the Chief Elder Elect for over the last seventy-five [75] to one hundred [100] years. Some of these customs are dying out.

The "CHIEF PRIEST" is assisted by all of the other "SUBORDINATE PRIESTS." They are "SUBORDINATES" only in rank, but not in social status, within the communities. The Chief Priest is "SELECTED" and "ELECTED" from, and by, the Subordinate Priests. He remains "CHIEF" unless he enters the "ORDER OF MONKS;" at which time he enters "...

> A LIFE OF COMPLETE MEDITATION AND SECLUSION FROM ALL OTHERS EXCEPT HIS PEERS IN THE ORDER...;"

and only "DEATH" can remove him. He will loose his rank, and will have to leave the communities.

> "FOR BREAKING ANY OF THE LAWS OF THE TEN COMMANDMENTS,"

or any of the other "...

> RELIGIOUS LAWS AND ORDINANCES OF THE SACRED [Holy] TORAH...."

There are "MONASTERIES" occupied by former "SINGLE PRIESTS" who have volunteered to enter into this type of seclusion. Priests joining the Monasteries become "MONKS," and must

> "...devote all of their time to prayers and other religious activities...."

They must "...

> occupy themselves in farming as an occupation in order that they may earn their own livelihood independent of the labors of the general communities...."

Any Monk of the religious order may withdraw from same upon his own desire, but can never be a leader in anything else again. A Falasha can become a member of the Priesthood, also a Monk, only if he is "...BORN OF THE CAST OF A KAHAIN..," the same being true for each profession any Falasha desires to follow; he or she must be of that CAST which the profession is assigned. All religious personnel of the MONASTERIES and SISTERHOODS must live apart from the general communities. Each religious order [Monks and Sisters] lives separate from the other Priests but do not live separate from the communities, whether married or single. Each community places great respect in all of the members of these two religious orders. For only Falashas of the very highest religious and personal background are permitted to enter such orders; of course, providing they are of the right "CASTE" and "TRIBE." The respect given the religious groups is due to the "SACRIFICES" the members therein must make in order that they could serve the general community unblemishly. They also have to do their share of the general community work. Their time-off from manual labor is devoted to prayer and other religious activities. Twenty-four [24] hours of each day of their lives are taken up with religious activities of their communities. The members of the Priesthood study the "SACRED TORAH" to such a degree that at least sixty-five percent [$65^0/_0$] of all of those who spend more than ten [10] years within can recite the complete TEXT almost word by word from their memory. I will venture to say that every Monk can do this fete; for the Monks devote much more of their time to the study of the SACRED TORAH than do the Priests. The Monks are the ones to be called upon to decide on any passage in the SACRED TORAH where a conflict of interpretation may arise in any of the communities. It is to be noted that unlike the Priests and Monks, the Sisters cannot engage in the administration of religious rights and rituals of any kind to be administered to the general community.

All of the "PRIESTS" are permitted to be married; and they are encouraged to do so, especially when they are young, and before they enter the Priesthood. The Sisters of the Sisterhood cannot marry while they are still active in the Sisterhood. However, there are no laws or rules that prohibit any of them from so doing after they have severed relationship with the Sisterhood. This condition is due to the fact that all members of the Sisterhood have to be "PHYSICALLY VIRGIN," a fact which all in the Falasha Communities have accepted. Therefore, they become for everyone:

> "symbols of the virgin women's honour, and a memory to all of the maidens that committed mass suicide rather than become concubines for the favors of the invading Christian and Moslem armies and missionaries in their conquest of Ethiopia, and their particular attempt to convert all Falashas."

The control of the relationship between male and female in terms of religion also relate to the wife of a Priest. For example; if a Priest's WIFE should die he is discouraged from marrying another woman. But should he prefer to remarry, without any exception to the rule whatsoever, he

> "must marry at all times a woman of a physically virgin state, and not of the Sisterhood at anytime in her entire life."

He cannot marry a WIDOWED or DIVORCED woman under any circumstance whatsoever; never.

The High Priest officiates at all of the "ORDINATIONS" of "SUBORDINATE PRIESTS." The High Priest and all of the Subordinate Priests have to be members of the "TRIBE OF LEVI." And their only qualifications must be based upon their BIRTH and EDUCATION [along religious lines-the study of the Most Holy Torah]. All of the Priests must be investigated back to their SEVENTH [7th] LINEAL ANCESTORS. And if there was any past ADULTEROUS LIFE by any of their grandparents SEVEN [7] GENERATIONS removed, those affected are rejected from entering the Priesthood, this being equally true in the case of LEPROSY. All of the Priests that satisfy the investigation become ready for their ORDINATION into the Priesthood [dissimilar to any RABBINICAL ASSEMBLY in the United States of America, with many major differences].

The ORDINATION RITUAL is of very serious involvement for the entire communities. An extract from one follows: After the selection of the CANDIDATE PRIEST from the TRIBE OF LEVI for the Priesthood he must "...

> appear with a young male lamb as a sacrifice for the forgiveness of his sins which he had committed in the past, and those of his living parents, equally for his ancestors seven generations into the past...."

He may sacrifice a male "GOAT" or male "OX" instead of a "LAMB." Which ever type selected:

"IT MUST BE THE FIRST BORN MALE OF THE MOTHER THAT BIRTH IT."

The sacrificial animal will be given to the Priests and/or Deacons to be raised. When the animal is of the proper age for this ritual it is slaughtered in the same manner as in all of the other cases where sacrifice is carried out. The complete outline for "SACRIFICIAL RITUALS" is already describe in Chapter III of this Volume. The "ASH" from the Ordination Sacrifice is not thrown away in the same manner of other sacrifices; instead, it must at all times take place as

"scattered at the four corners about the outside of the tent and altar,"

built solely for the purpose of the sacrifice. These rituals -

"must be performed where there is running water - a river and/or stream,"

[bottom of a hill]. Other extension of this area of the service I prefer to leave for only those who are still practicing Judaism according to the teachings of the Agaw Communities' High Priest, Subordinate Priests and Monks.

After the Ordination Sacrifice is completed the new Subordinate Priest must be ready to -

> "offer a young male lamb [ox or goat] to the general community as a symbol of his charity and love for the people - Israel, whom he desires to lead in religious and spiritual sacrifice and devotion to the one and only God - Ywh."[1]

He must SLAUGHTER the lamb with his own hands in the direction of the EAST GATE of the Community to which he will be assigned [review plan of average village on page 102 of this Volume. The "BODY" of the sacrificial animal [minus the entrails and extremities: feet, ears, head and genital organs, etc.] is distributed amongst the women and children of the community. The Community in return gives the "INITIATE" [new priest] gifts of FOOD and CLOTHING; but never a

---

1. Typical of "Abraham's sacrifice of a lamb instead of his son...," etc. [Gen.xxii: 1 - 13].

solitary "CENT" if he lives in a Communal Community. MONEY was given in Communities located in Gentile areas of Ethiopia where the economic system was either CAPITALISM or FEUDALISM, etc. The present "AFRICAN SOCIALIST ECONOMIC SYSTEM" has caused drastic revisions.

The Chief [or High] Priest thereafter performs the most solemn Ceremonial Act, which is called: "... Wrapping of the TURBAN of the Priest..." around the head of the new Priest. This is combined with the "...Passing of the LONG WHITE SHIRT of the new Priest...." The latter item is "...

> THE SYMBOL OF THE SPOTLESS LIFE A PRIEST MUST LIVE...."

He is shown that:

> "THERE IS NO DIRT APPEARING ON THE LONG WHITE SHIRT"

when he received it. Then he is further warned:

> "YOU RECEIVED A NEW SOUL IN THE SAME MANNER, SYMBOLICALLY, YOU MUST KEEP IT AS CLEAN AS YOU WILL KEEP YOUR OWN SOUL." [White does not indicate "purity" in the Western sense].

After the Wrapping of the Turban and the presentation of the Long White Shirt the High Priest offers "...PRAYERS FOR THE NEW PRIEST...." The High Priest proclaims that the new Priests

> "OFFICIALLY ORDAINED AS A FOLLOWER IN THE LINE OF ABRAHAM, JACOB, ISAAC, JOSEPH AND MOSES."

He is told by the High Priest:

> "You are bound by all of the Laws of the Ten Commandments and the Sacred Torah. It is your duty to give up your own life, rather than loose any of them; and if you are dying because of defending them, you are not permitted to use any force whatsoever to protect your physical person, but must call upon your God - YWH - for protection; for there are men such as our Chief Elder-Elect, who must do your fighting physically. Your duty is to lead us in our battles spiritually and morally against imperfection."

A Priest can be "DEFROCKED" for any violation of the "TEN COMMANDMENTS" of the most SACRED TORAH [Pentateuch, Holy Bible, Five Books Of Moses or Christians' Old Testament]. However his CASTE as a KAHAIN, or PRIEST, cannot be taken away from him; this he inherits geneologically according to the Falashas interpretation of the Hebrew Scriptures on religion. If he desires to "DIVORCE" his wife he must resign his active participation in the Priesthood and return to live as anyother male in his community. However, a "DIVORCED PRIEST" who automatically loses his office as a PRIEST also receives the name..."DÄBTÄRÄ"..." A LEARNED MAN."[1] This title allows him to practice many of the duties he had while he was a Priest, with only one exception. A "DÄBTÄRÄ" cannot perform religious sacraments and services, nor officiate at a SACRIFICE. Like all of the practicing SUBORDINATE PRIESTS, he can still prepare any

1. Equivalent to the "Priest-Scribe" of the Mysteries System of the Grand Lodge of Wa'at, Egypt.

FOOD for the Priests, and prepare [sharpen] the "SACRIFICIAL KNIVES" for any sacrifice. He must see that "...

> there is no rough edge on neither of the two sides of the Sacrificial Knife...."

And he must also "...

> keep the Religious Umbrellas of the Priests to be used in the Procession Of The Sacrifice in excellent condition, and free from uncleanliness...."

He can take part in most of the other activities of the synagogue which a lay Falasha does not even know to perform, nor is permitted to perform.

The "SISTERHOOD" is never visited by any male except a Subordinate Priest on an emergency. The "SISTERS" never reenter the general community amongst the other women unless they are on missions of mercy or teaching assignment with young girls, particularly with respect to the "DIETARY LAWS" and "LAWS OF CLEANLINESS" [Levitical Laws].[1] A SISTER upon leaving the SISTERHOOD holds no post directly or indirectly connected to it. But she does not lose any prestige as an ordinary lay woman upon her return to the community. She cannot make contact with the other Sisters in the Sisterhood when she returns to the general community as she surrenders her right to said contact upon her resignation, irrespective of the cause. However, she can generally hold the position of "NURSE" and/or "TEACHER" in her community because of the teaching and educational activities she learned while being a Sister. She can never be married and enter the Sisterhood, or marry after she has already entered; for once within the Sisterhood she..."MUST ALWAYS REMAIN A SPOTLESS PHYSICAL VIRGIN...." She can leave without stigma.

The "FALASHA SISTERHOOD" is not to be confused with that of the "CONVENT" of the Christian Religion, particularly the Roman Catholic Church and the Anglican Church, etc. The Falasha Sisters are never considered ..."MARRIED TO YWH"... as "NUNS" are "MARRIED TO JESUS CHRIST" in the Christian Religion. However, there are similarities in certain educational and teaching functions which both groups perform. Equally, the Falasha Sister is not considered to be "...PART OF THE RELIGIOUS COMMUNITY..." as in the case of the Christian "NUN" and or "SISTER." They do take care of the SICK, INFIRMED, WOMAN IN CHILD-BED, etc. similarly to their Christian counterparts. Her "Obligation of Duties" includies the following:

> "IF I SHOULD DEBASE THE HOLINESS OF MY BODY FOR THE SOLE PLEASURE AND GRATIFICATION OF MY PHYSICAL NEEDS; I SHALL NOT FAIL TO DISAVOW THE RELATIONSHIP I SHARE WITH MY SISTERS IN HONOUR OF THOSE WHO HAVE GIVEN THEIR LIVES FOR ALL OF US TO BE ALIVE IN GOD."[2]

---

1. Kosher regulations are extremely rigid in all of the Falasha communities throughout the world.
2. A Falasha Sister appeal to her God for strength and guidance in remaining pure as the "... honoured maidens in whose honour I serve...," etc., etc., etc., almost ad infinitum. She must surrender her entire life to the service of her people - Falashas/Kyla and God - Ywh/Jehovah.

THE HOUSE OF WORSHIP/SYNAGOGUE: Chapter Two, Part II

The House of Worship [SYNAGOGUE] or House of God - Ywh is constructed from specially prefabricated baked mud and straw bricks made by brick masons of the communities. The Synagogue is generally built ROUND, rather than SQUARE and/or RECTANGULAR as most synagogues in the United States of America. There are at least two [2] doors of entry to each synagogue. One door always faces "EAST," the other "WEST." The EAST DOOR is for the use of the Priests and Monks and should always point towards the direction of Jerusalem, even if said point is not in the East. The WEST DOOR is for the use of the general male population of the community "ONLY." The GENERAL COMMUNITY" in this case never include WOMEN, as "WOMEN" are never permitted inside any of the Synagogue [there is "Western" pressure to change]. Synagogues, with Monks assigned to them, are always constructed with a "QEDDESTA GEDDUSAN" or "HOLY OF HOLIES" built in the East Wall where the "ARK" and "SACRED TORAH" are also kept, this being located very near the EAST DOOR which is used by the Monks and the High Priest, but not by the Subordinate Priests normally. The servicing of the Most Holy Of Holies is performed by "SCRIBES, DEACONS" and "SUBORDINATE PRIESTS" only. The "MOST SACRED CEREMONIAL INSTRUMENTS" are kept in the Holy of Holies, along with the "RELIGIOUS UMBRELLAS" and "SACRED SCROLLS." Sometimes the High Priest also keeps his own special "PRIESTLY GARMENTS" in this chamber. The Holy of Holies in times gone by was generally built with at least a portion of "EARTH" imported from the "SINAI PENINSULA" in Egypt, Northeast Alkebu-lan ["Africa'] and/or "JERUSALEM" in Israel [Palestine], Western Asia. It was placed into the MORTAR that bound the bricks together, and did not have to be more than a spade full of earth in the entire mix of any portion of the mortar; for the purpose was just to have a part of the so-called PROMISED LAND to which the so-called "HOLY OF HOLIES" is always associated. Roman Catholics building new churches place saints' bones in altars; as per rumors.

Having already shown that the SACRED TORAH remains in the HOLY OF HOLIES, it is also important for you to know that no PRIEST may carry a SACRED TORAH to his home even for the purpose of study. The "SACRED SCRIBES," who write all of the "SACRED TORAHS," must have an "ARK" built into their house to place the SACRED TORAH they are working on; their "WIVES" must never touch it, or it will be "EXCLUDED FROM THE SYNAGOGUE" and destroyed. Any SACRED TORAH is declared "...UNCLEAN..." in the very same manner like a female who is capable of going to the "HOUSE OF UNCLEAN BLOOD" [house of menstruation].[1] A Priest may carry other religious articles to his home, but the same rule applies to his WIFE and anyother FEMALE as in the case of the SACRED TORAH. This rule is unchangeable.

1. Hebrew males are restrained from sexual intercourse with any woman menstruating at any time.

The "ALTAR" in the synagogue must always "FACE EAST" and/or "TOWARDS THE DIRECTION OF JERUSALEM." It is sometimes built from "FIELD STONES" and covered with a thick MARBLE-TYPE slab. This SLAB forms a table-top on which the SCROLL with the TEN COMMANDMENTS and passages of the "SACRED SCRIPTURES OF THE HOLY TORAH" are read during the regular services. ["Jewish Missionaries"are also trying to change this].

Sometimes the"ARK" is also constructed from "FIELD STONES." It must have the "LAWS OF THE TEN COMMANDMENTS" on a small slab of marble over the door where the SACRED TORAH is to be stored. This "DOOR" is always located at the front of the ARK; and it is always made from a PLAIN MARBLE [or other] STONE SLAB hinged to the wall of the Ark.

There is always a sizeable section prepared for the private use of the Priests and Deacons. It is set off for them to study and rest between services, or when they are in the synagogue due to other duties. It is very seldom ever open to the General [males alone] Community. It is cleaned and attended by the Subordinate Priests and Deacons themselves.

At a THREE [3] FEET distance off the exterior wall surrounding the Synagogue's front door there is a section marked off for WOMEN and FEMALE CHILDREN to attend and listen to the services; because FEMALES are never allowed to get closer to the Synagogue unless by some

> "very special order from the High Priest under an extreme emergency."

This is a condition which is reconciled by the theory which states that:

> "THE WOMEN ARE NOT REQUIRED TO ATTEND RELIGIOUS SERVICES;"

as they are considered to be "...

> clean in conscience by the mere possession of their precious womb, and by their giving birth, which causes all of their sins to be removed...."

On this point it is further believed that:

> "A woman, who has given birth to a child, is also forgiven for her sins by the mere fact that she has a womb, which in itself is the essence of the forgiveness."

It is to be noted that this "forgiveness" does not extend to any of the wrongs and/or truly mortal "sins in violation of the Ten Commandments and Laws of the Sacred Scriptures."

All MALES attending the Synagogue Services must BATHE [wash] themselves each time before they enter the door of the Synagogue building in the community. Each service on every day requires the same action on the part of the MALES, irrespective of "AGE;" so that if there are THREE [3] SERVICES in one day and a man must attend all THREE, he would have to take at least THREE [3] BATHS. All FEMALES coming within the "THREE [3] FEET LIMIT" around the "THREE FEET PERIMETER MARK-OFF" from the exterior wall of the Synagogue must also take a "THOUROUGH BATH" before approaching the service area.

The SYNAGOGUE is always draped with curtains all year around. The draperies are made of bright colors, and used on all days of festivities with but one exception. The exception is only

1. "Women's Movement" in the U.S.A. cannot fathom this concept of the African Goddess, etc.

on YUM-KIPPUR [Day of Attonement] - the most sacred of the High Holy Days of the Hebrew Religion, at which time the entire Synagogue is draped in WHITE. The main Altar remains draped in BLACK, while the Ark is covered in striped SKY BLUE and WHITE [there maybe changes now].

"LIGHTS" in the Synagogue are provided by means of "SESAME SEED OIL LAMPS." These LAMPS are kept lit on all occasions of Synagogue activities and services. Before the SABBATH DAY SERVICE" the LAMPS are lit at Sun-Fall [sundown Friday evening, equivalent to the European and European-American "Omeg Shabbath"] by a youngster who has not reached manhood [age twelve]. If any, or all, of these LAMPS should go out between the lighting on Sun-Fall Friday and Sun-Fall Saturday - "SABBATH" - the service must continue in total darkness rather than have a single LAMP relit. All FIRES or LIGHTS throughout all of the communities that go out during the SABBATH DAY cannot be relit, irrespective of the place in which a FIRE and/or LIGHT is. The DABTARAS [Learned Men] must make certain that all OIL LAMPS are filled before the beginning of Sun-Fall on Friday evening. They must see that the "WICKS" of the LAMPS are in good condition, also that they have been cleaned and trimmed. It is the Learned Men's Sacred Duty to

"GIVE THE PRAYERS FOR THE LIGHTING OF THE OIL LAMPS."

The Synagogue can be easily identified by any member of the communities, or a visitor, as it is generally built at the center of a community. It is always much larger than all of the other buildings within any of the villages of the communities, as shown on the following pages: 116 - 118 and 119, also the layout of a typical village on page 102 of this Volume.

The Synagogue's relationship to the very small sizes of the residential units does not signify that it is so enormous that it dwarfs the homes in any of the communities. Yet, it is generally built to accommodate a minimum of at least THIRTY [30] to approximately ONE HUNDRED-FIFTY [150] males at most. Such a synagogue, the larger size, is considered to be very large in modern times; but miniscule for the ancient times when the Falashas made up the vast majority of the Ethiopian population. The reason for the smaller synagogue is basically due to the method of having continuous services conducted on SABBATH and/or HIGH HOLY DAYS. In each service there must be at least "TEN [10] MEN" present. The reason is that a "MINION [quorum] OF LESS THAN TEN MEN" is contrary to the provisions called for in the SACRED TORAH to begin an official service in the Hebrew Religion; even if it is just for the purpose of reading the TEN COMMANDMENTS or saying the KADDISH [Prayers for the departed or deceased]. The completion of a "MINION" signals the beginning of the service. The "ELDERS" [all men][1] of the community or village are given their schedules on the hours in which their respective groups are to attend service. All of the men in the communities who are not ILL or FEEBLE must attend at least two

1. Only the "educated, wise" and "righteous elders" were/are allowed to lead Africans/Falashas in any of the numerous villages.

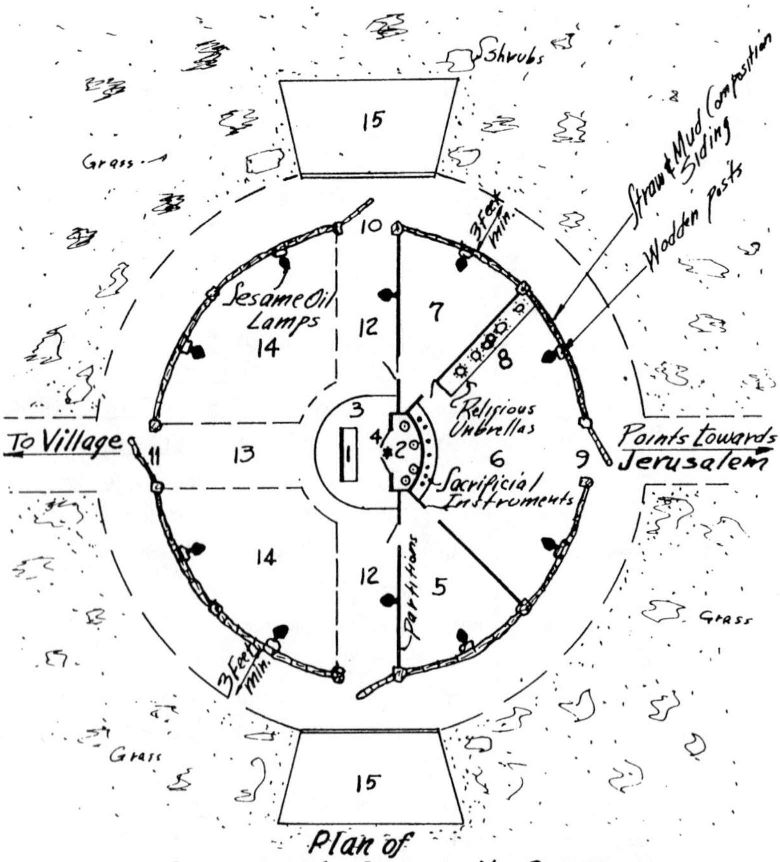

Plan of
Communal Community Synagouge

1. SLAB FOR READING OF TORAH	6. HOLY OF HOLIES	11. WEST DOOR
2. ARK FOR SACRED SCROLLS	7. PRIESTS STUDY	12. SERVICE ISLE
3. ALTAR AREA	8. RELIGIOUS RACK	13. ENTRANCE ISLE
4. ARK DOORS	9. SOUTH DOOR	14. SESAME OIL LAMPS
5. MONKS & CHIEF PRIEST STUDY	10. NORTH DOOR	15. AREA FOR WOMEN

* EVERLASTING LIGHT

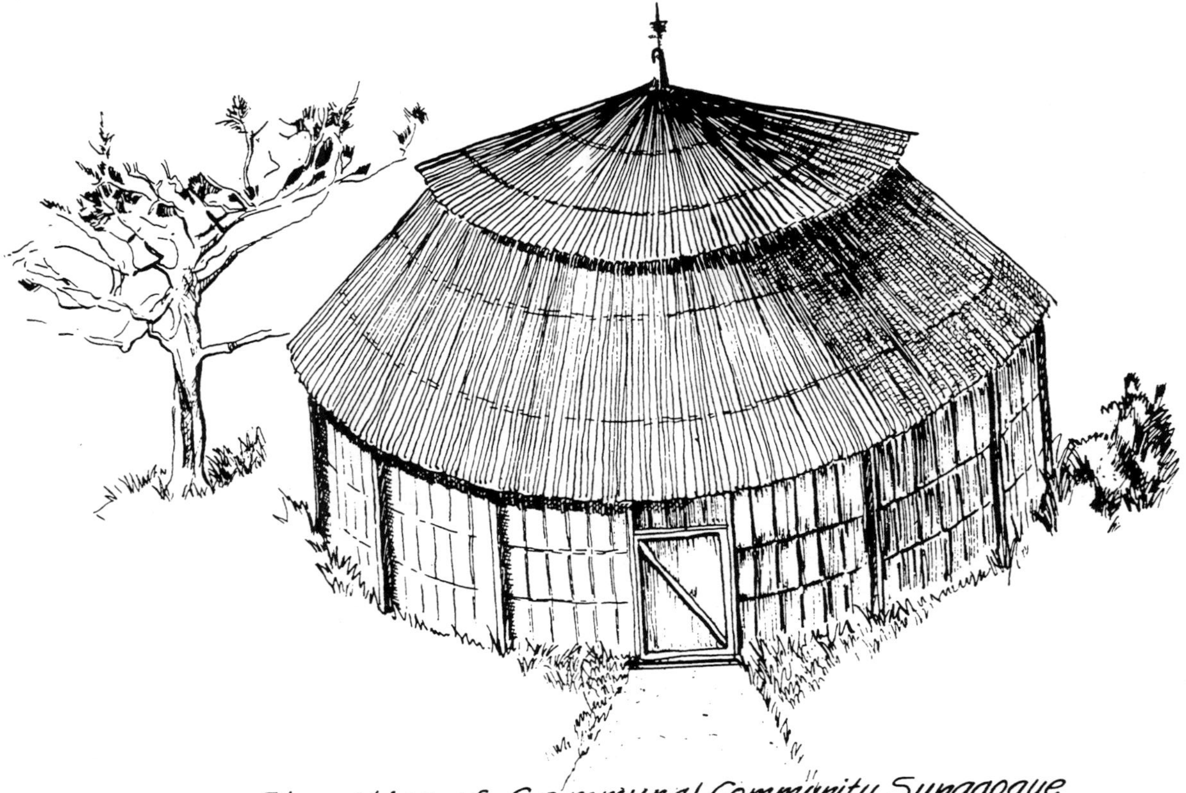

Elevation of Communal Community Synagogue

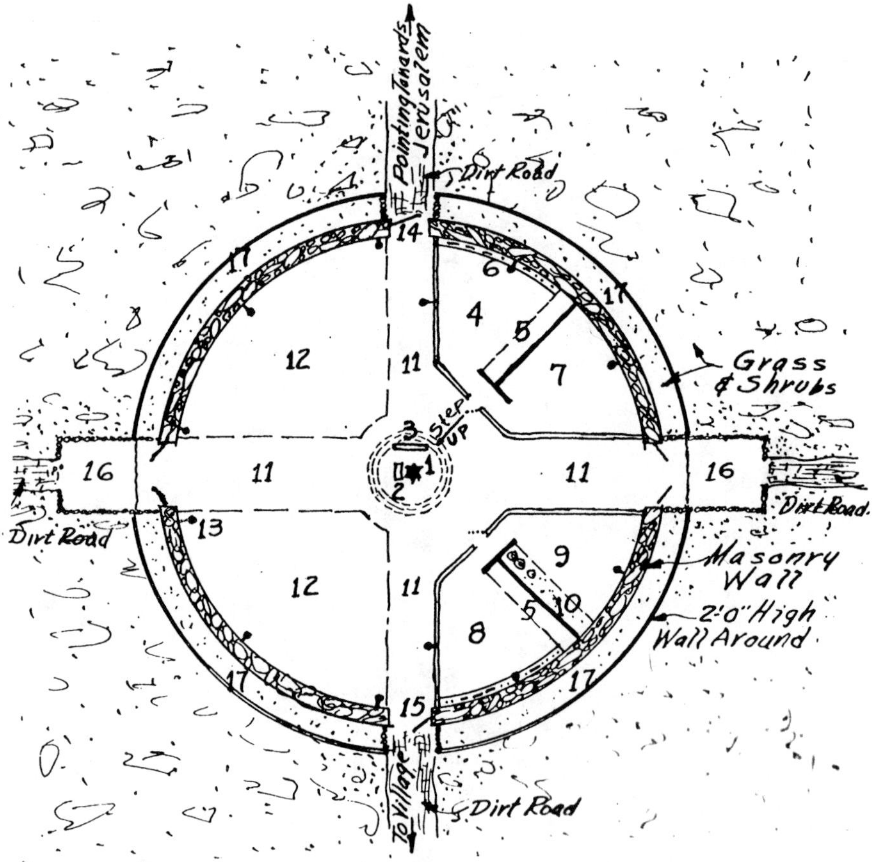

Plan of
GENERAL COMMUNITY SYNAGOGUE

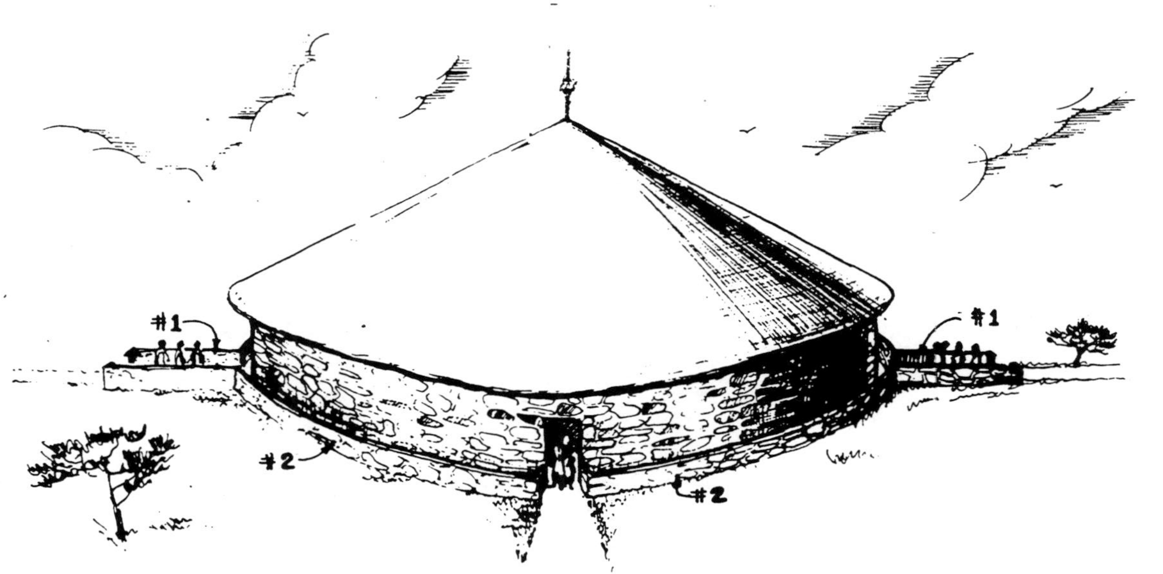

SYNAGOGUE

MUD COMPOSITION ROOF
WITH STONE WALLS

1.- WOMENS' SECTION
2.- WALL, 3 FEET FROM
SYNAGOGUE

[2] services on each Sabbath. On the Sabbath falling on a High Holy Day they are required to attend at least THREE [3] TIMES that day.

The "BRICK MASONS" and/or "CARPENTERS" must keep the SYNAGOGUE within their community on the top of their list of work to be done each day; of course except on the Sabbath. If there is no work to be done on the Synagogue in any single day the masons and carpenters are permitted to remove it from their list for at most "ONE [1] WEEK" only. Work to be completed on a synagogue must be taken care of before the masons and carpenters work on anyother project they may have for a given day. In Communal Communities the masons and carpenters do not receive any form of monetary compensation for their work, as they are required to work at any place in the communities where their services are needed and requested. However in the non-Communal Communities they receive monetary wages for their work even on the Synagogue.

Please take careful note of the fact that there are TWO [2] TYPES of "FLOOR PLAN" and "ELEVATION" for the Synagogue construction shown on the preceding four pages: 116-119. On the FLOOR PLAN showing the "ARK" in the center of the building, this is most befitting a Communal Society or Community [village]. Of course the other is generally the architectural preference in the non-Communal Communities. There is no special reason for the difference in architectural asthetics that your author can tell at this time. And I would not attempt to speculate as in the manner so common among "Western academicians" who use belief and hypothesis as "FACTS."

As we prepare to enter into another aspect of the historical and cultural heritage of the so-called "BLACK JEWS, FALASHAS," etc. it is necessary to bring back to your memory that the people who are living this life are the same people too many of us tend to deny as being KOSHER as European and European-American JEWS who practise a European-type TALMUDIC JUDAISM that differs basically in many areas. But, with all of these differences, it is the area of "RACE" that the breech is greatest; an emotional stimulus that is unheard of in the Falasha communities - Communal[1] and/or non-Communal.[2] This tern "...JEWISH RACE..," or "...SEMITIC RACE..," is only common amongst European and European-American "JEWISH" communities. For this reason throughout this work I must always bring to your eyes "SEMITES "[black, brown, yellow, white, and whatever else there is], all of whom look like anyother so-called "NEGRO JEWS" we have in the United States of America and all of the other nations of the North American and South American continents, the Caribbean Islands, and of course even in the Continent of Alkebu-lan ["Africa, Afrika," etc.]. Certainly the following picture on the next page shows many of the so-called "SEMITES" and "HAMITES" we hear so much about of late; and only the top FOUR [4] are considered "LOST JEWS." Is it strange that they look like any "NEGRO" in your home town, etc?

1. Not to be confused with "Communism," although Karl Marx made comments and overtures to it.
2. During the Empire - "feudalism" and "capitalism;" today "African Socialism," etc.

Sketch of Pharaoh AKHENATEN
(Berlin Museum Coll.)

**

Pharaoh Rameses II wearing the
CROWN OF THE ROYAL THRONE

Emperor Lidj Yasu of Ethiopia,
deposed by Ras Tafari Makonnen
(Emperor Haile Selassie).

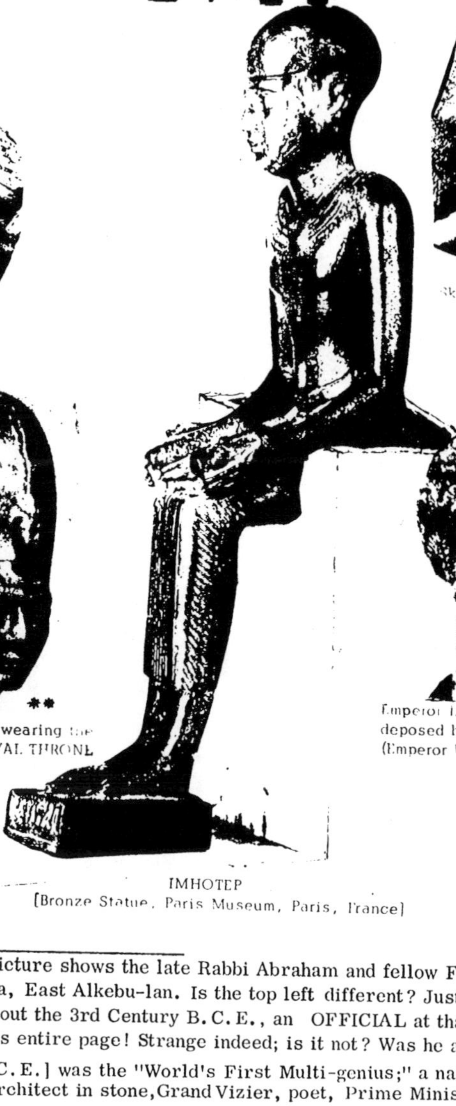

IMHOTEP
[Bronze Statue, Paris Museum, Paris, France]

Certainly the top center picture shows the late Rabbi Abraham and fellow Falasha students of Gondar Province, Ethiopia, East Alkebu-lan. Is the top left different? Just imagine that he was an ancient "GREEK" of about the 3rd Century B.C.E., an OFFICIAL at that; yet he is the only so-called "NEGRO" on this entire page! Strange indeed; is it not? Was he a "JEW?" Who knows!

Imhotep[ca. ? - 2875 B.C.E.] was the "World's First Multi-genius;" a native of Egypt, N.A. First known physician, architect in stone, Grand Vizier, poet, Prime Minister, etc.

COULD'NT THEY BE
"JEWS"?

ETHIOPIANS OUTSIDE DIRE-DIRE

[Is There Any BLACK JEW In This Picture?]

"SEMITES" AND "HAMITES" ONLY!

Ethiopians In A Market Scene; Axum,[1] Ethiopia, Africa.

ALL OF THEM "NEGROES" IN THE U. S. A.; TRUE?

1. The "World's largest outdoor market" is in Addis Ababa, the Capital City of Ethiopia, East Africa. Hundreds of thousands of people visit this market daily - from ca. 5:00 A.M. through 7:00 - 8:00 P.M., etc.

ORDER OF RELIGIOUS SERVICES: Chapter IV, Part Three.

The regular Daily Service [held in the same manner each day] begins with the BLESSING of the establishment of "...GOD'S [Ywh] HOUSE OF WORSHIP [Synagogue]...." The Priest thank God"...for all present to be here...;" and orders:

"LET GOD'S HOUSE OF WORSHIP BE FREE OF INEQUITIES."

He informs the congregation that:

"THE SERVICE IS NOW READY TO BEGIN."

The Priest then calis upon all who have experienced difficulties with any of their neighbours to -

"COME FORWARD AND GIVE AN EMBRACE OF FELLOWSHIP TO YOUR FOE."

While making the embrace [chest to chest, and side of face to side of face] and/or handshake, all the parties so doing must ask for "FORGIVENESS" from God, then "APOLOGIZE" to each others for their wrong-doings [sins]. After this has been done and all is clean in "BODY, MIND" and "SOUL," the main service gets on its way.

The CHIEF PRIEST [or HIGH PRIEST] turns his face towards the direction of "JERUSALEM," with the congregation doing likewise. He blesses the "ARK" and the "ALTAR;" and commands:

"LET THE ARK BE OPENED AND THE LAW OF THE PEOPLE -ISRAEL-
BE PLACED UPON THE TABLE OF THE ALTAR FOR ALL TO WITNESS."

The SACRED TORAH [Pentateuch, Five Books of Moses, Christians' Old Testament] is then removed from the ARK by two Subordinate Priests. They hold the SACRED TORAH high above their heads and the congregation sings the opening song of the service. At the end of the last stanza of the opening song the High Priest blesses the SACRED TORAH; then turning away from it he blesses the congregation. The SINGER [equivalent to the European-American Cantor or Kantor] comes forward to the ALTAR and receives the SACRED TORAH from the High Priest, thereby resting it on the TABLE OF THE ALTAR. The SINGER examines the first sentence in the BOOK OF GENESIS. Having assured himself of the true content, he proclaims the following:

"THE SACRED TORAH IS A TRUE ONE; IT CARRIES THE HOLY SCRIPTURES
AND THE LAWS OF OUR FOREFATHERS JUST AS THEY WERE GIVEN TO
MOSES ON THE MOUNT OF SINAI IN EGYPT LAND" [Northeast Africa].

All of the Subordinate Priests in attendance of the service are called upon, without exception, to

"COME FORWARD AND WITNESS THE PRESENCE OF THE SACRED LAWS;"

the Deacons following in turn, and all of the students of the Priesthood behind them. The High Priest reads the "TEN COMMANDMENTS" from the SACRED TORAH, and asks the Subordinate Priests the following question:

"ARE THESE THE SAME LAWS AND WORDS OF OUR GOD, THE GOD

OF ISRAEL[1] WHO GAVE THEN TO MOSES ON THE MOUNT OF SINAI?"

After they agree to the authenticity of the SACRED TORAH they return to their respective places in the Synagogue.

The "READING OF THE LAWS" follows. All of the members [males only] of the Synagogue's congregation come forward to read the "LAWS" and the "HOLY SCRIPTURE OF THE DAY" when each is called. They are called in the order of the chronological listing of the "TRIBES." The calling begins with the...HOUSE OF LEVI... [the caste of priest] and ends with the "TRIBE OF GAD" [the caste of scribes and teachers], as listed on page 39 of this Volume.

After the READING OF THE LAWS the "RELIGIOUS MUSICIANS" play "WIND AND STRING INSTRUMENTS, PRAISING GOD WHO SITS ON HIGH." This is done "...IN MEMORY OF KING DAVID...," who ordered his people:

> "COME TO THE GOD OF ISRAEL, PRAISING HIM WITH WIND AND STRING INSTRUMENTS TO THE HIGHEST, AND IN GLORY" [see page 126].

This music has what European-Americans generally call "...AN ORIENTAL TONE...," and is very similar to the music of the Yemenite Jews. However, it has a much deeper crying tone than that of the Yemenite religious brothers. Some of the tunes are typical of the music of other communities of the ORTHODOX [Coptic] CHRISTIANS all over Ethiopia. This is due to influence of the first group of Falashas who were compelled to convert to Christianity, thus carrying their music and songs into the "STRANGE FAITH" or "NEW RELIGION"- both names which earliest Christianity was called before the Council Of Trent and Council Of Antioch, etc.

The "RELIGIOUS MUSICIANS" are men [never women], all of whom are highly trained in "SACRED MUSIC." They must have very highly respected homes, and live moral lives almost in comparison to the Subordinate Priests and Däbtärä [Learned Men or former Priests]. They are also engaged in farming as a second profession in order to fulfill their working day when there is no service in the Synagogue or other religious functions where their music is needed. These two professions are their tasks, but the first one is their obligation due to their "CASTE," that of the TRIBE OF ZEBULUM.[2] Remember that we are dealing with a "theocracy."

On the days of "SACRIFICE" the service starts in the Synagogue and move to the "MOUNT OF THE SACRIFICE" where the ceremonies will be conducted. The "SACRIFICE SERVICE" is conducted completely in the Synagogue because the marchers [male only] in the "SACRIFICIAL PROCESSION" are technically considerd to be "...CONNECTED TO THE SYNAGOGUE..." by the presence of the "SACRIFICIAL TOOLS" in their midst during the procession. The "SACRIFICIAL TOOLS" are designated to be "...PHYSICALLY PARTS OF THE SYNAGOGUE;..." They

1. Meaning "the people;" not the geopolitical state created by the United Nations Organization.
2. The tribal structure of the earliest "Jewish People" is followed by Falasha communities.

ETHIOPIAN LITURGICAL WIND AND STRING INSTRUMENTS: PAST/PRESENT

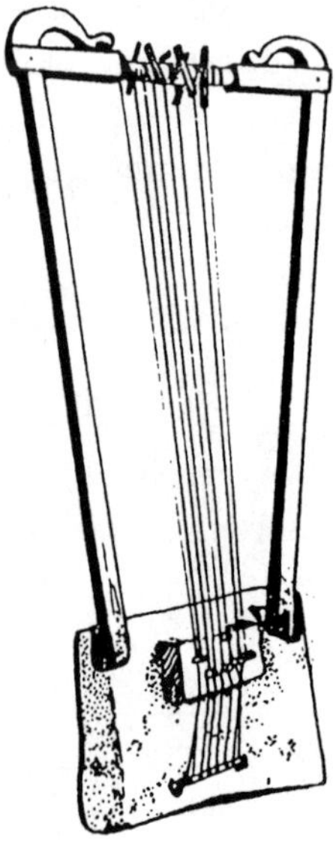

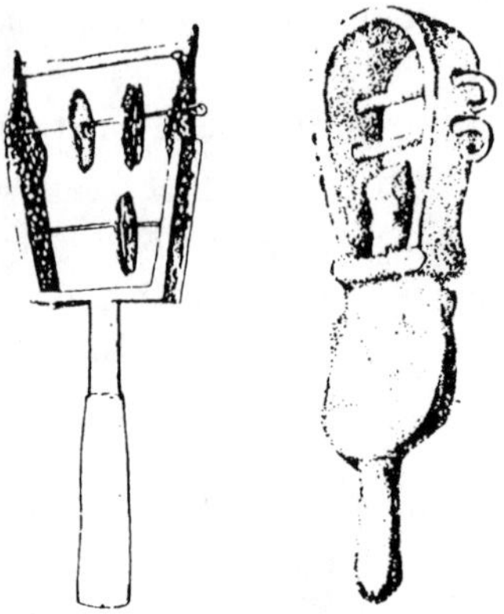

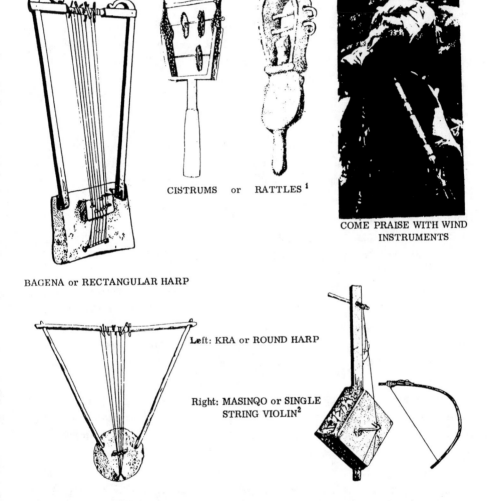

CISTRUMS or RATTLES [1]

COME PRAISE WITH WIND INSTRUMENTS

BAGENA or RECTANGULAR HARP

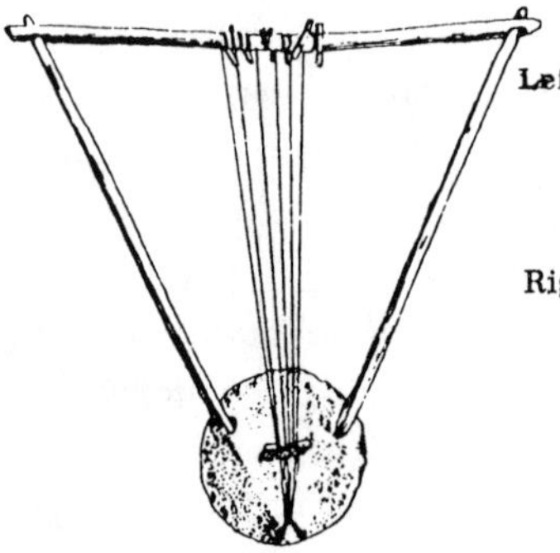

Left: KRA or ROUND HARP

Right: MASINQO or SINGLE STRING VIOLIN[2]

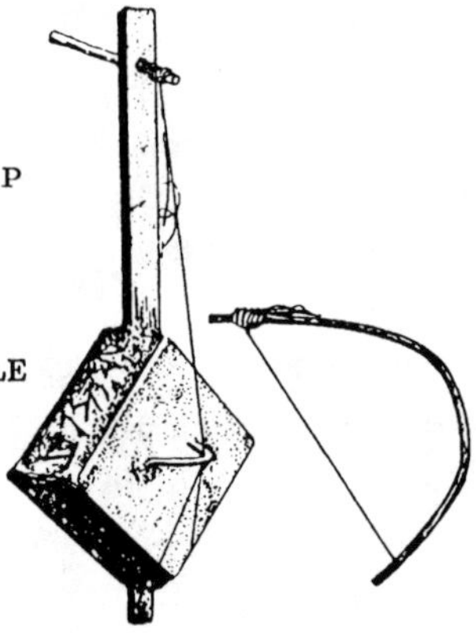

---

1. From the hands of the Cat-headed Goddess "BAST" or "BESS" of Pre-Christian Nile Valley [Blue and White] High-Cultures. These instruments are typical in other areas of Alkebu-lan also.
2. This instrument was played in Africa thousands of years before there was a single Greek alive.

also carry other INSTRUMENTS and POSSESSIONS that belong to the Synagogue, all of which have the same technical significance.

The "HIGH HOLY DAY SERVICE" commences with the "PRAYERS OF SACRIFICE." The Sacred Musicians render many chants having psychological effect, all of which causes a person to feel that he is in another world [euphoria]. On the High Holy Days the services are conducted entirely by the High Priest and the Monks. The Monks take the dominant role, and the Subordinate Priests act as their assistants. Each service from here on continues like all other regular services, but some of the prayers are different.

When this part of the High Holy Day is concluded the Monks leave the Synagogue and walk ahead of the procession to the MOUNT OF THE SACRIFICE where the SACRIFICIAL LAMB [or male ox] will be "SACRIFICED" [slaughtered] and the "BURNT OFFERINGS" made. The High Priest and all of the Subordinate Priests follow the Monks, they are followed by the Deacons, and they by the general congregation [males only]. Women are never permitted to be around the SYNAGOGUE or MOUNT when there is to be an "ANIMAL SACRIFICE." "WOMEN" and "BLOOD" are so closely associated in Falasha theosophy and theology that they are never permitted to be near the "SACRIFICIAL BLOOD OF THE OX" and/or "MALE LAMB." For Falashas believe that:

"A WOMAN'S BLOOD WOULD MAKE THE SACRIFICIAL BLOOD UNCLEAN."

Therefore, "WOMEN" must stay away from all activities connected with ANIMAL SACRIFICE.[1]

The "MONKS" always march at a distance of at least TWENTY [20] FEET in front of the congregation, as they are not allowed to mingle socially with the general population [men included]. Their lives are of constant "BATH FOR CLEANLINESS" and "PRAYERS OF MEDITATION," to the extent that it is very hard to understand them when they speak in their mumbling praying way. This is also due to the fact that they will not hold any conversation which is not connected in some way to the HOLY SCRIPTURES of the SACRED TORAH, etc.; all in the holiest of tradition.

Unlike the "MONKS" of the Roman Catholic Church those of the Falasha Communities [Communal and/or non-Communal] are not housed in "MONASTERIES," but instead live in single room houses high up on the side of mountains. They do not write any theological or theosophical works for the teaching of Judaism, this being the function of the TRIBE OF GAD - from whence the "RABBIS" [teachers] are taken. Remember that a "MONK" is still of the "CASTE" and "HOUSE" OF LEVI." And this does not change because of his dedication towards total devotion in prayer and meditation. He is not believe to have any holier connection with YWH than anyother PRIEST within the entire communities, irrespective of CASTE or TRIBE. The MONK is an HONOURED PRIEST because of his devotion; not because of his "SACREDNESS," etc., etc., etc.

1. Note that this was done by Abraham as a token of his willingness to sacrifice his own son for God Ywh/Jehovah according to Genesis, Chapter xxii, Verses 1 - 13.

RELIGIOUS SACRIFICES: Chapter IV, Part Four.

All of the members of the "PROCESSION OF THE SACRIFICE" must be dressed in "ALL WHITE," and with "OPEN STRAP SANDALS" on their feet. The type of CLOTHING and other garments used by the Falashas in the "PROCESSION OF THE SACRIFICE" is shown on pages 129 and 130 following. The general population of the Agaw People do not cover their head with any form of hat like the European-American and European "ORTHODOX JEWS," or wear "SHAWLS" as many do. The "PRIESTS" in ancient days had to wear a "TURBAN" when they were involved in carrying the "SACRIFICIAL LAMB" [Ox or Goat], and still do, as shown on page 129 following.

The "SACRIFICIAL KNIFE" is carried in the front of the procession of the "SACRIFICIAL SLAUGHTER." The "SACRIFICIAL ANIMAL" follows, carried by four turbaned Priests as I have shown on page 129. The Sacrificial Animal, if a LAMB, is carried on the shoulders of the four Subordinate Priests suspended from a center rod, which is tied to a front and rear cross-bar equally as shown on page 129 following. If it is an OX the weight prevents its being carried in the same manner; it is lead to the SACRIFICIAL area with the four Subordinate Priests at the end of a "TOW-ROPE" [a term from the Egyptian Mysteries System which Freemasonry adopted].

The type of terrain [landscape, running water with highland above] for the ANIMAL SACRIFICE is shown on page 130 following. On pages 130 and 132 a Falasha is shown grazing a few of the SACRIFICIAL ANIMALS on the "SACRIFICIAL GRASS," also outside a regular village.

Upon the arrival on the "MOUNT OF THE SACRIFICE," like that shown on page 130 where the Monks have already assembled, the Subordinate Priests gather around the Monks and the High Priest forming a circle. The High Priest offers "PRAYERS" for "...ALL OF THE WOMEN AND LITTLE CHILDREN...." He offers special PRAYERS for the "...WOMEN IN CHILD BED..." and in the "...HOUSE OF BLOOD...." He asks God - YWH - to "...

> Protect us from the Woman in Child Bed and House of Blood from mingling with that of the Sacrificial animal. Remember them for having made their own sacrifice by their presence in these houses. Forgive the souls of Your people - Israel - for having born of these ways, the sins caused by our not being able to be perfect as you had made us. Forgive us through this sacrifice we are making, although only symbolic of our forefather Abraham's willingness to sacrifice his own son; and like Abraham please take this Ox [lamb or goat] rather than the sons and daughters of our communities; spare our children - Israel....!"

The "DÄBTÄRÄ" [Learned Men or former Priests] and the SACRED MUSICIANS follow as they sing SONGS OF PRAYERS and of JOY TO YWH, etc. like the following:

> Halelujah, Halelujah, Halelujah is the cry our Father of fathers who have died in your honour, and in your praise; they are safe in your hands, and

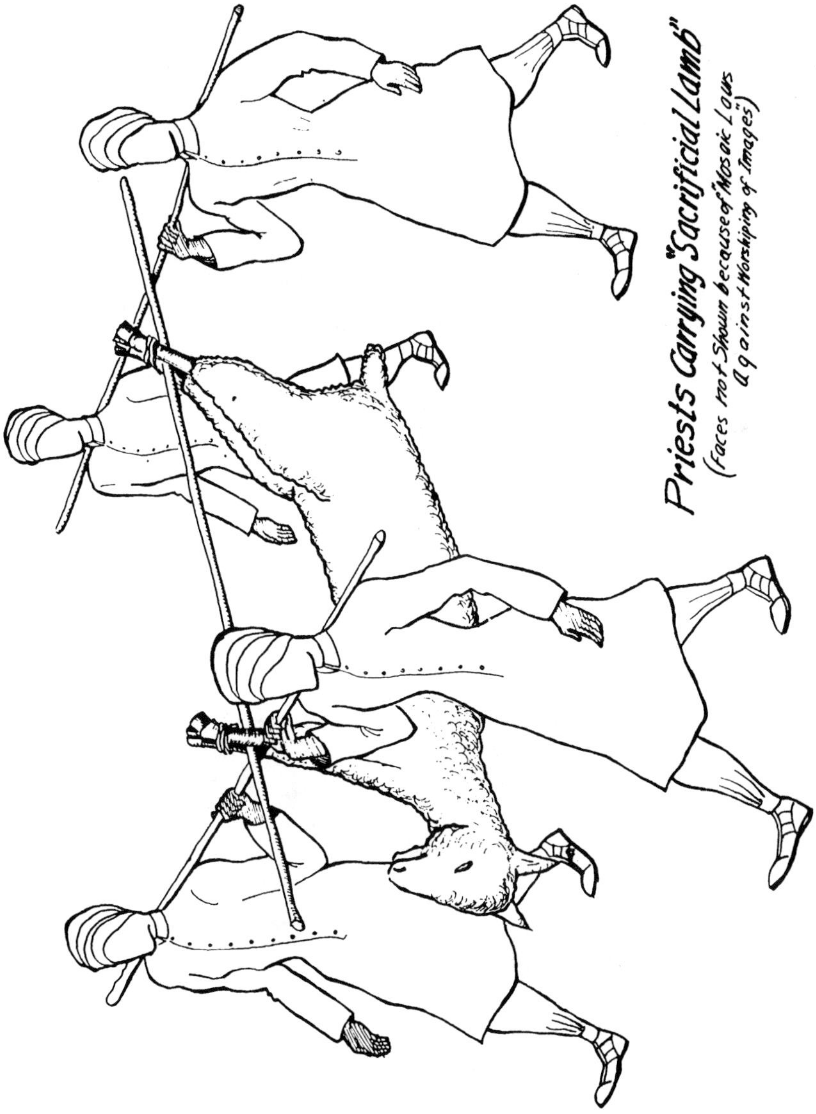

Priests Carrying "Sacrificial Lamb"
(Faces not Shown because of "Mosaic Laws Against Worshiping of Images")

Falashas Slaughtering The Sacrificial Ox
in a
non-Communal Community for the
"FEAST DAY"

Falasha Supervising Cattle
Feeding On The Sacrificial Grass.[1]

1. Note that Falashas are the only people allowed to feed their animals for any purpose whatever. To be kosher is compulsory for all Falashas in every Falasha village; no exception exist to this Law set down in the Book Of Leviticus of the Five Books Of Moses/Holy Torah.

COMPARATIVE ETHIOPIAN RELIGIOUS PERSONALITIES
OTHER THAN "FALASHAS - JEWS"

[These are Orthodox Coptic Christians]

DÄBTÄRÄ
Christian Priest

Peasant Christian of
Tigre

Right: Christian with
religious Staff

1. Ethiopian Church Authorities changed their denomination's title from Coptic Christian to "Orthodox Christian" over twenty years ago in a dispute centered over the amount of Coptics in Ethiopia against those in Egypt. Ethiopia had many times those in Egypt; thus demanded the Holy See.

Falashas Communal Village High On The Plains Overlooking
Glorious Lake Tana[1]

Taking Water From The Blue Nile[2]
That Begins At Lake Tana, Gondar

1. The Round Houses are typical in design of the Synagogue - the largest structure shown above.
2. One of the three sources of the Nile River - White, Blue and Atbarra - Uganda to Egypt, Africa.

protected by your gracious hereafter. Halelujah is your name; so be it."

The following words are repeated by the High Priest between each song:

> "Holy is the name of God our Creator, Maker of the Universe, Judge of all judges, Master of all masters, King of all kings, and Father of all of our fathers - Abraham, Jacob, Isaac, Joseph, Moses...,"

etc., etc., etc., and calling the names of noted and historic leaders of the Falashas past down through the centuries. This is also recited by the Monks in unison, and led by the Chief of Monks. It is to be noted that the naming of the sages, prophets and other creators of biblical Judaism [Hebrewism] can extend as long as the High Priest desires, as all of the names are from mental recall.

The CONGREGATION [all male] recites the prayers said by the High Priest, repeating his words in sentences. The SUBORDINATE PRIESTS also repeat after the High Priest along with the Congregation. There is a moment of silence following the proclamation of the High Priest:

> "IN HONOUR OF THE SACRIFICE MADE BY THE MAIDENS OF THE COMMUNITIES WHO DIED RATHER THAN SUBMIT IN DISGRACE."

The "Sacrifice" referred to in the above quotation was described in details to you before in this Volume, but it would be worthwhile repeating certain aspects here at a different level of participation on the part of the victims. Thus on THREE [3] occasions when the Falashas were in conflicts militarily and their enemies were about to capture them, thousands of their "MAIDENS" [girls and adult women] of the communities [all of whom were "PHYSICALLY VIRGINS"] marched to the top of a precipice and jumped over while shouting:

> "YWH SAVE US; YWH SAVE US; YWH SAVE US; YAAAWAAH,"

etc., etc., etc. Hundreds more Falasha women who were not "PHYSICALLY VIRGINS" did the same. The reason for the prayers is in honour of the "SACRIFICE OF THE VIRGIN GIRLS;" not the other "WOMEN," this due to the "PURITY OF THE SACRIFICE" to be performed after the ending of the PRAYERS. The "VIRGINS" qualified as being "PURE;" but not the other "WOMEN" who had already experienced "PHYSICAL SEXUAL INTERCOURSE" in their marriage, some of whom were even widowed at the time of their "SACRIFICE" or "SUICIDE." However, it must be understood that a "SPECIAL PRAYER" is always offered by MALE and FEMALE worshipers:

> "THE WOMEN OF THE SACRIFICE, AND IN HONOUR OF WOMANHOOD."

Silent and recital PRAYERS by everyone singularly, or in unison, are continued until about TWELVE [12:00] O'CLOCK high noon while the Sun appears to be in the center of the sky. This is the position in which the Sun must appear before the High Priest announces "...THE BEGINNING OF THE ANIMAL SACRIFICE...."[1] The Chief Monk bows his head towards JERUSALEM and

1. "Animal Sacrifice" is conducted on Rosh Hashana, Yum Kippur and Pesach on the top of a hill, at the foot of which there is running water that leads to other sources to the sea.

offers a "...PRAYER FOR THE SACRIFICE...." While offering this PRAYER the High Priest blows the "SHOFAR" [or "RAM'S HORN"] three times calling upon the People - "ISRAEL" - to...

"WITNESS THE SACRIFICE IN THE CLEANSING OF OUR SINS, AND IN THE GLORY OF YWH; AS TAUGHT US BY OUR FOREFATHER ABRAHAM."

On the High Holy Days - "ROSH HASHANAH [New Year], YUM KIPPUR [Day of Atonement] and "PESACH" [Passover] the "ANIMAL SACRIFICE" is held. In the Communal Communities alone this is true; not in the areas where Falashas reside amongst a Gentile majority. This is due to the fact that the Gentiles look negatively at the practice of "ANIMAL SACRIFICE."

If any "HOLY DAY" of the Sacrifice comes on the SABBATH the Sacrifice must be postponed for another day following; because the "SLAUGHTER" is considered to be "WORKING," and no "WORK" unless related to a question of "LIFE" and/or "DEATH" is involved. When such is the case there are "PRAYERS" of a very special nature to take the place of the Animal Sacrifice; these are called - "SACRIFICIAL PRAYERS."

Everyone taking part in the sacrifice MUST keep their "FAST" from Sun-Fall the previous day, and should not have tasted even "FLUID." This also includes "WATER" for washing ones mouth. They must take their "BATH" without allowing any "WATER" to enter their MOUTH in any amount whatever.

The "SACRIFICIAL ANIMAL MUST BE THE FIRST MALE BORN TO ITS MOTHER." It is taken from its MOTHER a few days - NINE - after it has been born and raised by the Subordinate Priests placed in charge of this task. The Sacrificial Animal, like those shown on page 130, is fed on "SACRIFICIAL GRASS" for SEVEN [7] DAYS before the final day of the "SACRIFICE," which "...MUST NOT BE MORE THAN ONE YEAR AND SIX MONTHS FOLLOWING ITS BIRTH." In wealthy non-Communal Communities where Falashas live separate from Gentiles it is generally a "SACRIFICIAL OX" that is slaughtered, as shown on page 130.

For the performance of the SACRIFICE the ANIMAL is held to a standing position while the High [Chief] Priest holds the "AMOLYE" [sack of salt] over its back, as the Monks recite the "PRAYER OF THE SLAUGHTER." At the ending of the PRAYER a Subordinate Priest, who also specializes in the SLAUGHTER, takes the "SACRIFICIAL KNIFE" and sticks it into the sack of "AMOYLE." The High Priest reads from "ABRAHAM'S SACRIFICE OF HIS SON TO YWH," etc. Upon his recitation the OX or LAMB, never a GOAT, is held by FOUR [4] SUBORDINATE SENIOR PRIESTS and placed upon the "SACRIFICIAL ALTAR." The ALTAR has a "STONE SLAB" upon which the ANIMAL rests. The SLAUGHTERER sticks the ANIMAL with the double-edge "SACRIFICIAL KNIFE" through the JUGGLER VEIN. The ANIMAL is turned upside down, with its head hanging down and allowed to drain of its "SACRIFICIAL BLOOD." This "BLOOD" is caught in the

1. This is the most ancient custom of Judaism practised in any group of Hebrews/Jews anywhere.

"SACRIFICIAL PAIL." When the "SACRIFICIAL BLOOD" is completely drained from the veins of the ANIMAL the ENTRAILS are taken out and placed with the other waste matter. All of the waste is turned into "BURNT ASH" far away from the "SACRIFICIAL ALTAR" at a place where there is running water. The BODY of the SACRIFICIAL ANIMAL is bisected into chunks after it is skinned, and the chunks placed into a brime of SALT and VINEGAR and MYRRHS while the "SOLEMN PRAYERS" for the preservation of "MEAT" are being said. The "SKIN" is turned over to the High Priest, who turns it over to a Subordinate Priest to be cured for the purpose of making "SACRED SCROLLS" and/or "SACRED TORAHS." The bisected BODY is turned over to the poor if the SACRIFICE was held in a non-Communal Community. It is turned over to the cooks [women] if the SACRIFICE is conducted in a Communal Community.

The "ALTAR OF THE SACRIFICE" is then "...thoroughly washed and cleaned of all blood-stains..." which may be remaining from the BLOOD of the Sacrificial Animal.[1] The High Priest must check the cleaning operation to see if there is "...any sign of blood..." which may have been overlooked by the cleaners. After the cleaning is checked the BURNT ASH is placed into a container and carried to the nearest "STREAM" or "RIVER," where all of it is then symbolically

"SCATTERED TO THE FOUR CORNERS OF THE EARTH."

To perform the "SCATTERING TO THE FOUR CORNERS OF THE EARTH" the "BURNT ASH" is thrown in the direction of the four points of the compass, namely: NORTH, SOUTH, EAST and WEST. It is thrown in a manner whereby some must enter the RIVER and/or STREAM that travels to the high seas, where it is believed to -

> "FLOW TO THE FOUR CORNERS OF THE WORLD, AND THEREBY COMPLETE THE SACRIFICE OF THE SACRIFICIAL ANIMAL ON THE SACRED ALTAR."

The "WORSHIPERS" prepare to leave the SACRIFICIAL ALTAR and sing a song of praise to the God of Israel - YWH; Thusly:

> "He has allowed us to wash away the sins of our enemies and those of our own. He has allowed us to follow the footsteps of our forefathers Abraham, Jacob, Isaac, Joseph, Moses [etc., etc., etc.]. He has allowed us to witness the symbolic sacrifice of the son of Abraham, which is represented in memory by our sacrifice; Halelujah, Halelujah, Halelujah; so shall the name of our God - YWH - be; so shall Israel."

The "SHOFAR" [one of the horns of the last ram from the sacrifice] is sounded for "TEN TIMES," and the "TEN COMMANDMENTS" are recited by all. The "SACRIFICIAL RECESSIONAL" then begins its return to the main building of the "SYNAGOGUE," because the "ANIMAL SACRFICE" is at this time completely finished so far as the SLAUGHTER and SPREADING of the Burnt Offering are concerned.[see page 308 for "Shofar" being blown by Rabbi W.B. Matthew].

1. Any blood whatsoever that is not of the slaughtered animal is not tolerated near the Altar of Sacrifice. This will cause the Sacrifice to be voided.

"THREE [3] WORSHIPERS" are left at the "SACRIFICIAL MOUNT" to make certain that:

"NOTHING UNCLEAN TOUCHES THE SACRIFICIAL ALTER
BEFORE SUN-FALL ON THE DAY OF THE SACRIFICE."

They must keep away all persons, and equally all animals, from coming near the "SACRIFICIAL ALTER" before Sun-Fall. The Falashas assigned this task are generally DÄBTÄRÄ and/or DEACONS; but "NEVER A FEMALE." If there is no QUORUM [10 men] it must be cancelled.

At "SUN-FALL" [sun down] the DÄBTÄRÄ and/or DEACONS return to the Synagogue for the last service of the day and notify the High Priest that:

"THE SACRIFICE IS KEPT HOLY; NOTHING INTRUDED ON THE SACRED ALTAR."

This completes the last "OFFICIAL ACT OF THE SACRIFICE" according to Falasha traditions.

The "SUN-FALL SERVICE OF THE SACRIFICE" mainly consists of "PRAYERS OF SACRIFICE AND FORGIVENESS" led by Subordinate Priests designated this task, and repeated by all of the Subordinate Priests and the General [male] Congregation in unison. The "SACRIFICIAL SERVICE" ends with the usual "BLESSING, EMBRACING, SHAKING OF HANDS and other "HOLY DAY GREETINGS"-SHABBATH SHALOM, etc.-PEACEFUL SABBATH or SABBATH OF PEACE. All of this soothes the Falashas to return to their normal living once more.

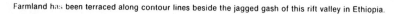

Farmland has been terraced along contour lines beside the jagged gash of this rift valley in Ethiopia.

RETRIBUTION FOR TORAH and COMMANDMENTS WRONGS: Chapter IV, Part Five.

"EXPULSION" [total banishment] from the Falasha Communities is the most serious of all of the punishments a Falasha can suffer. This is so because most of the Falashas will prefer "DEATH" than having to be chased out of their Community, and to hear that he/she is bannished -

" FOR THE REST OF YOUR LIVING DAYS GOD GAVE YOU."

They look with horror at the thought of having to leave their community and other brother and sister Falashas in total shame. Some of the cardinal "WRONGS" or "SINS" to cause any Falasha to be "EXPELLED" are as follows:

[1] Involvement in "PREMARITAL SEXUAL INTERCOURSE" is one of the most serious wrongs that an unmarried woman can commit.[1] Upon proof of this fact the woman will be brought up on charges for "immediate expulsion." She is banished from the community upon being proven guilty. The man responsible for her shame is equally expelled with her.

[2]"ADULTRY" by either spouse of a marriage is not forgivable. Upon being found guilty of this wrong immediate expulsion is certain. Adultry will be charged against a woman if her husband finds that she was not a physical virgin on the day of her first marriage. If so, an annulment is immediately granted him. The responsible man and the young woman are expelled from the community.

[3] "RAPE" is also punishable immediately by expulsion; but there are certain conditions in this wrong for which expulsion is not carried out. One of these conditions is due to the "innocent party" [victim] who would gain nothing by the expulsion of the guilty man from the community. This, of course, is if the rape was not committed maliciously, but with consent of a minor, or upon some extraordinary technicality. The latter condition is similar to "statutory rape" in the United States of America. Rape committed upon a virgin woman regardless of her age is dealt with in the above manner. If the rapist is an unmarried man he will be forced to marry the offended woman. If he is a married man and his wife refuses to have a polygamous life he will be charged with adultry and expelled from the community. If his wife refuses to take action against him, she too will be charged with adultry and expelled. Let it also be noted that within the past two [2] generations there has not been a single case of rape in the Falasha communities.

[4] "MURDER, STEALING" and "USING OF A WOMAN IN BLOOD" [menstruating] are also treated in the same natural course of trial, finding of guilt or innocence expulsion or denial of the charge, etc., etc., etc., ad infinitum.

In all cases of "IMMEDIATE EXPULSION" from any of the communities the parties so excluded are forced to leave only with the suit of clothing they are wearing at the time when they were found guilty of the wrong. At times expelled individuals would not be able to have their children of adult age join them in their exile; for any adult Falasha brought up religiously in the Falasha Communities will prefer to live with strangers than follow parents into exile be-

1. This is both biblical and cultural for Ethiopians of all religions. See "Adam and Eve" story.

cause of genealogical reason. The property of excluded persons is turned over for burning; as in any event it is condemned as the persons to whom it belonged; and no one would want to use of it in its state of disgrace. This is another area "JEWISH MISSIONARIES"[1] are trying to change.

The communities that operate on a non-communal economic basis treat the property of the excluded persons in the following manner: The poor members of neighbouring Gentile communities will be given all personal belongings; but real estate will be confiscated and turn over to the Elders for joint distribution among all. If there are children under adult age the money paid for the property will be divided between them. If there are no children the money from the real estate is distributed amongst the poor of the non-Communal Communities.

We continue looking at the causes or wrongs for expulsion in the Communal Communities:

> [5] For "VIOLATION OF LAWS AFFECTING THE SACRED TORAH" that are not enumerated in the Ten Commandments the punishments are much more liberal than those specified above. This is so, due to the fact that the violations is of customs rather than laws; for violations of the Ten Commandments are equally considered violations directly against God - YWH.
>
> [6] If a Falasha should be discovered "RIDING ON THE SABBATH" and the reason for so doing is unsatisfactory to the Council of the Priesthood, the offender will loose some of his rights in the communal system. That person may also be required to do more work than his usual six hours per day for as much as One Lunar Year or Ten Full Moons.
>
> [7] Any person "ACCEPTING UNCLEAN FOOD" [food not grown or prepared by Falashas] from anyone will be sent out of the communities for a period of seven days to cleanse himself of the wrong he or she committed. He would have to wash himself at a place where there is running water at least three times per day. He would have to go to the Synagogue and pray for one hour each morning for the seven days, and ask God: "...forgive me for using unclean food in my body...," etc., etc., etc. "...which you have loaned me...." After the seventh day of cleaning the person is allowed to return to his or her family [see plan of village on page 103 for review of the locations of the House of Uncleanliness, etc.]
>
> [8] "MARRIAGE TO A GENTILE" without the benefit of his or her conversion to the Hebrew Faith first is subject to immediate expulsion. I place this point here, for there is a possibility of acceptance if he or she can show that the Gentile was previously a Falasha. In this case they would be permitted to live outside the community walls for seven days. They, or he and she, will have to "...wash in the river [running water] for purification, and pray every morning...." The Falasha who never deserted prays in the Synagogue for "forgiveness for stealing the love of a Gentile." The "Gentile" [reconverting Falasha] will have to pray on the outside of the Synagogue even if a man "...for mercy and forgiveness for ever converting to another religion...." Any "reconverted Falasha male" is permitted to return to the community after the seventh day. But the converted FALASHA woman must pass her first oncoming MENSTRUAL PERIOD in the House of the Woman in Blood. She will have to await such time

1. Hadassah, as other Middle-Class Jewish organizations, has been trying to Europeanize/White-typed Falashas to Talmudic/Rabbinical Judaism from Torahdic Judaism: White-Jew-Washing.

as she is ready for this biological function; as she is considered "unclean" in this respect, returning from a community where the customs of this method of cleanliness is not observed. If it be a Falasha man, he may enter after the third moon. In the case of a woman, she has to pass through the House of Blood in order to remember that it is her "...duty to return to the House of the Woman in Blood three days before her menstrual period each month." While she is there the other women of the community, who are also passing their "blood," must explain to her the necessary functions which she has to perform while in such condition. They will advise her as to the type of prayers she will have to say; the things she will have to do upon her reentry in the general community, and in the home of her husband. She is told: "You cannot touch your husband's food upon your return from the House of Blood until he has given you permission to so do...," etc., etc., etc. The last step is the "Ritual Bath Of Purification" [migvah or Mitvah]. When she has completed this task she will be reunited with her husband, the other men, and women of the community. They will welcome her return to Judaism. She will not be made to suffer any humiliation or lasting stigma. It must be noted that she could not return if she had"...given birth to a child of a Gentile father...," or "...given her virginity to a Gentile man...."

[9] For "MISSING RELIGIOUS SERVICE," any man so guilty will be forced to "...attend all services for a period of time not less than than three Lunar Months duration...."

"GENTILE"[as used in the above sense] includes a FALASHA that "CONVERTED" to any religion and is returning to his or her own original "Hebrew [Jewish] Religion Of Birth." If it is not under this condition, then the above procedure is more rigidly constructed; and it is almost impossible for admittance of Gentiles who were never Falashas. Such a condition is dealt with in other sections of this work. Is it not strange that all of the "BLACK JEWS" shown in this Volume, excluding those from North and East Alkebu-lan and Asia have been placed into the same category of "CONVERTED GENTILES" by the vast majority of European-American [WHITE] Jews in the United States of America along with the vast majority of European [WHITE] Jews that presently dominate the government of Israel today?[1] The pictures of American Black Jews in EBONY MAGAZINE of more than a generation ago show many similarities with "Western Talmudic Judaism" more so than any other group of "BLACK JEWS" in the world; yet all of the others are rated on a higher plain of acceptance than the so-called "NEGRO AMERICAN JEWS " who prefer to be called by the proper name or title - ETHIOPIAN HEBREWS and/or ETHIOPIAN ISRAELITES, etc. Who is it that said:

"A SINGLE PICTURE IS WORTH A THOUSAND WORDS?"

1. The majority population of Israel/Palestine today is from Asia and Africa; most of them are of BLACK and BROWN skin. Yet European [WHITE] Jews dominate the Government of Israel.

SEMITIC CHARACTERISTICS: DON'T THESE JEWS HAVE IT TOO?

Rabbi Wentworth Matthew Blessing Table In Harlem's Synagogue Kitchen While Members Of The Congregation Listen In Silence.

Compare these two pictures with those on pages 177 - 178 with regards to the myth of a "Semitic Race." What makes the above Jews or Hebrews [Israelites] "Negroes" and others "Semites"? Is it not the same type of "White Racism" which discriminates against "White Jews, Christians," et al, and other non-White Anglo-Saxon Protestant Christians by the Ku Klux Klan of the United States of America?

THESE AT THE TOP ARE "KOSHER;" THE BOTTOM "UNKOSHER"

A NORTH AFRICAN JEW REGISTERING HIS WIFE AND CHILDREN IN PALESTINE/ISRAEL

THEY ARE ALL "BLACK JEWS" OF JUDAISM!

Above center:
Cochin Jew from
India, South Asia

Right and Left:
African-America[n]
Jews from Harle[m]
New York, N.Y.

AFRICAN-AMERICAN JEWS IN HARLEM, NEW YORK CITY, NEW YORK

HIGH HOLY DAYS CUSTOMS: Chapter IV, Part Six.

The chronological listing of the following DAYS and/or PERIODS is based upon their historical happenings; not according to their calendar appearances as most believers remember them; thus:

The "FEAST OF THE PASSOVER" or "PESACH" is held "...in memory of the flight of the Israelites out of Egypt [Northeast Africa] with [the African named] Moses to the Promised Land[1] in Western Asia ..." sometime around ca. 1236 B.C.E. to 1196 B.C.E., this being one of the highest of the Falashas and all other Jews "HOLY DAYS." It is symbolized by the "...eating of the unleavened bread..." made from "...a mixture of peas and wheat..." and "...baked in the sun while it rests upon stones in the wide open air...." No "YEAST" and/or "SALT" is permitted to be mixed in this bread. And it is only "...eaten after the Sun-Fall when the last service of the Feast of the Passover..." is completed. Note that Falashas can not eat anything before the last service of a High Holy Day or Fast Day, which is at Sun-Fall. At the time when the "Unleavened Bread" is to be eaten on the "Feast of the Passover" there is the recital of the story of the Israelites [Hebrews or Jews] flight out of Egypt by one of the students preparing to be confirmed - "BARMITZVAH" - as a man in the Hebrew Religion. There are many small gatherings throughout the communities where this story is being told. The Feast of the Passover comes on the "15th day of the First Moon." An "Animal Sacrifice" must be performed on this day.

The "DAY OF ATONEMENT" or "YUM KIPPUR" is the day when Falashas everywhere pray...

> "for the souls of the departed ones that they may be comfortable in the Hereafter; for the forgiveness of the sins of those who registered in the 'Book Of The Hereafter' to pass away in the present year; for the afflicted and those to become afflicted; for the sick and those to become ill; for the nations of the world that they have God's guidance in reaching decisions; and that they would cease making wars and live in peace and harmony; for the freedom of all colonial peoples, and for the salvation of the souls of the colonizers, for the cleansing of the souls of those who live in our communities, all other communities in Ethiopia, and of the entire world...," etc.

This is the highest of all High Holy Days of the Hebrew Religion. The Day Of Atonement comes on the "10th day of the Seventh Moon."

"RASH HASHANAH"[2] or "NEW YEAR" is symbolized by the "...calling of the people [Israel] of the communities..." up to the highest "MOUNT" to hear and "WITNESS" their obligations; the

"READING OF THE LAWS YWH GAVE TO MOSES ON MOUNT SINAI."

This is the only day of the year in which "WOMEN" and "GIRLS" [females] are permitted to at-

1. This was in fact the "land" upon which the Caanites [so-called "cursed negroes"] originated, etc.
2. There is no "O" in the Hebrew language written during the time of Prophet Isaiah, this being the only type known to the Falashas from ancient times; plus Aramaic by a few. The type of Hebrew language - "Sphardic" - used in Israel was developed by Moorish Jews in Sphard/Spain, Europe. It was during this period the currently used "Talmud" was developed, etc.

tend any "SERVICE ON THE MOUNT;" but they must leave before the "ANIMAL SACRIFICE" begins. "WOMEN" and "GIRLS" are permitted to attend this SERVICE because they too must always

"HEAR AND WITNESS THE LAWS," WHICH WILL GOVERN THEM.

Falashas believe that:

> WOMEN MUST KNOW WHY THEY HAVE TO ABIDE BY THE LAWS AND REGULATIONS THEIR COMMUNITY PLACES UPON THEM, AND UPON THE MEN EQUALLY. THIS WAY THEY CAN'T CLAIM NOT TO KNOW.

This day Falashas have FEASTING AND REJOICING, and equally PRAYERS FOR THE AGED, ILL, AFFLICTED, INSANE, etc. If there is any "LEPER" amongst them, he or she will be sent away after the "FEAST OF THE NEW YEAR." It must be borne in mind that the "LEPER" is given all assistance possible before leaving the community. He [or she] is given enough to keep him in supply, at least, for "ONE LUNAR MONTH." From this point onwards he must provide for himself in the best manner possible. The "LEPER" generally finds no acceptance in other Ethiopian communities. If he does not wish to give up his religious customs, he can live in a large "LEPER COLONY" located quite a distance away where he may continue his own religious life;[1] of course with some difficulty, as the "COLONY" is owned and operated by "Christian Missionaries." One must realize that the subject of the "EXCLUSION OF LEPERS" creates quite a great deal of differences of opinion, as many Falashas believe that the biblical provisions on the treatment of the "LEPERS" are too severe. However, there is very little any layman can do about changing this "BIBLICAL PROHIBITION" at present in a "THEOCRATIC SOCIETY" such as the Falashas have in Ethiopia, and have had for thousands of years since the period their fellow African Moses passed down the teachings of the LAWS and COMMANDMENTS in the Five Books [Of Moses [Pentateuch], Christian Old Testament, and part of the Holy Qur'an]. This does not exclude Falashas living outside of the Communities in Ethiopia; those of us who try to change the traditions of our people to meet the "MORAL VALUES" of European and European-American Talmudic Jews with their European oriented Anglo-Saxon White Protestant Christian Greek-centric socio-political "ETHICS." One has to remember that most of the Falashas are literalist where their "SACRED TORAH" is concerned; thus their "HIGH PRIEST" and "CHIEF MONK" will have the last words on the issue of the "TREATMENT OF LEPERS" in their communities according to their understanding of the SACRED TORAH and their TRADITIONS, CUSTOMS and TABOOS; the same as all other people in control of the leadership of all governments everywhere in the world today, as in the past.

Other "HIGH HOLY DAYS" are celebrated in somewhat similar activities to the customs practiced by European and European-American JEWS in Europe, the Americas and elsewhere. On

1. This historical fact is affected by the Revolutionary Government that took power in 1974 C.E.

these I will elaborate, as they will only prove to be very important; and because you can witness them in your own communities here in the United States of America. You can examine the list of "FEAST" and "HIGH HOLY" days of the Falashas in the following Chronological Chart:

LUNAR [Weekly, Monthly and Annual] FESTIVALS AND FAST DAYS, ETC.[1]

Day	Description	Agu, Gheeze, Amheric
1st Day.........	Festival of the New Moon................	Yäcäräqä bät
10th Day........	Festival of the Tenth....................	Asärt
29th Day........	Festival of theTwelfth..................	Asrä Hulät
	MONTHLY	
	Festival Arfe Asart	
	ANNUALLY	
	1st Moon.................	Somä Fasikä
14th Day........	Fast of the Passover	
15th - 21st Day..	Feast of the Passover...................	Fäsikä
	3rd Moon.................	Somä Tomäs
12th Day........	Feast of the Harvest....................	Mä', rär
	4th Moon.................	Somä äb
1st - 10th Day...	Fast of Tomas	
	5th Moon.................	Soma abt
1st - 17th Day...	Fast of Ab	
3rd Sabbath.....	Sabbath of Sabbaths......................	Yäsämbät sämbät
	6th Moon.................	Asärtu wäsämätu
6th Day.........	Feast of our Day of Atonement	
18th Day........	Festival of the 18th.....................	Asärtu wäsärmäntu
	7th Moon.................	Astäyo
1st Day.........	Festival of the Commemoration of Abraham...........................	Aberhäm Särräga
10th Day........	Day of Atonement	
15th - 22nd Day..	Feast of Tabernacles	
	8th Moon.................	Bä älä mäsällät
29th Day	Feast of the Suplication.................	Methellä

You will notice that the "MISSIONARY-TYPE" influence of European and European-American "JEWS" like Dr. Jacques Faitlovitch on the FALASHAS caused the celebration of a few High Holy Days and Feast Days that were not part of our experiences and development, the same being equally true for those days that were influenced by our stay in Ethiopia amongst the Coptic Christians. The same as European and European-American "Jews" who were influenced by "Christians," etc.

1. Before the experiences of other Jews with regards to the commemoration of the "Feast of Chanuka" and "Purim," the Falashas had already become separated from the greater body who later went North into Europe; thus no celebration of these Holy Days. The custom of "Animal Sacrifice" on Rosh Hashanah, Yum Kippur and Pesach tells how ancient the Falashas are by comparison to their European and European-American brother and sister counterparts. The "Sacrifice" dates back to the original Haribu/Jew - "Abraham" - and his son in the Genesis story, etc.

HEBREW [Jewish] and GREGORIAN CALENDAR 5371-72, ca. 1971-72 C.E.

ELUL 5731 -TISHRI 5732 — **SEPTEMBER 1971** — אלול תשל״א־תשרי תשל״ב

SUN.	MON.	TUE.	WED.	THU.	FRI.	SAT.
			1	2	3	4

TISHRI-ḤESHVAN 5732 — **OCTOBER 1971** — תשרי־חשון תשל״ב

SUN.	MON.	TUE.	WED.	THU.	FRI.	SAT.
					1	2

HESHVAN-KISLEV 5732 — **NOVEMBER 1971** — חשון־כסלו תשל ״ב

SUN.	MON.	TUE.	WED.	THU.	FRI.	SAT.
		2	3	4	5	6

KISLEV-TEVET 5732 — **DECEMBER 1971** — כסלו־טבת תשל״ב

SUN.	MON.	TUE.	WED.	THU.	FRI.	SAT.
			1	2	3	4

TEVET-SHEVAT 5732 — **JANUARY 1972** — טבת־שבט תשל״ב

SUN.	MON.	TUE.	WED.	THU.	FRI.	SAT.
						1

SHEVAT-ADAR 5732 — **FEBRUARY 1972** — שבט־אדר תשל״ב

SUN.	MON.	TUE.	WED.	THU.	FRI.	SAT.
			2	3	4	5

ADAR-NISAN 5732 — **MARCH 1972** — אדר־ניסן תשל״ב

SUN.	MON.	TUE.	WED.	THU.	FRI.	SAT.
			1	2	3	4

NISAN-IYAR 5732 — **APRIL 1972** — ניסן־אייר תשל״ב

SUN.	MON.	TUE.	WED.	THU.	FRI.	SAT.
						1

5732 — 5733
ABRIDGED HEBREW CALENDAR

5732	*1971*
Rosh Hashanah	Mon.-Tues., Sept. 20-21
Fast of Gedaliah	Wed., Sept. 22
Yom Kippur	Wed., Sept. 29
Sukkot	Mon.-Tues., Oct. 4-5
Hoshana Rabbah	Sun., Oct. 10
Shemini Atzeret	Mon., Oct. 11
Simḥat Torah	Tues., Oct. 12
•Rosh Ḥodesh Ḥeshvan	Wed., Oct. 20
•Rosh Ḥodesh Kislev	Fri., Nov. 19
Ḥanukkah	Mon., Dec. 13-Mon., Dec. 20
•Rosh Ḥodesh Tevet	Sun., Dec. 19
Asarah BeTevet	Tues., Dec. 28
	1972
Rosh Ḥodesh Shevat	Mon., Jan. 17
NWL ANNIVERSARY SABBATH	Fri., Jan. 21
Tu (15) BiShevat	Mon., Jan. 31
•Rosh Ḥodesh Adar	Wed., Feb. 16
Ta'anit Esther	Mon., Feb. 28
Purim	Tues., Feb. 29
Rosh Ḥodesh Nisan	Thurs., Mar. 16
Pesaḥ—1st days	Thurs.-Fri., Mar. 30-31
Pesaḥ—last days	Wed.-Thurs., Apr. 5-6
Yom HaSho'ah	Tues., Apr. 11
•Rosh Ḥodesh Iyar	Sat., Apr. 15
Yom Ha'atzma'ut	Wed., Apr. 19
Lag Ba'omer	Tues., May 2
Rosh Ḥodesh Sivan	Sun., May 14
Shavu'ot	Fri.-Sat., May 19-20
•Rosh Ḥodesh Tammuz	Tues., June 13
Shivah Asar BeTammuz	Thurs., June 29
Rosh Ḥodesh Av	Wed., July 12
Tishah Be'av	Thurs., July 20
•Rosh Ḥodesh Elul	Fri., Aug. 11
5733	
Rosh Hashanah	Sat.-Sun., Sept. 9-10
Yom Kippur	Mon., Sept. 18

• *Previous day is also observed as Rosh Hodesh.*

IYAR-SIVAN 5732 — **MAY 1972** — אייר־סיון תשל״ב

SUN.	MON.	TUE.	WED.	THU.	FRI.	SAT.
	1	2	3	4	5	6

SIVAN-TAMMUZ 5732 — **JUNE 1972** — סיון־תמוז תשל״ב

SUN.	MON.	TUE.	WED.	THU.	FRI.	SAT.
				1	2	3

TAMMUZ-AV 5732 — **JULY 1972** — תמוז־אב תשל״ב

SUN.	MON.	TUE.	WED.	THU.	FRI.	SAT.
						1

AV-ELUL 5732 — **AUGUST 1972** — אב־אלול תשל״ב

SUN.	MON.	TUE.	WED.	THU.	FRI.	SAT.
		1	2	3	4	5

ELUL 5732-TISHRI 5733 — **SEPTEMBER 1972** — אלול תשל״ב־תשרי תשל״ג

SUN.	MON.	TUE.	WED.	THU.	FRI.	SAT.
					1	2

1971

JANUARY

S	M	T	W	T	F	S
					1	2
3	4	5	6	7	8	9
10	11	12	13	14	15	16
17	18	19	20	21	22	23
24	25	26	27	28	29	30
31						

FEBRUARY

S	M	T	W	T	F	S
	1	2	3	4	5	6
7	8	9	10	11	12	13
14	15	16	17	18	19	20
21	22	23	24	25	26	27
28						

MARCH

S	M	T	W	T	F	S
	1	2	3	4	5	6
7	8	9	10	11	12	13
14	15	16	17	18	19	20
21	22	23	24	25	26	27
28	29	30	31			

APRIL

S	M	T	W	T	F	S
				1	2	3
4	5	6	7	8	9	10
11	12	13	14	15	16	17
18	19	20	21	22	23	24
25	26	27	28	29	30	

MAY

S	M	T	W	T	F	S
						1
2	3	4	5	6	7	8
9	10	11	12	13	14	15
16	17	18	19	20	21	22
23	24	25	26	27	28	29
30	31					

JUNE

S	M	T	W	T	F	S
		1	2	3	4	5
6	7	8	9	10	11	12
13	14	15	16	17	18	19
20	21	22	23	24	25	26
27	28	29	30			

JULY

S	M	T	W	T	F	S
				1	2	3
4	5	6	7	8	9	10
11	12	13	14	15	16	17
18	19	20	21	22	23	24
25	26	27	28	29	30	31

AUGUST

S	M	T	W	T	F	S
1	2	3	4	5	6	7
8	9	10	11	12	13	14
15	16	17	18	19	20	21
22	23	24	25	26	27	28
29	30	31				

SEPTEMBER

S	M	T	W	T	F	S
			1	2	3	4
5	6	7	8	9	10	11
12	13	14	15	16	17	18
19	20	21	22	23	24	25
26	27	28	29	30		

OCTOBER

S	M	T	W	T	F	S
					1	2
3	4	5	6	7	8	9
10	11	12	13	14	15	16
17	18	19	20	21	22	23
24	25	26	27	28	29	30
31						

NOVEMBER

S	M	T	W	T	F	S
	1	2	3	4	5	6
7	8	9	10	11	12	13
14	15	16	17	18	19	20
21	22	23	24	25	26	27
28	29	30				

DECEMBER

S	M	T	W	T	F	S
			1	2	3	4
5	6	7	8	9	10	11
12	13	14	15	16	17	18
19	20	21	22	23	24	25
26	27	28	29	30	31	

1972

JANUARY

S	M	T	W	T	F	S
						1
2	3	4	5	6	7	8
9	10	11	12	13	14	15
16	17	18	19	20	21	22
23	24	25	26	27	28	29
30	31					

FEBRUARY

S	M	T	W	T	F	S
		1	2	3	4	5
6	7	8	9	10	11	12
13	14	15	16	17	18	19
20	21	22	23	24	25	26
27	28	29				

MARCH

S	M	T	W	T	F	S
			1	2	3	4
5	6	7	8	9	10	11
12	13	14	15	16	17	18
19	20	21	22	23	24	25
26	27	28	29	30	31	

APRIL

S	M	T	W	T	F	S
						1
2	3	4	5	6	7	8
9	10	11	12	13	14	15
16	17	18	19	20	21	22
23	24	25	26	27	28	29
30						

MAY

S	M	T	W	T	F	S
	1	2	3	4	5	6
7	8	9	10	11	12	13
14	15	16	17	18	19	20
21	22	23	24	25	26	27
28	29	30	31			

JUNE

S	M	T	W	T	F	S
				1	2	3
4	5	6	7	8	9	10
11	12	13	14	15	16	17
18	19	20	21	22	23	24
25	26	27	28	29	30	

JULY

S	M	T	W	T	F	S
						1
2	3	4	5	6	7	8
9	10	11	12	13	14	15
16	17	18	19	20	21	22
23	24	25	26	27	28	29
30	31					

AUGUST

S	M	T	W	T	F	S
		1	2	3	4	5
6	7	8	9	10	11	12
13	14	15	16	17	18	19
20	21	22	23	24	25	26
27	28	29	30	31		

SEPTEMBER

S	M	T	W	T	F	S
					1	2
3	4	5	6	7	8	9
10	11	12	13	14	15	16
17	18	19	20	21	22	23
24	25	26	27	28	29	30

OCTOBER

S	M	T	W	T	F	S
1	2	3	4	5	6	7
8	9	10	11	12	13	14
15	16	17	18	19	20	21
22	23	24	25	26	27	28
29	30	31				

NOVEMBER

S	M	T	W	T	F	S
			1	2	3	4
5	6	7	8	9	10	11
12	13	14	15	16	17	18
19	20	21	22	23	24	25
26	27	28	29	30		

DECEMBER

S	M	T	W	T	F	S
					1	2
3	4	5	6	7	8	9
10	11	12	13	14	15	16
17	18	19	20	21	22	23
24	25	26	27	28	29	30
31						

National Women's League of America, New York. N.Y., 1972

Akhet, season of inundation.	*Peret*, springtime, appearance of crops.	*Shemu*, summer.
1. Thoth. or *tepy* January I	5. Tybi. May I	9. Pachons. September I
2. Paophi. February II	6. Mechir. June II	10. Payni. October II
3. Hathor. March III	7. Phamenoth. July III	11. Epiphi. November III
4. Choiak. April IIII	8. Pharmouthi. August IIII	12. Mesore. December IIII

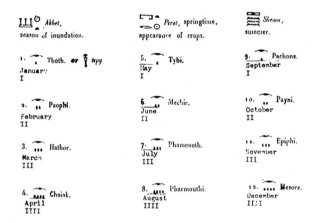

Divisions of the 4100 B.C.E. Egyptian, Meröwan and Nubian Nile Valley Nile Year and Solar Calendar compared to the Justinian and Gregorian Calendar along with the Hieroglyphic symbols..., etc.

ETHIOPIAN CALENDAR

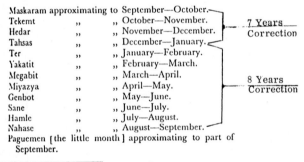

Maskaram	approximating to	September—October.	7 Years Correction
Tekemt	,, ,,	October—November.	
Hedar	,, ,,	November—December.	
Tahsas	,, ,,	December—January.	
Ter	,, ,,	January—February.	8 Years Correction
Yakatit	,, ,,	February—March.	
Megabit	,, ,,	March—April.	
Miyazya	,, ,,	April—May.	
Genbot	,, ,,	May—June.	
Sane	,, ,,	June—July.	
Hamle	,, ,,	July—August.	
Nahase	,, ,,	August—September.	

Paguemen [the little month] approximating to part of September.

1. September 11th - This is the equivalent of the 1st of Maskaram[or the Ethiopian "NEW YEAR"]. Since Ethiopia did not change her Calendar to suit the European Gregorian Calendar of the Nicean Council of ca. 325 C.E. [A.D.], you must subtract SEVEN YEARS between September and December, or EIGHT YEARS between January and August, in order to synchronize both. I have shown the Months of each comparatively. Note that the Ethiopian, Nubian and Egyptian are the same.
2. The FIRST DAY OF THE WEEK is Wednesday; thus the week is as follows: 1st Day - Rob or Wednesday; 2nd - Hamus or Thursday; 3rd - Arb or Friday; 4th - Kadamyit or Saturday; 5th - Ehud or Sunday; 6th - Sanyo or Monday; 7th - Makasanyo or Tuesday. All of the religions of the world based their Calendar partly on Solar and Lunar calculations; thus the Hebrew Passover and the Ethiopian Christian Easter are within the FIRST FULL MOON OF THE VERNAL EQUINOX; a fact known to very few.

Edward Ullendorf, one of the so-called "authority on the Falashas of Ethiopia," on page 111ff of his book - THE ETHIOPIANS, AN INTRODUCTION TO COUNTRY AND PEOPLE, Oxford University Press, London, 1960made this point very clear when he wrote the following:

> The present writer feels convinced that all the evidence available points to the conclusion that the Falashas are descendants of those elements in the Aksumite Kingdom who resisted conversion to Christianity. In that case their so-called Judaism is merely the reflection of those Hebraic and Judaic practices and beliefs which were implanted on parts of southwest Arabia in the first post-Christian centuries and subsequently brought into Abyssinia. If this opinion is correct, then the religious pattern of the Falashas—even though it will have undergone some change in the past 1,600 years—may well mirror to a considerable extent the religious syncretism of the pre-Christian Aksumite Kingdom. It is in their living testimony to the Judaized civilization of the south Arabian immigrants and their well-nigh complete cultural ascendancy over the Cushitic and other strata of the original African population of Ethiopia that we must seek the value and great interest of the Falashas today—and not in their rehabilitation as a long lost tribe of Israel (which is historically quite unwarranted). Like their Christian fellow-Ethiopians, the Falashas are stubborn adherents to fossilized Hebraic-Jewish beliefs, practices, and customs which were transplanted from South Arabia into the horn of Africa and which may here be studied in the authentic surroundings and atmosphere of a Semitized country.

But the Falashas estrangement from the body of what is today called "European and European-American [WHITE or SEMITIC] Jews" took place generations before the "...destruction of the last Temple in Jerusalem..." by the Romans in approximately ca. 47 - 30 B.C.E., which was at least[plus or minus] two thousand twenty-one [2021] years ago [ca. 47 B.C.E. ± 1974 C.E. = 2,021]. It must be remembered that most of the Falashas remained in Ethiopia when most of their fellow African Hebrews [Haribus, Israelites or Jews] left Ta-Merry [Sais, Qamt, Misrain or Egypt] during the "EXODUS" that began in ca. 1236 or 1234 B.C.E., at which time Pharaoh Rameses IInd reigned [ca. 1292 - 1232 B.C.E.] over Ta-Merry, a period known as the XIXth Dynasty [ca. 1340 - 1232 B.C.E.][1] Of course there are many European and European-American writers of varied disciplines who would prefer to have the origin of the Falashas dated later than this, which would be nearer to the reign of King Solomon of the Kingdom of Israel in the 10th Century B.C.E.[2] A review of the HISTORY and HERITAGE of the origin of the Agaw in Chapter II of this Volume should prove of great importance at this juncture.

---

1. For cross-referencing the periods related to the EXODUS, PASSOVER WITH MOSES, KING SOLOMON, etc. and the PHARAOHS of Egypt, Nubia, Ethiopia, Puanit, etc. see chronologies in Y. ben-Jochannan's BLACK MAN OF THE NILE AND HIS FAMILY, pages 171 through 202
2. This impact upon contemporary White Jewish theologians is suppressed, as they do not want anyone, even fellow White parishoners, realize "Judaism" is an outgrowth of African theosophy.

PRESENT RELIGIOUS TEACHINGS.
VIEWS ABOUT THE MESSIAH: Chapter V, Part One.

The BOOK OF ISAIAH in the Sacred Torah is the only basis for all of the views Falashas have on the subject of "A MESSIAH COMING TO SAVE ISRAEL," etc. This is the one and only true "BOOK" upon which the Falashas have accepted any theory about "...the coming [or appearance] of a Messiah..." in the future. This "REVELATION" by the Prophet Isaiah is accepted by all of the Falashas who still practise Torahdic and Talmudic Judaism the world over. And like all of the other practicing JEWS, the Falashas believe that:

> "The Messiah has never appeared on the face of this earth. He will never come to us in the manner he has so often been said to have already come into this world by the Christians."

We know that the evidence of world history today and in the past does not warrant the Falashas believing in any manner whatsoever that:

> 'The Messiah once appeared here on the planet Earth amongst the Israelites.'

Thus we refer to the "WRITINGS OF ISAIAH" with respect to the manner in which he said that the

> "Messiah will reveal himself upon coming into the world to His children Israel."

For Isaiah, in his own "BOOK," stated the following:

> "The Messiah will come and stop all of man's sins. There will be no more murder, lust of the flesh, war, stealing, coveting one's neighbour. There will be peace on earth among all mankind; and mankind shall live forever after without fear of death [paraphrased into current expressions].

Of course the Falashas are still asking; has any of these "PROPHECIES OF ISAIAH" ever come to pass? This question was never answered by any of the Christian Missionaries, local and/or foreign. Thus we remind them that it is in the Sacred Torah of the Hebrew Religion that the first mention of a " COMING OF THE MESSIAH" is written; and that the sources are the following:

Deuteronomy 18 : 15, 18 and 19; Malachai 3 : 1; Isaiah 41 : 2, 3 and 4;
Isaiah 9 : 6 and 7.

The answer is that:

THE PROPHECIES OF ISAIAH ARE STILL LEFT TO BE FULFILLED.

On the matter of the "...birth of the Messiah from the physical virgin womb of Mary..." [1] Falashas find ourselves asking questions which answers have not kept up with the facts as we see and know them to be. But we must repeat the following questions:

> "How can a woman give birth to a child and still remain physically a virgin?"
> "Why did she have labor pains like any other woman giving birth to a child?"
> "Why did this child not proclaimed himself to be GOD - YWH - until Rome

1. The origin of this story is found in the Egyptian teaching about the "Immaculate Conception," etc. story with respect to Isis.

saw fit to do so more than three hundred years after the child had grown into manhood, and then died?" Did Isaiah outline any of these teachings?

These and many other questions have been asked, and repeatedly the same meaningless responses are given by the so-called European and European-American "Christian Missionaries" who constantly try to prosetylize the Falashas. Their answers are hardly different to the local vintage of the African Orthodox [Coptic] Christian Missionaries. Their answers are always based upon belief. And since their answers are only based upon belief, the Falashas concluded long ago that:

IT IS NOT WORTHWHILE TO CHANGE ONE RELIGIOUS BELIEF FOR THAT OF ANOTHER, PARTICULARLY WHEN NEITHER HAS ANY HARD AND FAST PHYSICAL PROOF TO DISPLAY WHERE THE OTHER IS WRONG OR RIGHT.

With the above picture in mind, the Falashas reached the decision that:

"We must continue awaiting the first coming of the Messiah; and we must go along with the view that he is still coming; but, only as written in the Sacred Torah according to the teachings of the Prophet Isaiah."

All of this, if we are to believe in the "COMING OF THE MESSIAH" at all at this juncture, must refresh your memory that the author is not endorsing or denying any of the teachings and beliefs of his people - the AGAW/ FALASHAS/ BLACK JEWS, etc. - in Africa and/or the Americas.

On the position taken by most of the foreign so-called "CHRISTIAN MISSIONARIES" in Africa, and including even the local "AFRICAN CHRISTIAN MISSIONARIES," all over Ethiopia, that:

"THE JEWS KILLED JESUS CHRIST;"

we [Falashas and/or Black Jews] answered in the past, as we still do at present:

"We do not have any records which indicate that there was at anytime a fellow Jew in our midst by the name of Jesus, who was killed by any of our fore-parents because he claimed to be the Messiah. And we cannot find in any of our records that the people in Palestine were ever put to death in the manner prescribed by persons who accused our ancestors of this murder. We can not understand how Jews could have gained enough power to kill GOD - Messiah."

The Falashas found the above to be so full of lost links that we must flatly deny there ever existed such an incident. For if there was any "...KILLING OF GOD...," we are totally ignorant of it having taken place; as we have never known of "Our God ever being killed" by anyone.

Falashas cannot pass the blame to the Romans, who were colonizing Palestine at the time the Christians' "GOD - JOSHUA THE ANOINTED" or "JESUS THE CHRIST" - was supposed to have been "KILLED." How could we pass the blame when we cannot recall the incident? We cannot say it was not our ancestors who did the killing, but instead someone else; for we would have had to show when, and where, this lynching actually took place; and we would be at a lost to find such a case in our history - ORAL and/or WRITTEN - even hieroglyphically, etc.

In closing this chapter I can only state that "WE" [Falashas and Kylas] do accept the right of other people to hold to their own views on "...THE COMING OF THE MESSIAH..." and/or "...THE RETURN OF THE MESSIAH...."But these same people must also accept our right to reject all theories which state that "...THE MESSIAH CAME TO THE WORLD 1983 YEARS AGO, AND WAS BORN OF A VIRGIN MARY...," etc., etc., etc.[1] Since we are known to have rejected this theory, hopefully we shall not have to explain this matter any further to the "Christian Missionaries" already in, or coming to, Ethiopia for the expressly overt purpose of allegedly

"...CONVERTING THE HEATHEN FALASHAS TO CHRISTIANITY..."

a - la - European and European-American Roman Catholic and Protestant versions. This also applies to their Europeanized-African "CONVERTS," and equally for the local branch of the earliest Christian Order - the Ethiopian Orthodox [formerly Coptic] Christian Community.

The Moslem Missionaries of Ethiopia, and elsewhere, have placed the issue of "JESUS THE CHRIST" -[Messiah]- to us in a much different light. They say that:

> JESUS CHRIST WAS THE SECOND GREATEST PROPHET SENT BY AL'LAH; SECOND ONLY TO MOHAMET IBN ABDULLAH IN IMPORTANCE, BUT HIGHER THAN ABRAHAM AND MOSES."

They have also maintained that:

> THERE IS NO TRINITY OF JESUS CHRIST WITH AL'LAH, FOR JESUS CHRIST WAS NOT AL'LAH; BUT YOU MUST STILL ACCEPT HIM AS A PROPHET OF AL'LAH.

By accepting the Moslems position in preference to the Christians we would be confusing the facts; because Hebrews everywhere who practice Judaism have already rejected all religious propaganda from Roman Catholic and Protestant Christian sources which suggest that such a person called "JESUS CHRIST" ever lived among the Jews, and was killed by them. The same equally holds true for the Moslem's VERSION, in spite of the fact that HE was supposedly" ... of Hebrew parentage...," who were also "...of the line of David." But "Mary" was not of David!

We have already told our many friends who believe in JUSHUA THE ANOINTED [or Jesus the Christ"] as "GOD - JEHOVAH," and all that is said about "...HIS WORKS AND MIRACLES HE PERFORMED...," etc., etc., etc. according to the Christian HOLY SCRIPTURES [New Testament] and Moslem HOLY SCRIPTURES [Holy Qur'an], that:

> "We are willing to listen at all times to whatever you have to say about your God [Jesus Christ and/or Al'lah] and Religion; but you must be equally prepared to listen to what we have to say about our God [Ywh or Jehovah] and Religion - Judaism."

Needless to say, the issue always end in name calling at this point; and most often it even leads to violence when one does not agree to the opposite position of his or her belief in one of the major

1. In Hebrew/Jewish Culture and Heritage the child's lineage comes from the mother; never father.

three god-heads - YWH, JESUS CHRIST and/or AL'LAH. Not one African "GOD" that preceded them.

We have discovered that we cannot accomplish the above results requested; and that we must always be caught-up in conflicts with the "Christian" and "Moslem" missionaries in Alkebu-lan [Africa]. Sometimes these conflicts finish with physical combat, as in the years 1629, 1896, 1936 and 1957 C.E. when Falashas had to fight on the open battle field against Forced Conversion to Christianity and Islam. Might we add that "FORCED CONVERSION" is not totally a desire of the past Falashas had to fight. There are some diehards around today who are still deeply engaged in this type of activity. Some "Western Jews" are equally pressuring us to their Talmudism.

We, FALASHAS, say further that:

> "The Messiah, so far as we know through biblical records, wouldn't encourage wars; but we still see Christians and Moslems fighting wars of conversion upon us in the name of the Messiah Jesus Christ and Al'lah. And if wars are sanctioned by the Messiah, or Al'lah, we cannot accept either. The complete teachings about the Messiah in the Hebrew Sacred Torah are based upon peace and the abolition of immorality upon His arrival on the planet Earth. Not a single one of these truths, according to teachings of our Prophet Isaiah about the Messiah, has ever happened." [1]

It may be safely said that the above subject can occupy everyone of us from now until centuries yet to come without ever stopping to eat or sleep, and we still could not exhaust the beliefs, topics and/or materials to be added. So let your author conclude by saying:

> It is repulsive for anyone to expect Falashas to accept any religious belief which is contrary to our own. Since each religious belief is founded upon the same basis, which is by assumptions and related dogmas, also by personal experiences directly or indirectly, much of which many prefer to call "REVELATIONS FROM THE ONE AND ONLY TRUE GOD." Caution Please! [2]

Before we approach the following Chapter, let us not forget these remarks from a man who did not tell us the name of his GOD and/or RELIGION. He wrote this many hundred of years ago when "Jews/Hebrews," Moslems/Muslims, Christians, et al., were committing genocide on each in the name of "GOD" - Ywh/Jehovah, Jesus "the Christ," Al'lah, et al; thus:

> All Faith is false, all Faith is True
> Truth is the shattered mirrors strewn
> In myriad bits; while each believes
> his little bit the whole to own. [3]

---

1. Biblical Citations: The Coming Of The Messiah - Deuteronomy 18 : 15, 18, 19; Malachai 3 : 1; Isaiah 41 : 2, 3, 4; and Isaiah 9 : 6, 7 according to the Sacred [Holy] Torah [written by Jews].

2. The "Book Of Revelation" caused more suffering to Falashas because of Christian zealots.

3. From: THE KASIDAH of Haji Abu el-Yezdi, as translated into English by Sir Richard F. Burton. Christian, Moslem/Muslim and other prosetlizing missionaries should heed this very simple poem of historical significance. What drive is it that makes one man/woman feel that specially "chosen" above all other human beings that were made by the same God?; religious bigotry!, or racism?

GENERAL RELIGIOUS BELIEFS: Chapter V, Part Two.

Falashas believe in a place called "HELL," also in a place called "HEAVEN." "HELL," according to our Beta Israel "Learned Men/Sages, et al., is:

"A PLACE WHERE THE BODY IS BURRIED AFTER DEATH."

It is not the Christian Missionaries' "HELL" that is:

"A BOTTOMLESS PIT, FULL OF FIRE AND BRIMSTONE,"

we are threatened by if we do not fall for Christian Conversion propaganda. It is the place all of us are told of in the Resurrection Of The Dead in Hosea 13 : 13, 14; Ezra 37 : 11, 12; Job 14 : 5 - 14, 15; 19 : 26; Isaiah 35 : 10; and Ezekiel 37. Nevertheless, there is no doubt Ethiopian Christianity has influenced these two allegorical beliefs adopted by the Falashas; equally as European Christianity influenced the same thoughts - "GEHEDEN" and "GENEDEN" - amongst European and European-American Talmudic [Rabbinical] Jews, et al.

"HEAVEN" is The Place Of Everlasting Life - Genesis 5 : 24; 2 Kings 2 : 11; Hosea 13: 13, 14; Psalm 49 : 6, 9; 118 : 17; Proverbs 7 : 1, 3, 23; 6 : 23 - as per our Sacred Torah. But Falashas also described "HEAVEN" as:

A PLACE OF GLORY AND CONTENTMENT FOR THE CHILDREN OF ISRAEL
WHO LIVED AND DIED IN RIGHTEOUSNESS.

In this latter interpretation one can equally find commonality with the Christian VERSION of the Falashas' "HEAVEN." Why? Because Falashas were the first to be converted by force to the earliest Christian Church that came into Ethiopia over 1,802 years ago, and as such carried their own version into the Coptic [now Orthodox] Christian Church - which was called "The New Religion."

The paramount height of Falashas belief is in -

"THE ONE AND ONLY YWH [God] OF THE CHILDREN OF ISRAEL, THE MAKER OF HEAVEN AND EARTH: HE WHO MADE THE WORLD AND EVERYTHING IN IT DURING SIX DAYS, AND ON THE SEVENTH DAY - Sabbath - RESTED,"

as per the Creation Story - Genesis 1 : 1, 5; Ezekiel 14 : 6; Isaiah 28 : 11, 12; Ezekiel 36 : 26, 28; Ezekiel 14 : 26, 31; Jeremiah 31 : 31; Joel 2 : 28 - 39; and Malachai 1 : 2; etc., etc., etc.,

"AFTER ALL WAS WELL."

We can read more about this in detail in the SACRED WRITINGS AND TRADITIONS, Chapter V, Part Four, of the following texts.

"RESURRECTION OF THE DEAD" is another of the fundamental beliefs of the Falashas, the bibilical justification for same cited above being the basis; yet the following is also given as details relative to such belief. It is the period, according to the Most Holy and Most Sacred Torah,

" when all of the children of Israel will be called upon by Ywh to answer for all the sins all of us have committed in violation of the Ten Commandments and the Laws of the Comesh [Five Books Of Moshe]."

That during this period - DAY, WEEK, MONTH, YEAR - whatever:

"all shall go into Heaven; but only those who have lived clean religious life would be permitted the full freedom of Heaven; all sins shall be washed away; and all shall leave the place called Hell."

Here, in the above, we see that "HELL" is not a place where people are to be "BURNT" like roast meat according to the beliefs and teachings of most Christian Missionaries - even to the present day. This is the reason that Falashas cannot believe in an "...ANGRY GOD...." And we do not believe in a "GOD" who will enjoy seeing His people - ISRAEL, whom He also created, "...BURN FOREVER AND EVER WITHOUT END...." And we cannot, and do not, accept a "...HELL...." of the type described by the "Christian Missionaries" from Europe, Great Britain, European America, and even the local African vintage that began in Egypt and Nubia and transferred to Ethiopia under the name of the Coptic Christian Faith [Religion] more than one hundred and fifty [150] years before Rome became a Christian Nation in ca. 312 C.E. by virtue of a DECREE ordered by Emperor Constantine [then so called "Great"] to this effect.

The "DAY OF JUDGEMENT" or "RESURRECTION OF THE DEAD" could be said to mean the same thing in regards to Falashas belief, the biblical citations having been given before on page 152; yet so many are still preaching that it will be "...

the day [week, month, year, etc.] when Ywh shall appear on Earth, and all of mankind shall see Him, the wicked and the just alike. And He shall, on that day, call all of mankind to stand and represent themselves for the sins which they have committed. He shall set aside those who have been merciless; and those who showed mercy and worshiped Ywh will be sent directly to a place of Peace and Everlasting existence...."

The Kabbalistic "SAINTS" like Gavreel, Michareel and Owreel are still perpetuated by the Falashas; thus the "SANCTITY OF THE MONKS [Raddics]" who live to pass the ripe old age of THREE [3] SCORE AND TEN [70] and have devoted most of their entire lives to continuous praying and religious devotion..., and become that of "SAINTS." For, according to Falasha teachings, it is indeed a "VERY HUMBLE AND PIOUS PERSON" who becomes a "SAINT" in any of the communities comprised of the Agaw People. "SAINTS" are never made of MONKS after they have died. This is solely in the Christian custom. Instead, Falashas believe that:

"A SAINT MUST BE A LIVING MONK; AND HE MUST RECEIVE THIS HONOUR DURING HIS LIFETIME BY HIS OWN PEOPLE - ISRAEL" [as he lives, he so dies]

Unlike the Christians, it is not our belief that a "SAINT" goes to "HEAVEN" and "INTERCEDE" with God more so than anyone else. But Falashas do believe that:

"A SAINT WILL HAVE A POST IN HEAVEN ON THE DAY OF RESURRECTION ABOVE OTHER PEOPLE WHO HAVE NOT REACHED THIS LEVEL OF RELIGIOUS DEVELOPMENT AND INVOLVEMENT WITH YWH."

Falashas do not "PRAY TO SAINTS" when they are dead or alive; for we do not believe in "PRAYING" to the person of any human being for any reason whatsoever. Yet it is true that the "SAINTS" will be remembered in the Falasha Communities [communal or not] that they were religiously devoted human beings up to their death.

It is believed by Falashas that:

> THE OFFERING OF THE SACRIFICIAL LAMB OR OX CAUSES ALL OF THE PEOPLES OF THE WORD TO RECEIVE SOME FORGIVENESS GRANTED TO THEM BY GOD." [And that] "THE SACRIFICE WILL MEET THE APPROVAL OF ABRAHAM, ISAAC AND JACOB WHEN THEY APPEAR WITH MESSIAH ON THE DAY OF JUDGEMENT.

Falashas equally believe that:

> "All of the world's peoples will come under one rule in a land called Eden, where man shall see for the first time the manner in which he was created." [And that] "Man will be able to eat of the Forbidden Fruits in Eden, and shall not surely die." [Also, that] "Man will again return to a place where he shall not want for food; wear no clothing; have no sin; and never die."

> "There will be no New Born and the House Of Blood, and the House Of The Woman In Child-Bed will be forever destroyed. The Love man will have for women would be on a plain never before realized by man. None will feel the lust for each other which we now feel for the flesh."

> "God will on the Seventh Day After The Judgement show all of His children who have obeyed His laws, the manner in which the Heaven and the Earth was made. And He will allow them to visit the entire Universe before they will live in a place More Glorious Than Eden."

> "Animal Sacrifice on Yum Kippur will clean the communities from the uncleanliness of the Women In The House Of Blood and the House Of The Woman In Child-Bed."

> "Any person who committed Sexual Intercourse on Sabbath, or on the night before the Sabbath, and he [or she] attended the service, prayers shall never be received by Ywh. All who have committed this sin will have to live in a place where he will suffer from his lust for a period commensurate with his sin, and shall be without peace in the Hereafter for some time."

When a new Sacred Torah [Comesh, Pentateuch, Five Books Of Moses, etc.] is to be written it is believed that:

> GOD COMES INTO THE MIDST OF HIS INSPIRED RELIGIOUS SACRED SCRIBES AND LEAD THEM, AS IT IS NOT THE FREE WILL OF MAN TO THINK OF THE NEED FOR ANOTHER OF GOD'S SACRED WORKS.

> "Any person who has not taken a bath before attending the service will surely

cause the service to be rejected by God; and the prayers from such service would not be received by God. God will reject the prayers, for it is unclean; as all that is of God is good and clean."

"Water in a still place is not good for human use; for it is a reminder from God that He can stop the seas from rolling and the rivers from flowing. Thus it is that the Ash from the Sacrifice is thrown into the river or the stream to travel throughout the world and clean the sins of those who will not accept the religious Laws of the God of Israel."

"All persons,[1] whether Gentiles or Jews, will enter the House Of God; but those who have not followed His Holy Torah will have to make further qualifications to remain in Heaven, which is the House Of God, as they would not be able to maintain the Laws of Heaven."

"So far as Ywh is concerned there is but ONE RACE and that is the RACE OF ADAM AND EVE. From them male and female were made in all of their glorious colors and physical characteristics because of God's love for everything beautiful."

"Forced Conversion is one of the lowest of all sins; for God would not accept any person who was forced to recognize Him. God has not, in all of his greatest wisdom, issued any order to any man to force others to listen to the words of the Sacred Scriptures; as whenever God desires a person to come to His Sacred teachings in the Sacred Torah they will go freely and give themselves to His Faith, if they were not already members thereof. God will remove any person from our Faith if the Leaders of our faith are disobeying His words."

"The sufferings we [Falashas] had, and particularly the Mass Suicides the maidens made, were prearranged by God because we were not truthful and fair in many of our past deeds with Him; and thus it is that the sins of the Father will still fall upon his children for at least seven generations to follow him; but the sins of the mothers will not follow their children, instead will return to Hell with her sinful womb. There will be no sin left on a mother if she has born a child. A child cleans his [or her] mother of all her sins which she has ever committed, except adultry and other violations of any of the Ten Commandments."

"No child was ever BORN IN SIN; and every child is free from sin upon his [or her] arrival in this world; the type of sin attributed to adults. It is a sin that only God in His holiest wisdom understand. For a child is never guilty of sin until he [or she] reaches the age of reasoning, which is established in the Holy and Most Sacred Torah as twelve years of age. Confirmation [Bar-mitzvah] brings a child closer to Ywh that he can realize his responsibility for all of his own sins; and that he will not be able to pass his own responsibility for anything to others."

"A child should not be brought into this world solely for the labour of its parents. He [or she] shall be protected by his parents to the fullest until he has reached the biblical age of reasoning and maturity as a man - age twelve; for a child is like a fruit upon a tree which must be shed to make a new root for itself, or be consumed by something. But in the case of a child, whom we shall teach to

1. This is a point that Christian Religious Bigotry cannot fathom;" all persons will enter God's Grace," etc. The Judaeo-Christians believe they alone have the sole communication from "all of the World's peoples' God - Jesus."

HONOUR YOUR FATHER AND YOUR MOTHER THAT THE DAYS OF YWH CAN BE LONG UPON THIS EARTH, shall also realize that an adult human being is his best protection; next only to his One And Only God - YWH. Yet for sins committed as an adult, he too shall be consumed by Hell until the final preparation of the Hereafter on Judgement Day."

"The Chief [or High]Priest is the most sacred representative of YWH; but as such has no authority to pass any Law or Commandment which is not already listed in the Sacred Torah. Any High Priest, and all of the Subordinate Priests, the Chief Monk, and all of the Subordinate Monks, that disobey the Sacred Torah will equally remain in Hell for a period commensurate with his sin, or longer than others; for he, and they, knows more about the punishments he would receive for his violation of the Sacred Torah and the Ten Commandments of Ywh - the God Of Israel. Blessed be the God of the people - Israel. Blessed be EXODUS, Chapters 19 and 20 where the Laws of the Ten Commandments are written. Blessed be our Prophet Moses whom the Lord, God - YWH - gave them to pass down unto us Shema Israel [Hear us O Lord, God of Israel]. Blessed be the short Sacred Scrolls [mezuzahs] which bears the name of our mothers of at least seven generations back. Blessed be the name of the One And Only True God - YWH."

The "KADDISH" or "MOURNER'S PRAYER," unlike the custom among European and European-American Jews, is a "JOYOUS PRAYER;" not sorrowful as in the others usage. For Falashas believe in the "SWEETNESS OF DEATH." This does not mean that all Falashas are trying to die.[1] The Falashas explained this theosophical concept in the following manner:

JUST AS THE TABLE IS SPREAD WITH THE RITUAL FOODS OF HORSE-RADISH, WINE, MATZOHS [unleavened bread], THE MIXTURE OF LIVER AND WINE, THE HARD BOILED EGGS, SCALLIONS, WATER HEAVY WITH SALT, AND THE GOOD LAMB; WE ARE REMINDED THAT THE PASSOVER [Pesach] WAS OF DEATH; AND THAT THE DEAD WAS ALLOWED TO REMAIN WITH THE DEAD; AND THAT THE LIVING HAD TO CARRY ON WITH THE LIVING.

The above layout of the "SEDER" [Passover meal] is cited in the European and European-American Jews' HAGGADAH [narratives of the Passover], all of which has been imposed upon the younger Falasha Brothers and Sisters who have had contact with their fellow Jews of European origin while they were living in Israel because of one reason or another. Of course the contact with people such as Professor Dr. Jacques Faitlovich equally had its impact in this direction. But, let it be very clearly understood that Edward Ullendorf's comments - cited on page 147 of this volume, nor anything worse or better, could not make the Falashas' [my people] "JUDAISM" the type of "...RELIGIOUS SYNCRETISM..." he sees in his own RELIGIOUS BIGOTRY that must be in his own type of EUROPEAN and/or European-American RELIGIOUS SYNCRETISM, etc. Yet; it is not at all "STRANGE" that the WHITE JEW should assume that all other JEWS who differ to his way of practicing "JUDAISM" have to be WRONG, and he/she RIGHT. Moses, like

1. Neither does the repenting Christian hurry to meet his/her death for entrance in the Next World.

all of the others shown on this page, WAS, or IS, another African: Semite, if you are pleased!

NILE VALLEYS AFRICANS; NOT ONE A NEGRO

[Truly; Their ancestors wrote the "Commandments"]

And, is it not a fact that our brother Moses dealt with the foundation of the TEN COMMANDMENTS in Egypt, Northeast Africa before he passed them on to all of the Israelites? Certainly we must recognize the following from whence the ISRAELITES got our original LAWS, etc.:

EXTRACTS FROM THE "NEGATIVE CONFESSION 1

[1] I have not done iniquity.
[2] I have not committed robbery with violence.
[3] I have not done violence to no man.
[4] I have not committed theft.
[5] I have not slain man or woman.
[6] I have not made light the bushel.
[7] I have not acted deceitfully.
[8] I have not purloined the things which belonged to the God.
[9] I have not uttered falsehood.
[10] I have not carried away food.
[11] I have not uttered evil words.
[12] I have not attacked man.
[13] I have not killed the beasts which are the property of the Gods.
[14] I have not eaten my heart... i.e., done anything to my regret.
[15] I have not laid waste ploughed land.
[16] I have not pried into matters.
[17] I have not set my mouth against any man.
[18] I have not given way to anger concerning myself without cause.
[19] I have not defiled the wife of a man.
[20] I have not committed transgression against any party.
[21] I have not violated sacred times and seasons.
[22] I have not struck fear into any man.
[23] I have not been a man of anger.
[24] I have not made myself deaf to words of right and truth.
[25] I have not stirred up strife.
[26] I have not made no man weep.
[27] I have not committed acts of impurity or sodomy.
[28] I have not eaten my heart.
[29] I have not abused no man.

1. Sir E.A.W. Budge's EGYPTIAN MAGIC, pp. 108-109; BOOK OF THE DEAD, Chapt. CXXXV. There is a total of 147 "Negative Confessions" responding to "Commandments" in other works. The 42 are listed in the Tomb of Pharaoh Rameses IIIrd and VIth, Valley of the Kings, Luxor.

ABOUT THE SABBATH: Chapter V, Part Three.

The "Sabbath" is proclaimed to be....

> "the mother of the observance of the Laws Of God given to Moses; the mother of Love; the mother of Purity; the mother of Fertility; the mother of Flowers...,"

and a host of other superlatives. The Falashas point to the following citations from the Sacred Torah for their belief in the purpose of the "SABBATH" - Genesis 2 : 1, 3; Exodus 31 : 15, 16, 18, 32; Deuteronomy 29 : 29; Isaiah 58 : 13, 14; Daniel 7 : 25; Ezekiel 8 : 16; Numbers 15 : 32, 33; Psalm 1 : 1, 4; and Ezekiel 15 : 26. But the Monks described the "SABBATH" in the following manner:

> "Sabbath, with her powers, is the intruder and intercessor with Ywh for the forgiveness of the sins of His people - Israel. She is the interpleader between man and his God, for the happiness of those who have lived saintly lives. She is the interpleader between man and his God for the entrance of man's soul in the gates of Heaven. She has the power to cast her wrath against all who does not worship her in the manner set forth in the Sacred Torah."

The Monks place extra emphasis on the following citation; thus:

> "SABBATH'S ANGER IS SWEET, WHILE SHE IS STERN. HER LOVE IS DEEP, WHILE NOT LUSTFUL OF THE FLESH AS THE LOVE OF MAN. HER JUSTICE IS STRAIGHT-FORWARD, WHILE NOT CHANNELED AGAINST MERCY. HER EMBRACE IS WARM, WHILE NOT IN THE LUST LIKE MAN."

Among all religiously involved Falashas in Ethiopia and the Americas [including the Caribbean Islands] "SABBATH" is not considered just "...A DAY OF PRAYERS AND REST...." Instead, She is believed to be "...A DAY FOR MEDITATION BETWEEN MAN AND HIS GOD...." And that on this day "...WE ACTUALLY COME INTO DIRECT CONTACT WITH GOD...;" particularly for those who are "...CLEAN IN MIND, BODY AND SOUL...;" thus She is.

We, Falashas, also do not believe that:

> "Sabbath was made to be a day for listening to the Laws of Ywh which he gave to man." Instead that: "Sabbath is the day when the Laws of God must be recited as an incidental to the day itself. She is in herself that which makes the mind of man heavy with love and respect for his Creator, because Sabbath has a magical power which makes mere man realize that there is in existance a force [or forces] greater than himself. Said force is the ever-present God and Host of the people- Israel. God is Sabbath, and Sabbath God. Whenever Sabbath is misused and abused, we do the same to God; for one cannot be separated from the other, and if we should ever act against one, we will definitely act against the other and be guilty of committing a sin against both."

> "The Sabbath is the Holy Day, set aside by God for man to humble themselves to their Law-Giver and Creator; a day when we must deny all men, and place

ourselves in mind, body and spirit at the heals of our God and Father, Ruler of the Universe and His people - Israel."

Falashas are very serious about the above interpretations which they have formulated about the "SABBATH," and further believe that:

"The height of the Sabbath's GLORY cannot be expressed in words, even though so much has been written about her; but nothing comes higher than the expression which states - SABBATH IS THE PERSONAL REPRESENTATIVE OF THE ONE AND ONLY LIVING GOD OF ISRAEL UNTIL THE APPEARANCE OF HIS MESSIAH. She is the reminder to man that whatever life he enjoys on Earth can be taken away in the space of mere time; for man is but an imbicle if he defies God and His Sabbath."

"Sabbath's GLORY is one which words will never accurately describe, though many have so often tried. Sabbath is the greatest condition of the mind. It is Sabbath who gives to man God. And it is not God who gave to man Sabbath."

These latter citations are explained in the following interpretations; thus:

"If it was not for the Sabbath Day, any man would have continued to work and do all sorts of evil things,without anything to remind him that he has to stop and do the biddings of his Creator, who is the God and Host of the people - Israel. God cannot speak to man in anyother way than through His Holy Day, which is the Sabbath, and His Holy Words which is the Sabbath. Sabbath is the Day, and she is the Word of God, so being the Day and the Word she is GOD IN PERSON- and she stands to remind us of GOD IN HIS SPIRIT. God is in the Spirit of the Sabbath, and the Sabbath in GOD'S SPIRIT."

The feminine character attributed to the name of the "SABBATH" is not to be confused with the description of a mere EARTHLY WOMAN;[1] as Falashas believe that:

"By so doing, Sabbath will be debased from Her splendor and most spotless position in the Sacred Soul of men. For the WOMAN OF THE EARTH is full of lust, and sins equally with her man. Common WOMAN must pass through the unclean chambers of sin. WOMAN of mere mankind must purify from the common lowness of man; and she cannot enter the Holy Of Holies where the Sabbath rests herself. It is the Sabbath who intercedes into the WOMB of the pregnant WOMAN in order that her children may be born free from the SINS of man."

Therefore Falashas believe further on the last point; that:

"SABBATH MUST CLEAN EARTHLY WOMAN, JUST AS MAN IS CLEANSED."

"Sabbath is the Holy of Holies where the light of the world is to be stored, and all men in need of light must enter Her Holy Of Holies."

The brilliance of the "SABBATH" and the "HOLY OF HOLIES" is exemplified by Her power

"...to clean away the sins of the Woman In Child-Bed, and the Woman In The House Of Pleasant Blood from their uncleanliness...."[2]

The following is called the "HERALD OF THE SABBATH." It is recited by all Falashas in

1. Remember that Falashas do not care about any "Women's Liberation Movement" in their culture.
2. Every culture has its taboo about women's menstrual period, which include Falasha's.

their communities on the Sabbath Day; thus:

> "Sabbath is the GLORY of the world; She is the world; She is given to man by His God, and is God. God spoke His words through the Sabbath, and She became the words. There is no TRUTH greater that the Sabbath. For God gave the world Sabbath, and the world became Sabbath, and Sabbath the world. GLORY, GLORY, GLORY be the name of Ywh; Sabbath and Ywh are ONE; Sabbath and Messiah are ONE; Hallelujah, Hallelujah, Hallelujah- the God of Israel is the Sabbath. She is the Sabbath, and the Sabbath God. And I am the slave of Ywh, who is my master. Glory be the name of the Ever-Living God And Creator of His People - ISRAEL. It was so from the BEGINNING, and it shall be so at the ENDING. God and the Sabbath is the BEGINNING, and shall be the ENDING. As the SABBATH begin the WEEK, so did our GOD began the world.

The following song - "TRUSTING THE LORD," which was heard when the African-American Congregation headed by the late Rabbi Wentworth Matthew removed the Most Sacred Torah and marched with it around the Synagogue three times in memory of the honour of our late brothers - Abraham, Isaac and Jacob is typical of a closing song of our brothers and sisters at home.

" So the sign of the fire by night,
And the sign of the cloud by day;
Hov'ring o'er, just before
As the journey on their way.

Shall a guide and leader be,
Till the wild-er-ness be past
For the Lord our God in His own good time
Shall lead us to the light at last."

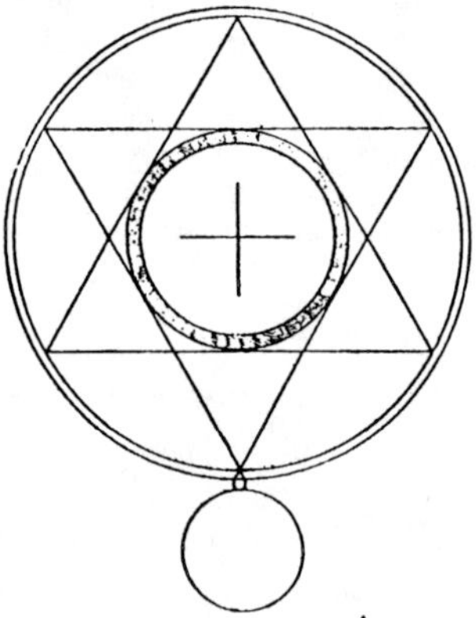

From Egypt[1]

---

1. "The Tuat and the Twelve Hours of the Night," hewn in stone in the Great Pyramid of Ghizeh. Certainly our fellow African brothers saw to it that in Egypt we were to receive our 'Star of David' so many Jews, Christians, Moslems/Muslims, et al., believe originated in Judaism.

SACRED WRITINGS AND TRADITIONS: Chapter V, Part Four.

Lower case [common] letters indicate WRITTEN and/or ORAL teachings; whereas Upper case [capital] letters indicate GOD'S - [YWH'S] - teaching and/or speaking. The WRITTEN works are taken from the Pentateuch [Comesh, Sacred Torah, Five Books Of Moses, etc.]; the ORAL teachings from handed down myths, allegories and historical traditions by generations of Falashas of the past and present. Other sources are also quoted and specifically identified.

At times it will be noted that there are some differences in the interpretation of the meaning of certain words from Hebrew to Yiddish, to Amheric, to Gheeze, to Agu and to English, etc. With regards to Agu, the original language of Ethiopia, and Gheeze - a former National Language of Ethiopia. It is the former which the Falashas mostly use when speaking to each others; yet, the common language of the nation is Amheric. Thus it is that at times either of the two might be used as reference or point of translation into English. This, of course, does not illiminate Gheeze - the religious language of the nation [somewhat in the status of Latin today;, a so-called "dead language"] use only for religious liturgical works. Because of these factors it will be necessary at times for your author to make further comments on certain pertinent points in details as we proceed in this Chapter and Part.

Amheric, Agu and Gheeze, like Hebrew and Aramaic, are direct languages; as such quite a few times words are translated in English to mean one thing, but the actual original means something else completely, this being particularly true in trying to convey feeling and/or thought from one language into another. For example, in English the following sentence would be considered standard grammar: "JOHN HAS A SON." The same sentence in the Agu and/or Gheeze language will be translated from the English language in the following literal transcription: 'TO JOHNATHAN - SON.'[1] At no time will the helping words - "HAS" and "A" - appear in the latter sentence. They are assumed, depending upon the word or words preceeding and following the subject. Your author's name is another point for an example: 'YOSEF ben-JOCHANNAN' or 'JOSEPH son JONATHAN.' English translation directly from the original word by word: 'JOSEPH THE SON OF JONATHAN.' The latter reverses the father and son relationship of the former.

I will quote only those points which I consider to be expressing the most paramount beliefs in our FALASHA communities, as it is impossible to show everything taught in the communities in this very short introduction of the heritage and history of my people - "FALASHAS" or "BLACK JEWS" - everywhere.

You will notice that some of the teachings in parts of this Chapter will have bearings on those already mentioned in previous chapters, and some in the following chapters and parts. Also, that

1. The same principle holds true for Hieratic writing - Hieroglyph - and other african writings.

some are extracted from the "BOOK OF MAGIC" [Magical Books] which were organized from the EGYPTIAN [Nile Valley Africans'] BOOK OF THE DEAD, PAPYRI, COFFIN TEXTS, PYRAMID TEXTS, OSIRIAN DRAMA, NEGATIVE CONFESSIONS, TEACHINGS OF AMEN-EM-EOPE, etc., etc., etc., most of which appears in the Sacred Torah as if they were originally created and developed by the Israelites or Jews. Many more are suppressed to date in the same Hebrew teachings from the time of the African from Egypt, Northeast Alkebu-lan named Moses to the present "SCHOLARS" shown below on this page:

Panel of Jewish Scholars Translating the Bible

Dr. Harry M. Orlinsky — Rabbi Solomon Grayzel — Rabbi Max Arzt

Photographs for The New York Times by JACK MANNING

Rabbi Bernard J. Bamberger — Dr. H. L. Ginsberg

On the following page the example of what happens in translation and transliteration by the above so-called "Panel of Jewish Scholars" is best observed; thus you can imagine what actually takes place from one language to another, and also others, etc., etc., etc. For extensive details of the above you are refered to pages xxix and xxx of my work - THE BLACK MAN'S RELIGION, AND EXTRACTS AND COMMENTS FROM THE HOLY BLACK BIBLE, Volume III;[1] and the original article by Edward B. Fiske, THE NEW YORK TIMES, Monday, May 21, 1973. Hopefully you will understand that the Bible says whatever its writers want it to say; and its truth is whatever the writers determine is truth as seen by themselves alone - Falasha scribes being no exception.

1. This Volume is divided in three sections: No I, II and III; an outline of the need of African Theosophy.

The...PANEL OF JEWISH SCHOLARS...,"etc. made"EZEKIEL 36:4" say what they wanted below:

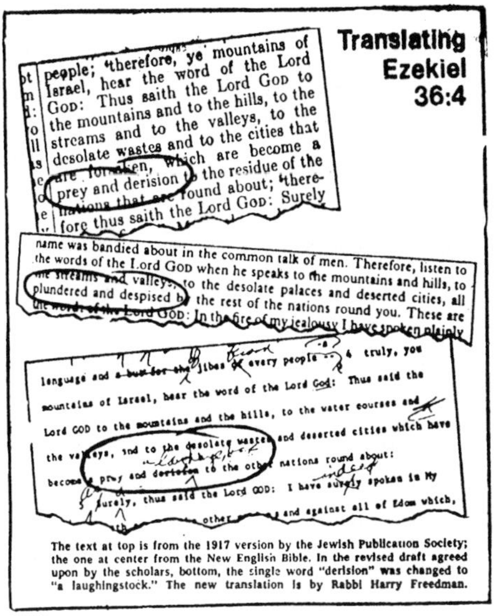

Translating Ezekiel 36:4

people; therefore, ye mountains of Israel, hear the word of the Lord GOD: Thus saith the Lord GOD to the mountains and to the hills, to the streams and to the valleys, to the desolate wastes and to the cities that are forsaken, which are become a prey and derision to the residue of the nations that are round about; therefore thus saith the Lord GOD: Surely

name was bandied about in the common talk of men. Therefore, listen to the words of the Lord GOD when he speaks to the mountains and hills, to the streams and valleys, to the desolate palaces and deserted cities, all plundered and despised by the rest of the nations round you. These are the words of the Lord GOD: In the fire of my jealousy I have spoken plainly

language and a butt for the jibes of every people — truly, you mountains of Israel, hear the word of the Lord God: Thus said the Lord GOD to the mountains and the hills, to the water courses and the valleys, and to the desolate wastes and deserted cities which have become a prey and derision to the other nations round about: surely, thus said the Lord GOD: I have surely spoken in My ... other ... and against all of Edom which,

The text at top is from the 1917 version by the Jewish Publication Society; the one at center from the New English Bible. In the revised draft agreed upon by the scholars, bottom, the single word "derision" was changed to "a laughingstock." The new translation is by Rabbi Harry Freedman.

You can see why your author decided to clarify the above points before entering the details of this part of Chapter V. This is also the reason why elaboration on the writings and teachings that differ to the European and European-American Jews about Judaism had to be detailed at this point. These comments deal with the historical development and interpretation of the recordings from the so-called "HOLY [Sacred] SCRIPTURES" as deciphered by Falasha religious leaders - MONKS, PRIESTS, DEACONS, ELDERS, RABBIS [teachers], WRITERS, ORAL HISTORIANS, etc.,of the past and the present. Whose "SACRED TORAH" is correct, above or below?

Rabbi McKethen, a representative of the Brooklyn group

All of the installments I have given are complete versions because the purpose for them was, and still is, as stated before and repeated at this juncture. Thus, I will continue showing only matters of importance that affect the picture of so-called "FALASHA" religion, culture and heritage according to their own TEACHINGS and IDEAS of foundations and fundamentals that created what is today called THEOSOPHY and THEOLOGY. You can better prepare yourself to understand these teachings which come to you from Falasha ORAL and WRITTEN traditions and experiences in Judaism, particularly when you compare them with your own VERSION of the HEBREW RELIGION according to European Jews ORAL and WRITTEN traditions, if such is yours; and of course if you are from a Judaeo, Christian, Islamic background. If you fail to follow this instruction in the following text, and/or have failed to do so in the previous text, you have already missed the beauty of the Falashas culture, heritage and history with regards to their own Judaic experience.

We are about to enter into the area of RELIGIOUSITY/THEOSOPHY that is basic to all of the religions of the world - "CREATION OF MAN," the Africans of the Nile Valley VERSION being the foundation of the JUDAEO-CHRISTIAN-ISLAMIC teachings in the Torah, Bible and Qur'an.

PICTORIAL SCENES OF CREATION AND HEAVEN IN HISTORY 1

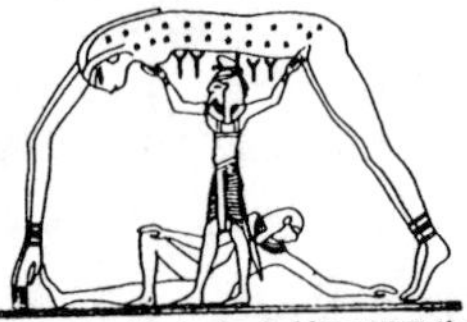

SHU - the Air God - holding NUT the Sky Goddess from the embrace of GEB - the Earth God lying on the horizontal. The stars on NUT indicate her celestial nature; the Y shape symbols indicate the Four Supports of Heaven and Evolution [Procreation].

Section of an early Christian concept of the Creation Of Eve out of Adam, and the Serpent Of Eden. [From a sarcophagus in the Lateran Museum, Rome, Italy]

CHNUM - the God Of Creation - fashions the First People on His Potter's Wheel.

Adam and Eve picking the Forbidden Fruit [From painting on the ceiling of the Cisteen Chapel, Rome],

[Egyptian conception of The Creation from a bas-relief depicting the birth of Pharaoh Amenhotep - father of Akhenaten - at Luxor or Thebes, Egypt][2]

---

1. See Y. ben-Jochannan's Black Man Of The Nile And His Family, 1981 Ed.; The Black Man's Religion and Extracts And Comments From The Holy Black Bible, Vol. I, p. 65.
2. See also Temple Of God Khnum at Esna, Egypt, Northeast Africa for other wall paintings of this.

The Falashas belief in the "CREATION OF THE WORLD AND MANKIND" comes from the Sacred Torah, particularly in the BOOK OF GENESIS [First Book of the Five Books Of Moses]. However, the following is also common ORAL TRADITIONAL TEACHING about this most basic of religious theosophy, theology and philosophy; thus:

> And it was the beginning of time, space and matter. Now the Earth was unformed and therefore nothing existed. Nothingness [darkness][1] was upon the face of time, for there was nothing [no light]; but there was water of the spirit of light. And God said to the Messiah and His assistant Messiah-Theodore;[2] WE SHALL CREATE A UNIVERSE. And God shone the light of His face over the waters of life and commanded that there be light, saying; LET THERE BE LIGHT, and there was light; and the light was very powerful, for the light was the universe; and the universe was the light. And this was the FIRST DAY.
>
> After God had seen the light, and the light was good, the Law Maker - God - said; THE LIGHT MUST BE SEPARATED FROM THE DARKNESS. And the light was separated from the darkness; and that which was of the dark remained in darkness; and that which was of the light became the light and remained of the light. God called the light DAY, and all that was of the light He called DAILY THINGS. And those things given to the DAY. God called the darkness NIGHT, and all that is of the darkness, NIGHTLY THINGS. And all that was of the night remained of the night by the command of the Law Giver.
>
> God called the period between light and closest to night EVENING. And that which was closest to the light from darkness God called MORNING. And the morning and the evening were both beautiful. For God had chosen this time to show the changing of his movements, which was planned for this universe and for God's most precious gift to come...MAN.
>
> God continued to prepare for the creation of man, as He set forth to create the other parts of the universe for this end. And God ordered; LET THERE BE A FIRMAMENT IN THE MIDST OF THE SEA, AND LET THE FIRMAMENT DIVIDE THE WATERS FROM THE WATERS. And the waters from the waters were divided, and everything was perfect. And this was the SECOND DAY."
>
> And God said; LET THE WATERS OF THE CREATION UNDER THE HEAVENS GATHER ITSELF TOGETHER AT PARTS OF THE UNIVERSE. AND LET LAND APPEAR WHERE NO WATER LIES, AND THE LAND, AND THE WATER REMAIN IN ITS STAND, AND THE LAND IN ITS STAND. And the dry land became; and the water remained; and all was good and perfect. God called the dry land EARTH, and the water around the earth He called SEA.
>
> God looked around and saw all was still perfect and began to prepare for man's food, and for man's peace, and for man's beauty. And God said; LET THE EARTH BRING FORTH SEEDS OF LIFE THROUGH THE GRASS, HERBS YIELDING SEEDS, FRUIT-TREES WITH FRUIT. AND THE SEEDS OF THE FRUIT AS THE TREE FROM WHENCE IT CAME. AND THE SEEDS OF THE TREE FROM WHENCE IT CAME, SCATTERING OVER THE EARTH. AND THE EARTH REVEALING THE TREE FROM

---

1. The equivalent word for African thoughts is without "Western" racist interpretaion of any type.
2. The typical Christian "TRINITY" is not intended here; none should be inferred by speculation.

THE SEEDS SCATTERED THEREON. AND THE EARTH BRINGING FORTH GRASS, AND THE SEED OF GRASS SCATTERING OVER THE EARTH, AND THE WATER FEEDING THE SEEDS OF THE GRASS AND FRUIT TREES. God looked around, and God saw that it was good, and looked up, and it was passed the evening, and the morning had gone. And this was the THIRD DAY.

God then said; LET THERE BE LIGHT IN THE FIRMAMENT OF HEAVEN, DIVIDING THE DAY FROM THE NIGHT. AND LET THEM BE SIGNS FOR THE SEASONS, AND DAYS, AND YEARS, AND FOR THE LIGHT ON THE EARTH. And God saw that it was good, and He said; LET THIS LIGHT IN THE FIRMAMENT SEPARATE ITSELF. AND THE MOST POWERFUL LIGHT RULE THE EARTH BY DAY, AND THE LESSER LIGHT THE EARTH BY NIGHT, AND THE LESSER LIGHT RULE THE STARS I NOW ORDER TO APPEAR. And God made the most powerful light rule the day, and the lesser the night and the stars. And it was good, and God saw it was good. And there was the evening, and the morning had passed. And this was the FOURTH DAY.

And God said; LET THE WATERS CONTAIN LIVING CREATURES, AND THE WATERS COVER THEM. AND LET THERE BE LIVING CREATURES OVER THE WATERS, AND THE WATERS FLOW UNDER THEM. LET THERE BE FOWL FLYING HIGH IN THE FIRMAMENT, AND WATER BENEATH THEM FOR THEIR THIRST TO QUENCH, AND THE LAND THEIR HOME AND THEIR FOOD. THE CREATURES OF THE SEA REMAINING OF THE SEA, EACH WITH ITS KIND, AND THE FOWLS EACH WITH ITS KIND. And it was good. And God looked around, and He was pleased. And God blessed them, saying; GO FORTH AND BE FRUITFUL, AND MULTIPLY, COVERING THE EARTH, AND FILLING THE SEAS. And this was also good. And God saw the morning passed and the evening gone. And this was the FIFTH DAY.[1]

And God said; LET THE EARTH BRING THE LIVING CREATURE OF ITS KIND CREEPING, DRAGGING ON STOMACH, WALKING ON FEET, WALKING AND FLYING, THE CATTLE, BEAST OF EARTH, SERPENT OF SEA AND EARTH, AND ALL THAT WHICH I DESIRE OF EARTH AND SEA. ALL AFTER ITS KIND TO MULTIPLY AS ITS KIND. And this was good, and God looked around Him and saw it was good, and God said; LET US MAKE MAN IN OUR OWN IMAGE, AFTER OUR OWN LIKENESS, WITH MANY COLORS WHICH IS BEAUTIFUL AS THE DARKNESS, AND AS THE LIGHT. AND THE DARKNESS TO BLEND WITH THE LIGHT, AND THE LIGHT TO BLEND WITH THE DARKNESS. AND LET THE BLENDING BE AS BEAUTIFUL AS THE LIGHT AND THE DARKNESS, AND THE DARKNESS BE MORE. LET MAN HAVE CONTROL OVER THE BEAST OF THE LAND, AND FOWL OF THE AIR, FISH OF THE SEA. AND THE FOWL, FISH, BEAST AND CATTLE BE IN THE DOMINION OF MAN. AND HE RULE OVER THEM, AND EVERYTHING ON EARTH. And the earth was carried to the rule of man, and all that was in it, and the sea, and the air, was carried under this rule, with beast and all other animals; fowl as cattle,fruit as trees, and all therein came under man's control. And God blessed them. And God said to the Makers of the Universe; THIS MAN MUST HAVE A COMPANION, THAT HE MUST CALL WOMAN. AND WOMAN MUST BE OF MAN, FROM MAN, AND LIKE MAN; BUT WILL NOT ACT AS MAN. And God made wo'man, and she was good, and as beautiful as was man. And she was distinguished from man, and man her, and her things hers, and man's things his. And man's things never woman's, and woman's never man's.

---

1. Remember there are various types of calendars, with different arrangements for week and month.

So be other things to each its kind. God blessed the man [male], and the woman [female], saying; BE FRUITFUL AS THE TREES SPREADING THEIR SEEDS, AND MULTIPLYING IN NUMBERS, AND REPLENISHING THE EARTH FROM WHENCE YOU CAME.[1] CONTROL THE EARTH AND THAT WHICH IS IN IT, AND SUBDUE ALL THAT IS ON IT FOR IT IS YOUR DOMINION, AND YOURS TO RULE. AND YOU, MAN, SHALL LEAD. AND YOU, WOMAN, SHALL FOLLOW. AND YOU, MAN, SHALL CARE AND PROTECT HER. AND YOU, WOMAN, SHALL NOURISH AND NURSE HIM. YOU SHALL BOTH LIVE AS ONE, AND YOU SHALL RULE AS ONE. And God looked around, and all was good, and all was perfect. And God saw it was good, and He was pleased. And God called upon the Messiah And they called upon Messiah Theodore,[2] and it was still good. And they who had agreed to make man, and woman, saw it was good, and they were pleased. And God said; I HAVE GIVEN YOU MY LIFE, AND HERB-SEEDS THAT COVERS THE EARTH TO CONTINUE, TREES AND THE SEEDS OF THE TREES, AND MORE TREES, AND THE BEAST AND THE FOWL OF THE AIR, THE FISH AND ALL CREATURES OF THE SEA. ALL THIS I HAVE GIVEN YOU, FOR YOU AND YOU, WHICH IS YOU IN OUR NAME. And it was so. And God saw everything that He had made was good and perfect, and He was pleased. And the Messiah was pleased. And the Messiah Theodore was pleased. And man was pleased. Man was asked if he needed more light. And man did not ask for more. The evening had passed, and the morning was already gone. And this was the SIXTH DAY.

And the Heaven, and the Earth was completed. And the Host of Heaven and Earth was finished. And the next morning came, which was after the Sixth Night. And God finished His work which He had created. God rested on this greatest of His days. And this was the SEVENTH DAY.

God blessed the Seventh Day, and hollowed it, because he was resting; for He was keeping the LAW for His people. He rested. All His work was completed, and God was satisfied.

God had formed MAN from the dust of the Earth; He had taken WOMAN from the rib of MAN, whom He had made from the dust of the Earth; and He had blown His breath into their bodies. Oh! Oh! Oh! Hallelujah be the name of God. He has created man from the dust of the Earth; and from the dust of the Earth man's rib was, in order to make woman; and man and woman became one, and the man one, all for the universe...etc., etc., etc.

The COVENANT OF HOLINESS [extracts from the Pentateuch] believed by the Falashas to have come from the teachings of the Hebrews in Israel, which was in fact taken from the teachings established in the "STONE CHEST'S RITUALS" that Moses had to learn when he was a mere student at the Grand Lodge of his fellow Africans of the Nile Valley High-Cultures,[3] follow after the chronological listing of the LODGES and the description of the STONE CHEST on page 168. As Jews, however, it is to Moses the Falashas prefer to believe God YWH handed down all of

1. From the First Book Of Moses, Chapter I: The origin of man [male] and woman [female], etc.
2. Falashas believe in a "MESSIAH THEODORE" who will come and rule over them for a period of "50 YEARS BEFORE THE MESSIAH" mentioned in the Book Of Isaiah in the Holy/Sacred Torah.
3. All of the ancient Haribu/Hebrews/"Jews," et al., were trained by Nile Valley Africans in the African/Egyptian Educational [Mysteries] System that provided the foundation of "Jewish Thought."

these teachings; but the evidence shows differently.

THE ARK OF THE COVENANT [1]

The Ark of the Covenant, built and set up by Moses in the wilderness, according to the Sacred volume—and which has not been seen—is precisely similar in all measurements to the "Stone Chest" still to be seen in the King's Chamber of the Great Pyramid, and which is undoubtedly the original, although the contents are gone. According to the *Ritual* it should have contained the "Coffined One," and we know that miniatures of this used to be carried around the Egyptian temples at Memphis on state occasions during their religious rites.

SUBORDINATE LODGES OF THE GRAND LODGE OF LUXOR [2]

1. Palestine [at Mt. Carmel]
2. Assyria [at Mt. Herman in Lebanon]
3. Babylon
4. Media [near the Red Sea]
5. India [at the banks of the Ganges River]
6. Burma
7. Athens
8. Rome [at Elea]
9. Croton
10. Rhodes
11. Delphi
12. Miletus
13. Cyprus
14. Corinth
15. Crete
16. Cush [[illegible]]
17. Monomotapa [South Africa]
18. Zimbabwe [Rhodesia]

LUXOR was destroyed by fire, burnt to the ground, in the year c. 548 B.C.E. It was set aflame by foreigners, who were jealous of the indigenous Africans ["Negroes," etc.] knowledge of the "MYSTERIES" taught in the Osirica - which included all of the above mentioned disciplines. [See John Kendrick's, ANCIENT EGYPT, Book II, p. 363; Eva B. Sandford's, THE MEDITERRANEAN WORLD, pp. 135 - 139; Yosef ben-Jochannan's, AFRICA: MOTHER OF "WESTERN CIVILIZATION", Chapter IX].

---

1. See Dr. Albert Churchward, Signs And Symbols Of Primordial Man, London, 1920, p. 296, etc.
2. See Yosef ben-Jochannan, Black Man Of The Nile And His Family, New York, 1972, p. 251, p. 273 of the Revised and Enlarged 1981 Edition. Note that there was a Subordinate Lodge established in Palestine/Judaea/Israel, etc., at "Mt. Carmel;" yet the myth of King Solomon having "created Freemasonry" that came out of the "African/Egyptian Mysteries System" at Wa'at, Egypt!

THE COVENANT WITH MOSES:
And God spoke to Moses, saying; SPEAK TO ALL THE CONGREGATION OF THE CHILDREN OF ISRAEL, SAYING UNTO THEM: YOU SHALL BE HOLY IN GOD'S NAME, FOR I, YOUR LORD, GOD AND CREATOR IS HOLY. YOU SHALL FEAR EACH AND EVERY MAN HIS FATHER AND MOTHER. YOU SHALL KEEP MY SABBATH. I AM YOUR GOD, YOUR CREATOR AND LAWGIVER. TURN NOT TO IDOLS, NOR MAKE NONE YOURSELF OF ANY MAN, NOT EVEN OF ME. MAKE NONE IN ANY FORM, FROM THE MATERIALS OF THE EARTH OR OF THE AIR I HAVE GIVEN YOU. AND MAKE NONE OF THE SMOLTEN IMAGES ABOUT YOU, NOR OF THE SMOLTEN GODS AROUND YOU. I AM YOUR GOD, YOUR LORD, YOUR LAWGIVER, AND YOUR CREATOR.[1]

GOD'S COVENANT WITH ISRAEL:
And Moses called the children of the congregation of Israel, saying; YOU HAVE WITNESSED, AS YOU HAVE SEEN, ALL THAT GOD HAS DONE IN YOUR PRESENCE AND SIGHT IN THE LAND OF EGYPT TO PHARAOH, HIS SERVANTS, HIS MAIDSWOMEN, HIS LAND. YOU HAVE ALSO WITNESSED THE TRIALS, SIGNS AND GREAT WONDERS. BUT YOUR LORD, GOD AND LAWGIVER HAS GIVEN YOU A BRAIN TO KNOW, EYES TO SEE, EARS TO HEAR, THIS DAY. I HAVE LED YOU FOR FORTY YEARS IN THE WILDERNESS, AND YOUR CLOTHING WAS NOT WAXEN, OLD AND STUCK ON YOU, NEITHER WERE YOUR SHOES TO YOUR FEET. YOU HAVE NOT EATEN BREAD, NEITHER HAVE YOU EATEN OF BAD, NOR DRANK OF WINE OR OTHER STRONG DRINKS, SO THAT YOU WILL RECOGNIZE I AM YOUR GOD AND HOST OF THE UNIVERSE. AND WHEN YOU CAME UNTO THIS PLACE SIHON THE KING OF HESHBON, AND OG THE KING OF BASHAN, HURLED THEIR EVIL EYES AGAINST US, AND WE SMOTE THEM. WE TOOK THEIR LAND AND GAVE IT TO THE REUBENITES FOR THEIR INHERITANCE AND TO THE GADITES AND TO THE HALF-TRIBES OF THE MANASSITES. WATCH WITH CARE THEREFORE THE WORDS OF THIS COVENANT OF YOUR LAND THEN, THAT YOU MAY MAKE ALL THAT YOU DO TO PROSPER.

GOD'S COVENANT WITH THE CHIEFS OF THE TRIBES:
YOU ARE STANDING IN THE PRESENCE OF YOUR LORD AND GOD, AND WITH YOUR CHIEFS AND HEADS OF THE TRIBES. YOU ARE WITH YOUR ELDERS AND YOUR OFFICERS. ALL THE MEN OF ISRAEL ARE PRESENT WITH THEIR WIVES AND CHILDREN. THE STRANGER IN THE CAMPS ARE ALSO PRESENT, FROM THE HEWER OF THE WOOD TO THE DRAWER OF THE WATER, THAT YOU SHOULD ENTER INTO THE COVENANT WITH THE LORD YOUR GOD, AND INTO THIS OATH WHICH THE LORD YOUR GOD MAKE WITH YOU THIS, THAT YOU MAY ESTABLISH THIS YOUR DAY AND THE DAY OF YOUR GOD UNTO HIMSELF IN THE NAME OF HIS PEOPLE. THAT HE MAY BE UNTO YOU AS A GOD, AS HE SPOKE UNTO YOU AND HE HAS SWORN UNTO YOUR FATHERS, ABRAHAM, ISAAC AND JACOB. NEITHER WITH YOU ALONE DO I MAKE THIS COVENANT AND OATH, BUT WITH HIM THAT STANDS HERE THIS DAY WITH US BEFORE OUR LORD, GOD AND LAWGIVER, ALSO WITH HIM THAT IS NOT HERE IN YOUR PRESENCE, FOR YOU KNOW THAT WE HAVE DWELT IN THE LAND OF EGYPT; AND WE CAME THROUGH THE MIDST OF THE NATIONS THROUGH WHICH WE HAVE PASSED,

1. The African/Egyptian "Creator God - Khnum" predated Ywh/Jehovah by thousands of years in history. The "Creation Story" of Jews, Christians and Moslems only dates back to ca. 3760 B.C.E.

AND THAT WE HAD RESTED ONLY ONCE IN ETHIOPIA WHERE WE HAD LEFT SOME OF OUR BRETHREN . YOU HAVE SEEN THE FALSE PEOPLE AND THEIR GODS OF STONES, WOOD, SMOLTEN SILVER AND GOLD; ALL OF WHICH YOU NOW MAKE A COVENANT AGAINST, IN THIS YEAR, LAND, AND FROM THE GOD OF THE PEOPLE AND THE CHILDREN OF THE HOUSE OF ISRAEL..., etc., etc., etc.

TEACHINGS FROM THE MAGICAL BOOKS [extracts on child-birth]:
And it came to pass that Adam was to have a child from his woman companion, Eve. And Eve was to have a child from her companion Adam. It also came to pass that the child was born, and the child bore the name of Cain. After Gain followed Abel, and also his youngest brother Seth. All was beautiful, and the work of God was completed. And God was satisfied; and God gave Adam more power over the domain of the Earth from whence he came, and whence he lived, and whence he returned.

But it also came to pass when Cain killed Abel, and was driven to the land of Nod. And the power given the seeds of Cain was to be sin; and the mark upon seeds from Cain is sin. Those who are of the seeds of Cain are to bear the ugly mark of sin forever and ever. And those that were of the seeds of Abel and Seth are to bear the beautiful mark of Godliness. And it was so, and it is so, and it will always be so.

It is as it was, and it is, and it will be, that I bring the name of this child of God, and of this man from Adam, and this woman from Adam, and all from this community. Naming him in honour of his fathers, and in the presence of his God [the child's name is inserted here], and upon the faith and belief of the people - Israel - I commit you to your Lord and God - Ywh.

And the blood sacrifice of the Woman In Child Bed is the sacrifice Eve made to Adam for her God. It was to be so, and it was ordered so. Hallelujah, from Adam and of Eve there is a [sex of the child inserted here] child [or children] born to the people of the House of Israel, and he [or she] is born free from sin. For of a child the sins of the world will challenge; but of the dead the sins of the world no longer liveth. Let us call upon the Lord our God and Creator that he witness the life; and that he make the life remain free from sin, that he watch over it and keep it in His Holy of Holies; and with the Sabbath of Sabbaths; and that he[or she, depending on the sex of the child] enter into Heaven on the Seventh Day after his[or her] soul slips into the Great Beyond. Oh Holy of Holies, Sabbath of Sabbaths, Lord God and Host of the children of Israel, it is beautiful all that you have created and all that you have made. It is peaceful all that you have done; it is joyful all that you have taught us. Be it then Oh God and Master Maker of the Universe and Giver of the Laws of your people - Israel..., etc., etc., etc.

READINGS FOR THE DEPARTED SOUL [Kaddish; from the Book Of The Departed Soul]:[1]
So was it created, so is it taken, so was it before, so is it now, and so shall it be forever more. The Lord our God and Host of the Universe gives life, and He takes life. He gives the breath from His body, and He takes it away as He alone had given it. Therefore as the body of this [sex of the child added

1. The African/Egyptian God of Resurrection - Osiris - dealt with the "Raising of the Dead" thousands of years before the Christian allegory about "Jesus' raising of Lazarus from the dead," etc.

here] child was given from the dust of the Earth, it hereby returns; and as the breath of this body's soul was given from the breath of its God and Creator, here has it returned. Hallelujah, Hallelujah, Hallelujah the Lord our God is ever present; He, and He alone, made man, and take man.

And all of the souls shall travel in Hell; but the righteous souls shall not dwell in Hell. And the unrighteous souls shall cry out to the righteous souls; REMEMBER ME AND TAKE ME ALONG. But the righteous souls cannot, and will not, for it is on the call of the Lord God and Host of the People - Israel. Then shall the righteous souls remain in Eden, and enter thereafter in the gates of Heaven, and shall live with God forever and ever. And they shall be blessed by the Holy of Holies; and they shall become of the Holy of Holies and the Sabbath of Sabbaths. Oh God and Redeemer, my soul awaits your call! Oh beautiful death, when shall I be called to enter into the House of my Father - the God of His people - Israel! It is better to be dead in the House of the Lord and of Life everlasting than live in sin everlasting. The death of the Lord is beautiful and sweet; but the life of mere man is bitter and of false sweetness.

I guess you will gather from the above extracts and quotations why it is that the Falashas and many other non-European and European-American [WHITE] Jews maintain the custom of not ... "MOURNING [crying] FOR THE DEPARTED"... in "KADDISH." But you can readily see that the teachings above and before set a psychological pattern whereby death is not considered to be "... MUCH MORE BEAUTIFUL THAN WORLDLY LIFE...;" but instead "...JUST ANOTHER STAGE OF LIFE...." Thus: LET THE DEAD BE OF THE DEAD, AND THE LIVING BE OF THE LIVING.

THE SEVENTH DAY PRAYER AFTER THE INTERNMENT OF THE DECEASED [extract from the Book Of The Departed Soul]:
And it came to pass that our brother [or sister] entered the gates of Hell but evil could not claim him, for he had lived a full life; and he had lived and married, using of the woman after marriage, and he has shown forth seeds of purity. [A woman would have the following said of her: she has married when she was virtuous of her virginity and brought forward children in purity]. He [or she] has now entered the gates of Heaven and live with our forefathers Abraham, Isaac and Jacob; and they with our Creator in the presence of the Messiah [and Messiah Theodore]. How beautiful have I experienced death; but how distasteful have I experienced wickedness of man on his earth which the Lord, God - YWH - of the House of the Children of Israel gave him. Glory, glory, glory be His name in the highest. His shall be the first and the first shall be His name. The last shall be His name, and His the last. From the dust of the Earth came Adam and Eve. And from the dust of the Earth came their seeds; and to the dust of the Earth shall they and their seeds return. It was so, it is so, and it shall always be so.

PRAYER OF THE WOMAN IN CHILD-BED[1] [extracts from oral traditional teachings]:
And it is the will of God. It was the function of my ancestral mother Eve; and it has always been the will of my mothers since. All women have, and all shall, sacrifice in the manner of my sacrifice. I have to make my sacrifice; and I am proud of the privilege given men. Blessed be the Sacrifice, and Blessed be the name of the Holy of Holies, and the Sabbath of Sabbaths that protect me, and walk me home to my God. I am the house of the life, and the life is my furnish-

1. This woman, although separated from the active community, remains in high esteem, physically.

ing. My womb is the Holy of Holies of the life. And my soul the conductor from the God of the children of Israel that creates this breath. Holy, Holy, Holy, Glory, Glory, Glory be the name of the God of His people - Israel. And by His name the children I bear shall increase the people - Israel. Blessed be the name of the God of my children - Israel.

PRAYER OF THE WOMAN IN THE HOUSE OF BLOOD [extracts from oral tradition]: For my body was unclean; and the Lord our God - YWH - has given me these days that I might cleanse myself, which is the house of my God and Creator of my body, as my soul. I shall be happy, and most proud, to cleanse and make pure that which the Lord my God has given me; for Holiness is Purity, as Cleanliness is Godliness. Blessed be the temple of my kind - the child of my mother - Eve.

I shall replenish Israel after I have cleansed myself. I shall use of the man, only with my clean body. Glory, Glory, Glory, it was always so, and it is so, and it shall always be so...,etc., etc., etc.

PRAYER OVER THE BATH FROM MALEDICTION BY THE WOMAN IN CHILD-BED AND THE WOMAN IN THE HOUSE OF BLOOD [from the Book On Cleanliness, or "Levitical Laws"]:
I have offered my sacrifice; I am cleansing myself of my sins and uncleanliness caused by the womb I have inherited from my mother Eve. Give me the wisdom that I shall keep your body you have given me clean as I am to keep it. I shall keep clean this body, and make a wholesome place where the sons and daughters of Israel may dwell until they have entered into the worldly life of mortal man, pending their return to our beginning.

Oh Holy of Holies and Sabbath of Sabbaths, clean my womb from the lust of man and make it a place from the purified soul of mankind. I ask of you Oh Sabbath of Sabbaths, you who are a woman-supreme to all women of cleanliness; you who never know uncleanliness; you who does not have to sacrifice, for you have not fallen to the lust of man. Oh! Glory, Glory, Glory be the name of the God of the children of Israel. I have been helped to cleanse my womb from the lust and the sin which it contained. I shall wash away all my impurities, and I shall again return to my manfolk of the children of the House of Israel; and I shall bear him more, for I am to multiply in abundance, increasing the people - Israel. It was so, and it is so, and it shall always be so; Blessed be the name of the God of the children - Israel.

PRAYER FOR THE ANIMAL SACRIFICE:
In the memory of the Sacrifice which Abraham made of his son I come to you my Father and God of the Universe.[1] This offering is but a lamb [or ox]; for it is your word that I shall offer my son as did our forefather Abraham. I offer with the love of my son, as my son will freely give on your command. Take as my son, keep as my son, receive as my son this humble offering O' Lord, God of our children - Israel.

I have received so much; but I can give but so little. I offer this lamb [or ox] in the name of Abraham. I offer life in your name, for you and to you alone belongs life.

---

1. This was said about God - Ptah, Amen-Ra, Amen, et al., for thousands of years along the Nile Valley and Great Lakes region before the origin of Ywh, Jesus and Al'lah, et al.

This lamb [or ox] is clean; and the blood of the woman in Child Bed or the House of Blood is not in the presence of the blood of the lamb, for no woman has entered in the presence of the Service of the Sacrifice; nor has she entered at the Service of the period of the Sacrifice; and she has not been a part of the Sacrifice on the mount. Lord, God and Maker of the Universe, Father of Abraham, Isaac and Jacob, take you my life and it shall be; spare me and it shall equally be.

The Burnt Ash is of the body of the lamb [or ox], and nothing unclean has touched it or passed over it. It is the First Male of its mother, who has given it at the eight day of its birth. It has been circumcised as a man does. It has been fed on the Sacrificial Grass ever since. It is a MALE, and it is of a clean birth. It has shown good skin; and neither it, or its mother, nor its mother's mother for seven generations before its birth, carried any sickness or uncleanliness not worthy for this Sacrifice.

The Sacrifice has heard the Sacred Musicians play their tunes; and your herald has sounded throughout Israel the people, for your Shofar [ram's horn from the last sacrifice before this one] has sounded and all your people - Israel - was warned of the Sacrifice of Abraham's son. Some have refused to recognize you; but those of us in your presence have listened. Oh Lord, God of your children - Israel, forgive them for they have taken unto worldly materials and prefer them. They have ignored your Laws and your People who follow them. They have said, and they are saying, that your Laws are old and outmoded. They have become, as they have claimed, too wise for the Laws by the standards which they have set for themselves in order that they may carry on their wicked deeds. They have made wars in your name; and they are still making wars in your name; yet, we say: Blessed Be The Name Of The One And Only Living God Of Your Children - Israel.

We offer ourselves in preference to the lamb [or ox] of Sacrifice to make them cease; we await your taking of our souls in your sacred bossom. [There is a period of silence for at least three minutes]. God, Father and Maker of the Universe we - ISRAEL ... have awaited your calling, but you have preferred our offering of this lamb [or ox] as our Sacrifice; and you have spared us from your wrath you hold for the wicked and those who preferred to wallow in sin and worldly pleasures. God, the One and Only True King of the People - Israel,[1] have mercy upon their wretched souls. Your words will prevail. It was so; it is so; and it shall always be so..., etc., etc., etc.

A MORNING PRAYER [before breakfast daily]:
God, Father, My one and only King and Host of your people - Israel - I have been blessed by your precious gift. Yesterday you allowed me to use your body, and retain my soul. Today you have allowed me to rise up one more time to spread the teachings of your WORD, and to be an example of your name. To live for you, and not for myself alone. To place material things below spiritual things; for you are the only everlasting, all others being only temporary.

I wake because of you, from the place of another world where I had slumbered into. You, and you alone, have protected me with your Holy of Holies and your Sabbath of Sabbaths; you have been my mother through my slumber; you who created Adam, made you Eve; and from them made you your children - Israel.

---

1. The "Chosen People" - Jews myth once again. This form or religious bigotry is the basis for Judaism, Christianity, Islam, and other religions directly related thereto.

I went to sleep and the Lord was there. I slept and the Lord was with me. I awoke and the Lord was there. I am fully conscious now, and I know that there is but one God, and He is still with me. Glory, Blessed, Hallelujah, the Lord and God and Lawmaker of the Universe and your children - Israel - lives with me. It was so; it is so; and it will always be so.

MID-NOON PRAYER [before lunch]:
I lived with the Lord from the break of my fast. I recognize the strength of the Lord my God. I must recognize my God and Creator. I have lived with Him, and breathe in the midst of His comforting arms. I shall now eat with His guidance; and I shall eat only that which you my Lord, God and Creator have directed me to eat, through the teachings of my forefathers before me. I shall not place anything whichis unclean in your body which have given me in a pure manner. So it was, so it is, and so it will always be.

EVENING PRAYER [before supper at Sun-Fall or sundown]:
I have worked a full day in the lust of man. I have not given myself completely to my God alone. I have worked to gain the love of my woman [if a woman praying she says: I have worked for the lust and favor of a man]. I have, therefore, sinned against you, for I have worked for worldly graces and not completely for your spiritual blessings. However, Lord, God and Host of your children - Israel, I have not broken neither of your Ten Commandments, for my lust was not of the evils of love. I have only thought of the woman [or women if he is married to more than one wife] who is my wife. The companion you have given me. [A woman say: I have always thought of the man who is my husband].

Contrary to foreign and local Christian Missionary propaganda, there has never been a case of "POLYANDRY" among the Falashas in all of their history. The Evening Prayer continues:

Now my God, My Creator, Creator of the Universe, King and Host of Israel,[1] I wish to eat of your meal, and at your table of the supper. I shall not waste of your food, for you have spared me to eat when many others are hungry. I have set a place at my table for the stranger at all meals; and I am hoping that he [or she] might appear and be taken out of his [her] hunger. I shall be to you, who already know, the giver of food to the hungry stranger before I shall be free of my own hunger; for I am full of the food of your grace; and I know that the food of the world can remain if you choose, and you have; and I will still be fed; but does the stranger know this of your presence? O' Father in your Heaven, God and Creator of Heaven and of Earth, your name shall be forever, and I shall live forever in your name, for I have remembered you always. When I have eaten, I lay me down into your arms; and you shall, as you always have, direct me as you desire. Take me home, or leave me here. It has always been your life, your food, your world. It was always so, it is still so, and it shall always be so. Blessed be the name of the Lord, the One and Only God of your children - Israel.

One has to remember that the Falashas, as all other religious groups that form a so-called "ETHNIC" ... socio-political compact around their THEOSOPHY and THEOLOGY, have created and developed many original TEACHINGS, TABOOS, TRADITIONS, etc. they [WE] have associated with JUDAISM or HEBREWISM down through the more than five thousand seven-hundred and

1. All "Creator God" concepts came from the "Created Universe" claim by each culture's Godhead.

forty-four [5,744] years of biblical history - from ca. 3759 B.C.E. [the year one - 1 - of the Hebrew or Jewish Calendar] to the present year 1983 C.E. of the Christian Calendar, or 5742 of the Hebrew Calendar. This is the reason why European and European-American TALMUDIC JUDAISM differs so greatly from the Africans and Asians' TORAHDIC JUDAISM. Yet Hebrews [or Jews] who practice the latest type of Judaism demand that those who practice the earlier type "MUST CONVERT" to their own style and/or VERSION of Eastern and/or Western European "ORTHODOXY." Needless to say that the vast majority of Falashas have not succumb thus far; and do not so plan for the future. A review of the article on pages xxxii and xxxiii of this volume with regards to the Falashas "RECONVERTING" to European and European-American [WHITE] Judaism a-la European style will perhaps make us forget that the BLACK ones on the following page are not equally Jews as the WHITE ones who control the Government of Israel. But maybe we are to forget that it is from scenes like the following that the Hebrews' SACRED TORAH became a reality. Yes, it was Africans like Moses and thousands before and after him that were educated along the banks of the Blue and White Nile who gave us the basis for GENESIS.

Yes, the scales of "JUSTICE" based upon a concept of a "GOD OF THE UNIVERSE" existed, and was practiced in Africa for thousand of years before the birth of the first Hebrew - Abraham - in about 1680 B.C.E.[1] The scene above is extracted from the PAPYRUS OF ANI and THE EGYPTIAN BOOK OF THE DEAD; both dates back to at least ca. 4100 B.C.E., which was at least three thousand four hundred [3,400] years before the first line of the SACRED TORAH was written [ca. 700 B.C.E. to 500 B.C.E.] as the Pentateuch or Chomesh [Five Books of Moses].

1. Nile Valley High-Cultures from Uganda to Egypt-created the foundation for Judaism. Check The Egyptian Book Of The Dead and Papyrus Of Ani.

ONLY TWO ON THIS PAGE IS NOT OF THE HEBREW RELIGION

3. Elder Harold Grey from Youngstown, Ohio, delivering a lecture.

YEMENITE BEAUTY

A COCHIN JEWISH G...

PLANES BROUGHT THOUSANDS OF YEMENITE JEWS TO ISRA...

Ethiopian Noble

Ethiopian Subject

Ethiopian Subject

ALL OF THESE BELOW ARE "SEMITES" AND/OR "HAMITES"[1]

Emperor Lidj Yasu of Ethiopia,
deposed by Ras Tafari Makonnen
(Emperor Haile Selassie).

A 3rd Century B. C. E.
Caucasian European

GREAT SPHINX OF GHIZEH

Amharan Women Of
Royal Status In Addis

Rabbi Abraham and Falasa
("Jewish") students of Gondar, Ethiopia (East Africa)

1. Both "Semites" and "Hamites" came from Judaism's racist teachings in the First Book of the Five Books Of Moses/Genesis, all of which deals with the "Great Deluge" detailed in R. Graves and R. Patai's Hebrew Myths: The Story Of Genesis, MacGraw-Hill, Co., New York, 1972, p. 220.

YES!!!ALL OF THESE ARE OF THE "SEMITIC" AND "HAMITIC" RACE

An"Hamitic" Vendor In The Market

Tigreno Religious Drummer

Ethiopian Christians At An Easter Festival

Amharan Religious Official

Father and Daughter Ethiopians In Traditional Garments

ETHIOPIA'S "BLACK MESSIAH"[1]
[Why is this image missing from African churches today?]

JESUS "The Christ": LORD OF THE UNIVERSE
by
Ethiopian Artist - Walda-Maryan - 17th Century, C.E./A.D.

1. This "Black Mesaiah" existed for hundreds of years before Mantegna and Michaelangelo drew their first "White Mesaiah" during the 15th and 16th Century C.E./A.D. The latter for Pope Julius II of the Roman Catholic Christian Church - from 1509 to 1511 C.E./A.D. See pp. , - , etc. of Y. ben-Jochannan, Our Black Seminarians And Black Clergy Without A Black Theology, and The Black Man's Religion and Extracts And Comments From The Holy Black Bible [3 Vols. under one cover]. The "Black Madonna" appears in the above works, and equally in Y. ben-Jochannan, Black Man Of The Nile And His Family, pp. 491-493 [1981 Revised and Enlarged Edition]. Why is a "straight nose" not African as it is European? See Y. ben-Jochannan, They All Look Alike! All Of Them?, Vol. I and II, for African people with noses longer and straighter than millions of White People.

THE FALASHA FAMILY,
STRUCTURE AND FUNCTION: Chapter VI, Part One.

Like all other Black Hebrews [or Jews] throughout the entire world A [so-called] "FALASHA" FAMILY is the center of his worldly living, and everything must be centered around his family life. Because of this truth we must open the family pattern at the beginning of two people's [male and female] union in infancy up to the time when it becomes a family unit with children, father, mother, grandparents and ancestors, etc., etc., etc., ad infinitum.

The selection of the opposite sex [female] in the Falasha communal communities [other types are not considered here] is generally conducted in the following manner: When a girl reaches of her twelfth [12th] birth anniversary [birthday] she is proclaimed by her parents and the entire community to be of marriageable age and ready for courtship. In many of the villages she can take unto herself a husband at this age. However, you must remember that at this time a Falasha girl at age fourteen [14] is similarly developed physically as a twenty [20] year old girl in the United States of America. At the age of 14 the usual manner of selection of a mate by her parents and the "match-maker" begins. This practice is dominant in all of the communities for the pairing-off of the boys and girls; age 16 for the boys and 12 for the girls.[1]

If the girl is living in a community which is based upon the general economic scheme of the national government of Ethiopia, her parents and those of the selected boy, also the match-maker, plan for the marriage arrangements. If she is living in a communal economic type of society, which is the most common amongst Falashas and Kylas, her match-making at the age of 12 is made by the Elders, the parents of the selected boy and those of the selected girl. The parents act as advisors to the Council of Elders on the marriage plans.

A boy is eligible for marriage after the celebration of his twelveth [12th] birth anniversary [birthday]. Before his marriage, he must make his Confirmation [Barmitzvah] in the Hebrew Faith [religion]. The age 12 is given by the Sacred Torah [Five Books Of Moses] to establish the time of reasoning for one's self, and the reaching of manhood from that of a boy. After his Confirmation the young man is entitled to get married. But a young man generally becomes engaged in the same manner described in the situation of the girl. He would not be allowed to marry until he is about seventeen [17] years of age. At this age the average Falasha male resembles a twenty [20] to twenty - three [23] year old African-American young man.

You have already seen that for a marriage to take place under general religious tradition the girl must be at least twelve [12] years of age, and the boy fourteen [14] years of age. However, this would be misleading to leave what is just said at that; for the actual truth is that the average

1. Typical of agrarian societies of tropical or hot climates people often marry in their mid-teens.

normal marrying age in the communal communities is fourteen [14] for girls and seventeen [17] for boys. These ages are considered by the Council of Elders to be "safe age limits;" the period when a young man and young woman are deemed "...

> able to decipher the normal problems and economics of their society. It is the age when they can undertake the responsibility of raising their children with the necessary Hebrew religious education, which the children of the communities must have and know...," etc.

Before there is any "courtship" permitted, the two parties so interested must submit themselves to the Council of Elders for a complete examination of their families' background. They are also examined for the detection of communicable diseases like "leprosy" and "yaws." The examination of the females are never done by male Elders; neither are the males examined by matured women. The couple is also questioned for any trace of mental incompetence.

If the parents had not selected a match for their son and/or daughter at the age prescribed when they had such authority and responsibility, then the youngsters can select their own mate whenever they have arrived at age sixteen [16] for the female and nineteen [19] for the male as described above. The selection can be made by either the male or female. What this also means is that a female can be the aggressor in letting the male know that she is in love with him, and that she would like to have him court her for the purpose of matrimony. This is normally the case when families do not facilitate a match for their marriageable daughter by her twelfth [12th] birthday or son at his fourteenth [14] birthday.[1]

COURTSHIP AND MARRIAGE: Chapter VI, Part Two.

We have seen from the last section we read that a young man or woman may be the aggressor in making their affection known to each other. We are now going to follow a young couple from the time when one makes the offer and it is accepted by the other. Both parties have agreed they are feeling sufficiently infatuated spiritually and physically with each other and they go directly to his and her parents, telling them what they had agreed upon. The respective parents get in touch with each other and set a date when they can meet together with the "Marriage [Match] Maker." The Marriage Maker is the man who advises the parents on the wisdom or lack of wisdom of the selection made by the loveones. He is the person who will make all suggestions to the parents to the length of time he thinks the youths should court each other before getting married. The Marriage Maker never receives any renumeration if he lives in a communal community. He is paid in the non-communal communities.

The first match-making meeting takes place in absence of the young man and young woman

1. Parental approval must precede all marriages in all Falasha communities or there can be no marriage whatsoever. Parents have control of their children from birth all the way to death.

who are planning to begin courting each other. A second meeting is called if the families have agreed on the wisdom of the selection. By the way, the young man cannot be rejected for any reason other than for contagious desease and mental illness, or if the young woman decided to become a member of the Sisterhood instead. Also, the young man cannot be rejected unless he planned to join the Priesthood if he is of the Tribe Of LEVI,[1] or if he was afflicted by a mental or contagious disease. Either party must be rejected if there was any case of "ADULTRY" ever committed in either of their immediate families. This refers to their mothers [from whom they inherited their Hebrew origin], father, grandparents for seven generations back, etc. At this second meeting the man is told:

> "...you have been accepted by your suitor's parents. You are, therefore, entitled to visit your fiancee after sunrise to before sundown any and every day except on the Sabbath and High Holy Days...."

The time of Sunrise to Sunfall is about 7 : 00 A.M. to 6 : 00 P.M. This is more or less the normal time when the sun rises and sets over Ethiopia in the sections where most of the Agaw [Falasha and Kyla] communities are located. The sun-lit day begins when the SUN has risen over the great [highest] peak of the communities; and the sun-dark night begins when the SUN has subsided behind the lowest mountain peak.

Let us follow the young man in his glee on the way to visit his sweetheart [you may call her whatever name you feel suits the situation]. When he arrives at the door of her house he calls her father and announces his arrival. The girl's father, if he is at home, appears at the door and gives the young man a great embrace around his shoulders and invites him to "...enter my son in love...." He [the young suitor] calls upon the girl's mother, who is anxiously waiting beside her daughter. He kisses the girl's mother on her forehead. He cannot kiss the girl in any manner whatsoever. Remember that at no time until the date of their marriage will the young man be entitled to kiss his intended bride anywhere; and that these two people are not in an American community. Ethiopians kiss the side of each other face three times on each meeting.

Her father announces:

> "My house is open to the young people in love. All business of the household must be concerned only with this matter of my son of love and my daughter."

The male suitor is allowed, at the most, two hours of courtship-calling each time. May I interrupt by stating that the hours a suitor generally calls on his intended is around the two last hours before the Sun-Fall.

The seating arrangement of the fiances is with the girl's father and mother seated in the center chairs; the girl on the side of her father, and the boy on the side of the girl's mother.

1. This "tribe" provides the scribes for the Falashas. They alone write new Sacred/Holy Works.

Her father generally asks the boy about his parents, and about the health of the older folks in his family. Then he explains the general health of the girl, her mother, grandparents and himself. After this is over, they entertain any conversational subject involving only the two young people in love. The girl's parents never interfere from this point on. They only sit and listen most attentively. They will only interfere if the conversation begins to touch on any sexual topic which is not on a very high educational level. It is only natural that the parents should speak if they were asked questions by either of the two fiances. The visit is completed at the end of the hours allowed the young man for his courting. The goodbye greeting is somewhat similar to the arrival greeting; thus:"Salam" [Shalom or Peace]. It is always said upon the entry of any house, and upon leaving. It is the greeting anywhere for meeting and leaving. After the suitor bids goodbye to the family of the girl he may take any course of action he may have planned.

From this "...first official visit..." the young man [boy] pays the young woman [girl], she is considered "...officially engaged..." to the young suitor. He has the right to prevent all other men in the communities from speaking to her, if he has any belief that his interest in her may be damaged. She, in return, has the same prestigious right against any other woman in the communities whom she believes challenges her chance of being married to the young man. From the first official visit of the suitor the girl is placed under the strictest surveillance. She is not allowed to meet the young man in any other place than in her home; or at a place where there are grown adults of her blood relation, at least an aunt or uncle. No other relative further away in kinship is considered; not even her uncle's and/or aunt's children of mature age.

The courtship does not permit any "Western" type premarital form of love-making. No kissing, necking or petting is permitted under any circumstance. This rule was ordered because of the temptation which such practices cause, thereby resulting in a girl losing her "physical state of virginity." For if a girl loses her "PHYSICAL VIRGINITY" before her first marriage, the right of her intended allows him to have the marriage annuled when he discovers her condition. She will be charged with being an ADULTERESS, and thereby suffer immediate expulsion from the community. The responsible male is equally expelled. The latter rule against petting, etc., eliminates a high degree of the temptation which results in the loss of "PHYSICAL VIRGINITY." I must state now that this rule is very effective, only because the girls have always lived by it most religiously. Historically the percentage of girls being sent away from any community due to the above reason is so very low it is almost nonexistent. We do not take census on anything of this nature in such cases; but if we did, it would read something like 99.99⁰/₀ of all Falasha girls throughout all of the communities on their first marriage are "PHYSICALLY A VIRGIN." It

1. Falashas do not accept "the rupture of the hymen by biological accident" theory as a just excuse for a girl's lack of virginity on her bridal night.

is a rare occasion indeed to hear of physically unvirtuous cases; and whenever there has been one, the entire population talks about it for such a long time that any stranger would believe there was about to be a catastrophic dilemma in that particular community. All of the Falasha Mothers place a sort of "RESTRICTIVE COVENANT" on their daughters for quite some time whenever such an incident occurs.

The parties in a courtship must attend "Marriage Counseling Classes" conducted under the auspices of the Council Of Elders. They must take classes in "RELIGIOUS EDUCATION FOR THE FAMILY" conducted by the Subordinate Priests. The girl has to attend classes conducted under the guidance of the Sisterhood. She will learn the needs for the birth of an expected new-born child and other matters pertaining to child-bearing and child-raising after child-birth. The type of instruction she receives covers her entire community LIFE and INVOLVEMENT. It includes education, health and dietary laws, laws on cleanliness, etc.

The next step for the prospective bride and groom is meeting with the "Young Married Couples Group." There the girl will go to the men and the boy will go to the women. They are told everything pertaining to a family's sex life, beginning with physical sexual intercourse to the do's and don'ts which come before and after the girl's menstrual periods. The girl is instructed by the men on the manner in which a man expects his wife to act; and the boy is instructed by the women on the things a woman expects of her man. The group then meets jointly with the two fiances [bride and groom]. They are allowed to ask questions directed to either sex partner of the Young Married Couples Group. These meetings take place in the open air at evenings, generally on early moonlit nights.

The period of the Woman In The House Of Blood is explained, and its reasons evaluated. The girl is told that:

> "Nobody in the community will ever look down upon you with shame while you are in either the House Of Blood or the House Of The Woman In Child-bed, because such houses are places of honour in the community; and you should be proud that the mercy of God has credited you with the honour of producing children of Israel."

He is told that:

> "Your expectant bride in these conditions is unclean only in the sense that she cannot be used sexually; but she is spotless and free from any sin due to that uncleanliness; and whatever comes from her during such times is due to the will of the God of His people - Israel." [1]

This is but one of the many reasons why a woman in the House Of Blood would sit and speak to a passing Falasha male or female and not feel ashamed of her condition. In such situations she

1. This isolation is total to the point where husband and wife do not share a common bed at such occrrences. Falashas consider any form of sex play during this period utterly unclean and ungodly.

feels proud that she should be so fortunate to be reproductive once more.

The young man is told:

> "You are the head of the household, and as such you are responsible for the protection of your family; and you must at all times maintain this responsibility. You must treat your wife in the manner whereby she would be more than willing to obey your commands."

She is further instructed that:

> "You must always obey your husband;as your devotion to him is one of foundation and not of leadership. You are the administratrix of all matters not connected with the duties of the head of the household. You must not wear the garments of your husband in private nor in public; equally you must not allow him to use any of your garments likewise."

They are both told:

> "The seal of matrimony is not always a happy one in the eyes of man; but it is the most glorious in the eyesight of the father of all men, the God of His people - Israel. For it is God's delight to have His children binded together; and anyone who destroys His pleasure by committing adultry must suffer in obscurity [hell] and shall never enter the hereafter [Gates of Heaven] with the rest of the people from the communities of the children of Israel."

The young couple is instructed on many other pertinent points of the marriage life they are about to enter. They are told why they must make their marriage as happy as they possibly can. The Young Marriage Couple Group wishes them -

> " a great future full of religious devotion, an abundance of children to strengthen the bonds our people, and long life to enjoy your descendants."

The marriage engagement is never concluded in less than one [1] year and six [6] months to a maximum of two [2] years and nine [9] months. Under no circumstance can a wedding take place before one [1] full year of at least ten [10] Lunar months of courtship.

The marriage is performed with other young people being equally married. These couples are lined up in what is called "The Marriage Festival Procession,"[1] which is one of the greatest of all pageants of the entire year in any Falasha community. It is a scene of beauty which no other can surpass; at least this is what the Falashas believe. The description that follows is based upon a Marriage Festival Procession[2] in any one of the communal communities. In the other non-communal communities there is but one difference than in the communal communities; that is, the non-communal societies have to enjoy whatever the individual couple and their families can afford to spend towards their own marriage; whereas in the communal communities the entire adult male and female population evenly contribute to the marriage of all of the brides and grooms to be joined in the Bond of Holy Matrimony.

---

1. Due to the ever-diminishing number of Falashas in Ethiopia the procession is very limited now.
2. This pageant is for the glory of the brides; it celebrates their chastity and virtue, etc.

A week is set aside for all marriages pending to be performed and celebrated. This week is called "THE MARRIAGE FESTIVAL." It can take place in any month except July to September, which is "NISAM." Musicians, cooks, bakers, carpenters and all other needed craftsmen must contribute their services to the preparation of the MARRIAGE FESTIVAL. The entire population concentrates on nothing else but this festivity. The preparations begin three or four days before the actual "PROCESSION" begins. These three days are set aside for the preparations of the various foods, drinks, etc. of the festivities - which involve washing, peeling, cooking, pickling, baking, bottling, etc. In some communities as much as five days used to be required for these tasks.

On the beginning of the first day of the "MARRIAGE FEAST" and "MARRIAGE FESTIVITIES," which comes on the first day of the week [Sunday], Falashas from various villages gather around a special place in one of the villages where the festivities are to be held. Not a single person is specifically invited to the MARRIAGE FESTIVAL, which belongs to all of the Falashas in all of the communities. It is a week of general feasting in which all of the members of the communities must observe and help to make a gala and most successful event. This custom is sadly leaving the Falasha scene by virtue of economic pressures forced upon my people through the efforts of the Central Government of Ethiopia and the Jewish "missionaries" who are trying desperately to make Falashas European-type "Jews" like themselves; except for "color" and/or "race."

The brides and grooms are lined up in two separate rows according to sex - males on one side and female on the other, the way they will march in the "MARRIAGE PROCESSION." They march from the center of the designated village in single file to the outside of the House Of Worship [Synagogue]. They continue until they are directly at the "ALTAR" erected on the outside under a "CANOPY." Each couple meets at the Altar as their names are called by the High Priest [Tellek Kahain]. The High Priest follows by reading the "MARRIAGE BLESSINGS." He asks each couple:

> "IS IT YOUR WISH TO BE JOINED IN HOLY WEDLOCK? DO YOU KNOW OF ANY REASON WHY YOU SHOULD NOT BE JOINED TOGETHER IN THE MANNER FOR WHICH YOU ARE BOTH HERE?"[1]

When all of the brides and grooms have passed the Altar, having answered the questions, the High Priest turns and asks the entire gathering:

> "DOES ANYONE AMONG YOU KNOW ANY REASON WHY ANY OF THE RESPECTIVE COUPLES GATHERED HERE SHOULD NOT BE JOINED TOGETHER IN THE HOLY SEA OF MATRIMONY AS PER YWH's LAW?"

He pauses for about five [5] minutes at least to await the voice of the stranger who has come to make an objection. If there be no objection the High Priest has certain Subordinate Priests [Kahain] take each couple's hands and place them crosswise, thereby forming a symbolic union between both parties. He then recites the "MARRIAGE VOW " while each Subordinate Priest rests

1. This is only traditional, as there is no record of anyone taking advantage of this opportunity.

his hands on the heads of a bride and groom symbolic of the biblical marriage of Jacob's own grandchildren and blessing of them. The MARRIAGE VOW is very similar to your own VOW recited by rabbis and ministers in "Western" societies of Europe, Great Britain and the Americas. The congregation recites special prayers in unisence with the High Priest leading them. He blesses the couples, and the entire congregation sings the "SONG OF THE NEWLY-WEDS." The festivities are proclaimed to be open, and all members of the communities follow the "MARRIAGE RECESSION MARCH" back to the center of the designated village for the MARRIAGE FESTIVAL [review layout of normal communal village on page 102 of this Volume]. Each couple's parents are congratulated by the opposite spouse's parents. The couples return to their individual homes to become involve in -

"THE MOST SOLEM OFFICIAL SANCTION OF THE MARRIAGE ACT"

because a marriage is not considered COMPLETED by the mere ceremonial activities. Each couple must make their marriage "OFFICIAL" by their participation in PHYSICAL SEXUAL INTERCOURSE, which is for all purposes:

"THE FINAL ACT OF OFFICIAL SANCTION OF THE SOLEM
MARRIAGE VOW BETWEEN THE BRIDE AND GROOM."

Just before Sun-Fall [sundown] on the day of the MARRIAGE SERVICES the father [or male guardian] of each bride takes her to the home of her respective husband. Her father leaves her in the custody of her husband. There, at the home of the husband's family, she must surrender her body to her husband. He "...MUST PHYSICALLY USE OF HER...;" and he "...MUST PROVE TO HIS SATISFACTION THAT THE GIRL WAS VIRTUOUS AS SHE CLAIMED TO BE...." If she is found to be "VIRTUOUS" her husband tells his father. But his father tells her father if she had been "...FOUND OTHERWISE...." All "HELL" breaks loose if she is found "UN-CHASTE."[1]

On the following morning the girls' fathers and general population [or congregation] gather at the center of the designated village to hear of the "PROOFS." If the girls were found to be "VIRTUOUS" the fathers of the boys walk to the fathers of the girls and embrace each others affectionately; then they do likewise to the girls' mothers. If a girl was "FOUND TO BE IN EFFECT OTHERWISE only" the father of the boy calls upon his son to tell the High Priest about the manner in which he found her. The High Priest immediately summons her parents to remove her from the company of the others, and to produce her for "EXPULSION PROCEEDINGS" on the day after the first ensuing Sabbath. Generally all wives produce their "PROOF CLOTH" or "PROOF SKIN." It is considered "...PROOF WHEN THE MALE GENITAL ORGAN ON CONTACT IS NOT ABLE TO PENETRATE THE HYMEN...," and by "...THE SPATTERING OF BLOODSTAINS FROM THE VAGINA ON THE WHITE LAMB'S SKIN..." that is placed under the bride during the

1. This tradition has been attacked by "Westerners" as "male chauvinism," etc. But does not in any way bother Falasha theosophy and culture, etc.

"PHYSICAL ACT OF SEXUAL INTERCOURSE." It is solely the groom that decides how she was found. She has the right to a "...PHYSICAL EXAMINATION BY A MIDWIFE..." if she feels that the groom has lied when, and if, he claims that:

"SHE WAS NOT VIRTUOUS; AS I FOUND HER TO BE UNCLEAN."

The MARRIAGE FESTIVITIES get underway after the PROOFS are submitted to the fathers and they notify the High Priest, who in turn proclaims the "PROOFS" to the general population that congratulates the parents of the brides and grooms. Immediately following these last two acts, drinking, dancing, story-telling, eating, teasing of the brides and grooms about life, etc. become the order of the five [5] days ahead. No drunkards are permitted; thus the grape wine is rationed sparingly. If any person shows sign of so becoming, he or she would be refused any more of the wine spirits. The drinks are of beer and natural fermented wine with no additives as in WINES made in the United States of America- even by Jews. There is roast meat from cattle, goats, sheep and fowl. The MARRIAGE FESTIVITIES become that much more exciting as the days roll along to the end of the Sixth [6th] Day. All kinds of Kosher food find their way to the stomachs.

There is one day of interruption when the MARRIAGE FESTIVITIES must come to a definite stand-still. That day is the "...FIRST SABBATH AFTER THE MARRIAGES...," which is in fact the Seventh [7th] Day after the MARRIAGE CEREMONIES." This is caused by the fact that the first day of the weddings begins on Sunday - the first day of the week, And "...THE MARRIAGE FESTIVAL MUST LAST FOR NO MORE THAN SEVEN [7] DAYS..."- all inclusive of religious obligations. This figuring brings us up to the SABBATH DAY. No dancing, marriage or drinking is permitted on the SABBATH DAY, not even the burial of the deceased; therefore the "MARRIAGE FESTIVITIES" must be interrupted from Sun-Fall FRIDAY to Sun-Fall SATURDAY for the SABBATH SERVICE, which equally marks the end of the "MARRIAGE FESTIVAL; etc.

On this "FIRST SABBATH" after the MARRIAGE CEREMONIES the new brides and grooms must attend the "FIRST SERVICE OF THE YOUNG MARRIED COUPLES GROUP" and receive "THE BLESSINGS FOR THE EXPECTED CHILDREN TO ENTER THE MIDST OF YOUR FAMILY." Following the "BLESSINGS" the service is typical of all regular Sabbath Day Services.

After the service ends the High Priest [Tellek Kahain], Monks [Maokse] and the Subordinate Priests [Kahain] congratulate the husbands for their "...WONDERFUL CHOICES...," and the wives for the "...SPOTLESS LIFE..." they have lived until their marriage.[1] The wives are instructed that they must always"...

> CARRY ON THE HONOUR OF WOMANHOOD TO YOUR DAUGHTERS IN THE MEMORY OF THE VIRTUOUS MAIDENS WHO COMMITTED MASS SACRIFICE [suicides] RATHER THAN LAY DOWN THEIR BODIES FOR

1. Polygamy is legal even though it is seldom followed; particularly in contemporary N.W. Itiopi.

THE PLEASURE OF THE SOLDIERS OF THE GENTILE AND MOSLEM ARMIES. AND TEACH YOUR SONS TO CHERISH THIS HONOUR AMONG OUR MOTHERS, DAUGHTERS, SISTERS, GRANDMOTHERS, AND ALL OTHER WOMEN, EVEN THOSE YET UNBORN AND TO COME...."

On the last day of the MARRIAGE FESTIVAL festivities - the CLEAN-UP DAY, which is the day following the "SERVICE OF THE YOUNG MARRIED COUPLES GROUP [Sunday]," the woman [or girls]-to-be "... EXPELLED FROM THE COMMUNITIES FOREVER..." is called to confront her [or their] accuser [s] and the general population - who will hear the charges and evidence. She is told to "...

LOOK AT THE OTHER GIRLS WHO WERE NOT WILLING TO LOSE THEIR HONOUR AS YOU HAVE DONE IN DISGRACE DUE TO LUST...."

After the charges are read, and she cannot offer any acceptable justification for her unfaithfulness to her suitor, she is ordered to "...

REVEAL THE NAME OF THE MAN WHO DEFILED YOU...."

Then she, along with the man that committed the "rape" on her, is by forceful means ordered to -

"LEAVE THIS COMMUNITY, AND ALL OF THE FALASHA COMMUNITIES, WITH NOTHING MORE THAN WHAT YOU ARE PRESENTLY WEARING; NEVER TO RETURN AGAIN, EVEN WHEN YOU ARE DEAD."

After they [she and the man that defiled her chastity] have passed through the gate of the village the aftermath of the MARRIAGE FESTIVITIES continue for the last day, with the musicians and the story tellers [court jesters] at their best until the entire festivities come to an end at Sun-Fall. This, because the communities have purged themselves by the honour of the VIRTUOUS WOMEN who maintained their PHYSICAL VIRGINITY TO THE DAY OF MARRIAGE, and because of the "EXPULSION OF THE GIRL [or girls] WHO DISHONOURED HER SUITOR [s]." The following day is kind of a BACK TO NORMAL TIME in all of the villages of the communities, the time when everyone must be back to the business of their full tasks assigned them according to TRIBE and/or CASTE, etc.

When everything subsides and the communities have recovered from the festivities, each BRIDE returns to the home of her husband's family -

"TO REMAIN FOREVER UNTIL HER FINAL BREATH."

In fact, at this stage she is -

"THE DAUGHTER OF HER HUSBAND'S ENTIRE FAMILY."

And at all times she must -

"TAKE ORDERS FROM HIS PARENTS LIKE HE HAS TO DO."

The eldest male member of the household of her husband's parents would still be considered the "HEAD OF THE HOUSEHOLD OF THE ENTIRE FAMILY," she and her husband included. In otherwords, she becomes a true "...DAUGHTER OF LOVE BY MY SON..." which I mentioned at the outset of the MEETING and COURTSHIP of the two people in my demonstration of a Falasha couple.

If the in-laws home is too small to accommodate the incoming bride a new house is added to the existing home by the craftsmen of the village at no cost, providing it is a communal society; the craftsmen must be paid in money if it is a Falasha village in the Gentile or Moslem areas. At all times the sole "AUTHORITY" of the eldest male in the family-unit also extends to this new household, even when the house is detatched from the main building of the in-laws.[1]

The traditional design [style or trend] of the building plans of a new house for a new couple in the communal communities must meet the following details; thus: A room for the husband and wife alone, and one for the expectant "...MALE CHILD...." However, it is only natural to understand that if a girl arrives first she is not thrown away. Moreover, since girls outnumber boys by a ratio . of at least 5 to 1 in Falasha communities, there is adequate assurance that there will be more than enough GIRLS to go around. Next is a "...

> ROOM FOR THE WIFE TO WITHDRAW WHEN SHE IS MAKING PREPARATIONS FOR HER DEPARTURE TO THE HOUSE OF THE WOMAN IN BLOOD;"

this period being estimated as at least -

> "THREE DAYS BEFORE THE BEGINNING OF THE MENSTRUAL FLOW."

You have followed the COURTSHIP and MARRIAGE in a Falasha community. Would you have liked to try it? Do you think that the girl who loses her PHYSICAL VIRGINITY before her first marriage should be treated as she is in our Falasha communities, which is very similar to other "African communities" in this respect? Do you have an equal taboo in your own communtty where you live with regards to "PHYSICAL VIRGINITY" and "MARRIAGE" as "A WAY OF LIFE," etc.

These TRADITIONS I have mentioned are so old that they have become the basic foundation, along with the SACRED TORAH, upon which Falasha Communities live and die. The concepts for them are from very ancient teachings; and they revert back to periods even before there was the first BOOK in the SACRED TORAH during biblical times, even before there was the earthly Father of ISRAEL and/or JUDAISM,...ABRAHAM or AVRM [Abrm, etc.]. Since they are pre-biblical TRADITIONS, and you also profess biblical leanings, it is certain that you will understand the above reporting I have done on this aspect of the cultural heritage of my people - the so-called "FALASHAS OF ETHIOPIA, EAST AFRICA," correctly the - AGAW OF ITIOPI, ALKEBU-LAN.

What you have just read is very common amongst many of the other cultural groups of Ethiopia in terms of the pressures on the females during the period before their "FIRST MARRIAGE."

1. Every Falasha woman must live where there is a Falasha man to protect her; thus there is no single woman living alone by herself. She must be connected to a family unit.

CHILD-BEARING AND CHILD-BIRTH: Chapter VI, Part Three.

After the courtship and the marriage comes the pregnancy. When it has been acertained the expectant mother is permitted to continue enjoying her husband sexually until the seventh [7th] month of said pregnancy. But, at the end of the seventh month "...SEXUAL INTERCOURSE MUST CEASE... " according to Falasha morality, religiousity and obstetrical care. The expectant mother must withdraw to her own quarters from this period until her first labor pains begin, or the fluid in her placenta erupts and discharges.

At the beginning of her first labor pains she is carried to the HOUSE OF THE WOMAN IN PLEASANT BLOOD [yäräs gogo]. This House is located on the outside of the West Gate of the community, as shown on the plan of the village on page 103 of this Volume.Upon leaving her home for this House the expectant mother will be escorted by a pair of well-trained MIDWIVES - normally members of the Sisterhood. The midwives and the expectant mother MUST remain at the House Of The Woman In Pleasant Blood until the delivery of the child.

While in the latter House the expectant mother is permitted to "...EAT ANYTHING EXCEPT MEAT...." The reason for her not being able to eat "MEAT" is based upon the "BLOOD SACRIFICE" she would be making. The Falashas evaluation of this point is that:

> "THE BLOOD FROM THE MEAT AND THE WOMAN DELIVERING A BABY WOULD BE BLENDED TOGETHER; THEREFORE, THEY WOULD BE REJECTED BY THE SABBATH OF SABBATHS, FOR THEY WOULD BE UNCLEAN."[2]

This point is strictly theosophical; and it was developed by the LEARNED MEN [Däbtärä] just as European and European-American rabbis [learned men] developed theosophical teachings based upon their own interpretations of the Sacred Torah and influence from their Christian and other Gentile countrymen and countrywomen -- here in the United States of America is the best example.

There is a messenger assigned to each expectant mother in the House Of The Woman In Pleasant Blood, also for the Woman In The House Of Child Bed. The messenger, who is always a male, cannot enter the House with the expectant mother and the midwives. His major duty is to carry food from the community to the midwives and women in the two Houses. He also runs other errands which are directly in connection with the midwives'functions. His last mission in all cases is "...

THE ANNOUNCING OF THE BIRTH OF THE NEW-BORN CHILD TO ALL...."

If the child is a MALE the messenger enters the community through the East Gate. He walks to the center of the community, and he calls the women of the community to gather around him and announce the "BIRTH OF A BOY." The women shout words of joy for the new -born male child

1. This conclusion is of Falasha Theosophy; which, of course, does not ape "Western Philosophy."

twelve separate times; thus:

"OUT OF THE HOUSE OF THE WOMAN IN CHILD-BED A SON."
[Yarakat goolo kis sat]

If a female child is born the messenger enters the community from the West Gate. He walks to the center of the community. He calls the women to gather around, and then publishes the news of the BIRTH OF A GIRL. The women shout words of their joy for the birth of the new-born female for nine [9] times; thus:

"OUT OF THE HOUSE OF THE WOMAN IN CHILD-BED A DAUGHTER."
[Yäräkät goolo kis sätä].

After the day of the infant's birth the mother must remain at the House Of The Woman In Pleasant Blood for forty [40] days if a MALE was born, forty-one [41] days if a FEMALE is born.

If a boy is born the midwives and the messenger take the infant to the Mohel [the religious surgeon]. The Mohel CIRCUMCISES the boy on the eighth [8th] day after his birth. The infant's father must be present at the "CIRCUMCISION;" but he is not permitted to stand nearer than twelve [12] feet from the Mohel and the boy during the CIRCUMCISION RITUAL; even if touching the little fellow meant the difference between his life and death.

If a girl is born, she will be carried to a woman on the day selected by her mother to have an "EXCISION" made. A man is never permitted to make, or even be present at, the "EXCISION." The operation consists of pricking the outside of the girl's VULVA at a distance of at least one-quarter [1/4] inch into the entrance of the orifice of the vagina. No disturbance of the HYMEN; none!

The philosophy and theosophy behind the "EXCISION" is one of a series of special developments that is typical only to the communities of Ethiopian Hebrews [Kylas, Falashas or Black Jews]. It is unknown amongst Hebrews in the West - Europe, Great Britain and the Americas. It is symbolized in the historical "HONOUR OF THE MAIDENS" who committed "MASS SACRIFICE [or suicide] RATHER THAN SUBMIT THEIR BODIES TO THE INVADING GENTILE AND MOSLEM ARMIES THAT RAVAGEDWESTERN ETHIOPIA" in past wars. It is also a reminder of the VIRGIN'S obligation -

"TO REMAIN PHYSICALLY PURE IN BODY BEFORE HER FIRST MARRIAGE."[1]

If the "EXCISION" did not take when it was made on the infant girl, she will have to take another at the age of nine [9]. The "EXCISION" is also proof to the men of the community that she is a member Falasha. This latter point does not mean that she will have to exhibit herself to the men in order that she might prove her status in the community. What it does mean is that upon her first marriage the man who becomes her husband will have "PROOF" that he is not going to

"....USE OF THE BODY OF AN UNCLEAN WOMAN...."

1. Chastity, as a major principle Falasha morality is frowned upon by the "Women's [white] Movement."

At the end of the fortieth to forty-first day during the new mother must remain in the House Of The Woman In Pleasant Blood she must take a thorough RITUAL BATH [Mikvah]. She will leave this HOUSE at midday and take a walk with her new-born child around any area not closer than three [3] feet perimeter about the community. She must await the Sun Fall [sundown] of that day. At the beginning of the Sun Fall she leaves her position and proceeds to enter the House Of The Woman In Child-Bed [woman lying]. After she enters this latter House, she must place her child to rest and immediately take a "BATH OF PURIFICATION." This "BATH" is prepared from certain HERBS and ROOTS of many trees and also of sweet scented flowers [zaze]. After she has done this, she will return to her baby and prayer for her "SOUL" and that of the infant. She thank God - YWH - for allowing her to pass through the "HOLY OF THE HOLIES" and the "SEA OF THE SABBATH OF SABBATHS." The "SABBATH OF SABBATHS" in this instance refers to

"....THE DIFFERENCE BETWEEN LIFE AND DEATH...."

In this House the mother remains for twelve [12] days if the infant is a boy, and fourteen [14] days if it is a girl. This waiting period is called "THE PERIOD OF CLEANLINESS AND REST." It is a "PERIOD" whereby the community can prepare to have a post-natal midwife at the mother's home, to provide for her and help with the care of the infant if she is a first-timer. There is also a female attendant who will be sent to take care of the family for at least thirty [30] days in order that the new mother would be able to give her entire devotion to the care of her child.

Some of the above and following TRADITIONS have passed away in many villages frequented by missionaries - both Jewish and Christians - who forced their own VERSIONS of morality, culture, prenatal and postnatal care on our people. I know I am repeating; but the fact of the destruction of another African group and their cultural heritage by virtue of "CULTURAL GENOCIDE" always need repeating with respect to the danger signs. This is the case with the so-called "WHITE JEWS" always trying to change these TRADITIONAL CUSTOMS of the Agaw, and in place add their own VERSIONS and TRADITIONS as God-given "INTELLIGENCE." But the beautiful TRADITIONS of my people will continue so long as those of us who are aware of what is being done to destroy them defend them;[1] even when we may have gone away ourselves because of various reasons.

If the new mother has any flow of blood after the twelveth [12th] day or fourteenth [14th] day, she is suppose to remain in the House Of The Woman In Child-Bed. She would have to remain there under treatment for at least three [3] days after the blood has stopped.[2] If she is in proper health, which is required of her, she will start to prepare herself for her return to the community and retake her place amongst her people.

1. You must be mindful that Falasha Traditions in many instances have no equivalent examples.
2. The biblical prohibition is in the Book Of Leviticus of the Holy Torah, which Falashas follow.

She has to wash herself completely again at the beginning of Sun-Fall with the same kind of sweet-scented Zäze [herb] bath as she had done when she was to be transferred from the House Of The Woman In Pleasant Blood. She must also shave her hair, and wash all of the clothing she used while living in the two houses awaiting her baby's birth, and after its birth.

After she has completed the above duties, she will proceed to a special place outside the West Door of the Synagogue marked-off for women. Here she prays to God for the favor He has granted her in allowing -

> "my child to pass through the Holy Of Holies of my womb and into this world."

She thanks God - YWH -

> "for the honour of allowing me to bear a son [or daughter] for a man of Israel."

She also asks God to -

> "take my life rather than that of my child in any emergency, for I have lived and enjoyed all the fruits of joy, which was climaxed by my producing a life into this world of Israel."

She further requests that -

> "the father of my child continue to guide me as he has always done to this day."

That both she and the father of the child -

> "be remembered by the Sabbath Of Sabbaths, when they are to enter the Hereafter...;" and that "...our children be at our side on that wonderful day of judgment...," and complete with "...Our Father's Prayer...."

After she has completed the prayers mentioned above, she starts on her journey of reentering the community. Upon entering the community she is met by her husband and his family. The oldest member of her husband's family takes the child from her and delivers it to her husband. This is the first time that her husband has ever placed his hands on his little infant son [or daughter]. The women of the community again render the shouts of the "NEW-BORN" mentioned before, for the same amount of times necessary for the sex of the infant.

The infant is carried to the home of its parents for the first time.[1] Here a Subordinate Priest, relatives and friends would be at the house awaiting the arrival of the New-Born. When the mother enters the door she is hugged by the mother of her husband.[2] Her mother thanks her for the new joy she has brought into the family. Both families became one by virtue of the commonly shared child.

The Priest calls the family and friends to gather around the infant for the reading of prayers from the MAGICAL BOOKS [ärdě'ět]. Different pages are read, each to suit the sex of the infant. Next, the Priest blesses the home and the infant. He makes a speech on the need of affection which the child requires. He reminds the family that:

---

1. The child's sex determines which set of grandparents will see it first; and who will name it.
2. Sometimes the mother sees the child after most of her family members have seen it.

"You are still required to bring up the child in the strictest manner in which any Hebrew child must be brought up." [They sing an Ethiopian Lullabye.]

Now the Priest bids the gathering "salam" [shalom, peace or goodbye]. The Family and friends continue their get-together as long as they desire within the day.

The infant is turned over to the supervision of the post-natal midwife for the period mentioned above. He [or she] is returned to the full control of his mother after such time as is necessary for post-natal care.

From the instance when the child is returned to the control of the parents they are completely responsible for his [or her] training and upbringing.

Before the mother can return to any sexual activities with her husband she must await the passing of **24** menstrual periods after the birth of her child. This means she would have to return to the House Of Blood for at least 24 times before she can resume physical sexual intercourse with her husband. It includes all of the forty to forty-one days there after her child's birth

After she starts sexual relations with her husband she may become pregnant again, and the entire procedure outlined above would be repeated on each succeeding occasion.

REARING OF THE CHILD: Chapter VI, Part Four.

The child is the center of the family's orientation in the communal communities. Due to its being the center of attraction, it requires certain specific rules under which it must be guided. This set of rules is laid down by the head of the household [the oldest member of the family] who is always, at least generally, a grandparent of the new-born infant child.

In this arrangement the child has also to obey the father and mother of its natural birth.[1] The child is corrected by the mother if it is a girl. If it is a boy he is corrected by the father. This is generally opposite to the "Western" rule which states that:

> "The girl is the closest to her father, and the boy closest to his mother;"

this I have already shown in Chapter V under the heading of "Teachings On Morals By Falashas."

The "Western philosophy" governing the theory in the last paragraph above is as follows:

> The girl will be able to prepare for her father in the event of the death of her mother. Whereas, the boy would be able to protect his mother at the death of his father.

It is also believed that:

> "The dominant sex in a child comes from the opposite sex of the parents."[2]

For example, this is the basic belief:

> "The girl-child receives her sex from her father; and the boy-child receives his sex from his mother."

1. The grandparents have more rights of control over the child than even the natural parents, et al.
2. Scientific reasoning does not play any part in this theosophical reasoning "from God - Ywh."

All of this is contrary to Falasha morals and ethics, as shown in Chapter V, pages 152 - 157.

The "AUTHORITY" of the household can be shifted from the oldest member therein to the child's father. This is the general custom in the communities.

The first thing the child is taught in the line of education is his [or her] religious indoctrination - that which is comprised of prayers for eating, drinking, sleeping and all other natural functions of the child's biological needs. After prayers the child is taught the "TEN COMMANDMENTS" until it could be rehearsed from memory. The "GOD OF THE UNIVERSE" prayer is also taught with the TEN COMMANDMENTS jointly. This training starts about the SECOND [2] YEAR of the child's formalized education. At about the FOURTH [4th] and FIFTH [5th] YEAR the child should be able to rehearse the above teachings. You may safely state that the child learns to respect God - YWH - before he [or she] learns to respect his [or her] own natural parents.

The child is introduced to the social graces of the communities at AGE FOUR [4]. These graces consist of teaching the need for respect of all children older than him-[or her] self; and that all grown adults are superior in respect to older children; also, that at all times older adults must be obeyed in preference to older children, etc.

The child is taught that:

> "Your father and mother by birth are only the medium through which a child must enter the world; but all of the men and women in the community have the same authority to guide a child."

The child is further told that:

> "Upon this [latter] basis you will be corrected verbally and physically by adults if you are ever unruly."

The children of the communities are brought together at this tender age of FOUR [4] to be taught the reasons for the paramount respect of the Priests. They are told that:

> "The Priests are the holders of the Laws Of God; and as such you must follow the teachings of the Priests above your own parents on all religious matters; but follow your parents above anyone else on all other matters."

Dietary habits, sleeping habits, and all of the necessary cleanliness, etc. are taught at age TWO [2] up to age NINE [9] YEARS for all children.[1]

The formal age of education begins at FOUR [4]. At this age the children have at least TWO [2] HOURS of schooling per day. The FIRST [1st] HOUR in the morning religious stories are taught. Stories such as the "PASSOVER, JOSEPH IN EGYPT, KING SOLOMON AND THE QUEEN OF SHEBA " and others of the major myths. They are told in a manner feasible to their tender minds. The SECOND [2nd] HOUR in the afternoon the children are taught the names of things and places surrounding their community, and about the community in which they live. Things such

1. They are subject to the control of all adults of the communities. Age 12 marks adulthood for all.

as poisonous bushes and weeds, names of animals, birds, trees, and others which children this AGE-GROUP would be normally interested to know about.

As the children progress in age their religious and secular educational training increase. The children remain in this system of education until they are about SIX [6] YEARS of age. After they have passed the minor age limit they are expected to attend the general public school of the local Government. That is only if there is one nearby the community where the children live. The Government Schools must be very near the community, because Falasha children must eat food which is cooked only by Falashas in their communities. They must also return to their communities by Sun-Fall at the latest each day. They must wash themselves thoroughly before reentering their communities each day at a place set aside for this purpose [review Plan Of Communal Village, Chapter III, page 102].

At the government's schools Falasha children learn all methods of education available to any of the other Ethiopian children. There is no SPECIAL EXCLUSION and/or DISCRIMINATION against Falasha children in the government's schools today. Recently a few of the schools have gone out of their way to establish methods whereby Falasha children would not have to use anything, or act in any manner, contrary to their religious customs and traditions.

Sometimes there are schools nearby the communities which Falasha children alone attend;[1] but these situations are very rare indeed. The general procedure is to send the Falasha school children to the nearest government operated school. These children in the communities who are unable to enter government schools because of one reason or another are given instruction by other Falasha children in upper grades when they return to the communities following their regular school hours. There are a few formal schools in the communities, but they cannot keep up with the new facilities afforded the children of the government schools. And as a direct result of this they are generally as much as TWO [2] GRADES behind the children in the government owned/operated schools.[2] To offset this gross difference the students in the communities' schools meet with those who are attending government schools and do their homework together. This condition at present is gradually decreasing; but it has contributed to the amount of Falashas who are now returning from government colleges to their own communities. In the past these students were taking jobs with the Ethiopian Government in Addis Ababa upon graduation, and they remained in their positions without ever returning to visit their communities. Only once in a while one of them would return to visit his family, or to take a brother or sister away to college upon his own return to his government post. I have already stated that this practice is not general today, for the situation is rapidly reversing itself. The reason for the difference in attitude can-

1. The former Imperial Government of Ethiopia treated Falashas with "benign neglect" constantly.
2. Religious knowledge is superior to Secular knowledge among Falashas everywhere on earth.

not be attributed to any specific cause. However, it is the general community's belief that:

> "Falasha students have met with such success, and received so many honours at the government colleges, that we are now realizing that we must return and bring our own schools up to par with the government's; for as such we will be that much better off socially, politically and economically."

It must be equally noted that Falasha students who majored in engineering and science courses have seen the need for many changes to meet the so-called "INDUSTRIAL REVOLUTION" that is presently under way in all of Ethiopia. But most, if not all, of them are very careful to remind themselves that no pressure will be tolerated to force changes upon the communities whenever the Elders and Priests have ruled that they will ruin the religious life of our people. They realize that their people would be left in an uncompromising position if they are caught lagging behind the rest of the Ethiopian poor who are moving to rid themselves of the FEUDAL SYSTEM imposed upon them by the Central Government's monarchist landlords. Yet, they equally realize that the COMMUNAL AGRICULTURAL SYSTEM their ancestors created has basic merits which any industrial economy they follow must adopt; as it is certain that even the "CAPITALIST SYSTEM OF THE UNITED STATES OF AMERICA" cannot satisfy the communal way of life that is necessary for their religious obligations as they interpret them.

Falashas attend schools of higher learning when they have finished lower grade government schools. However, an insignificant amount does this today. The children of the Falasha communities are not responsible for this dilemma, because they are anxious for higher educational opportunities as children in the United States of America their own ages are, the same being equally true for children in Europe and Great Britain. The parents of the Falasha children who feel that...

"FURTHER SECULAR EDUCATION WILL ALIENATE US FROM OUR RELIGION"...

are the same ones who are equally responsible for so many that refused to take advantage of certain scholarships awarded unusually bright Falasha students; particularly girls.

A few Falasha students who are standouts in local and international prestige are men such as the late Professor Tamrat Emannuel. He served as the Cultural Attache of the Ethiopian Embassy, Paris, France shortly following World War II, and was once an Examiner in the Ministry of Education in Addis Ababa. He was also the one, and only, Head-Professor and Director of the HEBREW INSTITUTE in Addis Ababa, Ethiopia -which is presently defunct. Another was the late Hon. Atto [Mr.] Taddese Yakob,[1] who was Director of Customs of the Ethiopian Government. He was noted for his "TREATISE ON THE LEAGUE OF NATIONS." These two, and a host of other Falashas, held cabinet positions in the Royal Government of the Empire and Kingdom of Ethiopia.

1. He is currently encarcerated because of his role in leading Falashas to Israel and back home.

There were jobs in government where Falasha graduates could not secure functional positions due to discrimination, as it must be remembered that the KEBRA NEGASTE [Ethiopian Chronicle Of Kings] recites that:

> "ALL OF THE KINGS OF ETHIOPIA MUST BE LINEALLY DESCENDANTS OF THE HOUSE OF EMPEROR MENELIK Ist, SON OF KING SOLOMON OF ISRAEL AND QUEEN MAKEDA OF ETHIOPIA [EMPRESS OF SHEBA]."

If such is not the case, the absense of said "HEBREW ORIGIN" legally deny anyone the right of rule under the Ethiopian "GOVERNMENT'S RIGHT OF SUCCESSION."[1] This is a fact that equally forced the former Emperor, His Imperial Majesty Haile Selassie Ist, to reject Israel's proposal that the Falashas "...

RETURN TO ISRAEL IN MASS MIGRATION...."

WOMEN IN THE COMMUNITY: Chapter VI, Part Five.

Apart from religious restrictions and duties a Falasha woman can take part in all of the activities her man enjoys. She can enter, or open, any conversation in public or private. She can give her opinion or decision on any subject which her husband or family has initiated. She can take part in any skill where extreme physical force is not a necessity. She is a full and equal partner in all social intercourse within her community.

The highlight of a Falasha woman's life is her activities with other women and their communal groups [equivalent to the Synagogue's women auxiliary]. In these groups she takes part in the making of varied items for the Sisterhood and her Synagogue. She also makes various items for the aged and the infirmed. In the women's groups she also relaxes from her daily tasks with the social activities developed by themselves.

She joins committees for rendering assistance to families when they are without their woman of the household. This is particularly true during the period when the woman of the household had to go to the HOUSE OF BLOOD or HOUSE OF CHILD-BED. This committee also prepares for the entrance of the "NEW BORN INFANTS" by making clothing and other necessities for them.

She takes part in many sports in which her man does not take part. One of the major activities of which she is denied is "HORSEBACK RIDING." However, married women are not forbidden from this sport, even though they do not engage in it. This sport, like a few others where there are body contacts, is restricted to all maidens for the purpose of protecting their PHYSICAL VIRGINITY.[1] Due to this restriction the women are not verse in the skill of riding; therefore, you will not find one amongst them who can sit on a horse in very fast motion. Horse racing is one of the biggest events in Falasha entertainments, also of the entire Empire of Ethiopia.

---

1. Falashas don't accept any modern medical theory with regards to "ruptured hymen;" sex alone.

The wives of the Subordinate Priests take part in all of the activities the other women of the community enjoy. They are generally the initiators of most of the women's activities; and they also maintain a higher educational standard than most of the other women, because they are required to keep abreast of their husbands in almost everyone of the areas of activities in which they engage themselves. One of a Priest wife's activities is the constant research in the field of education, both religiously and secularly. Therefore, it is understandable why the wives of the Priests are generally further advanced in education than the other women of the Falasha communities. They are equally the women of the communities after whom most of the other women model their lives and that of their daughters. Quite naturally many of the young girls would also like to become the wife of a Priest, as this is one of a few ways in which she can obtain a higher education than the average girl can without having to attend one of the government's schools away from her village. On this point it is to be remembered that there is but a very minute amount of Falasha women who ever leave their communities for any purpose whatsoever. The women of the Falasha communities will not travel to places where there are no Falasha men to look out for their physical and general welfare. Before we leave this area, it should be noted that:

"A PRIEST CAN ONLY HAVE ONE WIFE AS LONG AS HE LIVES."

A "divorced" or "annuled" Falasha woman in the community retains her respect and status she had before the dissolution of her marriage. However, if the DIVORCE was due to ADULTRY she would be "EXPELLED" from any community. Also, if the "ANNULMENT" was due to her loss of "PHYSICAL VIRGIN STATUS" before her first marriage she would be equally "EXPELLED" from any community. These two points have been elaborated upon in details before in Chapter VI, "Courtship And Marriage," pages 180 - 190.

A woman who has never given birth to a child after SEVEN [7] YEARS of marriage is considered "BARREN" [unable to bare a child]. She could secure an annulment of the marriage if her husband consents. This does not mean that she must have given birth to a "BOY CHILD," as is the case in a Mohammedan [Moslem or Islamic] marriage.[1] Any birth whatsoever will remove this ineligibility from the woman's right to annulment on the claim of being "BARREN." Yet - her husband can initiate the action independently, even without her consent.

Each woman of the Falasha communitiy wears a "NECKLACE"[2] [string of beeds] before and following her marriage. This NECKLACE shows the woman's marital status. Any man in the community can detect a woman's marital status by noticing the color and design of the NECKLACE she is wearing. If she is wearing a "red composition" necklace she is married; if "red and black" she is a widow or divorced person; and if "varied in other colors" she is a maiden. It would be

1. About one-half, or more, of the Ethiopian population are Moslems; maybe the majority!
2. Signs and Symbols are still part of the Falashas communication system even to this very day.

worthwhile for you to know that the man does not wear any symbol to show his marital status. Many of the villages of the various communities today have abondoned even the custom of the woman wearing the "STATUS NECKLACE." And some Falashas can be seen wearing the so-called "MARRIAGE RING" and/or "WEDDING BAND" introduced to them by "Jewish Missionaries."

The women of the Falasha communities, communal or non-communal, are very proud of their husbands, and always can be heard boasting about their love for each others. Each woman takes great pride in her "CLEANLINESS" and "METHODS OF PURITY." She believes that:

> "The Falasha woman living in non-Falasha communities are unable to be as clean, because they had to adopt customs that are contrary to the Levitical Laws of the Sacred Torah, Chapters 12 and 13."

She also maintains that:

> "The special ritual bath of purification a Falasha woman must take after child bearing is required of all women whatever they may be; or the woman so failing to wash would remain unclean of her blood."

She always consider herself to be the criteria for all womanhood, and a center of the community. Her theory on this latter point is that:

> "I must give birth to the men of the communities; thus it is my power over them, because I become responsible for their very existence."

If you understand Falasha tradition and culture you will know that she is absolutely right in this latter theory; because the men in the communities treat their women with such grace and respect that they are correct to feel the way they do in this case. A man in the community would be almost lynch if he should sit at any time while a woman awaits a seat in his presence. All of the men MUST at all times protect their women before themselves in all emergencies, the same being true for all of the children under the age of maturity ["twelve years old" according to the Sacred and Most Holy Torah].

Women in the communities have rejected the introduction of BRASSIERES, GIRDLES, HAIR PIECES and other forms of such femenities used by women of the so-called "Western World" [Europe, Great Britain and the Americas].[1] The theory which the women of the Falasha communities placed behind their rejection of sold distortion of their actual physical appearence is that:

> "these things are false, and make the woman lie to herself and her husband. They tend to create conditions for permiscuity and adultry. They show distaste for the manner in which nature has formed human beings. And it is vulgar for a woman to purposefully point her breast in a position whereby she would be personally attracted; and as a result of said action cause men to notice her, when they would not have done so normally."[2]

The physical appearance of the women of the Falasha communities is similar in dresswear

---

1. So-called "Christian Missionaries" have tried to introduce these "western clothes" to Falashas.
2. Jews, Christians, Moslems, et al, do not condemn these sexy contrivances of distortion, etc

to other women all over Ethiopia and other parts of Alkebu-lan [Africa], but with one exception. Many women of Gentile communities throughout Ethiopia at times dress in so-called "Western" clothes, particularly in dresses with low cut neck that show the outline of the breasts. This type of dresses is definitely banned by Falasha women inside and outside of their own communities. Dresses which stop less than THREE [3] INCHES above the ankles are never worn by Falasha women. Their colors are varied; but white dominates. Most of the materials used in making them are generally hand-woven. It is customary to have them embroidered with yellow and green on a white background, some spots of red are also common in the basic designs. These colors are arranged in a manner whereby the dresses would not have to look drastically gaudy in appearance. Materials used in the dresses MUST have been produced in the communities where Falashas live. A type of SHAWL is also worn in the higher regions of Ethiopia by women of every cultural group to break the rather bleak climate that sometimes cover the Highlands of Ethiopia around the Rift Mountain Range. The average Falasha woman's WARDROBE consists of at least THREE [3] to FOUR [4] DRESSES, plus SHAWLS and UNDERWEARS. She has quite an abundance of UNDERWEARS; because Falasha women, like Falasha men, are required to change their entire garment at least once every day. The latter point is even written in the traditional laws and customs of the Agaw people, all of which comes from the interpretations out of the Levitical Law On Cleanliness in the Sacred Torah. And since the Falasha woman must take a minimum of at least TWO [2] BATHS each day in order to keep her body clean, they are not considered to be the same as those she must take when in the HOUSE OF THE WOMAN IN PLEASANT BLOOD - which is called "RITUAL BATH" or "MIGVAH."[1] This is one of the many reasons outsiders refer to the men and women of the Falasha communities as the "...DON'T TOUCH ME PEOPLE...." It's insulting.

A Falasha Woman's grooming, particularly her "HAIRDOS," is ordinary to most of the women of the general community of Ethiopia, and equally typical of hundreds more throughout all of Alkebu-lan [Africa]- some of whom I have shown on the following two pages. Of course each woman tries to develop her own special styles. Some of the "HAIRDOS" in the present AFRICAN-AMERICAN [Black] COMMUNITIES today in the United States of America had their origin amongst the Falasha women as well as women from other parts of the continent of Alkebu-lan. The following "HAIRDOS" speak for themselves. They are from Central Africa - ZAIRE;[2] Northeast Africa - EGYPT [or TA-MERRY] and ZETI [or NUBIA]; West Africa - NIGERIA [or OYO; East Africa, also SOUTH AFRICA [or MONOMOTAPA]; and the UNITED STATES OF AMERICA. The only Falasha on the following two pages is No 7. But the only so-called "NEGRO WOMAN" is the only African-American WOMAN - No.1. Strange, is it not? Like the other women of Ethiopia and other parts

1. There are "migvahs" in every Orthodox [white] Jewish communities in the United States of America
2. The original name for this African nation is NZAIDE; Zaire is the name of a major river in NZAIDE.

ETHIOPIAN WOMEN HAIR-DOOS[1]

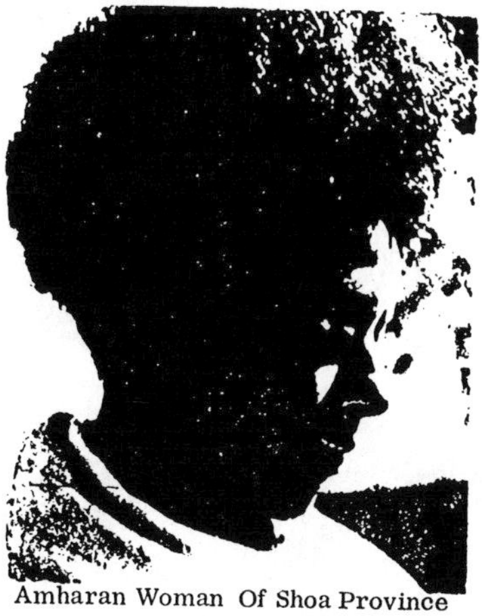

Amharan Woman Of Shoa Province

Galla Women In The Market

Tigreno mother and child at Atsbi

Tigreno woman of the City of Tigre

How Are They Different To Their Ancient Indigenous Egyptian Sisters ?

Note that not a single one of the above women is considered a so-called "NEGRO" by any of the European and European-American anthropologists, ethnologists, palaeontologists, etc.; they are classified as "SEMITIC, ITIOPIC, NILOTIC, CUSHITIC, HAMITIC, SUDANIC," etc. Moreso, they are of "a different race"; this is what we are still being told by so-called White Liberal Africanists who equally hold to the same for other African peoples of the South Pacific Islands.

ONLY ONE IS A "NEGRO"! THE OTHERS ARE "HAMITES, SEMITES", ETC. ? [1]

1] Ida Smith, U.S.A.; 2]Malagasian; 3]Sudanese of the Nile Valley area; 4] Ann Zingha, Queen of Matamba [Nzaide or Zaire]; 5]Bronze Head of Oyo [Nigeria]; 6] Zulu Princess, Monomotapa; 7] The only Falasha and 8] Selassie'sdaughter; 9]Mangbetou, Queen of Nzaide; 10]Tusi Princess, Rwanda. Who made these classification: White racist academicians or religious bigots of Western Society?

"HAMITIC-SEMITIC WOMEN"!!! AND THEIR NILE VALLEY STYLES HAIR-DO[1]

Two Ethiopian Young Women. Which One Is The Semite; Or The Hamite????

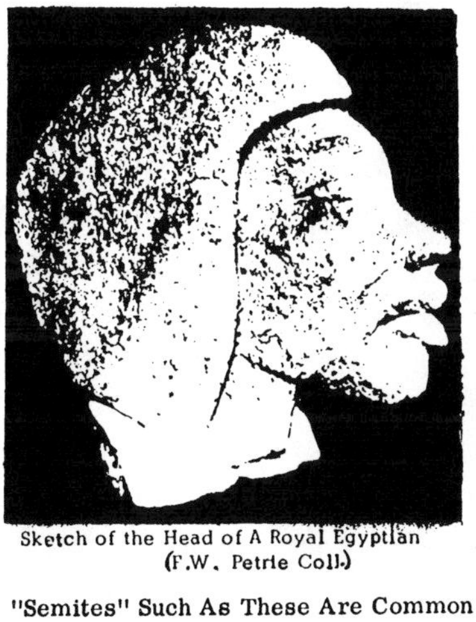

Sketch of the Head of A Royal Egyptian
(F.W. Petrie Coll.)

Egyptian Woman

"Semites" Such As These Are Common All Over The Harlems Of The Black World[1]

1. Throughout this and the following Report there are African/Black Women of Papua New Guinea, the United States of America and the rest of the "Americas", Africa, etc. who are typical of these: "They All Look Alike"! This is what we were told before by "Western Academia".

of Alkebu-lan Falasha women use certain types of FACIAL MAKE-UP, but no LIP STICK and/ or EYEBROW PENCIL PAINT. Any painting of a Falasha woman's face is strictly for religious services only. Why? Because she believes that:

> "Any form of mechanical beauty for the purpose of making myself appear attractive just for the purpose of causing a man's attention is unfair to myself, and deceiving to the man. This is beyond what I owe my people."

The Falasha woman washes herself with an extract from a root named "ZAZE." It is also used to sprinkle her clothing, and to keep her body from bad odor which she might develop during her daily task in the hot sun. It is also used in the RITUAL BATH OF PURIFICATION I have mentioned before. It has the same significance in this manner as a DOUCHE has to the American woman after the completion of her menstrual period. This root-extract has a fragrance somewhat similar to the Jasmin flower.

Women of our Falasha communities never permit NECKING, PETTING and any other form of PHYSICAL EXPRESSION OF LOVE while they are in public places; whether it be from their husband or fiancee. This is strictly taboo in all of the African High-Cultures known to this author.

When a man wishes to greet a Falasha woman on the streets of the village he must do so by mere words. If she is in the presence of her husband he MUST greet her husband first; then with the husband's permission he may continue further to greet her. He is permitted to shake her hands by the wrist, she in return responding in like manner. The two hands make contact with the palms covering the ball of the hands with heal to heal and the grasp of the fingers around the wrist. The HANDCLASP GREETING method is the same when two men meet. When a woman meets another woman the greeting is made by throwing their arms around each others and giving a warm embrace; also by giving each others a cheek to cheek [side of face] press three times.

A woman can study any professional art or science and practice same; providing she does not have to use garments designated for men only. Also, providing it would not cause possible bodily harm to her, or require extreme physical exertion on her part. But most of all, providing she does not have any children under the minimum age of maturity as prescribed by biblical law and tradition, which is normally at age TWELVE [12].[1] Any job outside of her community which requires that she does not return before Sun Fall [sundown] is not acceptable under any condition.

We have seen the Falasha woman in most of the living conditions she faces in her daily routine. She is very much like all of the other women of her country, except that certain religious obligations separate her from many of the activities they indulge in, which because of said restrictions she is set aside; not to any discomfort on her part. For the Falasha woman is a very happy woman in her religious devotion to her husband, children, and definitely her God - YWH.

1. Between ages 12 - 13 is the actual time of maturity for a Falasha boy to manhood/Barmitzvah.

MONOGAMY AND POLYGAMY: Chapter VI, Part Six.

On the question of POLYGAMY vs. MONOGAMY the Falashas quote as their justification the LEVITICAL LAWS ON CLEANLINESS; thus:

> "When the woman-kind is ill of blood, she must not be used; but the other must replace her. Three [3] days before and after her blood is isolated."

Falashas have concluded that this means -

> "there is more than one wife required in a household according to the Torah."

But, it is equally a warning to the men that they -

> "should not use of any woman during her menstrual period; at any time."

The Law further states very clearly that:

> "Under no circumstance is a Falasha man allowed with a Woman In Blood."

This shows that there is more than one wife required in a household. It is further accepted by all of the Falashas in all of the communities, communal and non-communal, that:

> "THE SACRED AND MOST HOLY TORAH SANCTIONS POLYGAMY." [1]

When we read about the HEBREW PROPHETS and SAGES of the past in any section of the most SACRED TORAH [Hebrew Bible, Five Books Of Moses, Pentateuch, and even Old Testament] we find that they were married to many wives, thereby maintaining POLYGAMOUS UNIONS. Abraham, Isaac, Jacob, Joseph, Moses and other biblical personalities had many wives. Of course the master of this practise [according to the same source], was KING SOLOMON of Israel. He had at least "...ONE THOUSAND WIVES AND CONCUBINES...." This is shown in the religious book of our past history. And that was done by the man Hebrew and Christian, equally Moslem, Religious History claimed to have been "...THE WISEST KING THAT EVER LIVED...." But if he was "...THE WISEST KING THAT EVER LIVED...," then we can understand the reason why the Falasha, Yemenite and Cochin Jews maintain the biblical practise of POLYGAMY; for it is the conduct of "WISE MEN"- according to the MOST SACRED SCRIPTURES of biblical history by the above mentioned people - so-called "Israelites" and/or "God's [Ywh or Jehovah] Chosen."

Polygamy has been totally maligned by most of the "JEWS" throughout European-American and European societies. But it must be remembered that JEWS and CHRISTIANS [who are now looking at this practise with scorn] ancestors not to long ago practised the same type of POLYGAMY. Christians all the way up to the Nineteenth [19th] Century C.E. in European-America, like the "MORMONS," practised it legally. For it was not until the late Nineteenth [19th] Century C.E. that the MORMONS, or LATTER DAY SAINTS, in the United States of America were ...PROHIBITED FROM PRACTISING POLYGAMY..." in any State of the United States Of America ac-

1. The relationship of a man with more than one legal wife among Falashas is accepted at all times.

cording to "CONGRESSIONAL ACT. March 3, 1887; U.S.R.S1. SUPP. 568; and U.S. SUPREME COURT CASE, 186 U.S.1. Jews in the Americas, Great Britain and Europe practised POLYGAMY at least up to the Ninth [9th] Century C.E. in Germany when Rabbean Gershom made the following announcement:

> "I AM GIVING UP ONE OF MY TWO WIVES AND ACCEPTING THE PRACTISE OF MONOGAMY, WHICH IS THE CUSTOM OF THE GERMAN STATE."

This was not only the "...custom of the German State..." at that period in European Christian development, it was the beginning of the outgrowth of the effects of the industrialization that was raping Western Europe and Great Britain; the so-called "Christian Church" and its officialdom being no exception to the rule of accomodation brought on by the capitalist economic revolution.

Falashas answer those who say;

> "POLYGAMY IS THE PRACTISE OF MEN WHO EXPLOIT THEIR WOMEN,"

with the following rebuttal:

> "The women of Falasha communities who live in polygamous unions are the only persons who decide whether there is to be polygamy in their own household. It is the woman's right to accept or reject any polygamous union in her household. If she rejects such a suggestion on the part of her husband he must abide by it, and cannot show her any outward expression of his displeasure with her decision. If there are many wives in the household, they must all agree unanimously before another wife can be added to their household."

There is no extra portion of money [or share] which a husband receives because he has a polygamous union. You will remember it is already shown that -

> 'Falashas in the communal societies share and share alike, communally. Each adult is entitled to one adult share only. And no person shall deal away his [or her] share to anyone for any special favor whatever."

Therefore, it can be readily seen that the husband of a POLYGAMOUS UNION has no material gain from such a marital status [see Chapter VIII, "Economics Of The Communities," pages 220-229, and elsewhere in this Volume].

Let us look at this subject from another perspective. There are amongst our communities a ratio of at least 5 - 6 females to 1 male in the total Falasha population - both communal and non-communal. And since BARREN WOMEN and/or CHILDLESS WOMEN[1] are not so highly cared for, this creates an extra amount of women who would not be able to marry if MONOGAMY was the custom of all Falashas. Plus, we have the fact that:

> "UNMARRIED WOMEN IN FALASHA COMMUNITIES CANNOT LIVE IN HOMES BY THEMSELVES" [shack-up like millions of Western women].

Another point to be considered is that a Falasha woman who had "SEXUAL INTERCOURSE" before the benefit of a "FIRST MARRIAGE" is disgraced and "EXPELLED FROM HER COMMUNITY," etc.

---

1. These women are still considered the most respectable; no stigma of disgrace do they suffer.

There is still another angle in which to look at this issue; the latter condition is never tolerated in any of the Falasha communities, neither in many hundreds of other African communal and non-communal communities in Alkebu-lan [Africa or Afrika]. This type of punishment is not easy to risk [review "EXPULSION" or "EXCOMMUNICATION," Chapter VI, pages 181 - 190].

The people of our Falasha communities also defend their POLYGAMOUS behavior by stating, without any remorse whatever, that:

> "There is no law against polygamy in the Sacred Torah, neither is there any on monogamy. But there are many directed suggestions in the same Sacred Torah and Holy Scriptures which support polygamy against monogamy."

Upon these biblical suggestions Falashas based our POLYGAMOUS practise as a moral right as much as is the practise of MONOGAMY. Again, everyone should refresh our memory with the "LEVITICAL LAWS ON CLEANLINESS" [review Chapter VI "Child Bearing and Child-Birth," pages 191 - 195].

We know that the homes of "POLYGAMOUS MARRIAGES" are happy and stable in the Falasha communities in spite of all that is said unfavorably about POLYGAMY by the inexperienced opposition. But it has never, and can never, be truthfully said that:

> there are as many broken homes in cultures where polygamy is the order of marriage as in "Western Societies" where practicing monogamy is the only legal manner of marriage.

It is also noted that the amount of MURDERS and other SERIOUS CRIMES OF VIOLENCE related to adultery in the "Western Monogamous Societies" are almost non- existant in Alkebu-lan where polygamy is the legal and traditional manner of marriage. In all of the Falasha/Kyla Communities where there are POLYGAMOUS MARRIAGES the woman maintains her female role and respect. She is never "KICKED" and/or otherwise "STRUCK" by her man in the marriage.

In POLYGAMOUS Falasha societies there isn't any need for "VICE COURTS;" for there is not a single "LEGAL" and/or "ILLEGAL HOUSE OF PROSTITUTION" and/or "PROSTITUTE." You cannot find a solitary "PROSTITUTE" among the Falasha Women in any of the Falasha communities, communal or non-communal. This cannot be said for a single "Western Society" the size of the Falasha communities in any section of Europe. The same holds true for those in the "Americas."

We have never in all of history planned any legislation which would require any special form of MARITAL STATUS affecting "POLYGAMOUS MARRIAGE" and/or "MONOGAMOUS MARRIAGE." We leave the method of MARITAL SELECTION to the individuals interested in deciding under which MARITAL CUSTOM they desire to pursue-"Polygamy" or "Monogamy;" never "Polyandry."

There is but one restriction on "POLYGAMY" in our Falasha communities, which states that:

1. Polygamy is illegally practised every day by most European and European-American societies. The difference being "legally." Most divorces are "Third Party" action complaints.

"NO MAN WHO HAS EVER HAD A MARRIAGE FAILURE IS PERMITTED TO HAVE A MULTIPLE MARRIAGE. NO MAN CAN SHOW SPECIAL FAVORITISM TO ANY OF HIS WIVES WHICH IS NOT EQUALLY SHARED BY ALL OF THE OTHERS. A POLYGAMOUS UNION IS FEMALE CONTROL."

Whenever there is a POLYGAMOUS UNION the amount of WIVES never total more than three [3] to four [4] in any family. The average [general] "MULTIPLE UNION" has two [2] wives per family; but the majority of the Falashas have maintained "MONOGAMOUS UNIONS" for the most part in non-communal communities. The latter trend relates back to the historical periods when Falasha families had to be on the move in order to evade conquering armies of so-called "Christian Missionaries" and so-called "Moslem Missionaries" from Europe, European-America and Asia, most of whom were sent by their respective national government or national church body.

The women in a POLYGAMOUS UNION share the duties of their household equally. Also, they must at all times jointly -

"arrange the manner in which each will use and share in the sexual activities of their husband throughout the marriage. There is no Chief Wife among them."

This arrangement is made -

"to suit the order in which each wife will have to leave her household and go into the House Of The Woman In Blood each month."[1]

Children of POLYGAMOUS UNIONS must take orders from all of the wives in the various households in which their father is the husband. The WIFE from whence the child, or the children, is physicaly born is called by the child [or children] - "MOTHER OF MY NATIVITY." All of the other wives in the household are called - "MOTHER OF MY FATHER'S MARRRIAGE." And all of the wives in such unions can correct any child in the family. When an order is given by either of the wives to any of the children of the common father, no other wife can change it without consultation with the wife making the order unless there is a question of life and/or death involved.

There are many other details involving the question and issue of "POLYGAMY vs. MONOGAMY;" but they would need a special treatise on the subject to adequately cover all of the minute details necessary to have in so extensive and delicate a subject. This Volume certainly is not the place for such an analytical undertaking. However, it should be quite clear at this juncture that the moral issue of which is correct strictly hinges upon one's own personal upbringing in religion and/or cultural enviornment. There is no easy answer to give to either side of the pros and cons of the issue; for each acts most of the time upon strict emotionalism; and each does not want to be "...CONFUSED BY THE FACTS..." after having "...MADE UP His/Her MIND...," etc., etc., etc. Unfortunately European and European-American Jews have adopted their fellow Europeans and European-Americans of the Christian Religion MONOGAMISTIC practise as their own custom.

1. Falasha women are not "sexually clean" but 10 - 12 days out of each 28 - 31 days of each month.

DEATH AND BURIAL: Chapter VI, Part Seven.

Whenever a Falasha has passed on to the "GREAT BEYOND" or "HEREAFTER" there is no "MOURNING OF THE DEAD" because he or she is parting with the communities. There is a lot of "REJOICING" and "MUSICAL CHANTING" instead. This method of behavior is due to the biblical teachings in the Sacred Torah; thus:

"REJOICE THE PASSING OF THE SOUL OF THE DEPARTED; BUT MOURN THE COMING OF THE NEW BORN."

This latter interpretation has been given a theosophical basis and explanation by the Priests; thus:

"THE DEPARTED SOUL IS ON ITS WAY TO GOD'S ABODE: THE DEPARTED HAS NO FURTHER PAIN OR SUFFERING TO BEAR; WHEREAS THE NEW BORN FACES A WORLD OF TROUBLE, DESPAIR AND UNNECESSARY SUFFERING BECAUSE OF MAN'S DISOBEDIENCE OF GOD'S SACRED TORAH AND HIS TEN COMMANDMENTS AS HANDED DOWN TO MOSES ON MT. SINAI."

There is "MOURNING OF THE DEAD" in some of the non-communal Falasha communities of the Lake Tana district, because said Falashas in those regions were influenced by the Gentiles amongst whom they live as a minority group just as the European Jews in Europe and America.

When a man is about to die in a communal community a Subordinate Priest is summoned to his beside. This Priest thereafter summons THREE [3] ELDERS to accompany him to the house of the dying man. ONE [1] of the THREE ELDERS acts as the "CONFESSOR" while the other TWO and the Priest await him outside of the dying man's home. At the end of the "CONFESSION" the Elder who took it notifies the Priest and the other two Elders of the man's readiness; thus:

"HE IS READY TO RECEIVE HIS BLESSING FOR THE PREPARATION OF THE JOURNEY OF HIS DEPARTING SOUL TO THE HEREAFTER WITH GOD."

Before the "BLESSING" is administered the dying MAN is asked to make what would appear to be his "LAST WILL." This so-called "WILL" is nothing more than a directive to his wife or wives on the method of how their children should be raised, and how his personal belongings should be distributed if he is in a non-communal community. However, in the non-communal communities Falashas make "LAST WILL AND TESTIMONIES" that are very similar to those made in the United States of America by the so-called "BLACK [Falasha] JEWS" of the Harlems, etc. For in such communities any Falasha can own and pass on real estate and personal property to his/her heirs and next-of-kin, unlike in the communal communities.

After the "WILL" has been made the Priest asks the Elder-Confessor:

"HAS THE DYING MAN MADE A FULL CONFESSION OF HIS PAST SINS AND COMPLETE LIFE? HAS HE ACKNOWLEDGE HIS FINAL STATE WITH YWH?"

If the Elder-Confessor answers in the affirmative, the Priest reminds the Elder- Confessor that:

"The confession of a dying man is an extraordinarily private matter, and a Religious Sacrifice to his God; therefore, you must never devulge a single word of its contents to anyone, including your own dear mother."

The Elder-Confessor is then required to assure the dying man that:

"I have passed on the secrets of your confession to the Sabbath of Sabbaths, and she has received it safely in her bossom for you; no earthly man shall ever hear a single word of any part of it again."

The Priest asks the dying man:

"Do you wish to appoint a male guardian for your children? Is it your desire that special prayers of any kind or songs shall be done before you have departed to the Great Beyond? Do you have any special messages for your wife and children?"

After the dying man answers the interrogations the Priest-Confessor assures him that:

"They shall be immediately dealt with; and they shall be carried out in the exact manner which you have described and directed to me."

At this point the Priest takes the LEFT and RIGHT hands of the dying man and place them on the dying man's stomach; holding them with his right hand, he gives "PRAYERS FOR A DEPARTING SOUL." These Prayers are continued at intervals of at least ONE EVERY ONE/QUARTER OF AN HOUR. When it appears that the dying man is about to take his last breath the Priest begins to chant the "PRAYER OF A SOUL IN TRAVEL." This Prayer is continued until the dying man has passed away. After he had been pronounced officially dead by the Priest and the Three Elders the Priest chants the "PRAYER OF THE DEPARTED SOUL AND SPIRIT." The Priest and Three Elders chant the "FAREWELL SONG" for the passing of the dead. When they have all concluded the Priest orders:

"THIS BODY MUST BE RETURNED TO THE EARTH FROM WHENCE IT CAME BEFORE SUN-FALL THIS VERY DAY IN ACCORDANCE WITH THE HOLY TORAH."

If it is on a Sabbath Day or High Holy Day the body will remain to be inturned before Sun-Fall on the following day.

Four [4] Male Attendants from the community are summoned for the purpose of " washing the departed soul's remains." The Attendants also dress the deceased and place him in his coffin. The coffin is made from a plain piece of woven cloth; if a Priest, Deacon, Sister or Learned Man the coffin is made from plain box wood and provided with [4] four rope handles. The clothing of the deceased is made from a plain piece of white material shaped as a robe or shroud--with a split down the back and a black tassel on the side; or with no tassel if the deceased was not married.

If a woman or girl is the deceased Four [4] Female Attendants are summoned to act as her washers and dressers; for under no circumstance whatever can a person of one sex wash the body of the opposite sex. The Female Attendants do not carry the body to its resting place. The

1. Hebrew customs/traditions dictate when, and how, a deceased person must be burried, etc.

Male Attendants take the body of the deceased woman and/or man in their coffin or wrap to the outside of the community's village where the BURIAL GROUND is located [review Plan Of Communal Village at the beginning of Chapter III, page 102]. The body of the deceased is burried far from the community if he or she committed SUICIDE because of any reason.

The Attendants must dig a hole at least Seven [7] Feet long, Four [4] Feet wide, and Seven [7] Feet deep to receive the coffin with its remains of the departed. This hole cannot be dugged by any Gentile who may be in the vicinity at the time of the burial; neither can the body be covered by any Gentile; nor can it be lowered into the grave by a Gentile. At all times, and under all circumstances, the body of any Falasha must be lowered and covered by FOUR FALASHA MALE ATTENDANTS designated for this type of function; and only them. If any other person should perform any of these functions it is believed that:

> "THE SOUL OF THE DECEASED WILL NEVER REST IN THE HEREAFTER; AND HIS [or her] SOUL WILL REMAIN IN UNEASINESS UNTIL THE DAY OF RESURRECTION."

This reason is based upon the fact that:

> "THE GENTILE CANNOT PERFORM THE NECESSARY RITUALS AND WASH HIMSELF AS PRESCRIBED BY THE LEVITICAL LAWS ON CLEANLINESS. THEREFORE A GENTILE IS NOT ALLOWED TO HANDLE ANY PART OR PARTICIPLE ON CONTACT WITH A DECEASED FALASHA REMAINS."

There isn't any funeral procession with family and friends following the coffin. No one worries about the body of the deceased, because "...the soul..." of any Falasha in any community is -

> "already on its way into the Nether World [hereafter]; and the body passed into uselessness, where it will remain until judgement."

After the body has been inturned and completely covered with earth a small tree or shrub is planted at the head of the grave. There isn't any other sign or mark placed on the grave to create any means by which it could be identified from any of the others that preceded it; for no one will ever visit this grave or any other at anytime in the future unless it is a Burial Attendant passing by in the course of another internment.

When the complete burial is over the Four Attendants must remain on the outside of the community in a house prepared for them for a period of SEVEN [7] DAYS. There all of them must -

> "pray for the children and wife of the deceased...,"[also for]"...the cleansing of our own soul....' Because Falashas say that "...we have caused our own bodies to be of the dead by our handling of the dead...," etc., etc., etc.

There they must also perform "RITUAL BATHS." These "BATHS" are made from "river water," and "sweet-scented herbs..." added[1]. At the end of the SEVENTH [7th] DAY the last one is made. The "BATHS" are used for the purpose of disinfecting the body, and to create a sweet scent. After

1. Falashas, according to Torahdic traditions, cannot cremate or embalm the deceased. This is a very serious prohibition. Thus there is no ancient remain of any Falasha for examination, etc.

the attendants have completed their BATHS they must "...

> wash all of their clothing and hang them to dry, thereafter remain in the house prepared for the burial attendants until the clothing is completely dried...."

Upon such time that their clothing is dried they must -

> "shave all of their hair off their head and face, then scrub completely."

Following all of this, at Sun-Fall on the SEVENTH [7th] DAY after the burial they will be ready to prepare to "...

> reenter the community from the West Gate...;" [but they will have to] " visit the synagogue and pray...," [before they can enter the community; therefore] "...they cannot enter from the synagogue directly into their homes before Sun Fall..." [as it is considered] "...the time when the sun Falls behind the lowest mountain peak of the community that the last of the 7th Day is completed...."

After the Burial Attendants have reentered the community they must -

> "continue directly to the home of the deceased family..."[where they will be served] "...dried peas and hot black coffee."

The family of the deceased then assures them that they are completely satisfied that their departed member is properly burried. The Attendants in turn assure the family that:

> "The deceased has been placed away in the customary manner, in the customary place of the departed body; and his ..."[or her] "...soul has started upon its journey, for we encountered not a single obstruction; and because there was no one who was not a matured son of our people - ISRAEL - who helped with the washing, clothing, boxing, carrying, digging, lowering and covering the deceased; nor at anytime was anyone other than our protectors of the children of ISRAEL allowed to violate the sacred dust from whence he [or she] came, and whence he has returned."

The entire family present takes turn individually in thanking the FOUR BURIAL ATTENDANTS for their "...

> services to the God of Israel, His people, and the departed soul to rest his body in the sacred soil from whence the birth he experienced took place...."

In communities having a non-communal system economy the Attendants, must be paid. This payment is generally a few pounds of meat from a young calf - OX -which has been killed especially for such a purpose to rejoice the passing of the soul to God. Some rich families of the few non-communal communities give the attendants money for their families, also other presents which they could not otherwise afford but directly are in need of.

In all communities, communal or non-communal, there is a "PRAYER PERIOD" of at least "SEVEN DAYS FROM THE DAY OF THE PASSING OF THE DECEASED," which is equal to the date when the deceased was buried; unless the deceased died on a Sabbath or High Holy Day. These

---

1. Most of these laws and traditions go back to the "Falashas" experience in Egypt and Nubia, etc.

Seven [7] Days are considered to be -

> "the time it takes the body to travel and give up the soul...." [Also] "...for the soul to travel from the body to, and into, heaven."

The final day is called "REMEMBERANCE DAY" or "TÄZKÄR." This day must be observed by all of the members of the entire immediate family of the deceased. The membership of the observing family includes the wife or wives, husband, children[irrespective of age], grandparents, aunts and uncles, and all first cousins; all other relatives further away from the deceased may attend, but are not required to be there. At the observance the Subordinate Priest [Kähäin] reads from the MAGICAL BOOK [Arde,et]. He reads the following section:

> "And it was the seventh day. And God rested His body, Spirit and Soul; so shall man rest his body, Spirit and Soul. Man shall rest in Heaven with his Creator. For God made man from the dust of the earth around and about him. And God blew the breath of life into man's body. And God took that which He had temporarily loan to man, in order that he may return to the better home at the place where he shall see his forefathers - Abraham, Jacob, Isaac and others unknown. There was light given by our Father who is God. And the light was given in darkness, and out of this darkness came light. And man was from this light and back to this darkness shall man's body return. And to this light shall man's soul ascend. Therefore I say to you there is no death; and no eternal darkness for the people - Israel. There is but one place for the worthy children of Israel; that place is in the House of God, which is my house. By the Sabbath of Sabbaths the soul of the departed has entered the gates of the Kingdom of God. Rejoyce our children of Israel, for man must return to his Creator - the God of His Chosen People - Israel. Amen."

After reading the MAGICAL BOOK, with regards to the "Departed Soul" which has been shown to you in the above quotations, you should be able to understand why there isn't any "...mourning of the passing of the dead..." among the Falashas in Ethiopia; the same is not true for those living in the Americas. If you have not reached such a conclusion, let me explain some of the finer points in the above quotations that may have eluded you because of the major differences in culture. Note carefully that "DEATH" is never referred to as anything more than "...THE PASSING OF THE SOUL..." The living persons' mind is always kept from thinking of the"...DECEASED BODY IN THE GROUND..." as in the "Western" burial sermons.[1] The psychology behind this is that the mind will follow "... THE PLACE WHERE THE BODY IS..." considered to be.[2] And the mind will be restful and happy if the "...DEATH PLACE..." is shown to be one superior to the ever-present world of life in which the mind presently exists, especially when the person is trained to this theosophical theory from the inception of his or her religious experience -which in most cases begin at the date of birth. The "PLACE" or "RESTING SPOT OF THE BODY" is called "EDEN;" and the "LAST PLACE WHERE THE SOUL REMAINS" is called "HEAVEN." If the entire MAGICAL BOOK is read by you, you will get the feelings of being in a new world situation should you surrender

1. The Sacred Torah gives all of the necessary regulations for burrying any Falasha - male/female.
2. Egyptian theology places the body with the Ka and/or ba in the Nether World/Next World, etc.

your total mind to the words being spoken, as does the average Falasha. And if it is read by one of the Subordinate Priests of any of the Falasha communities you will be carried away like most of the Falashas do, as the Priests are dramatists in this art. They will make you accept the theory which states that:

> "THE SOUL OF A PERSON IS BETTER-OFF WHEN THE PERSON IS DEAD THAN ALIVE; FOR THERE IS NO MOURNING AND NO SIN IN GOD'S HOME."

You can see [if you are willing to free your own mind from its present influence your own culture has upon it] the reason why there is no "MOURNING THE DEAD" amongst the Falashas and other African and Asian so-called "BLACK JEWS" [the same being true when they leave their native homeland and migrate to cultures where the opposite is common] is indoctrination, and also belief.

The next day the family of the departed must attend a special "HIGH HOLY SERVICE" to thank the God of the People [Israel] for His mercy in "...RECEIVING THE DEPARTED'S SOUL...." At the service the Priest announces the -

> "Feast for the Departed Soul of [name] who has arrived into the world of the unknown with our ancestors - Abraham, Jacob and Isaac," et al.

This FEAST is climaxed with the slaughtering of a male lamb or ox, and the cooking and eating of the meat between the family and neighbours who desire to come and join-in with the others. At the commencement of the FEAST the Priest must leave; therefore he expresses his appreciation

> "to those who have witnessed the blessings in the Service Of The Soul Of The Departed, our brother [name of the person, or a sister] - Chosen of the God of His people - Israel....Amen."

This is done because the Priest does not eat of such food, therefore he must leave and return to his own residence.

After the FEAST the family of the widow [if the deceased was a married man] and the family of the deceased husband get together and arrange to assist the widow and her children, if any. They decide among themselves whether or not the widow goes to her parents home or remains at the parents of the deceased husband where she had always lived from the day of their marriage. This is done with the widow's consent, and in her presence.

The widow is not permitted to marry for a period of at least ONE LUNAR YEAR following the day her husband was interned. It is said to be -

> "a period of respect which the soul of the departed spirit is entitled to have."

This also goes for the husband if he is a widower. The widow can marry the brother of her deceased husband if he does not already have a wife. She cannot marry into a polygamous family if she has any children by her deceased husband under the age of NINE [9] for a girl and TWELVE [12] for a boy [see rules governing "Confirmation" or "Barmitzvah"].

If a "MALE GUARDIAN" was appointed before the departing of her husband - the deceased, then the eldest brother of her deceased husband will take charge of the effects of the family. But if there was no brother of the deceased, then the eldest son will take care of the household if he is at the "AGE OF MANHOOD," this age being "TWELVE [12] YEARS OF AGE" according to the Sacred Torah. Of course this does not mean that the boy can disobey his mother or tell her what to do when she does not care to do something he does not like. What it does mean is the boy must protect his mother to the best of his ability as the deceased HEAD OF THE FAMILY would have done was he alive. He will be responsible for her safety while she remains single in his deceased father's honour.

The widow cannot marry a man less than SEVEN [7] YEARS her junior. If she is a very young woman her next husband cannot be less than "TWENTY-FOUR [24] YEARS OF AGE," regardless if he is more than the "SEVEN YEARS HER JUNIOR," due to the respect she owes her children and the memory of her deceased husband. She cannot live alone with her children, nor by herself. She "MUST BE ATTACHED TO A FAMILY UNIT WHERE THERE IS A FULL-FLEDGE MALE;" even if the male figure is only her paternal or maternal grandparent, or the grandparent of her children. And if there is no grandparent, then she must remain with her in-laws or return to her parents' home if they are alive. If neither of these conditions exist, she must live with some family related to her children's father [her deceased husband] where there will be a MAN to protect her along with her eldest son.

In neither of the above situations the family with whom the widow lives will be allowed to interfere with any suitor who will respectfully call upon her, or anyone who might desire to take her at some social function before Sun-Fall on any day except the Sabbath or a High Holy Day. However they may, and can, refuse to allow their grandchildren to live in the house of the new husband if they have any just reason; because their paternal grandparents are considered to have as much interest in their grandchildren as their deceased father had when he was alive.

The widow MUST wear her MARITAL STATUS NECKLACE following "...

> the beginning of the Seven Days after her husband internment at the place of rest...."

She must at all times demand respect for herself and her children. She would be always considered the "...WIFE OF THE DECEASED HUSBAND..." until she has remaried. She is required to carry on the religious training of the children as it was when their father was alive.

At the end of the first year of the burial of her deceased husband the widow must give a PRAYER FOR THE SACRIFICE, and ask that she be "...

> spared from having to remary, and thereby desicrate the memory of the soul

of my departed husband, and myself, and that of our children...."

This PRAYER will continue for SEVEN [7] DAYS. It will be the last of the PRAYERS she has to make in the interest of her deceased husband.

At the end of the second year [if the widow is not already remarried] she gives a "PRAYER OF SACRIFICE." She ask that if she remarries she will have the power to divorce her husband and save herself from shame and disgrace, rather than have him bismirsh the name of the deceased.. That she will prefer SUICIDE [sacrifice] rather than drag the name of her children in the gutter through the conduct of a sinful husband. She further asks that:

> "I will be able to summon enough strength in order to avoid remarrying until my youngest child is already married."

In the latter request above the widow owes no obligation, for she does not have to wait on the marriage of her children before she can remarry. However, it is generally the custom to do so; and most widows in the communal communities ask for this type of "STRENGTH." Most of the women in all types of Falasha communities try to have only one man in their entire love-life, particularly when they have children - <u>whether minors or adults</u>.

From the SECOND [2nd] YEAR onwards the widow takes her place in society without any other special obligations caused by the death of her husband and his memory. She conducts herself in the manner exemplified by any other Falasha woman of her status! <u>She can marry any man who has been married before; never a man who has never been married before.</u> If she chooses to remarry she will receive special respect, which will be as high as that received by the <u>Sisters</u> of the <u>Falasha Sisterhood</u>. She has the right to requisition any man in the community to assist her in any need that she may have if she has not remarried; except of course less than moral and/or traditional conduct of any sort, or for condoning any of her sins she may have committed.[1]

If you have not already turned back to review certain aspects of <u>Chapter III</u> as I have suggested before, you should do so at this moment and reexamine the relationship of the community to the functions of the burial and the location of the houses where the attendants must live and go through their RITUALS. The layout is titled "SCHEMATIC PLAN OF A COMMUNAL VILLAGE." Take special note of Items 11, 12, 13, 1 and 10 in this order. These numbers follow a sequence of the travel which the FOUR BURIAL ATTENDANTS must take when they are to burry the deceased. This plate was made solely for showing the basically different requirements of a Falasha village to that of other Ethiopian villages of indigenous people other than those who practice the Hebrew religion, such as we have seen in the pictures showing the Christian churches and priests. However, modern Falasha villages since the latter part of the 1950's C.E. may vary somewhat from

1. See Y. ben-Jochannan's African Origins Of The Major "Western Religions" for the basic traditions. The only people that go to the cemetary beside the grave diggers. They are highly revered.

that outlined in Chapter III. Thus any of the villages that differ to this one may have certain minor changes. All of them MUST have all of the basic items and housing shown in this one, and they MUST be similarly located in the sense of position on the compass. It would be wise for you to look at the other features of the "PLAN;" for you will need to recall other points of interest on it as you go along in the following Chapters of this Volume.

YES! SHE TOO IS AN AFRICAN WOMAN LIKE HER FALASHA SISTERS[1]

YES! HE TOO IS A FALASHA MAN LIKE HIS HARLEM BROTHERS[2]

YES! A RABBI TOO!

1. When will it be that the European and European-American realize that African People are as common amongst each others as European People are amongst each others? Who knows? Race!
2. He suffered untold persecution from European-American Jews because of his "black skin," etc. Yet there are too many African Hebrews/Israelites/Jews awaiting to be approved by "White Jews."

ECONOMICS OF THE COMMUNITIES: Chapter VII.

The working day of a Falasha is TEN [10] HOURS, THREE [3] HOURS of which he must devote to praying only. Working is not permitted on the Sabbath or High Holy Day, except for cases where "LIFE" or "DEATH" is in the ballance. The prayers are said in three separate periods per day. ONE in the morning before going to work, ONE at noon before having lunch, and the last ONE at the beginning of Sun-Fall before eating dinner.

The chief occupation of the Falashas is agriculture. Both the "modern" and the "traditional" methods of farming and grazing are used side by side in Ethiopia. The "Old," which the European and European-American academicians insultingly called "PRIMITIVE," is much more in use than the "Modern" or "New." This is not a serious problem, because mass production is not needed in the communal communities. However it was an important factor in the non-communal societies where Falashas were only SQUATTERS and/or SHARE-CROPPERS for their feudal landlords of the Christian and Moslem population that dominated the regions where they lived.

The Falashas in the communal communities produce only those things which they need; not for economic competition with the general population of Ethiopia, though some of their products do reach the local market places nearby [see page 123 of this Volume. Because the top soil of the land where the Falashas live is in very good condition on the plateaus of the Rift Valley - irrigation and vegetation also follow in excellent condition, this we can observe in the picture on page 136. The latter condition is due to the constant rainfall and back-draining of the water on the land in this area of the Ethiopian "HIGHLANDS," which is not equally true all over the country. This back-draining helps to create a natural irrigation system in certain areas of Begemder Province where most of the Falashas [not Kylas] live - as shown on the MAP OF ETHIOPIA, page 49.

The land in the communal communities must "...LAY FARROW [workless] FOR ONE [1] YEAR AFTER EACH SEVENTH [7th] YEAR..." as prescribed in the Sacred Torah. This is done by working sections of the land while other sections lay at "FARROW."[1] After each LUNAR YEAR a new section starts its working out of "FARROW" as another begins its "FARROW." At the end of the year when a portion of land is to LAY FARROW, vegetation on it is never reaped at the time of harvest. It is left to rot in order that the land [or soil] would be enriched by it. At the end of the year when the land has completely layed at rest the vegetation, which has grown during that period of FARROW, is plowed under with the top soil and made to amalgamate, thereby creating an under-layer of rich fertilized soil for future planting. This method has a scientific basis. And it has been proven by modern science that it is one of the best method of agriculture for re-fertilization in all of Ethiopia. The only reason why it is not much more widespread anymore

1. This too is expressed throughout certain Books Of Moses: "And on the seventh year the land must lay farrow" or "rest," etc.

throughout Europe, Great Britain and the Americas is that it takes too much time for processing, therefore hindering its abundant usage in those continents and nations where MASS PRODUCTION is gravely needed. It is to be noted that this too is called "PRIMITIVE SUBSISTENCE FARMING" by European and European-American academicians - historians, missionaries and entreprenuers - who make their livelihood writing about "Africa" [Alkebu-lan] and "Africans" [indigenous people].

There is also the "JUBILEE YEAR," which comes at the FORTY-NINTH [7X7] YEAR following the last one. In the period of the Jubilee Year all of the domesticated animals and birds are freed so that they may wander in the hills and other parts of the farm and pasture land of the communities. Members of the communities at this period must allow all visitors to use whatever they have found in the fields. The Jubilee Year is described in the following words:

"THE YEAR OF NATIONAL REJOICING AND PRAYERS FOR FREEDOM FROM PESTILENCE, FAMINE, PERSECUTION, WAR AND ALL DEGRADATION."

The [illegible] Year preceeding the Jubilee Year there is quite a strain placed upon the land due to the need for storing grains and other foods which come from the land alone. In the year of preparations every grain bin and other means of storage are used. In the Jubilee Year not even the animals are taken care of unless there are some emergencies which may cause them to loose their lives. If there is a dry spell during the Jubilee Year the animals are driven down to the flats to be watered periodically.

Next in importance is the "POTTERY INDUSTRY," which is dominated by the Falasha women.[1] Their artistic abilities have surpassed that of the men in this field to such an extent that there is no present example of which I can show you any close similarity between their works. The designs of the potteries are generally of various subjects and colors; but never of the face of persons at anytime, which we can observe on the following page. This latter rule is from one Law of the TEN COMMANDMENTS in the Sacred Torah that forbids the "... MAKING OF GRAVEN IMAGES...." and the "... WORSHIP OF FALSE GODS...." The vases generally have flowers or landscape designs. They are sold to Moslem and other Gentile communities at many markets and/or traded on the barter system to other communal and non-communal communities. Whatever the system in non-Falasha areas, the returns must be in items which do not violate the LEVITICAL LAWS ON CLEANLINESS AND DIETARY FOODS. Generally purchases by the Falashas from Gentiles, Moslems, and others, consist of tools for agriculture and other needs for farming and grazing.

"WEAVING OF CLOTH" is another of the important industries of the Falasha communities.[2] Falasha garments are woven by the women in the communities; and they are sometimes sold at very high prices because they are made from the best of fabrics available throughout all of Ethi-

1. Like the West African Women, Falasha Women have dominated domestic commerce everywhere.
2. Falashas are very competent silversmiths and goldsmiths beside being farmers of note, etc.

ALKEBU-LANIAN/"AFRICAN" ARTISTRY [1]

FALASHA
WATER VASE

1. Except for "Western Scholars'" racism; what is the difference between this work and that of the ancient Africans/Egyptians, Nubians, Meroites, Puanites, et al., of the Nile Valley and Great Lakes region of Alkebu-lan/"Africa"? Nothing is different.

opia; thus many find their way even into the better stores of the Capital City, Addis Ababa. It takes as much as one week to make a Falasha woman's dress, many more for a Sabbath Dress of a special type. This should give you an idea of the time and artistic touches put into each piece of material. "QUALITY ABOVE QUANTITY" is the motto. The artistic weaving and symetrical styling in the basket on page 224 following is proof of the Falashas outstanding craftsmanship in weaving.[1]

All "TRADING" by the Falashas is made at nearby Gentile and Moslem communities, because Falashas are not permitted to travel on the Sabbath; neither are they who live in communal communities permitted to sleep in the homes of Gentiles, Moslems and others. These rules have made it almost impossible to travel any long distance from the communities. This even holds true for the use of animals in any distance that would cause them to be away on the Sabbath. The animals must be in the communal communities by Sun-Fall on Friday to Sun-Fall on Saturday [Sabbath] like the human beings. Remember this: "Thou Shall Not Violate The Sabbath Day." From where?

The method of distribution of wealth earned from the sale of the above products of the communal communities is on a COMMUNAL ECONOMIC SYSTEM. Thus; if a Falasha has ten children, he is entitled to TEN CHILDREN'S SHARES. Therefore, it is seen that EACH CHILD is entitled to ONE CHILD'S SHARE. The above is also true when we say that this system goes for the adults; except that an "ADULT'S SHARE is larger than that of a CHILD'S SHARE. When the entire profit of the community is ascertained the number of people [adults and children] in the community is divided into the total amount of profit. Each of these "EQUAL SHARES" is assessed with a total of "TWENTY PERCENT [20 %] COMMUNITY TAX." The money from the TAX on each "COMMUNAL SHARE" is placed into the budget for the community in the event of any emergency, and to pay for the land if it is leased, also for the National Government's physical protection against intruders...like Christian and Moslem "missionaries." Food in the communal communities is also distributed in the same manner. The "HUNTERS," who hunt for the entire community like the "FISHERMEN" do, have to divide their catches in equal shares for old and young alike.

At this point you should be reminded that the Falashas living in non-communal communities must conform to the economic structures of all of the Gentile and Moslem areas in which they live. Because of this fact, it is impossible to detail their economic way of life. Of course, even the communal communities find certain pressures daily that impose changes on their type of COMMUNAL ECONOMIC SYSTEM. Quite different from the tourist historians' reports! ?

The type of EMPLOYMENT in the communal communities is no criteria to explain the need for any EXTRA and/or SPECIAL shares. Only persons who are ill, or in need of very special

1. This basket was drawn by Mike Portilla - an architect and long-time friend of your author.

ALKEBU-LANIAN/"AFRICAN" ARTISTRY [1]

FALASHA BASKET

1. Typical of the artistry seen all over the Continent of Alkebu-lan/"Africa;" yet called "Primitive Art" when it is originated in West and Central Africa, etc. Once again it is so-called "Western Scholarship" making the difference between "primitive" and "modern," etc.

and extraordinary care will receive more shares than others; this of course having been approved by the Elders, Deacons, Priests and others within the communities. There is no need to believe that the Falashas would take advantage of this system, because they have developed its technique to such an extent that now they have accepted it with a THEOSOPHICALLY RELIGIOUS BASIS that is fundamental to their PHILOSOPHY OF THE THEOCRATIC SOCIETY which they have.[1] Therefore the Falasha system is not only ECONOMIC; it is equally RELIGIOUSLY CENTERED under a common theocracy that is conditioned by the teachings in the SACRED TORAH as regards to the One And Only God - JEHOVAH - of the Chosen People - ISRAEL. Falashas at home cannot separate one from the other - secular from religious, and do not even try. The "COMMANDMENT" Falashas associate with their ECONOMIC SYSTEM is the following:

"YOU MUST LOVE YOUR NEIGHBOUR AS YOU LOVE YOURSELF."[2]

But, more than this, review the entire TEN COMMANDMENTS on page xL... along with their African origin in the accompanying NEGATIVE CONFESSIONS on the same page.[3]

This type of ECONOMY has been used throughout the entire continent of Alkebu-lan [Africa or Afrika] at one time or another before, and since, the arrival of the Asians and Europeans as conquerors. It has been more than THREE HUNDRED YEARS since some of the Falasha communities have returned to this system of economics. Our foreparents returned to this form of economic system after fleeing to the hills to escape persecution and genocide at the hands of the Christian and Moslem armies, because they were convinced it was the best manner in which to practice the teachings of the Sacred Torah and the Laws of the Ten Commandments; particularly that which states:

"YOU MUST LOVE YOUR NEIGHBOUR AS YOU LOVE YOURSELF."

We say that:

> "It will be impossible to love our neighbour as ourselves unless we live in the manner whereby each would have alike, and use alike in similar conditions."

Of course this does not mean that we will all have the same taste and/or desire. But it does mean that we would have to maintain an ECONOMIC SYSTEM whereby all of our Agaw [Falasha] People would be able to live on the same land in peace and harmony, and together with the non-Jews surrounding us. Those of us who found it necessary to live outside of the communal communities have Our Own Ideology that best suits Our Specific Circumstances in the area of economics.[4]

It must be noted that the ECONOMIC SYSTEM used in the non-communal Falasha communities

---

1. A "theocracy is no better or worse than any other system of government in the Western World."
2. Note that "Thou, Thy, Thine," etc. are all from "Old English;" and that Falashas do not speak or write in any language that can be literarily translated in such terms. No "speaking in tongues."
3. See comments on the origin of the "Ten Commandments" from the "Forty-two Negative Confessions" in Y. ben-Jochannan's African Origins Of The Major "Western Religions," Chapter IV.
4. The best name for the economic system of the vast majority of Falashas is "communalism."

is similar to that of other parts of Ethiopia's general Gentile and Moslem population. Formerly from NEO-FEUDALISM and FEUDALISM to CAPITALISM. There were the SUPER RICH and the EXTREMELY POOR to be found in the latter communities, the communal communities class structure being non-existant. Yet, they too have an extreme "CASTE SYSTEM" laid down in the Sacred Torah[1] with respect to the "HEBREW [ISRAELITE or JEWISH] TRIBES [see The Fallacy Of A "Jewish Race," Chapter One, page 39 for a review of Tribes]. Changed by the 1974 Revolution.

In all forms of Falasha communities' ECONOMY the Priests and the Monks, even though they are of the HIGHEST CASTE, must toil the fields for their own livelihood; but some of them become SCRIBES [writers of new Sacred Torah]. Some of them also act as INSTRUCTORS OF RELIGION during their spare time. There isn't any special pay for the Priests due to their work in the Synagogue. The religious writings state that:

"THERE SHOULD BE NO MONEY PAID FOR THE TEACHINGS OF THE WORDS OF GOD."

The Sisters of the Sisterhood are also made to work and support themselves; and they too [like the Priests] are only entitled to "ONE SHARE PER PERSON" just as any other member of the communities. The Priests [Kähäin], Monks [Mäoske], Learned Men [Däbtärä] and Sisters are considered as mere "...

> men and women of Sacrifice for the Kingdom of God; and as such, they are not permitted to receive money for their services to God and Israel...."

At this juncture it would be worthwhile to review General Religious Beliefs, Chapter V, Part Two, pages 152 - 157 of this Volume.

WOMEN occupy the same importance in the ECONOMIC SYSTEM of the communities as do their men; therefore their SHARES are the same in value as those of the men. Each woman is entitled to an "ADULT PERSON'S SHARE" just as each man. Most of the domestic industries are handled by the women, while the farming is handled by the men. In some communities the women in the fields with their men do similar work, except hewing trees and ploughing, etc.

The "WORKING DAY" for the women is approximately $4^1/_2$ hours. The other hours are spent in their homes with their small children, and making preparations for their husbands and other men upon their return from the field or other endeavours.

The only "MONEY" in the communal communities is that which is used for trade with the outside Gentile and Moslem communities, and for sending members of the communities to the nearby government and/or private schools if there is any in the surrounding Gentile and Moslem areas. Taxes to the Central Government in Addis Ababa also require that the Falashas have money.

1. The Class Structure of earliest "Judaism" goes hand-in-hand with "Capitalism" and "Feudalism." From its inception Judaism taught about "I" above the collective "WE," etc.

The Falasha communities should not be called "SOCIALISTIC" or any of the other modern names generally given to "Western" forms of ECONOMIC SYSTEM. The term "COMMUNAL SYSTEM" is the proper description; which means:

> "The living and sharing alike in everything, including one's own privacy."

The rudimentary "COMMUNAL SOCIETY" is not outmoded, for we have seen a truly steady decrease of ILL FEELINGS and/or LACK OF LOVE for one's brethren in our communal communities. And today we [Falashas] can happily say that:

> SUCH TYPE OF SINS HARDLY EXIST IN FALASHA COMMUNAL COMMUNITIES WITHIN THE NATION OF ETHIOPIA TODAY.

Of course, neither communal nor anyother type of Falasha agricultural economic system applies to "BLACK [Falasha] JEWS" in the United States of America. The latter is primarily capitalistic.

Christians will notice some similarity with our communal communities and the interpretation of their theory of THE LAST SUPPER; where Jesus "the Christ" [the son of two Jewish parents - Joseph and Mary] is said to -

> "break bread and drank wine, which he shared alike with his disciples."

The Mohammedans [Moslems or Muslims] have also stated that:

> "the Falashas system is very much similar to the methods planned by Prophet Mohamet ibn Abdullah to convince the wealthy people of his time on earth on the need for reforms to a better economic system for the masses."

All of these and other references must have some bearing on the type of "COMMUNAL ECONOMIC SYSTEM" we [Falashas] have in our communities of Northwest Ethiopia, East Alkebu-lan; particularly outside the vicinity of Gondar, as shown by the arrows on the map of Ethiopia on page 49 of this Volume. But they all fall short of the entire goal, because Our [Falashas] objective in our communal economic system cannot be separated from our religious concepts, activities and faith in Jehovah and Judaism [or Hebrewism]. This is due to the fact that whatever we do in economics within our Falasha communities must be expressed in terms of BIBLICAL PHILOSOPHY according to the Sacred [Hebrew] Torah and its Nile Valley sources that were centered in the "MYSTERIES SYSTEM" of the Grand Lodge of Wa'at,[1] which permeated the Sanhedrin School that used them to create the SACRED TORAH [Pentateuch, Five Books Of Moses or Christian Old Testament] which began in ca. 700 B.C.E. and was completed in ca. 500 B.C.E. The Sacred Torah is the basis for Falasha achievements and any progress we have made in the past, are making now at present, and will make in the future. We, as Falashas everywhere, and in Ethiopia particularly, therefore maintain:

> "It takes a religious philosophy [such as ours] to be able to produce the same type of communal economic system where everyone share alike accordingly."

---

1. See Y. ben-Jochannan's Black Man Of The Nile And His Family, 1981 [Revised and Enlarged Edition], and G.G.M. James' Stolen Legacy, New York, 1954 for details of Greek plagiarisms.

There isn't any other society practicing our form of economics except those in the communal vilages of the sections of the continent of Alkebu-lan [Africa or Afrika] where the Europeans and European-Americans have not been able to corrupt under their capitalist form of colonialism. Those groups of other indigenous African communities using this method have been doing so even before the existence of Falasha communities in Ethiopia, East Alkebu-lan. But there is a great deal of differences which could be pointed out between the two groups and their systems, solely upon the basis of preference and interpretation of whose "GOD" said why, what, how, etc.

The raising of domestic animals, such as sheep and goats, is another means of creating income for the communal communities. Cattle raising is also a growing enterprise. However, it is to be carefully noted that the last three items are for local Falasha communal communities consumption rather than for trade with other Ethiopian communities. Yet, there is very limited trading in these items outside of the communities. The herds of cattle, flocks of goats and sheep, bring much in revenue because of the good health of the animals. All of this is due to the geographic location of the Falasha communal communities - which benifits our annimals. This is equally what people in other communities badly need. Thus, there is very little sickness ever encountered by Falasha animals; and as a result, they bring higher prices than other animals in the many markets in the Gentile and Moslem regions. Changes have taken place under the new Marxist Regine.

All "SLAUGHTERING OF ANIMALS" is performed in the communities. Any animal that "... died from natural cause or accident..." is never traded or eaten by Falashas. However, if anyone else outside would care to have such an animal he may take it free of charge; but only if it had strayed beyond the limits of our Falasha communities before it died there; otherwise it would be burnt and/or buried. Meat for Falasha consumption must meet Kosher Dietary Regulations.

"AGRICULTURAL PRODUCTS" of the Communal Communities range in great varieties. Some of the food products are very similar to those of other tropical countries in the so-called "Western Hemisphere." Sweet potatoes [white and yellow], Yams, Bananas, Tomatoes, Onions and all spices, etc. are also in abundance to meet the needs of the communities in the communal areas. Of course all of these vegetables and fruits are common throughout the general Ethiopian countryside where there is farming.

"BARTERING" is conducted between Communal Communites, and equally a limited amount with non-Communal Communities, of the Falasha people. Such "BARTERING" was also conducted on a very low scale between Falashas and the neighbouring Gentile and Moslem peoples. When "BARTERING" is conducted with the Gentiles and Moslems the goods received in exchange "...

shall not be food products or anyother form of items which could be unclean

1. Your author must remind everyone that he is not a practicing "Falasha/Jew" in any sense today.

if they were made by Falashas. They must conform with all of the prohibitions of the Levitical Laws On Cleanliness and Dietary Foods...."

All products or goods of any sort can be transferred from communal to non-communal societies, and vice versa. There is no restrictive law against products from one Falasha community going from and/or entering another; providing each community is a 100% Falasha Community; and that"...

"no non-Falasha touches any food or water product prepared by Falashas...,"

if they are covered by Dietary and Cleanliness prohibitions.

THE FALASHA COMMUNITIES DURING THE ITALIAN FACISTS OCCUPATION OF ETHIOPIA IN WORLD WAR II: Chapter VIII.

Like all other tyrants of history the people of the Falasha communities [Communal and Non-communal] have had to contend with the murderer - Il Duce Benito Mussolini - was coldly and bluntly greeted in a similar manner as the other "masters of genocide" before him. For we had surviv-ed the extermination threats of the tyrants preceeding Mussolini, and were certain that we would outlast him in his effort to accomplish what others before him had woefully failed to complete. Of course our experiences were in many aspects equal to that of all of the other African brothers and sisters who suffered the same "HELL" and "INFAMY" of Asian and European imposed "SLAVERY" and "COLONIALISM" down through the centuries, and even to this present day in too many places in Alkebu-lan/"Africa," etc.

Mussolini's urge for conquest which he expressed to the United States of America's Representative Mr. Kirk - according to U.S DIPLOMATIC PAPERS, 1935, I, 740 - 1 states the following:

> Italy had prepared an exhaustive statement of her case which would be laid before the League of Nations. When that was presented the League would have to choose between Italy and Abyssinia. If Abyssinia were ejected from the League Italy would proceed with her plans in Abyssinia which . . . could then be regarded as having the character of high police measures enforced by arms. Abyssinia would by a brief demonstration of force be convinced of the power of Italy, the impression of the victory of Adowa would be wiped out and the undertaking would develop into a colonial enterprise...

It had the full blessings by the then existing "Holy Father of the Roman Catholic Church" in Italy during Mussolini's heydays. This "INFALABLE" person was no other than Pope Pius XIth, who when blessing the Fascist armies[1] reminded them that they, each and everyone of them, were

"on a mission to spread the truth of Christianity and the Sign of the Cross,"

etc., etc., etc. He told them that:

---

1. This Pope is constantly praised for having "saved many [white] Jews from the Nazis;" but, nothing is being said for the thousands of [black] Jews he caused to be murdered in Ethiopia.

"You have a job to bring civilization to the natives of Ethiopia...," and that, "...you have to carry to the heathens of Ethiopia the words of God, and the only True Faith, which is the Holy Christian Religion."

The one major fact Pope Pius XIth carefully forgot to tell the Fascists was that Ethiopia had an organized government and High-Culture before the existence of Rome in history; equally an organized "CHRISTIAN RELIGION" before Constantine ["The Great"] made Rome the first European "CHRISTIAN NATION" in ca. 312 C.E. [A.D.]; the same fact being true even for Greece. The same "CHRISTIAN RELIGION" with its only "HOLY BLACK FAMILY - JOSEPH, MARY and JESUS "the annointed," as shown on the following page. This dipiction was derived from the one original "BLACK MADONNA AND CHILD" - Isis and Horus [in death father Osiris] - of Ta-Merry [Egypt, Kimit, Qamt, Mizrain, etc.] in ca. 4100 B.C.E.- as shown on the page following the above.[1] Pope Pius XIth had equally forgotten that the Greeks and Romans received all of their basic understandings that eventually made it possible to use the mathematics and science which ultimately produced the weapons and poison gas he blessed to exterminate ..."the natives of Ethiopia." They were the descendants of the people who taught Hipocrates, Herodotus, Socrates, Plato, et al.; just like the African [BLACK] Semite below whose TREATISE ON MEDICINE Hypocrates copied and used to learn from more than 2,200 years following his death:[2]

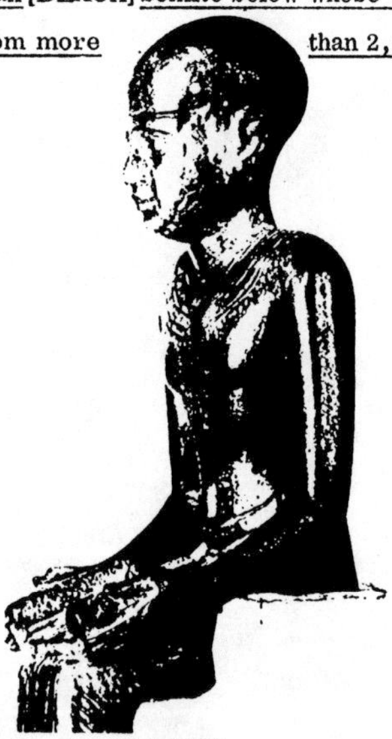

IMHOTEP
[Bronze Statue, Paris Museum, Paris, France]
Physician, Prime Minister, Grand Vizer, Poet, Magician, Architect and Builder of the STEP PYRAMID OF SAKHARA for Pharaoh Djoser - IIIrd Dynasty, 2780 BCE

1. See Section Two, page 394; Y. ben-Jochannan's BLACK MAN OF THE NILE AND HIS FAMILY, pp. 85 - 191 for further details on the "Semitic Black African" above on this page [use 1981 Edition].

2. Ibid, pp. 371 - 373 revealed numerous treatises on African Medicine eons older than Hipocrates.

1. Religious dignitaries of the Orthodox Christian [Coptic] Church with Religious Canopy; 2 Priest

1 2

3

4 5

reading religious text; 3 Holy Family; 4 One of Three Wise Men; 5 Mary carrying Jesus the Christ.

ISIS AND HORUS OF "AFRICA" BECAME THE WHITE "SEMITIC-CAUCASIAN" JESUS AND MARY OF EUROPE[1]

ISIS and the Infant HORUS,
BLACK MADONNA & CHILD
(F.W. Petrie Coll.)

Ethiopia's Jesus Christ

The BLACK MESSIAH!!!

Italy's White Madonna and Her Child - Asian Jesus Christ

Mary Nursing The "Christ-Child"

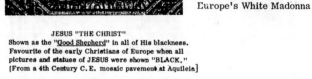

JESUS "THE CHRIST"
Shown as the "Good Shepherd" in all of His blackness. Favourite of the early Christians of Europe when all pictures and statues of JESUS were shown "BLACK." [From a 4th Century C.E. mosaic pavement at Aquileia]

Europe's White Madonna

1. See Y.ben-Jochannan's THE BLACK MAN'S RELIGION, Volume II, pages xvii - 19 for details, THE BLACK SEMINARIANS AND BLACK CLERGY WITHOUT A BLACK THEOLOGY, and CULTURAL GENOCIDE IN THE BLACK AND AFRICAN STUDIES CURRICULUM, 1973.

All that is said about the Greeks and Romans learning from the Egyptians is equally applicable to their learning from the indigenous "BLACKS" of Meröwe, Ta-Nehisi [Nubia or Zeti], Punt [or Puanit, Somali] and Ethiopia [Itiopi or Axum]. For these taught them philosophy, architecture [See pages 67-90], literature [see page XXXIX], law [see page XI] and most of the other disciplines. Egypt in those ancient days was the "Ta-Merry" of the same indigenous "BLACK" [negro, native, african, etc.] "POPULATION" to whom Pope Pius XIth was planning to carry what he had considered to be "CIVILIZATION" and/or "CHRISTIANITY." It was the Egypt that was cultivated and originally occupied by the Africans of whom Benito Mussolini told the following to DeBono on March 8, 1935 C.E.

> It is my profound conviction that, we being obliged to take the initiative of operations at the end of October or the end of September, you ought to have a combined force of 300,000 men (including about 100,000 black troops from the two colonies) . . . You ask for three divisions by the end of October; I intend to send you ten, I repeat, ten: five from the regular army, five of volunteer formations of Blackshirts, who will be carefully selected and trained. These divisions of Blackshirts will be the guarantee that the undertaking will obtain popular support . . . In view of the possible international controversies (League of Nations, etc.) it is wise to speed up our tempo. For the lack of a few thousand men we lost Adowa! I will never commit that error. I am willing to err in excess, but not in deficiency. [DeBono, ANNO XIII, 123]

Obviously, he did not remember that his own brand of "CHRISTIANITY" - a-la European style - was basically designed from its earliest days - [from its inception in Egypt] - by three "AFRICAN FATHERS OF THE CHURCH" [Roman Catholic Church]; namely:

> "TERTULLIAN" [from Carthage], "ST CYPRIAN" [from Carthage], and "ST. AUGUSTINE" [from Numidia]; all three of whom lived during the 2nd, 3rd or 5th Century C.E. or A.D.; and all three were no different than their fellow "native [African] pagans" that became "POPE OF THE ROMAN CATHOLIC CHRISTIAN CHURCH," namely: MELCHIADES, LEO and VICTOR.

Lastly, he even forgot that Ethiopia became officially "...A CHRISTIAN NATION..." more than one hundred and twenty-four [124] years - ca. 188 C.E. - before Rome in ca. 312 C.E./A.D., etc.

The Falasha communities destined to suffer hardest in the invasion were those which could not under any circumstance whatsoever accept that the "CHRISTIANS' GOD - JESUS CHRIST" - was in fact the "MESSIAH" promised by the "PROPHET ISAIAH" of the Hebrew or Judaic Religion and/or "Way Of Life." The "COPTS" or "COPTICS," presently called "ORTHODOX CHRISTIANS," the oldest of the Christian Community's Followers of Jesus "the Christ" in Christendom, and also the Moslem [Muslim, Mohammadan, etc.] - who have accepted "JESUS" as a "PROPHET" in their Religion or Way Of Life - "ISLAM or MOHAMMADISM," did not have the same problem.

1. See Chapter IX of Y. ben-Jochannan's Black Man Of The Nile And His Family; G.G.M. James' Stolen Legacy; and C. Anta Diop's African Origin Of Civilization: Myth Or Reality?

Therefore this left the Falashas "holding the barrel;" for we were/are Hebrews, and as such could not accept the Roman Catholics' Christian God - Jesus Christ - in any form whatsoever. Such acceptance would have meant accepting those things which were/are completely in conflict with our own religious teachings, development and belief. It must be also stated that the Roman Catholic Christian Church had always tried to bring the Coptic Christian Church of North and East Africa under its domination for many centuries following the Nicene Council of Bishops in ca. 325 C.E. This issue was brought to a head in the Seventeenth [17th] Century C.E. with the Priestly Wars" on the northern borders of Ethiopia. These said priests and their missionary staff engaged in military scuffels with us consistently, which was due to their continued efforts in trying to force all of us [Falashas] into "CONVERSION" and full acceptance of Christianity a-la European style. It got so bad one time that the late Emperor Menelik IInd was forced to supply the Falashas with military protection against the Jesuits and other Christian [Protestant] and Moslem missionaries. This situation of consistent raiding of Ethiopia's borders for the sole purpose of gaining Falasha "...CONVERTS TO CHRISTIANITY..." and "...ISLAM..." was stopped when Emperor Menelik IInd's military forces defeated the Italian armies at the BATTLE OF ADOWA in 1896 C.E., which also stopped the English from linking their "...CAPE TO CAIRO..." colonialist expansion dream for "...TOTAL CONTROL AND PARTITION OF AFRICA...." But this is what the Italian people, the Popes of the Roman Catholic Church and Kings of Italy that followed could not forget; thus they were determined to reverse that defeat by the conquest of the Kingdom and Empire of Ethiopia un-under the leadership of Benito Mussolini and his Facist armies. In order to better understand the frustration of the European colonialist forces in their failure to defeat Emperor Menelik IInd, I have included the maps on pages 243-244 that speak for themselves [review pages 48 and 50 of this Volume for added details].[1]

While the so-called "LEAGUE OF NATIONS" was meeting in Geneva, Switzerland in the year 1934 C.E. Il Duce Benito Mussolini sent Marshall Grazziano and his holy SEARCH AND KILL SQUADRONS of Fascist raiders with thousands upon thousands of poison gas bombs to drop on the sovereign territory of the Kingdom and Empire of Ethiopia to exterminate the Ethiopian people. These raids continued most persistently and consistently without the least outcry by the so-called "CIVILIZED NATIONS OF THE FREE WORLD," which of course included Italy. They were monstrous and barbaric to the enth degree; for the people of Ethiopia had nothing with which to defend ourselves against these "poison gas bombs" attacks. Thus it is that the Ethiopian Government was forced to apply to the so-called "FREEDOM LOVING NATIONS" of the League of Nations that previously proclaimed their friendship for the Emperor - Haile Selassie Ist - and the Ethiopian

1. See Sir Edward Hertslett's The Map Of Africa By Treaty, Vol. I - Extracts follow from p 245; P.T. Moon's Imperialism And World Politics, 1932; and J.Scott-Keltie's The Berlin Conference.

people as a whole.[1] But Ethiopians very soon after the Emperor's appeal found out that the League of Nations was nothing more than the creation of the new haven for the same groups of WHITE RACIST IMPERIALISTS and COLONIALISTS that PARTITIONED Africa at the Berlin Conference[2] of ca. 1884-1885 C.E. and reinforced their demography of "Africa" again in 1896 C.E. at what they preferred to call this time the "BRUSSELS CONFERENCE." England, Ethiopia's so-called "CLOSEST FRIENDLY NATION," had refused to sell Ethiopia ammunitions of any kind. The United States of America under the leadership of its hyprocritial "LIBERAL" President Franklin Delano Roosevelt - [who supposedly was a "friend of the Negroes"] - placed restrictions amounting to an embargo against all materials going to Ethiopia, and equally threatened all African-Americans who tried to give aid to their Ethiopian brothers and sisters against the genocide the Italians were imposing upon all of the people in Ethiopia. Roosevelt even made it punishable by "...the loss of American citizenship..." for anyone who dared to fight in the Ethiopian army, but made no such restriction against Americans of Italian and/or other European ancestry from going to help Italy and her Fascist Italian missionaries and military combine against Ethiopia; all of whom were part of the German-Italian-Japanese Axis that eventually murdered American soldiers and civilians.

Ethiopia was then forced to appeal once more to the same LEAGUE OF NATIONS that was still controlled by her same enemies in Europe and European-America. This time it was to secure actual "SANCTIONS AGAINST THE ITALIAN GOVERNMENT" that was invading her soil and committing all forms of genocide upon the entire Ethiopian population. All members and observing delegations at the League of Nations had refused to lend an ear to the words of the representatives sent before them by the Emperor of Ethiopia. Then the Emperor Haile Selassie Ist - "the Lion of Judah," etc., etc., etc. - was forced to make a personal appearance before the joint membership of this body of "...CIVILIZED NATIONS..." to state Ethiopia's case and position.[3] The following few pages are facts that influenced Emperor Selassie's entire speech, a speech that made the Japanese delegation call it "...one of the most historically significant speech ever made by the head of any member state in any world body of nations...." When the speech of the Emperor was concluded, and it was asked if any member state had wished to change their previous position on the main question, all members present remained pat as they were the first time when the Emperor's representatives had appeared before them on the same appeal. However, there was to come a major change in position by a few nations who felt disgusted with the atrocities and acts of genocide by

1. This include Christians, Moslems, Jews, Atheists, et al., of Ethiopian nationality or birth, etc.
2. See Sir J. Scott-Keltie, THE PARTITION OF AFRICA, London, 1920; Sir Edward Hertslett, THE MAP OF AFRICA BY TREATY, London, 1900, 3 vols.; Gorge Padmore AFRICA: BRITAIN'S THIRD EMPIRE, New York, 1947; Parker T. Moom IMPERIALISM AND WORLD POLITICS, New York, 1936; and Walter Rodney, HOW EUROPE UNDERDEVELOPED AFRICA, New York, 1978.
3. Do not forget that Ethiopia virtually mothered Egypt; not the other way around.

the Italian armies, for their use of the "INTERNATIONALLY OUTLAWED POISON GASES" on the Ethiopian armies and civilian population. These nations were the respective governments of the Kingdom of Sweden, Kingdom of Czechoslovakia and the Union of Soviet Socialist Republics [formerly the Kingdom of Russia]. They asked for another full compliment of the General Assembly for "...immediate reprisals against Mussolini..." and the murderers he sent into Ethiopia. But that was impossible, for all of the alleged "...friends of Ethiopia..."had to show their loyalty to their WHITE RACIST IMPERIALIST COLONIAL POLICY throughout the European and European-American colonies in Asia, Africa and the Americas. The colonial powers and all of their backers were forced to be together because Italy represented their own IMPERIALIST SYSTEM, also a new chance of getting at the natural resources of Ethiopia which they themselves were always seeking in the past and had aluded them. England and other nations of the European continent had tried to conquer Ethiopia for colonial pusposes many times during the Nineteenth [19th] Century C.E.; and as an existing colonizer could not oppose "COLONIALISM" or "IMPERIALISM" in Africa, Asia and the Americas, even in the Caribbean and Pacific Islands. Ethiopia had to fight a highly mechanized Italian army and air force using conventional and poison gas bombs with her national "POLICE FORCE." I wish to emphasize that it was nothing more than an outdated so-called "POLICE FORCE" which Ethiopia had when she was attacked by the Italian armed forces. But, even with that wretched "POLICE FORCE" the Ethiopians had engaged the Italian armies and air force in one of the most courageous battles that history has ever been able to record. The Ethiopians defeated their Italian invaders in many engagements on the ground; but they were doomed to failure, as they had no appreciable air force of their own; and the invaders were free to roam Ethiopia's air space as they wanted; plus the fact that the Ethiopians had no MUSTARD [poison] GAS of their own, and no protection against it. The Ethiopian Government in Addis Ababa had tried repeatedly to purchase protection from the "Western Nations" who had; but they would not sell, because at that time they were close friends of the so-called "AXIS POWERS"- Mussolini's ITALY, Hitler's GERMANY, and later on Hirohito's JAPAN. Little did they know that what the Emperor had told them about his victory, while their heads would roll, would have been so very close to our own hardships. The Emperor had told them:

> "when there would be no kings left in Europe due to this crisis, I will still be Emperor of Ethiopia if you fail to come to the aid of the world's oldest nation."

He also warned all of them:

> "when kings and queens would be running and hiding [their hides] from their own subjects, I will be welcomed home by my people in the tradition of peacemaker;"

but they had equally ignored him.

---

1. The United States of America placed an embargo on all materials intended for Ethiopia; never one on anything going to Italy. The present Ethiopian Government cannot easily forget this.

As was expected, the main Ethiopian armies were forced to retreat due to the superior mechanized might and support of the Italian Air Force. Since this retreat took place on the northern and northeastern borders of the country, it meant that the Falashas would be directly involved in the conflict. We already had many Falashas who had volunteered to fight in the Ethiopian Armed Forces, all of whom were giving great account of themselves, just as all other Gentile and Moslem, etc. Ethiopians were doing. But this retreat also meant that the entire Falasha communities would be forced to fight "guerilla warfare," if we were to exist following the end of this conflict. The key Falashas knew what they had done in the past, and what they had to do in the present crisis, therefore they did not hesitate to get their plans and activities underway.

Falasha women were taken up to the hideaways their men had prepared for them through caves and mountain ranges where it was impossible for the enemy's air armada to spot them. After the women were placed safely in the caves between these mountain ranges the livestocks were carried up, and those that there was no time to transport were chased off the land so that the enemy could not have their use. They had collected enough food for this adventurous battle for mere life and survival against "...CONVERSION TO ROMAN CATHOLICISM..." and submission to further European and European-American Imperialism in "Africa."

On the mountains my people courageously agreed to form "...small guerilla units to sabotage the efforts of the enemy's troops movements...." Falasha maidens and married women alike also volunteered, as was to be expected from their own records in our struggles for survival against enemies of the past. With no military training whatsoever in the methods of warfare, Falashas began attacking the "enemy" where they felt it worse; for they had set a special bounty price on each and every Falasha man, woman and child's head. However, the girls in our units had once again made a "CODE OF ETHICS" amongst themselves. This "CODE" stated:

> Death by suicide above captivity. Fight to death, above allowing our bodies to be raped by the Gentile armies. Death by suicide, rather than conversion whenever captivity is unavoidable. Death by suicide, rather than disgrace.

The oaths in this "CODE" were rigidly adhered to; not a single girl violated the first one any time.

Again we were to experience our "VIRTUOUS WOMEN" committing "MASS SACRIFICES" rather than submit their virginity to the Gentile armies.They had defended their integrity in a similar manner in the past under our Great Chief Elders - GEDEON and RADA'I. It was a pity to see these young women making the "SUPREME SACRIFICE OF DEATH" before they even had a chance to enjoy their lives. Gladly and gallantly they had "SACRIFICED" themselves, nevertheless. Yet, it was this sense of determination that kept us from being totally exterminated by the Italian armies and air force. To the Falasha women this was a "GREATER HONOUR" than living

1. Where are the works by "Western" Jewish writers decrying these acts of a "holocaust" directed against their fellow Jews of "black skin"? Of course, of other human beings of "black skin"?

and always rembering that they had been "RAPED" and lost their "PARAMOUNT PRIDE" of first marriage while not being "VIRTUOUS" [Virgin]. A woman in any Falasha community who had been so mistreated could never hold her head as high as she would have wanted by her own standard of MORALS and traditional CUSTOMS. She would have "...died a million deaths..." worse than what she was doing when she joined in committing "MASS SACRIFICES" over the mountain cliffs in preference to becoming the harlots and prostitutes of the conquering Italian armies. This type of "SACRIFICE" [suicide] was/is an honour to our women. They, themselves, without coersion from the men, made these "LAWS" and "OATHS" from past generations; and they have stuck by them. This is our women's sense of morality; and it cannot be adequately judged by any person or persons who do not have the experience of what it means to us[1] [a review of pages 96 and 97 would be worthwhile at this juncture].

When a Falasha man or boy was caught by the enemy they could not tell him apart from any of the other Ethiopians who could have been Moslem, Christian, or of a local religion. But the method the enemy developed for just this purpose was to take a "...PIECE OF FAT PORK...," uncooked at that, and try to push it into the mouth of such a Falasha male who refused to recognize "JESUS CHRIST" as his "GOD." This form of atrocity, of course, resulted in violent reactions from Jews of Europe who were devoted to their religious practises; and naturally, it held the same effect on the Falashas - Jews of Africa. Whenever an Ethiopian was found to be a "JEW" he was shown a "CHRISTIAN CRUCIFIX," a "PICTURE OF JESUS CHRIST" according to Michaelangelo's Sixteenth [16th] Century C.E. VERSION of a blonde, blue-eye and golden hair European he painted for Pope Julius IInd, and also a picture of Pope Pius XIth demanding to be called "THE HOLY FATHER." The captured Falashas were told:

> "You would be given your freedom and a god position with the army if you would only accept Jesus Christ as your only Saviour, and the Pope as your only earthly intermidiary with God. If you fail to do either, you will be placed to your death before sun down today."

Everyone of those Falashas who were captured tried to fight back against the overwhelming odds of such conditions; and they were all slaughtered by the Italian enemy. This peeved the "enemy;" for he was unable to find a new method to bring about "CONVERTS TO CHRISTIANITY" for their own European VERSION as ordered by Pope Pius XIth. This was equally true to a great extent among many of the Moslems and Christians, and equally to the last man amongst those of local religions European and European-American missionaries generally call "PAGANISM" and/or "ANIMISM." But the enemy Italians were not so much interested in the COPTIC CHRISTIAN POPULATION as they were the FALASHA [Hebrew or Jewish] POPULATION; for his plan was that it would be easy

1. This might be difficult for "Western women" to understand, but not other African/Asian women.

to change Ethiopians from being "COPTICS" by CONVERSION to Roman Catholicism, because both of them had the same GOD - Jesus Christ, However, the AGAW [Falasha, Black Jew, Beta Israel, etc.] and Moslems [Muslims or Mohammedans] were placed into different categories. And because of such, they were specifically commanded to "...CONVERT, OR BE PUNISHED...,"etc. The methods of punishment, or shall we say torture, ranged from MUSTARD [poison] GAS BATHS to eventually DRAGGING BEHIND ARMY TANKS. Those Falashas, all men and boys, who were resisting "CONVERSION TO ROMAN CATHOLICISM" were therefore forced to adopt some sort of a system of "MORAL CODE" which was similar to those their women and young girls of the communities were using. It was decided that they would use their women folks CODE; but with the exception of the "VIRTUOUS" clause, as the latter could not affect them - since the enemy did not bring any women from Italy to be used by the Falasha males.

There was in Ethiopia at the beginning of the ITALIAN-ETHIOPIAN WAR in 1934 C.E., where at least 800,000 Falashas[1] existed throughout the entire nation of Ethiopia, East Africa, a growing and beautiful Falasha culture and religion-"HEBREWISM" or "JUDAISM." We saw ourselves reduced to a mere 90,000 after the end of the WAR and the retreat of the enemy Italian armies from Ethiopia before the allied forces and the Ethiopian guerilla in 1942 C.E. The hollocaust was ended.

Let me explain to you a little about the enemy's retreat; and how Falashas were able to laugh and cry happy tears even though they were in such a state of horror. In 1942 C.E. the "Jewish Brigade" from Palestine came to Ethiopia as a part of the Royal British armies of the North African Command [campaign]. They were so happy that they almost forgot there was a war to be continued. Our Falasha women and men had nothing more than kisses, love and prayers for their fellow co-religionists. Falashas even attributed their arrival to the following:

> "It was a definite act of God to send Jews like ourselves to help repulse the enemy, and to stop the atrocities which we were all suffering, like that which other Jews in Europe are facing."

It was the first time in our history that Falasha maidens had ever let themselves relax to any extent whereby they could find themselves KISSING men who were not their own husbands or very close male relatives. Historically they could not remember any period when they were invaded by friendly invaders. Unfortunately, at that time they did not know that in 1974 C.E. they would have to be "CONVERTING" to their own Hebrew or Jewish Religion when they entered the political State of Israel where their fellow rescuing Jews of the Jewish Brigade had returned after the war [review article on pages xiv - xv, xxx - xxxi and xxxii - xxxiii of this Volume].

When the cleaning-up job was completed, and there wasn't one more enemy Italian soldier to be found as the Jewish Brigade prepared to leave Ethiopia to meet the Germans in other parts of

1. Why did'nt White American "Jews" rally against Italian Fascism by Mussolini and Pius XIth?

North and Northeast "Africa," many Falashas were so much enthused with their brother Jews that they joined the Brigade as "SCOUTS" and continued with them all the way into Europe; and many even went all the way to Palestine. Some of the Falashas who lived to go to the "PROMISED LAND" they had always dreamt of returning to may be still living there in very OLD AGE. Today PALESTINE is a new political entity called the STATE OF ISRAEL. Many of our girls and young women wanted to go along fighting with the Jewish Brigade like our men and young boys but they could not because the "Western Nations" did not have, and could not see, their women fighting on the battlefield with their men. I hope that any man still thinking this way will never have to meet an army of women against an army of men if the women are fighting to protect their honour, and said honour is their "PHYSICAL VIRGINITY" or "VIRTUOUSNESS." I can tell you from firsthand experiences that the most determined human animal there is in this entire world is a Falasha woman fighting to maintain her PHYSICAL VIRGINITY or any other criteria of her DIGNITY, if she is brought up to believe that such criteria means that her entire MORALITY OF LIFE and GOD'S FAITH depended upon the manner in which she "SURRENDERS HERSELF" in loosing either. Any good book on the HISTORY OF THE AMAZON WOMEN ARMY of the Fons of Dahomey, West Africa should equally help in understanding this last point. Such was the case of our Falasha women and other women of the Gentile and Moslem population; and certainly it was no different for the Ethiopian women of other local Ethiopian religions where the people neither worship Jehovah, Jesus Christ and/or Al'lah. Therefore, I must take my hat off to each and every woman of Ethiopian cultural pride; this I am only repeating, as it was equally said by a stranded British military correspondent who was saved by a scouting detail of Falasha women that almost disected him, believing first that he was one of the Italian invaders.

After the Ethiopian Government was reborn; and after Emperor Haile Selassie Ist returned to Ethiopia from Great Britain where he fled into exile; Falashas, like all other Ethiopians, began searching for their families and friends who were still around. It was pitiful for one to see the bodies lying all about the countryside of Ethiopia disfigured in every dimension from the MUSTARD [poison] GAS and other instruments of torture applied by the Italian enemy in their attempt at exterminating selected sections of the Ethiopian people. The land was scorched by the POISON GAS BOMBS used by the enemy. The people were starving everywhere; and the livestocks, whatever was left of them, were scattered all over the mountains - those which were not already killed ruthlessly by the enemy - both as food and to starve the population into submission.

Falashas had returned to our communal communities and rebuilt our homes from whatever could be found to begin. In other words, we had to start life all over again because all that we had was gone. Some Falashas had bare rags on their backs, which represented the only luxuries they could see, muchless touch, around them for miles upon miles.

A ROLL CALL was made in each of the communal communities for a check on our human losses, the result being more than 740,000 of the original 800,000 [plus] Falashas dead and/or missing from the communal communities alone; and still others from non-communal areas - including those living in Gentile and Moslem cities in other sections of Ethiopia; this is not including others who fled into Sudan, Kenya and Uganda. Thousands more were not counted in the census.

Our loss in numbers did not discourage those of us who remained; for we had something which the Italian armies with their MUSTARD GAS and other means of ATROCITIES could not steal - our "SACRED [Holy] TORAH." The SACRED TORAH, literally dozens of them had been burried, each in a separate cave under earth and stones. The SACRED TORAH had remained THE BASIS OF STRENGTH and COURAGE;[1] added to the fact that WE could still look at OURSELVES, which include MOTHER, DAUGHTER and other WOMEN FOLK straight into their eyes and shout with greatest joy about anyone of them:

THIS IS OUR WOMAN OF INTEGRITY, AND THE MOTHER OF OUR REBIRTH.

With that foundation Falashas dug out of the rut; and like all of the other Ethiopians we have made tremendous gains since we first began. Those who see us [the Falashas] now and conclude that we are "...

FAR BEHIND ALL OF THE PEOPLE OF [so-called] BLACK AFRICA...,"

should have seen us in 1935 C.E. to 1942 C.E., and they would have instead say the following:

> 'THE FALASHAS ARE FAR INFRONT OF WHAT WAS TO BE EXPECTED OF THEM AFTER THE SLAUGHTEROUS ORDEALS OF GENOCIDE THEY HAVE SURVIVED UNDER THE ITALIAN FACIST ARMIES INVASION AND OCCUPATION OF ETHIOPIA ON THE ORDER OF BENITO MUSSOLINI, KING VICTOR EMMANUEL IInd, POPE PIUS XIth AND THEIR NAZI COHORTS IN ADOLF HITLER'S GERMANY.'

As His Imperial Majesty Emperor Haile Selassie Ist had so wisely predicted, and as it came to pass, the Ethiopian people regained control of their national government. But in the meantime the KINGS and QUEENS, as other MONARCHISTS in Europe, all of whom had failed to heed Ethiopia's cries at their "LEAGUE OF NATIONS," were running all over the face of the globe without a place to call "HOME." Also, the pleasure was to witness what happened to Dictator [Il Duce] Benito Mussolini. The same Italian people who had so gallantly proclaimed and hailed Il Duce and Adolf Hitler were after Il Duce's neck. Hitler had already "COMMITTED SUICIDE;" as the Europeans have said. But Il Duce was finally caught by his own one-time worshipers; and they too.

> HANGED HIM UPSIDE-DOWN IN PUBLIC DISGRACE WHILE OTHERS SPAT ALL OVER HIM IN THE PUBLIC SQUARE WHERE HE HAD ONCE PROCLAIMED HIMSELF INVINCIBLE.

---

1. Why are we not hearing anything from European-American Jews about this "holocaust"?

Haile Selassie Ist, the former Ras or Governor Tafari Makonen, was back on his throne in Addis Ababa, Ethiopia's Capital City, siting as HIS IMPERIAL MAJESTY - THE KING AND EMPEROR OF ETHIOPIA, LION OF JUDAH..., etc., etc., etc. But most of all the kings and queens who scoffed at him from their palaces in Europe were receiving INTERNATIONAL WELFARE where-ever they were scattered all over the world penniless. They were living upon the CHARITABLE DONATIONS of Great Britain and the United States of America. England was to follow a few years later to live equally upon the CHARITIES given her by the United States of America. The people, of whom they once ruled mercilessly, wanted no more of them and kicked them out of power. The prophecy was fulfilled and the Emperor was victorious. The Africans had come through once more, and are still going forward with the rest of the colonial peoples to complete freedom from Western imperialism, colonialism and local neo-colonialism; with uncompromising complete self-government for all as our main goal. Even Haile Selassie Ist suffered the fate of many uprisings by the Ethiopian people he had deserted; finally having been overthrown himself in 1974 C.E./A.D.

A CHRONOLOGY OF THE ITALIAN-ETHIOPIAN WAR OF 1934 - 1942 C.E.

Dec. 9, 1934 At Wai Wai [Wal Wal] Italian armies from the colony of Italian Somaliland attacked Ethiopian troops on Ethiopia's northern borders.

Dec. 10, 1934 Aksum, the Holy City of Ethiopia, invaded by Italian forces.

May 3, 1935 Emperor Haile Selassie Ist and family fled Ethiopia, from Addis Ababa to Jibuti in the colony called "French Somaliland," and was taken by a British Cruiser to Palestine [today called "Eretz - State of - Israel" or "Palestine"].

May 5, 1935 Il Duce Benito Mussolini, with the blessings of Pope Pius XIth and King Victor Emmanuel IInd, decreed "...the successful end of the Italo-Ethiopian War" in favor of the Fascists.

May 9, 1935 King Victor Emmanuel IInd of Italy declared and proclaimed himself "...EMPEROR OF ETHIOPIA..." with the blessings of Pope Pius XIth - the "Representative of God on Earth."

May 10, 1935 Persecution of the Falashas begins. It must be remembered that the entire Ethiopian population also suffered from the Facists. [But to date they have not condemned Pius XIth bigotry]

Aug. 4, 1942 The JEWISH BRIGADE of the British North African Command, along with the Ethiopian Army and Guerilla forces, forced the Italian invaders and colonialists in Ethiopia to surrender.

The above data is far from complete. The only reason for this limited list is due to the need to understand the sequence of the events related to the main point for presenting this very short synopsis of the ITALIAN-ETHIOPIAN WAR[1] and its effect upon the Falashas and their communities. The following data gives the background incidents which led to the above "Chronology."

1. See League of Nations proceedings relative to the "Wal-Wal Incident"... Italy vs Ethiopia, etc.

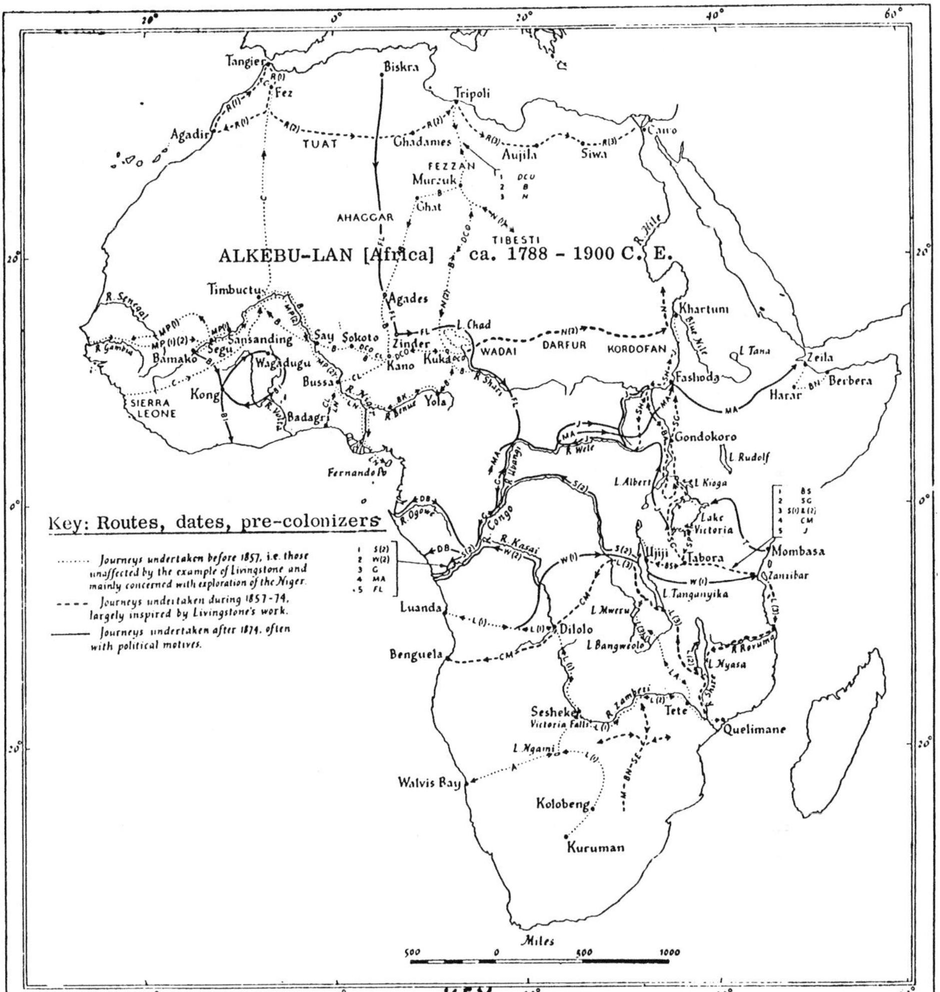

KEY

THE MAJOR IMPERIAL PRE-COLONIALIST SO-CALLED "EXPLORERS" WHO CHARTED THE CONTINENT OF ALKEBU-LAN [Africa] FOR ARMIES, MISSIONARIES AND ENTREPRENUERS

MP(1)	Mungo Park 1795-7	BN	Burton 1854-5	S(1)	Stanley 1871-2
MP(2)	" " 1805-6	BS	Burton & Speke 1857-9	S(2)	" 1874-7
LA	Lacerda 1798-9	SP	Speke 1858	CM	Cameron 1873-4
DCO	Expedition of Denham, Clapperton & Oudney 1823-5	SG	Speke & Grant 1860-3	DB	De Brazza 1875-9
C	Caillé 1827-9	BA	Baker 1862	J	Junker 1879-86
CL	Clapperton & R. Lander 1825-7	R(1)	Rohlfs 1862	W(1)	Von Wissmann 1880-3
LN	R. & J. Lander 1830	R(2)	" 1864	W(2)	" 1884-5
L(1)	Livingstone 1841-56	R(3)	" 1869	T	Thomson 1883
L(2)	" 1858-64	M	Mauch 1860-72	G	Grenfell 1885
L(3)	" 1866-73	BN	Baines 1869-72	BI	Binger 1889-90
B	Barth 1850-6	N(1)	Nachtigal 1869	MA	Marchand 1898
A	Andersson 1850	N(2)	" 1870-4	FL	Foureau-Lamy expedition 1898-1900
BK	Baikie 1854	SE	Selous 1872-92		
		SH	Schweinfurth 1868-71		

NORTHEAST AFRICA DURING THE HEIGHT OF EUROPEAN COLONIALISM, ETC.
[This map, etc. from "The Map Of Africa By Treaty" as modified by ben-Jochannan]

THE EUROPEAN IMPERIALIST ADVANCE IN NORTH-EAST AFRICA WHICH CAUSED THE BATTLE OF ADOWA [1896] AND WAL-WAL INCIDENT [1935]. THE SPREAD OF EUROPEAN COLONIALISM IN NORTH-EAST "AFRICA" ca. 1865 - 1914 C.E.

Note: Colonial expansion in North Africa was simultaneous with all of the other areas of the continent. The Turks, for example, maintained their so-called "... SUZERAINTY..." until 1914 in Egypt, which the British made a "PROTECTORATE" after World War I - ca. 1914 - 1918

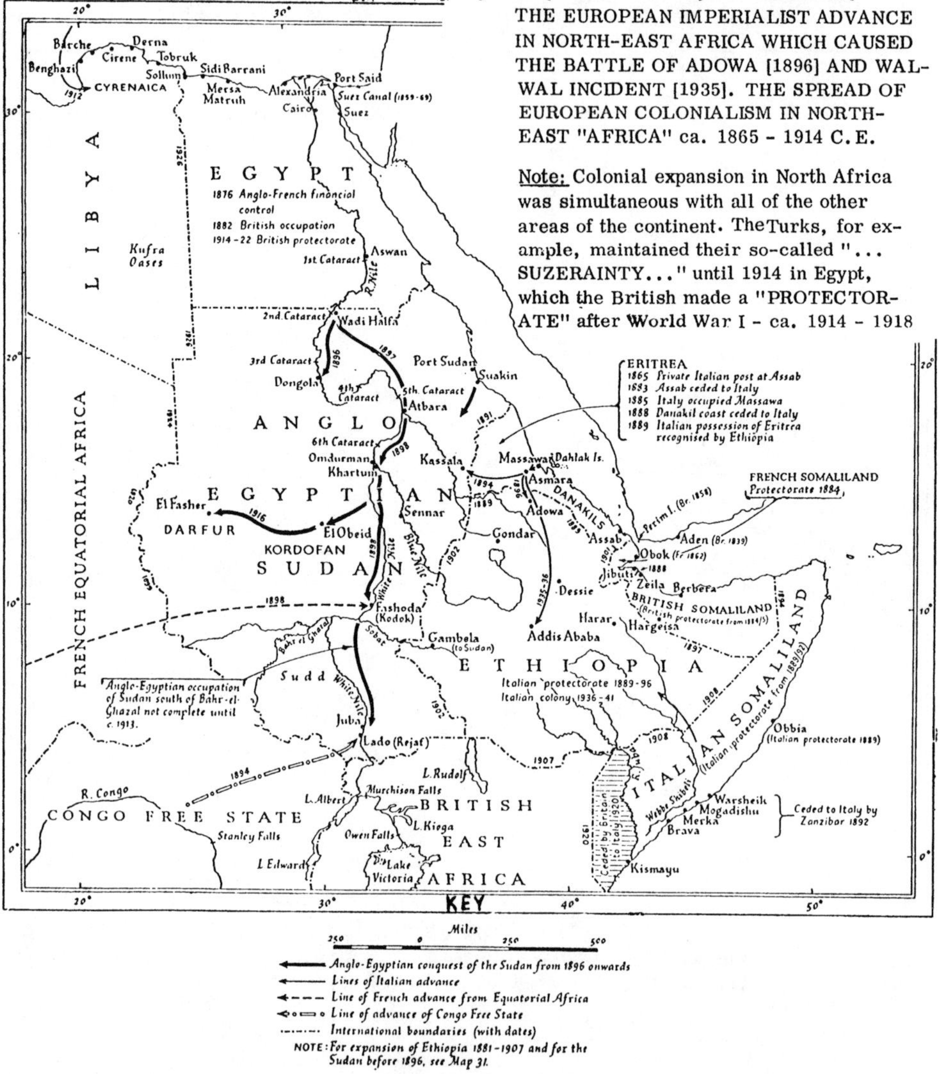

This map should reflect British colonialism in Egypt until 1936 C.E. through the so-called "Anglo-Egyptian Treaty of 1936 A.D.," which allowed Britain in Egypt until 1954 C.E. This form of colonialism was endorsed by churches, synagogues, mosques, etc. all over Europe and America. All who backs "Eritrean Independence from Ethiopia" should study this period of Ethiopian history.

EUROPEAN COLONIALISM IN MOTHER ALKEBU-LAN/"AFRICA"

[All of it by Christians, Jews, Atheists, et al]

ABYSSINIA, &c.[1]

LIST OF TREATIES, &c.

[For convenience of reference, all the Treaties concluded by Great Britain and Italy with ABYSSINIA, SHOA, ETHIOPIA, ASSAB, AUSSA, DANAKILS, and ZULA are inserted under the general heading of ABYSSINIA, &c. The General Agreement of 1906 between Great Britain, France, and Italy respecting Abyssinia is also inserted under this heading, but the Protocols concluded between Great Britain and Italy respecting Abyssinia, Massowah, &c., appear under the heading of GREAT BRITAIN AND ITALY.] The Emperor of Ethiopia acceded to the "Brussels Act" of 2nd July, 1890, on the 16th September, 1890.

ABYSSINIA AND FRANCE.

[illegible] Mar., 1897.	Convention	France and Abyssinia.	Frontier of Coastal Zone.

ABYSSINIA, &c., AND GREAT BRITAIN.

16 Nov., 1841.	Treaty	Shoa and Great Britain.	Friendship, &c.
2 Nov., 1849.	Treaty	Abyssinia and Great Britain.	Friendship, &c.
3 June, 1884.	Treaty	Ethiopia and Great Britain and Egypt.	Bogos, &c. ....
17 Aug., 1888.	Declaration	Abolition. British Consular Jurisdiction at Massowah. See Great Britain and Italy, p. 947.	
14 May, 1897.	Treaty	Ethiopia and Great Britain	Frontiers of British Protectorate on Somali Coast.
4 June, 1897.	Exchange of Notes.	Ethiopia and Great Britain.	Do. do.
15 May, 1902.	Treaty	Ethiopia and Great Britain.	Frontier between Soudan and Ethiopia.
15 May, 1902.	Treaty	Ethiopia, Great Britain and Italy.	Frontiers between Ethiopia and Eritrea and Soudan and Eritrea.
29 Jan. / 1 Feb., 1903.	Exchange of Notes.	Great Britain and Italy.	Frontier between Abyssinia and the East Africa Protectorate. (See Great Britain and Italy.)
27 June, 1903.	Description	Soudan-Abyssinian Frontier	
13 Dec., 1906.	Agreement	Great Britain, France, and Italy.	Abyssinia ....
6 Dec., 1907.	Agreement	Ethiopia and Great Britain.	Frontiers between British East Africa, Uganda, and Ethiopia.
9 Mar., 1894.	Concession	Ethiopian Railway Company	
25 Dec., 1899.	Concession	Wallaga Mining Company	

ABYSSINIA, DANAKILS, &c., AND ITALY.*

10 Feb., 1859.	Treaty	Ethiopia and Sardinia	Commerce ....
15 Nov., 1869.	Convention	Assab and Italy	Sale of Territory.

1. See Sir Edward Hertslett, THE MAP OF AFRICA BY TREATY, London, 1890, etc., Vol. I, II and II, was the "Official Historian" for Queen Victoria of Great Britain, the most powerful of the monarchs of the Berlin and Brussels Conference and Act, etc.

11 Mar., 1870.	Convention....	Assab and Italy	Sale of Territory. 1
30 Dec., 1879.	Convention....	Raheita and Italy	Cession of Islands.
15 Mar., 1880.	Convention	Raheita and Italy	Cession of Islands.
15 May, 1880.	Convention....	Danakils and Italy	Cession of Territory.
15 May, 1880.	Declaration....	Danakils and Italy	Cession of Territory.
20 Sept., 1880.	Convention....	Raheita and Italy	Protection ....
15 Mar., 1883.	Treaty...........	Assab (Danakils) and Italy.	Cession, Ablis (Aussa), &c.
21 May, 1883.	Treaty...........	Shoa and Italy...........	Boundaries, &c.
3 Feb., 1885.	Proclamation	Italy	Occupation of Massowah.
7 July, 1887.	Convention....	Aussa (Danakils) and Italy.	Road. Assab to Mt. Musalli.
10 Aug., 1887.	Convention....	Aussa (Danakils) and Italy.	Assab - Aussa - Shoa Road.
20 Oct., 1887.	Treaty...........	Shoa and Italy...........	Alliance ....
2 Aug., 1888.	Notification	Italy	Protectorate over Zula.
9 Dec., 1888.	Treaty...........	Aussa (Danakils) and Italy.	Italian Sovereignty.
2 May, 1889.	Treaty...........	Ethiopia and Italy	Boundaries. Foreign Relations.
1 Oct., 1889.	Additional Convention.	Ethiopia and Italy	Boundaries, &c.
12 Oct., 1889.	Notification	Conduct of Ethiopian Foreign Affairs by Italy.	
6 Dec., 1889.	Notification	Italy	Protectorate over Aussa (Danakils).
26 Oct., 1896.	Treaty...........	Abyssinia and Italy....	Frontiers (Art. 4).
10 July, 1900.	Treaty...........	Ethiopia and Italy	Delimitation. Eritrean Frontier.
15 May, 1902.	Treaty...........	Ethiopia, Great Britain and Italy.	Frontiers between Ethiopia and Eritrea and Soudan and Eritrea.
16 May, 1908.	Convention & Additional Act	Ethiopia and Italy....	Frontier. Italian Somaliland (Benadir) and Ethiopia.
16 May, 1908.	Convention....	Ethiopia and Italy....	Frontier. Eritrea (Danakil Coast) and Ethiopia. 2

* See Declaration of 13th December, 1906, annexed to Agreement of that date between Great Britain, France, and Italy respecting Abyssinia as to communication by Italian Government of its frontier Treaties with Lugh, Raheita, and the Danakils. 3

1. See Sir Edward Hertslett's THE MAP OF AFRICA BY TREATY, Vol. II [1895, 1900, 1910], 1969, pp. 419 - 420. Note that the above listing did not include wars fought; nor the reasons for the various treaties, conventions, declarations, exchanges of notes, agreements, concessions, etc. Thus it must be remembered that in ca. 1896 C.E./A.D. it became necessary for Emperor Menelik IInd to repress an invasion by the Italians on Ethiopian territories, and finally defeated them in the world renown "Battle of Adowa." You have already read details about this battle in the general text on Ethiopia, East Africa.

2. Don't forget for one milisecond the role of the United States of America in support of its fellow European [WHITE] imperial colonialists that raped the indigenous African [BLACK] colonials of their riches from the natural resources all over the continent of Alkebu-lan/"Africa."

3. All of the above "conventions, declarations, treaties, proclamations, notifications, acts," etc. were innitiated, discussed, voted and made "International Law" without the input of one solitary African nation, or African person, from any of the three "independent African nations" at the time: Ethiopia, Haiti and Liberia. Haiti located in the Caribbean Sea; the vast majority of her people being of African origin and/or birth at that period, etc.

Boundary.]

TREATY. Ethiopia and Italy. 2nd May, 1889.[1]

(Translation.)

His Majesty Humbert I, King of Italy, and His Majesty Menelek II, King of Kings of Ethiopia, in order to render profitable and secure the peace between the two Kingdoms of Italy and Ethiopia, have decided to conclude a Treaty of Friendship and Commerce:

And His Majesty the King of Italy, having sent as his Representative and Envoy Extraordinary to His Majesty King Menelek Count Antonelli, &c., whose powers have been duly recognized, and His Majesty King Menelek, negotiating in his own name as King of Kings of Ethiopia, have concluded and do conclude the following Articles:—

Art. I.—*Perpetual Peace and Friendship.*

Art. II.—*Appointment of Diplomatic and Consular Officers.*

Boundary between Italy and Ethiopia.

Art. III.†—In order to remove any doubt as to the limits of the territory over which the two Contracting Parties exercise sovereign rights, a Special Commission, composed of two Italian and two Ethiopian Delegates, shall trace with permanent landmarks a boundary-line, the leading features of which shall be as follows:—

(*a.*) The boundary between Italy and Ethiopia shall follow the high table-land.

(*b.*) Starting from the country of Afrafali, the villages of Halai, Soganeiti, and Asmara shall be within the Italian boundary.

(*c.*) Adi Nefas and Adi Johannes, in the direction of the Bogos tribe, shall be within the Italian boundary.

(*d.*) From Adi Johannes the boundary between Italy and Ethiopia shall be marked by a straight line running east and west.

Convent of Debra Bizen.

Art. IV.—The Convent of Debra Bizen, with all its property, shall remain in the possession of the Ethiopian Government, who shall not, however, be able to make use of it for military purposes.

Art. V.—*Customs Dues payable by Caravans. 8 per cent. ad valorem.*

Freedom of Commerce in Arms and Ammunition through Massowah for King Menelek.

Art. VI.—Commerce in arms and ammunition to and from Ethiopia shall be free to pass through Massowah only for King Menelek, who will be bound to make a regular application to that effect to the Italian authorities, furnished with the Royal seal.

The caravans, arms, and ammunition will travel under the protection and with the escort of Italian soldiers as far as the Ethiopian frontier.

Art. VII.—*Freedom of Travel and Commerce. Armed Men prohibited from crossing Frontier to intimidate or molest Inhabitants.*

Art. VIII.—*Freedom of Commerce with Natives in Italy and Ethiopia.*

Art. IX.—*Religious Liberty guaranteed.*

Art. X.—*Jurisdiction. Disputes and Lawsuits between Italians in Ethiopia to be settled by Italian Authorities at Massowah or their Delegates. Disputes between Italian and Ethiopians to be settled by Italian Authorities at Massowah, or by Italian and Ethiopian Delegates.*

Art. XI.—*Disposal of Effects of Italians dying in Ethiopia and of Ethiopians dying in Italy.*

Art. XII.—*Jurisdiction. Italians accused of a Crime to be judged by the Italian Authorities at Massowah. Ethiopians accused of a Crime*

---

1. "Abyssinia" is a very despised word/name placed upon Ethiopia by the Arab Moslems when they colonizing East and North Africa during their "Jihads" or "Holy Wars," etc. in 639 C.E., etc.

committed in Italian Territory to be tried by Ethiopian Authorities. [Altered by Art. IX of Additional Convention of 1st October, 1889.

Art. XIII.—*Extradition of Criminals.*

Art. XIV.—*Prevention of Slave Trade. No Caravan of Slaves to be allowed to pass through King Menelek's Territories.*

Map Shewing

THE ITALIAN POSSESSIONS ON THE DANAKIL COAST

ACCORDING TO

THE TREATY BETWEEN ITALY AND THE SULTAN OF AUSSA

OF

9th Decr 1888.

NO MAP WAS ATTACHED TO THE TREATY OF THE 9TH DECR 1888.

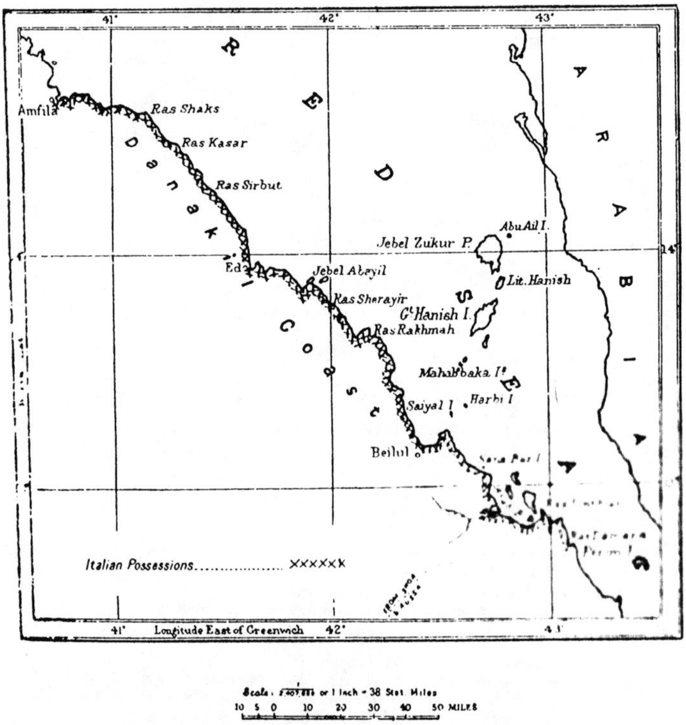

Art. XV.—*Validity of Treaty in the whole of the Empire.*

Art. XVI.—*Power of either Party to modify Treaty after 5 years, on giving a year's notice. Concessions of Territory to be unalterable.*

Negotiations of Ethiopia with Foreign Powers to be made through Italian Government.

Art. XVII.—His Majesty the King of Kings of Ethiopia consents to avail himself of the Italian Government for any negotiations which he may enter into with the other Powers or Governments* (*per tutte le trattazioni di affari che avesse con altre potenze o governi*). [1]

Preferential Treatment to Italians in Ethiopia in regard to the establishment of Houses of Commerce or Manufactures.

Art. XVIII.—If at any time His Majesty the King of Ethiopia should have the intention of granting special privileges to subjects of a third State in regard to the establishment of houses of commerce or manufactures in Ethiopia, he shall always give preference, when all other conditions are equal, to Italians. [2]

Art. XIX.—*Both Italian and Amharic Texts of Treaty to be considered Official, and of the same authority.*

Ratification of Treaty.

Art. XX.—The present Treaty shall be ratified.†

In faith of which Count Pietro Antonelli, in the name of His Majesty the King of Italy, and His Majesty Menelek, King of Kings of Ethiopia, in his own name, have signed and sealed the present Trèaty in the encampment of Uccialli, on the 25th Mazzia, 1881, corresponding to the 2nd May, 1889.

For His Majesty the King of Italy,
(L.S.) PIETRO ANTONELLI.
(Imperial Seal of Ethiopia.)

* Notified to British Government, 12th October, 1889.
† Ratified by the King of Italy, 29th September, 1889.

---

1. It must be noted that King [Emperor] Menelik II was unalterably adverse to the "SLAVE TRADE:" This is the opposite of the common rumors against all African emperors, kings, chiefs and other hands of government which the European and European-American missionaries spread.

Just emagine that Ethiopia, under the leadership of this same king and emperor, had to battle Italy just SEVEN [7] SHORT YEARS later over violations of these same provisions. This was the cause for the BATTLE OF ADOWA, which was THIRTY-NINE [39] YEARS later revenged by Il Duce Benito Mussolini, King Victor Emmanuel IInd and Pope Pius XIth in the October 3, 1935 invasion of the Kingdom and Empire of Ethiopia. Yet all of the above treaties had been signed.

The ratification of the above TREATY at the Encampment of Uccialli was hardly a fact before Italian military personel was moved westwards from the coastline area shown on the map on page 248 of this volume, which the Italians claimed to have received from the so-called "SULTAN OF AUSSA." The issue is that the SULTAN had seized the same territory when the Arabs were invading most of the Northeast, East and Southeast coastline of Alkebu-lan, all of which began with their first "JIHAD " [Holy War] in ca. 640 C.E. or 18 A.H. [After the Hejira, Hagira, etc.].

What we have seen here is the common conduct of conquerors distributing amongst themselves all the "SPOILS" of their conquest; their own "International Legalization" of same; and more than that - their insistance their ruthless butchered victims acquise to their wanton acts of genocide and international piracy as being"...a blessing from God Almighty... [Ywh Jesus and/or Al'lah].

2. This "power play" was with the full endorsement of the United States of America. Sad enough, most Americans - including "African-Americans," will swear their country was not involved.

AFRICA: BEGINNING OF PARTITION ca. 1830 TO END OF PARTITION ca. 1885.

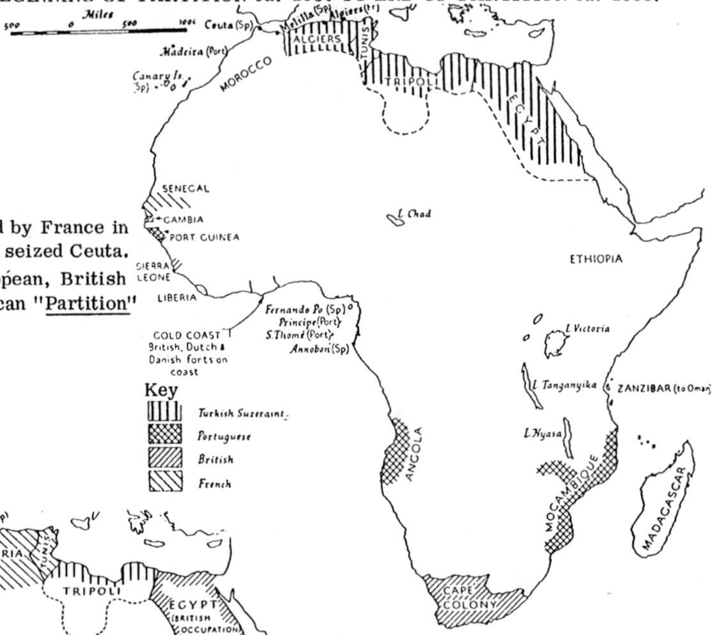

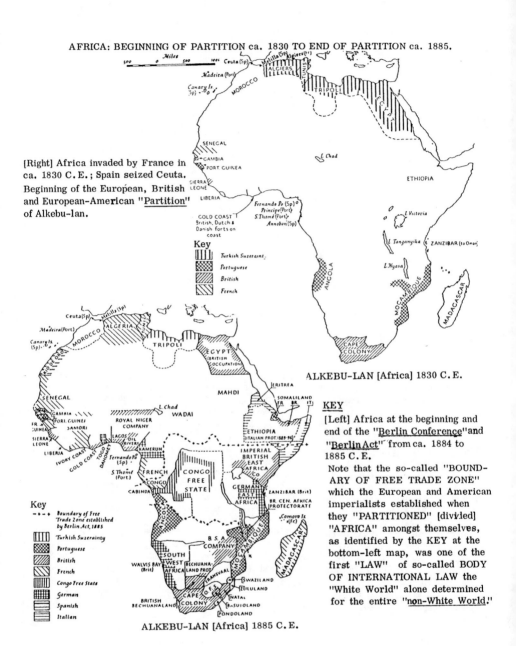

[Right] Africa invaded by France in ca. 1830 C.E.; Spain seized Ceuta. Beginning of the European, British and European-American "Partition" of Alkebu-lan.

ALKEBU-LAN [Africa] 1830 C.E.

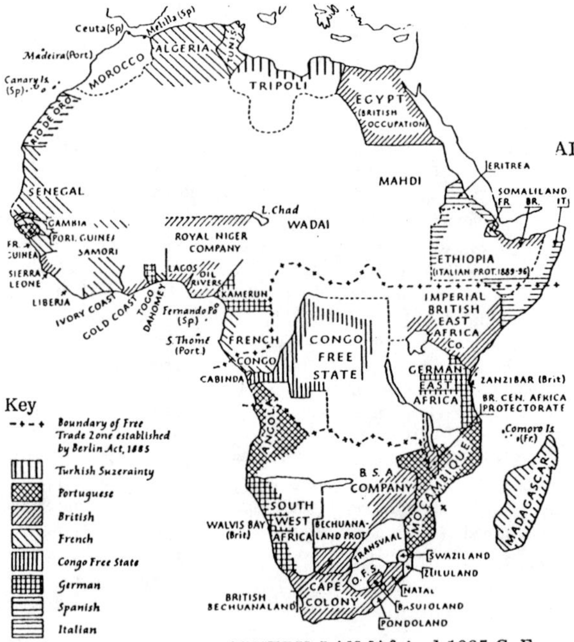

KEY

[Left] Africa at the beginning and end of the "Berlin Conference" and "Berlin Act" from ca. 1884 to 1885 C.E.

Note that the so-called "BOUNDARY OF FREE TRADE ZONE" which the European and American imperialists established when they "PARTITIONED" [divided] "AFRICA" amongst themselves, as identified by the KEY at the bottom-left map, was one of the first "LAW" of so-called BODY OF INTERNATIONAL LAW the "White World" alone determined for the entire "non-White World."

ALKEBU-LAN [Africa] 1885 C.E.

THE UNITED STATES OF AMERICA: PARTNER IN AFRICA'S PARTITION

—GENERAL ACT of the Conference of Berlin, relative to the Development of Trade and Civilization in Africa; the free Navigation of the Rivers Congo, Niger, &c.; the Suppression of the Slave Trade by Sea and Land; the occupation of Territory on the African Coasts, &c. Signed at Berlin, 26th February, 1885.[1]

(Translation.)

In the Name of Almighty God.

Preamble.

HER Majesty the Queen of the United Kingdom of Great Britain and Ireland, Empress of India; His Majesty the German Emperor, King of Prussia; His Majesty the Emperor of Austria, King of Bohemia, &c., and Apostolic King of Hungary; His Majesty the King of the Belgians; His Majesty the King of Denmark; His Majesty the King of Spain; the President of the United States of America; the President of the French Republic; His Majesty the King of Italy; His Majesty the King of the Netherlands, Grand Duke of Luxemburg, &c.; His Majesty the King of Portugal and the Algarves, &c.; His Majesty the Emperor of all the Russias; His Majesty the King of Sweden and Norway, &c.; and His Majesty the Emperor of the Ottomans, wishing, in a spirit of good and mutual accord, to regulate the conditions most favourable to the development of trade and civilization in certain regions of Africa, and to assure to all nations the advantages of free navigation on the two chief rivers of Africa flowing into the Atlantic Ocean; being desirous, on the other hand, to obviate the misunderstanding and disputes which might in future arise from new acts of occupation ("prises de possession") on the coast of Africa; and concerned, at the same time, as to the means of furthering the moral and material well-being of the native populations, have resolved, on the invitation addressed to them by the Imperial Government of Germany, in agreement with the Government of the French Republic, to meet for those purposes in Conference at Berlin, and have appointed as their Plenipotentiaries, to wit:—

Her Majesty the Queen of the United Kingdom of Great Britain and Ireland, Empress of India, Sir Edward Baldwin Malet, her Ambassador Extraordinary and Plenipotentiary at the Court of His Majesty the German Emperor, King of Prussia;

His Majesty the German Emperor, King of Prussia, Otho, Prince von Bismarck, his President of the Prussian Council of Ministers, Chancellor of the Empire; Paul, Count von Hatzfeldt, his Minister of State and Secretary of State for Foreign Affairs; Auguste Busch, his Acting Privy Councillor of Legation and Under-Secretary of State for Foreign Affairs; and Henri von Kusserow, Privy Councillor of Legation in the Department for Foreign Affairs;

His Majesty the Emperor of Austria, King of Bohemia, &c., and Apostolic King of Hungary, Emeric, Count Széchényi de Sarvari Felsö-Vidék, Chamberlain and Acting Privy Councillor, his Ambassador Extraordinary and Plenipotentiary at the Court of His Majesty the German Emperor, King of Prussia;

His Majesty the King of the Belgians, Gabriel Auguste Count van der Straten-Ponthoz, Envoy Extraordinary and Minister Plenipotentiary at the Court of His Majesty the German Emperor, King of Prussia; and Auguste Baron Lambermont, Minister of State, Envoy Extraordinary and Minister Plenipotentiary;

His Majesty the King of Denmark, Émile de Vind, Chamberlain, his Envoy Extraordinary and Minister Plenipotentiary at the Court of His Majesty the German Emperor, King of Prussia;

1. These documents prove that the U.S.A. was directly involved in the colonization and partition of Alkebu-lan/"Africa" from France's invasion of Cueta, Morocco, N.A, in 1830 C.E. to 1983 C.E.

His Majesty the King of Spain, Don Francisco Merry y Colom, Count Benomar, his Envoy Extraordinary and Minister Plenipotentiary at the Court of His Majesty the German Emperor, King of Prussia;

The President of the United States of America, John H. Kasson,[1] Envoy Extraordinary and Minister Plenipotentiary of the United States of America at the Court of His Majesty the German Emperor, King of Prussia, and Henry S. Sandford, ex-Minister;

The President of the French Republic, Alphonse, Baron de Courcel, Ambassador Extraordinary and Plenipotentiary of France at the Court of His Majesty the German Emperor King of Prussia;

His Majesty the King of Italy, Edward, Count de Launay, his Ambassador Extraordinary and Plenipotentiary at the Court of His Majesty the German Emperor, King of Prussia;

His Majesty the King of the Netherlands, Grand Duke of Luxemburg, Frederick Philippe, Jonkheer van der Hoeven his Envoy Extraordinary and Minister Plenipotentiary at the Court of His Majesty the German Emperor, King of Prussia;

His Majesty the King of Portugal and the Algarves, &c., Da Serra Gomes, Marquis de Penafiel, Peer of the Realm, his Envoy Extraordinary and Minister Plenipotentiary at the Court of His Majesty the German Emperor, King of Prussia, and Antoine de Serpa Pimentel, Councillor of State and Peer of the Realm;

His Majesty the Emperor of All the Russias, Pierre, Count Kapnist, Privy Councillor, his Envoy Extraordinary and Minister Plenipotentiary at the Court of His Majesty the King of the Netherlands;

His Majesty the King of Sweden and Norway, &c., Gillis, Baron Bilt, Lieutenant-General, his Envoy Extraordinary and Minister Plenipotentiary at the Court of His Majesty the German Emperor, King of Prussia;

His Majesty the Emperor of the Ottomans, Méhémed Saïd Pasha, Vizir and High Dignitary, his Envoy Extraordinary and Plenipotentiary at the Court of His Majesty the German Emperor, King of Prussia;[2]

Who, being provided with full powers, which have been found in good and due form, have successively discussed and adopted :—

---

1. It is not necessary to show the entire "PREAMBLE." The sole purpose for showing this much is to let the reader know that the United States of America's loud disclaimer over the last eighty-nine [89] years about not being involved with the "...PARTITION OF AFRICA..." is documented in Volume II of Sir Edward Hertslett's semi-official book - THE MAP OF AFRICA BY TREATY, London, 1900 [3 Volumes]. In this work even President Ulyses S. Grant's colonial activities are documented! One such activity is shown in all of the documents bearing his name and signature. Other works in which this part of the role of the United States of America in the BERLIN and BRUSSELS fiasco, with respect to the "PARTITION OF AFRICA," are the following: Sir J. Scott-Keltie, THE BERLIN CONFERENCE, London, 1900; THE PARTITION OF AFRICA, London, 1915; Parker T. Moon, IMPERIALISM AND WORLD POLITICS, New York, 1927; and George Padmore, AFRICA: BRITAIN'S THIRD EMPIRE, New York, 1957.

2. The United States of America supported all of the atrocities imposed upon the indigenous Africans by fellow European and British imperialist nations. Even GENOCIDE they engaged in from 1776 C.E. through the present period of neo-colonialism - 1983 C.E./A.D.

THE UNITED STATES OF AMERICA'S SLAVEHOLDER ROLE REPUDIATED!

—DECLARATIONS exchanged between the United States of America and the International Association of the Congo. Washington, 22nd April, 1884.[1]

Declaration of the Association.

The International Association of the Congo hereby declares that by Treaties with the legitimate Sovereigns in the basins of the Congo and of the Niadi-Kialum and in adjacent territories upon the Atlantic there has been ceded to it territory for the use and benefit of Free States established and being established under the care and supervision of the said Association in the said basins and adjacent territories, to which cession the said Free States of right succeed.

Flag.

That the said International Association has adopted for itself and for the said Free States, as their standard the flag of the International African Association, being a blue flag with a golden star in the centre.

No Import Duties to be levied.

That the said Association and the said States have resolved to levy no Custom House duties upon goods or articles or merchandize imported into their territories or brought by the route which has been constructed around the Congo cataracts ; this they have done with the view of enabling commerce to penetrate into Equatorial Africa.

Right to Buy, Sell, or Lease Lands and Buildings.

That they guarantee to foreigners settling in their territories the right to purchase, sell, or lease lands and buildings situated therein ; to establish commercial houses, and to carry on trade upon the sole condition that they shall obey the laws.

Most-favoured-nation Treatment.

They pledge themselves, moreover, never to grant to the citizens of one nation any advantages without immediately extending the same to the citizens of all other nations ;

The Slave Trade.

And to do all in their power to prevent the Slave Trade.

In testimony whereof Henry S. Sanford, duly empowered therefor by the said Association, acting for itself and for the said Free States, has hereunto set his hand and affixed his seal this 22nd day of April, 1884, in the city of Washington.

(L.S.) H. S. SANFORD.

DECLARATION OF THE UNITED STATES

Recognition of Flag of the Association.

Frederick T. Frelinghuysen, Secretary of State, duly empowered therefor by the President of the United States of America, and pursuant to the advice and consent of the Senate, heretofore given, acknowledges the receipt of the foregoing Notification from the International Association of the Congo, and declares that, in harmony with the traditional policy of the United States, which enjoins a proper regard for the com-

1. The proof of the United States of America's role as a colonialist power in Africa documented.

mercial interests of their citizens, while at the same time avoiding interference with controversies between other Powers as well as alliances with foreign nations, the Government of the United States announces its sympathy with and approval of the humane and benevolent purposes of the International Association of the Congo, administering, as it does, the interests of the Free States there established, and will order the officers of the United States, both on land and sea, to recognize the flag of the International African Association as the flag of a friendly Government.

In testimony whereof he has hereunto set his hand and affixed his seal this 22nd day of April, A.D. 1884, in the city of Washington.

(L.S.) FREDERICK T. FRELINGHUYSEN.

References to the above documents are in the "Berlin Act, 26th February, 1885 and Brussels Act, 2nd July, 1890. Explanations and further documentation are also available in Sir Edward Hertslett's THE MAP OF AFRICA BY TREATY,[1] pages 468, 488, 602 and 614, etc.

—*PROTOCOL. Ratifications of General Act of Berlin Conference of 26th February, 1885. Berlin, 19th April, 1886.*

Ratifications (with the exception of the United States of America) deposited at the Berlin Foreign Office.

(Translation.)

All the Powers who took part in the Conference of Berlin having, with the exception of the United States of America, ratified the General Act of that Conference, signed at Berlin on the 26th February, 1885, and having delivered their ratifications to the Government of the German Empire, which has deposited them in the Imperial archives, and has so informed the other Signatory Powers, the Undersigned, authorized to this effect by their respective Governments, have met together at the Berlin Foreign Office to draw up the Act of Deposit of these ratifications, in the manner agreed upon by Article XXXVIII of the said General Act.

Count Bismarck explained in a few words the object of the meeting to which he had invited the Representatives of the Powers who had ratified the General Act of the 26th February, 1885. He read Article XXXVIII of the General Act, and observed that the delay provided for by the first paragraph of the said Article had been prolonged, by common consent, at the request of the Government of Austria-Hungary.

Count Bismarck having then formally declared that the General Act had not been ratified by the Government of the United States of America, recalled to mind that this eventuality had been foreseen at the time of the deliberations of the Conference of Berlin, as shown in Annex No. 3 to the Protocol No. 9, and particularly in the extract of the Protocol of the sitting of the Conference of the 31st January, 1885, which forms Annex No. 6 to the said Annex No. 3. He consequently expressed the opinion that the United States of America enter into the category of Powers who may adhere later to the stipulations of the General Act, in the manner and to the effect determined by Article XXXVII of that Act; all the stipulations contained in the General Act would, however, remain in full force and vigour among all the other Signatory Powers of the said Act, and would bind them reciprocally by virtue of their respective ratifications.

The Representatives of Austria-Hungary, Belgium, Denmark,

1. This work is never used in Higher Education, in spite of the fact that the author was the "Official Historian" for Queen Victoria of Great Britain, the worst of the imperial colonialists.

Spain, France, Great Britain, Italy, Holland, Portugal, Russia, Sweden and Norway, and Turkey having declared that they concurred in this view, and that they were authorized to complete, under the conditions explained by Count Bismarck, the formality provided for in Article XXXVIII of the General Act, the ratifications were produced, and after being examined and found in good and due form, Count Bismarck declared that the documents would, in conformity with the conditions of Article XXXVIII, remain deposited in the archives of the Government of the German Empire.

The other members of the meeting took formal note of this deposit.

In witness whereof the present Protocol has been drawn up, a certified copy of which shall be communicated by the Government of the German Empire to each of the other Powers who have ratified the General Act of the 26th February, 1885.

Done at Berlin, read, and approved on the 19th April, 1886.

[Here follow the signatures.]

Note that the United States of America's ratification was missing from this document, but it was given at the Brussels Conference; that it was not held back because of opposition, but due to the fact that the Congress had already acted in the affirmative, thus it only waited upon the endorsement of the Senate and the President for final action. Like the distortion of Ethiopia's history as presented in the picture below, the distortion of the U.S.A.'s role in "AFRICA" is known.

[Right] Frontpiece to the book published by Father Alvarez in 1540 C.E. - AUTHENTIC REPORT ON THE LANDS OF PRESTER JOHN - following his return from the embassy of the years ca. 1520 - 1526 C.E.[1]

1. This is another example of the type of "authentic history" Europeans wrote about Africa, etc.

–PROTOCOL of a Meeting held at the Foreign Office at Brussels, respecting the Ratifications of the General Act of the Brussels Conference. 2nd *July*, 1891.

(Translation.)

Present:

[Here appear the names of the Representatives.]

Ratifications.

THE Undersigned met at the Foreign Office at Brussels, in order to proceed to the execution of Article XCIX of the General Act of the Brussels Conference.

Production, Examination, and Deposit of Ratifications of certain Powers. (Germany, Belgium, Denmark, Spain, Congo, Great Britain, Italy, Netherlands, Persia, Sweden and Norway, and Zanzibar.)

Baron Lambermont, one of the Representatives of Belgium, read the said Article and the penultimate paragraph of the Declaration. He announced to the meeting that the Government of His Majesty the King of the Belgians had received the ratifications of His Majesty the Emperor of Germany King of Prussia; of His Majesty the King of the Belgians; of His Majesty the King of Denmark; of His Majesty the King of Spain, and in his name of Her Majesty the Queen-Regent; of His Majesty the Sovereign of the Independent State of the Congo; of Her Majesty the Queen of the United Kingdom of Great Britain and Ireland, Empress of India; of His Majesty the King of Italy; of Her Majesty the Queen of the Netherlands, and in her name Her Majesty the Queen-Regent; of His Majesty the Shah of Persia; of His Majesty the King of Sweden and Norway; and of His Highness the Sultan of Zanzibar.

The said ratifications were produced, examined, and found in good and due form. These documents, in conformity with the provisions of Article XCIX, will remain deposited in the archives of the Belgian Government.

The Representatives of the above-mentioned Powers acknowledged to the Representatives of Belgium the fact of depòsit.

Austria-Hungary.

His Excellency Count Khevenhüller-Metsch declared that His Majesty the Emperor of Austria-Hungary, his august Sovereign, had signed the ratification of the General Act (   ) and of the Declaration of the 2nd July, 1890 (p. 517), that they have been dispatched, and will be, on their arrival in a day or two, deposited at the Belgian Foreign Office.

Turkey.

His Excellency Carathéodory Effendi declared that His Majesty the Emperor of the Ottomans, his august Sovereign, had also signed his ratifications, and that it has been dispatched. His Excellency recalled attention to the reserve which his Government had made on the subject of the use of Turkish characters in the case provided for in Article XXXIV of the General Act, a reserve which had been brought to the notice of all the Signatory Governments, and had encountered no objection.

The Representatives of the Powers took note of their Excellencies' declarations.

Russia.

His Excellency Prince Ouroussoff declared that His Majesty the Emperor of all the Russias, his august Sovereign, had signed the ratification, but his Excellency considered that it was proper to defer its deposit until the moment when the execution of the General Act should be definitely assured.

United States.[1]

His Excellency Mr. Terrell declared that he was not officially authorized to speak at this meeting, being without instructions on the subject from his Government. He was present merely in response to the courteous invitation he had received.

Nevertheless, he thought he might say that the question of the ratification of the Brussels General Act was still before the Senate of the United States, which was not then in Session, but which would meet towards the beginning of the month of December next.

His Excellency added unofficially, and merely for the information of the Representatives of the Powers, that the Government of the United States wishing to show the profound interest taken by them in the success of this great work, had concluded an arrangement with the Congo State with the express object of rendering possible the ratification of the Brussels General Act ( ) by the other Signatory Powers.

The fact that Mr. Terrell stated that the United States of America's actions and imputs into the Brussels Conference "...was not officially authorized..." at the time of his actual meeting, which is recorded above, when reading the many RESOLUTIONS ratified by most of the member nations at the Berlin Conference and the Brussels Conference one can not help but see the constant roles of her representatives - Henry Casson at Berlin and Edwin Terrell above - as advocates of the "PARTITION OF AFRICA." Volume I, II and III of Sir Edward Hertslett's THE MAP OF AFRICA BY TREATY, London, 1900 prove this position, all of which is supported by Sir J. Scott-Keltie's THE BERLIN CONFERENCE, London, and THE PARTITION OF AFRICA, London.

—*PROTOCOL recording the Ratification by the United States of America of the General Act of Brussels of 2nd July,* 1890. *Signed at Brussels, 2nd February,* 1892.

(Translation.)

Ratifications. United States.

On the 2nd February, 1892, in conformity with Article XCIX of the General Act of the 2nd July, 1890 ( ), and with the unanimous decision of the Signatory Powers prolonging till the 2nd February, 1892, in favour of the United States, the period fixed by the said Article XCIX, the Undersigned, Envoy Extraordinary and Minister Plenipotentiary of the United States of America, deposited in the hands of the Belgian Minister for Foreign Affairs the Ratification by the President of the United States of the said General Act.

At his Excellency's request the following Resolution, whereby the Senate of the United States consented to the Ratification of the President, was inserted in the present Protocol :—

"Resolved (two-thirds of the Senators present concurring therein),

"That the Senate advise and consent to the ratification of the General Act signed at Brussels on the 2nd July, 1890 ( ), by the Plenipotentiaries of the United States and other Powers, for the

---

1. In political science courses in all of the major "Institutions Of Higher Learning" it is the teaching that the United States of America was not involved in the "Partition Of Africa." Not a solitary word of the above reaches the average student; yet this was/is "official Record."

suppression of the African Slave Trade, and for other purposes.

"Resolved further: That the Senate advise and consent to the acceptance of the partial ratification of the said General Act on the part of the French Republic, and to the stipulations relative thereto, as set forth in the Protocol signed at Brussels on the 2nd January, 1892.

"Resolved further, as a part of this act of ratification: That the United States of America, having neither Possessions nor Protectorates in Africa, hereby disclaims any intention in ratifying this Treaty, to indicate any interest whatsoever in the Possessions or Protectorates established or claimed on that Continent by the other Powers, or any approval of the wisdom, expediency, or lawfulness thereof, and does not join in any expressions in the said General Act which might be construed as such a declaration or acknowledgment; and, for this reason, that it is desirable that a copy of this Resolution be inserted in the Protocol to be drawn up at the time of the exchange of the ratifications of this Treaty on the part of the United States."[1]

The above Resolution of the Senate of the United-States having been textually communicated in advance by the Government of Belgium to all the Signatory Powers of the General Act, the latter have assented to its insertion in the present Protocol, which shall remain annexed to the Protocol of the 2nd January, 1892.

An official notification to this effect was made to the United States Minister.

The Ratification of the President of the United States having been found in good and due form, notification of its deposit was made to his Excellency Mr. Edwin H. Terrell. It will be retained in the archives of the Belgian Foreign Office.[2]

On proceeding to the signature of the present Protocol, the Minister for Foreign Affairs of His Majesty the King of the Belgians announced that the Representative of Russia, in his note expressing the assent of his Government, expressed the opinion that it was desirable that, in the Protocol, a French translation should accompany the English text of the Resolution of the Senate of the United States of America, and that, in any case, the absence of such translation should not form a precedent.

A certified copy of the present Protocol will be sent by the Belgian Government to the Signatory Powers of the General Act.

Done at Brussels, the 2nd February, 1892.

PRINCE DE CHIMAY, *Minister for Foreign Affairs.*

EDWIN H. TERRELL, *Envoy Extraordinary and Minister Plenipotentiary of the United States of America.*

---

1. The hypocritic disclaimer by the United States of America in this paragraph did not change the fact that her envoy Edwin Terrell participated on behalf of the same United States of America in all deliberations, votes, panel discussions and decision-making resolutions. The fact that the United States of America had no actual "POSSESSION" or "PROTECTORATE" did not stop her from treating the Republic of Liberia, West Africa as one under the pretext of "PROTECTING AMERICAN CITIZENS' LIVES." The jig saw puzzle created at both the Berlin Conference and Brussels Conference was with the full participation of the United States of America. This included running boundary lines[literally]through buildings, ethnical groups, etc. and sectioning them off between their fellow European and British colonialists and imperialists. The end result is shown on the map on the following page: THE COLONIAL EMPIRE IN 1914.

2. The role of the United States of America is seen in this document as a co-conspirator in the "Partition Of Africa." In many cases it was the innitiator of the most vile forms of imperialism in the Republic of Liberia, West Africa - its protege.

AFRICA: BEGINNING OF THE "SLAVE TRADE" AND THE FINAL "PARTITION" IN 1918 C.E.

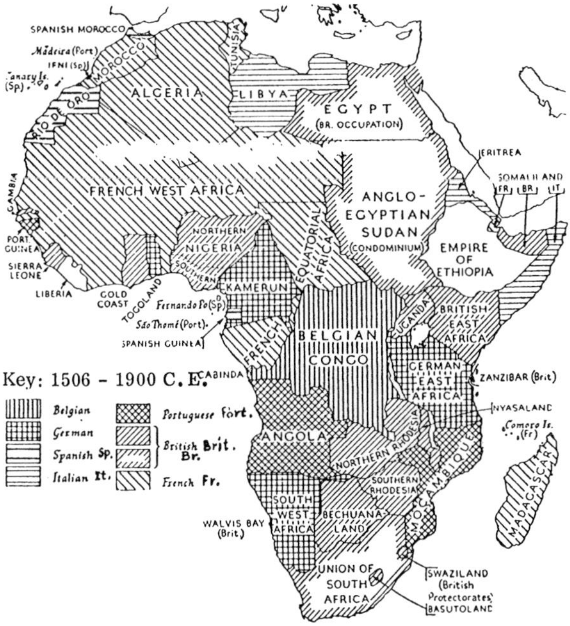

[Top Left] Africa as "Partitioned" at the Berlin Conference and extended at the Brussels Conference ca. 1886-1896 C.E. The political "JIG SAW" that helped to trigger the beginning of the Ist World War. The basic terms: "Protectorate, Condominium," etc. are European and British colonialist semantics which were equally created by the United States of America in consort with the others already mentioned.

[Bottom] The infamous "SLAVE TRADE" and the SLAVE TRADERS.[1] European and European-American "Christians" across the "Middle Passage" [Atlantic Ocean and Caribbean Sea] and Asian "Moslems" across the Red Sea and Indian Ocean. The colonizers who came to Africa, allegedly "...to stop the Arab slave traders and their trade to the East...," began their own that even surpassed the Arabs' in brutality and genocide. More than 200,000,000 Africans were exterminated between the Moslem Asians and Christian Europeans, European-Americans and Britishers. Note that the Moors in Spain were the first Africans to be made slaves of the Europeans in 1506 C.E.[1] under the auspices of the Roman Catholic [Christian] Church with Rev. Bartolome de lasCasas and Pope Julius IInd and Martin V.

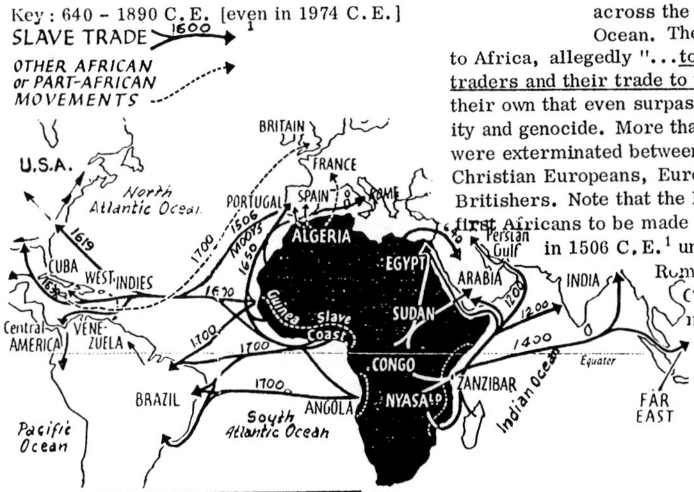

1. See Bartolome de LasCasas, HISTORIA de los INDIAS, Madrid, 1675 A.D., for details of his, and others, role in the beginning of the "Slave Trade" to the Caribbean Islands and elsewhere.

-*DECLARATION. Portugal and Congo. Approval of Report of Boundary Commissioners of 26th June,* 1893. *Lunda Region. Brussels, 24th March,* 1894.

(Translation.)

DECLARATION signed at Brussels, 24th March, 1894, conveying the approval by the Governments of the Independent State of the Congo and of His Most Faithful Majesty of the tracing of the frontier executed by their Commissioners in the region of Lunda, in execution of the Convention concluded at Lisbon 25th May, 1891.

Declaration.

The Governments of the Independent State of the Congo and of His Most Faithful Majesty, having received the report of the delimitation works carried out on the spot by the Commissioners charged by them, in the terms of Article II of the Convention signed at Lisbon, 25th May, 1891 , to execute the tracing of the boundary in accordance with Article I of the above-mentioned Convention, and having taken cognizance of the procès-verbal of the 26th June, 1893, signed, subject to ratification, at Loanda, have decided to approve and ratify respectively this procès-verbal of the 26th June, 1893, in the following terms :—

The year eighteen hundred and ninety-three, the twenty-sixth day of the month of June,

We, George Grenfell, missionary of the English Baptist Mission, and Jayme Lobo de Brito Godins, Governor-General *ad interim* of the province of Angola ;

The above "Declaration" continues for at least two more pages; yet, it is the military and political roles of the so-called "Christian Missionary" from Great Britain mentioned - "George Grenfell" - that I wish to specifically identify. He, like all of his kind from Europe and the entire European-Americas, aided and abeted the "PARTITION OF AFRICA" along with their fellow imperialists, colonialists and entreprenuers. This documentary proof, unlike those in which there is only certain commentary without hard evidence, shows without any doubt whatsoever the role of the "missionary" in the so-called "Congo Free State." Henry Nevinson's book - A MODERN SLAVERY - speaks very much of this imperialist and one Mr. Ron. It deals with how the indigenous "African People" of Nzaide or Zaire [Congo] were dismembered and left to live as examples of what would happen to the others who did not meet their quota of rubber-sap and mineral ore to be shipped to Great Britain, the United States of America and Europe to enrichen further the upper-class of these countries.[1] We remember that the so-called "White Fathers" were equally involved; besides their own pockets being filled, their own sponsor - the Roman Catholic Church - was also enriched beyond comprehension in this type of "PACIFICATION AND CIVILIZATION OF THE NATIVE HEATHENS AND CANNIBALS." The following map from Sir Edward Hertslett's THE MAP OF AFRICA BY TREATY should make us understand what was at stake in the "Congo" was the same thing at stake in "Ethiopia" when the Italians twice invaded this Promise Land[see The Map Africa By Treaty, pages 596 and 597 for further details].

1. More than forty million Africans suffered genocide at the hands of Christians, Moslems, et al., in the Congo Free State, today's Nzaide; at least 35,000,000 more than Jews of Hitler's Nazism.

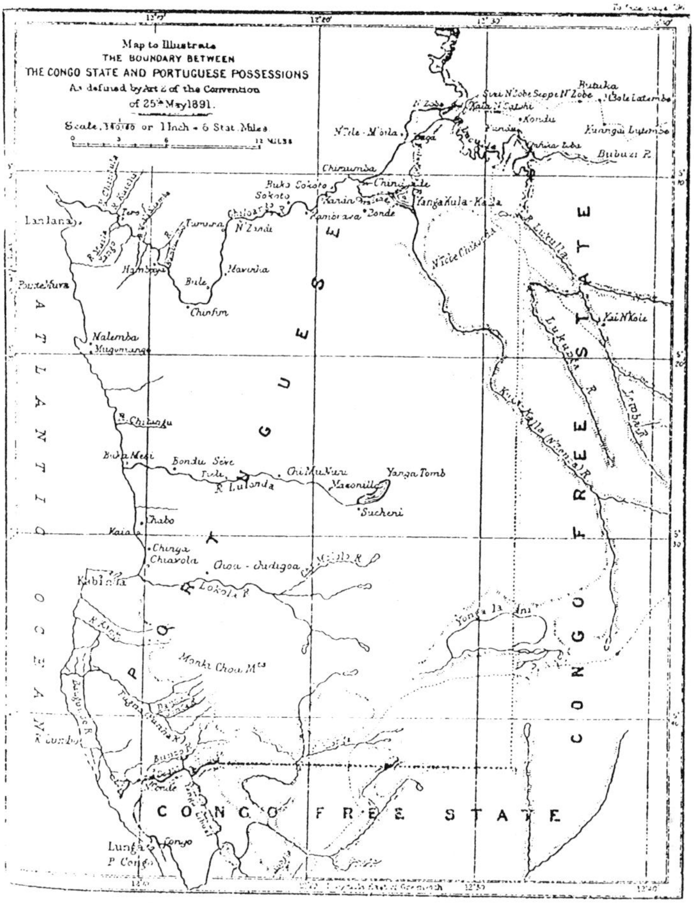

The map above was extracted from one published in the PORTUGUESE WHITE BOOK for 1891 C.E.[1] It is cited to have no official character, and in certain details it cannot be reconciled with the wording of the Convention of 5/25/1891. It is no different than most of the other maps that were produced at the Berlin and Brussels Conference. Why? Because the Europeans, Britons and European-Americans who sat and "PARTITIONED AFRICA" from 1830 to 1896 C.E. were unfamiliar with most of the continent of "AFRICA" all through that period. They placed rivers, mountains, jungles, etc. where no such things were in fact. They even created "PIGMIES, HOTTENTOTS, NEGROES, BANTUS, BUSHMEN." etc.

1. The Portuguese were the racist culprits that created "negroes" for their "negroland" of the 17th Century, C.E./A.D. See R. Moore's The Name Negro, Its Origin And Evil Use, New York, 1961.

ALKEBU-LAN ca. 1749 C.E.

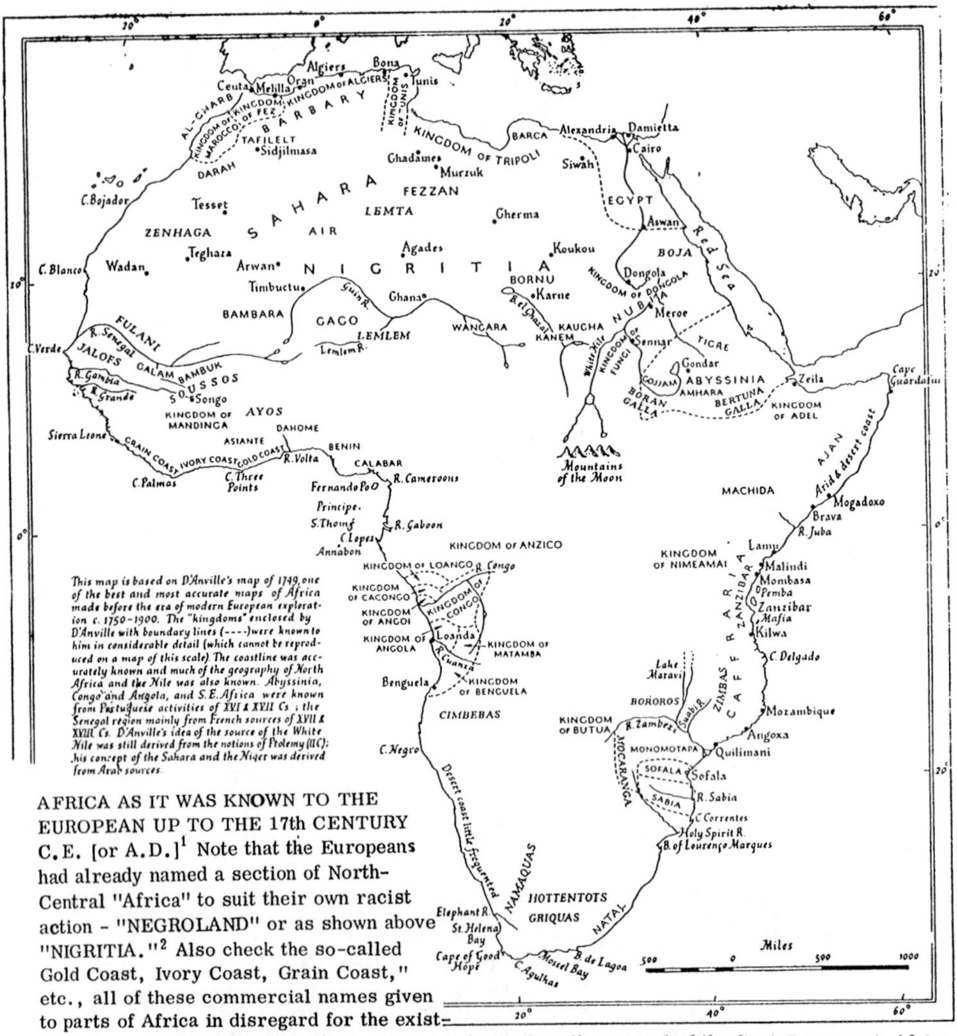

AFRICA AS IT WAS KNOWN TO THE EUROPEAN UP TO THE 17th CENTURY C.E. [or A.D.][1] Note that the Europeans had already named a section of North-Central "Africa" to suit their own racist action - "NEGROLAND" or as shown above "NIGRITIA."[2] Also check the so-called Gold Coast, Ivory Coast, Grain Coast," etc., all of these commercial names given to parts of Africa in disregard for the exist- Africa names the indigenous Africans already had before the arrival of the first European in Africa.

1 The correct name of the continent - "ALKEBU-LAN" - is added to this map by the author. It is also in brackets ["Africa"] the name the Greeks gave to it in approximately ca. 500 B.C.E. For further details with respect to this academic point see p. 24 of this Volume.

2. See Richard B. Moore, The Name Negro, Its Origin And Evil Use, New York, 1961 for an extensive detailing of the racist development of the words "Negro" and "Negroland," etc.

"Africa"as known to Europeans in the mid-18th century

[Top] The map at the top of this page demonstrates the total ignorance of the Europeans and European-Americans about "Africa" and "Africans" even until the 18th Century C.E./A.D. Yet, most of the opinions of negative value we have about Africa and African people were formulated upon misinformation such as this.

[Bottom] The colonial picture of the European and European-American imperialists and colonialists' "PARTITION" of the Asian and African peoples and lands amongst themselves is quite vivid in this map. It was at the "BERLIN CONFERENCE" and "BRUSSELS CONFERENCE" that "AFRICA" became the "jig saw" abortion disected along rivers, mountain ranges, lakes, etc. Boundary lines were even drawn through homes; and families found themselves partly in one European colony or another.

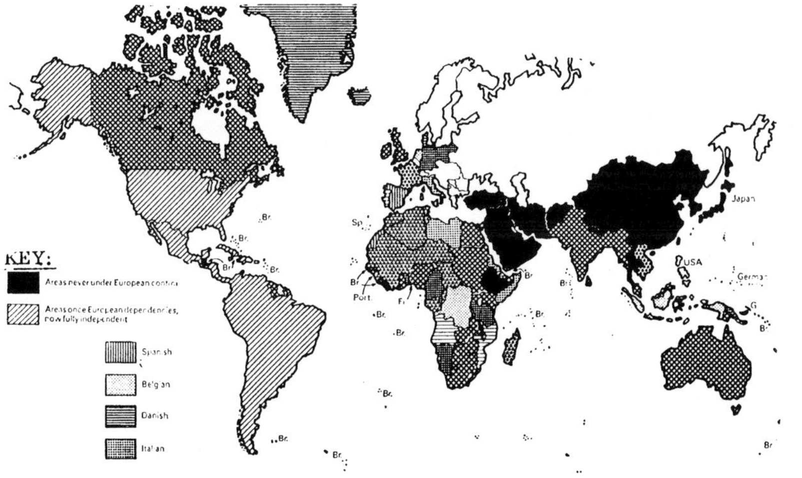

The Colonial Empires in 1914

THE PARTITION OF AFRICAN LANDS, JANUARY 1895

as of the

BERLIN ACT and BRUSSELS ACT 1900
[Estimated Census Dominates Here]

	Area, Square Miles.	Population.	Inhabitants to a Square Mile.
British Africa :			
Gambia	4,120	60,000	15
Sierra Leone	27,730	480,000	17
Gold Coast	52,990	1,800,000	38
Lagos and Yoruba	21,100	3,000,000	142
Niger Territories	375,190	24,380,000	65
British Guinea	481,130	29,720,000	62
Cape Colony (with Walvisch Bay)	225,690	1,800,000	8
Natal	16,740	550,000	33
Zulu and Tonga Lands	11,540	200,000	18
Basutoland	10,290	220,000	21
British Bechuanaland	54,610	60,400	1.1
Bechuanaland Protectorate	117,860	100,000	0.9
Matabili and Mashona Lands	252,880	400,000	1.6
British Central Africa	285,900	3,000,000	10
British South Africa	975,510	6,330,400	6.5
Zanzibar and Pemba	960	210,000	219
British East Africa, to 6° N. and 30° E.	449.570	4,500,000	10
Upper Nile Basin to 10° N.	218,110	1,858,000	8.5
Somali Land	67,000	200,000	3
Sokotra	1,380	10,000	7
British East Africa	737,020	6,778,000	9
British Africa—*cont.*—			
Mauritius and Dependencies	1,090	395,000	363
St. Helena, Ascension, and Tristan da Cunha	130	4,300	32
TOTAL BRITISH AFRICA	2,194,880	43,227,700	20
French Africa :			
Algeria	309,580	4,175,000	13.5
Tunis	50,840	1,500,000	30
Sahara (part of)	1,683,550	2,500,000	1.5
Senegambia	112,820	2,050,000	18
Western Sudan (part of)	290,150	4,900,000	17
Ivory Coast, etc.	64,420	650,000	10
Dahome	14,140	600,000	42
French Congo to 10° N.	496,920	8,950,000	18
Bagirmi	65,650	1,000,000	23
Tajura Bay (Obok and Jibati)	8,640	30,000	3.4
Madagascar and Dependencies	228,560	3,500,000	15
Comoros	760	62,000	81
Réunion	760	172,000	221
Total French Africa	3,326,790	30,089,000	9.6
Portuguese Africa :			
Portuguese Guinea	14,370	200,000	14
Cape Verde Islands	1,490	111,000	74
St. Thomé and Principe	420	21,000	50
Kabinda (Congo)	2,030	30,000	15
Angola	515,670	3,610,000	7
Mozambique	292,750	1,500,000	5
Total Portuguese Africa	826,730	5,472,000	6.6
Spanish Africa :			
Ceuta, etc. (Morocco)	30	16,000	533
Sahara (part of)	150,100	100,000	0.7
Canaries	2,820	292,000	104
Gulf of Guinea	884	35,000	40
Total Spanish Africa	153,834	443,000	3
German Africa :			
Togoland	19,660	800,000	40
Cameroons (Kamerun)	193,370	4,570,000	24
South-West Africa	320,540	200,000	0.6
East Africa	351,040	2,800,000	8
Total German Africa	884,810	8,370,000	9.4
Italian Africa :			
Eritrea (with Kasala)	84,950	450,000	5
Somal and Galla Lands	277,330	800,000	2.5
Abyssinia	155,920	3,600,000	23
Part of Egyptian Sudan	30,680	300.000	10
Total Italian Africa	548,880	5,150,000	8
Congo State (Belgian)	905,090	16,300,000	18
Boer Republics	177,750	763,000	4
TOTAL EUROPEAN AFRICA	9,018,760	112,545,700	12
Morocco	154,500	6,000,000	39
Tripoli, Barka, and Fezzan	338,470	1,000,000	3
Egypt	349,170	7,600,000	22
The Madhi's Territories, to 10° N.	609,300	5,800,000	9
The Eastern Sahara (Tibesti, etc.)	673,230	60,000	0.1
Wadai and Kanem	100,000	2,730,000	
Mosi and other unappropriated territories in the Western Sudan	155,650	2,800,000	18
Liberia	51,970	1,000,000	19
Lakes (not included above)[1]	70,480	...	...
ALL AFRICA	11,621,530	130,535,700	12

The above table was compiled by E. G. Ravenstein, F.R.G.S.; figures being submitted in most cases by the Berlin and Brussels Committee On Land And Population Distribution Of The Continent Of Africa. Note that both Edwin Terrel and Henry Casson represented the United States of America in the capacity of "Minister Plenipotentiary...." You will also note that these figures represent the "PARTITION" on the previous page. Do not forget that the representatives and governments that participated in these acts of genocide on Africans were Christians, Jews, etc.

"AFRICA" IN COLONIAL RETREAT - 1922 - 1936 C.E.

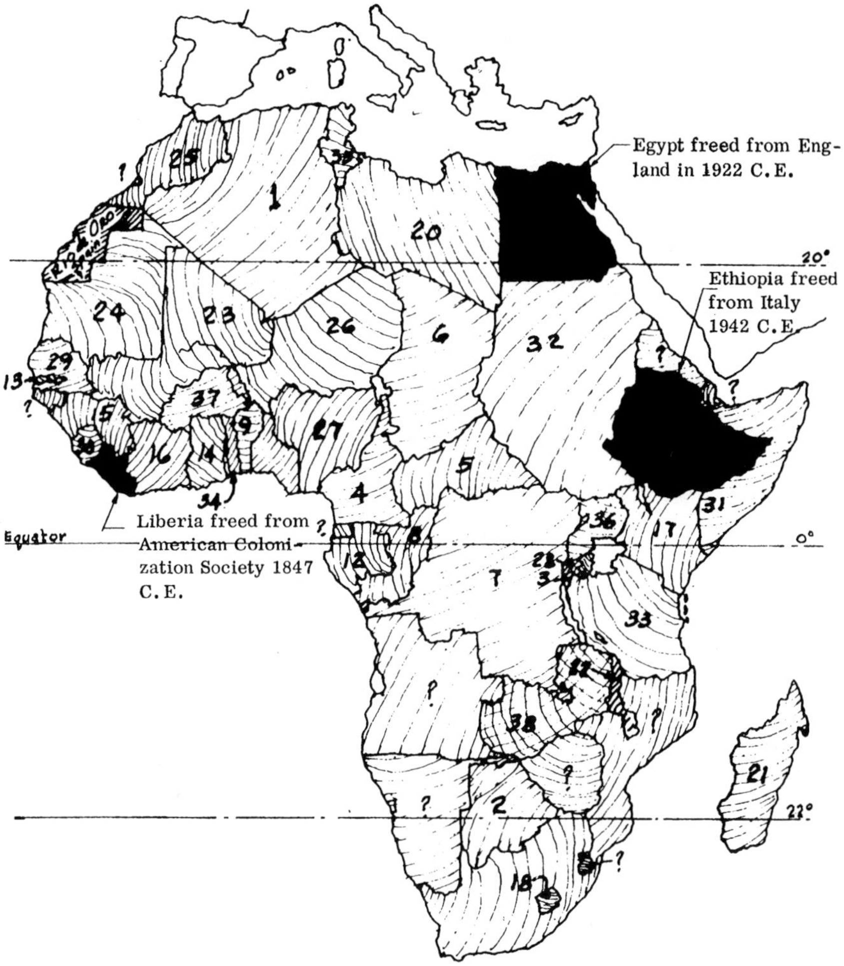
Egypt freed from England in 1922 C.E.
Ethiopia freed from Italy 1942 C.E.
Liberia freed from American Colonization Society 1847 C.E.
Equator
20°
0°
23°

KEY:
Independent States shown solid black ■. Colonial States shown cross-hatched/No. [2]
Note that the "African People" do not consider the WHITE RACIST governments in Azania [South Africa], Zimbabwe [Rhodesia], Ngola [Angola], Monomotapa [Mozambique]and Guinea Bissau [Portuguese Guinea] to be "INDEPENDENT NATIONS." Except for "South Africa" and "Southwest Africa," along with the Arab "colonies of Northwest and Northeast Africa," there is not a semblance of "independence" in all of these nations; the "Gold Coast Revolution" under Dr. K. Nkrumah change it all.

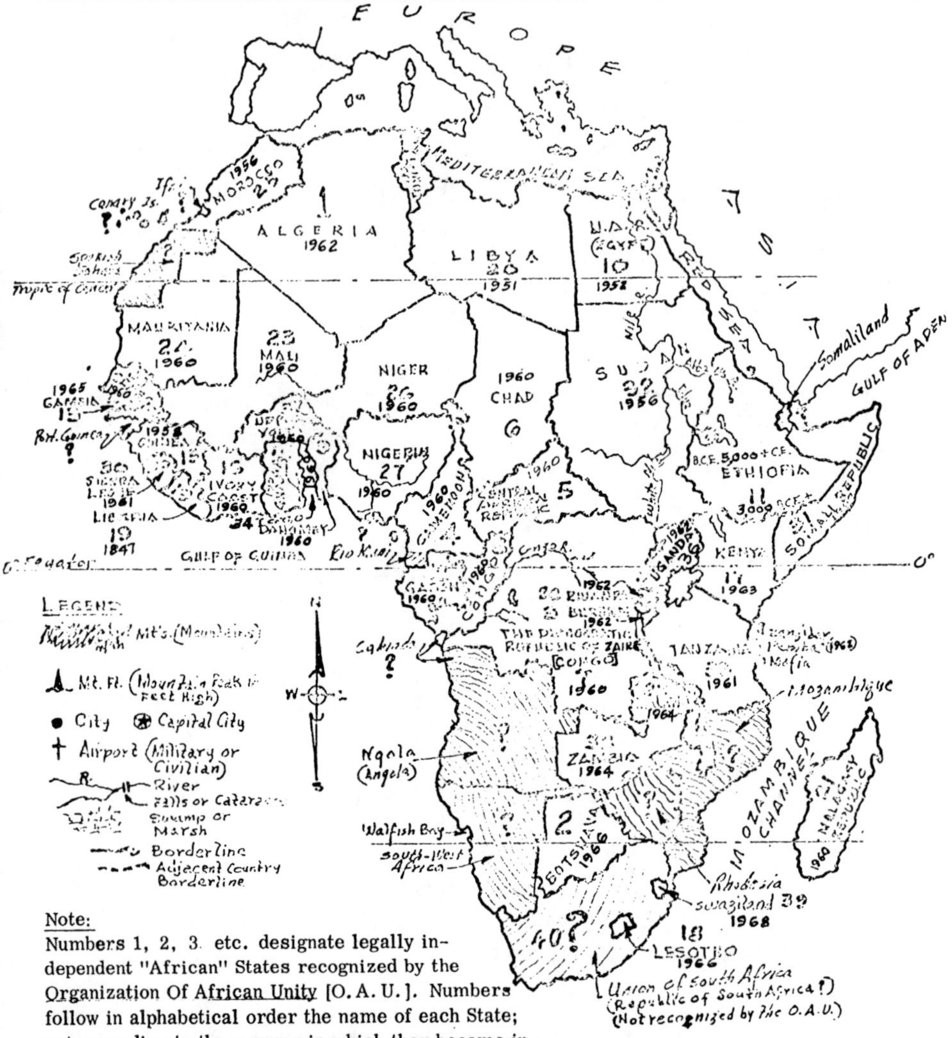

Note:
Numbers 1, 2, 3. etc. designate legally independent "African" States recognized by the Organization Of African Unity [O. A. U.]. Numbers follow in alphabetical order the name of each State; not according to the manner in which they became independent of their European colonialists.

KEY MAP OF INDEPENDENT and COLONIAL "AFRICA"
1951 - 1974 C. E.

39 Independent,	10.8 Mil. Sq. Mi.,	291.4 Mil. Pop.	as of the beginning of 1974.
9 Colonies ,	1.1 Mil. Sq. Mi.,	23.3 Mil. Pop.	as of the beginning of 1974.
Total: 48 Nations ,	11.9 " " " ,	314.7 " "	" " " " " " .

PAN-AFRICAN FREEDOM FROM NKRUMAH'S GHANA IN 1957 C.E.

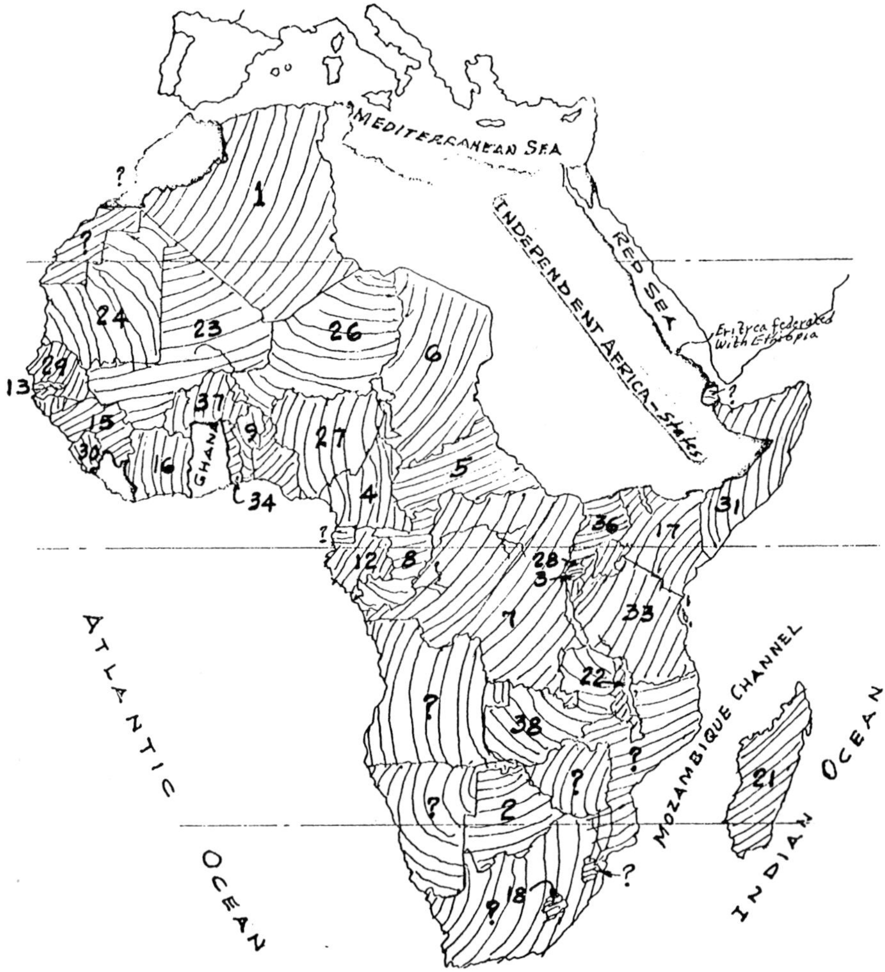

COLONIZATION IN AFRICA IN RETREAT - 1957 C.E.

[Arab-Asian Colnialism Is Next On The African Agenda]

Independent Africa:	States	8,	Area:	3.0 Mil.	Sq.	Mi.
Present Colonial :	"	40,	"	8.9	"	"
Total	"	48,	"	11.9	"	"

Independent Population: 77.9 Mil.; Colonial 236.80 Mil.

Total Population 314.7 Millions

1. Afri^ans are too quiet about Arab-Moslem colonialism, racism and religious bigotry in Africa; at the same instance condemning the same genocide by Europeans and European-Americans. Think.

ARAB-MOSLEM COLONIALISM ATTACKED. .OIL AND THE PAN-AFRICANISTS

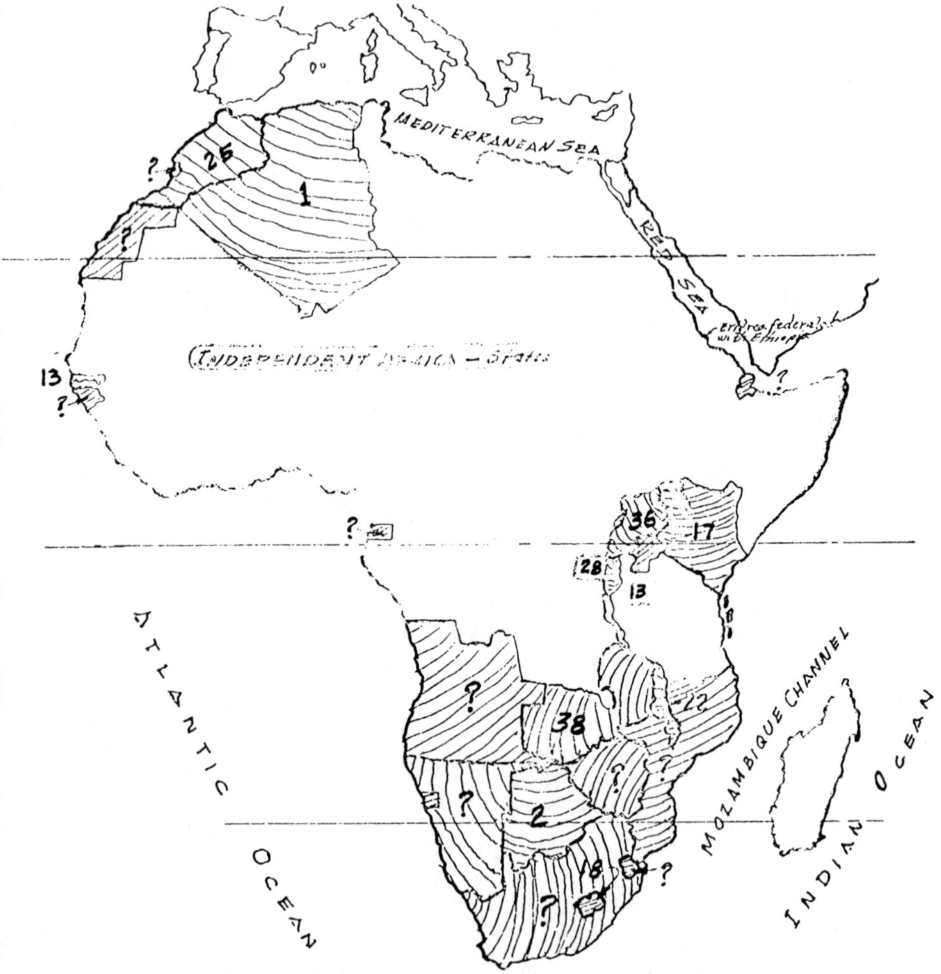

COLONIZATION IN AFRICA IN RETREAT - 1961 C. E.

[When Will Arabs In Africa Become Plain Africans!]

Independent Africa:	States	28,	Area	8.6	Square	Miles
Present Colonial :	"	20,	"	3.3	"	"
Total	"	48	"	11.9	"	"

Independent Population: 244.2 Mil.; Colonial 70.5 Mil.

Total Population: 314.7 Millions

THE MYTH OF ARAB-MOSLEM "FREE" NORTH AFRICANS"? WHY!

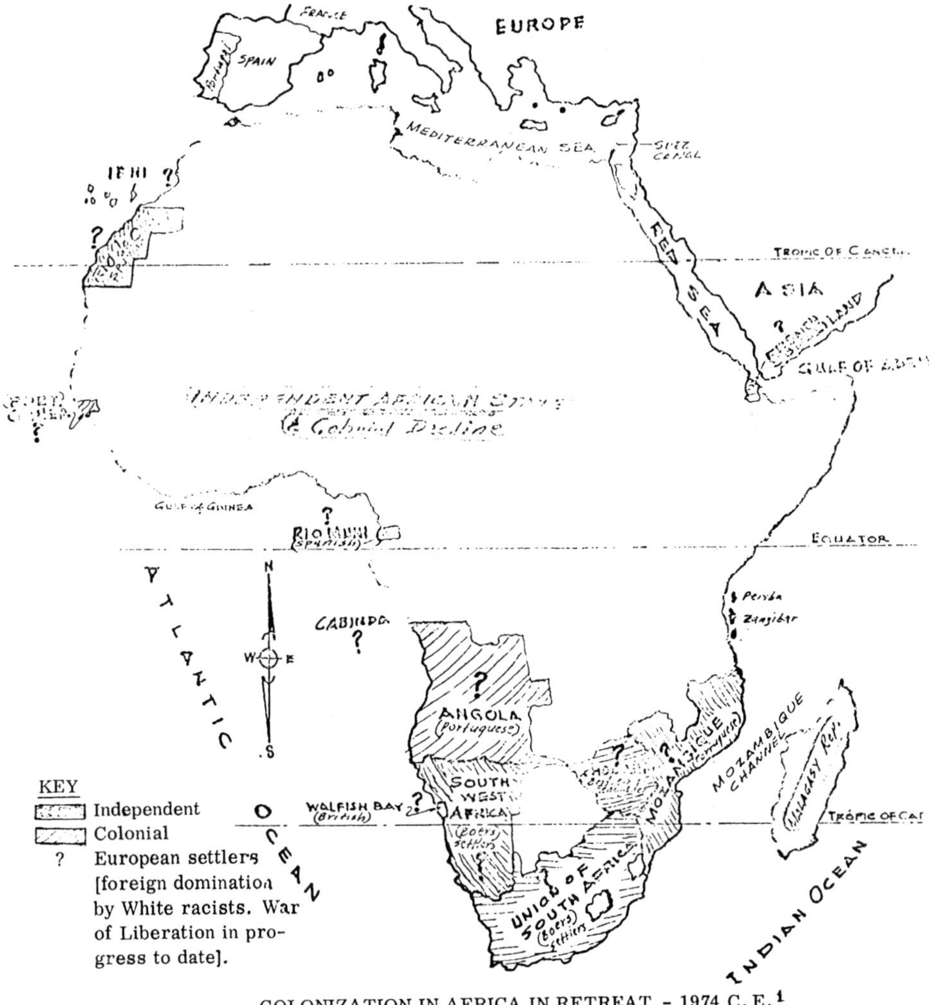

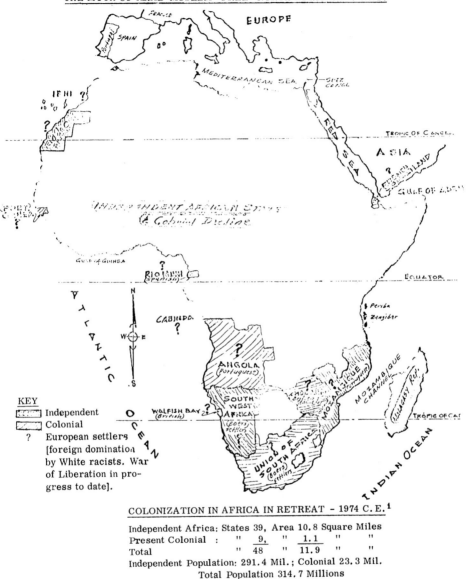

COLONIZATION IN AFRICA IN RETREAT - 1974 C.E.[1]

Independent Africa:	States	39,	Area	10.8	Square	Miles
Present Colonial :	"	9,	"	1.1	"	"
Total	"	48	"	11.9	"	"

Independent Population: 291.4 Mil.; Colonial 23.3 Mil.

Total Population 314.7 Millions

1. The maps stop here because of the last "Population Census Of Africa" in 1974 C.E./A.D. And because a true census was never made of Africans in the interior limits of colonial states.

FALASHAS VIEWS ON THE STATE OF ISRAEL: Chapter IX.

The coming into being of the newly recreated political State of [Eretz] Israel has raised many questions so far as the Falashas are concerned, both at home in Ethiopia and abroad - in the Americas and the Caribbean Islands. At home the question of greatest concern among ourselves was/is:

"Are we [Falashas] going to try another Exodus to Israel, as in past experiences?"

Abroad, among the White Zionist Jews, it was/is:

> What are we going to do with those Black Jews of Ethiopia if all of them should suddenly decide to return to Israel on the theory of the right of biblical return?

The answer appears in the article on page xxxi of this Volume; thus: "...they" [Falashas]"must go through the process of converting...," etc., etc., etc.; all of which I have already underlined.

On the first question Falashas have concluded that:

"We are not contemplating any mass EXODUS as we had tried in previous times."

The reason is obvious to those who know our history and heritage. They know that when we tried a "...MASS EXODUS..." in the past we were almost exterminated from the face of the earth by bad weather and wars with the Jesuit Priests-led so-called "Christian Missionaries" with whom we came in contact while on our attempted return to the so-called "PROMISED LAND." The other factor during the past two occassions is that the people of Ethiopia also knew that the Agaw [or Falashas] are not being "PERSECUTED" any longer in Ethiopia on a governmental basis. Even most of the Christians and Moslems recently have avoided such inhuman acts. Therefore, there would have been no specific reason other than religiou to have caused any sudden "MASS EXODUS" [migration] to the newly created European and European-American political State of Israel by the Falashas. Or, if the local religious bigots could exceed governmental control once more.

However, the Falashas view the above answers to the first question as being not the full basis for the lack of a movement for migrating to the European and European-American State of Israel. The fundamental point was the matter of finding a method whereby Falashas could have traveled to Palestine [presently "Israel"][1] without having to live in any manner different than they were accustomed. You would recall the reason why many Falashas had to leave ancient Israel in the first place, which was because they were dissatisfied with their king and political rule; and that was sometime after "...the destruction of the First Temple in Jerusalem...." The following reasons must be added: 1] Falashas had to respect the laws against using food prepared by Gentiles; 2] They could not travel to Palestine by foot without having to eat food prepared by people who were not Hebrews; 3] They had no other means of travel, and the officials of the political State of Israel

1. The issue of the correct name of the former land "Canaan" is of no concern to this author here.

were not interested in transporting them by air as they had done to other Hebrew groups in other parts of the so-called "WHITE WORLD;" 4]They claimed that we [Falashas] were not in need of urgent aid, therefore it was not necessary to give us such consideration; 5]The Falashas accepted this reasoning, but most of us living outside of Ethiopia had seen the fallacy of such a concession, also the deep-seated racism that initiated it, needless to mention its inherent religious bigotry.

Another crucial point was the fact that there was no special movement of any "ZIONIST" tendency in the communities of Ethiopia. Black [Falasha] Jews of Ethiopia and other parts of the African continent were not included in the European and European-American "ZIONIST SCHEME" of thinking, therefore no effort was made to include us. Thus the only "ZIONIST" feeling which remained, or has since developed, in the Hebrew communities in Ethiopia was through our religious teachings and convictions resulting therefrom. And the fact that the name FALASHA itself had [illegible] that we are -

[illegible] in the land [on which we are presently living] - Ethiopia."

It equally forces us to believe that:

"We have to return to our homeland according to the orders of God."

The second question was partly answered in "THE FALLACY OF A JEWISH RACE," Chapter 1, pages 1 - 41 of this Volume. However, the second question calls for further clarification by the Falashas, particularly with reference to our feelings about Eretz Israel. For it must be remembered that the Falashas have a stake in Israel which is just as valid like any other group of Jews anywhere, regardless of where they came from and whether they are professed "ZIONIST" or not. This is further true when we look at the percentage of Falashas who were living in Palestine under the so-called "BRITISH [self-proclaimed] MANDATE" and we find that many of them also fought against the British occupation with various units, including the murderous "STERN GANG" and "IGRUNI." But when the British withdrew from Palestine European, European-American and European-Asian born Jews in residence declared themselves "...A NATION." We found that said fellow Falashas went along with the general movement of their fellow Jews and tried to join the "HAGANAH" that became the "ISRAELI ARMY" much later on in 1947 C.E. They fought side by side with their Jewish comrades from Europe, the Americas, Asia and North Africa. Now, after looking at these facts herein stated, it is only natural that we must also ask some questions of our own; thus:

> 1. What purpose is the second question above to serve? 2. What must we take such questions to mean? 3. Why must Falashas be "super-Jews?"

We answered ourselves by saying:

We have taken it to mean that we are rejected on the sole basis of our being darker in pigment than the majority of Jews in Israel; and because of the general disrespect shown peoples of the homogeneous population of Africa, which is held by the major populace of the so-called 'Western Nations'.

This condition is also due to the systems of culture in which "Western Jews" live. Some of them even believe that any and everything the "Western Nations" have to offer to the new political State of Eretz Israel is SUPERB. But that which is offered by Jews of the so-called "Eastern Nations" and Africa is "INFERIOR." What is actually happening is that the "WESTERN JEWS" are looking at the political State of Israel through prejudice mechanical eyes. They have not taken time out to notice that the contributions of the DARK-SKIN [black] JEWS of Yemen, India, Egypt, Sudan and Ethiopia in the field of ANCIENT JUDAIC HISTORY AND CULTURE were, and still are, of most vital importance to the survival and growth of the political State of Israel. We, the rejected ALL-BLACK JEWS of Ethiopia and elsewhere, have maintained certain CUSTOMS and TRADITIONS of the biblical Hebrew "WAY OF LIFE" which would make the "ORTHODOX JEWS" of European and European-American TALMUDIC JUDAISM appear to be "REFORM JEWS" when we are placed side by side [review Chapter IV, Part One through Part Six, "Present Religious Practices And Customs," pages 109 - 147 of this Volume].

However, it must be noted that the question, truly; what are we going to do with the Black Jews of Ethiopia.. originates only with so-called "SEMITIC/CAUCASIAN JEWS" from "Western Communities;" and that such communities are most common in the United States of America. When Falashas travel in South and Central America, Asia, Europe and Africa and meet other Jews we are seldom, if ever, reminded of the fact that we are of a different "COLOR" and/or "RACE" than they are.[1] Needless to mention, this situation is reversed in the United States of America. Even when an African-American meets the average European-American Jewish person in the United States of America, thereby starting some sort of conversation and it is discovered that he or she is a so-called "NEGRO JEW," a sudden silence generally follows; and it is equally broken with:

"YOU KNOW, THIS IS THE FIRST TIME I HAVE EVER MET A NEGRO JEW!"

The fact is that the African-American "JEW" and/or "ISRAELITE" [Falasha] is not ashamed in the least of his or her BLACK COLOR, THICK LIPS, BROAD NOSE and WOOLLY HAIR; nothing of which has anything to do with "NEGROISM" and/or "NEGROPHOBIA." We are definitely certain that our COLOR and HAIR have at worse the equivalent value to that of any other human being on the face of this planet - EARTH. What we have objected to in the above conduct is the method of RACIST aproach that exposes such stereotype reaction. For it is very clear that this type of aproach is never made to "WHITE JEWS" who came to these United States of America

1. See Yosef ben-Jochannan's Cultural Genocide In The Black And African Studies Curriculum, Alkebu-lan Books Associates, New York, 1973 for details on this aspect of the issue.

from some of the most "underdeveloped, backward and primitive" parts of Europe. This type of RACIAL DISCRIMINATION adds to the doubts in Falashas minds on '...the possibility of our being able to live in the political State of Isreal with people who look at us not as plain Jews and/ or human beings, but as a special type of Jews and/or special type of human beings, solely on the basis of our BLACK SKIN, THICK LIPS, WOO¯ LY HAIR...,' etc., etc., etc., ad infinitum.

On the matter of RACIAL DISCRIMINATION Falashas received a grave set back in the "LOVE" they were steadfastly developing for the new political State of Israel when our fellow BLACK and/ or BROWN [darker-skinned] brothers and sisters from Cochin, India [see pages xxxix and 12] were racistly greeted with the following remark by European and European-American [WHITE] Jews:

"BLACK BREAD IS FOR BLACK JEWS, AND WHITE BREAD IS FOR WHITE JEWS."

This news was reported in THE NEW YORK TIMES, March 31, 1952 from an article dispatched by Dana Schmid in Tel Aviv, State of Israel on March 30, 1952 C.E. The reaction to said bigotry made members of the entire Falasha communities throughout the entire world extremely angry at the manipulators of the White Jewish population of the political State of Israel. This statement made many African-American "FALASHAS" who were already purchasing thousands of dollars of ISRAELI BONDS hesitate from so doing further. It even drove those of us BLACK JEWS who were members of "ZIONIST ORGANIZATIONS" in the Americas, and particularly in the United States of America, to stand for our slavation solely with the AFRICAN NATIONALIST and PAN-AFRICANIST groups whose first "GOAL" was/is "...THE FREEDOM OF ALL OF AFRICA FROM EUROPEAN AND EUROPEAN-AMERICAN IMPERIALISM AND COLONIALISM...," and to forget about the possibility of our being able to live side by side with WHITE [Caucasian] RACIST JEWS from the Americas, Great Britain and Europe in the so-called PROMISED LAND. Many so-called "LIBERAL JEWS" have since tried to argue-down this racist act with the following disclaimer:

"THIS IS NOT THE OFFICIAL POLICY OF THE GOVERNMENT OF ISRAEL."

This may be true; but the fact remains that the peoples of other nations, not only Jewish, look at this remark as an open rejection on the part of WHITE JEWS against those of BLACK, BROWN and YELLOW pigment. Moreover, there are no restrictions of official policy by the Israeli Government placed against such racism reoccuring in the State of Israel, thereby causing Falashas to look at the WHITE ISRAELIS unfavorably. This of course did not mean that many more Falashas would not have liked to enter the political State of Israel and live with their fellow JEWS, irrespective of pigment of skin. Neither did it mean that some Falashas would not have assisted Israel if there became a need for them in some conflict where Israel's independence was threatened. What it does indicate to date is that each time something of this sort occurs, that many more Falashas -

1. Since this incident many Falashas had to return to Ethiopia because of "white racism in Israel." The type carried from Europe, Britain, Australia, North and South America by "White Jews.

LIKE MYSELF - would feel that '...there isn't any need to continue the belief that JUDAISM, particularly as practised by White Jews, is the hope of man's salvation...;' and that '...there is no use trying to return to a PROMISED LAND where those who control it do not want the first Black Jew therein....' The fact that the political State of Israel has claimed to be -

"A PLACE FOR ALL JEWS WHO DESIRE TO RETURN TO THEIR HOMELAND,"

under the BIBLICAL teachings of the so-called -

"RIGHT OF BIBLICAL RETURN TO THE PROMISED LAND" [Israel],

is another point to be reckoned with as it affects the interest of the Falashas. But, of course, the rejection of the BLACK ISRAELITE JEWS from Chicago, Illinois - the United States of America in 1970 - 74 is just another of the same replay of the 1952 C.E. "BLACK BREAD FOR BLACK JEWS AND WHITE BREAD FOR WHITE JEWS" racist and bigoted religious drama Israeli style.

The political State of Israel has also stated to all of mankind that she is a "DEMOCRACY." Thus, the peoples who heard her are looking forward for demonstrations in the truth of said declaration. The Arab nations around her will rightfully utilize the above statement with respect to the above wrongs, as evidence that the State of Israel was not formed for the purpose which her leaders had claimed, but as the Arabs have charged. But regardless of how you, anyone else, or this writer will try to defend the political State of Israel on this issue, we will not be able to morally or intellectually use the most common argument that follows to vindicate Jewish racism:

"As a democracy the State of Israel is entitled to make many mistakes."

For most White Jews therein should be aware of what such "MISTAKES" developed into under an Adolph Hitler in Germany and Benito Mussolini in Ethiopia with regards to BLACK, WHITE, BROWN, YELLOW and RED peoples of the Hebrew or Jewish Faith [Religion or Way of Life].

Many Falashas are still willing at this moment to migrate to the political State of Israel,[1] even with the existing fear that they have acquired by the above conduct of White Israelis. However, you will recall that the Government of the State of Israel gave as one of its reasons for not being in a hurry to have Falashas migrate in mass numbers as it accepts Russian Jews was that we have a "...SPECIAL DISEASE ...," which was never identified or named. Moreover this position made no sense, because the Government of the State of Israel had received thousands of European Jews riddled with TUBERCOLOSIS from all over the continent, and still others with "VARIOUS TYPE OF SPECIAL DISEASES" developed in the concentration camps of Europe, and elsewhere. Were these WHITE JEWS from Europe told that '...BECAUSE OF YOUR DISEASE YOU DO NOT HAVE THE RIGHT OF BIBLICAL RETURN TO THE PROMISED LAND? The answer is an emphatic "...NO...." In this respect we need to review pages xxxiii - xl of this Volume.

---

1. This is in spite of the fact that most White Jews demand that "Falashas reconvert to Judaism;" but never the same for one solitary "White Jew" from the Soviet Union.

Let us look at the late Dr. David Horowitz and his UNITED ISRAEL WORLD UNION organization's activities a while. Here you will find in this movement [almost defunct] that its primary purpose is to "...CONVERT..." all possible "WHITE [Caucasian] AMERICANS" to the Hebrew Religion, also the so-called "AMERICAN INDIANS" on the basis that they are the so-called "LOST TRIBES." Of course the Falashas were/are equally the "LOST TRIBES." This group of "WHITE" American Jews was never turned dowm from entry into the State of Israel, where their leader also passed away. Instead their late leader was highly respected, and was accepted with full honour amongst the intellectual groups of the State of Israel. Dr. Horowitz's organization, which was located at 507 Fifth Avenue, New York City, New York never received the type of rejection which the greater body of White Jews applied in the case of organizations of the Black Jews of Harlem, New York City, New York and other parts of the United States of America, though these Falashas have a long history of continued allegiance to the Hebrew Faith that compares with any other Hebrew group inside and/or outside the State of Israel. Dr. Horowitz's group went out of their way to "...CONVERT... European-[WHITE]-Americans...," but to date they have not done a single thing to "...CONVERT..." the first African-[BLACK]-American. Dr. Horowitz, as so many other White Jews, even claimed that:

> "THE AMERICAN INDIANS AND THE ENGLISH [a mixture of Anglo-Saxon, Norman and Scandanavian peoples of Europe] ARE THE LOST TRIBES."

Of course not a single so-called "...AMERICAN NEGRO..." was converted because he or she was even remotely considered a "...MEMBER OF THE LOST TRIBES...." Could it be that the Doctor's own WHITE color did not match the BLACK color of the African-Americans; thus not a single one of them could possible qualify as a member of "...THE LOST TRIBES...?" But the members of "...THE [White Caucasian] LOST TRIBES...,"every last one of them that migrated with Doctor Horowitz to the political State of Israel, were fully accepted as "JEWS" in every quarter of Israeli society; even among the so-called "ORTHODOX JEWS" from Europe and European-America.

Regardless of the issue about the Northern Europeans above, my people leave me with the following impression whenever I ask them about the "ZIONIST" question; and that is they are always sympathetic to their biblical ancestral homeland[1] and that they will always try their best to gain unqualified entrance into the political State of Israel whenever they would be fully accepted, because it is not their desire to enter any country where they are not wanted. They have also stated:

> "We will not go to the State of Israel, if we have to be a burden on the Government."

Their position reflects the fact that they are not looking for favors; as all that they have ever requested is a "...PIECE OF FARMLAND..." where they can work in the same manner which they are accoustomed. They are not asking for a "...PIECE OF LAND..." that is already cleared-off

1. They were/are refering to a theocratic government; not a capitalist republic or "democracy."

by others; but instead, they are asking for "...ANY PIECE OF THE WILDERNESS..." where they can make a fresh start, because they have had quite a lot of experiences in making fresh starts of this kind throughout their history.[1]

It was the hope of the BLACK [Israelite or Falasha] JEWS in Ethiopia, East Africa, the Caribbean Islands, the Americas and elsewhere that they may be able to witness the attitude of the JEWS who control the political State of Israel [those who put up the bulk of the monies from [white] Europe, Great Britain and the United States of America], in their own regards become much more humanitarian for the comfort of all concerned in this latter question. They had hoped that the day would have soon come when not only Falashas would have been fully welcomed in the State/Eretz Israel, but anyone else who might have needed a place of "REFUGE" and/or "HAVEN" could have find a home in the so-called PROMISED LAND mentioned in the Sacred Torah. Let us not forget to remind ourselves that we Jews told the entire world in our Sacred Torah and other Sacred Writings that our biblical forefathers wrote the following:

> "AND GOD'S [Ywh, Jehovah, etc.] PEOPLE SHALL RETURN TO THE PROMISED LAND BEFORE THE END OF TIME." [And that] "GOD CREATED MANKIND."

This certainly means that Jews, or anyone else who follows YWH'S teachings and/or Commandments, will return to the "PROMISED LAND." Therefore, why should anyone try to disassociate the State of Israel from the natural "...RIGHT OF RETURN..." of the Falashas, or all other persons of whom the above biblical quotations refer? Or are we to legislate against the "SACRED WRITINGS OF THE PROPHETS" whenever our own personal materialistic interests and racial ego are affected? Probably God - YWH - did not make anyone else but "WHITE [Caucasian-Semitic] JEWS" before and/or after the so-called "...GREAT DELUGE..." or "...FLOOD...!" And maybe God - YWH - is in fact a "RACIST" and/or "RELIGIOUS BIGOT" who despise anyone except certain "...CHOSEN [White Caucasian-Semitic] PEOPLE...," even though at times he brought to be a "...wicked pharaoh that enslaved thy people - Israel...;" a very "...brutal Prime Minister named Hanaan that tried to turn the king against thy people - Israel...;" a colonialist "...King Herod that enslaved thy people - Israel...; ' a master of genocide "...Adolph Hitler, who made lampshades out of thy people - Israel...;" but not a notorious master exterminator '...Benito Mussolini, who tried to exterminate all of thy people - Israel [Falashas]...,' because they were/are of BLACK SKIN and from "AFRICA !" This analysis will get me the "Anti-Semitic" stamp.

Yes, they are still BLACK-SKINNED; and many of us still have so-called "CURSED NEGRO FEATURES: THICK LIPS, BROAD NOSTRILS, WOOLLY HAIR," etc. the same as described on page 2 of this Volume. But WE are equally the descendants of the same "CURSED CANAANITES"

1. Falashas were not only refused land in Israel, they were made to feel unwanted there. Why! Nothing else but the same type of "racism and religious bigotry" Jews suffer under Nazism/Fascism.

whose land was confiscated by OUR COUSINS that descended from the "UNCURSED SHEMITES" and "JAPHITES" - in the allegorical story written in the FIRST BOOK OF MOSES [otherwise called GENESIS]. However, let us not forget that it was in the "CURSED LAND" of the "CURSED NEGROES" of the Blue Nile Valley and White Nile Valley and Great Lakes regions of Alkebu-lan ["Africa" and/or "Afrika"], from Zimbabwe at the South to Kimit's Great Sea [Mediterranean] at the North, that the "CAUCASIAN-WHITE-SEMITIC JEWS" received their first introduction into "CIVILIZATION" and "THE BOOK." And that even the so-called "STAR OF DAVID"[or "Mogen David"] is still from "THE TUAT AND THE TWELVE HOURS OF THE NIGHT" symbol [see page 179] the Hebrew People adapted from the indigenous BLACK African named "MOSES," who [allegedly]"..

RECEIVED THE TEN COMMANDMENTS FROM GOD ON MOUNT HOREB...," after all of them, plus another THIRTY-TWO [32] MORE"!- in the indigenous Africans' NEGATIVE CONFESSIONS, which he had to learn the first day he entered school - "THE MYSTERIES SYSTEM" - that was centered in the GRAND LODGE OF WA'AT. But, is it not equally true that the same "CURSED DESCENDANTS OF HAM" produced most of the so-called "PROVERBS" attributed to King Solomon of the Kingdom of Israel, some of which I have shown below ?

THE COMPARATIVE WORKS

The Teachings of Amen-em-ope Pharoah of Egypt (1405-1370)	The so-called "Proverbs" of King Solomon of Israel (976-936)?
Give thine ear, and hear what I say, And apply thine heart to apprehend;	Incline thine ear, and hear my words, And apply, thine heart to apprehend;
It is good for thee to place them in thine heart, Let the rest in the casket of the belly. That they may act as a peg upon thy tongue.	For it is pleasant if thou keep them in thy belly, That they may be fixed upon thy lips. .....
Consider these thirty chapters; They delight, they instruct. Knowledge how to answer him that speaketh, And how to carry back a report to one that sent it.	Have I not written for thee thirty sayings, Of counsels and knowledge! That thou mayest make known truth to him that speaketh. .....
Beware of robbing the poor, And of oppressing the afflicted.	Rob not the poor for he is poor, Neither oppress the lowly in the gate. .....

Associate not with a passionate man, Nor approach him for conversations; Leap not to cleave to such a one, That the terror carry thee not away.	Associate not with a passionate man, Nor go with a wrathful man, Lest thou learn his ways, And get a snare to thy soul.
.....	.....
A scribe who is skillful in his business Findeth himself worthy to be a courtier.	A man who is skillful in his business Shall stand before kings.

The so-called "PROVERBS" above were used even during the time Moses and all of the other Hebrews [Haribu and Israelites] that were privileged to go to school [LODGE] in Egypt, Nubia, Ethiopia and Punt amongst their indigenous "FELLOW BLACK-AFRICAN" students and teachers. Note that these teachings were later taught in the SUBORDINATE LODGES all around the known world of the time of King Solomon of the Kingdom of Israel. That which he attended was called "MOUNT CARMEL." Of course one should not be surprise about the rejection of these facts; for we have seen them denied even in the MASONIC ORDER where it is taught that "FREE MASONRY came from the HOUSE OF SOLOMON." Yet in their RITUALS they constantly refer to the GRAND LODGE OF WA'AT [Thebes or Luxor] in AFRICA on the bank of the Nile River. It is because of these reasons that a list of the SUBORDINATE LODGES that existed thousands of years before, during, and hundreds following the reign of King Solomon - ca. 976-936 B.C.E.:

SUBORDINATE LODGES OF THE GRAND LODGE OF LUXOR[1]

1. Palestine [at Mt. Carmel]	10. Rhodes
2. Assyria [at Mt. Herman in Lebanon]	11. Delphi
3. Babylon	12. Miletus
4. Media [near the Red Sea]	13. Cyprus
5. India [at the banks of the Ganges River]	14. Corinth
6. Burma	15. Crete
7. Athens	16. Cush [Itiopi, Ethiopia]
8. Rome [at Elea]	17. Monomotapa [South Africa]
9. Croton	18. Zimbabwe [Rhodesia]

LUXOR was destroyed by fire, burnt to the ground, in the year c. 548 B.C.E. It was set aflame by foreigners who were jealous of the indigenous Africans ["Negroes,"et al] knowledge of the "MYSTERIES" taught in the Osirica - which included all of the above mentioned disciplines. [See John Kendrick's, ANCIENT EGYPT, Book II, p. 363; Eva B. Sandford's, THE MEDITERRANEAN WORLD, pp. 135 - 139; Yosef ben-Jochannan's, AFRICA: MOTHER OF "WESTERN CIVILIZATION", Chapter IX].

2,400 The Temple of Kharnak, the most pompteous of the Chapters of the Grand Lodge of Luxor's Secret Society where the Mysteries were taught, was built at a distance of 1/2 mile from the Grand Lodge. Separated each 12 feet on both sides of an isle stood a double row of sphinxes. The width of the isle was 60 feet When in its perfection this entrance presented one of the most magnificent walkways i[illegible] able

1. These lodges were under the control of Africans from the beginning and end of the entire Blue and White Nile Valley and Great Lakes Region, etc.

THEY EXISTED BEFORE JEHOVAH, JESUS CHRIST, AL'LAH, ET AL., OF THE TORAH, NEW TESTAMENT AND QUR'AN, ETC.

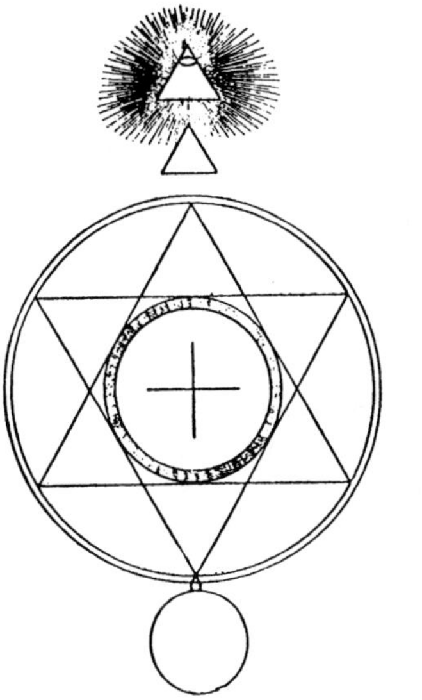

From Egypt

"The Tuat and the Twelve Hours of the Night," hewn in stone in the Great Pyramid of Gizeh.[2] In the Christian doctrine the twelve gates of heaven were taken from this.

AFRICAN SYMBOLS[1] ADAPTED BY THE WESTERN WORLD

Swatzthika (Swastika adopted by Adolph Hitler's Nazi party in Germany) imposed upon the *Sunburst* (Rā or Rē).

Star of Amenta (adopted by the Muslims as the Fertile Crescent of Al-'la. Also widely used by the Freemasons).

Double Right-Angle Pyramid or *Square* (another Masonic emblem, symbolizing the "squaring of man's deeds").

Double Right-Angle Pyramid: House of Fire, House of the Nether World, House of Amenta, House of Heaven (adopted by every civilization of the "Western World" as a symbol of "Strength" and the "Reaching out into the Heavens" to the God Jehobah, an offspring of the God Rā or Rē).

The *Ankh*: Key of Life (the original Cross, corrupted by the Christians of Rome).

The *Cross* (symbol of death; adopted by European Christians and by those of North Africa for Jesus of Nazareth).

Rā (the center dot) *in his Pole Star* (the Double Pyramid adopted by the Hebrews, or Jews, as the Star of David).

The *Ever-Seeing Eye of Horus* (adopted by the United States on its legal tender).

Tears from the Ever-Seeing Eye of Horus, being received by the

Sepulcup (adopted by Christians as the Chalice, or cup to be used during the Eucharist).

---

1. Note that the symbols listed under the title "African Symbols Adopted By The Western World" are all shown in the Africans of the Nile Valley [BLUE and WHITE] High-Cultures' papyri and inscriptions inside and outside of pyramids, temples, stalae, oblisks, etc. It is obvious where the so-called "STAR OF DAVID, CHRISTIAN CROSS, MOSLEM CRESCENT," etc. had their origin. This symbol from "EGYPT" had an origin of more than 2,000 years before the first Hebrew or Jew - "Abraham" - was born in Chaldea in ca. 1755 C.E., which is more than 3,755 years before the birth of the Christians' God - " JESUS CHRIST" - in ca. 1 C.E., and 4,325 years before the birth of Prophet Mohamet ibn Abdullah. A careful examination of the indigenous Africans writings in the BOOK OF THE DEAD, PAPYRUS OF ANI, OSIRIAN DRAMA, PYRAMID TEXT, COFFIN TEXT, NEGATIVE CONFESSIONS, etc., etc., etc. will reveal all of the symbols above [in: BLACK WORLD, February 1974 issue - "Fundamental Steps To Historical Analysis: An Interview With Yosef ben-Jochannan," by Carole A. Parks, pages 62-72].
2. For extensive details on this see Albert Churchward, SIGNS AND SYMBOLS OF PRIMORDIAL MAN, London, 1928, and Godfrey Higgins, ANACALYPSIS, London, 1836 [2 Volumes].

THE DEFUNCT "HEBREW INSTITUTE" OF ETHIOPIA: Chapter X.

The "Hebrew Institute" of Ethiopia is presently defunct; but a reflection on it is of very grave importance here in this work. The importance will be seen by the mere fact of the work that it undertook to do amongst the Hebrew communities of Ethiopia, and the extension of relations with the African-American Hebrew communities in the Americas and the Caribbean Islands.

The Hebrew Institute was founded by private individuals in Ethiopia, who were at that time given official sanction by the government. It was believed that the Hebrew Institute may have helped to encourage Falashas to enter the higher schools of learning in the major cities of Ethiopia without having fear of breaking the Levitical Dietary Laws and Rules of Cleanliness and Health which the Sacred Torah's HOLY SCRIPTURES impose upon each and every practicing Beta Israel, commonly called "Falashas" or "Black Jews/Black Hebrews/Black Israelites," etc. of Ethiopia.

The Government of Ethiopia had donated "...free land..." to the Hebrew Institute and allocated a few thousand dollars to its building fund and treasury. The rest of the money came from a very small group of White Jewish intellectuals who called themselves the "AMERICAN PRO-FALASHA COMMITTEE," and other individuals who made up informal groupings in Italy and Ethiopia; many of whom were not even Jews.

The director of the Hebrew Institute was the late Honourable Professor Tamrat Emmanuel, who was later on appointed to the diplomatic post as "Cultural Attache" of His Majesty Haile Selassie's Government in the Embassy at Paris, France. Professor Tamrat explained that he had "...

> intended to try and introduce the acceptance of the Rabbinical Talmud of the European Jews to the Falasha Priesthood as a mean of common teaching...."

He thought that "...

> this would be the most excellent idea, because it would certainly cause much more interest in my task by the entire Falasha Communities; this is providing that I am able to have the Elders and Priests interested in the work...."

He also felt that "...

> the Hebrew Institute can branch out in its subjects and enter other fields related to religion, and also courses in science as it develops...."

The Hebrew Institute was opened in 1945 C.E., just subsequent to the end of World War II, and was doing very well; yet, it was at the same instance seen to be heading for failure. This was due to the lack of interest which the Falashas were showing when Professor Tamrat introduced his European and European-American Jews' Rabbinical Talmud.[1] Ninety percent of its enrollment was already Gentiles, and the remaining ten percent was mainly Falashas living

1. The Talmud is only an attempt to have one standardized version of the Torah; nothing else. This too was the work of European Jews. The current one being that of Moses ben-Maimonides in Spain.

amongst Gentiles in the major cities of Ethiopia that were very far from the basic concentration of the Falasha communities. This was realized as a very bad trend; for the purpose of the Hebrew Institute was to bridge the gap between European and European-American Jews and the African and African-American Jews, besides give to the Falashas at least and introduction into the Liberal Arts that were available to the average Ethiopian student on the college level. One could already see that the supply of African Jews in the larger cities of Ethiopia was not sufficient to maintain the already low ten percent ratio. In other words, the Hebrew Institute had to depend upon people who would have been least affected by the type of general education it was geared and/or prepared to impart.

The Hebrew Institute continued until 1949 C.E., even when the enrollment had fallen off to thirty-four percent of minimum capacity it functioned. This period when the Institute reached this very low figure of enrollment there were only FIVE [5] FALASHAS from the general Falasha communities, and the only reason why these FIVE were attending was because Professor Tamrat was a close friend of their families.

Another reason why the Falashas refused to support the Hebrew Institute was the same for their having refused to support any other institution outside of their Falasha communities; as they would have had to travel on Sabbath, and eat "unclean food" which was not even prepared by Falashas. The Institute had no eating facilities; and it did not have any dormitories either, because its treasury could not afford these necessities. However, it was the plan of the Director to have these facilities added when the Institute became financially able to support them.

The fact of financial support being turned down by European and European-American [Western] Hebrew communities was also responsible for the failure of the Hebrew Institute. We had asked Hebrew [Jewish or Israelite] communities outside of Ethiopia for "...old books and other old school supplies...." We received absolutely nothing from most of these communities, except from the very small Hebrew Community in Italy. This Italian Jewish Community helped because they were also the first to become instrumental in the founding of the Hebrew Institute. One of their members, Mr. Vituroso, had come to Ethiopia during and after the Italian armies invasion and occupation, and he made contact with the Falashas in our communities. By his memory, and the memorablias he took back to Italy, made Italian Jews of his community feel obligated to help.[1]

A last minute appeal was made by the Hebrew Institute's Officers to the Ethiopian Government for aid. The Government was willing to give some more, but refused to cover all of its needs, even though there was a pressing need for technical schools throughout Ethiopia. The officers were told if they could gather enough technical instructors from any part of the world

1. Guilt feelings played a major role in the Italians [Christians, Jews, et al] attitude toward the Falashas for their former Fascist Government's attrocities against all Ethiopians; Falashas mostly.

they would have all the funds which they needed to keep the Institute's doors open. We knew that this meant the Institute had the possibility of becoming one of the most important schools in the entire country of Ethiopia. The officers set forth to contact different European and European-American Jewish individuals and organizations, because they were always told that "there are many Western Jews who are always willing to travel abroad and teach other Jews. . . ." Thus it was upon this latter information they acted, along with many of us in the United States of America who were living here for a goodly number of years but only to discover that it was just another rumor like all of the others before. Out of TEN THOUSAND [10,000] LETTERS mailed to different so-called individual "FRIENDS" and "JEWISH ORGANIZATIONS" for aid, the combined effort recieved "ONE HUNDRED AND TWENTY-FIVE [125] REPLIES," with only "THREE [3] ACCEPTANCE." We needed at least FIFTEEN [15] TECHNICAL INSTRUCTORS, and at least SIX [6] MATHEMATICS TEACHERS. The Institute was again on the path of failure, for its measily staff had very few men who were prepared in the technical sciences and/or trades. The few that it did have in these fields were experts connected to the Ethiopian government's scientific development projects. They could not be spared to the Institute in the daytime; not even to take time to establish the courses until the incoming people could arrive. Therefore, the Institute would have been forced to give courses in their fields at night. But the Institute also ran into trouble because no kind of school in Ethiopia was geared for evening education. The Falashas in Ethiopia could not have fathom the new method of this peculiar educational system; having classes at night. Any rapid change of this sort that would change the status quo in Ethiopia was never accepted by the people, particularly amongst the Falashas of the communal communities with their hundreds of religious prohibitions against almost everything that does not appear in the Sacred Torah as a directive from God - YWH [who is otherwise called "Jehovah, Adanoi, Elohenu," etc.]

With their backs up against the wall the officers decided that it was best to close the Hebrew Institute in the condition it was. That was the wisest move, because there was enough in the treasury to return monies to those who had used almost every penney they had to start it. The payments were made, and all was settled in a very short period of time; but the "Hebrew Institute" that began in 1945 C.E. was defunct in less than FIVE [5] YEARS duration - 1949 C.E.; sadly so!

Let us look at some of the courses which the Hebrew Institute was offering, and planning to offer. From this you will see the great loss which the Falashas have suffered in Ethiopia, and in other Hebrew communities the world over. Do not forget for one momemnt that the communities the Hebrew Institute was designed to service were, and still are, theocratic. Thus you will understand why the following courses were compulsory:

1. The Torah and the Hebrew People.

2. The Geography and History of the Sacred Torah.
3. Present Judaism as practised around the world.
4. The Zionist Movement of the World and its leaders.
5. Hebrews of world renown in the field of Science and the Arts: an examination of their contributions.
6. Methods of closer relationship between Ethiopian and other Hebrew groups around the world.
7. The Talmud and the people who wrote it.

There was also included a course of which was common to the Ethiopian scene with respect to the treatment of Falashas by the majority of the Ethiopians who were not of the Hebrew Faith; thus:

8. The history of the persecution of the Jews around the world down through the ages - from biblical times to the present.

Although this course [No. 8] was an "ELECTIVE" in the program, it was very highly recommended. The major danger was its references to the Egyptians and Israelites as "separate races of people." This was the fault of the origin of the textbooks in the U.S.A. by "White Jews."

We have not given up hope that someone will be able to start another Hebrew Institute not too far in the near future; this time in the middle of the communal communites of Gondar vicinity where the vast majority of the Falashas are to be found in Ethiopia. As a matter of fact, there is an "AMERICAN PRO-FALASHA COMMITTEE, Inc."[1] and its "STANDING COMMITTEE" that is led by Rabbi Hailu Moshe Paris [already shown on page xxxviii].They are planning activities on methods to secure enough money and books to start a "New Hebrew Institute." This time they will not make the same mistake of having the "Institute" located in Addis Ababa, the Capital City of Ethiopia, which is more than TWO to THREE HUNDRED MILES from the nearest Falasha community. They will have it at a place where all qualified Falashas can attend without having to stay away from their communities at nights. They will have food and other necessities of life which will be prepared and serviced by Falashas on the premises of the Institute. Local instructors from the general Ethiopian population of professionals will be engaged. And the base finance will be from the Falasha communities income-producing exports to other Ethiopian communities.

With this new venture they will not have to waste money on Jews from other lands who are versed in the "WESTERN RABBINICAL TALMUD." Since they intend to make the New Hebrew Institute a center for training young priests as well; thus they will need a specialist in the field of the "Hebrew Religion" as practise all over the world today; but not with the main emphasis on the "Western Version;" instead, upon their own biblical "Jewish Traditions." I too hope that this opportunity we had in the Hebrew Institute will again become a reality. And it would seem that Rabbi Paris' group is certain that they can bridge the gap of ignorance and superstition in this

1. When it was at top strength during the 1930's, and 1947 - 1967, etc. it did not render any type of meaningful assistance to Falashas anywhere in Ethiopia, or elsewhere outside of Ethiopia.

method of contact with "Western [WHITE] Jews." I believe you will agree that people can better understand each others if they only know each others. I also realize that you may feel you do not know enough about us [Falashas], and we about you. But this conclusion if allowed to remain, far from the truth as it is, will only cause further racism and religious bigotry on our part. European and European-American Jews know African and African-American Jews as much as their Christian counterparts who come to "AFRICA" as so-called "CHRISTIAN MISSIONARIES." Yet, there are dozens of European and European-American "JEWISH MISSIONARIES" to Ethiopia trying to convert Falashas into TALMUDIC [rabbinical] JEWS. Thus they believe, we will become "KOSHER SEMITES" a-la Caucasian European style. But these will equally fail, no more and no less than their European and European-American "CHRISTIAN MISSIONARIES" have also failed. Because, just as the ancient traditions dwell in the AKHSUM [Axum] STELAE, of which all of us witness below, that much a determination is built into the tradition of the biblical origin among the Falashas and their original form of TORAHDIC JUDAISM; and Falashas will hold on to them.

The tallest stelae is SIXTY-THREE FEET high. The window designs appear to be set in a framework of timber one above the other. This type of design is common to ancient Ethiopian architecture. Note the false door technique at the foot as in the pyramids all along the Nile Valley.

FALASHA VIEWS ON WORLD TENSION: Chapter XI.

These days it is very hard to write on any phase of religious teachings without hurting the political sensitivity of certain persons and/or governments. This writer shall not try to avoid such, as I can not help from calling the facts as my people see them, all of which will be further emphasized in Volume Two of this project. Yet, I will give answers only to the questions which are most often asked of me about my people - the so-called "FALASHAS." These answers are not my own, instead they represent some of the reactions of my people - FALASHAS and/or BLACK JEWS - in many lands. The order in which they are treated indicates their popularity; they are:

1. For whom will the Falshas fight in the event of a war with any "Western" capitalist nation against an "Eastern" communist nation?

2. What do the Falashas think about communism, since they have a somewhat similar economic order in some of their communities?

3. Would the Falashas fight for Israel against the Arabs?

4. What do the Falashas think about our [the United States of America is meant] democracy?

5. What do the Falashas think about aid from the United States [of America] to Ethiopia?

I take to give my people's reactions to the questions listed above because they are the only ones which I think present the greatest challenge to a very insecurely frightened people. Remember that I am not giving an analysis of conclusions,or suggestions,for any action on your part; this I have done in Volume Two. The questions are answered in the chronological order listed above.

1. Falashas would fight for Ethiopia whenever this nation is in a conflict, whether it is with the "West" or "East." It is only natural that they will fight for the country where they are living. The masses of people in any country do not fight because they have analyzed the "RIGHT" and "WRONG" in a conflict in which their nation is involved. The Falashas fall into this same pattern politically. The leaders tell us that this or that nation is against our interest, and that of our nation's; therefore, we go to fight with and for our "GOD" and our "NATION" as a unity. This is the case here of your own GOD and COUNTRY. We would not fight for philosophies, because we have our own. And we cannot very well avoid fighting for the COUNTRY in which we are living, even if we did not care too; this is providing we do not wish to be sentenced to at least a jail term, probably death.

2. On the matter of "COMMUNISM," the Falashas answer by saying that: We are not prepared to evaluate the paramount points. We cannot give an unbias opinion of the subject, because all of the information we have received about it came from those who are in bias disagreement with everything communism stands for. The few of us who have studied Marx and/or Lenin's works will not disturb our people in their communities over what

1. European-American White Jews have for decades looked at the Beta Israel/Falashas [so-called "primitive people"] practicing a very elementary form of "Judaism;" which they are trying to stop.

we have read. We feel that our system is as good as any other system which we have encountered - this includes both "COMMUNISM" and "CAPITALISM," etc. It needs no changes unless we see them fit; at such time we shall change to any other system we deem beneficial for ourselves, and not because someone tells us this or that is good, bad and/or indifferent.

About the resemblance of the Falashas economic system and that of "communism" or "socialism" we are not frightened; none whatsoever. We have practiced the "economic system in our communal societies" for centuries after centuries before the birth of Marx and Lenin. We copied this economic system from our indigenous African brothers and sisters in other African "communal societies," some of which existed before Judaism itself. We do know that there is a distinct difference in our method of distribution of wealth and the way it is done in "Marxist" or "Communist Nations" system of economics. First of all, we cater to the theory of "...a share of equality to all regardless of field of endeavor; and to a man's need above his ability to produce...." Whereas in Marxism, Leninism and/or Maoism there is catering to a man "...according to his ability to produce..."material wealth. We based our reasoning for our [Falasha] COMMUNAL economic system of distribution of material wealth on one of the major "Laws" of the TEN COMMANDMENTS... ; thus: "You must love your neighbour as you love yourself..." Whereas the Marxist, Maoist and Leninist avocates based their method of distribution of material wealth upon their own version of "...Scientific Economic Statistical Theory Of Productive Capacity And Value...." "COMMUNISM," as we see it, is not a "TYPICAL RELIGION;" but our Falasha communities are "RELIGIOUS" in their very theocratic foundation. We do not rationalize the "RIGHT" and/or "WRONG" of the policies laid down in the Hebrew "SACRED TORAH," which is not "SCIENTIFIC," but instead religious faith based in theosophy and theology. And whereas the communists make rationalizations on all of their policies, we accept a "DIVINE GUIDANCE THEORY" in ours. The communists accept a "...PLANNED SCIENTIFIC THEORY OF ANALYZATION..." for their community guidance. We, on the other hand, accept "...FAITH IN GOD AND OURSELVES FOR OUR GUIDING FORCE...." We do not believe that Falashas should be asked to join the "FEAR BRIGADE," as the "communist vs. capitalist" battle is not any of our making; neither are we in a position to end it.

3. Falashas cannot fight for the political State of Israel if they are living in Ethiopia during any conflict between Israel and her neighbour Arab Nations. Another important point is that the Arab Nations also include the sympathies of most Moslem Nations and Peoples. The Moslems[or Muslims] represent more than forty [40] to forty-five [45] percent of the entire population of Ethiopia. Still another point to be considered is the fact that the Moslems consider "...the present Israelis are merely Europeans...," but the

1. Your author's response is the conclusion of a "Committee of Falashas" who live in the Motherland - Ethiopia, the Caribbean Islands, North and South America. No single person speaks for us.

Black Jews are the real Jews of the territory called Palestine..."[see Ali ben-Pasha's pamphlet, THE EUROPEAN INVASION OF PALESTINE, published simultaneously in Egypt and Sudan in 1949 C.E.; also other Moslem writers'works]. You will note the importance of this latter point from the reaction of the Moslems in the "1947 WAR" between the Asian Arab nations and the predominantly controlled European and European-American and British Jewish nation. This reaction was felt in Ethiopia in the same manner as it was felt in the middle-Eastern States of the Moslem world. Yet the FALASHAS [JEWS OF ETHIOPIA] were treated with the same respect which we were accoustomed to receive from our Moslem brothers and sisters of Ethiopia. The Moslems made it very clear to the Falashas that they "...ARE NOT ENGAGED IN ANY CONFLICT WITH THE FALSHAS OR ANY ASIAN JEWS...;" but that they "...ARE ENGAGED IN A BATTLE MENTALLY, SPIRITUALLY AND PHYSICALLY AGAINST THE EUROPEAN INVADERS IN PALESTINE THAT ARE NO DIFFERENT TO THE INVADERS OF ETHIOPIA FROM ca.1934 - 1935 C.E. to 1942 C.E."

It was very difficult for the Falashas to decide what steps to take, if any; and with whom they were to align themselves. This difficulty came from the fact that we are Jews, and at the same time we are rejected by the greater body of European [WHITE] Jews who were fighting for the British colonial holding in "Palestine," and are now fighting for the political "State of Israel." Another point or hurdle we had to climb was the fact that the Moslems and Falashas in Ethiopia were getting along fine, as could possibly be expected under the trying circumstances war naturally imposes upon victor and vanquished, we do not ignore individual acts of religious bigotry.

We finally decided that:

AS A GENERAL BODY WE CAN NOT MAKE A MOVE, EVEN IF WE WANTED, BECAUSE THE GOVERNMENT OF ETHIOPIA WILL NOT ALLOW ITS SUBJECTS [citizens] TO INTERFERE WITH THE DOMESTIC AFFAIRS OF OTHER SOVEREIGN NATIONS, PROVIDING THAT ETHIOPIA HERSELF IS NOT INVOLVED IN THE SPECIFIC CONFLICT [This seems to be equally true of the new power/"derge"].

We took a further step, the position that"...any Falasha willing to aid the Israelis cause because of religious leanings may do so by going to the State of Israel and joining their brothers and sisters; but those of us at home in Ethiopia will not hold any conflict whatsoever with our fellow citizens of the Moslem Faith living in Ethiopia." Nor shall we go against Mother Ethiopia."

The fact is that many Falashas went to Israel and fought in the war against the Arab nations. All who were living there before the WAR began went into the conflict voluntarily on the side of their religious brothers and sisters. It is sad to say that their REWARD was no better than for the Africans who fought for the "...INDPENDENCE OF [white] AMERICA..." with General George Washington against General Cornwallis and England in 1773 - 1776 C.E. - and the other Africans who fought against IT with Cornwallis and wound-up in Nova Scotia, Canada, England and Siera Leon, West Africa [see any history book of the "War of Independence" between both].

This position of the Falashas should cause you to review Chapter I of this Volume, particularly the beginning page titled: THE FALLACY OF A JEWISH RACE. It also calls for a counter-question from the Falashas; thus:

> 'IF WE ARE NOT ETHNICALLY JEWS, AND ONLY PICKED UP BY THE WAYSIDE; WHY SHOULD WE FIGHT FOR THE POLITICAL STATE OF ISRAEL?'

Added to this:

> 'IF WE SHOULD FIGHT FOR THE POLITICAL STATE OF ISRAEL, WE WOULD NOT BE ABLE TO MAINTAIN OUR POSITION OF BEING OPPOSED TO ANY STATE THAT IS NOT THEOCRATIC.'

Remember that we have never in our history accepted political governments, regardless by whom they are sponsored. Next, most of us are from strictly biblically religious groups! Thus we can not accept most of the practices which have become a part of the political government in Israel; Thus such as the eating of "PORK" in some sections, and the selling of same in the stores; driving of busses on the Sabbath; working on High Holy Days; etc., etc., etc. Falashas can be closely fitted to Yemenite Orthodox philosophy on these matters, moreso than with any other group in the political State of Israel today. In other words, Falashas believe that:

> THE THEOCRACY OF ISREAL IS TO BE REBORN ACCORDINGLY FOR THE SACRED HEBREW TORAH, AND NOT FOR THE EMULATION OF PRESENT-DAY WESTERN MATERIALISTIC PHILOSOPHIES/SYSTEMS.

> 4. About the word "DEMOCRACY," and the practices we observe therein, we are unable to see any common relationship with the two. We look at the word "DEMOCRACY" as an idea which every group hold to suite their own position and interest. If you explain what is meant by "DEMOCRACY" to any Falasha, he [or she] would immediately tell you: "WE HAVE OUR OWN SYSTEM OF DEMOCRACY." You would likely respond to him: OURS IS FAR SUPERIOR TO YOURS.' The term is, therefore, quite controversial in itself without clarifications which forces one to the dictionaries for individual interpretations.

By "DEMOCRACY" my hosts and hostesses have always meant the equivalent of "...Capitalism and a two party electoral system within a republican form of government...." FALASHAS, on the other hand, know that "...we can have democracy under a King, Queen or Emperor...." We also know that "...representation of the people, and by the people, does not have to mean a two party system...." Because we feel that "...we are completely represented in our own system; yet there are no political parties or political candidates..."[review Falasha Electoral System: Chapter III, Part Two, pages 101 - 108 of this Volume].

Another point we feel is lacking is the situation highlighted in Volume One of this project on the question of "COLOR" and "RELIGIOUS" distinctions. We make no hipocritical claim about

1. Beta Israel/Falashas should no more fight against Ethiopia than American Jews fight against the United States of America and Israel. Ethiopia is the native homeland of the African Jews/Falashas.

our "COMMUNAL SYSTEM." We say that "...all is welcome in our community, providing he or she observes the rules and Laws of the Sacred Hebrew Torah, the Ten Commandments and the mores and customs of our society...." This applies to people of all shades of skin pigment, geographic origin, etc., etc., etc.; whereas European-American "DEMOCRACY" excludes a person who wishes to practice all of its laws and abide by all of its cultural values. And due to his or her "...color of skin... " and/or "...religion... " he or she cannot enjoy European and European-American [WHITE] Democracy. Falashas have no better reason to accept Capitalist Democracy than we have found to accept Socialist ["communist"] Democracy. Both systems Falashas have watched with respect, and both we have rejected from employing in our communal communities, for none would work in any of our theocratically religious established economic systems. Thus, we say:

> Your democracy encourages Christian Missionaries coming into Africa. We are against such practises; for such has only led to grave conflicts of violence and other disturbances in our homes. It has ruined many of our homes by turning one against the other religiously.
>
> Your democracy had, and is still supporting the powers of colonialism in Africa. And since we are predominantly African Nationalists, we are unable to see the difference between your democracy and other European states in regards to our interests in Africa.
>
> The voting position of your democracy on the question of the North African States and the Union of South Africa in the United Nations Organization has made us in the Falasha Communities the world over wonder what does your Constitution really means in its writings as against your alleged execution of it in practice?

You would have to consider the fact that you are seeing your own version of "DEMOCRACY" by the way it affects you from within; and my people are seeing it from outside in the manner it is presented to them by your conduct. In "DEMOCRACIES" there are special practices for home consumption, and others for foreign export. Those for foreign export are bitter and bad; they are loaded with ".. the Great White Father protecting his Little Black Children..." policies. We resent this type of double identity; and we are certain that you would have done the same if the power was in our hands and we were doing to you what you are doing to us. In other words, every man's "DEMOCRACY" is as good as the other man's as far as each man thinks; especially when their ideals of life are based upon different goals and philosophies.

> 5. The alleged former "AID" to the Ethiopian Government affected Falashas very little, if any. Most of the Falashas [US] have been living apart from the general Ethiopian population so long that we have developed somewhat of "an independent state within a state...." Our moral conduct at home is quite in contrast to that of the Gentile and/or Moslem population of Ethiopia. We could

---

1. Even in ancient Greece there was no such thing as a "Democracy of the People," who mostly slaves in every sense of this word. By the way; the vast majority of the people were less than free.

not, therefore, feel any direct effect of the "...AID..." which the United States of America was using to prompt-up the Emperor and Monarchists,

We must realize that the United States of America was not giving Ethiopia, or any other nation of "Independent Africa," a single thing. Ethiopia made "TREATIES" and "CONTRACTS" with the Government of the United States of America and American business enterprises. "PROFITS" go to each concern in these agreements; each receiving no more than its share according to the "CONTRACTS." It was not a system of..."AID"... like that given to the European and British nations during the existence of "LEND LEASE" and the "MARSHALL PLAN." Ethiopia must PAY, and PAY she must heavily, for all assistances which she recived from any European, British and European-American nation. She will either PAY in natural resources or by the PROFITS from them. She has to relinquish some of her national prestige in terms of "...SPHERE OF INFLUENCE PACTS..." in return for any "...AID..." she received. Again, we assure you that no government whatsoever helps another for mere philantrophical and altruistic motives. Governments help each others only when it is advantageous for so doing. "Western Nations" must now turn to their former "...AFRICAN COLONIES" and "...POSSESSIONS, PROTECTORATES...," etc. and try to assist them in the redevelopment of the lands which they themselves destroyed commencing in the Sixteenth [16th] Century C.E. and up to the present Twentieth [20th] Century C.E.;[1] that is if they are to continue having any place to secure their needed natural resources, and to dump their excess mass production. Spanish and Portuguese-Speaking America are both fast becoming industrially independent; and Asia has taken back her own powers from the hands of the "Western Colonialist and Imperialist Nations;" therefore the only logical market is the 11,300,000 Square Miles of Alkebu-lan ["Africa"] and its more than 400,000,000 indigenous [BLACK'] people. But this was when the Africans were not in control of their own "DEVELOPMENT;" and when "NEO-COLONIALISM" was the order of day in the minds of too many "African Heads of State." Today is a different day, different time and a different generation mentally.

The United Nations Technical Assistance Program [of which Ethiopia is a member] is to be credited for many major projects in Ethiopia today which were government sponsored. "POINT FOUR PROJECTS" operated on the greater percentage of Ethiopian money and labour. The only "POINT FOUR AID" given to the Ethiopian nation was provision for some technical advisers on certain specific equipments and projects bought from the United States of America of which the Ethiopian people were not familiar. This does not mean that Ethiopia had no specialists of her own; but that Ethiopia is not as highly developed industrially to undertake certain projects independently without some assistance from other coutries that met their industrial development

1. See Walter Rodney, HOW EUROPE UNDERDEVELOPED AFRICA, london, 1972, in which he detailed a type of "Western Genocide" against Africans not being told in "Western" history books.

objectives - such as Sweden, the U.S.A., the U.S.S.R, Peoples Republic of China, Japan, West and East Germany, and a few others. The U.S.A. made its own "on the backs of enslaved Africans."

You will note from your own experience that when you give something you expect something in return, even if it is only good will. It does not have to be material gains, for sometimes the gaining of a friend in a strategic position is much more important than gaining a million dollars. Your nation is presently in search of gaining both of these things today. Ethiopia is in search of gaining both of these things also. Remember, then, that in this field of searching no one has a monopoly; for if any nation had, it would not be looking for friends today.

There is an old saying amongst the indigenous [BLACK] African people - Falashas too; thus:

> YOU CANNOT EVERLASTINGLY WHIP A MAN IF YOU ARE IN HIS HOUSE CARESSING HIS WIFE, ALL OF WHICH SHE RESENTS. BUT YOU CAN CONTINUE TO WHIP HIM IF SHE ACCEPTS YOUR ADVANCES AND CARESSES, AS SHE WILL WORK AGAINST HIM.

Can you see any bearing on this subject in the latter maxim? I assure you that there is a strong relationship to the above and the following from THE KADISH by Abu el-Yezdi [English translation by Sir Richard F. Burton]: thus:

All faith is false, all faith is true
  Truth is the shattered mirrors strewn
In myriad bits; while each believes
  his little bit the whole to own.[1]

The strength in which you author brings this chapter to a close is demonstrated in the above carving of the ancient ETHIOPIAN LION in a rock at Angiarro, which was formerly called "... WOLLO...." This picture was taken from T. Lefebure's VOYAGE en ABYSSINE, and is currently on display by a photo in the Bibliotheque Nationale of Paris, France. "TRUTH" is the rock-hewn Ethiopian lion one believes he[or she] saw, and swore he had seen "...speeding across the plains...;" yet its solid rock-mass was as immoveable as its rock-mountain source. TRUTH is also seen in the following "...FACES OF THE SEMITES..." on the next page - 292:

1. Your author's presentation of his fellow Beta Israel [Ethiopian Jews, African]/Black Jews'position on history, heritage, etc. ad infinitum, expressed by a Falasha "Council of Elders," etc.

Faces and Colors
of
"JEWS" AROUND THE WORLD"
[Their mothers were Jews; thus they]

YEMEN

SPAIN

CHINA

TRINIDAD
West Indies, Indep.

ETHIOPIA

NIGERIA

FORREST HILLS
New York City
USA

ISRAEL

BRAZIL

Yosef ben-Jochannan's

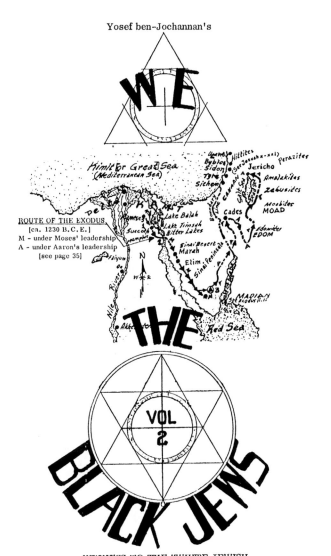

WE THE BLACK JEWS

VOL 2

WITNESS TO THE "WHITE JEWISH RACE" MYTH

All To The Memory Of The Late Honourable
Rabbi Wentworth B. Matthew, "Dean Of African American
Rabbis Throughout The Americas And Caribbean Islands"

DEDICATED TO ALL WHO BELIEVE THAT THEIR GOD-HEAD CREATED ALL OF MANKIND WITH THE SAME PERFECTION HE, OR SHE, ORIGINATED FROM PRO-CREATION; AND THAT THE ONLY SOURCE BY WHICH MANKIND REPRODUCE THEMSELVES - SEXUAL INTERCOURSE - IS EQUALLY SACRED AND GODLY.

Yosef A. A. ben-Jochannan
1983 C.E.

The Black Jews of Harlem[1]

Who Decides Their Jewishness? Is There A Jewish Race?
What Color Is The "Jewish Race"?

1. See front cover of Howard Brotz's book, THE BLACK JEWS OF HARLEM. All three of these rabbis have died since this picture was taken at Harlem's East River, 135th Street, New York, N.Y.

AMERICA'S BLACK JEWS

More than 100,000 Negroes now proclaim their loyalty to ancient Hebrew religion

AMERICA'S Black Jews, whose numbers exceed 100,000, are not integrated officially into any of the three main divisions of Jewry, but their strict observance of the ancient Hebrew *mitzvot* (commandments) proclaim their loyalty to the ancient religion.

The Commandment Keepers, founded in Harlem 38 years ago, is probably the largest and best-known Negro Jewish group in the United States. The sect has 1,100 registered members, practically all of whom are Negroes. Use of the word Negro, however, is forbidden. Black Jews are insulted when so categorized.

"We abhor the word Negro," says Rabbi Wentworth Arthur Matthew, aggressive, African-born spiritual leader of the group. "I am not a Negro, never have been. I am an Afra-American and so are all of my children. Today we have 16 million colored Americans. Tomorrow we will have 16 million Black Jews."

The existence of this sect has led to spirited discussion by Jewish scholars over their right to classification as Jews. For five years, Rabbi Irving Block,[1] of New York's reform Brotherhood Synagogue, has been trying to get the Commandment Keepers recognized by the main body of Jewry. "Any group of people," he states, "who say they are Jewish and who follow the practices and traditions of Judaism are Jews."

Another prominent reform rabbi welcomes the sect into Jewry and chides white Jews who scoff at its authenticity. "Some of our Jews," he says, "have not awakened to the fact that we are Jews by conviction and not by blood. There is no Jewish race and black as well as white Jews are equally members of the Jewish people."

The Commandment Keepers maintain close spiritual and sentimental ties to Ethiopia, where some 60,000 Black Jews, called Falasha, live. Like the Falashas of Ethiopia, the Commandment Keepers claim to be descendants of King Solomon and the Queen of Sheba.

The Harlem Jews live an austere communal life according to the precepts of the Talmud. They eat the traditional *matzoh* during Passover, meticulously maintain kosher kitchens in their homes and buy their meat from kosher butchers. Like white Jews, they are awaiting the coming of a Messiah who will usher in a Messianic Age.

---

1. B.C.E. means "Before the Christian Era." This term is used in preference to B.C. or "Before Christ;" as it presents a problem to the Jewish reader who does not believe Christ existed.
2. Punt/Puanit, Ethiopia/Kush or Cush, Sudan/Ta-Nehisi and Egypt/Ta-Merry had their own "beginning of the world" theories and myths for thousands of years before the birth of the first Haribu/ Hebrew or Jew named "Avrm/Abraham," and biblical "Adam and Eve," etc.

What you have just read comes from the so-called "NEGRO JEWS," written by another "White Jew." Surely most of my readers have heard about "NEGRO" or "COLORED JEWS" living in Old Harlem,[1] New York City, New York and Brooklyn, New York City, New York, equally The Bronx, New York City, New York. These groups of Jews, Israelites as most prefer to be called, are set aside from the main body of WHITE JEWS - who originally came from Europe and their descendants born in the United States of America. Their living apart is no accident, but instead planned with the intent of remaining in the same manner in which it now stands forever. JEWS of lighter [WHITE] complexion must maintain this set-up if they intend to enjoy the pleasures of being "Pure Hebrews" as most generally claim, or "Pure Whites" as others prefer saying. Still others yet have claimed to be of some kind of a "Pure Semite Ethnic Stock." Yet all is like any other European or European-American Christian, Moslem, Druid, Mormon, and even Atheist. Therefore, you can see why the Falashas' descendants in the United States of America must remain SEGREGATED from the general body of Jews of light pigmentation. This SEGREGATION is obvious, since those Jews who profess their "SEMITIC RACIAL STOCK" and "WHITE PURITY" theories can not accept the BLACK FALASHAS as full brothers and sisters in every respect, as it would mean that those who claimed "RACIAL PURITY" would not be able to make such a claim anymore. This would also mean that they would have had to refer back to the BOOK OF GENESIS in their SACRED TORAH [Pentateuch, Five Books Of Moses. Comesh, Old Testament, etc.] and practise what our ancestors have written. They/Our "Biblical Forefathers/Ancestors" - wrote:

> "AND GOD CREATED MAN FROM THE DUST OF THE EARTH, AND BLEW THE BREATH OF LIFE INTO HIM. THEN GOD TOOK A RIB FROM THIS MAN HE HAD CREATED AND MADE HIM A COMPANION. GOD CALLED THE MAN ADAM AND THE WOMAN EVE...,"etc., almost ad infinitum.

This most WHITE JEWS have conveniently denied, because they know too well that they have now discovered they are from a "SPECIAL RACE OF WHITE SEMITES," and as such they must remain separate from all of the BLACK, BROWN, YELLOW and RED JEWS of the world; thus equally maintaining that "NON-WHITE JEWS ARE CONVERTS TO JUDAISM." Of course by whom, when and where they cannot document, and very poorly try to hypothesize.

Let me take one of these "BLACK JEWISH COMMUNITIES OF AMERICA" and visit it with you. This group we are about to visit is known to most Americans who are familiar with the existence of "BLACK JEWS" and/or "BLACK ISRAELITES," originally "ETHIOPIAN ROYAL HEBREWS" of the "COMMANDMENT KEEPERS SYNAGOGUE, Inc.," whose center of Community Group Life was not too long ago located at Lenox Avenue on the Northeast corner of 128th Street, HARLEM, New York City, New York one flight up and over a drug store [pharmacy] on the street level. This

1. See R. B. Moore, The Name Negro, Its Origin And Evil Use, New York, 1961, for details, etc.

group and Synagogue have since moved to a new location at the west side of Mount Morris [Mall] Park, 123rd Street and Mount Morris Park West [or Fifth Avenue]; still in the general Harlem area. The old Synagogue occupied the 2nd and 3rd floors of an old converted tenement building. Behind all of the stained-glass windows was the HOUSE OF WORSHIP. You could not miss this place, due to the signs on the many glass window panels. The correct name of the congregation also appeared on the windows, thus: COMMANDMENT KEEPERS CONGREGATION OF ROYAL ETHIOPIAN HEBREWS, Inc. On "SPECIAL" or "HIGH HOLY DAY" temporary announcements also appeared on the panels.

Let us take the trip to our African-American Hebrew brothers and sisters and their leader at the former home at 128th Street. We travel by taxi, bus or automobile; the Subway is the fastest. We arrive at the above address, and we notice the signs on the windows. We agree that this must be the correct destination. We look for the entrance, only to find that it is on the side street located slightly east of Lenox Avenue and 128th Street. We open the wooden door and notice that there is a flight of stairs which we must climb, and knowing that we must if we wish to go up we start to mount the stairs. Now that we have reached the first landing, it is obvious that we are standing directly in front of a door with the sign "SYNAGOGUE." We enter because the door is always open on the SABBATH [Saturday] - the last day of every week, SUNDAY being the first day. Excuse me. I am sorry I did not tell you that we are visiting on the SABBATH SERVICE in order that we could have a full view of most of the customs [religious and otherwise] on one of the MOST, if not the MOST, important day of any Hebrew Calendar since the first one in ca. 700 B.C.E. [or B.C.] when the first SACRED TORAH [Pentateuch, Comesh, Old Testament, Five Books Of Moses, etc.] was begun, to its completion in ca. 500 B.C.E.; not ca. 5734 B.C.E. - the World Of Genesis!

We enter this place and immediately get the feelings we are in the section where the various "COMMITTEES" meet, because we cannot see the regular type of seats used in WHITE SYNAGOGUES of the downtown New York City areas. However, we turn our heads to the right of us and notice that there is an "ARK" and an "ALTAR" [see page 303] at the front of the room located at the east wall. We then say to ourselves: 'We must be in the place of worship itself.' We further observe that there is an upright piano at the right side of the Ark and Altar. Someone said in a very low voice: "This place is very small; it can only hold about 250 persons in any service." You agree; and I agree with all of you. However, you will notice that the members always make room for all visitors, as you look around the Synagogue and see many WHITE people seated [as shown on the following page].

1. B.C.E. means "Before The Christian Era." This term is used in preference to B.C. or Before Christ; it presents a problem to the Jewish reader who does not believe in the Christians' Jesus.
2. Punt/Puanit, Ethiopia/Kush, Sudan/Ta-Nehisi and Egypt/Ta-Merry had "Beginning Of The World" allegories and myths for thousands of years before the birth of the first Jew - Abraham.

"BLACK" OR "WHITE:" THEY ARE ALL "JEWS/ISRAELITES" TODAY![1]

White Jews often visit Commandment Keepers and take part in service. Congregation follows main features of Jewish worship. Service has carefully-prescribed ritual.

Just Imagine They Must Be Told They Are Rejected Because Their Parents Were/Are Not "Pure White Semitic Jews" a-la?

1. Yes; but only the visiting "White Jews" are covered by "The Law Of Return" in White Racist Israel by God Ywh!

By this time it is getting closer to the beginning of the SABBATH SERVICE, because we can see that the pianist has arrived at the piano and is playing many hymns. Her assistant walks directly over to us and welcome us to the SERVICE. She asks:

"Is there any way in which I may be of help to you before the Rabbi enters?"

All of us agree that we are alright, and that everything is in good order. But, actually you are a little uneasy because you do not know these people - and how they may yet react to your being in their midst. You feel, probably for the first time, like a BLACK person feels in an all WHITE congregation; it is your very first experience. But, do you not feel you are exactly like the rest of those who always say that "...SOMETHING IS WRONG WITH THE NEGROES...?" Maybe this is what you have told yourself, even later all during the late Reverend Martin Luther King, Jr.'s "CIVIL RIGHTS MARCHES" of the 1960's C.E. Of course not Minister Malcolm X, whom you feared.

By this time the gathering is much larger, and the members are reaching for their prayer shawls [talaces], prayer books, etc. You also notice that everyone keeps on their hats. You are asked to take a "PRAYER CAP" if you are a man and do not have on a head gear of any kind. You are also given a PRAYER SHAWL if you are not Hebrew and have any of your own. The person next to you hands you a PRAYER BOOK. You open the BOOK and notice that it is written from RIGHT to LEFT instead of the usual LEFT to RIGHT that you are accoustom to use. You also notice that it was not donated by any rich member like it generally is in downtown synagogues. You ask yourself:

"Why don't the people of wealth in this congregation help the poor ones?"

But then you will also notice that everyone you have seen coming into this HOUSE OF WORSHIP[1] is of a moderate class from the type of clothing they are wearing. You have answered your own self by your own observation.

Everyone stands; and naturally you followed the crowd and did likewise. Then you hear a voice coming from back of where you are standing, and you turn around to look in the direction of the voice in order that you might observe what is taking place. You become a little relax because it is Rabbi Wentworth Matthew leading a procession with the SACRED TORAH clutched in both hands and laying on his right bossom and shoulder, followed closely by the Kantor and the Elders of the Synagogue. all of whom are chanting in an apparently strange language - "Hebrew."

By this time it is getting closer for the Rabbi to reach where you are standing as the procession follows the isle in the direction from East to West; the procession going from the Altar and Ark in the East towards the congregation in the West, as shown on the following page - 301.

1. Called "Synagogue School, Sabbath House," etc.; but never Temple until the up-coming "Third Temple" is built in Jerusalem. The last "Temple" was destroyed by the Roman colonialists in ca. 3831 H.C. or ca. 70 C.E.

"Shamoi Adanoi, Adanoi Heroit/Blessed Be God, God Liveth Forever," Is His Message.
WHAT IS IT ABOUT HIS COLOR AND "RACE" THAT DISQUALIFY HIM AS A JEW?

Leading procession of synagogue elders, Rabbi Matthew holds Torah or holy scroll and chants "Amen–Hallelujah." At Sabbath service in Commandment Keepers Harlem synagogue.

---

1. The man who made WHITE RABBIS by the dozens prove that "BLACK ANTI-SEMITISM" is no more extensive than "WHITE SEMITIC ANTI-BLACKISM" throughout the United States of America.
Born June 23, 1892, Lagos, Nigeria; Died December 10, 1973, New York, N.Y.

At the Ark Of The Covenant With God,[1] we are witnessing Rabbi Wentworth Matthew chanting

"THE BLESSING OF THE ARK AND THE LAWS IN ITS PORTALS;"

then equally "BLESSES" the congregation; and the congregation follows by rendering the Opening Song. From here on the SABBATH SERVICE is conducted in the manner that is very similar to any other HEBREW SERVICE of which you are normally accustomed; this is if you are a JEW. At certain points in the SERVICE you will notice a few traditional moves that you are not familiar with; this is due to the mixture of African and European formats of Judaism inherent among African and African-American JEWISH CUSTOMS and TRADITIONS. All of this is caused by "CULTURAL CARRY-OVERS AND ABSORPTIONS" within JUDAISM in the "Western [WHITE] World."

If you are a male of more than twelve [12] years of age in appearance you would observe the man next to you asking:

"ARE YOU AN ISRAELITE OF FULL AGE TO READ THE SACRED TORAH?"

And if you say yes; he will advise you that:

"YOU HAVE THE RIGHT TO GO UP AND READ THE LAWS WHEN THE TIME COMES FOR YOUR TRIBAL GROUP TO BE CALLED TO READ THE TORAH."

He then asks you for "...YOUR HEBREW NAME...." You give it; and he carries it to one of the Elders up at the Ark. You notice that the note is placed on the Altar in front of the Kantor [singer, crier, etc.]. You are by now quite nervous, because you will have to read the LAWS in the presence of all of these people. But why? You do not know if they are using the same type of Hebrew Language which you are accustomed to read in your synagogue downtown. Well!, your own "TRIBAL GROUP" is ready to read the LAWS, and you are the first to lead off from your group. You are the first, because of a most basically fundamental custom among Hebrew/Jewish people:

"the stranger [or visitor] must always be served first according to the rules of this congregation and all Falasha congregations the world over, which is required by the Sacred Torah."

You walk up, and look down upon the Sacred Torah; lo and behold you find that it is the same as the Sacred Scroll[2] you are accustomed to read in your own synagogue downtown. You further observe that it was WRITTEN, EDITED, PRINTED and PUBLISHED by a Hebrew [or Jewish] firm which is composed solely of white-skinned Jews. You read the LAWS; and you receive the regular handshake which everyone of the others received after reading the LAWS. Upon your return to your seat you begin to feel a little more relaxed, because now you know that you are becoming an actual part of this congregation due to your personal participation. For those of you who did not participate in this manner, you will feel involved because one of your travel companions on the tour participated freely of the fellowship extended in taking of the most precious possession of

1. See Y. ben-Jochannan's Black Man Of The Nile And His Family, p. 305, for the African original.
2. The Holy Torah or Old Testament was originally written in the form of a "Scroll" of lamb skin.

FALASHA RABBIS IN THE U.S.A. REJECTED BY THEIR WHITE BRETHRENS.[1] WHY? BECAUSE OF WHITE SEMITIC RACISM AND RELIGIOUS BIGOTRY.

Rabbi Matthew is assisted by elders and other rabbis

Visiting rabbinical student Alvin Block addresses congregation. "I am not a stranger among you," he said, "for I am one of you. We are all Jews together. We have a united goal and that goal is Judaism. We are all children of the God of Israel."

---

1. Rabbi Block's expression of brotherhood in 1947 C.E./A.D. is still not shared by most of his fellow WHITE RABBIS. Yes! A BLACK JEW is still "...a stranger among you..."[White Jew]; for he or she is not "...one of you. We are " [not] " all Jews together...." Why? Racism. This date, more than seven [7] years, means nothing in terms of Black-White Jewish harmony, etc.

any Israelite Synagogue - THE READING OF THE LAWS OF THE SACRED TORAH ON THE ALTAR OF THE SABBATH, ALONG WITH THE TEN COMMANDMENTS MOSES RECEIVED AT MOUNT HOREB [Sinai] FROM JEHOVAH. Remember, from the same downtown "Holy Torah."

The SABBATH SERVICE continues in the manner of which you are accustomed and then gradually draws to a close. The congregation, including yourself, begins to sing the "Parting Song" - "SHALOM ALECHEM" - as Rabbi Matthew blesses the congregation through the power of "The One And Only True God - Ywh - Of Israel." You are told by someone:

> "Hold your position until the Rabbi, Kantor and Elders leave the Synagogue and enter the Vestry. Following this you can talk to the Rabbi in his office.

After the recession enters the Vestry you are immediately notified that:

> "Rabbi Matthew would like to meet you personally, along with the entire group of new faces in the midst of our congregation - The Commandment Keepers.

Before you could get the chance to visit the Rabbi, you find that you are receiving questions from old and young alike. Some of the questions you are asked are the following:

> "Are you living very far from our congregation? What is your name? Will you visit us often? Would you like to become a member of this congregation; if you are an Israelite? Will you have lunch with us? May I visit your synagogue on a Sabbath, if it is not too far, because I will have to walk there?

There will be many more such questions asked of you. The LOVE in a Falasha [BLACK JEW] Synagogue could produce no less than this. "LOVE" and "FOOD" you will be offered amongst any African and African-American group involved with any religion of an African beginning or base - such as TORAHDIC JUDAISM, JUDAEO-CHRISTIANITY, YORUBAISM, VOODOOISM, ISLAM, etc.

Someone holds your hand and lead you into a specific direction, while saying to you:

> "Come to meet the Rabbi now, it is your turn. He will be going to visit the sick in the hospitals, or maybe some other activities in the course of his duties."

You enter the Rabbi's study and you are greeted by him:

> "I am Rabbi Wentworth Matthew; what may I ask is your name?"

You tell your name. He responds once more:

> "Will you give us the honour of returning to Sabbath Service again?"

He then asks you about your own Rabbi, for it is quite possible that they may have attended the same conference at one time or another; or maybe your Rabbi is one of the very few WHITE RABBIS that invited Rabbi Matthew to meet and participate with his group downtown. Your conversation with the learned Rabbi covers almost every and anything; from religion down to the "kitchen sink." Both of you agree that you will have to be getting on the way of your other commitments for the rest of the day, and you bade each others love: SHALOM, SHABBATH SHALOM [Peace, Peace of the Sabbath]. You are about to leave the Commandment Keepers Congregation Of

Royal Ethiopian Hebrews, Inc...," Harlem's Black [never "Negro" or "Colored"] Hebrews/Jews.

We make our exit through the same door we had entered and down the stairs we go. You open the street level exit door and leave the building on West 128th Street, Harlem, New York City, New York. Now you are feeling a little different sensation than that you had when you entered, for you had experienced a new chapter in your life; and you may be now convinced that these people are just like me in almost every manner, except for color, and maybe facial characteristics. If you are "WHITE" you might say:

> 'I don't see why we should continue excluding these Black Jews from the greater body of Judaism in this country solely on the basis that some of us wish to maintain the color line of racial prejudice around us.'

Then you recall one of the "PSALMS OF SOLOMON," which he coopted from the indigenous African scribe - "Amen-em-eope" [see page 355 of Chapter] - that reads:

> "My hair is woolly, and my color as swarthy as the robes of my father's kingdom; therefore I am Black and comely...," etc., etc., etc. [see "Fallacy of Racial Jews;" for similar biblical quotations see page 400 of this section

Do not call my people here in the United States of America "NEGRO JEWS" or "COLORED JEWS;" because a "NEGRO" or "COLORED" nomenclature is rejected in toto by each and every consciously self-respecting African - Jew, Gentile, Moslem, Yoruba, Voodooist, etc. included. The reason for the rejection of this term is obvious, as shown on the 17th Century C.E. Map Of Africa before the Portuguese changed their term "NIGRITIA" to the point where the British could relabel the area of West "Africa" by the imperialist name "NEGROLAND" and the indigenous African people - "NEGROES." The Map Of Africa showing "NEGROLAND" appears on page 34 of Chapter One; take note. It is the SLAVE MASTER'S insult to his SLAVES: BLACK JEWS, ETHIOPIAN JEWS, AFRICAN-AMERICAN JEWS, ISRAELITES, AGAW, and other titles which WE shall tell you to call US are the only correct names acceptable to US; not what anyone else said it should be because he/she has been calling US that for over the last three to four hundred years. Every man or woman has the right to name his or her self. We, Agaw or "Israelites, have never in all of history changed our group's name to "NEGRO;" that is the work of the Portuguese slavers whom historian Richard B. Moore took to task in his most timely book - THE NAME NEGRO, ITS ORIGIN AND EVIL USE, New York, 1961.

You can find BLACK JEWS in other communities such as Philadelphia and Pittsburgh, Pa.; Cleveland and Youngston, Ohio; Boston, Mass.; and Chicago, Ill.; all of whom comprises a total population in the United States of America of at least 95,000 to 110,000 members. They are in the majority composed of descendants of Falashas that arrived here in the United States of America by way of the Caribbean Islands within the last five [5] generations. There are very few amongst the

1. Racism permeates the Jewish, Christian, Moslem, etc. "Sacred Scriptures;" even the so-called "Image of God" shown in the picture bibles and tracts for Saturday and Sunday schools, etc.

congregations who were converted to, or born in, the "Christian Faith," and have returned to their "Mother's Faith."[1] Yet some are by the result of inter-religious marriage of the past, which is restricted and forbidden unless the convert joined a "HEBREW" group prior to the marriage; this being the same experience of the JEWS in, and of, Europe and South Africa noted in Chapter One.

The homes of the African-American JEWS of these communities in the United States of America are of very strict religious order. The women follow the "LEVITICAL LAWS OF THE UNCLEAN PERIOD" to the letter, and refrain from the room of their husbands upon such time that they are "UNCLEAN." The withdrawal to another room from the husband takes the place of the "HOUSE OF THE WOMAN OF UNCLEAN BLOOD" used in Falasha communities in Ethiopia [review Chapter VI, Child-Bearing and Child-Birth, pages 191 - 195 of Chapter One].

All members of the African-American [BLACK] Hebrew communities throughout the Americas must learn HARIBU/HEBREW and attend at least one HEBREW SCHOOL. They must study the religious life and history of their people - both ISRAELITES and AGAW. Each and everyone of the boys and girls are encouraged to complete a college education. They do not work on the Sabbath or any High Holy Day. These customs are "carry-overs" from their Torahdic experience in Africa.

In the homes of the African-American Jews the SABBATH is rigidly observed. From Sun-Down FRIDAY until Sun-down SATURDAY [Sabbath] there would be no gas burning or light shining on this day or any High Holy Day, and no hot food eaten. Their homes are furnished with all of the necessities and so-called "religious regalias" required of a religious family of an Orthodox Hebrew Home and Way Of Life. These items are purchased from European-American [WHITE] Hebrews [Jews]. "Kosher foods" must be eaten by all. The products to prepare such foods, like meats of every kind, are bought from "Kosher stores" uptown and downtown - all of them WHITE JEWS owned. Not a single African-American [BLACK] Jew has his own Kosher restaurant, delicatesen, or butcher shop which serves only "KOSHER FOODS." This alone indicates the extent of the dependency of the BLACK JEWS in the United States of America upon the WHITE JEWS; even for their very sustenance of life in too many cases; thus the further irony in Black-White Judaism U.S.A.

I am hoping that you would pay your brother and sister African-American Israelites [Jews, Hebrews, etc.] a visit and live a few hours with them, allowing them to equally live a few hours with you. They are very anxious to make friends with you in the community where they live, thereby helping to eliminate the lack of understanding existing amongst African-American and European and European-American Jews living in the United States of America and the Caribbean Islands.

African-Americans who are not of the Hebrew Religion, Culture and/or Way Of Life think it very strange to see "BLACK" people who are "JEWS." They have been for so long, studied by other

1. Jews, all over the world where they have lived, had/have taken local women converts into Judaism. Most of Europe's Jews have their own "Kharzak's Past," which they would like to forget.

European-American [Jewish, Christian, Atheist, etc.] racist "Scholars" [propagandists] who state:

"ALL JEWS HAVE WHITE SKIN AND ARE SEMITIC-CAUCASIAN,"

to the extent that most of them are shocked upon meeting any "AFRICAN-AMERICAN JEW" or "AFRICAN-CARIBBEAN JEW," much less an "AFRICAN JEW." There is presently a campaign against this sort of ignorance, and an uprooting of its sources. And as a result of this type of data in this volume the information is gradually changing. I am hoping that this Chapter will further help to bridge the gap between the spread of such ignorance in the BLACK and WHITE communities of the downtown and uptown areas, thereby eliminating some of the superstitions about the African-American Jews, thus causing the removal of the barriers set up by racist European-American Jews to bar these African [BLACK] Jews from the major body of the "Hebrew Community in America." Make friends now, because you may have to live with them one day in the State of Israel.[1] Why not be somewhat understanding before you have to be shocked by their presence in Israel as a part of the majority population. But remember, "BLACK JEWS" are not begging to be accepted. They have offered their "HANDS OF FRIENDSHIP." They are not "NON-VIOLENT." They will not "...TURN THE OTHER CHEEK..." when mistreated, much less when struck. They strongly believe in the teachings their fellow African Hebrew - MOSES - learnt from their fellow indigenous Africans of Ta-Merry, Ta-Nehisi, Meröe,[2] Itiopi, Punt, etc. all along the Blue and White Nile River Valley; particularly the following:

"AN EYE FOR AN EYE, AND A TOOTH FOR A TOOTH."

But the same Africans of the Nile Valley and Great Lakes regions also taught the following:

"THE PRINCIPLE OF THE LAW OF THE GREATEST GOOD AND OPPOSITES,"

which the Greeks copied under the title:

"... SUMMUM BONUM...."

The detailed outline of this issue on pages 313 - 338 in my book - BLACK MAN OF THE NILE AND HIS FAMILY - should refresh your memory on this point. Thus it is that the African Hebrews or Agaw people [Beta Israel or Falasha] have taught, and still teach, and will continue teaching:

"AN EYE FOR AN EYE, AND A TOOTH FOR A TOOTH;"

but only if it conforms to:

"THE LAW OF THE GREATEST GOOD."

It is indeed unfortunate that the END equally comes to many who use their own life as a model and foundation for thousands and/or millions who would have otherwise just drifted along through life's travails. Such a human person this entire chapter in effect deals with. And such a person it was the misfortune of the living to see passed by as he entered the PROMISED LAND of the world

---

1. This has become a fact for over one generation now! Black Jews from Chicago, Ill. are in Israel
2. Meroe once existed between Ta-Nehisi [Sudan] and Ta-Merry [Egypt] for centuries in antiquity.

of "WORTHY ANCESTRAL SPIRITS - the NETHER WORLD or HEREAFTER. Who Was He? Yes!,

"THE DEAN OF AFRICAN -AMERICAN [Black] HEBREWS."

Sounding the shofar or ram's horn, Rabbi Matthew signals beginning of *Yom Kippur*, the holiest day of Jewish year. On Yom Kippur, Jews fast all day, confess their sins and repent.

Performing taslic, traditional ceremony of Orthodox Jews, Commandment Keepers pray on bank of Harlem River. Ceremony, which follows regular service, must be held near flowing water. On Jewish holy days, no Commandment Keeper works.

---

t. He was the first Rabbi/Teacher/Leader of the first African/Black Synagogue in the United States of America. Most of the "noted Black rabbis" today were trained by his student-rabbis of the early 1920's to the present. He was indeed..."The Dean Of Black Rabbis"... in the U.S.A.!

The type of RACISM and RELIGIOUS BIGOTRY displayed by the "WHITE [?] JEWS" in the highest places of the United States of America's Talmudic [Rabbinical] Judaism with regards to the "DEAN OF AMERICAN BLACK JEWS" life was also displayed in his death in December, 1973. For a White Rabbi of equal status had passed away any place in the United States of America, irrespective of how much of a controversial figure he was, his death would have been cause for the greatest concern among the entire Jewish community. But the "BLACK COLOR" of Rabbi Matthew was to permit no so such concern in White Racist Judaism a-la European-America. The following is the manner in which the Harlem-based local newspaper mentioned his passing away; yet, he was the commonly proclaimed "Dean Of American Black Rabbis." Would the N. Y. Amsterdam News[1] give just a few lines of almost meaningless space if any of the merely noted BLACK MINISTERS, much less a BISHOP and or DEAN, had passed away? Certainly not! But RACISM and RELIGIOUS BIGOTRY have been a tradition African-Americans, particularly the "NEGROES" and "COLORED" among us, adapted with a mastery and vengeance to be expressed in every detail against our own selves. If the "GREAT WHITE FATHER" failed to endorse anyone of us - from Denmark Vesey and Nat Turner all the way to Malcolm X and Marcus Moziah Garvey [including hundreds of others] - we too must do likewise. But before we read the passing remarks by the local tabloid, let us not fail to remember that "MOSES" of the Pentateuch/Torah was an "AFRICAN" just like the late Rabbi Wentworth Matthew. Of course many of us would prefer to become members of the so-called "DEVIL'S RELIGION" rather than accept this fact. For is it not true that we have also learned to say:

"A NIGGER [meaning an African-American] AIN'T SHIT"

because of our conditioning by our SEMITIC and CAUCASIAN sociology, paleontology, anthropology, ethnology, history, etc. teachers and professors whom we call our own "AUTHORITY IN BLACK AND AFRICAN STUDIES" courses and textbooks - such as Loreen Katz, Basil Davidson, Herbert Aptheker, Daniel Moyniham, Robert July, et al.; but fail to recognize our own John H. Clarke, John G. Jackson, Cyril L. R. James, George G. M. James, Joel A. Rogers, and many others? Yes! Rabbi Wentworth Matthew's demise was more than entitled to a mere passing remark; at least from a local tabloid in his own community where he worked and transformed literally thousands into meaningful and worthwhile "AFRICAN-AMERICANS;" all of them even to realize that

"BLACK HAS BEEN ALWAYS BEAUTIFUL"

long before the buttons and ribbons of the so-called "Black Liberation Flag" that was coopted from the late Honourable Marcus Moziah Garvey's "TRI-COLORS OF AFRICA" flag of the Universal Negro Improvement Association [U.N.I.A.], of which Rabbi Matthew was a noted supporter. Yes,

1. Too many Africans/Blacks have been taught to be anti-any religious group which is not "Christian."

the following was the Amsterdam News final salute to the African-American Jews noted "Dean of Rabbis." This was ten years before the television spectacular about Ethiopian Jews on June 5, 1983.[1]

N. Y. AMSTERDAM NEWS Sat., Dec. 15, 1973 — C-9

RABBI WENTWORTH ARTHUR MATTHEW

Rabbi Matthew, The Organizer

Rabbi Wentworth Arthur Matthew, Black Dean of the Black Hebrews in the Western Hemosphere and Africa, died last Monday in Harlem Hospital after a long illness.

Rabbi Matthew was born June 23, 1892 in the city of Lagos, Nigeria, West Africa. At an early age he migrated, with his family, to the West Indian island of St. Kitts.

Marries

After completing his high school education he emegrated to the United States at the age of twenty-one. Here he met and married Miss Florence Liburd of Nevis, W.I. From that union four children were born.

Rabbi Matthew studied and was graduated from the University of Berlin from which he received a degree in anthropology and socialogy. He attended the Hebrew Theological Semonary in 1929 where is won his degree. He also attended the Institute of Chiropratic in Pennsylvania.

Hebrew Temple

Rabbi Matthew organized the Commandment Keeper Ethiopian Hebrew Congregation in 1929. This has grown into the largest Falasha Hebrew organization in the world.

He also organized the Hebrew Rabbinnical College, which has sent out Rabbis, teachers, and students to Hebrew Temples throughout the world. He also organized a Talmud Torah for children. He set up The sons and daughters of Culture.

Rabbi Matthew also built a Hebrew community which included a farm in Babylon Long Island, to teach young men and women the art of self preservation from the earth and its products.

Rabbi Matthew was one of the early pioneer fighters for civil rights for Blacks. He founght beside Marcus Garvey for the rights of the Black man.

Survivors

He was married for fifty seven years to Florence Matthew who survives him.

Rabbi Matthew is also survived by two sons, Arthur and Samuel Matthew. His grandson, whom he ordained as the youngest Rabbi in the world, Rabbi David Dore. Nine grandchildren and nine great grandchildren.

Rabbi Matthew was buried in the Frederick Douglas Cemetery in a section for Black Hebrews.

1. Channel 4 NBC, TV, 6/4/83 Monitor Show, 10:$_{00}$ P.M., presented "The Black Jews of Ethiopia/Falashas" without a solitary comment by an Ethiopian/Black Jew as commentator to counteract the racist distortions of the true history of the Beta Israel/Ethiopian [Black] Hebrews or Jews, etc.

An aspect of the major teachings of the Dean of African-American Hebrew Rabbis was: "Don't make assumptions solely upon biblical["sacred]scriptures." Many of his students heeded not; thus:

Most Africans[1] feel immigration will not solve the U.S. race problem

BY ERA BELL THOMPSON

Classes for children of Hebrew Israelites are held on porch until school is built. "We will not bring up illiterates," say parents who spend most of time clearing (right) fast-growing bush from 300-acre farm near Gbartala, Liberia. Some 200 members of Chicago-based Center have immigrated to Africa in past two years. "We get all the help possible from the government and people," they say, but biggest barrier is language. They need text books and tools

1. These too were/are the result of those who broke away from Rabbi Matthew's African Nationalism in Judaism to live among European-Jews in Israel/Palestine, but failed to reach there.

In the previous article I can hear the late Dean Of African-American Hebrew Rabbis warning his followers of "...THE SWEET SOUND OF THE MASTER'S VOICE OF DESENTION..." as Era Bell Thompson attempted to make us believe that she knows what "...most Africans feel..." about "...immigration..." with regards to the "...U.S. race problem...." For if migration and immigration by force to the Americas to become "SLAVES" mentally and physically can solve African-[BLACK]-Americans problem; why not '...RE-IMMIGRATION...' back to the world's richest piece of real estate - the only true "PROMISED LAND" for all people who are aware of their "AFRICANESS?" Era Bell Thompson failed to realize that it is not the Black/African People's return, or immigration, is the trouble; but instead the fact of what European and European-American colonialist and imperialist so-called "ENTREPRENEURS" who have migrated to the same so-called "AFRICA" have done to both the Africans at home and those abroad - even those who are directly in "...THE U.S. RACE PROBLEM...." with the Era Bell Thompsons.

Sad it is indeed that many who were with the African Hebrews below chose to move on to the so-called "PROMISED LAND" in the political State of Israel where it became necessary for their racist and religiously bigoted fellow Jews [Israelites, Hebrews] to have their Knesset [Parliament or Senate][1] meet to decide whether or not they are indeed KOSHER "JEWS," which is never the case NON-KOSHER JEWS from Russia who are totally ignorant of the first word of the first of anything stated in the Sacred Torah confront. Is this too "BLACK/NEGRO ANTI-SEMITISM?" Tell!

Wood-burning stove is tended by Naomi, 23, pretty ex-receptionist who admits she never knew how to cook before coming to Africa Group ...

1. To the very moment while this manuscript was being edited the Israeli Knesset was racistly continuing its official refusal to treat the Beta Israel/"Falashas" with the same "Right of return" it assures "Soviet Jewry," who for the most part know very little about "Judaism."

BACK HOME IN THEIR ONLY TRUE "PROMISED LAND"!

[Why Should They Leave Africa For Israel?]

WELCOME IN AFRICA Continued

Youngest camper is two-week-old Zivah, held by niece of Abe Yahhoo, 51, ex-foundry worker whose mother, Mrs. Mattie Buie, at 73 is oldest member of group. Twelve babies were born to immigrants during first 13 months

The recent immigration of over a hundred so-called Black Jews from the Abeta Israel Center in Chicago to a farm 100 miles into the Liberian bush was more religious than racial. Claiming to be one of the lost tribes of Israel, they came under Divine direction and in so doing, are fulfilling their own prophecy of black immigration before "America's ultimate destruction in 1970." Negroes can escape the disaster, warns their leaflet, by "keeping the laws of God."

What they did not escape was a bad press in the States and the fears and suspicions of neighbors in their adopted land.

The press, they said, has hurt their movement, so they proceeded to set the record straight. 1) They are not starving. Soul food gardens flourish; oranges are a cent a piece and they can buy a whole stock of bananas for a quarter. 2) They are not riffraff. "We may not be farmers, but among us are teachers, secretaries, postal clerks and machinists." And, although wearing skull caps and beards may seem strange to a predominantly Christian society, they are neither Black Muslims nor racists, they say, nailing Lie Number Three.

"When people return home after being away so long, they go through a period of adjustment," explained a youthful spokesman, waving toward blue tents and makeshift houses. "Of course it looks bad, compared with the nice homes we left behind us. But come back in a couple of years and you won't know this place."

The Israel Hebrews have expressed their intentions of becoming citizens, but they have not availed themselves of the presidential prerogative which would waive the two-year probationary period and entitle them to an immigrant's allowance provided for in the Liberian Constitution. Instead, they paid the government $1 an acre for a 500 acre farm and vowed: "We are here to stay."

The above article, which goes back to EBONY magazine of ca. 1969 C.E. [or A.D.],[1] deals with a type of African People who are as sturdy and as stubborn as the very ancient pre-Christian Itiopian archaeological statue adjacent to it. Just imagine, their ancestors created "JUDAISM!"

1. The sensational manner in which Ebony treated this historical event is typical, but unfortunate, of most - if not all - "Negro/Colored" tabloids, which should have been reporting from an African/ Black perspective. Ebony's owners appear to be oblivious to their own African heritage.

HOME, SWEET HOME, IN MOTHER ALKEBU-LAN/"AFRICA"!

Blowing of Shofar at sundown Friday (above) marks beginning of Sabbath at immigrant camp. Bamboo and woven mat houses (left) are replacing tents brought from America. Group now has generator for electricity and well water to drink.

The following Chapter should be of major importance to those who believe that all of the so-called "BLACK JEWS" are standing still awaiting their acceptance by "WHITE JEWS" in the so-called "PROMISED LAND" of Western Asia - the political State of Israel [formerly "Palestine"].

FALASHAS IN THE UNITED STATES OF AMERICA AND AFRICAN NATIONALISM:

A Falasha "AFRICAN NATIONALIST" is a person who looks at the issue of AFRICAN NATIONALISM, which is not to be mistaken with the 1960's "Black Nationalist Movement," with a very deep sense of emotion and combined intellect. He, or she, does not allow one to separate itself from the other. He, from this point also she when reasonable, is not a so-called "EXTREMIST" in any sense of the term; and due to this precaution has not become a typical "RACIST;" RACIST in the sense of believing that FALASHAS ARE MEMBERS OF A CHOSEN [superior] PEOPLE. He has rejected any such notion; but instead holds to the view that:

"FALASHAS ARE JUST ORDINARY MEMBERS OF THE HUMAN FAMILY,"

which is generally classified as the "HUMAN RACE", the latter being a creation of "Western [European and European-American] academicians." Whenever he uses the term "RACE," he gives it the meaning of a geographic cultural group. His designation of this term has nothing to do with one's COLOR OF SKIN or PHYSICAL CHARACTERISTICS. However, he will prefer not to use the term in any manner whatsoever. More-so, what is the "White Semitic Jewish Race"?

The successes of the so-called GOLD COAST [later Ghana] GOVERNMENT, the Africans' Prime Minister Dr. Kwame Nkrumah and his fight against the Imperial British Colonial Government, surely have given much more drive to FALASHA NATIONALISM for Africa in the United States of America and abroad. Just the mere idea of reading about our Brother and Sister [like the late Dr. Nkrumah]

> Africans in the Gold Coast resisting the oppressive rule of the British Imperial Colonial Government, and Western-type economic physical spiritual slavery generally

brought to all of the Falasha communities [my people] inside and outside of Alkebu-lan the will to fight under one common bond, towards one common goal, and for one common destiny. This purpose and destiny are still the main criterias involved in the Most Holy and Sacred duty towards

> "unconditional independence of all of 'Africa;' with Africans administering each and every African government over each and every inch of African soil, and for each and every African interest above all others living on the continent."

The political effect of the people of Alkebu-lan with their "NON-VIOLENT RESISTENCE MOVEMENT" against the racist and religiously bigoted ruling coalition of Jews and Christians in South Africa was/is another "feather in the cap" of my people and yours - the Falashas. Some of us could not help directly, but we raised our heads high with pride and joy when we saw that all of our African People could also rise up from where they had/have been trampled-down for centuries by the imperial colonialist "Western Powers." We, "FALASHAS," have also noticed in all of these triumphs that we have never had the cooperation of the WHITE HEBREW groups of the "West" - Europe, Great Britain and the United States of America; of course not excluding many of the European-American Central and South American governments. This was not the case of the BLACK HEBREWS when the WHITE HEBREWS from Europe were fighting the British colonialists in Palestine for their own "...INDEPENDENCE...." Yet, without help from WHITE HEBREWS, today we have AFRICAN [Black] HEBREWS who were/are fighting against the same British Imperial Colonial Government in one of the colonies the British created - "SOUTH AFRICA" [correctly "Monomotapa"], ZIMBABWE [colonialist "Rhodesia"] having freed itself in 1981. Is it a coincident why we do not receive aid from our WHITE HEBREW brothers and sisters of the so-called "WEST;" or is it intentional? To these questions you already have the answers; and nothing I could ever say will change your mind. You can not allow yourself to be confused by the facts, particularly when you have already reached your conclusion on African People; thus:

> "they are all alike, shiftless, lazy, oversexed and inferior in every other respect to any European and/or European-American - Christian or Jewish."

The fact that we call some of them "FALASHAS" and/or "BLACK JEWS" do not alter any of this.

Due to the contents of the last chapter we have just passed through Falashas living in the Americas, Caribbean Islands and Europe are forced to recognize a definite bond between themselves and other AFRICAN [Black] PEOPLE who still inhabit the great continent of Alkebu-lan. We must conclude that since we were set aside and segregated into a certain color and facial appearance called "NEGRO RACE," we must reestablish our honour amongst men by, and through, these same African People with whom we are identified, remembering of course that there is only one ALKEBU-LAN or "AFRICA," and it is very "BLACK." Thus no need to use the term "BLACK AFRICA;" anything else is NEO-COLONIAL SUBTERFUGE directed at further dividing African/Black People from their total liberation from the descendants of those that enslaved us at the Berlin and/ or Brussels Conference of 1884-1896 C.E.[1] in order to seized our more than 11.3 MILLION SQUARE MILES of the world's richest piece of REAL ESTATE - Our African/Black Birthright.

The AFRICAN NATIONALIST MOVEMENTS in the Americas and the Caribbean Islands are not a new factor; and many of you have heard of them in at least one of their few forms. For it was this "AFRICAN NATIONALIST FEELING" which was responsible for forcing President Abe Lincoln's administration to acquire land in the African-Caribbean Republic of Haiti [originally "Hayte," the Spaniards' "Hispaniola"] for the resettlement of African-Americans who were enslaved, and finally freed, in the United States of America; African People who were totally uncomfortable living in the midst of their former slavemasters and slavemistresses while having to remember their physical enslavement who suffered constantly by the mental enslavement of the same people. This same "AFRICAN NATIONALIST FEELING" was mostly felt in the Americas and Caribbean Islands when the late Honourable Marcus Moziah Garvey -"President-General Designate of the Universal Negro Improvement Association [U.N.I.A.] and African Communities League"- started his "AFRICAN NATIONALIST MOVEMENT" in 1900 C.E. in Jamaica [then the so-called "British West Indies," B.W.I.] and 1916 C.E. in Harlem, New York City, New York. This was the same U.N.I.A., and other AFRICAN NATIONALIST MOVEMENTS, that reached its zenith in the era of the "ITALIAN-ETHIOPIAN WAR" of 1934-35 to 1942 C.E. Yes, it was the same Mr. Garvey who was FEARED and finally SUPPRESSED and BANISHED by the United States of America because of his teachings of an AFRICAN NATIONALISM that reminded African People of every class and creed:

"AFRICA IS FOR THE AFRICANS, THOSE AT HOME AND THOSE ABROAD."

His SUPPRESSION and BANISHMENT had stiffled the power of any strong expression of outward protest in the form of AFRICAN NATIONALISM in the Western Hemisphere until the latter 1950's-1960's C.E. However the spirit of the AFRICAN NATIONALIST MOVEMENTS kept on developing amongst Mr. Garvey's "LIONS" and "CUBS" that followed, all of whom he spoke about, as AFRICAN NATIONALISM began regaining new adherents. Amongst the OLD and NEW members

1. See colonialist role of the U.S.A. in Sir E. Hertslett's The Map Of Africa By Treaty, Vol. 3 of 3.

are a very large number of African-American HEBREWS or ISRAELITES [Jews if you prefer] residing in the United States of America, and of course thousands more in the other nations of the Americas and the Caribbean Islands. You will find these Hebrew or Israelite brothers and sisters of yours and mine following the AFRICAN NATIONALIST MOVEMENT in various ways and commitments. Some are so-called "EXTREMIST" in their thinking, very much like the former "... STERN GANG..." and "...IGRUNI..." of the anti-British Palestinian Jewish [Zionist] Movement of pre-Israeli Independence. Yet, others are notedly "INTELLECTUAL" in their participation. Some are willing to go at this very moment to "MOTHER ALKEBU-LAN," as so many others have already done and are doing, to help their fellow African People on a person to person basis; if it was not for certain very well contrived "RED TAPE" designed to discourage African-[BLACK] Americans from developing any close ties with their African brothers and sisters in the Mother Continent - Alkebu-lan. Their conduct is nothing WORSE nor BETTER than those European and European-American HEBREWS or ISRAELITES who did likewise in the case of their fellow Jews in Palestine to establish the political State of Israel from the JEWISH NATIONALIST DREAM projected a few hundred years ago, which Hertzl reminded others to make a reality; even remembering further that Alkebu-lan ["Africa"] was considered at one time for a "...HOMELAND OF THE EUROPEAN JEWS...." Today we, AFRICAN-AMERICAN HEBREWS, are also contributing money and other material and moral aid to our African brothers and sisters who are feeling and suffering from the oppression of both the European and European-American imperialists of the Christian and Jewish faiths. But others yet take a "...HANDS-OFF POLICY..." between Asian Arabs and European Jews in their power struggle for "...THE CURSED LAND OF THE CANAANITES...," the "SACRED LAND" of the descendants of the so-called "...BLACK CURSE NOAH PLACED UPON HIS YOUNGEST SON'S [HAM] CHILDREN - THE NEGROES...." [see the "CURSE" on page 2, Volume I, and page 338 following].[1]

This volume makes it necessary to have a REAPRAISAL OF THE BLACK-WHITE JEWISH QUESTION," which is the subject title of the following Chapter In this we can very well see that the type of involvement African-American and African-Caribbean HEBREWS and/or ISRAELITES need to be into for our own SURVIVAL is not that of European and European-American controlled WHITE-SEMITIC-CAUCASIAN ZIONISM, but instead "AFRICAN NATIONALISM" at least, and "PAN-AFRICANISM" at best. The humiliating experiences of the BLACK JEWS from South and West Asia, North Africa, East Africa, as elsewhere should be enough reason to justify this stance; needless to mention the RACIST REJECTION and RELIGIOUS EXCLUSION we suffer here in the United States of America from our fellow Jews who clamor to be of a different COLOR and RACE.

1. See R. Graves and R. Patai's Hebrew Myths: The Story Of Genesis, pp. 120 - 122, etc. for details, and Kautsky's Are The Jews A Race, in which he questions the "Jewish Race" myth, etc.

A REAPPRAISAL OF THE BLACK-WHITE "JEWISH QUESTION":

I must reemphasize the fact that all of my writings to date are complete with emotion. This is equally true for the facts, objectively and subjectively, that I have found to be necessary in order to analyze the documents for the historical basis I have used in my hypotheses. My action will provide the reader with a visual understanding of history; for it is without justification that history has to be boringly placid. This I can very easily accomplish, as I do not attempt to hide the interest from whence I write. Thus, I do not try to imply that I can ever write an "UNBIAS HISTORY" of how the "AFRICAN PEOPLE" in any period of their life suffered from their exclusion in text books written on so-called "WORLD HISTORY" by European and European-American "historians" and "academicians" - including "biblical scholars" and "sages."

It is due to this exclusiveness that I find it necessary to keep in touch with the so-called "AVERAGE NEGROES" who spend much of their time listening to the "STREET CORNER SPEAKERS" at "MARCUS GARVEY AND MALCOLM X SQUARE,"[1] West 125th Street and Seventh Avenue, Harlem New York City, New York; and equally those who frequented the former "CHOCK FULL O'NUTS" restaurants at West 135th and Lenox Avenue and West 125th Street and Seventh Avenue, Harlem, New York City, New York. From these areas and points of interest, along with the COMMUNION one shares with his fellow Africans, any BLACK PROFESSIONAL can continue within the context of his or her unspoiled "BLACKNESS" that maintains the root-base of his [or her] "academic authority" and "independence."

The text of the "BLACK JEWS" has been seriously affected by the behavior on my part that reflects all that has been said above. For I have been able to hear from the so-called "AVERAGE BLACK JEW" whose interest is generally not represented by the "BLACK RABBIS" who try constantly to negotiate any type of acceptance by "WHITE TALMUDIC [Rabbinical] JUDAISM." Negotiations for a combined BLACK-WHITE JEWISH COMMUNITY being also futile.

I am equally cognizant of the fact that my own educational "BRAINWASHING" in "Western Judaeo-Christian Greek-centric" institutions must have had some sort of adverse influence on the way I react to "WHITE [Caucasian-Semitic-Indo-European-Aryan] TALMUDIC JUDAISM." Naturally the conditioned "Negro mind" can not understand this position. For such a "MIND" remains harnessed to the Judaeo-Christian mystique that detailed everything "BAD" and/or "SINFUL" in terms of "BLACKNESS," "WHITENESS" being the complete opposite - "GOOD" and/or "RIGHTEOUS." Thus "BLACK" is the symbol of "IMPURITY" and "UNGODLINESS;" whereas "WHITE" is the symbol of "PURITY" and "GODLINESS." This is equally carried over into the relationship between "BLACK-WHITE JEWS" as it is with "BLACK-WHITE CHRISTIANS." Thus the "BLACKNESS" of a "Jew, Christian, Moslem," etc. makes him or

1. Officially renamed "African Square" in May 1983 C.E. by a Proclamation. Seventh Avenue in Harlem is now "Adam Clayton Powell, Jr. Boulevard," honouring Harlem's late Congressman.

her that less "KOSHER" than the "WHITENESS" of a fellow co-religionist "Jew, Christian, Moslem," etc. The shades between "BLACK" and "WHITE" make one equally as "BAD" or "GOOD," depending upon what point between the center and the extreme ends one is located.

Unfortunately "BLACK JEWS," as a general rule, have failed to deal with the above fact honestly and forthrightly in any challenge to their fellow co-religionist "WHITE JEWS" in fear of being called "ANTI-SEMITE," to the extent that the latter expresses the belief that:

"MOST BLACK JEWS WANT TO AMALGAMATE WITH WHITE JEWS."

The fact is that the vast majority of the non-clerical "BLACK JEWS" could hate nothing else worse, as they are for the most part still dedicated to Garveyite "PAN-AFRICANISM," rather than Hertzlite "EUROPEAN-AMERICAN ZIONISM" which a mere handful of the total community have succumb to for the sake of a few dollars they receive on spacely occasions. And of course the recipients of these measly handouts must first become "NEGRO JEWS" by way of "CONVERSION" [see Volume One, page xxx.] before they can receive the first penny.

The context of the following remarks, documents, hypotheses, quotations, etc. from varied sources will enrage many who must maintain their hypocritical image of "unemotionalism," even though they suffer daily from intense "EMOTIONALISM" as a result of their second-class position within so-called "LIBERAL JUDAISM" with its "LILY WHITE SEMITE" syndrome.

The brutal fact is that the "BLACK JEWS" of the "HARLEMS" of the entire world must face the reality that THE ONLY FORM OF "JUDAISM" that is valid for them is that which they OWN, CONTROL and OPERATE like all other so-called "RACIAL" or "ETHNIC" JEWS do in their own separately RACIST and RELIGIOUSLY BIGOTED communities. For although their God-Head - "YWH, JEHOVAH, ADNOI," or whatever else HE, SHE, IT and/or THEY are/ is called - has been said to be a "COLORLESS SPIRIT" in most of the so-called "SACRED SCRIPTURES WRITTEN BY GOD-INSPIRED SCRIBES," Black Jews MUST realize that their co-religionist White Jews image of their God-Head is for all good and purpose the same as their own:

"WHITE, CAUCASIAN, SEMITE, INDO-EUROPEAN."[1]

The Black Jews must decide whether or not their PROMISED LAND should be somewhere in ALKEBU-LAN [Africa, Ortegya, Ethiopia, etc.] or in ASIA. Being "AFRICANS" however; why is the PROMISED LAND for the Black Jews not around the area where mankind has been proven to have existed - "CREATED"-ca. 1,750,000 before Genesis' "ADAM AND EVE IN THE GARDEN OF EDEN" sometime during ca. 3670 B.C.E. or 5,742 years ago? [see page 55].

We, Black Jews, need to realize that the allegorical myth about "ADAM AND EVE" is as real as the story about "MOSES" receiving "THE TEN COMMANDMENTS ON MT. HOREB, in

1. Western man created "races" to make himself the best of all men - the "Chosen People," etc.

SINAI, Northeast Alkebu-lan sometime around 1190 B.C.E. But this reality is only applicable to those Jews, Christians and Moslems [Muslims] who have maintained their brainwashing through parental guidance and/or conversion in these directions; as they were taught, only through the hearsay or written folklore one finds in the Book Of Genesis and/or the Book Of Exodus in the PENTATEUCH [Holy Torah, Old Testament, etc.]. Yet the fact still remains that the Black Jews among White Jews are more-so inferior than Black Christians among White Christians and Black Moslems among White Moslems, etc. The following article on page 321 extracted from page L 45 of THE NEW YORK TIMES gives adequate support for my conclusion. For irrespective of the underlying reason or reasons which caused the predominant community of White Christians to vote for this "BLACK CHRISTIAN CLERGYMAN" - the Reverend Dr. Sterling Carey - it is one hundred [100 $^0/_0$] percent better than any step ever made by most White Jews towards Black Jews any place in the Americas in any period of their existence in the so-called "New World." What is evident here is that the White Christians have at least recognized their fellow co-religionist Black Christians to the extent of having them in some of the clerical assemblies, of which not a single case exist in any branch of WHITE European Talmudic[or Rabbinical]Judaism. There is no doubt, even the PROMISED LAND is segregated.

Dr. Carey's reference to the role of the White Christian churches and White Christians involved in colonialism, imperialism and genocide along-side their European-American cartels is typical of what takes place between White Jewish Synagogue and White Jews. But is it not strange that not a single White Jewish leader of a single White Jewish Synagogue has openly condemned the role of European-American dollar-colonialism in any part of Alkebu-lan [Africa, etc.] to date? Obviously it must mean that not a single White Jewish Synagogue has any financial investment in "American Corporations" operating in "Africa" today. This is providing we are all foolish enough to believe in fairy tales. Certainly not one of them made the first condemnation of a solitary White Jewish corporation in the so-called "Republic Of South Africa" engaged in systematic genocide against the indigenous "African People" they too have misnamed "BANTUS, HOTTENTOTS, BUSHMEN" and "BUSHWOMEN." Of course we are not to mention any of this without being subject to the label of "ANTI-SEMITE." But any active or inactive "BLACK JEW" who runs from this form of character assassination is worse than the perpetrators of the genocide directed against the indigenous "African People" in their [our] own PROMISED LAND - Alkebu-lan [Africa or Afrika]. Of course Dr. Carey cannot go this far out.

The text following Dr. Carey's remarks is only the beginning of a very brief insite into the malady of the BLACK-WHITE JEWISH CONFRONTATION presently existing in the Americas and the Caribbean Islands today, which is no different than the past 200 or more years.

Church Groups Hit Corporations

By ELEANOR BLAU

Major religious groups are stepping up their stockholder challenges against certain practices of American corporations. The increased activity involves an issue they have confronted for three years—investments in white-ruled African areas—as well as new issues.

This month, for example, a coalition of nine church groups, including the National Council of Churches, announced that it was filing stockholder resolutions with nine corporations requesting data on equal employment for women and racial minorities.

The Rev. Dr. Lucius Walker Jr., associate general secretary of the National Council of Churches' Church and Society Division, said:

"Churches are multibillion-dollar investors in corporate America and recognize they have a basic obligation to look at the social bottom line as well as the financial bottom line of companies in which they invest."

More Resolutions Planned

In the next few weeks, various groups plan to file resolutions on matters including strip mining, the energy crisis, the presence of the International Telephone and Telegraph Corporation in Chile, and the role of investors in the Philippines.

Previously, most church proxy efforts had involved areas of southern Africa. Last year, various members of a church coalition filed 17 resolutions, of which 11 called for data on companies' involvements in South Africa.

Seven of the 11 companies agreed to issue such reports to all their shareholders, so the resolutions were withdrawn. Rev. W. Sterling Cary, president of the National Council of Churches, called that a "small victory."

Dr. Cary announced recently that the coalition on southern Africa was filing 22 stockholder resolutions this year in an expansion of its three-year-old activities.

The resolutions included, for the first time, appeals to companies doing business in Mozambique, Portuguese Guinea, (known by nationalists now as Guinea-Bissau) and border areas of South Africa.

United Press International

Dr. Sterling Cary, the president of the National Council of Churches, told of South African resolutions.

The Bethlehem Steel Corporation was urged to pull out of Mozambique. The Exxon Corporation was asked to end its contract with Portugal, from which Guinea-Bissau declared independence last September.

Border Acts at Issue

And a Canadian company, Alcan, Ltd., as well as the Foote Mineral Company of Philadelphia, were asked to cancel plans to invest in a South African border area. Church spokesmen said the white South African Government was developing such areas to reduce the concentration of black workers in cities, and offering incentives such as exemptions from minimum-wage restrictions.

In this month's action the church groups said they were calling on the Ford Motor Company, the General Electric Company, the General Motors Corporation, the Goodyear Tire and Rubber Company, the International Business Machines Corporation, the Kresge Corporation, the Polaroid Corporation, Sears, Roebuck & Co., and the Xerox Corporation to give their shareholders data already required by the Federal Government's Equal Employment Opportunity Commission.

The groups filing the employment resolutions are the Unitarian, Episcopal, United Presbyterian and American Baptist Churches; the Women's and National Divisions of the Methodist Church, the Roman Catholic Franciscan Friars of the Atonement; the National Council of Churches and a local parish, the Central Presbyterian Church, at 593 Park Avenue.

Timothy Smith, director of this as well as the African project said representatives would try to meet with the management of each of the companies in hope of winning agreements that would preclude a proxy fight.

"It's ironic that we actually have more information about those companies [illegible] South Africa than we do on their domestic activities," Mr. Smith remarked in an interview.

When I first considered making a critical analysis of the FALASHAS, my people at home in Alkebu-lan [in Volume One] and abroad in the Americas and Caribbean Islands [in Volume Two], I had to realize that the vast majority of my reading audience will more than likely be African-Americans of the "CHRISTIAN RELIGION," and of course many of the "MUSLIM" or "MOSLEM RELIGION." For this reason I equally had to use the most common "...HOLY SCRIPTURES..." of which they are acquainted as my base of reference with regards to the "FIRST BOOK OF MOSES [Genesis]" and "SECOND BOOK OF MOSES [Exodus]." Of course some BLACK JEWS may argue that it should be the PENTATEUCH, while BLACK MUSLIMS or MOSLEMS would demand that it be the QUR'AN.[1] Yet, the fact still remains that it is in the "AUTHORIZED VERSION OF THE KING JAMES BIBLE" references are made to make it appear that the Christians' GOD - Jushua [Jesus] Crystos [Christ or The Anointed] - was present when the Hebrew or Israelites' GOD - Ywh [or Jehovah] supposedly said some 5743 [ca. 3760 B.C.E. + 1983 C.E.] years ago:

[Gen. I:26]...."LET US MAKE MAN IN OUR OWN IMAGE,"

etc., etc., etc. All of this was years before I read the preceding article by the Right Honourable Reverend Sterling Carey. However, Dr. Carey's article moved me to reconsider my original presentation of the critical analysis that follows. It also imposed upon me an obligation to reexamine the role of the European and European-American [WHITE] Jews in COLONIALISM and FACISM in Africa, particularly in "SOUTH AFRICA [Monomotapa]" with regards to the daily oppression and acts of genocide against the indigenous "Africans" in their own "PROMISED LAND" the WHITE RACIST Christians, Jews, Moslems, Atheists and others exploit daily. This is further sharpened when I walk through the "DIAMOND CENTER" around the Avenue of the Americas and the streets bordering the 40's to 50's in New York City, New York. Thus it is that I had to face the evidence of the HARD FACTS of the SYSTEMATICAL EXTERMINATION of the indigenous African majority by the European and European-American minority, and ask myself the following:

> WHY IS THERE NO OUTCRY FROM THE SO-CALLED "RESPONSIBLE NEGROES" AGAINST AFRICAN GENOCIDE IN SOUTH AFRICA BY WHITE JEWS AS THERE IS AGAINST WHITE CHRISTIANS, MOSLEMS, ATHEISTS AND OTHERS? WHY?

I had to agree that at least a segment of the "CHRISTIAN COMMUNITY" [in part] recognizes in public its shameful and inexcusable "UN-CHRISTIAN" conduct in the ruthlessly repressive exploitation of the indigenous African People in their own PROMISED LAND - Azania [the so-called "Republic of South Africa"]. This can not in any manner whatsoever be said in the case of the vile "UN-JUDAIC" conduct of the White Jews who help in the exploitation and extermination of the indigenous Africans, much of which profit find its way into the coffers of many synagogues and other Jewish istitution in Europe, European-America and Israel as it does in Christian Churches and other

1. The first part of this work was written by an Ethiopian scholar - Hatzaad Khobad ibn-Rhabad.

institutions of Christendom; the Arab Moslems of North Africa being no exception in this respect.

Anyone reading Volume Two of this project [from this juncture unwards] should find it very easy to understand, at least after reading the preceding Chapter "...Falashas In The United States of America...;" as it is the hypocracy of RACISM and RELIGIOUS BIGOTRY centered in Talmudic [Rabbinical] Judaism that this Chapter and Volume highlights. But, why does your author hold to this conclusion? Because it should be obvious that the so-called "NEGRO" and/or "BLACK" Jews in the United States of America practise a type of TALMUDIC [Rabbinical] JUDAISM that is very similar to the so-called "SEMITIC" or "WHITE CAUCASIAN" Jews; yet, the "BLACK" Jews of Ethiopia, Yemen, India, and elsewhere, are tolerated by the "WHITE" Jews, even in the political State of Israel. But the same is not true for the "BLACK JEWS" living in the United States of America and the Caribbean Islands. Could it not be a question of "RACISM" and "RELIGIOUS BIGOTRY" on the part of the WHITE JEWS who are constantly protesting about

"...RISING NEGRO [and/or Black] ANTI-SEMITISM IN THE GHETTOS...?"

This writer, formerly a practicing so-called "BLACK JEW" myself, is definitely convinced it is nothing else but just that - RACIST RELIGIOUS BIGOTRY. For WHITE JEWS in the Western Hemisphere - the United States of America and the rest of North America [Mexico and Canada], Central America, South America and the Caribbean Islands, the same as WHITE Christians and WHITE Moslems, for the most part, see themselves as "...A RACE OF PEOPLE..." who are distinctly "SEPARATE" from their co-religionist BLACK JEWS anywhere, much less the so-called "...AMERICAN NEGRO JEWS..." in the United States of America who are not even tolerated.

Behind the SECRET DOORS of the above citations it is necessary for BLACK JEWS to uncover and bring to the open scrutiny of the general community of man these forms of JEWISH RACISM and JEWISH RELIGIOUS BIGOTRY, as BLACK CHRISTIANS like Dr. Carey, BLACK MOSLEMS like the late al Haji Malik Shabaaz [Malcolm Little - X],[1] and other BLACK PEOPLE of all other religions have done and are still doing. The BLACK JEWS or ISRAELITES, etc. are more than duty bound in this regards. WE are sacredly obligated for OUR own survival and prosperity to remove all of this form of CANCER in TALMUDIC [Rabbinical] JUDAISM that is knawing away culturally and physically at OUR African People both at home in Alkebu-lan and outside in the so-called "DIASPORA." Just imagine, even the pet expressions we use to designate our own involvements we adapted from old cast-off Jewish socio-political slogans and cliches[2] like the following;

"DIASPORA, GHETTO, INNER-CITY, PROPORTIONAL REPRESENTATION" [quota system in disguise], INTEGRATION, CULTURALLY DEPRIVED," etc.;

the last one being the real hooker. Whose "CULTURE" is Black People "DEPRIVED" of not hav-

1. There is a strong suspicion that his encounter with Zionist Racism caused his assassination.
2. When will African/Black People in the U.S.A. refuse Jewish scholars nomenclatures for us!

ing? Who said it is worthwhile wanting? Why is it that "BLACK SOCIOLOGISTS" have not pointed out that White People, Jews included, are "CULTURALLY DEPRIVED" of their [our] BLACK HERITAGE and HISTORY that brought them into "CIVILIZED LIVING" for the first time when they left Asia and entered Alkebu-lan in search of FOOD, CLOTHING, SHELTER and WISDOM - in short "HAVEN" and "HEAVEN." All of this is providing European and European-American Jews, in fact, do have a claim to the "HARIBU RELIGION" that received its first LAWS, THEOSOPHY OF MONOTHEISM and SCRIPTURES from the indigenous [BLACK] Africans of the Nile Valley, particularly those in Ta-Merry and Ta-Nehisi, such as Moses [ca. 1316 - 1196 B.C.E. ?] who copied "...THE PRINCIPLE OF MONOTHEISM" [One And Only True God]...from Pharaoh Akhenaten/Amenhotep IVth, ca. 1412 - 1356 B.C.E., before the birth of Moses in Ta-Merry. A collage of Akhenaten and family appears in Volume One, page xxxix of this work].

From this juncture to the end of this Volume it is with the MYTHS, ALLEGORIES and DISTORTIONS of Jewish history with regards to the "JEWISH" or HEBREW RELIGION/WAY OF LIFE mystique your author shall concern himself. This analysis will not cater to any group or organization. Even the "BLACK JEWS" it defends to some degree, will receive their [OUR] share of scrutiny and criticism with regards to their [OUR] role and behavior in the overall "AFRICAN [Black] COMMUNITY" in the "Western Hemisphere" [the Americas and the Caribbean Islands]. For ending this Chapter, I am reminded of the following from Rabbi Hailu Moshe Paris' article titled "African Christianity and the Black Madonna"[1] in Albert B. Cleage, Jr., BLACK CHRISTIAN NATIONALISM: NEW DIRECTIONS FOR THE BLACK CHURCH, New York, 1972, page 281:

> "........................... It would be my hope also that in the areas of the Middle East where the Sephardim—the Afro-Asian Jews—have once again become a powerful force, they will be able to reinterpret the tradition of Moses in the light of other reinterpretations of religions in that area, so that they will become part of the twentieth century. Hopefully they will relate to the history of the twentieth cenury and to the African peoples in the Afro-Asian world, in America, and in Europe. Christianity—the European version that is controlled by the European churches and institutions—will have to be redefined by Europeans for European usage and existence. In the African context, the Black American will redefine his Christianity, or Islam, or Judaism in light of the reinterpretations that are going on in Africa and in the greater Eastern world. With this, I believe, once again will arise the ascendancy of African heritage and tradition in these religions, and there will be a balanced world culture. This will not be an egocentric culture, but will basically be an

1. Your author recommends this book to be included in your library as one of your treasures. It is unfortunate that Cleage, as other Black Nationalist Clergy, can not produce their own Black Bible.

Afro-Asian-centered culture, which I believe will lead all of us back to a more even and peaceful world. If not in our time, at least in the time of our children. Possibly the twenty-first-century man will truly be a part of a brotherhood, and all will live in peace. Amen.

HEBREWS [Jews], CHRISTIANS, MOSLEMS, ETC. ALL OF THEM ARE HERE BELOW

JUST IMAGINE ONLY TWO OF THE ABOVE ARE "NEGROES," AND FROM HARLEM!!! BUT, THEY ARE ALL "JEWS" - SEMITES, HAMITES, NILOTS, NILO-HAMITES, ETC.

[Ethiopian snapshots taken by Robert Johnson in 1974 C.C./A.D.]

Rabbi Paris' AMEN, I am almost certain, was not a call to the ancient God of said name in Egypt.

The so-called "BLACK-WHITE" and/or "JEWISH-NEGRO, BLACK-JEWISH" [ad infinitum] "CONFRONTATION" we are still hearing so much about of late, which began during the late 1960's, increasingly demands some sort of honestly meaningful open dialouge with respect to [1]: What is a "JEW" from a biblical standpoint? [2]: Why European and European-American [White, Caucasian or Semitic] JEWS reject from their communities African and African-American [Black, Negro, Falasha] JEWS? [3]: Why is there a JEWISH-CHRISTIAN-MOSLEM [Muslim] CONFRONTATION among African [BLACK] Americans, including millions of many other RELIGIONS in the United States of America?

This writer once believed that I had sufficiently dealt with the issue of the origin, development and characteristics of the so-called "BLACK ["Negro, Colored, African, Ethiopian," etc.] JEW" in the first pamphlet [Volume I] NOSOTROS HEBREOS NEGRO [in English; WE THE BLACK JEWS, 1934-1938], I wrote for a community of African Jews who, at that time, inhabitated a few of the islands in the Caribbean Sea and mainland South and Central America. I began writing it in 1934, and finally published it in 1938 C.E. in Spanish. It was prompted by the imposition of the growth of WHITE RACISM and Jewish, Christian RELIGIOUS BIGOTRY I witnessed taking place as they disrupted the somewhat relatively non-RACIST atmosphere of the existing "RACIAL HARMONY" in the Puerto Rican [African-Indian - Carib-European][1] HIGH-CULTURE the United States of America inherited when the Americans seized Puerto Rico from Spain during the SPANISH-AMERICAN WAR in 1896 C.E. But I have been convinced by my many friends, professional colleagues, students and family [some of whom are my severest critics] that a revised and much more up-to-date version of WE THE BLACK JEWS had to be my next project following the completion of the three volumes extension to THE BLACK MAN'S RELIGION [Vol. II, "The Need For A Black Bible;" Vol. III, "The Myth Of Genesis And Exodus, And The Exclusion Of Their African Origin;" also, "Extracts And Comments From The Holy Black Bible"].[2] However, in this undertaking I realized that only extracts from the original pamphlet in Spanish will be adequate for the current situation of the so-called "NEGRO [Black] JEWS" in the Americas -the main issue which everyone concern desires that I address myself - should be included. Thus I began this task with particular emphasis on the BLACK [Ethiopian or so-called "Negro"] JEWS in the United States of America.

What I will attempt to accomplish is to relate RABBINICAL mythology, allegory, historiography, folklore, socio-political dynamics, theosophy, theology and philosophy, etc. as edited and projected with all of the so-called "MODERN CONCEPTS" of the present political

1. This is a major myth in all of Spanish-speaking "America" today. Puerto Rico is racist too!
2. Its a very important study dealing with the racist nature of Judaism, Christianity and Islam.

"JEWISH STATE" [Israel] and the so-called "JEWS" that are of solely "Caucasian, Indo-European, Semitic, White, Aryan, European, European-American," etc. "RACIAL STOCK" with respect to their effect upon the BLACK JEWS. In so doing many ugly citations must be exposed and dealt with; and certainly the cry of "REVERSE RACISM" and "NEGRO ANTI-SEMITISM" should be expected to be very loud and persistent from many quarters, particularly from the so-called "INTEGRATED NEGROES" and other "COLORED FOLKS." Nevertheless, I will try to be as objective as is humanly possible; however, bearing in mind that I too have a very personal interest on both sides of the subject matter, thus being "BLACK" and "AFRICAN," as well as a former adherent of the "HEBREW [Jewish or Israelite] RELIGION" [Faith or Way Of Life] and its TORAHDIC teachings.

Of course the sideline issue of being able to consider one self as a "DUAL CITIZEN" of both Israel and the United States of America, and having the same extended to any state or nation in Alkebu-lan ["AFRICA"][1]and the United States of America, while remaining a WHITE or BLACK Jew simultaneously, will take us back to certain historics from the beginning of "EUROPEAN ZIONISM" with Theodore Hertzl in Europe and AFRICAN NATIONALISM or PAN-AFRICANISM" with John Chilembwe and Dr. Edward Wilmot Blyden in Alkebu-lan. This analysis will demonstrate that "PAN-AFRICANISM" always equally existed alongside "EUROPEAN ZIONISM." However, there will be no attempt to write a historical analysis or critique of European [White, Caucasian, Semitic, etc.] JUDAISM and its European-American offspring. References to EUROPEAN/TALMUDIC JUDAISM will be mainly for historical background to show that IT, as ITS "EUROPEAN-AMERICAN" counterpart throughout the Americas and the Caribbean Islands, has no more validity for acceptance in JUDAEO-CHRISTIAN AMERICAN religious politics than AFRICAN and AFRICAN-AMERICAN PAN-AFRICANISM with regards to a homeland away from Europe and European-America for both White JEWS and Black JEWS alike.

The first step in all of what I have stated so far is to be able to observe that all existing biblical history is ETHNOCENTRIC, RACIST, EGOCENTRIC and SELF-SERVING. That the authors, or so-called "GOD-INSPIRED HOLY SCRIBES," wrote what they probably believed to be TRUE as the FACTS related to INCIDENTS they described in their mythological and allegorical stories in the PENTATEUCH [Holy Torah, Five Books Of Moses, Old Testament, etc.] But most of all, that we see the writers of the so-called "HOLY SCRIPTURES" of every religion as human beings like anyone of us today - people born of MAN and WOMAN, subjected to all of the frailties of the HUMAN BEINGS of their era and MORTALS who died because of either violent termination by murder or orderly transition due to age or other deterioration

1. I use "Africa" instead of Alkebu-lan in many of my works although I project "Alkebu-lan."

of the cells and body.

The second step is that we, all of mankind, should realize that "GOD" [regardless of the name in each religion] is a concept based solely in BELIEF. And as such, let us realize that each GOD is as TRUE or FALSE as the other.[1] If this can be effectively achieve the following evidence, facts, documents and pictures I have submitted for your analysis should prove to be of very interesting reading so far as their revelation in this JUDAEO-CHRISTIAN GREEK-ORIENTED SOCIETY [civilization] is concerned.[2]

Most of all, I sincerely hope that this very short PRELUDE will assist in making the African Americans, particularly, realize that their sociological or political condition in the Americas is not based upon differences in RELIGION, but more-so due to "RACE" and/or "COLOR OF SKIN." Thus a "BLACK JEW" is no more acceptable socio-politically to any "WHITE JEW" than a "BLACK CHRISTIAN" to a "WHITE CHRISTIAN," equally any "BLACK MOSLEM" to a "WHITE MOSLEM," etc. all the way down to its most illogical conclusion. It is due to this reason that the author of this Volume decided to revise and add another dimension to my very first historical work I wrote in 1936 C.E. and published in 1938 C.E./A.D. under the title - NOSOTROS HEBREOS NEGRO [We The Black Jews] - which was further enhanced by the prodding of BLACK PEOPLE of varied forms of religions who read one or more of my books. The following picture and extract begin the exposition of the naked truth:

Falasha Jewish students of Ethiopia and their teacher, Rabbi Abraham

Turning to modern anthropology one finds confirming evidence. Ratzel
[See J.A. Rogers' Sex And Race, New York, 1954]

1. Take note of "The Kasidah Of Abu el-Yezdi" [as transl. by Sir R.F. Burton, Vol. I of this work].
2. It was not until the Greeks, Romans, and other Europeans met the Africans that they became "civilized." See works by Homer and other Greeks of antiquity.

says: "The entire Semitic and Hamitic population of Africa has...a mulatto character which extends to the Semites outside of Africa."[6] Prof. Elliott Smith in "Human History," similarly states: "Every kind of intermingling has taken place between the original groups of the Negro, Hamitic and Semitic peoples."[7]

In the Sudan, Upper Egypt, and North Africa there are Jews whose color and features are indistinguishable from Negroes. The Jews outside Africa retain, large numbers of them, their Negroid traits.

Fishberg traces the physical resemblance between the white Jews and the black ones. Speaking of the color prejudice among Jews in India he says: "The white Jews keep aloof and do not associate with their (black) co-religionists." Of the latter he says: "Such persons also have a Jewish physiognomy, which is so specific that one would be inclined to believe that they are of mixed blood, were they not so cruelly maltreated by their white co-religionists and treated as black Jews."

[6] History of Mankind. Vol. II, p. 246.
[7] p. 143. London, 1934.

[FOUNDATION]: The most fundamental teaching in Judaism, Christianity and Islam lies in the allegorical myth about THE CREATION OF THE WORLD and the making of ADAM AND EVE IN THE GARDEN OF EDEN - BY JEHOVAH [God, Jesus the Christ, Al'lah, etc.] This story was written about two thousand four hundred and eighty-three [2,483] years ago - ca. 700 B.C.-1983C.E. all of which we find in the FIRST BOOK OF MOSES [otherwise known as "GENESIS"] of the PENTATEUCH [Holy Torah, Old Testament, etc.] Yet this FOLKLORE, the most fundamental area of the theosophy upon which JUDAISM, CHRISTIANITY and ISLAM are still based, makes the followers of either religion believe they have the ONE and FINAL word on "HOW THE WORLD AND EVERYTHING THEREIN WAS CREATED." No other people!

When we look back at the fact that FIVE THOUSAND SEVEN HUNDRED AND FORTY-THREE [5,743]YEARS ago, relatively speaking, is modern in terms of time,[2] and that many High-Cultures with their religions had been created, reached their zenith, and moved on into oblivion before the JUDAEO-CHRISTIAN-ISLAMIC..."BEGINNING OF THE WORLD"..., we will understand that RELIGION is the culmination of the glorification of a people's heritage and the deification and worship of their heroes and heroines. Also, that no amount of logical explanation or reasoning is as material to RELIGION as is BELIEF and FAITH.[3] Thus, we must be willing to understand that a RELIGIOUS individual is more often than not conditioned to accept only that which pays HOMAGE and VALIDITY to his or her GOD-HEAD; and even to their CO-BELIEVERS and their "HOLY LAND" [Axum, Luxor, Jerusalem, Mecca, Bethlehem, Mt. Fujiama, Kilamanjaro, Blue Mountain, etc.]

1. See A. Walter, Negro-Caucasian Mixing In All Ages and All Lands, New York, 1967, p. 3.
2. Equivalent to 3760 B.C.E., at least 340 years after the beginning of the Ist Dynasty of Egypt.
3. A private experience of expectation beyond logical deduction.

From this point onwards it should be very easy to understand why this author is not interested in whether or not my readers accept the RELIGIOUS tenets of the main personalities in this volume - the AGAW or KAYLA [Kyla, Falasha, Falassa, Black Jews, "Negro" Jews, Ethiopian Jews, African Jews, Beta Israelis, etc.] of Alkebu-lan.[1] But, who are the so-called "FALASHAS OF ETHIOPIA, EAST AFRICA?" What is their source [or sources] of origin? Are they any more or less authentically "JEWS, ISRAELITES" or "HEBREWS" than their European, British and European-American [WHITE] co-religionists in Europe, Great Britain, European-America and/or Israel in Western Asia? And more specifically; in what manner does the AGAW's TORAHDIC CUSTOMS AND PRACTICES of the HEBREW [Jewish] RELIGION [Way Of Life] differ to their co-religionists of Europe's and European-America's RABBINICAL TALMUD-TORAH CUSTOMS AND PRACTICES? Of course there are numerous other related areas of concern to be considered, and will be answered forthrightly and historically in this Volume - the same as I have done in all of my other published volumes on Africans.

This is a further attempt on my part at bringing to the African [BLACK] People other historical insights into their heritage, irrespective of who outside of this so-called..."ETHNIC GROUP" or "RACE" does not like whatever is being revealed; as there is no intent to appease anyone's sensibility, neither to be extra sensitive of any possible repercussion. The main objective is "TRUTH," as your author finds it in its virgin state.

We are now at the point where we can establish the historical origin of a religious assembleage of people called "HARIBU, HEBREWS, ISRAELITES" and/or "JEWS." Equally, we are at the juncture where we must identify their very first "HOMELAND" which the God-Head "YWH" [Jehovah]... allegedly... "GAVE HIS CHOSEN PEOPLE"..., etc. And again we must fall back on the first source in which the earliest account of the "HARIBU" or "JEWS" involved is recorded, equally their RELIGIOUS BELIEF; and when their High-Culture or nation called "PALESTINE" or "ISRAEL," and also "JUDEA," was created. The original source is the so-called "FIVE BOOKS OF MOSES" [Pentateuch, Holy Torah or Old Testament] of 700-500 B.C.E.

The first observation of this source - FIVE BOOKS OF MOSES [Pentateuch] - is its date of origin. In this regards we find that it was not written until ca. 700 Before The Christian Era [B.C.E. or B.C.] and ca. 500 B.C.E.;[1] less than 2,483 years ago.

The second observation is that the main master author to whom the FIVE BOOKS OF MOSES have been attributed - the African [Egyptian] named "MOSES"[2] - never saw the first

1. See Y. ben-Jochannan's Chronology Of The Bible: Challenge To The Standard Version, Alkebu-lan Books Associates, New York, 1972, p. FOUR, for further details, etc.
2. There is not one solitary piece of evidence in any Egyptian writing that there ever existed a Moses any time throughout Nile Valley history and culture of antiquity.

nor last draft of the manuscript, much less the finished "SCROLL" or "FIVE BOOKS" he allegedly wrote and/or dictated. Moreover, the <u>master author</u> - "MOSES" [or MOSHE] - died or disappeared into oblivion more than five hundred [500] years before the actual first page of the beginning of his FIRST BOOK [Genesis] was written. Of course we are told that the entire group of so-called...

"GOD-INSPIRED HOLY SCRIPTURES [Five Books Of Moses], WRITTEN BY GOD-INSPIRED AND MOST HOLY SCRIBES"...

were passed down from God - YWH - himself in Hebrew to Moses; who in turn passed it on to the Rabbis and Great Scribes of the SANHEDRIN; who equally passed it down to their fellow Hebrew [Jewish] Scribes living in Egypt that began its translation into Greek in ca. 700 B.C.E., and completed it in ca. 500 B.C.E. under the name - "PENTATEUCH;" and then it was passed down to others who translated it into a much more common class of Greek with added testimonies for the Christians under the name - "KOIÑE BIBLE" - in ca. 100 of the Christian Era [C.E. or A.D.] following its beginning in ca. 50 C.E.; and lastly, it passed on down to others called Moslems, who revised it into Arabic during the Seventh Century C.E. or the First Century After The Hijira [or 1 A.H.] and called it "HOLY QUR'AN. Those so-called "God Inspired Sacred Words" - became the first basic literature - "Holy Scriptures" of

'THE JUDAEO-CHRISTIAN-ISLAMIC MYSTIQUE.'

The third and final observation deals with the "LAND, NATION, CONTINENT," and most of all the "PEOPLE" and/or "RACE," where the source - "FIVE BOOKS OF MOSES" - actually originated. But it is just at this juncture that there is difficulty to understand how this type of investigation generally engenders objection on the part of certain theologians, rabbis, priests, ministers, imams, and even the congregations of any religion remotely related to the so-called "JUDAEO-CHRISTIAN-ISLAMIC MYSTIQUE" - the theosophy of people answering to the nomenclature - "JEW" and/or "ISRAELITE, CHRISTIAN, MOSLEM" and/or "MUSLIM - exists.

We now commence our safari of the first observation into the background of the HARIBU or ISRAELITES [Black, Brown, Yellow, White, etc.] origin from the birth of their <u>first</u> [No. 1] <u>Patriarch</u> - "ABRAHAM" - [Abrm, Avrm, etc.],[1] of whom the FIRST BOOK [<u>Genesis</u>] of THE FIVE BOOKS OF MOSES [Pentateuch], <u>Chapter XI</u>, Verses 10 - 28 states:

The generations of Shem and of Terah, the father of Abram

10 ¶ These *are* the generations of Shem: Shem *was* an hundred years old, and begat Arphaxad two years after the flood:

11 And Shem lived after he begat Arphaxad five hundred years, and begat sons and daughters.

12 And Arphaxad lived five and thirty years, and begat Salah:

13 And Arphaxad lived after he begat Salah four hundred and three years, and begat sons and daughters.

14 And Salah lived thirty years, and begat Eber:

15 And Salah lived after he begat Eber four hundred and three years, and begat sons and daughters.

1. He was born in ca. 1775 B.C.E. or ca. 1975 after "The Creation of Adam," while the Africans along the Nile River were already in their XIIIth Dynasty that foreigners destroyed.

16 And Eber lived four and thirty years, and begat Peleg:
17 And Eber lived after he begat Peleg four hundred and thirty years, and begat sons and daughters.
18 And Peleg lived thirty years, and begat Reu:
19 And Peleg lived after he begat Reu two hundred and nine years, and begat sons and daughters.
20 And Reu lived two and thirty years, and begat Serug:
21 And Reu lived after he begat Serug two hundred and seven years, and begat sons and daughters.
22 And Serug lived thirty years, and begat Nahor:
23 And Serug lived after he begat Nahor two hundred years, and begat sons and daughters.
24 And Nahor lived nine and twenty years, and begat Terah:
25 And Nahor lived after he begat Terah an hundred and nineteen years, and begat sons and daughters.
26 And Terah lived seventy years, and begat Abram, Nahor, and Haran.
27 ¶ Now these *are* the generations of Terah: Terah begat Abram, Nahor, and Haran; and Haran begat Lot.
28 And Haran died before his father Terah in the land of his nativity, in Ur of the Chaldees.

The family of Abraham continues in the same source in the following manner according to Genesis, Chapter XI, Verses 29 - 32:

29 And Abram and Nahor took them wives: the name of Abram's wife *was* Sarai; and the name of Nahor's wife, Milcah, the daughter of Haran, the father of Milcah, and the father of Iscah.
30 But Sarai was barren; she *had* no child.

Terah goes from Ur to Haran

31 And Terah took Abram his son, and Lot the son of Haran his son's son, and Sarai his daughter in law, his son Abram's wife; and they went forth with them from Ur of the Chaldees, to go into the land of Canaan; and they came unto Haran, and dwelt there.
32 And the days of Terah were two hundred and five years: and Terah died in Haran.

Here we can see that the ghost writers, all of whom wrote in the name of Moses, established the sting which even today forces one to believe that their stories are of the so-called

"GOD-INSPIRED SACRED SCRIPTURES,"

etc. God is "JEHOVAH" if one is a Jew, JESUS ["the Christ"]if one is a Christian, and "AL'-LAH" if one is a Moslem [Muslim]; all of the other "GODS" of all of the other religions of the entire world are DAMNED and THRUSTED into the wilds of "CULTIC" and "DEMONIC" obscurity under the label - "PAGAN IDOLS." The "LAND" over which so much bloodshed is still being spilled daily, even as your author writes these words, was called "PALESTINE," which later on became "ISRAEL" and "JUDEA" following a "CIVIL WAR" between "GOD'S [allegedly] CHOSEN PEOPLE." The same "LAND" the Lord, God - "YWH" or "JEHOVAH" - once also called upon Abraham and gave him. It was equally the "LAND" known as "CANAAN" the same "Lord, God"YWH" - had already given the "CANAANITES" He allegedly made because of a "CURSE" His representative - "NOE" or "NOAH" - placed upon one of his own three sons - "HAM" [see Gen.IX:20-25; pp. 337 - 338 this Volume]. Thus Genesis, Chapt. XII, Verses 1 - 9:

God calls Abram, and blesses him with a promise of Christ

12 NOW the LORD had said unto Abram, Get thee out of thy country, and from thy kindred, and from thy father's house, unto a land that I will shew thee:
2 And I will make of thee a great nation, and I will bless thee, and make thy name great; and thou shalt be a blessing:
3 And I will bless them that bless thee, and curse him that curseth thee: and in thee shall all families of the earth be blessed.

He departs with Lot from Haran

4 So Abram departed, as the LORD had spoken unto him; and Lot went with him: and Abram *was* seventy and five years old when he departed out of Haran.
5 And Abram took Sarai his wife, and Lot his brother's son, and all their substance that they had

gathered, and the {souls / persons} that they had gotten in Haran; and they went forth to go into the land of Canaan; and into the land of Canaan they came.

He journeys through Canaan, which is promised him in a vision

6 ¶ And Abram passed through the land unto the place of Sichem, unto the {plain / oak} of Moreh. And the Canaanite *was* then in the land.

7 And the LORD appeared unto Abram, and said, Unto thy seed will I give this land: and there builded he an altar unto the LORD, who appeared unto him.

8 And he removed from thence unto a mountain on the east of Beth-el, and pitched his tent, *having* Beth-el on the west, and Hai on the east: and there he builded an altar unto the LORD, and called upon the name of the LORD.

9 And Abram journeyed, going on still toward the {south. / Negeb.}

The so-called "GOD-INSPIRED HOLY SCRIBES" who [allegedly] wrote the FIVE BOOKS OF MOSES hastily moved their characters and stories in such a manner that within two paragraphs hundreds of years and thousands of peoples passed off the scene into oblivion if they were not Israelites [Jews, etc.]. Thus it is in the next paragraph ABRAHAM quickly fled the "HOLY LAND" Ywh took away from the Canaanites and gave to him for another HOLY LAND in Alkebu-lan, which the indigenous African [BLACK] People called "TA-MERRY, QAMT, SAIS, KIMIT," etc. Just remember that it was the "HOLY LAND" of the so-called "Cursed Blacks" the descendants of "CANAANITES." This "HOLY LAND" was later to be renamed "MIZRAIN" [Egypt] according to the same "GOD-INSPIRED SACRED SCRIBES" who attributed their own facts to the "FIVE BOOKS OF MOSES," particularly the very "FIRST BOOK [Genesis] in this case. But we also find ABRAHAM being driven into "MIZRAIN," Northeast Alkebu-lan [Africa, etc.] from the desert of Western Asia [today's so-called "Middle East"] in search of basic "FOOD, CLOTHING, SHELTER" and "LEARNING" from the same "CURSED BLACKS" whose other "HOLY LAND" he had to abandon The "SACRED SCRIBES" recorded this allegorical story in the following extract from GENESIS, Chapter XII, Verses 10 - 11; thus:

He is driven by a famine into Egypt

10 ¶ And there was a famine in the land: and Abram went down into Egypt to sojourn there; for the famine *was* grievous in the land.

11 And it came to pass, when he was come near to enter into Egypt, that he said unto Sarai his wife, Behold now, I know that thou *art* a fair woman to look upon:

What we have just seen is the original PERSONALITY or "PATRIARCH" around whom the the entire JUDAEO, CHRISTIAN, ISLAMIC "Religions" or "Way of Life" is based. So far he - "ABRAHAM" - is an indigenous Asian, who had to flee his native homeland in Asia to seek haven among the indigenous people of Alkebu-lan [Africa, Ethiopia, etc.] as shown on page 339 of this Volume] upon the command of his own GOD - Ywh or Jehovah. Thus, biblically speaking, it was solely in Asia and Alkebu-lan/Africa the entire drama relative to the first of the HARIBU, ISRAELITES, JEWS, etc., back to the very "FIRST HUMAN BEING - ADAM" - took place.[1] This biblical FACT removes EUROPE and all other CONTINENTS of the world [planet Earth] from consideration with respect to the "ORIGIN OF THE ISRAELITE [Jewish] PEOPLE

1. Do we need another reason to show why White Jews, Christians and Moslems whitened this?

AND NATION" or "HOLY [Promised] LAND," etc., etc., etc., ad infinitum.

The second observation deals with a period which covered more than four hundred [400] years, from "ABRAHAM'S ENTRANCE INTO MIZRAIN [Egypt]" in ca. 1675 or 1670 B.C.E. - during the XIVth Dynasty - to the conflict between the African worshipers of the God known as "YWH" with Moses and their fellow African worshipers of the God known as "AMEN-RA" with Pharaoh [Head of the Great House, or King] Rameses IInd sometime between ca. 1298 - 1232 B.C.E.; and following this, up to forty [40] years later at Mount Horeb [or Sinai] in ca. 1192 B.C.E., where Moses allegedly -

"LED THE ISRAELITE CHILDREN FROM THEIR CAPTIVITY."[1]

The third observation brings us directly into the crux of the origin of LITERARY JUDAISM - the first written materials the JEWS came in contact with, and from which they coopted their basic theories for the THEOSOPHY, THEOLOGY and PHILOSOPHY they used in producing what they finally called "FIVE BOOKS OF MOSES." The body of their original literature noted above speaks of Moses' identity. And we must assume HE was similar to most, if not all, of the other "ISRAELITES" or "JEWS" of HIS era - ca. 1316 - 1196 B.C.E. In this respect the SECOND BOOK OF MOSES [Exodus], Chapter II, Verses 11 - 20 shows "MOSES" murdering one of his fellow indigenous "EGYPTIANS" or "AFRICANS;"[2] repudiating his fellow "EGYPTIAN JEW" because he questioned MOSES' right to commit "MURDER" on anyone [all of this before he reached Mt. Sinai]; fleeing to escape prosecution as a COMMON FUGITIVE from justice; and finally, MARRYING the woman - "ZIPPORAH" - that identified him to be the same as any other so-called "NEGRO" like all of the other "AFRICANS OF EGYPT" - "AN EGYPTIAN"- according to her own response to her father - "REUEL" - [the High-Priest of Midian] - in the following extract from EXODUS, Chapter II, Verse 11 - 20.

He slays an Egyptian

11 ¶ And it came to pass in those days, when Moses was grown, that he went out unto his brethren, and looked on their burdens: and he spied an Egyptian smiting an Hebrew, one of his brethren.

12 And he looked this way and that way, and when he saw that *there was* no man, he slew the Egyptian, and hid him in the sand.

He reproves a Hebrew

13 And when he went out the second day, behold, two men of the Hebrews strove together: and he said to him that did the wrong, Wherefore smitest thou thy fellow?

14 And he said, Who made thee a prince and a judge over us? intendest thou to kill me, as thou killedst the Egyptian? And Moses feared, and said, Surely this thing is known.

He flees into Midian

15 Now when Pharaoh heard this thing, he sought to slay Moses. But Moses fled from the face of Pharaoh, and dwelt in the land of Midian: and he sat down by a well.

16 Now the priest of Midian had seven daughters: and they came and drew *water*, and filled the troughs to water their father's flock.

17 And the shepherds came and drove them away:

1. See Exodus, Chapter XII, Verses 31 - 42, and Y. ben-Jochannan's Black Man Of The Family Chapter I, pp. 3 - 72 for further detailed information.
2. There was no physical difference between an indigenous Ethiopian, Puanit, Sudanese, Egyptian, etc., racially; this being manufactured in the racist western minds much later on as shown in the semitic and hamitic syndrome of the equally infamous "Noah and his sons" allegory, etc.

but Moses stood up and helped them, and watered
their flock.
18 And when they came to Reuel their father, he
said, How *is it that* ye are come so soon to day?
19 And they said, An Egyptian delivered us out of
the hand of the shepherds, and also drew *water*
enough for us, and watered the flock.
20 And he said unto his daughters, And where *is*
he? why *is* it *that* ye have left the man? call him, that
he may eat bread.

Certainly the RACIST and RELIGIOUSLY BIGOTED manner in which the so-called "FIVE BOOKS OF MOSES" have been translated from HEBREW to GREEK, GREEK to LATIN, and also GREEK and LATIN to ENGLISH, etc. make most of us JEWS, CHRISTIANS and MOSLEMS [Muslims] believe that the "ISRAELITES" and "EGYPTIANS" of the PENTATEUCH [Torah/Five Books of Moses, etc.] were of 'DIFFERENT COLORS" and "RACES." Thus the use of the term "ISRAELITES" during the era of "MOSES," as if there was at anytime before said period any "LAND" and or "NATION" called "ISRAEL" in Asia or Alkebu-lan. For the fact is that the "NATION" called "ISRAEL" in actual biblical time came about over one hundred [100] years following the disappearance or death of MOSES in the Sinai Peninsula of Northeast, N.E. Alkebu-lan ["Africa"].[1] Remember that Sinai always belonged to Ta-Merry [Mizrain, Egypt].

If we are to continue accepting the "HARIBU, ISRAELITES" or "JEWS" as a religious group in Mizrain [Egypt] up to the so-called "EXODUS" in approximately 1236 B.C.E., also as a national political entity; then we must be equally prepared to accept that the so-called "NEGRO AMERICANS" and/or "COLORED AMERICANS" [properly African-Americans] in the United States of America comprise a 'SEPARATE NATION OF PEOPLE,' as so many have claimed; of course with rebuttal from the "integrationists" and "amalgamationists." For there is a direct correlationship between the biblical status of the so-called "ISRAELITE IN EGYPT" as "SLAVES" and the so-called "NEGRO IN THE UNITED STATES OF AMERICA" equally as "SLAVES." In Egypt, Northeast Alkebu-lan [Africa] the "OPPRESSORS" of the "ISRAELITES" were called "PHARAOH;" whereas the "OPPRESSORS" of the "NEGROES" in the United States of America were, and still are, called "PRESIDENT." But, the relationship between "OPPRESSORS" and "SLAVES" in either situation was the same. Yet we are taught in "Western" educational institutions that the "OPPRESSORS" and the "OPPRESSED" in the latter case were of distinctly different so-called "RACES." Yet only the GOD-HEAD between the African followers of "AMEN-RA" and those who followed "YWH" were different.

I have taken note of the fact that many of the TRANSLATIONS and VERSIONS[2] of the so-called "FIVE BOOKS OF MOSES" give different accounts of "MOSES' AGE." In the TRANS-

---

1. See Numbers, Chapter xxvi, Verses 12 - 17; Map on p. 383 of this Volume and Maps on p. 35 of Y. ben-Jochannan's The Black Man's Religion, Vol. II: The Myth Of Genesis And Exodus, And The Exclusion Of Their African Origin; for further detailed clarification of this biblical personality.
2. This key word - "VERSION" [s] - constantly escapes people. It does not say "ORIGINAL" and/ or "TRUTH," etc.

LATION and VERSION I am using in this Volume - THE HOLY BIBLE - [Clarified Edition, The Complete Text Of The AUTHORIZED KING JAMES VERSION[1] to which is added approximately parallel readings from the AMERICAN STANDARD VERSION and the REVISED STANDARD VERSION, Consolidated Book Publishers, Chicago, Illinois, 1957, EXODUS [2nd Book], Chapter VII, Verse 7 gives the following date:

His age

7 And Moses *was* fourscore years old, and Aaron fourscore and three years old, when they spake unto Pharaoh.

Because of the disjointed manner in which the so-called "GOD-INSPIRED SCRIBES" recorded their stories in the FIVE BOOKS OF MOSES, we have to turn to the FOURTH BOOK OF MOSES [Numbers] Chapter XII, Verse 1 for the validation of "MOSES' MARRIAGE TO AN ETHIOPIAN [Cushite, Abyssinian, Habbasha, Black, "Negro," etc.] WOMAN;" thus the following:

God rebukes the sedition of Miriam and Aaron

12 AND Miriam and Aaron spake against Moses because of the {Ethiopian / Cushite} woman whom he had married: for he had married an Ethiopian woman.

Of course "...AN ETHIOPIAN..." today in the United States of America's racist educational system, both religious and secular, is of ANOTHER "RACE" than the so-called "NEGRO [Black] AMERICAN" and/or "COLORED AMERICAN"...who is generally called "BOY, GIRL, AUNT" or "UNCLE" irrespective of age; and of course even "NIGGER" by himself. Who else today! ?

It is equally in the FOURTH BOOK OF MOSES that there is sufficient proof that "MOSES," his brother "AARON" and his sister "MIRIAM" were not in any manner "WHITE" like any European of the past or of the present. For Numbers, Chapter XII, Verses 1 - 11 were written by the same so-called Jewish "GOD-INSPIRED SCRIBES" to show what happened to Moses' sister - "MIRIAM" - when she protested his marriage to a fellow AFRICAN [Black, Ethiopian, "Negro," Cushite, etc.] HEBREW, ISRAELITE or JEW; thus the following:

God rebukes the sedition of Miriam and Aaron

12 AND Miriam and Aaron spake against Moses because of the {Ethiopian / Cushite} woman whom he had married: for he had married an Ethiopian woman.

2 And they said, Hath the LORD indeed spoken only by Moses? hath he not spoken also by us? And the LORD heard *it*.

3 (Now the man Moses *was* very meek, above all the men which *were* upon the face of the earth.)

4 And the LORD spake suddenly unto Moses, and unto Aaron, and unto Miriam, Come out ye three unto the {tabernacle of the congregation. / tent of meeting.} And they three came out.

5 And the LORD came down in the pillar of the cloud, and stood *in* the door of the tabernacle, and called Aaron and Miriam: and they both came forth.

6 And he said, Hear now my words: If there be a prophet among you, *I* the LORD will make myself known unto him in a vision, *and* will speak unto him in a dream.

7 My servant Moses *is* not so, who *is* faithful in all mine house.

8 With him will I speak mouth to mouth, {even / clearly,} {apparently,} and not in dark speeches; and the similitude of the LORD shall he behold: wherefore then were ye not afraid to speak against my servant Moses?

1. Sir Francis Bacon and 47 other men created this Version of the notorious King James of England concept of "Christian Holy Bible." James was originally Roman Catholic in teachings, etc.

is half consumed when he cometh out of his mother's womb.

13 And Moses cried unto the LORD, saying, Heal her now, O God, I beseech thee.

14 ¶ And the LORD said unto Moses, If her father had but spit in her face, should she not be ashamed seven days? let her be shut out from the camp seven days, and after that let her be received in *again*.

15 And Miriam was shut out from the camp seven days: and the people journeyed not till Miriam was brought in *again*.

16 And afterward the people removed from Hazeroth, and pitched in the wilderness of Paran.

9 And the anger of the LORD was kindled against them; and he departed.

Miriam's leprosy is healed though God commands her to be shut out of the host

10 And the cloud departed from off the tabernacle; and, behold, Miriam *became* leprous, *white* as snow: and Aaron looked upon Miriam, and, behold, *she was* leprous.

11 And Aaron said unto Moses, Alas, my lord, I beseech thee, lay not the sin upon us, wherein we have done foolishly, and wherein we have sinned.

What the author of this Volume has done so far is to use the allegedly HOLY SCRIPTURES, which were supposedly "WRITTEN BY GOD-INSPIRED HOLY SCRIBES," to validate the existence of JEWS in other parts of Alkebu-lan besides "TA-MERRY" [Egypt or Mizrain] during the period when Moses was born and lived in Alkebu-lan. For in order to have had a marriage between "MOSES" and "AN ETHIOPIAN WOMAN," which is recorded in the ETHIOPIAN BIBLE as... "THE DAUGHTER OF THE HIGH PRIEST OF THE LAND OF THE AGAW PEOPLE"..., there had to be many "PRIESTS" and "CONGREGATIONS" of so-called "NEGRO JEWS" in Ethiopia during "MOSES'" lifetime, before his birth, and of course after his death, all of whom were the ancestors and/or foreparents of the current AGAW of Ethiopia, East Alkebu-lan - whose images appear throughout Volume One and Volume Two. Thus we have:

"AND, BEHOLD, MIRIAM BECAME LEPROUS, WHITE AS SNOW."

But if "MIRIAM" - Moses' sister - was already "WHITE;" how was it possible for her to have

"BECAME LEPROUS, WHITE AS SNOW?"

It was possible because the so-called "modern" RACIST and RELIGIOUS BIGOTS who translated the FIVE BOOKS OF MOSES to suit their own VERSIONS made it so. It has nothing whatsoever to do with any type of a "GOD" anywhere that turned "WHITE" to "WHITE" racially.

Let us approach the issue from the RACIST precedence established in the "modern editors" story about NOAH [Noe], his three sons: "SHEM [Sem], HAM[t] and JAPHET, and the so-called "BLACK CURSE" he allegedly placed upon his grandson's ["CANAAN"] children and all of their descendants forever, according to the following from the 1st Book Of Moses/GENESIS, Chapter IX, Verses 10 - 25:

Noah plants a vineyard, gets drunk and is mocked by his son, Ham

20 And Noah {began *to be* an husbandman, and he / was the first tiller of the soil. He} planted a vineyard:

21 And he drank of the wine, and was drunken; and he was uncovered within his tent.

22 And Ham, the father of Canaan, saw the nakedness of his father, and told his two brethren without.

23 And Shem and Japheth took a garment, and laid *it* upon both their shoulders, and went backward, and covered the nakedness of their father; and their faces *were* backward, and they saw not their father's nakedness.

24 And Noah awoke from his wine, and knew what his {younger / youngest} son had done unto him.

1. See Graves and Patai's Hebrew Myths: The Story Of Genesis, New York, 1961, pp. 120 - 123.

He curses Canaan,

25 And he said, Cursed *be* Canaan; a servant of servants shall he be unto his brethren.

Let us not be fooled by the mildness of the above "CURSE." In the following VERSION... written during the Sixth [6th] Century, C.E. by another set of "God-Inspired Scribes" and/or European "Jewish Scholars"... [all of whom seemed to have forgotten their own "BLACK" or "NEGRO HERITAGE"] the real RACIST BIGOTRY translated into the original story is also brought to the surface for your critical analysis. Thus they wrote:

> Now I cannot beget the fourth son whose children I would have ordered to serve you and your brothers! Therefore it must be Canaan, your first born, whom they enslave. And since you have disabled me...doing ugly things in blackness of night, Canaan's children shall be born ugly and black! Moreover, because you twisted your head around to see my nakedness, your grandchildren's hair shall be twisted into kinks, and their eyes red; again because your lips jested at my misfortune, theirs shall swell; and because you neglected my nakedness, they shall go naked, and their male members shall be shamefully elongated! Men of this race are called Negroes, their forefather Canaan commanded them to love theft and fornication, to be banded together in hatred of their masters and never to tell the truth.[1]

If we scrutinize "NOAH'S GENERATION" from the following in GENESIS, Chapter X, Verses 1 - 19 we should find that even into "ASSYRIA" his African descendants - the "SONS OF CUSH" [Ethiopians] - amalgamated their numbers with the ASSYRIANS while they were building the cities of ASSYRIA and establishing their EDUCATIONAL SYSTEM which all of the Asians of the area were already using, including the so-called "ISRAELITES," all of whom is specifically detailed in Verses 6 - 19 by "GOD'S INSPIRED SACRED SCRIBES," etc.[2]

The generations of Noah

10 NOW these *are* the generations of the sons of Noah, Shem, Ham, and Japheth: and unto them were sons born after the flood.

The sons of Japheth

2 The sons of Japheth; Gomer, and Magog, and Madai, and Javan, and Tubal, and Meshech, and Tiras.

3 And the sons of Gomer; Ashkenaz, and Riphath, and Togarmah.

4 And the sons of Javan; Elishah, and Tarshish, Kittim, and Dodanim.

5 {By these were the isles of the Gentiles divided}
{From these the coastland peoples spread}
in their lands; every one after his tongue, after their families, in their nations.

The sons of Ham

6 ¶ And the sons of Ham; Cush, and Mizraim, and Phut, and Canaan.

7 And the sons of Cush; Seba, and Havilah, and Sabtah, and Raamah, and Sabtechah: and the sons of Raamah; Sheba, and Dedan.

1. See R. Graves and R. Patai's Hebrew Myths: The Story Of Genesis, New York, 1964/1971, pp. 120 - 123; Y. ben-Jochannan's Black Man Of The Nile And His Family, New York, 1981, p. 11.
2. African "Sacred Scribes" wrote the "WORD" thousands of years before Adam and Eve existed anywhere in literature - religious or secular, etc.

Nimrod, the first monarch

8 And Cush begat Nimrod: he {began to be a / was the first on}
{mighty one in the earth. / earth to be a mighty man.}
9 He was a mighty hunter before the LORD: wherefore it is said, Even as Nimrod the mighty hunter
before the LORD.
10 And the beginning of his kingdom was Babel,
and Erech, and Accad, and Calneh, in the land of
Shinar.
11 Out of that land {went forth Asshur, / he went into Assyria,} and
builded Nineveh, and the city Rehoboth, and Calah,
12 And Resen between Nineveh and Calah: the
same *is* a great city.
13 And Mizraim begat Ludim, and Anamim, and
Lehabim, and Naphtuhim,
14 And Pathrusim, and Casluhim, (out of whom
came Philistim,) and Caphtorim.
15 ¶ And Canaan begat Sidon his firstborn, and
Heth,
16 And the Jebusite, and the Amorite, and the
Girgasite,
17 And the Hivite, and the Arkite, and the Sinite,
18 And the Arvadite, and the Zemarite, and the
Hamathite: and afterward were the families of the
Canaanites spread abroad.
19 And the border of the Canaanites was from
Sidon, as thou comest to Gerar, unto Gaza; as thou
goest, unto Sodom, and Gomorrah, and Admah, and
Zeboim, even unto Lasha.

It is rather strange that Jehovah - the JEWISH GOD-HEAD - could have found no other place/ "HOLY LAND" to keep His biblically "CHOSEN PEOPLE" [Jews] but in that of the so-called "HAMITES'" descendants - the so-called "NEGROES." But JEHOVAH constantly led His very own "CHOSEN PEOPLE" into the "LAND" of Ethiopia. "ETHIOPIA" during the ancient periods of biblical history was once the name of the entire continent called "Africa" today, as shown in the footnote of the following map from page xxvi in one of my books - BLACK MAN OF THE NILE AND HIS FAMILY, the origin of its source being "R. NORDEN'S BOOK OF MAPS, London, 1688 A.D. Please do not forget it was also "the land to the south of Egypt," etc. historically.

MAP
Of AFRICA.
1688.

AFRICA, by the Ancients, was called *Olympia*, *Hesperia*, *Oceania*, *Coryphe*, *Ammonia*, *Ortygia*, and *Æthiopia*. By the *Greeks* and *Romans*, *Lybia* and *Africa*. By the *Æthiopians* and *Moors*, *Alkebu-lan*.

You have noted the period in which the biblical JEWS were speaking of ETHIOPIA they were also referring to the entire continent. This was due to the vastness of the Ethiopian Kingdom/Empire, and the abundance of her indigenous BLACK ["Negro," etc.] PEOPLE everywhere in their biblical "WORLD" [see pages 382-383]. A partial view of the "EMPIRE OF ETHIOPIA" follows:

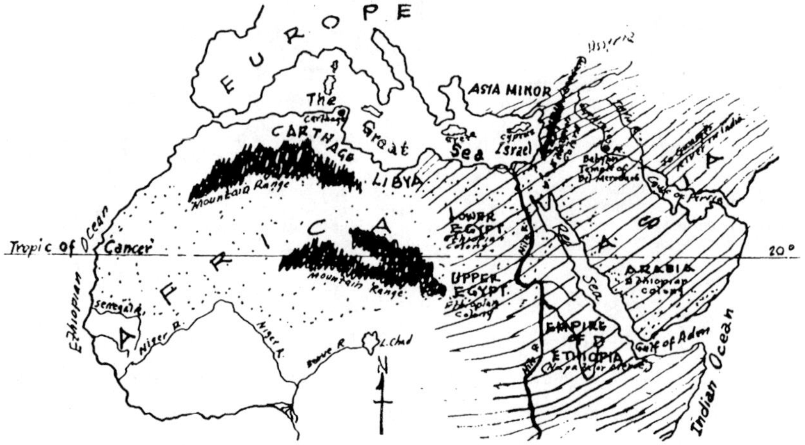

EMPIRE OF ETHIOPIA
850 - 650 B. C. E.
[Note: Ethiopian conquest of Ta-Merry (Egypt or Mizrain) in ca.750 B.C.E. during the reign of Pharaoh Sheskonk IIIrd. Withdrew under Pharaoh Psamthick I of the XXVIth Dynasty]

For those who would prefer to present an image of the ETHIOPIANS being other than the so-called "NEGROES SOUTH OF THE SAHARA" we have heard so much about, let it not be because the so-called "AFRICANIST AUTHORITIES" stated that the so-called "NEGROES" they have created are not aware of the fact that their aim is to belittle the so-called "NEGROES CONQUEST OF EGYPT" in about 750 B.C.E., which was during the reign of Pharaoh Oroskon IIIrd [also called SHESHONK in the Pentateuch]. We must equally remember that... it was not until the reign of Pharaoh Psamthik Ist of the XXVIth Dynasty [650 BCE] did the Ethiopians withdrew from Ta-Merry [Egypt, Qamt , etc.] without a fight. But, why did the Ethiopians withdrew? Because of the cowardice of the "CHOSEN PEOPLE" of Israel, who failed to fight against the Assyrians as agreed upon between Ethiopia and Israel in a TREATY to this effect. The failure of the ISRAELITES to fight the ASSYRIANS caused the latter's entry as conquerors into Ta-Merry. Yet the ETHIOPIANS remained for quite a long period after in Assyria until they were driven back south by King Essarhadden, who restored the TEMPLE OF BEL-MERODACH at Babylon as Assyria's second capital. Of course the stay of the Ethiopians in ISRAEL at such an early date in biblical history, we are to believe, had no physical effect between the LILY-WHITE "CHOSEN ISRAELITES" and the JET BLACK "CURSED NEGRO ETHIOPIANS" that amalgamated freely with each others. This, definitely, is assuming that they were of different "RACES." At least this is what we are being asked to believe by the so-called "LIBERAL AFRICANIST HISTORIANS," who only write "UNBIAS" accounts of WORLD HISTORY a-la European and European-American [White Semitic-Caucasian] style.

What we have witnessed in the two exhibits on the previous pages [339-340] is that the "NEGROES" or "ETHIOPIANS" were totally involved with JEWS and NON-JEWS of the major geo-political area we now call "THE MIDDLE EAST." The "HOLY BIBLE," supposedly also

"WRITTEN BY GOD-INSPIRED SCRIBES,"

tells us that the extent of this relationship between these Africans and Asians even included the Ethiopian Kings [PHARAOHS] accepting Jewish "refugees" and "captives" all over the entire "ETHIOPIAN EMPIRE" that stretched all the way across the Persian Gulf, even into India in Southern Asia. This "Negro Empire" also included the "KINGDOM OF YEMEN" - the "LAND" on the southwestern tip of the Arabian Peninsula where the "JEWS" came to secure haven as they "FLED THEIR ASSYRIAN OPPRESSORS AND SLAVEMASTERS." This, even as late as the year ca. 70 C.E. - following the destruction of the SECOND JEWISH COMMONWEALTH OF [ancient] ISRAEL, many of the Jews of the tribal groupings called "BENJAMIN" and/or "JUDAH" fled to the KINGDOM OF YEMEN where they received the protection of their cursed "NEGRO" brothers and sisters. This debt is being somewhat repaid today. Many remained in ISRAEL, but others found their way as far as the West Coast of Alkebu-lan into the KINGDOM and EMPIRE of Ghana, Mele, Songhai, Edoh, Mauritania, Nzaide, etc. much later.

All of the above information and artifacts in the form of maps and pictures gave rise to J.J. Williams' book - HEBREWISM OF WEST AFRICA: FROM THE NILE TO THE NIGER WITH THE JEWS, London, 1930 in which he states the following on pages 145 - 146:

THE DIASPORA

If at all there was a primitive Semitic stock, its earliest habitat is a matter of conjecture. Nowhere, not even in Arabia, were the people of Semitic speech indigenous to the soil. It seems probable that at divers periods in remote antiquity they had migrated from somewhere in Central Asia." [68]

Pure Race Non-existent.

Eugene Pittard, Professor of Anthropology at the University of Geneva, after a careful study of the subject, was led to the conclusion that such a thing as a pure race is non-existent to-day, and that even at the period commonly known as the beginning of historical times, practically every nation was already an ethnic complex. Thus he asserts, for example: "Primitive races became mixed from the time that the wanderings of humanity over the continents became intensive. Up till the Mesolithic, Western Europe knew only Dolichocephals —of different types, it is true. The arrival of the first Brachyce-

---

1. Typical of the colonialist mind is that everything of substance had to come into Africa by some method other than being indigenous; this author being no different in his "missionary" zeal.

phals profoundly disturbed this relative unity. From that day forward—and the mingling increased progressively as time goes on—it is impossible to speak of pure races as regards Europe."[69]

Ethnic Permanency Impossible.

Professor Dixon is quite of the same opinion. He writes: "By migration and conquest the original racial factors, whatever they were, have been so interwoven and blended that the vast majority of all living men must have a complex racial ancestry, and such a thing as a pure race can hardly be expected to live."[70] And again: "There is not a race in all history that has remained permanently unchanged, although the rate and degree of change have varied. Some races have retained their fundamental characteristics for millenia with but slight modifications, whereas others have, as a result of the incorporation of new factors, ceased to exist, because by virtue of such amalgamation they have become something else."[71]

Jewish People.

Concerning the Jews, Professor Pittard expresses this view: "I do not know what specialists think about the influence that may be attributed to the Jewish people in the general history of the Oriental peoples. It seems to me that if we take into consideration the two kingdoms of Judah and Israel only, the influence would appear to be a small one. Can we not say that it is thanks to their very dispersion that the Jews, in certain circumstances, have been more or less important factors in History as a whole? It has developed upon individuals and groups and not on the nation to exercise a frequently decisive influence. For anthropologists, though they may consider certain Jews to be inspired by the Israelitish racial idea, all Jews are very far from belonging to the 'Jewish race.' There is no such thing, said Renan, as a Jewish type—there are Jewish types. Nothing would be more true. We cannot consider the Jews to-day—not even in Palestine, because the Sionist movement has imported all kinds and conditions of Israelites—as constituting a homogeneous ethnic group. The Jews belong to a religious and social community to which, in every period, individuals of different races have attached themselves. These Judaized people have come from every kind of ethnic stratum, such as the Falashas of Abyssinia and the Germans of Germanic type; or the Tamils—Black Jews—of India, and the Khazars, who are supposed to be of Turki race."[72]

Ethnic Complex.

A little later the same author ascribes the large number of Jews scattered throughout the world at present not merely to "a natural excess of births over deaths during historic times," but rather to "the incorporation of other more or less large populations," and adds: "On many occasions entire groups have become Judaized and thus contributed their numbers and their eugenic qualities to the Israelite contingent."[73]

[68] Margolis and Marx, *History of the Jewish People,* p. 3.

[69] Eugene Pittard, *Race and History,* London, 1926, p. 17. Note:—Dawson makes the observation: "The pure race is at best a scientific abstraction, and the generalisations, in which many anthropologists still indulge, regarding the fixed types of racial psychology, which lie at the root of all historical cultures, are mere speculations, often influenced by modern national prejudices. From the first we have to deal, not with pure races, but with regional types which are the products of social and cultural influences."—*The Age of the Gods,* p. 21 f.

[70] Dixon, *Racial History of Man,* Introduction, p. 4. Note:—Professor Dixon thus defines his terms. "From the standpoint of the anthropologist . . .

a race is a biological group, based on community of physical characters." For peoples characterized on the one hand by linguistic, or on the other hand by cultural, historical, or political unity, he employs the terms "stock" and "nation."—l. c. p. 3.

[71] Idem, p. 503.
[72] Pittard, *Race and History*, p. 337.
[73] Idem, p. 339. Note:—Friedrich Hertz insists: "A most remarkable instance of racial compound is the Jews. . . . Besides Semites and Hittites, the Amorites, who probably were Aryans, formed a component part of the Jewish stock.

Of course J. J. Williams overlooked the basic religious foundation of West African High-Cultures equally as much as he was blinded to the origins of what seemed to him as "HEBREWISMS" in this area of "AFRICA"-much of which had already produced the THEOSOPHICAL and THEOLOGICAL concepts we now call JUDAISM, CHRISTIANITY and ISLAM. All of this began before the arrival of the first AFRICAN and/or ASIAN "JEW" in Western Alkebulan/"Africa." Williams, typical of "Christian Missionaries," believed "Jews created theosophy."

If we had stopped at this juncture of our "safari" into the origins and development of the so-called "BLACK JEWS," we would have dealt with quite enough factual data to effectively conclude that there could be no doubt there was no separation between the "Africans" who worshiped "AMEN-RA" and those who worshiped "YWH" solely on the basis of "RACE, COLOR" or "SOCIO-POLITICAL STATUS," unless one is blinded by his [or her] own religious bigotry and/or racial syndrome caused by the so-called "CHOSEN PEOPLE" myth and "GOD'S HOLY SCRIBES" and "SACRED SCRIPTURES" allegorical propaganda common in Judaeo-Christian-Islamic mysticism - all of which if we challenge becomes "Black Revisionist History" for some.

The basic historical foundation of the origin of the AGAW [Kyla, Falasha, etc.] biblically has been indisputably established. And of course one could use much more extensive quotations from the same "FIVE BOOKS OF MOSES" to further authenticate their so-called "JEWISHNESS" and/or "KOSHER STATUS." However, we must consider other sources for about the "AFRICAN JEWS" relationship to those other AFRICANS of much more ancient religions, those who created the "AFRICAN MYSTERIES SYSTEM" that became the foundation upon which all JUDAEO-CHRISTIAN-ISLAMIC theosophy, theology and philosophy are based. For further fine detailing of these sources my other works listed on the Copyright Page of Volume One are also recommended, along with the others I have mentioned throughout these two volumes.

[VALIDITY?] When an Agaw say "GOD" or "YWH" [Jehovah]; what does he, or she, mean? Is it not the same identity was meant when the Egyptian "Sun Worshiper" of ancient times said "AMEN-RA;" or our contemporary Kikuyu of the Republic of Kenya, East Africa today say "NGAI;" and a Yoruba of the Republic of Nigeria, West Africa say "OLODUMARE"? Certainly it is the same "ONE AND ONLY GOD" - Ywh, Jesus the Christ, Al'lah, et al. - who told their

"African Soul Brother" - "MOSES" - in EXODUS, Chapter III, Verse 14, to:

> " tell them when they ask you who sent you,
> I Am That I Am... [Eyeya ashe eyeya];"

who also told the other Africans from whom Moses copied this saying that was so very common in the teachings of the MYSTERIES SYSTEM all along the High-Cultures of the ancient Nile Valley, Atbara River and Great Lakes regions of North, Northeast and Central Alkebu-lan, even for thousands of years before someone came up with the allegorical story about "Adam and Eve in the Garden of Eden" and all of the other stories related therefrom.

From the knowledge of the rites of CONCEPTION, DELIVERY of the child conceived, CIRCUMCISION of the male or EXCISION of the female, CONFORMATION into the High-Culture and/or religion, coming of age of PUBERTY, MARRIAGE, and finally DEATH; it was, and it still is, one of RELIGIOUS RITUALISTIC CONFORMITY in the experience of the indigenous AFRICAN SOCIETIES before, during and since the advent of JUDAISM, CHRISTIANITY and ISLAM. Certainly these "RITES" are not exclusive only to these areas of Alkebu-lan. In this respect the "THIRD BOOK OF MOSES," otherwise known as "LEVITICUS," mainly deals with prohibitions for health, cleanliness, food preparation and preservation, family and sexual regulations, etc., etc., etc., all of which the indigenous Africans of Ta-Merry [Egypt, etc.] and other High-Cultures taught their fellow RELIGIONISTS, including JEWS, before there was the first "JEWISH [Holy] HOMELAND" by any name whatsoever. However, it is suggested that a full review of the entire set of the fundamental Forty-two [42]"Negative Confessions" developed by the Africans of the Nile Valley and Great Lakes regions,[2] more than two thousand [2,000] years before Moses' birth in Alkebu-lan ["Africa"], be read in order to fathom how far into these areas of RELIGION and MAGIC the predecessors of Judaeo-Christian-Islamic THEOSOPHY, THEOLOGY and PHILOSOPHY ventured; even before the allegorical folklore about... "Adam and Eve in the Garden of Eden"...was a hypothesis in the mind of the first Jew.[1]

On page 274 of Albert B. Cleage, Jr's book - BLACK CHRISTIAN NATIONALISM: NEW DIRECTIONS FOR THE BLACK CHURCH - Rabbi Hailu Paris, Religious Director of Education for Congregation Mount Horeb, Bronx, New York City, New York and Chairman of the American Pro-Falasha Committee, 507 Fifth Avenue, New York City, N. Y., states:

> In these highlands of Ethiopia there are a people called the Agaw, who have lived in the Hebraic tradition from ancient times. Their language is of the most ancient

1. See Y. ben-Jochannan's African Origins Of The Major "Western Religions: Judaism, Christianity And Islam," Alkebu-lan Books Associates, New York, 1972, pp. 68 - 69.
2. See walls of the Tomb of Rameses VI, Valley of Kings, Luxor [Wa'at or Thebes, etc.], Egypt, Northeast Alkebu-lan/Africa; no relationship to Pharaoh Rameses II who allegedly chased "the Hebrew [Israelite] children/people out of Egypt...," etc. as per the Book Of Exodus, etc.

times. It is called *Karinya* in the Kushite dialect. These people with the Jews who came back to Africa created a new culture and new way of life. That way of life was called by the westerners *Falasha,* or Ethiopian Jewish life. In the eleventh century B.C.E., this land was called Abyssinia by the Europeans, a corruption of the Arabic term *habasha,* which means "a people of mixtures." The Ethiopians renamed the land Ethiopia when Haile Selassie first became emperor. To that area came a tribe from Yemen in 200 B.C.E., a tribe called the Ahgessahn. This ancient Sabean tribe—because Sabea was the ancient kingdom of South Arabia before the Arab conquest and before the Mohammedan religion had taken over—had migrated to the highlands of Ethiopia. They brought with them the writings, trades, arts, and crafts that were then current in Arabia. About the third century B.C.E., they formed a kingdom, the capital of which was known as Aksum. Why was Aksum important? The Ethiopians believed that the local kings of Ethiopia were descended from Solomon, King of Israel, and that the Tabernacle of the Law of God—that is, the Ark of the Covenant—had been brought from Jerusalem to Aksum by Menelik, Solomon's first-born son. They believed that God had transferred his place of abode on earth from the ancient city of Jerusalem to Aksum, the ecclesiastical and political capital of Ethiopia.

Rabbi Hailu Paris, himself an Ethiopian and JEW [a so-called "Falasha"], had already covered the issue of the "AFRICAN ORIGIN OF JUDAISM" in the beginning of his task - which was to write about the African [Black] People in the "JUDAEO-CHRISTIAN-ISLAMIC" experience, all of which he stated in his direct comments on the "BLACK JEWS" under the chapter title he gave the name - "AFRICA AND THE BIBLE." But in all of his detailing with the PRO and CON of the history of the AGAW as written by African-American historians, and definitely more-so by European and European-American Christian and Jewish missionaries,[1] it is still suggested that each reader becomes much more acquainted with the facts they are taught by AGAW historians and theologians orally, and in written form.

Rabbi Paris speaks only of the "TABERNACLE OF THE LAW OF GOD" [which is otherwise known as the "ARK OF THE COVENANT"] that was allegedly transported into Ethiopia from ISRAEL with King Solomon's son- "EMPEROR MENELIK Ist," whose mother was the greatest monarch of her time - "EMPRESS MAKEDA" [commonly called "QUEEN OF SHEBA" because her EMPIRE OF ETHIOPIA also included the "KINGDOM OF YEMEN" or "SHEBA," sometimes said to have been the capital instead of the name of a country], in about ca. 970 B.C.E. as the sole "origin of the Agaw in Ethiopia." This is the same period European and

1. Most of whom assume status as "Authority" on Africa and Africans after a few visits to the continent of Africa; no African being equally complimented upon visiting Europe or the Americas.

European-American so-called "AFRICANISTS" always use in terms of their super knowledge of

"THE DATE OF ORIGIN OF THE FALASHAS IN JUDAISM."

In validating this type of belief and/or hypothesis on the part of a typical European-American "AFRICANIST" we have the following from pages ix - x of the "Introduction" in one of the popularly used book in White Jewish circles - FALASHA ANTHOLOGY: THE BLACK JEWS OF ETHIOPIA, by Professor Wolf Leslau, Schocken Books, New York, 1951:

Falasha Research

IN SOME REGIONS north of Lake Tana in Ethiopia lives a population of Jewish faith called Falashas. Their historical origin and racial affinities present many difficult problems. Were they originally Jewish immigrants? If so, whence and when did they come to Ethiopia? Or are they a segment of the indigenous population of Ethiopia converted to Judaism? If so, by whom were they converted and when? These questions have occupied all who have dealt with the Falashas.

The name Falasha can best be explained as deriving from the Ethiopic *fälläsä,* "to emigrate." The Falashas of the villages of the region of Gondar do not use this name in speaking of themselves. They say either ***beta Isra'el,*** "the House of Israel," or just *Isra'el,* or use the Cushitic term *ḳayla.*[1] It would seem, therefore, that the term originated among the older native population as a designation for these foreign immigrants and was not invented by the latter themselves.

The sources for our knowledge of the Falashas are of various kinds. Among the oldest testimonies to the existence of Jews in Ethiopia are the reports of Jewish travelers like Eldad Haddani (ninth century), Benjamin of Tudela (twelfth century), Elijah of Ferrara (fifteenth century), and others. Most of these accounts report things of legendary character that lack historical basis, and are presumably based on hearsay. Ethiopia was known throughout the Middle Ages as the country of Prester John and was supposed to be the habitat of the Ten Tribes. This idea excited the curiosity of travelers who vaguely related that there were Jews living in Ethiopia or that Jews had come thither from other countries. There is a more reliable source of information available in the Ethiopian royal chronicles but they unfortunately give no information about the religion or the cultural or social conditions of the Falashas, dwelling only on the campaigns of the Ethiopian kings against them. We will revert to these events later.

When James Bruce mentioned the Falashas in his important work on Ethiopia [2] the curiosity of the western world was at once aroused. Specialists subsequently were further intrigued by the report about these people brought home by the Frenchman Antoine d'Abbadie in 1840. But it was the initiative of English missionaries like Flad, Stern, and others,[3] who saw a promising field for their activities in that quarter, that gave greatest impetus to the study of the Falashas.[4] At the same time Jewish circles also became conscious of the advisability of establishing contact with this forgotten component of their people, and the *Jewish Chronicle*

---

1. Yemenite Jews, for centuries, dealt with "Falashas" without any "difficultproblems" about their "historical origin and racial affinities," etc. European Jews cannot help but find. Why?; racism!

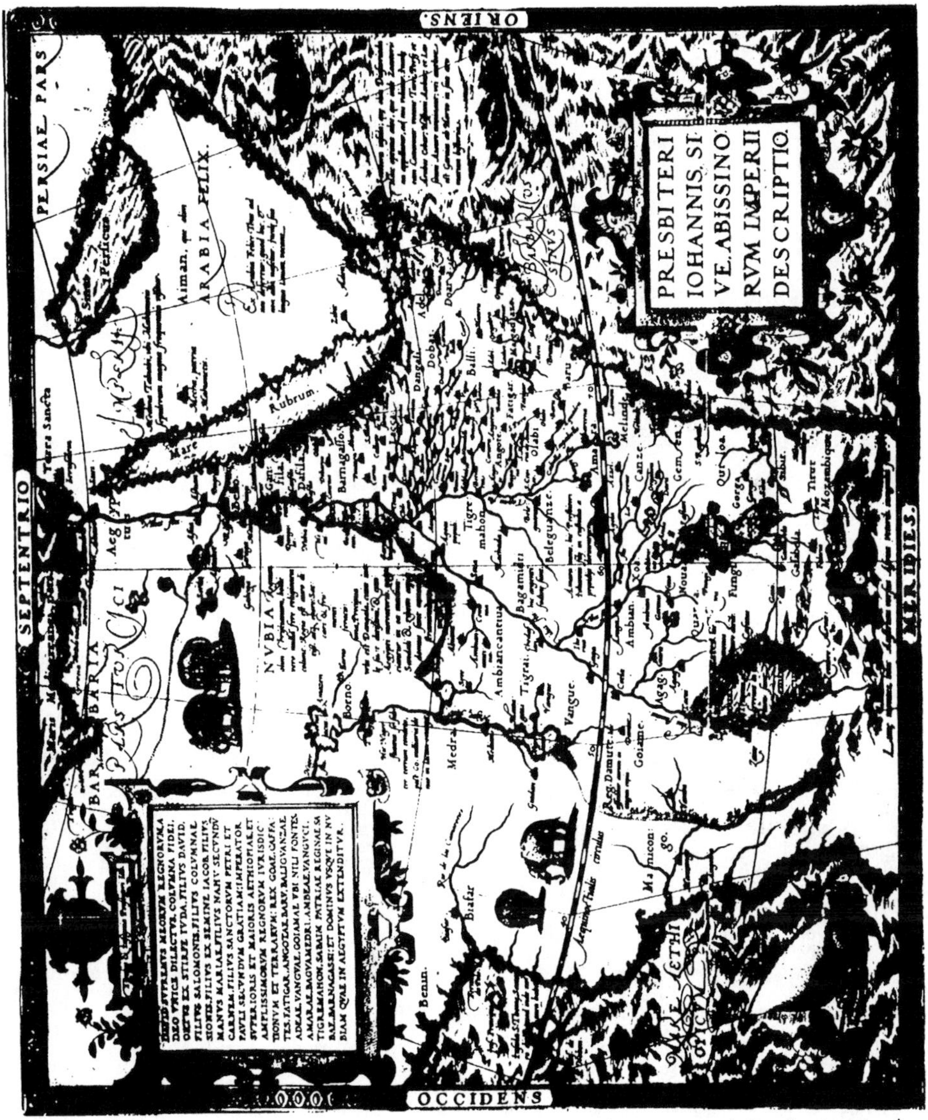

"DESCRIPTION OF ABYSSINIA, EMPIRE OF PRESTOR JOHN, " Anvers 1570 A.D., by Ortelus.[1]

---

1. Note that in 1508 - 1540 A.D. Emperor Lebna-Dengel David IInd was the reigning monarch; and that the "Ethiopian Ocean" was not yet replaced by the "Atlantic Ocean." Who writes history for all African people? And, by whose "authority"? Here is a typical example of "White History" for all.

> of London urged that efforts be made to do this. The Alliance Israélite Universelle sent the noted Semitist Joseph Halévy to Ethiopia to investigate the situation.[5] His positive assertions that Jews were indeed to be found in Ethiopia was, however, received with incredulity in some Jewish quarters, and a countermission headed by a Rabbi Nahoum was dispatched.[6] In 1905 interest was again stimulated by the report of Jacques Faitlowitch who had visited the Falashas in that year.[7] Pro-Falasha committees were created in several countries, including the United States, with the purpose of restoring these people to the general body of Israel.

Unlike Professor Wolf Leslau's confusion over WHICH or WHAT European or European-American "CHRISTIAN MISSIONARIES" or "JEWISH TRAVELERS" wrote about the AGAW..., the FIVE BOOKS OF MOSES [Pentateuch, Holy Torah, Old Testament] had already established the origin of the AGAW [Agu] or KYLA people...the so-called "FALASHA" or "FALASSA" - as being connected with the first body of JEWS there ever was. But Professor Leslau's CONFUSION, as is his CONCLUSION, shows that he follows the same line of all the other European and European-American historians, cultural anthropologists, ethnologists, egyptologists, archeologists, paleontologists, etc. who make it their life's pride to write about the so-called

"PRIMITIVE PEOPLES OF DARKEST AFRICA SOUTH OF THE SAHARA - THE BANTUS" -

after having spent anywhere from one day to one year in Alkebu-lan; which, of course, supposedly qualified them as the sole -

"AUTHORITY ON AFRICA AND THE AFRICAN NATIVES."

For example: Professor Leslau could not understand that among the AGAW there are distinctions in worship and rituals within their African-Asian TORAHDIC or JUDAIC religiousity. Thus it is that he could not give the commonly known historical difference between the KYLAS and the so-called "FALASHAS" although both were, and are, part of the entire "BETA ISRAEL [Agaw] COMMUNITY of Ethiopia, East Alkebu-lan ["Africa"]. This is not different to the distinction made between "ORTHODOX, CONSERVATIVE, RECONSTRUCTIONIST, REFORM," etc. "WHITE JEWISH COMMUNITIES" throughout the United States of America, Europe, Great Britain, and even the State of Israel in Western Asia - the so-called "Middle East." Thus it is that Professor Leslau found it necessary to comment:

"Their" [Falasha] "historical origin and racial affinities present many difficult problems."

Who had the... "DIFFICULT PROBLEMS"! Why did he? The AGAW presented absolutely not a single 'PROBLEM' to themselves for being what they are - "BLACK JEWS" or "AFRICAN JEWS"..., etc. And, this should be the same for anyone else who comes to their community

1. How does a professor from a racist and bigoted religious institution avoid his/her own bigotry!

and enjoy their hospitality. The person, or persons, who suffered any such "PROBLEMS" because he, and/or she, met an AGAW [Falasha] in his, and/or her, own indigenous homeland - ETHIOPIA -can only blame the background culture of RACISM and RELIGIOUS BIGOTRY from whence he, and/or she, came in the so-called "Western World" - Europe, Great Britain and European-America. Why don't the WHITE-CAUCASIAN-SEMITIC Polish, Turkish and European-American, etc., also most of all the golden hair blonde JEWS of Germany, Sweden and Denmark, etc.,...

"HISTORICAL ORIGIN AND RACIAL AFFINITIES
PRESENT MANY DIFFICULT PROBLEMS"...

to the Agaw, Yemenite, Cochin and other Black, Brown and Yellow HEBREWS [Jews] or ISRAELITES inside and outside of the State of Israel today? The answer should be obvious, for European and European-American [WHITE or SEMITIC] Jews see themselves as all other "Caucasian" and/or "Indo-European Aryan People" who indulge in "RACIAL SUPERIORITY," who function upon same as all others of the so-called "SILENT WHITE MAJORITY" of the "Western Culture" they have labeled "WESTERN CIVILIZATION." Their MORAL VALUE is based upon "COLOR" and "RACE" distinctions as criterias amounting to life and death considerations. Thus except for Adolph Hitler and his Nazis the GERMAN JEWS were as patriotic to the German Republic on the issue of "RACE"[1] as is the AMERICAN JEWS to the United States of America on the same issue. This is somewhat the same condition that allows so-called "DUAL CITIZENSHIP" on the part of European-American JEWS with respect to the State of Israel and the United States of America, a situation frowned upon by every kind of White People of every religious groupings when African-Americans of any religion and/or socio-political order demand the same privilege from the United States of America for any African nation controlled by their fellow African [BLACK] People in Alkebu-lan. It is equally the same MORALITY which drives a WHITE JEW to move as far as he, or she, can out of the so-called "WHITE [Jewish, Christian, Atheist, etc.] NEIGHBOURHOOD" whenever the first BLACK FACE appears as a tenant, irrespective of the fact that said "FACE" belongs to a BLACK JEW, BLACK CHRISTIAN, BLACK MOSLEM, BLACK YORUBA,[2] etc. Yes! This is the same reason why Professor Wolf Leslau should not have been confused over what he is accustomed in the United States of America, and what he had extended in mind when he too saw the Agaw - "BLACK JEWS, NEGRO JEWS, BETA ISRA'EL," etc. - of the world's oldest empire - ETHIOPIA [Itiopi, Kush, Cush, Habbasha, Abyssinia, etc.] that predated Israel.

[DIOSPORA and RACISM]: When WE THE BLACK JEWS was originally written and published

1. Created and developed by Europeans/Whites to hide their own inferiority complexes about others.
2. Let us not forget that not a solitary "religion" is any better or worse than another one, except in the mind of the "religious bigot" so holding to his/her own religious fanaticism, etc.

for the first time at San Juan, Puerto Rico in 1938 C.E. as "NOSOTROS HEBREOS NEGRO," I was under the belief that the tenets in the FIVE BOOKS OF MOSES made my fellow JEWS different and apart from "RACISM" and "RELIGIOUS BIGOTRY." This was due to the closed Hebraic background and indoctrination under which I was raised by my family. But it was not too long before I reached my maturity I was forced to observe the painful reality that there is/was a fundamental distinction throughout the Americas and the Caribbean Islands with respect to "COLOR" and "RACE" [one's physical characteristics] between BLACK JEWS and WHITE JEWS, and was made to understand that the BLACK JEWS are "INFERIOR" to the WHITE JEWS. In the United States of America I found that this area of distinction between BLACK and WHITE Jews was even further-reaching than it was in all of the Islands of the Caribbean Sea, South and Central America, and even Mexico and Canada at the southern and northern borders of the United States of America in North America.

For the first time in my young life I was to realize that White Jews, irrespective of those with KINKY HAIR, THICK LIPS and SWARTHY COLOR that exposed their "AFRICAN [black] HERITAGE" from the four hundred [400] plus years of their infancy as "SLAVES" among the so-called "NEGROES OF EGYPT, NUBIA, MEROE, ETHIOPIA," etc. used their RELIGIOUS and CULTURAL identity with the HEBREW RELIGION and TRADITION to maintain their so-called distinct "ETHNIC GROUP" or "SEMITIC RACE" status, which most preferred to use at that time to distinguish themselves from other European and European-American so-called WHITE ANGLO-SAXON PROTESTANT CHRISTIANS and WHITE ROMAN CATHOLIC CHRISTIANS. Of course all of this was at a period when WHITE JEWS were not considered "CAUCASIAN" or "WHITE," and as such could not enter public places catering to -

"MEMBERS OF THE WHITE RACE ONLY."

During this same period White Jews, along with Black People of every religion there were, and still are, were demanding of White Anglo-Saxon Protestant Christians:

"WE WANT PROPORTIONAL REPRESENTATION": A QUOTA SYSTEM!

We have only to return to our personal files, much less our public libraries and old newspapers, particularly those going back to the 1940's C.E. before the so-called "BROWN-ISAAC BILL" passed the City Council of New York City, New York. For it was this "BILL" that established the national pattern for the removal of "COLOR, RELIGION, RACE" and/or "NATIONALITY" as prerequisites for entering public and private places doing business with the general public - including colleges, hospitals, restaurants, etc. - some of which were then owned by WHITE JEWS who did not accept non-WHITES, the vast majority being owned by most WHITE CHRISTIANS who barred BLACKS generally, and equally WHITE JEWS. The irony of it all is that Earl Brown is a "BLACK CHRISTIAN," and Stanley Isaac was a "WHITE JEW." It is also ironic, because their "BILL" did nothing whatsoever for the RACIST and RELIGIOUSLY BIGOTED minds of either group which both men represented, and for whom their "BILL" was mainly intended to help physically and spiritually. Just look at the CHURCH and SYNAGOGUE of God today and judge for yourself. Thus as late as the writing of this Volume there is still a so-called "BLACK-WHITE CONFRONTATION" in every facet of the entire United States of America's High-Culture ["civilization"], New York City being no exception to the general rule. This situation between BLACKS and WHITES, irrespective of religious affiliation, is most rampant to the point of a stand-off in which each group is afraid of visiting the others so-called "NEIGHBOURHOOD" after sundown; in some areas even during the middle of the day. The above facts are best demonstrated in Shlomo Katz's edited book - NEGRO AND JEW: AN ENCOUNTER IN AMERICA, The Macmillan Company, New York, Collier-Macmillan Limited, London, 1967. For example, on pages xi - xii of the "Introduction" the following extract appears:

> THE VOICE on the phone trembled with indignation. "Where do you live? I bet you live in a safe white neighborhood and have your office in a safe area in mid-Manhattan. Do you know what it means to fear attack every time you walk down the street? If you did, you wouldn't talk that way.... You're just another Jewish self-hater.... You don't care what happens to your own people...." and the voice trailed off into incoherent hysteria.
>
> This phone call was but the first after I had published a letter in a liberal Jewish periodical shortly after some Negro rioting during which numerous Jewish stores were sacked. The letter protested an editorial that, it seemed to me, was hectoring, and that smugly boasted how "we," Jews, that is, had all along stood "in the front ranks" of the struggle for Negro rights, and vaguely threatened that unless "responsible" Negro leadership ("if there are responsible Negro leaders") puts a stop to outbreaks of violence "we," while remaining liberal, might nevertheless be driven to some sort of agonizing reappraisal.
>
> For nearly a week after the first call my line was busy. The anonymous callers would always begin with a reasonable appeal for understanding the plight of Jews living or conducting their businesses within or on the margins of Negro ghettos, their sense of insecurity, the violence they were subject to. Then would follow bitterly sarcastic requests for advice as to what they should do under the circumstances, and finally a deluge of vituperation, sometimes accompanied by threats. On a few occasions the callers would put their argument on a personal level: "What's the matter? Aren't you scared of Negro hoodlums and muggers?" But all attempts to answer this question with statements that I was indeed very much afraid of muggers and hoodlums, but not especially so because they were black; that I was probably more afraid of white anti-Jewish violence; and that any Jew of our generation, remembering what the white Germans, in cooperation

with other European whites, did to us within our own memory, could he, must not, allow himself to fall into the trap of associating anti-Semitism and its concomitant violence with Negroes in particular were wasted effort, for the voices on the phone were genuinely urgent with fear and confusion and anger, and, above all, with surprise. Beneath the furious taunts of "nigger lover," "self-hater," "traitor," could be discerned the bewilderment of people caught unawares. How could this happen in America? How could this happen to us who are relatively recent newcomers to the American scene and are not part of the Negro-white tragedy that has been in the making for three centuries?

In the course of our long history, and especially during the past nineteen centuries of dispersion, we Jews have come in contact, for better or for worse, with many peoples. We have been in Spain and in Poland, in Germany and in Russia, in France and in Rumania. But it was not until we came to America in substantial numbers that we encountered the black race. In the dim beginnings of our history the problem of Negro-Jewish relations had briefly cropped up in the somewhat ominous and vaguely outlined story of Moses and the Cushite wife he had taken, how his brother and sister, Aaron and Miriam, resented this alliance, and how they were punished for it. But this encounter, wrapped in the fog of mythology, had no followup. Here and there a Negro appears peripherally in ancient Jewish history, in the entourage of King David, for instance, but this contact is ephemeral. Our encounters, our loves and hates, unfolded their destinies in the European and Mediterranean world.

The two pages of extract shown above sufficiently established the pattern of the general tenor of Katz's entire book. But the agony in the above extract is the PREJUDICIAL position in which it began, which was designed to validate Katz and his so-called "27 Negro[1] and Jewish Commentators"...

"CANDID EXAMINATION OF NEGRO ANTI-SEMITISM
AND THE CONSEQUENT JEWISH REACTION..."

written on the cover of the book as the added sub-title. However what Katz, and equally all of the so-called "27 Prominent Negro and Jewish Commentators" [particularly the White ones], wanted to do with the so-called "BLACK-WHITE CONFRONTATION" was to set aside WHITE JEWS as being untouched by the RACISM and RELIGIOUS BIGOTRY that brought about the so-called "NEGRO ANTI-SEMITISM" in the first place in this entire so-called "JUDAEO-CHRISTIAN WESTERN CIVILIZATION." But they failed, miserably so, to note that even their most disgusting term- NEGRO- is a racist label attached to AFRICAN [never "Negro"] PEOPLE without their consent. Whereas, "JEW" is a term that was equally applied to a RELIGIOUS GROUP OF PEOPLE without the stigma of a RACIAL connotation until said group began using

1. The "27 Prominent Negro Commentators, apparently, knew nothing about the fact that even the title of the book they were crawling in was/is racistly inspired. What is a "negro/Negro"?

it as such for their own advantage. It is as if saying:

'I SAW A WHITE MAN, A JEW, AND A NEGRO.'

In fact, only the WHITE MAN states an identity of a human being on face value. What is "A NEGRO"? Is it a MAN, WOMAN, CHILD, GOD, DOG, IT," etc.? Katz and his team of super "27 [etc.] Commentators" forgot that there are thousands upon thousands of BLACK or AFRICAN-AMERICAN [Falasha, etc.] JEWS throughout the Americas who can prove their "JEWISHNESS" as much as Katz and/or any other "WHITE JEW" - man, woman or child. Here too is the basic problem the BLACK JEWS and WHITE JEWS in the United States of America have consistently failed to deal with, much less solve. Thus the STAND-OFF or CONFRONTATION between BLACK JEWS and WHITE JEWS as it is with BLACK CHRISTIANS and WHITE CHRISTIANS, and as it is with BLACK and WHITE everything else. Yet BLACK JEWS were seen collecting monies to send for their fellow co-religionists in the State of Israel during each and every "WAR" the Israelis had with their Arab Moslem neighbours since 1947. And certainly BLACK JEWS and BROWN JEWS from Ethiopia, East Alkebu-lan and Yemen, Western Asia fought with the STERN GANG and IGRUNI for Israel's independence. To them the following extract from Gustav Saron and Louis Holtz's book, THE JEWS IN SOUTH AFRICA, Oxford University Press, London [etc], 1955, "Introduction," page xiii is quite a revelation, but not in any sense whatsoever a surprise:[1]

> A second major influence upon South African Jewry came from England, both in religious matters, as many of the leading ministers and rabbis in South Africa have come from England, and generally through contact with Anglo-Jewry's life and institutions. This was to be expected as first the Cape and Natal, and later the whole of South Africa, have developed within the British Empire and Commonwealth, and South African life as a whole has been greatly influenced by British ways and institutions.
>
> Jewish life in South Africa represents, indeed, a unique blend, resulting from the interaction of *Litvak* and English elements with the emergent South African way of life. Naturally, among the South African-born descendants of the immigrants the older traditions have grown weaker. The South African Jew of today is not only taller, more broad-shouldered and more open-air-minded than his forebears, but he exhibits many of the psychological characteristics of his fellow South Africans.

Katz's "27[etc.] Commentators" praised the contributors of the "CONTRIBUTIONS" certain White Jews gave to carefully selected so-called "NEGRO CAUSES" throughout the United States of America's history in which "JEWS" and "NEGROES" came in contact with each other often. But they failed to mention that said "CONTRIBUTIONS" then, and now, were/are solely "FINANCIAL INVESTMENTS" that guaranteed White Jewish socio-political and major economic

1. White Jews in the so-called "Republic of South Africa" treat the indigenous African people in every way commensurate with the same Hitlerite Nazism they protested against in Germany, etc.

growth in the general BLACK and WHITE Judaeo-Christian communities. For each "CONTRIBUTION" was, and/or is, primarily used to finance passive "NEGRO" and/or "COLORED" front organizations to break down segregated so-called "White Protestant" and "Roman Catholic" CHRISTIAN INSTITUTIONS of every type that originally barred both BLACKS and WHITES who were outside of their select groupings. The end result was, as it still is, that the so-called "NEGROES," irrespective of religious affiliation, became the visible antagonists; thus the so-called "WHITE [today including Jews] BACKLASH." Yet it is almost one of the major sins for a BLACK PERSON, even BLACK JEW, to ever mention "WHITE JEWISH BACKLASH" except behind closed doors with intimate friends before the label of "NEGRO ANTI-SEMITISM" starts flying all over the so-called "NEGRO GHETTOS" by WHITE JEWS and their amalgamated "NON-VIOLENT INTEGRATED NEGROES" and "COLORED FOLKS."

It will be quite interesting if the following extract from the Song Of Solomon, Chapter I, Verses 1 - 6 would return to its original wording, all in context to Katz's "27 Negro and Jewish Commentators." Thus we read from the "God Inspired [Jewish] Scribes" this bit of racism:

The church's love for Christ

THE song of songs, which *is* Solomon's.

2 Let him kiss me with the kisses of his mouth: for thy love *is* better than wine.

3 Because of the savour of thy good ointments thy name *is as* ointment poured forth, therefore do the virgins love thee.

4 Draw me, we will run after thee: the king hath brought me into his chambers: we will be glad and rejoice in thee, we will {remember / extol} thy love more than wine: {the upright / rightly do they} love thee.

She confesses her deformity,

5 I *am* black, but comely, O ye daughters of Jerusalem, as the tents of Kedar, as the curtains of Solomon.

6 Look not upon me, because I *am* {black, / swarthy,} because the sun hath {looked upon / scorched} me: my mother's children were angry with me; they made me the keeper of the vineyards; *but* mine own vineyard have I not kept.

Is it not strange that the editors of the above - allegedly another group of "God's Inspired Scribes" - found it necessary to manipulate "GOD'S WORDS" to suit their own racial sensitivities among their so-called "GOD-FEARING" Christians, Jews, and other Judaeo-Christian believers? Just imagine that a "QUEEN" [Sheba or Makeda] all the way from "ETHIOPIA," East Alkebu-lan ["Africa" - geographically located only fifteen [15] degrees due north of the "Equatorial Line"] became "BLACK" and/or "SWARTHY" solely because she was once

"THE KEEPER OF THE VINEYARDS" [1]

for someone else. But we equally saw that the same editors post-dated JESUS "the Christ's" chronological appearance to relate back to the era of King Solomon and Queen Makeda, both of whom reigned more than nine hundred [900] years before "Jesus" was declared "born." I am

---

1. Were these racists and religious bigots who wrote this pre-Hitlerian diatribe any-the-less guilty of cultural and racial genocide than the Ku Klux Klan, Calvinist Christian, Mormom, Jewish, etc. zealots of the 1900's C.E./A.D. ? Why!

SOLOMON'S "WISEST MAN THAT EVER LIVED" REPUTATION QUESTIONED

THE COMPARATIVE WORKS[1]

970 BCE ?	1000 BCE ?
ISRAEL (Asia-Minor)	EGYPT (Nortn-Africa)
PROVERBS XXII. 17-XXIII. 14;	THE TEACHINGS OF AMEN-EM-OPE
The "teachings of King Solomon" of Israel	Pharoah of Egypt
1. Incline thine ear, and hear my words, And apply thine heart to apprehend; For it is pleasant if thou keep them in thy belly, That thy may be fixed like a peg upon thy lips.	1a. Give thine ear, and hear what I say, And apply thine heart to apprehend; It is good for thee to place them in thine heart, Let them rest in the casket of thy belly. That they may act as a peg upon thy tongue.
2. Have I not written for thee thirty sayings Of counsels and knowledge! That thou mayest make known truth to him that speaketh.	2a. Consider these thirty chapters; They delight, they instruct. Knowledge how to answer him that speaketh, And how to carry back a report to one that sent him.
3. Rob not the poor for he is poor, Neither oppress the lowly in the gate.	3a. Beware of robbing the poor, And of oppressing the afflicted.
4. Associate not with a passionate man, Nor go with a wrathful man, Lest thou learn his ways And get a snare to thy soul.	4a. Associate not with a passionate man, Nor approach him for conversations: Leap not to cleave to such a one, That the terror carry thee not away
5. A man who is skillful in his business Shall stand before Kings.	5a. A scribe who is skillful in his business Findeth himself worthy to be a courtier.

The above comparisons are but a choice few of the selected sayings of the entire so-called "PROVERBS OF KING SOLOMON" of Israel, which have been earmarked for cross reference. However, the entire PSALMS ["Songs of Solomon"],[2] and all of the HOLY TORAH generally, are full of direct copies of works written WORD-FOR-WORD as their African [Egyptian, Nubian, Ethiopian, Meroite, etc.] sayings and teachings. This should not be supprising to anyone, since Moses and most of the earliest Haribus [Hebrews or Israelites later on] in GENESIS and EXODUS were all Africans. They were all born in Ta-Merry, Ethiopia [the Falashas], and Ta-Nehisi [Nubia]. Even the theory of "MONOTEISM," the belief of "ONE GOD" above all others, was taught in Ta-Nehisi [Nubia], Ta-Merry [Egypt], and Itiopi [Ethiopia] before the birth of Moses by the Pharaoh Akhenaten [Amen-hotep IV], c. 1370-1352 B.C.E. Moses did not live until the reign of Pharaoh Rameses I, c. 1340-1320 B.C.E. or Seti I. c. 1318-1298 B.C.E.

---

1. See Yosef ben-Jochannan's Black Man Of The Nile And His Family, pp. 102 - 103, also the Revised and Enlarged Edition for further detailed information and other references.
2. In spite of the above fact there are rabbis who cannot accept that "PSALMS" were equally copied from African scribes' works; one even wrote his finding to the contrary, which you have already read in the previous Volume.

certain that there is no problem reading this VERSION of biblical racism in any ALL WHITE SYNAGOGUE; and most definitely it will find no opposition even in the BLACK SYNAGOGUES of which I am familiar. Yet, was it not KING SOLOMON who made the comment relating to his own "BLACK" and/or "SWARTHY" color of skin? The ancient text, particularly the only ETHIOPIAN TEXT, identifies SOLOMON as the one who made this comment. Of course it does not make any difference which one of these two biblical characters made the statement; neither would be acceptable with a "BLACK" or "SWARTHY SKIN"[1] in the average SYNAGOGUE, TEMPLE, CHURCH and other HOUSES OF WORSHIP throughout the United States of America in all BLACK and/or WHITE communities. Why? Because RACISM and RELIGIOUS BIGOTRY in any "WESTERN [European and European-American] CIVILIZATION" are part and parcel of its entire fabric. Not a single person, irrespective of RELIGIOUS, RACIAL, NATIONAL, SEX, etc. designation, can escape it.

Going back to the main direction of our "safari" we find that Howard M. Brotz took a similar position on the "BLACK-WHITE CONFRONTATION" issue when he too joined-in to dispel the idea of the African-American "JEWS" kosher status, as such being a kind of a Shlomo Katz in his own book he gave the following title--THE BLACK JEWS OF HARLEM: NEGRO NATIONALISM AND THE DILEMMAS OF NEGRO LEADERSHIP, Schocken Books, New York, 1970. Thus on page viii, under "Acknowledgment," he ended with the following impudent comment:

> "To this, however, I would say to him that whenever I use the term Negro it is almost, if not quite, what he means by Ethiopian Hebrew."

The "HIM" to whom Katz referred was no other than the late Honourable Rabbi Wentworth B. Matthew of the Commandment Keepers Congregation of Ethiopian Hebrews in Harlem, New York City, New York. But in other words, what he was also saying is; if I told any WHITE man that my name is "YOSEF" and he feels it should have been "JOHN," then I have to accept YOSEF and JOHN to be synonymous.[2] Yet, on the other side of the coin; if I called any Jewish and/or Christian WHITE man "ABRAHAM" and his name is instead "MOSES " he has the right to ignore anything I said, and ABRAHAM and MOSES will never become synonymous with each other. The similarity in these two examples is in every sense equal to the word "NEGRO" as a name for AFRICAN-[Black]-AMERICANS who rejected this term which their ancestors' European slavemasters attached to them. It is equally the reason why the so-called "American Negro" or"Colored American" is a "MOOR" in Spain, "CARTHAGENIAN" in Morocco, "HOTTENTOT" and/or "BUSHMAN" in South Africa's racist [for Whites only] so-called

1. A catch-phrase. But what color is "swarthy"? This is another typical example "biblical racism."
2. African-American are changing their European slavemasters' names for their Arab slavemasters.

"Republic," "BANTU" in most of Central and Southern Africa [from East to West Coast], "NILOT" along the Egyptian, Sudanese and Ethiopian extension of the Nile River valleys, and "HAMITIC" or "NEGROID-CAUCASIAN-SEMITIC" [and whatever else] in North and Northeast Africa, etc. according to the so-called modern "WHITE AFRICANISTS" who wrote most of the books presently being used in most of the so-called "AFRICAN" and/or "BLACK STUDIES" curriculums throughout "NEGRO [colored], WHITE" and/or "NEGRO-WHITE" institutions of learning [religious and secular] in the United States of America.

Commenting further on pages 11 and 12 in his book Brotz wrote the following about one of the best known and best loved AFRICAN HEBREWS of the Ethiopian Hebrew Community of Harlem, New York City, New York during the 1920's and 1930's, of whom he had to have met solely upon hearsay or written propaganda; as Rabbi Ford left the USA for Ethiopia in the 1930's:[1]

> Perhaps the most interesting and important of all these early figures was a man named Arnold Ford, whose origins and ultimate destiny are shrouded in the usual obscurity that attends new prophets. The testimony of those who knew him personally is that he was a man of unusual intelligence. It is certain that he studied Hebrew with some immigrant teacher and was a key link in transmitting whatever approximations there are to Talmudic Judaism in the practices of these sects. Like many of the Black Jews, he was attracted to the "Back to Africa" movement (see Chapter IV, pp. 99-104) of Marcus Garvey which had such a spectacular rise during the early twenties. He was the musical director of Liberty Hall, the headquarters of the Garvey movement in New York. Garveyism did not coincide exactly with his own outlook, for Garvey rejected his counsel to adopt Judaism as the Negro's religion. Nonetheless, in its militancy, its glorification of blackness, its elevation of Africa as the source of all civilization, Garveyism articulated much of what these people were thinking and seeking; and when the Garvey movement collapsed, the nationalistic impulse beneath it survived in these religious sects. Legend or hearsay has it that Ford, tiring of Judaism, emigrated in the early thirties to Africa where he became a Muslim and where he subsequently died. As this was in the midst of the depression and passage money would be rather scarce, it is equally possible and even more plausible that he emigrated not to Africa but to Detroit, and that the W. Fard, Ford, or Farrad who founded the Islamic cult in that city and Arnold Ford were one and the same.[16] This, of course, can be only speculative.

1. Quite a goodly number of African-Americans left the U.S.A. during said period for other lands - "Africa."

Brotz "...speculative..." genius must be treated as purposely misleading to discredit Rabbi Ford.

> In any event, with the disappearance of Ford from the, New York scene, the mantle has fallen and remains to the present day on the shoulders of Wentworth A. Matthew, who is the vocal and most charming leader of Harlem's largest Black Jewish congregation. This is the Commandment Keepers Congregation of the Living God or, as they often refer to themselves from the name of their lodge, the Royal Order of Ethiopian Hebrews, the Sons and Daughters of Culture, Inc. The nucleus of Matthew's group has been, like Garvey himself, West Indian. West Indians who had enjoyed greater freedom and independence tended to look down upon the Southern Negro, at least until fairly recently, as servile and lacking in reserve, dignity, and self-control. Whenever Matthew uses the term "Negro,"[1] which he always pronounces in a derisive manner, or "the colored people in this country," as a way of distinguishing themselves from Negroes, he evokes this regional distinction.

Of course Brotz had to fan the fire of the good old Napoleonic technique of "divide and conquer" when he found it necessary to insert his own bit of RACISM with regards to the open rift between the so-called "WEST INDIANS" and "AMERICAN NEGROES," which I have carefully underlined. But Brotz carefully forgot that in the same "UNIVERSAL NEGRO IMPROVEMENT ASSOCIATION [U.N.I.A.]" founded by the late Honourable Marcus Moziah Garvey[2] there were many top-ranking positions in the executive arm of the organization held by officers who were African-Americans; whereas, not a single African-Caribbean ["West Indian"] held any position as an officer in the "NIAGRA MOVEMENT" [or National Association for the Advancement of Colored People - N.A.A.C.P. which it later on became] as constituted by the two WHITE JEWS - Joel and Arthur Spingarm - who established it for their good COLORED PEOPLE 'most of whom by 1920 C.E. and up to this present day became the main resisters against "BLACK ZIONISM" and/or "PAN-AFRICANISM" - the so-called "BACK TO AFRICA MOVEMENT" of the 1920's to the present time; the movement from which the TRI-COLOR FLAG OF AFRICA with its RED, BLACK and GREEN colors, was born, the FLAG that is presently called "THE AFRICAN LIBERATION FLAG" by young African-Americans who believed that the "New Left Black Militants" brought it about.[2] He conveniently forgot that Mr. Garvey,[3] like all of the other Africans, African-Americans,

1. Brotz, like so many other White Jewish "authorities on the Negro," became a God too! Why?
2. See Amy Jacques Garvey [ed.], PHILOSOPHY AND OPINIONS OF MARCUS GARVEY, London, 1924, Volumes I and II for further details.
3. Born at Saint Anne's Bay, Jamaica, British "West Indies" he became a fighter for his fellow Africans everywhere, no less than Theodore Hertzl for European Jews, et al.

African-Caribbeans, African-Europeans and whatever other African People there were/are knew that the origin of the term "NEGRO" had no truly historical background beyond the sixteenth [16th] or seventeenth [17th] century C.E., at which time the Portuguese and other European pirates, "Christian missionaries," slavers and plain old colonialist so-called "entrepreneurs" renamed a section of the former Ghana, Mele [Mali] and Songhai [Songhay] kingdoms and empires of West Alkebu-lan [Africa]..."NEGROLAND."[1] But maybe Brotz expected that African People should equally call themselves "IVORY COASTERS" and "SLAVE COASTERS" because his European and European-American [Jewish, Christian, Atheist, etc.] forefathers renamed sections of "West Africa" such labels as "IVORY COAST" and "SLAVE COAST." Thus it is that this tragedy reflects greatest in the fact that the late Honourable Marcus Moziah Garvey could not convince the membership and most of the official staff of the U.N.I.A. that the term "NEGRO" and/or "COLORED" was an insult to themselves, as their ancestors' slavemasters brainwashing of them had already received its basic goal - the DE-AFRICANIZATION of the Africans and the CREATION of the concepts of CULTURAL GENOCIDE that made the present descendants of the Africans ['slaves'] develop an internalized "HATRED" that now consumes their mental state of being more than one hundred and seventeen [117] years following their so-called "EMANCIPATION" from the enslavement their ancestors suffered under the "PHARAOHS" [presidents] of European-America and European-Great Britain. All of this we can best observe in the "Negroes" and "Colored Folks'" LILY-WHITE HEAVEN and LILY-WHITE HOLY FAMILY demonstrated and advertised in their churches of one hundred [100 $^{0}/_{0}$] percent all JET BLACK COMMUNITIES their benefactors gave the name "NEGRO GHETTOS" and/or "INNER CITIES," etc.

On the rear cover of Katz's book - NEGRO AND JEW - , etc. - the following appears:

In
NEGRO AND JEW
An Encounter in America

27

prominent Negro and Jewish commentators
speak out on one of the most troubling issues of our time:

---

1. See Y. ben-Jochannan's BLACK MAN OF THE NILE AND HIS FAMILY, pages 24 and 34 for maps and details relative to this aspect of African-American historical heritage; also Y. ben-Jochannan's AFRICA: MOTHER OF "WESTERN CIVILIZATION," Alkebu-lan Books Associates, New York, 1971, pages 690 - 691 for other maps and details with respect to the intercourse that existed between Northwestern and Western Alkebu-lan during said period. Richard B. Moore, The Name Negro, Its Origin And Evil Use, New York, 1961 must be added.

the existence of black anti-Semitism in American life.

They are:

Joel Carmichael	Paul Jacobs
Arthur A. Cohen	Horace M. Kallen
Jacob Cohen	C. Eric Lincoln
Lucy S. Dawidowicz	Will Maslow
Howard Fast	Floyd B. McKissick
Myron M. Fenster	Aryeh Neier
Leslie A. Fiedler	Maurice Samuel
Roland B. Gittelsohn	Steven S. Schwarzschild
Jacob Glatstein	Ben B. Seligman
B. Z. Goldberg	William Stringfellow
Harry Golden	Marie Syrkin
Ben Halpern	Gus Tyler
Arthur A. Hertzberg	Herbert Weiner

Jacob J. Weinstein

Since there is no label to each of the above names that would identify the carefully selected "NEGRO COMMENTATORS" from the "JEWISH COMMENTATORS;" and since it is that the so-called "NEGRO" has been forced to accept his [or her] ancestors' slavemasters' JEWISH, CHRISTIAN and MOSLEM "NAMES" and other "IDENTIFICATIONS" as God-given nomenclatures; it is obvious that at least twenty-one [21] of the twenty-seven [27] so-called "COMMENTATORS," according to the appearance of names, are "WHITE JEWS." It would have been quite adequate to have heard from many more so-called "NEGROES" - at least half of the total - than only six [6], natural integrationists [possibly "Christians"] - as C. Eric Lincoln and Floyd B. McKissick, the latter having been the leader of an organization - THE CONGRESS OF RACIAL EQUALITY [C.O.R.E.] - once dedicated to "INTEGRATING THE RACES" throughout the United States of America, which almost became defunct when its predominately WHITE JEWISH underwriters refused to further fund its operations because its young "BLACK POWER" advocates under the leadership of Roy Innis decided to make it truly representative of the aspirations of its predominantly so-called "NEGRO MEMBERSHIP." Certainly at least one [1] so-called "NEGRO [Black] JEW" could have been found to speak of "WHITE [Semitic] JEWISH ANTI-NEGROISM [Blackism]."But, are we to understand that neo-"SEMITISM" is racial instead of linguistic and/or cultural? Is it not true that one can look like a so-called "NEGRO" and equally be so-called "SEMITIC?" And, that one can look like a so-called "SWEDISH BLONDE" and equally be a so-called "SEMITE"? There are names identifiable as "JEWISH;" but which ones are identifiable as "NEGRO" and/or "COLORED" in the above list? This is one of the points of which BLACKS who are proud of their AFRI-

1. Blacks carry the names of their Christian, Jewish, Moslem, etc. slavemasters everywhere.

CAN HERITAGE try to make WHITE so-called "LIBERALS" and "CONSERVATIVES" understand about the word "NEGRO" and/or "COLORED," but of which they have refused to hear. Here too we have another example of the "TOKEN NIGGER AT THE DOOR" representing the entire African-[BLACK]-American community.

How could the above disprove the Hebrew origin of the BLACK JEWS like this author's grand-uncle - the late Professor Tamrat Emmanuel - who, according to Professor Wolf Leslau's book - FALASHA ANTHOLOGY: THE BLACK JEWS OF ETHIOPIA, page x, was

"a man of noble character and one of the finest scholars in Ethiopia?"

Yet, Professor Tamrat Emmanuel in the middle of the "HARLEMS" of the United States of America could not be separated from any "AFRICAN-AMERICAN JEW" and/or "BLACK" Christian, Black Moslem [Muslim], etc., as he too would have been identified as a "NEGRO" by any White Jew, White Christian, White Moslem, etc. But is it not equally true that many thousands of WHITE JEWS with their KINKY HAIR, THICK LIPS, BROAD NOSES and "SWARTHY" SKIN would be labeled "NEGRO" and/or "COLORED" if they were residents of any of the so-called "NEGRO GHETTOS" throughout the United States of America, and even among the Agaw [Falasha] in Ethiopia, East Alkebu-lan and the State of Israel, West Asia see pages 11 - 16?

[CO-RELIGIONISTS IN ONE GOD]: In Prophet Elijah Muhammad's book - MESSAGE TO THE BLACKMAN IN AMERICA, Muhammad's Temple No. 2, Chicago, Illinois - he deals with the basic points that turned him around from Judaeo-Christianity to "AL'LAH" and Judaeo/White Christian - "ISLAM." Although this author is knowledgable of Islam, equally as I am with Judaism and Judaeo-Christianity, Yorubaism, Bhuddism, etc., and cannot accept either as my salvation to the human problems that confront me, I can still empathize with the "NATION OF ISLAM" [so-called "Black Muslim"] in the United States of America from Prophet Elijah [Poole] Muhammed's position in the following on page 27 of his book.

> How many non-Muslims will we find who do not believe in God as being One God? Regardless of the trinity belief preached by the Christians, they (the Christians) claim and agree that Allah (God) is One God. They make fools of themselves when they reject Islam and the Muslims five principles of belief: One God, His Prophets, His Books, the Resurrection, The Judgment. How, then, did they (the Christians) go astray believing in three Gods? Nevertheless, they make one of the three the Father of the other two—and these remaining two the equal of the Father.
>
> The so-called Negroes have been led into the gravest of errors in the knowledge of God (Allah) and the true religion (Islam) by their white slave-masters. They (the so-called Negroes) have been robbed more than any other people on the planet Earth. If they will only read and listen to the simplest of truths of which I write and speak have three essentials in it: power, light and life.

I have the same type of empathy and conviction about the following in Administrator and Minister Albert B. Cleage, Jr's. book - BLACK CHRISTIAN NATIONALISM: NEW DIRECTIONS FOR THE BLACK CHURCH, William Morrow and Company, Inc., New York, 1972, page xii:[1]

> Black people have been excluded from real participation in American society by firmly entrenched white institutional racism. Even so, we have been corrupted by an individualistic and materialistic white value system because we have tried to identify. But white hatred and hostility have saved us. White people would not let us in when we demanded integration so, in a sense, we have preserved our soul. A unique Black experience makes us different from white people. The separateness which the white man has forced on us is now our basic hope for the future. On the one hand it has preserved our African heritage, and on the other it has provided a basis for the power which is essential to our survival. Black Christian Nationalism seeks to build upon this black separateness.

What I am saying in my recognition of these two noted African-Americans' dialouge with respect to the reason that LED them to their conclusion to become whatever they are religiously, is that the conduct of their fellow "AMERICAN CITIZENS" - [White] Jews, Christians, Moslems, Ethical Culturists, Atheists, Communists, Socialists, etc. - racist "ANTI-NEGRO" and/or "ANTI-BLACK" conduct forced them to develop their own "RACIAL" dimensions in RELIGION, which is of course counter RELIGIOUS only if the "CHOSEN PEOPLE'S" racist myth and bigoted allegory were not a part of every RELIGION known to mankind in every "Western Civilization" [High-Culture] today.

The BLACK [or so-called "Negro"] JEW is driven to reject his WHITE JEWISH fellow co-religionists on the same basis, thus the following from Rabbi Hailu Paris' writings under the heading "Africa And The Bible" - in Albert B. Cleage, Jr's book - BLACK CHRISTIAN NATIONALISM: NEW DIRECTIONS FOR THE BLACK CHURCH, page 265:

> In their universal religion all Africans believed in the one God, the Great Ancestor or the Eternal Being of the universe. Africans of today who have not been disturbed by the religions of Judaism, Christianity, or Islam still worship the one great God and still have many deities to worship and to ceremonize over. We would like to show the connection between that which many people think is Egyptian or Hebraic religion and its African antecedents.

1. He changed his name to Jeramogi Agyemeon; later, even his religious title to "Patriarch."
2. Your author was once loosely associated with him; not believing he would adopt the "White Bible" [the King James Version of the European Sacred Scriptures from 1611 C.E./A.D., etc.

> The Hebrews had gotten much of their history, custom, and religion—one may say even their god—from the ancient Egyptians. In predynastic Egypt we see that the Egyptians had certain family clans and tribes that had their own emblem, a beast or bird whose unique powers were accredited to the social unit. Such designations as "the lion people," "the hippo people," and "the harpoon people" were properly used to identify these units. It appears that at least some of these emblems were carried over from an earlier hunting tradition whereby sympathetic magic—animal qualities of strength, speed, and cunning—was bestowed on the hunter. When agriculture became the dominant pursuit of most of the Egyptian people, these emblems were given more functional qualities, familiar to history in such forms as Annibus, the jackal-headed god of embalming; Sikmet, the warlike, lioness goddess; Ophof, the ibis-headed god of wisdom. From this we can see a similarity in the Old Testament in that the ancient Israelites, when they came into the land of Canaan and made it the land of Israel, divided their tribes into twelve units, or peoples, or clans, and those twelve units or clans were designated also by an emblem and a symbol.

What Rabbi Paris did not say is that the "EGYPTIANS" reached their zenith upon the teachings they received from their fellow African ancestors and contemporaries from Central and Southern Alkebu-lan. Yet, he said enough to offset the ANTI-BLACK [African] propaganda from the so-called 'noted European and European-American Judaeo-Christian and Jewish scholars, theologians, missionaries and clergymen' who constantly write from their racist and religiously bigoted theories of PURE WHITENESS with respect to the origin and development of "JUDAISM, CHRISTIANITY" and "JUDAEO-CHRISTIANITY." Joel A. Rogers added to Rabbi Paris' contention with the following from his book - SEX AND RACE, Helga Rogers, New York, 1954, Volume III, page 94:

> Dr. Hans Guenther in his "Rassenkunde des Judischen Volkes," does the same. His work is illustrated with portraits of Negroid Jews of Europe and elsewhere. As was already said he compares a portrait of Abraham Plattje, a Hottentot, with that of Benjamin Disraeli, Jewish Prime Minister of England.[8] The resemblance is striking. Guenther, it is said, did this to depreciate the Jew but since we do not concede that Negro ancestry is a disgrace we cannot consider that Guenther's alleged aim has been achieved.
>
> Count Adam Gurowski of Poland, who visited the United States in 1857, said similarly, "Numbers of Jews have the greatest resemblance to the American mulattoes. Sallow carnation complexion, thick lips, crisped black hair. Of all the Jewish population scattered over the globe one-fourth dwells in Poland. I am, therefore, well acquainted with their features. On my arrival in this country (The United States) I took every light-colored mulatto for a Jew."[9]

Measurements of the skulls of Polish Jews in Whitechapel, London, revealed that about 30 per cent of them were Negroid.[10]

The Negro strain is apparent among a considerable number of American Jews. Some Jewish women go to Negro hair-dressing parlors to have their hair straightened. The Island of Jamaica has a considerable number of mulatto Jews, also.

[8] pp. 90-95, 99-115, 143-148. Munich, 1930.
[9] America and Europe, p. 177. N. Y., 1857.
[10] Man, Vols. 5-6. No. 55, p. 93.

Additional Bibliography:
Williams, J. J. Hebrewisms of West Africa. N. Y., 1930.
Wheless, J. Is it God's Word? N. Y., 1926.
Wheless, J. Forgery in Christianity. N. Y., 1930.
Scribner's Maga Apr., May, June, July, 1929, for West African Jews. Additional data and sources in Rogers, J. A. Nature Knows No Color Line. pp. 122, 130, 140-142.

[JEWISH RACE ?]: Obviously the White Jews - including Karl Marx and Friederich Engels - of Europe, until Adolph Hitler's Nazis of the German Republic met them with the worse form of bestiality in Europe's history, were in every sense the same in thinking towards AFRICAN PEOPLE like all of the other Germans of the Christian Religion. Their contemporaries within the United States of America, who have never suffered [for the most part] any of the bestiality of their fellow European Jews, or even like the present African Jews with whom they live, nevertheless think and act like the vast majority of their fellow WHITE AMERICANS who are Christians, Moslems, Atheists, etc. We can say that all of this is similar to any woman's shocking pains she suffers in delivering her offspring, which she quickly forgets when her own little one is finally born. The corollary is paraphrased in the following African saying:

> "The rejected dog that finally gets past the door quickly pulls in its tail after entering the house; thus it very quickly identify itself with its owner as a full partner of the residence; biting everyone."

Unfortunately the so-called "NEGRO JEW" can neither "pull in" his [or her] "tail," nor change his [or her] color. Even if he [or she] becomes "JOHN" from "JONAS," or even "BLACK" from "SCHWARTZ," the so-called "NEGRO [Black] JEW" will remain equally as "BLACK" as all of his [or her] fellow BLACK Muslim [Moslem], Christian, Yoruba, Mormon, Christian Holiness, Jehovah Witness, Christian Scientist, Ethical Culturist, etc. But WHITE JEWS in the City of Bostom were/are able to become "WALKER" from "WALINSKY," in Mississippi "GREEN" from "GREENBERG," and melt into the WHITE ANGLO-SAXON PROTESTANT CHRISTIAN and/or ROMAN CATHOLIC populations in order to move the rest of their numbers from the squalor of their so-called "NEGRO GHETTOS" of the "Americas."[1]

Maybe the "Christian Race, Moslem Race, Protestant Race, Roman Catholic Race," and all of the other kinds of RELIGIOUS RACE one hears so much about lately, will become realities as is the so-called "JEWISH RACE;" then will the so-called Voodoo Race, Witch-

1. The basic insecurity of White Jews having to live as "non-Caucasian" makes many succumb to the pressures of "White Racism" against anyone African/Black to maintain their White posture.

craft Race and Black Magic Race become synonymous with the other so-called "Negro Race." But sad it is that even a "RELIGIOUS RACE" the so-called "Negroes" and "Colored People" can not accept if there is not a single "WHITE" Christian or Jew involve. Why? Because Africans reduced to "NEGROES" and/or "COLORED FOLKS" cannot survive in anything in which they are the sole participants and owners; at least this is what most of them believe. They are the only people I am aware of in the world today who accept being JOBBERS, but never think of being owners of the JOBS that need the JOBBERS. The BLACK JEWS find themselves locked-up in the same mental illness, and as such are always seeking handouts and endorsement in everything they do from their co-religionist "WHITE JEWS." This was the fate of the now defunct "Organization Hazaad Harishon" that deserted the Black Hebrew Community in Harlem and became converted "NEGRO JEWS" to White [Semitic] Talmudic Judaism in hopes of receiving total acceptance with charity from European-American JEWS that ignored all of their older generations. Yet this same so-called "NEGRO JEWISH COMMUNITY" acted as a kind of buffer between the greater BLACK COMMUNITY and the predominantly WHITE JEWISH-controlled Teachers Union during the "COMMUNITY CONTROL" confrontation between BLACKS and WHITES of the late 1960's C.E. in the City of New York, particularly at the height of the "BLACK POWER MOVEMENT" confrontation with the Jewish WHITE POWER MOVEMENTS like the so-called "JEWISH DEFENSE LEAGUE" and other Zionist cohorts.

Professor George E. Simmonds of Malcolm-King College, Harlem, New York City, New York pointed out the following in the book he co-authored with myself - THE BLACK MAN'S NORTH AND EAST AFRICA, Alkebu-lan Books Associates, New York, 1971, page 81:

> Since Dr. Louis S.B. Leakey's finding of Zinjanthropus boisie, there have been other datings of man-like creatures found in East Africa. Findings have taken place in such countries as Ethiopia, one dated by the University of Chicago to be ca. 4,000,000 years old; and in Kenya, one dated by Harvard University to ca. 5,000,000 years old. These two finds were published in the New York Times, the first one on May 1, 1969; the latter on February 19, 1971.[1]
>
> Here we are able to see Africa as the mother of mankind and Queen of the earth.[2] Not only did AFRICA give birth to the human family, she also gave the world an over abundance of natural resources unmatched anywhere.
>
> Secondly: AFRICA gave the sons who "NAMED THE HEAVENLY BODIES. Great African astrologers also NAMED THE SUN, MOON, STARS, and PLANETS..." says Lucian [one of Europe's "greatest" ancient writers]. Thus, Count C.F. Volney of France in 1791 wrote in his book, THE RUINS:[3]
>
> " There a people, now forgotten, discovered, while others

1. See example on p. 383 of this Volume for positive proof. Note "Europeanization" of the African fossil-man/woman, etc.
2. See references to Goddess Hathor, the very first Queen of the Earth, etc. in history.
3. See Count C. F. Volney's Ruin Of Empire, London, 1792, 1901, etc., p xvii, etc., etc., etc.

> were yet barbarians, the elements of the arts and sciences. A race of men now rejected from society for their sable skin and frizzled hair, founded on the study of the laws of nature, those civil and religious systems which still govern the universe.

All of these "THINGS" the Africans accomplished while the Europeans [Volney's ancestors] and others were yet "barbarians." But we are not taught any of these "THINGS" in school; it is always the reverse [or opposite] according to our instructors of today, in order to maintain the same old stereotype myths and teachings of "the black man's racial and cultural inferiority to the white man."

It is very sad, however, that "TALMUDIC [Rabbinic] JUDAISM" all over the United States of America has been blinded to everything stated by Professor Simmonds above, and even by Count C.F. Volney whom he quoted. Yet Volney's"...FRIZZLED HAIR..." Africans were/are no different than the Agaw or Kayla [so-called Falasha Jews] shown in Harvey Gilroy's article in THE NEW YORK TIMES, Friday, March 4, 1955, an extract of which appears on the following page 367. The entire analysis related to this picture and story is given on page 68 of my book - BLACK MAN OF THE NILE AND HIS FAMILY - I mentioned before in this later work. On the following page -367- the Agaw at the top with his WHITE JEWISH teacher in the State of Israel is supposedly a "DIFFERENT TYPE OF JEW THAN THE BLACK JEWS" [so-called "Negro Jews"] at the bottom of the page - the teacher and her student in Harlem, New York City, New York. This is part of the story of the so-called dilemma of "NEGRO ANTI-SEMITISM" and "THE ORIGIN OF THE BLACK JEWS IN THE AMERICAS." And, certainly it dictates that Shlomo Katz and his so-called "27 PROMINENT NEGRO AND JEWISH COMMENTATORS" who "SPEAK OUT ON ONE OF THE MOST TROUBLING ISSUES OF OUR TIME: THE EXISTENCE OF BLACK ANTI-SEMITISM IN AMERICAN LIFE" needed to examine these pictures, and even go to the site where the teachings were taking place, before they wrote their own ANTI-BLACK ["Negro"] propaganda which equally discriminated against "BLACK SEMITES" - a sort of "WHITE SEMITIC ANTI-BLACK SEMITISM." Strange, is it not? But maybe my citing these examples would qualify me as an "ARCH ANTI-SEMITE," etc.

Note that the BLACK JEW of Ethiopia became a "...DARK-SKINNED JEWISH YOUTH..." in the State of Israel; but the BLACK JEW in the Harlems of the United States of America became a"...NEGRO JEWISH YOUTH..." in the "NEGRO GHETTO;" strange, is it not? The following pictures on the next two pages are in themselves prima facie evidence that RACISM is at the bottom of the BLACK-WHITE JEWISH CONFRONTATION that permeated the need for the so-called "NEGRO ANTI-SEMITISM" in the face of "JEWISH ANTI-NEGROISM." Or, are we to ignore the fact that there is a mark difference between standards for Black and

White JEWS all over the world, the State of Israel's "PROMISED LAND" not excluded? Just only imagine that the "JEWS" at the bottom are "NEGROES;" not a single one at the top! Why so?

THE NEW YORK TIMES, FRIDAY, MARCH 4, 1955.

Falasha Jews From Ethiopia Studying in Israel

Their Tribe Practices Judaism According to Law of Moses

By HARRY GILROY
Special to The New York Times.

KFAR BATYA, Israel, Feb. 25 —Twelve young Falasha Jews, who might be taken as living proof of the legend that today's Ethiopians descend from Solomon and the Queen of Sheba, are studying at this children's village.

They come from a tribe, numbering 50,000, scattered over Ethiopia. The tribe is called Falasha, which in the Amharic tongue means "stranger." Its members practice Judaism according to the law of Moses, but have no tradition about later feasts such as Hanukkah and Purim.

The youngsters are here for two years of training. They are in a beautiful farm school adjoining Raanana on the Sharon plain—established and operated by the Women's Mizrachi Organization of America. Hadassah, the American Women Zionists, is aiding the project through Youth Aliyah, to which it contributes.

Isazah Adomic, 16-year-old leader of Falasha youngsters studying at Kfar Batya in Israel, serves Malka Avraham. Another Falasha student and an Israeli friend await their turns.

The Agaw [Falashas] existed before Solomon and Sheba, during their reign, and following their death to the present day. "Moses married the daughter of the High-Priest of Ethiopia - an Ethiopian woman;" all of this in the teaching and tradition of Cush.

At prayer: Members of the choir, wearing prayer shawls, await signal. Other [Negro] Jewish communities are set up in Philadelphia, Brooklyn, Pittsburgh, Chicago and Youngstown, Ohio.

ONLY THE BLACK JEWS MUST "RECONVERT TO JUDAISM" ?

Hebrew is official language of Israel and youngsters learn language at school. Here dark-skinned Jewish youth gets instruction in writing on the blackboard.

ONE AFRICAN, THE OTHER EUROPEAN
BLACK JEW and WHITE JEWISH TEACHER in ISRAEL

Is it not strange that "BLACK" became "DARK-SKINNED"[1] unlike "BLACK" as "NEGRO" below? But, is the teacher a 'LIGHT-SKINNED' or 'WHITE SEMITIC CAUCASIAN ?'
[See Channel 4, WNBC's Monitor: The Black Jews Of Ethiopia, 6/4/83, 10:00 PM]

Alphabet lessons. Children of the Commandment Keepers Congregation [are] taught Hebrew.

A "DARK-SKINNED JEWISH YOUTH" is a "NEGRO JEWISH YOUTH" in Harlem; quite unlike his African fellow "BLACK JEW" above. Strange, is it not? Maybe!

If the Brotz's, Katz's, Leslaus and other White Jews who are protesting their so-called... dilemma of "NEGRO ANTI-SEMITISM" cannot understand the basic cause for same after having examining the above pictures and comments; then, they will have to ask the question and also deal with the so-called "PROBLEM" for centuries yet to come and pass. Truth is "GOD."

1. Dr. M.D.W. Jeffries perpetuated the "dark-skinned Caucasian" syndrome. See the first chapters of Y. ben-Jochannan's Black Man Of The Nile And His Family, 1972 and 1981 editions

[NEW RELIGIOUS FRONTIER]: The major error the Black Rabbis in the United States of America continue making is the same for Black Ministers, except for a very few like Walimu Jaramogi Agyeman [formerly Reverend Albert A. Cleage, Jr.] and his BLACK CHRISTIAN NATIONALIST [B.C.N.] movement and/or the late Prophet Elijah Mohammad [once Elijah Poole] and his NATION OF ISLAM [the so-called "Black Muslims"] were trying to make their ancestors' slavemasters and slavemistresses' descendants grant them KOSHER APPROVAL in their own religiousity. And in so doing they have adapted their own God-Head's AUTHORITY to suit their own Black Image, Color and Race as is common among the White Clergy. But Judaism's God-Head still remains a LILY-WHITE SPIRIT named "YWH [Jehovah]," even among the Black Jews; thus without "IMAGE" and "RACE." Why? Because Black Jews are still dominated mentally by the White-Caucasian-Semitic versions of the FIVE BOOKS OF MOSES they always purchase from White Jewish publishing houses with the purest Lily-White God-inspired Sacred Scribes, not one of which has ever hired a single Black Jew on its editorial staff to revise a single word in any of its versions of the so-called "FIVE BOOKS OF MOSES [HOLY TORAH, PENTATEUCH, OLD TESTAMENT]. Thus the "MOSES" in Black synagogues presented by Jewish artists and sculptors is as LILY-WHITE and GOLDEN HAIR as their Christian contemporaries' LILY-WHITE "JESUS" and the "HOLY FAMILY" - Joseph and Mary, and even the animals in the manger with snow on the roof in the middle of the one hundred and ten [110] degrees heat in the Israelis Asian desert, all of which we find in most of the religious institutions of all of the Black Communities throughout the entire so-called Western World and/or "Western Civilization."

[MONEY; THE ROOT OF EVIL]: No one in his or her right mind that is cognizant of the true structure of the BLACK [Ethiopian] JEWISH COMMUNITY within the United States of America, and the other nations of the Americas, is not aware of the main struggle for the thrust Black Rabbis have forstered in creating their hopes for an amalgamation with their White co-religionist clergymen. It is plainly and simply "MONEY" that is the main stumbling block on either side of the BLACK-WHITE JEWISH amalgamation issue. Both sides approach the issue from the point of how much I will gain, or how much I will loose, financially. Of course this will be vehemiently denied by both sides. And, we are bound to hear that their rejection of either's proposal is based upon the -

"SACRED SCRIPTURES PASSED DOWN TO THE HOLY PROPHETS." [1]

But this is the same reason why the Black Baptist Christian Ministers were called to task by certain so-called "Black Left Militants" to be "... TARRED AND FEATHERED...." For any

1. Designated as such by Jewish scribes for a Jewish Theocracy of which they were principals. No other people were obligated to this if they so desired not to adhere to any aspect of it.

BLACK CLERGY [male or female] is like a MINOR GOD and/or GODDESS in his and or her church, and among his or her congregation owing or beholding to no one above his or her Board of [Holy and Sacred] Trustees which is for the most part only ceremonial. Most of the time he is not even beholding to such a ceremonial body as a Board of Trustees. The Black Rabbi is equally set in his synagogue amongst his BLACK congregation. Yet he hungers for the day when he will be accepted as an equal among his WHITE co-religionists in their LILY-WHITE [Semitic-Caucasian] RABBINICAL ASSEMBLIES; anyone of them. Thus he is often willing to change from "EXTREME ORTHODOX" to "ULTRA REFORM" out of desperation for acceptance into European and/or European-American TALMUDIC [Rabbinical] JUDAISM. But Black Rabbis continue claiming to be like their original source - their AGAW [Beta Isra'el, Falasha, etc.] ancestors of Ethiopia, East Alkebu-lan [Africa]; though they have utterly failed to follow Ethiopian TORAHDIC TRADITIONS like "ANIMAL SACRIFICE" on Yum Kippur, Rosh Hashanah and Pesach - the most sacred Hebrew [Jewish] HIGH HOLY DAYS of the Old Hebrew Calendar, all of which most of the rabbis and prophets of TALMUDIC JUDAISM condemned.

[ACCOMMODATION or CAPITULATION?]: By adopting all of the "FEAST DAYS" - such as "CHANUKAH" [Feast Of Lights], which have been experienced by the ancestors of certain other JEWS that were not among the AGAW, KYLA, YEMENITES, COCHIM, KARAITES, etc., and only practised by European and European-American WHITE JEWS, the BLACK JEWS in the United States of America definitely violated their fellow AFRICAN JEWS of the past and of the present most sacred bond of unity since the EXODUS and the following DESTRUCTION OF THE FIRST TEMPLE IN JERUSALEM. Thus they have become followers of European and European-American TALMUDIC [Rabbinical] JUDAISM that relates mainly from the DESTRUCTION OF THE SECOND TEMPLE IN JERUSALEM, but more likely the so-called THIRD TEMPLE.[1] In so doing they have allowed their WHITE co-religionists to believe that BLACK Jews depend upon them for everything JUDAIC; even for their minor "HOLY DAYS" and so-called "RABBINICAL" and "TALMUDIC" scholars who constantly create NEW PENTATEUCHS.

The most serious error Black Jews in the Americas made is their acceptance of the White Jews' RABBINICAL TALMUD[2] as the STANDARD VERSION of the PENTATEUCH [Holy Torah, Five Books of Moses, Old Testament, etc.]. This is contrary to the teachings and traditions of TORAHDIC theosophy, theology and philosophy of which the Agaw follow. For example; the FIVE BOOKS OF MOSES [Pentateuch, Holy Torah, Old Testament] teach that:

"YOU SHALL NOT BOIL THE MEAT IN ITS MOTHER'S MILK."

But, the European and European-American RABBINICAL TALMUD expanded the above to read:

1. The argument continues on the amount of temples destroyed by the conquerors of Palestine.
2. The current "Talmud" in use is that written by Moses ben-Maimonides [Egyptian] in Spain.

"YOU SHALL NOT EAT MEAT WITH MILK, NOR MIX THEM ON THE SAME DISH."

The Agaw have never accepted their European and European-American co-religionists' RABBINICAL TALMUD as the replacement of the HOLY TORAH [Pentateuch or Five Books Of Moses] from their beginning with their fellow biblical Hebrews until this very day, and give no reason to believe that they will anytime soon in the future. They continue in spite of the inhuman treatment and pressure brought to bear upon them by psuedo European and European-American Jewish missionary organizations; even like HADASSAH, which has been most active in sending Agaw boys and girls to the State of Israel for their 'European-Americanized' VERSION of Judaeo-Semitic Rabbinical Talmudic Hebrewism commonly used among White Jews of Europe, Great Britain, European-America and the State of Israel in Western Asia [the so-called "Middle East"]. The Agaw boys and girls subjected to this type of Jewish Missionary brainwashing are typical of those shown on pages 367-68 of this Volume. Is it strange that not a single one of their fellow BLACK JEWS of the Harlems of the United States of America was sent by the same Jewish missionaries to the State of Israel for the same type of brainwashing? It should not be if you have lived in any part of the so-called "Western World," particularly among WHITES of any religion within the United States of America. Of course the ancient 'TORAHDIC TRADITIONS OF THE HEBREW RELIGION'[1] practised for thousands of years by the Agaw community in Ethiopia, East Alkebu-lan [Africa] have been deemed to be a kind of "TREF" and/or "UN-KOSHER"[untouchable], even by some of the turn-coat members of the so-called "ETHIOPIAN HEBREWS" in the United States of America that adopted the white TALMUDIC form of JUDAISM a la RABBINICAL STYLE. In otherwords, even the biblical tradition of "ANIMAL SACRIFICE" practised by the Agaw must come to a sudden halt to satisfy the angelic thirst of European, European-American and African-American JEWS; and of course to the satisfaction of the same groupings of angels of the Christian Religion and their other Judaeo-Christian off-shoots, all of whom received SPECIAL COMMUNICATION from the on high that only their VERSION of worshiping the "GREAT I AM - GOD" [Ywh, Jesus, Al'lah] is correct. This type of dictatorship the Agaw will ignore in difference to the Jewish, Christian and Moslem missionaries with their TALMUD, NEW TESTAMENT and HOLY QUR'AN of any and all VERSIONS, even if "NEGRO JEWS" are among the missionaries. For the Agaw cannot accept the Hellenic version of African Philosophy; called "Greek Philosophy" today, nor Arab allegory and European mythology, all of which crept into TALMUDIC JUDAISM for many centuries when European and European-American JEWS were forced to live among other Europeans and Asians of the Judaeo-Christian and Islamic religions. Thus the Agaw [Falasha]

1. The "Talmud" is an attempt to standardize the interpretation of the Holy Torah by Western Jews. The Falashas insist on using the Torah as written - literally word-for-word, etc.

will never visit the grave, nor place a head-stone to mark the resting place of the deceased. They remember their TORAHDIC instruction that commands of them:

"LET THE DEAD BE WITH THE DEAD, AND THE LIVING BE WITH THE LIVING."[1]

Neither will the Agaw worship the heroes and heroines of European and European-American JEWS who adopted European, British and European-American CULTURAL, POLITICAL and ECONOMIC traditions that became what is today called "WESTERN CIVILIZATION" and/or "THE AMERICAN WAY OF LIFE," also "WESTERN DEMOCRACY." For the Agaw's strength lies in the one principle that is most absent from their African-[BLACK]-American Hebrew brothers community in the United States of America, must less in their European-[WHITE]-American brothers community. And this is what they have maintained for thousands of years:

PRIDE IN SELF,

which they have also boosted very much with the same vigorous determination as they refused to succumb to the pressures from Jewish, Christian and Moslem "missionaries," et al.

"AUTHORITY IN SELF."

Their own "Holy and Most Sacred God-Inspired Scribes" wrote, and still write, like the "Holy and Most Sacred God-Inspired Scribes" of the WHITE JEWS of Europe, Great Britain, the Americas [including the Caribbean Islands] and European-Asia [the modern political State of Israel included]; thus unlike the "BLACK JEWS" in the Americas they are independent.

[BLACK JEWISH GHETTO?]: The so-called "Negro Ghetto" is as much Black Jewish as it is Black Christian, Black Moslem [Muslim], Black Yoruba, etc. And all of the Black Synagogues are forced into the same so-called "Negro Ghetto" pattern as the buildings in which the Black Jewish parishoners live.[2] Thus the BLACK JEWS are confronted daily with the same Jewish, Christian, Judaeo-Christian, Atheist WHITE and/or SEMITIC retail merchants, bank representatives, school teachers, landlords, numbersmen, drug pushers and distributors, addicts, loan sharks, pawn brokers and general economic pimps and prostitutes as their fellow African-Americans who are of the Christian, Moslem, Yoruba, Voodoo, etc. religious traditions and/or "way of life." They are equally policed by the same absentee racists and/or grafters who do not spend a single second of extra time in the so-called "Negro Ghetto" beyond their minimun tour of duty daily. And because of all of these maladies BLACK JEWS are as frustrated and foundationless as their fellow AFRICAN-[Black]-AMERICANS of all of the other religions; and even like those who have no religion whatsoever.

1. This philosophical concept should baffle African/Black Americans, who go to extremes in providing elaborate funerals that last at least three to six days duration; sometimes even more.
2. This tern was transferred to African/Black people by White/Jewish sociologists in academia.

[FEARFUL or PASSIVE ?]: Are the so-called "Negro Jews" PASSIVE; or are they FEARFUL of speaking out against their entrapment? This is a critical question which BLACK JEWS are constantly confronted with by their other BLACK-[African]-AMERICANS. As one who once traveled this road; can I not tell the naked truth about this question? Certainly it is nothing else but "FEAR." "FEAR" of whom, or what? "FEAR" of not being approved by OUR WHITE co-religionists for futher financial [charitable] aid and other types of handout.[1] In most cases "FEAR" of failure of not securing OUR first proposal submitted for a grant. Worse of all; the "FEAR" of the word...NO..., when everything WE planned depended upon said handout.

I dealt with this aspect of the BLACK JEWS in Volume I of the three volumes THE BLACK MAN'S RELIGION [African Origins Of The Major "Western Religions: Judaism, Christianity and Islam"], Chapter THREE and FIVE, Alkebu-lan Books Associates, New York, 1970 in detail. A review of these two chapters will prove most beneficial following this Volume; equally an examination of Volume II - The Myth Of Genesis And Exodus, And The Exclusion Of Their African Origin, also Volume III - The Need For A Black Bible. Both Volume II and Volume III were published in February, 1974 C.E. by the same publisher as Volume I. The accompanying volume - Comments And Extracts From The Holy Black Bible - should prove equally as important in furthering your understanding of the role of BLACK [AFRICAN] PEOPLE in the origin and development of Judaism, Christianity, Islam and their predecessor religions.

The "FEAR" complex or syndrome is further exaggerated by the fact that everything most BLACK JEWS in the United States of America must use in OUR religious functions have to be purchased from WHITE JEWS, even all of OUR KOSHER FOOD PRODUCTS needed for OUR own sustenance - almost including the very breath that keeps US alive daily. But, only imagine that I was once caught-up in this web of religious fanaticism as a member of the only so-called "CHOSEN PEOPLE" - the BLACK ONES of course - myth and allegory, racism and bigotry!

[DOUBLE INDEMNITY]: The Black Jews must pay DOUBLE for everything in this "Judaeo-Christian White Caucasian-Semitic Indo-European Aryan" United States of America. First for being "BLACK" and/or "AFRICAN;" and second, for being "JEWISH" and/or forever "NON-ZIONIST." Thus the Black Jews encounter "HELL" from both "WHITE JEWS" and "WHITE CHRISTIANS" alike. And whereas "WHITE JEWS" enter the Judaeo-Christian Anglo-Saxon and Mediterranean Protestant and Roman Catholic WHITE WESTERN WORLD [civilization] with only one strike against them, their BLACK CO-RELIGIONISTS enter with three strikes against them. The so-called "THIRD STRIKE" is having to be rejected by their own so-called CO-RELIGIONIST WHITE JEWS because of their BLACK SKIN, WOOLLY HAIR, BROAD

1. This is the main reason the "responsible Negro leaders" can never challenge White Liberals.

NOSES, THICK LIPS and all of the other aspect of the their physical being; and all of which the so-called WHITE ANGLO-SAXON PROTESTANT and WHITE MEDITERRANEAN ROMAN CATHOLIC "Christians, Atheists," et al., equally abhors.

How, then, could"BLACK JEWS" in good conscience - withstand this form of bedlam without rebelling mentally and physically like all of the other BLACKS of their community? Only because, beside the silence of the BLACK JEWS there is in the background a kind of fiendish desire for punishment and an over-zealous religious devotion to fanaticism. But BLACK JEWS have to be cynical in order to maintain an ounce of sanity in the so-called "CROSS-FIRE" between White Christians and White Jews, they being directly in the middle and not knowing on which side to lean, much less take. With all of this they still find no comfort among BLACK Christians, BLACK Moslems, and all of the other BLACK religious groups there are in the overall BLACK COMMUNITY, because most of them can not understand other Black People who are not equally "JEWISH" or "HEBREW" like they are; thus their further religious dilemma. Note however, that the vast majority of European-Americans [WHITES] of every religion there is, including JUDAISM, cannot understand either; all due to the total ignorance in which their so-called "RELIGIOUS LEADERS" have kept them about ALKEBU-LAN [Africa] and BLACK [African] PEOPLE generally, and all due to their leaders selfish reasons for becoming richer.

[THE OTHER SIDE]: Father Joseph J. Williams' book - HEBREWISMS OF WEST AFRICA: FROM THE NILE TO THE NIGER WITH THE JEWS, Bilbo and Tannen, New York, 1967-70 [originally published in 1930] opened a whole new aspect to the origin, development and practise of what he designated as "HEBREWISMS OF WEST AFRICA." Of course the title of this Jesuit's book suggests that what he identified as "HEBREWISMS" must have been just that. But he, like most of his fellow so-called "CHRISTIAN MISSIONARIES" from Europe, Great Britain and European-America that were his contemporaries, those before and following him, could not find that his so-called "HEBREWISMS" were among the indigenous AFRICANS of every last part of the continent the Greeks and Romans called "AFRICA" before the birth of the very first HARIBU, HEBREW, ISRAELITE or JEW named "ABRAHAM" or "ABRM [Avrm, etc.]." All of these so-called "HEBREWISMS" are common to the so-called "TRADITIONAL RELIGIONS OF WEST AFRICA," and all of "AFRICA." Thus we find the following on page 54 of his book:

> "This stool we give gladly. It does not contain our soul as our Golden Stool does, but it contains all the love of us Queen-Mothers and of our women. The spirit of this love we have bound to the stool with silver fetters just as we are accustomed to bind our own spirits to the base of our stools.

---

1. Unless it has a "Judaeo" and/or "Judaeo-Christian Missionary" label the White racists and religious bigots of Judaism, Christianity and Islam must condemn it as "pagan, heathen, foreign," etc.

> "We in Ashanti here have a law which decrees that it is the daughters of a Queen who alone can transmit royal blood, and that the children of a king cannot be heirs to that stool. This law has given us women a power in this land so that we have a saying which runs:
>
> 'It is the woman who bears the man,'
>
> (i. e. the king). We hear that her law is not so, nevertheless we have great joy in sending her our congratulations, and we pray the great God Nyankopon, on whom men lean and do not fall, whose day of worship is a Saturday, and whom the Ashanti serve just as she serves Him, that He may give the King's child and her husband long life and happiness, and finally, when she sits upon this silver stool, which the women of Ashanti have made for their white Queen-Mother, may she call us to mind.
>
> "(Signed) Amma Sewa Akota,
>
> "X her mark." [52]

[52] Rattray, *Ashanti*, p. 294.

The good Reverend Williams seems to have forgotten that almost all of the African High-Cultures, up to the present, indicates a MATRIARCHIAL LINEAGE from top [the king and queen] to bottom of the heredity scale. But the established patterns of JUDAEO-CHRISTIAN and JEWISH RACISM, also RELIGIOUS BIGOTRY, that drive the so-called "MISSIONARIES" who come to "Africa" do not allow any tolerance for the type of information the evidence disclosed about the Ashante Kingdom of West Africa. This does not change the fact that most European and American JEWS give the impression that "CIRCUMCISION" for religious and health purposes started with their biblical ancestors, when in fact it was practised for thousands of years throughout the continent of Alkebu-lan [Africa] before the name of "ADAM" and his God YWH were in history. But J. J. Williams, S. J., like all of the other European, British and American so-called "Christian Missionaries" and others who wrote, and are still writing,[1] on the religious experiences [so-called "Traditional Religions"] of all indigenous Africans had to connect whatever "JEWISH" and/or "CHRISTIAN" slavemasters, entrepreneurs, missionaries and all of their descendants he could assign to the origin of what they decided must have been "HEBREWISMS OF WEST AFRICA: FROM THE NILE TO THE NIGER WITH THE JEWS." Yet the "JEWS" of whom they addressed themselves are not the so-called FALASHAS or BLACK JEWS of Ethiopia, East Africa, but instead the so-called WHITE SEMITIC-CAUCASIAN JEWS.

The height of all we have read in J. J. Williams' remarks is topped by the coalition between European, British and European-American JEWS and CHRISTIANS in the so-called "Republic of [White] South Africa," of which insufficient studies are made by indigenous Africans about their systematic extermination by European [WHITE] People like these who seized all of their land and natural resources. All of this should be enough to shed a different light on the

1. All of them forgot that "Hebrewism" got its beginning in Africa's Puanit, Itiopi, Ta-Nehisi and Ta-Merry. Cross-reference the Holy Torah with the Book Of The Dead for the proof.

following extract from Gustav Saron and Louis Hotz's book - THE JEWS IN SOUTH AFRICA: A HISTORY,[1] Oxford University Press, Cape Town , London, New York, 1955, pages xiii - xiv of the "Introduction:"

> A second major influence upon South African Jewry came from England, both in religious matters, as many of the leading ministers and rabbis in South Africa have come from England, and generally through contact with Anglo-Jewry's life and institutions. This was to be expected as first the Cape and Natal, and later the whole of South Africa, have developed within the British Empire and Commonwealth, and South African life as a whole has been greatly influenced by British ways and institutions.
>
> Jewish life in South Africa represents, indeed, a unique blend, resulting from the interaction of *Litvak* and English elements with the emergent South African way of life. Naturally, among the South African-born descendants of the immigrants the older traditions have grown weaker. The South African Jew of today is not only taller, more broad-shouldered and more open-air-minded than his forebears, but he exhibits many of the psychological characteristics of his fellow South Africans.
>
> What properly belongs to the history of South African Jewry? Should it deal only with the corporate life and activities of the Jewish group, both in its internal domestic aspects and its interactions with the general community? Or should it include the contributions made by Jewish individuals to the general life of the country in commerce, industry, civic affairs, politics, art, literature, and related fields?
>
> The writers in this volume have regarded both aspects as falling within its scope. They have, therefore, recorded the contributions made to the general welfare by outstanding individuals, and have also described the group life of the Jewish community in such fields as Jewish religion, education, and philanthropy. In the earlier period, roughly between 1800 and 1880, when the Jewish community was small and its group life rather restricted in expression, the interest in individuals predominates. From the time, however, that their numbers increased through immigration, attention is directed towards them more as a group.
>
> Many themes are discussed, such as the circumstances that brought the Jewish immigrants to South Africa; how they adapted themselves to it, economically and culturally, and in other ways; what influence they had upon its general progress; how far they built up their own group life and institutions. The various factors are recorded which made the pattern, never static, of the relations between them and the other elements of the South African population, more particularly the English- and Afrikaans-speaking groups. Their association with Jewish communities abroad, and the impact of world Jewish events upon them, are also described; for despite its geographical remoteness, South African Jewry has never been isolated but has always retained a lively interest in events affecting the welfare of the Jewish people as a whole.
>
> It may be helpful to the reader, especially one not familiar with South Africa, to be given a brief account of the general pattern of Jewish development in this country, so as to assist him to see the separate essays of this book in their proper framework.
>
> The chronicle falls into several well-defined periods. In the first 150 years, from the beginnings of European settlement until about 1800, small numbers of Jews settled in South Africa. Comparatively little is known about them. Their record does not strictly belong to Jewish history, as they did not profess Judaism, in some cases, no doubt.

1. In spite of this firsthand evidence, the acts of genocide by White Jews on Africans continue. Why!

> because the constitution of the Dutch East India Company required that all its servants and settlers should be Protestants.
>
> The second period began at the turn of the nineteenth century and continued until about 1870. We encounter a growing number of professing Jews, some of whom played a notable part in the general life of the country. We also see the early beginnings of Jewish communal life. In Cape Town, in 1841, in Grahamstown in 1843, in Port Elizabeth in 1857, and gradually further inland, small groups of Jews, faithful to their ancestral traditions, formed themselves into congregations, consecrated separate burial-grounds, built synagogues, established philanthropic institutions, and laid the foundations of a corporate Jewish life. By 1870 the relatively few Jews in the country were scattered over a wide area and were to be found in the most out-of-the-way places. Their contribution and achievements were often greater than their small numbers would lead us to expect. Some of them or their descendants were assimilated into the general population and lost their identity as Jews, a fact attributable to their small and scattered numbers, the scarcity of Jewish women whom they could marry, and the almost complete lack of spiritual ministration. Nevertheless, the first foundations of a Jewish community were laid during that period.

Is it at all strange that the question of the kosher "JEWISHNESS" of the White Jews of South Africa's "Pure White Race Society" has never been challenged by the Kosher Jew-Makers in the State of Israel as they are doing with respect to the Black Jews from Harlem, New York City, New York and those of Chicago, Illinois? Yet all three groups male members were without females - "MOTHERS" - for their children, and as such had to take upon themselves the WOMEN of other religions when they migrated from one country to another; this being no different for all of the JEWS of the entire world, those in Israel today being no exception. Or, are we saying that the mode of transportation used in the migration of the so-called "NEGRO JEWS" to the United States of America makes them less than the European "WHITE JEWS" to the colony of South Africa? The reader should pay very special attention to the underscored sentences above, which I have done for emphasis on the main points relative to the commonality of the problem the WHITE JEWS of South Africa had like the BLACK JEWS of Harlem, New York City and Chicago in the United States of America.

"Well Hush My Mouth!...,"[1] maybe Shlomo Katz and his "...27 Negro and Jewish Commentators..." would like to do some re-editing of their condemnation of so-called "NEGRO ANTI-SEMITISM" or "BLACK ANTI-SEMITISM" after reading the above about the structure of integration and amalgamation between European and European-American WHITE Jews, Christians, and others, in the Hitlerite system presently called "APARTHEID."[2] A LILY WHITE SYSTEM in a BLACK LAND in which WHITE JEWS are FULL PARTNERS with the

1. A very common slang used in the African-American community when clowning in misbelief about a particular rumor.

2. The almost paramoidial attack on former President Idi Amin of Uganda, East Africa White Jews of every branch of Judaism, and even some Black Jews; nothing even approaching it as White Jews.

OPPRESSORS of the indigenous BLACK PEOPLE that comprise more than Seventy [70] Percent of the entire population; this being typical in every part of "AFRICA" where WHITE [?!] Jews and Christians live as settlers. The fact that the acts of GENOCIDE are as common there in the so-called "REPUBLIC OF SOUTH AFRICA" as they were in Adolph Hitler's GERMANY of the 1930's seem not to disturb the WHITE JEWISH COMMUNITY any more so than they tend to disturb the conscience of the WHITE CHRISTIAN COMMUNITY. Facts such as these are too glaring for a BLACK JEW not to question the logic of remaining with the greater HEBREW and/or WORLD JEWISH COMMUNITY instead of joining with the AFRICAN NATIONALIST MOVEMENT called "PAN-AFRICANISM" today. But we are to believe that Katz and his gang of "27 Negro And Jewish Commentators" were not already acquainted with all of the facts revealed above in the quotation from Saron and Holtz's book. Comic Red Buttons[1] would have given the answer in the following manner:

"STRANGE THINGS ARE HAPPENING!."

Of course they are not so very "strange" here in the United States of America, neither in all of Europe and Great Britain, nor South and Central America.[2] The pattern of the WHITE JEWS integration and amalgamation into WHITE Anglo-Saxon Protestant and WHITE Roman Catholic societies with respect to the normal "ANTI-BLACK " [African, Negro, Colored, etc.] activities of the general WHITE community is not new, strange or unusual, but instead the common rule. For wherever WHITE JEWS and WHITE CHRISTIANS reside in every European, European-American and British dominated colonial and neo-colonial entities in Alkebu-lan [Africa] and the Caribbean Islands - Puerto Rico and the U.S. Virgin Islands included, equally South and Central America, and of course Asia and the Pacific Islands, there always exist a sort of "GENTLEMEN'S AGREEMENT" between all of the WHITES, irrespective of religious affiliation, shade of whiteness and economic status;all to the detriment of the indigenous people: BLACK, BROWN, YELLOW, RED[3] and whatever other color classification of people there is. The purpose of the accommodation is the partition and control of the indigenous peoples' HOLY LAND and SACRED NATURAL RESOURCES along with their GOD-INSPIRED LABOR, all of which they lost by virtue of violence through the GOD-INSPIRED "GUN POWDER and CANNON" which they are told are bad for them; as "VIOLENCE DOES NOT PROVE/SOLVE ANYTHING?"

Maybe one should examine the facts stated above, but never mention that they exist so long as a single WHITE JEW is involved as any other WHITE colonialist, imperialist and general exploiter in the Christian Religion and other religious affiliations. Of course this would equal-

1. The late movie, radio, television and stage personality of the 1950's and 1960's, etc. A.D./CE.
2. The prevailing myth is that South and Central America are free of U.S. type "racism," etc.
3. A designation for the indigenous people of the continent European misnomered "Red Indians."

ly exclude the notorious role British Prime Minister Benjamin Disraeli [first Earl of Beaconsfield, 1804 - 1881] who was in charge of English imperialism and colonialism, also the slave trading and mass genocide against the African and Asian peoples during 1868, and then again from 1874 through 1880 C.E. But before the howling begins over any of these relations, please be reminded that the British Imperial Government was involved in the trading of African people as SLAVES long after the "Lord Chief Justice Mansfield Decision" against the very continuance of "SLAVERY ON ENGLISH SOIL" in 1772 C.E., all of which survived through the two Disraeli's goverments.[1] Are we expected to believe that such RACISM and RELIGIOUS BIGOTRY are not common in the case of how Central Harlem, South Bronx, Grand Central Parkway, Eastern Parkway, all in the City of New York, New York. became predominantly BLACK as WHITE JEWS and WHITE CHRISTIANS exited in extreme haste as the BLACK FACES - Jews, Christians, Moslems, Voodooists, Yorubas, etc. moved into their neighborhoods? And certainly when the "FOR SALE" signs went up faster than "NEGROES" could have even think of moving into so-called WHITE JEWISH and WHITE CHRISTIAN neighborhoods; and after the first "NEGRO" [professional, skilled or unskilled] entered one neighborhood or paused for one second of fresh air and the community start fleeing to the suburbs? Should this equally be overlooked by BLACK JEWS more-so than their fellow BLACK AMERICANS who are not of the Hebrew [Jewish] Religion? Maybe BLACK JEWS should equally agree to the prevailing diatribe in WHITE AMERICA'S collection of racist myths and other cliches about

"THE SUDDEN DEVALUATION OF PROPERTY WHEN THE NEGROES [Jews, Christians, Moslems, Yorubas] MOVE IN."[2]

Yet, no one prepared the same "NEGRO JEWS" to understand how the rents and mortgages tripled for the same so-called "DEVALUATED PROPERTY" when the so-called "NEGROES MOVED IN." "MOVED INTO" buildings that were/are at least seventy-five [75] to One hundred [100] years old. I guess that FOREST HILLS, CARNARSIE, and LEFRAK CITY, only to mention a mere few of the neighborhoods that violently protested the entrance of "NEGROES MOVING IN," are to be equally illiminated from criticism by BLACK JEWS and/or BLACK CHRISTIANS; because "YOU KNOW, ALL THEY DO IS COLLECT WELFARE." The "ALL" include "BLACK JEWS" as well as "BLACK CHRISTIANS, BLACK MOSLEMS," etc. But the victims in all of these cases, like their persecuting WHITE oppressors, are supposedly the

"DESCENDANTS OF ADAM AND EVE: AND MADE BY GOD!"

At least this is the propaganda one hears in synagogues, churches, mosques, etc., each and every Friday, Saturday and Sunday so-called...SABBATH DAY...by rabbis, priests, imams,

1. Africans are expected to ignore Disareli's acts of genocide; not "Amin's murder" of a Jew.
2. See various studies by the former Harlem Youth Unlimited and Associated Community Team.

ministers, and other members of the standardized clergy. Or, is it that BLACK JEWS too know

"GOD [Ywh, Jesus, Al'lah, et al.] MADE ADAM AND EVE," [1]

from whom all of mankind descended except any and all of those who come from "Darkest Africa!"

BLACK PEOPLE OF ANY RELIGION?

Since the opposite is said to have been "GOD'S TRUTH;" then "Semites, Japhites, Canaanites - the descendants of Ham called "NEGROES," etc. are, at least, genetically and racially

BIBLICAL FIRST COUSINS.

But someone must have forgotten to edit this out of the FIVE BOOKS OF MOSES. If not true, then the entire JUDAEO, CHRISTIAN, ISLAMIC religions are based in nothing else but the most fraudulently while contrived ALLEGORICAL STORIES and RITUALS designed to establish for all of their so-called THEOLOGIANS, THEOSOPHERS, RABBIS, MINISTERS, IMAMS, et al., total control over the minds of the maximum numbers of mankind, all of whom to be ruled in total ignorance forever. By the way religious institutions are operated today, added to just how they were manipulated in the past with all of the political jingoisms therein, one should have no doubt whatsoever that not a single God - "I AM THAT I AM" - would want to ever enter any of them. Just imagine that Jehovah is told upon entry into one of His so-called PURE LILY-WHITE SYNAGOGUES that the reason there is not a single one of His so-called "NEGRO JEWS" He made praising Him along with their co-religionist "WHITE JEWS" is due to the problem of

> 'THE NEGRO JEWS INFERIOR COLOR OF SKIN, TEXTURE OF HAIR [Kinky and Woolly], THICK LIPS, BROAD NOSES AND GENERALLY INCONGRUOUS PHYSICAL CHARACTERISTICS!

God - I AM THE I AM - Jehovah, Jesus the Christ, Al'lah, et al.,[2] is shocked! But can you also imagine that He finally brings Himself together, realizing that this Most Holy PURE LILY WHITE SEMITIC-CAUCASIAN Congregation was carrying out the details of His own Sacred Scriptures written by His own God-Inspired Scribes, and responds with the following appraisal?

> This is absolutely religious of all of you My Purely and Lily-White Chosen People. You are truly following My teachings to the letter. I, your Lord and God, the I Am That I Am, recognize one of My Negative Confessions you are now calling Ten Commandments;[3] that which states: "You must love your neighbour [Negroes or Coloreds included] as you love yourself.'

Obviously all of the Judaeo, Christian, Islamic "PROPHETS," from Moses of the Hebrews all the way to Paul of the Christians and Mohamet ibn Abdullah of the Moslems [Muslims], must have gloated in the above remarks by the I AM THAT I AM; as they must have equally taught their followers, according to their "Most Holy and Sacred Scriptures written

1. Jews, Christians, Moslems, et al., demand that everyone accept this folklore.
2. What about Olodumare, Ngai, Unkulunkulu, Shango, Voodum, et al?; these are equally "Gods."
3. Refer to the "Osirian Drama" in the Egyptian Book Of The Dead for the original version.

by God-Inspired Scribes" alone, that:

'GOD [Ywh, Jesus, Al'lah] CREATED THE BEASTS; THEN HE CREATED MAN; AND THEN MADE WOMAN FROM MAN'S RIB!'

From this juncture onwards the "man - ADAM" and the "woman - EVE" God created and/or made in the "Garden of Eden" begot "CAIN, ABEL and SETH," who [minus Abel] in turn begot

'ONLY WHITE CAUCASIAN-SEMITIC INDO-EUROPEAN ARYAN JEWS, CHRISTIANS AND MOSLEMS; NOT ONE A "NEGRO."'

How could the "One And Only True God" [whatever you choose to call Him, Her, They, It, etc.] have created all of the STARS and PLANETS [worlds] in all of the GALAXIES, even those beyond the comprehension of mankind, and not be conscious of His so-called NEGRO [Black] JEWS as He is of His SEMITIC [White] JEWS? Why did such a "God" allowed His "NEGRO JEWS" to be made or created by a "CURSE" from one of His messengers that violated His trust by becoming drunk from drinking too much "WINE" [Sneaky Pete]? One has to wonder, because when the so-called "Day Of Judgment" finally comes about the following account of the "CURSE" God [Jehovah, Jesus, Al'lah, etc.] allowed Noah [Noe] to pass on his own son's - HAM - descendants will be placed before Him for review in the following version:

> Now I cannot beget the fourth son whose children I would have ordered to serve you and your brothers! Therefore it must be Canaan, your first born, whom they enslave. And since you have disabled me...doing ugly things in blackness of night, Canaan's children shall be born ugly and black! Moreover, because you twisted your head around to see my nakedness, your grandchildren's hair shall be twisted into kinks, and their eyes red; again because your lips jested at my misfortune, theirs shall swell; and because you neglected my nakedness, they shall go naked, and their male members shall be shamefully elongated! Men of this race are called Negroes, their forefather Canaan commanded them to love theft and fornication, to be banded together in hatred of their masters and never to tell the truth."[1]

Would God not ask the following after reading what His own "Inspired Scribes" wrote and passed down to Moses and others:

'When did I give Noe [Noah] power to turn the people I made from one color into another? And, when did I made it possible to have all kinds of races coming out of the two people - Adam and Eve - I created and made in the Garden Of Eden more than five thousand seven hundred and fifty-four years ago, according to my calendar?'

Is it not "strange" that the same "GARDEN OF EDEN" God was speaking about included Alkebu-lan [Ethiopia, Cush, Mizrain, Egypt, Punt, Somalia, etc.]? For example; GENESIS, Chapter II, Verses 8 - 16 describe the geography of the "GARDEN OF EDEN" as follows:

1. See Y. ben-Jochannan's Black Man Of The Nile And His Family, pp. 3 - 72, and R. Graves and R. Patai's Hebrew Myths: The Story Of Genesis, pp. 120 - 123 for further comments.

The garden of Eden, and the river thereof.

8 ¶ And the LORD God planted a garden eastward in Eden; and there he put the man whom he had formed.

9 And out of the ground made the LORD God to grow every tree that is pleasant to the sight, and good for food; the tree of life also in the midst of the garden, and the tree of knowledge of good and evil.

10 And a river went out of Eden to water the garden; and from thence it was parted, and became into four heads.

11 The name of the first *is* Pison: that *is* it which compasseth the whole land of Havilah, where *there is* gold;

12 And the gold of that land *is* good; there *is* bdellium and the onyx stone.

13 And the name of the second river *is* Gihon: the same *is* it that compasseth the whole land of Ethiopia.

14 And the name of the third river *is* Hiddekel: that *is* it which goeth toward the east of Assyria. And the fourth river *is* Euphrates.

15 And the LORD God took the man, and put him into the garden of Eden to dress it and to keep it.

16 And the LORD God commanded the man, saying, Of every tree of the garden thou mayest freely eat:

The following map shows the boundaries in Alkebu-lan and Asia according to the above description of the so-called "Garden Of Eden," not one square inch of which is located in any part of the continent called "EUROPE." ETHIOPIA in this sense represents the name "AFRICA," this you can verify once again on the MAP OF AFRICA on page 24 of Volume One.

RIVERS AND LANDS OF THE "GARDEN OF EDEN" [1]
[All According To The Pentateuch/Torah]
ca. 1 H.C., 3760 B.C.E., 4382 B.H.

1. It is quite obvious that the "second river"..."GIHOU"...that "compasseth the whole land of Ethiopia" began in Uganda, Central-East Alkebu-lan/Africa and the "High-lands of Ethiopia," East Africa [or any other name by which this continent has been called historically] shown on the map above. Did "God Ywh/Jehovah" forget this fact too! Do we need another miraculous story to realize that the Hebrew or Jewish scribes were ignorant of detailed geography with regards to the continent of Africa?

The map on the previous page makes us imagine that the "BLACK [Negro] JEWS" of Alkebu-lan had to have been part of the entire plan "God" had for His GARDEN OF EDEN. But this is contrary to the "CURSE" syndrome we were taught by the "TALMUDIC SCHOLARS" of Sixth Century C.E. Europe. Probably GOD - Jehovah, Jesus "the Christ," Al'lah, et al., will correct His former, and present, earthly representatives - Grand Rabbis, Holiness the Popes, Grand Imams, Presiding Bishops, et al., by showing them the following map of the "GARDEN OF EDEN" in Alkebu-lan and one of the first "MAN/WOMAN" created or made more than ONE MILLION SEVEN HUNDRED AND FIFTY THOUSAND [1,750,000] YEARS before "ADAM AND EVE IN THE GARDEN OF EDEN" of Asia mentioned in the FIRST BOOK OF MOSES [Genesis] of the HOLY TORAH:

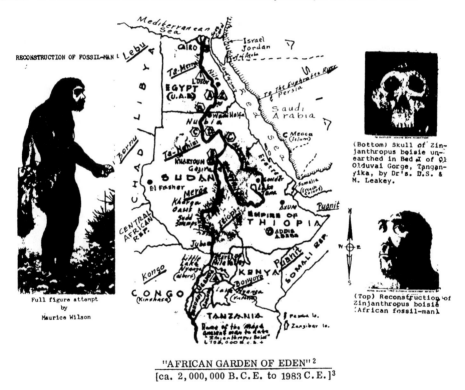

RECONSTRUCTION OF FOSSIL-MAN[1]

Full figure attempt
by
Maurice Wilson

(Bottom) Skull of Zinjanthropus boisie unearthed in Bed I of Olduvai Gorge, Tanganyika, by Dr's. D.S. & M. Leakey.

(Top) Reconstruction of Zinjanthropus boisie [African fossil-man]

"AFRICAN GARDEN OF EDEN"[2]
[ca. 2,000,000 B.C.E. to 1983 C.E.][3]

---

1. Note the racist attempt to make the African fossil-man/woman appear to be European in so-called "AFRICA SOUTH OF THE SAHARA." Why was "Zinjanthropus boise" not shown with the so-called "NEGROID FEATURES" [thick lips, broad nose, kinky or woolly hair, black color, etc.] commonly assigned to "Natives South of the Sahara" in "Darkest Africa" where he was originated?
2. The "Garden of Eden" was created by Jewish scribes using Hebrew allegory and/or myth, etc.
3. Another African fossil-human called "Lucy" predates Zinjanthropus boise by 3,000,000 years.

Is it not "strange" that God allowed us to find all kinds of prehistoric Africans in Alkebu-lan that date back millions of years before He created "Adam and Eve in the Garden Of Eden," but not a single fragment of the bones of Adam, Eve, Noah, Abraham, Jacob, Isaac, Joseph, Moses, nor anyone else from the BOOK OF GENESIS of the FIVE BOOKS OF MOSES [Pentateuch or Old Testament] which allegedly dates back only to no more than... Five Thousand Seven Hundred and Forty-two [5,743] Years ago or ca. 3670 B.C.E., was found to date? Just imagine that this "GARDEN OF EDEN" is located in almost dead-center of the Black Jews'

'DARKEST AFRICA, SOUTH OF THE SAHARA AMONGST SAVAGE PAGAN BANTU NEGROES!'

The area encircled with the large enclosure is about the middle of Central Alkebu-lan. The small circle is the approximate location of "BED I" where one of the oldest "AFRICAN FOSSIL-HUMAN" called "Zinjanthropus boisie"[1] [woman/man?] was unearthed, being at least one million seven hundred and fifty thousand [1,750,000] years old, a picture of which I have shown on the previous page. Is it not strange that IT should be unearthed in the homeland of the so-called "BLACK [Negro] JEWS?" Naturally "God's Inspired Sacred Scribes" must have forgotten to mention "Zinjanthropus boisie" and all of the other fossil-men/women found in Alkebu-lan in their Most Sacred and Holy Scriptures they wrote in their FIVE BOOKS OF MOSES, particularly in the FIRST BOOK [Genesis]. Or, could it be that God decided to make "BLACK JEWS" and other "BLACK AFRICANS" millions of years before HE decided it was time to make "WHITE JEWS" and other Semitic-Caucasian WHITE EUROPEANS in Europe, Britain and European-America?[2] Review GENESIS, Chapter II, Verse 13. But, maybe it is true:

"GOD WORKS IN A MYSTERIOUS WAY, HIS WONDERS NEVER TO CEASE."

More than this; God must have also forgotten His LILY-WHITE Anglo-Saxon Protestants and SLIGHTLY BROWNISH-WHITE Alpine-Mediterranean Roman Catholics when he was making BLACK-WHITE and/or WHITE-BLACK Etruscans and Greek Druids that migrated to and from Alkebu-lan and Europe a few hundred years before He made any type of EUROPEAN Jews.[3]

Maybe the maps [pp. 52-53] and historical evidence will make us take a closer look at the Kosher Jew Makers who barred BLACK [Negro] JEWS from Chicago, Illinois and other parts of the United States of America in Israel, but allow WHITE [Caucasian] JEWS from all over the Soviet Union [Russia] to enter freely - even to pay all of their expenses to travel. All of

1. See Y. ben-Jochannan's BLACK MAN OF THE NILE AND HIS FAMILY, pages 73 - 98.
2. Ibid. Review the entire chapter. See ben-Jochanan's CULTURAL GENOCIDE IN THE BLACK AND AFRICAN STUDIES CURRICULUM, pages 38 - 57, and 104 - 114.
3. See ben-Jochannan and G.E. Simmond's THE BLACK MAN'S NORTH and EAST AFRICA, p. 8.

this because of a "CHOSEN" Jewish Mother that is supposedly the source of all ... "JEWS"... without whom one cannot be considered a "JEW," short of the CONVERSION route. But in which case does a EUROPEAN JEW has to prove his or her "JEWISHNESS" before the Kosher Certifiers? NONE. All that any European, European-American, British or Israeli WHITE CAUCASIAN has to say is:

"I AM A JEW; MY MOTHER WAS [IS] A [White Semitic] JEW;"

and "open sesame" he [or she]is welcome into the State of Israel and all of the other WHITE controlled Reform, Reconstructionist, Conservative, Orthodox, Jewish Science, etc. and/or other TALMUDIC [Rabbinical] COMMUNITIES there are anywhere; even among "JEWS [White] FOR JESUS." But why no question beyond the declaration of her WHITE JEWISHNESS from a WHITE JEWISH WOMAN? Because those who are in charge of establishing KOSHER JEWISHNESS the KOSHER JEW CERTIFIERS - equally consider themselves in all of their teachings:

'WHITE CAUCASIAN-SEMITIC INDO-EUROPEAN ARYAN JEWS.'

The Agaw and/or Kylas [the so-called "Falasha" or "Ethiopian Jew" - properly in Hebrew "Beta Isra'el or "Children Of The House Of Israel"],according to the "Full Jew Certifiers" were

"CONVERTED TO JUDAISM BY JEWISH TRAVELERS OR
MERCHANTS PASSING THROUGH ETHIOPIA SOMETIME
DURING THE MIDDLE AGES."

Of course none of the latter-day Holy and Most Inspired Scribes who wrote this type of diatribe ever took time to ask the Agaw and/or Kyla about their own history relative to their Hebrew origin. Thus, only by "CONVERSION" can a "BLACK PERSON" become a "JEW" in the eyes of the Kosher Certifiers Of Jewishness. And thus; be it resolved that "BLACK [Negro] JEWS" will only work as SERVANTS in the WHITE [Semitic] JEWS' Hereafter, as do the BLACK [Negro] CHRISTIANS in the WHITE [Caucasian] CHRISTIANS' Heaven. Just take a second and look at your picture Bible [Pentateuch, Koiñe Bible, and Holy whatever else]. Is it not also resolved that:

"I AM A JEW; MY MOTHER WAS [IS] A [BLACK SEMITIC] JEW?" THUS KOSHER!

European and European-American TALMUDIC [Rabbinical] JUDAISM only requires that:

"ONE'S MOTHER BE A JEW"

in order to establish one's self as a "Jew." Then, and only then, short of the "CONVERSION" route, should one say that he or she is a "JEW." Of course all of this is only on paper. It is on paper like the United States of America's DECLARATION OF INDEPENDENCE," which states the following:

"BE IT RESOLVED THAT ALL MEN ARE CREATED EQUALLY,[1]

---

1. This refers only to "All White Men;" but not one solitary African/Black man or woman. Even Thomas Jefferson was a racist slave owner when he wrote this. He sired many slaves too.

etc., etc., etc. Let us note that while "All Men " who wrote this were still RESOLVING all that they had to be "RESOLVED," all before the ink of the first "RESOLUTION" was dried, they were equally taking good stack of the fact that their SLAVE FARMS and COTTON PLANTATIONS were not involved in the "BE IT" anything other than remain in STATUS QUO: the dehumanized Africans bound in chains "RESOLVED" to a life of "THREE-FIFTHS" of a person. "All Men" were equally no more, and no less, created by God as He did His One And Only

"CHOSEN PEOPLE - THE ISRAELITES;"

who, by the standards of those in charge of Kosher Jewishness all over the planet Earth today

'WERE, AND MUST STILL BE, LILY-WHITE CAUCASIAN-SEMITES.'

It was stated at the outset of this Volume that this writer was not interested in name calling. You have seen that my declaration is correct. But more than this, you can also observe why I had to drop my own affiliation with "WESTERN TALMUDIC [Rabbinical] JUDAISM." For the RACISM and RELIGIOUS BIGOTRY that permeate all types of the branches of "Western Judaism" - from ORTHODOX to REFORM - should make any "BLACK JEW" realize that he or she is not wanted or tolerated amongst "WHITE JEWS." And TALMUDIC JUDAISM as a religious institution, regardless of form in Europe, Great Britain and European-America, is as much a part of the ECONOMIC, POLITICAL and SOCIAL fibre of the governmental system that allows IT to operate "TAX FREE" as the people who manipulate IT as a part of the unholy marriage between Church [JUDAISM, CHRISTIANITY] and State [UNITED STATES OF AMERICA, GREAT BRITAIN, etc.]. The only exceptions for either religion and ITS manipulators are in their methodology of rituals, names of their God-Head, and choice of the foreigners' military power they support from their European-American base. And of course each military power or alliance is basically established to commit GENOCIDE upon any nation, and upon any person - the so-called "...ENEMY[1]...," all...

"FOR GOD, MAN, AND COUNTRY;"

Thou [You] Shall Not Kill" being conveniently sidetracked with "An Eye For An Eye, And A Tooth For A Tooth" whenever one's [MY] military alliance seems to be the possible victor. All of this quickly becomes...

"TURN THE OTHER CHEEK, SAYETH THE LORD" ..

whenever one's military alliance is about to become the victim. Is it not equally true for all of the BLACK JEWS who supported the WHITE JEWS in their wars against the ARAB MOSLEMS? CONVENIENT is not the word in this case; HYPOCRACY is much more appropriate and to the point of this type of THEOSOPHY, THEOLOGY and PHILOSOPHY in European and European-

1. Anyone whose interest violently conflicts with another person's - religious or secular.

American JUDAEO-CHRISTIAN religiousity. But, are we not conditioned in our PENTATEUCH [Five Books Of Moses, Holy Torah, Old Testament], KOIÑE BIBLE [New Testament] and HOLY QUR'AN [Koran] to be...

"MY GOD IS BETTER THAN YOUR GOD"

believers? And, do we not inflate our ego with the usual...

"MY PEOPLE ARE BETTER THAN YOUR PEOPLE"

myth? Certainly we do, and of course I am not addressing myself to you who know that you are the only...

"GOD'S CHOSEN PEOPLE, SAVED AND SINLESS ANGELS"...

awaiting His - God's [Ywh, Jesus, Al'lah, and maybe others] -

"JUDGMENT DAY TO ENTER HIS KINGDOM;"

Black Jews included. I am addressing those like myself:

BLACK, WHITE, BROWN, YELLOW, RED, ETC. - FIRE WORSHIPERS, SUN WORSHIPERS, YORUBAS,..., ETC.,

all of whom are not egotistical enough to assume that only we know when the entire universe and all of its galaxies were created or made, and as such we can refuse to recognize the IN-PERFECTION within RELIGIOUS INSTITUTIONS we have created and will defend even to our death to protect our clerical and administrative positions that first and foremost react to the following truth:

"MONEY IS, IN FACT, GOD EVERYWHERE;"

in the synagogue, church, mosque, bank, "white house," educational institution, labor union, marriage ceremony, labor room, funeral home, and even when someone say to... Black-White-Brown-Yellow-Red, etc., etc., etc.,... all of us..., one final day:

"DUST TO DUST, ASHES TO ASHES; AS HE [she] CAME, SO HE [she] GOES;"

Amen [GOD] Ra

Ethiopian [like Harlemite] Vendors in Debre Market

CONCLUSION:

What you have just read is a revised and updated version of how the author - formerly a practicing BLACK [African or Ethiopian] JEW - understood the socio-political and economic confrontation between BLACK-WHITE JEWISH relationship during the 1930's, which has since deteriorated to a very loathsome dimension following the vanguard of the African People unto the battle field to protect themselves from European, British and European-American colonialism and neo-colonialism politically and economically. This took place as the Africans began their take-over of the reign of their own government of former colonies held by the British, European and European-American imperialists and colonialists from 1830 C.E. when the French invaders conquered and occupied Cueta, Morocco in North Alkebu-lan [Africa]; and from 1884 - 1885 C.E. at the meeting of the "Berlin Conference" of European, British and European-American imperialists who declared their "BERLIN ACT" of political, military and economic control - "PARTITION" - of all of Alkebu-lan, except the Empire of Ethiopia and the Republic of Liberia; and up to 1957 C.E. when the late Honourable African Patriot Dr. Kwame Nkrumah ["Osagyefo"] freed the so-called "Gold Coast Crown Colony, Northern Territories [including the Kingdom Of Ashante]" and the indigenous "African People" politically [and to a great extent economically] from British contrived slavery and genocide on Africans.

The 1960's, from the wanton killing of a fourteen [14] year old African-American youngster by the name of "Powell" by a New York City, New York Police Lieutenant named Giligan in the German-American Community of Yorkville, 86th Street and Lexington Avenue, New York City, New York; the assassination of Moslem Minister Malcolm X in Upper Manhattan's Au-Audubon Ballroom, New York City [Harlem vicinity], New York; the assassination of the Most Reverend Dr. Martin Luther King, Jr. in Nashville, Tennessee by James Earl Ray; and of course the re-Africanization [BLACK] processing of "Negroes" into "Black Power" advocates that arose during the same period to combat the so-called "non-violent integration" and "amalgamation -minded Negroes" and "Colored Folks" who wanted to pray for everything they needed and hustle for what they wanted, found the so-called NEGRO [African, Ethiopian, even "Black"] JEWS without any political leadership whatsoever. And because of this dilemma most [excluding myself even as early as this period] were caught in a bind of not knowing just which side to take in the so-called "Black-White Confrontation" that demanded either of the following roles for each Black man, Black woman and/or Black child:

> 'Connection with the so-called non-violent integrationists; with the Black Power Movement that demanded a few states in the southern part of the United States of America to form an independent Black nation; or with

> the African Nationalist [Pan-African] "Back To Africa" Movement made popular by the late Honourable African Patriot Marcus Moziah Garvey.

And in spite of the fact that they were constantly hearing the following African Nationalists [not to be confused with the "Black Nationalists" who wanted a nation within the United States of America] like the noted deceased and living, such as...

> Carlos Cooks,[1] Authur Reed,[1] Bessie Philips,[1] John Dash,[1] Eddie [Pork Chop] Davis, James Thornhill, Professor Louis Michaux,[1] Professor George E. Simmonds, the Brath brothers, Arnold Lewis, James Lawson and countless others...

before, during, and even following the demise of the 1960's so-called "Militant New Left Black Liberation Movement."

The plight of "WHITE PEOPLE" generally, particularly following the death of their most celebrated "BLACK HOPE" - the Reverend Dr. Martin Luther King, Jr., made the basically "WHITE JEWISH" source of "NEGRO" and/or "COLORED" front organizations dedicated to the amalgamation of the races withdrew their financial support from all that began taking a forthright "AFRICAN" and/or "BLACK NATIONALIST" stand.[2] As, even the wearing of the "DASHIKI" and the cut of the woolly hair in the so-called "AFRO STYLE" frightened the formerly so-called "LIBERAL WHITES" almost out of their wits. This experience between BLACK and WHITE JEWS, equally as with BLACK CHRISTIANS and WHITE CHRISTIANS, was to reap a so-called BLACK-WHITE [Jewish] "BACKLASH" or "BLACK ANTI-SEMITISM" and "WHITE SEMITIC ANTI-BLACKISM" as it did between BLACK and WHITE CHRISTIANS and others. And becasue "BLACK [so-called "Negro" and/or "colored"] JEWS" did not have the type of free access to the communication media as "WHITE JEWS" - who owned and controlled dozens throughout European-America, it was only natural that the propaganda machinery was going to sink the former "NEGROES" and "COLOREDS" turned "INSTANT BLACKS." And equally, those who remained loyally "NEGROES" and/or "COLOREDS" with their processed hair and mind had to continue their servitude to their financial godfathers and godmothers who still underwrite their jobs and social organizations, even their CHURCHES and their GODS - Ywh and Jesus "the Christ;" Al'lah not being popular among the "Responsible Negro Leaders."

While all of the above was taking place the BLACK [Ethiopian, Israelite, Colored and/or whatever else they call themselves to this present day] JEWS remained so much aloof and passive that they were soon forgotten by both sides as ever having existed. But, why did they take the position of "FENCE STRADLERS"? Because of the same reason I too was once subjected to - "FEAR" - all of my youth as an "ETHIOPIAN [Black] JEW," etc. "FEAR" of not

1. Indication of those who passed away to rest forever after having served Africa with dignity.
2. See Y. ben-Jochannan's The Black Marxists vs The Black Nationalists: A Debate Resurrected for details on the difference between Black Nationalism and African Nationalism, etc.

being recognized by their fellow co-religionist White [!] Jews, and "FEAR" of their own African [BLACK] People of other religions [particularly the powerful majority of Black Christians] for generally ignoring their kinship and fellowship. Black Jews "FEARS" had to be basically paranoid [not by choice] by circumstances of "COLOR, RACISM" and "RELIGIOUS BIGOTRY," all of which they developed from their readings in the PENTATEUCH about their "Chosen People" status, and also from their adaption of the so-called European-American "Capital Free Enterprise System" they have made synonymous with the HOLY TALMUDIC [Rabbinical] JUDAISM they have adapted. This they have done, and all in their thrust for recognition by their fellow co-religionists... "WHITE JEWS." Thus their failure to realize that all WHITE JEWS in the United States of America are full partners of their fellow Europeans and Britons who are of various creeds and dogmas of the CHRISTIAN RELIGION, also of other religions, and even those of no religion whatsoever.

Not being able to "STRADDLE THE FENCE" is one of my major weaknesses and/or sins, second only to what other frailty of mine I cannot say at this instance. For I had to look at the reality of the "BLACK-WHITE CONFRONTATION" issue so far as I stood, and as I still stand today. As a so-called "BLACK [Ethiopian or African] JEW" at that time, I discovered that I too had to ask myself:

"WHAT IS BEING ATTACKED; MY JEWISHNESS, OR MY BLACKNESS?"

Needless to mention which one; but if you are a stranger to the so-called "American Way Of Life," it had to be my BLACKNESS. As such; what was my choice? Or; did I have a choice? Naturally the "DIE" had been casted without my ever having anything whatsoever to do with the direction I had to go; that is providing I was to be of sound mind, spirit and body - "BLACKNESS." My alliance with all who suffered because of the same reason I had/have to suffer in this land was compulsory. There was absolutely no other direction for this proud African to travel.

It was obvious to me, and I am certain it should be to any logically thinking BLACK person, "JEWISH" or not, that for the "BLACK JEWS" possibility of being receive in a welcome manner their chances would be at least one million [1,000,000] times greater in any nation controlled by indigenous Africans of any religion than in the State of Israel controlled by European and European-American JEWS. This fact cannot be avoided. It cannot be swept under the rug and it disappears into outer space to greet the astronauts. It cannot be talked away in integrated social gatherings. It must be dealt with honestly and courageously, irrespective of the resultant label of "NEGRO ANTI-SEMITE" to follow.

The WHITE JEWS, the few BLACK JEWS, and the vast majority of BROWN and YELLOW JEWS who have gone, and are still going to the State of Israel are for all purposes products of the representative culture [with all of its positives and negatives] whence they were born, raised, educated and/or worked. Since the politically and financially dominant groups inside and outside the State of Israel are "WHITE [Semitic-Caucasian] EUROPEAN-AMERICAN JEWS," and a few from Germany and England; what chance would a BLACK JEW from any land have among said combination of "WHITE JEWS" in control more than he [or she] has at present elsewhere? NONE WHATSOEVER. The "carry-overs" each so-called "RACIAL" and/or "ETHNIC" grouping of "JEWS" in the State of Israel took into this nation are exactly full of the extent of the RACISM and RELIGIOUS BIGOTRY they had before they left their country of origin. The controllers, mostly from the United States of America and a very few from Great Britain and Germany, are representatives of this general rule rather than the exception. All of us should remember when the Cochim Jews were told by White Jews in Israel:

"BLACK BREAD IS FOR BLACK JEWS, AND WHITE BREAD IS FOR WHITE JEWS ONLY," [1]

which caused so many of them to return to India - their homeland they once left to settle among their fellow co-religionists in the "PROMISED LAND" Jehovah equally gave them [see page 273].

Thus the major question that is always brought forward to a PRACTICING or an apparently NON-PRACTICING "Jew:"

"WHOSE SIDE ARE YOU ON, THE ISRAELIS OR THE ARABS?"

Yours truly usual response,..."NEITHER"..., inevitably encounters from the "Pro-Israelites [or Israelis], Arab Moslems [or Muslims], Black Nationalists, Jew Haters, Moslem Haters," and other sympathizers and supporters alike - their full wrath. But I am reminded that the Arabs came to North Africa with their "JIHADS" [Holy Wars] about 640 A.D./C.E. or 18 A.H.; and that thousands of White Jews came with their fellow imperialist and colonialist Christian Europeans,[2] and later on European-Americans, who still hold vast amounts of colonial territories in Alkebu-lan today. How then can I...BLACK JEW, BLACK CHRISTIAN, BLACK MOSLEM, BLACK AFRICAN NATIONALIST, BLACK VOODOOIST, BLACK SUN WORSHIPER, BLACK FIRE WORSHIPER," and/or BLACK whatever else worshiper of whatsoever other religions they are on this planet Earth, take a "PRO" or "CON" position between these combatants; WHITE JEWS and BROWN MOSLEMS, neither one of whom gives a damned and even care less that I ever existed, or now exist, except as their perverbially designated

"HEWER OF WOOD, AND DRAWER OF WATER?"

It is totally impossible to end this major "conclusion" without citing the following article that appeared on the Front Page of the DETROIT FREE PRESS, Monday, January 21, 1974 - which was brought to my attention by my associate Mr. Clarence Harris of the COMMITTEE

---

1. See documentation in Volume One. This, supposedly, is not proof of "White Racist Zionism."
2. If the Africans truly are the missionaries most of today's religious bigotry might have been non-existent.

FOR STUDENTS RIGHT, Detroit, Michigan on the same date given before:

Man Tells How Demons Tormented His Family [1]

AP Photo

THE EXORCIST, Father Patzelt: "The devil obviously was angered . . ."

SAN FRANCISCO —(AP) — A man who claims his family was freed from attacks of demons through the Roman Catholic rites of exorcism says they couldn't have managed "without the Lord helping us."

The man, a 28-year-old airline employe, described his experience in an interview with the San Francisco Examiner on condition his name not be used. The interview was published Saturday.

HE SAID he was born in Britain, raised as an orthodox Jew and was converted to Roman Catholicism after the exorcism, an involved religious process, last summer.

A resident of this area for 13 years, he lives with his 26-year-old wife, a native of the area, and their two-year-old son in suburban Daly City. He said his wife was raised in the Catholic faith.

The Rev. Karl Patzelt, who conducted the exorcism, reported Friday on what he called the young family's triumph over satanic forces.

The inexplicable happenings first occurred in the spring of 1972, the airline worker said. The activity appeared to stop after 10 weeks, but started up with renewed fury in May 1973.

"It seemed he (Satan) had a whole army of demons with him," the man said. "The activity would happen all over the house at the same time."

He said the devil would set objects on fire, throw things, and steal things. One time a bite was inexplicably taken from a sandwich his wife was preparing, he said.

THE TORMENT was physical, too, he said.

"They would put a force around our necks and press until we couldn't breathe. The harder we prayed, the harder we were hit," the man said.

"I don't think we could have stood it without the Lord helping us," he added. "It was beyond what we could take ourselves, way beyond."

The family contacted Father Patzelt last summer and after a report to the archbishop, the priest received permission for exorcism rites.

"After the archbishop got the report, the attacks grew worse in number and severity," the priest said. "The devil obviously was angered that he had been exposed."

Father Patzelt said the family was attacked by Satan, but not possessed like the girl in the film "The Exorcist."

The priest conducted 14 exorcism sessions in 29 days until mid-September.

"Then there was a tremendous peace in the house . . . Since then we have been at peace," the airlines worker said.

Certainly you must be wondering about my reason for citing this appearently disconnected article to the text of the main issue in this Volume! But it is indeed connected to the entire text just as much as the following "BLACK MADONNA AND CHILD OF MURIA" that is commonly known as "THE QUEEN OF THE PYRENEES,"[2] and which is always taught as being purely LILY-WHITE in institutions of learning throughout European-America, all of which in spite of her JET BLACK MAJESTY. When we look at her on the following page you might see in her face the basis for the mythological, theosophical and theological aspects you also read in the TEXTS of Genesis and Exodus in the so-called FIVE BOOKS OF MOSES - the main source of information relative to BLACK, WHITE, BROWN, YELLOW, RED "JEWS" and their heritage based upon "FAITH" and "BELIEF," equally as they apply to those of the people of the article dealing with the so-called "EXORCIST" and "THE QUEEN OF THE PYRENEES." Amen!

1. "Exorcism" is equally professed in the Holy Torah; but it is "witchcraft" in African religion.
2. See Y. ben-Jochannan's Black Man Of The Nile And His Family, 1981 Revised Edition.

THE "BLACK MADONNA AND CHILD"!
[Isis and Horus]

Queen of the Pyrenees

Most of all, however, we can observe the so-called "VOODOOISM" and "MYSTICISM" of the so-called "WITCH DOCTOR'S PAGANISM" in this JUDAEO-CHRISTIAN [Roman Catholic] act of object "PRIMITIVISM" the so-called "CHRISTIAN MISSIONARIES"[even the mother Roman Catholic Church][1]. vociferously condemned before they were taught its power. But is it not "strange" that not a single person suffered the need for the RITE OF EXORCISM in the Roman Church until the so-called "BLACK MAGICAL CHANTS OF WITCHCRAFT" were witnessed in a moving picture by like name,"THE EXORCIST," was recently released and shown to the general public. And did we not see the HolyRoman Catholic Church that adapted many of the MAGICAL TEACHINGS AND RITUALS practised when the WORSHIP OF ISIS - the AFRICAN GODDESS and "FIRST VIRGIN MOTHER"- was still the main religion of Rome and Greece even up with early Christianity and Judaism, both of which became "JUDAEO-CHRISTIANITY." This type of reaction to "BLACK [African, "Negro" and/or "Colored"] MAGIC" or "WITCHCRAFT" that had its beginning in the AFRICAN MYSTERIES SYSTEM thousands of years before Judaism and Christianity were in existence anywhere was brought into both JUDAISM and CHRISTIANITY by so-called "BLACK [Negro/Colored] JEWS" hundreds of years be-

1. This branch of "Christendom" started the Slave Trade from Africa to the West Indies.

THE FIRST "BLACK MADONNA" WORSHIPED IN ROME, EUROPE
[Before The Birth Of Jesus Christ 1983 Years Ago]

A SCENE FROM THE HERCULANEUM WORSHIP OF ISIS. This form of worship of the first Virgin Mother was common among the ancient Greeks and Romans in Greece and Rome for hundreds of years before, and up to, the adoption of "African Christianity" by the Roman Emperor Constantine "the great" in ca. 312 C.E. upon his rise to the throne. [From a fresco dating back to the pre-Christian Era in Rome]

fore Reverend Joseph J. Williams, S.J. recognized it in "WEST AFRICA" and called it by error "HEBREWISMS." It is presently defined by many so-called "modern psychologists" as:

"THE POWER OF SUGGESTION, AND TELEPATHIC GUIDANCE."

The "ROMAN CATHOLIC PRIEST," also known as the "EXORCIST," along with his Holy "ARCHBISHOP" that authorized the act of "EXORCISM" which the Roman Catholic Church, Protestant Church, Talmudic [Rabbinical] Judaism, and all of the other "Judaeo-Christian-Greek Philosophy" oriented religions of the so-called "Western World," need to take refresher courses in "EXORCISM" in the Republic of Haiti and other Islands of the Caribbean Sea, any French-speaking nation of Western Alkebu-lan, Brazil in South America, and many other countries all over the world from the indigenous peoples whose religion most European and European-American Christians, Jews, et al., still call:

"PRIMITIVE PAGAN RELIGIONS OF THE DEVIL."

Of course these religions and their priests and priestesses will continue being the very best

"CHARLATANS, CULTISTS, DEMONOLOGISTS, WITCH DOCTORS, QUACKS,"

etc. by their students who came and studied their concepts of "EXORCISM" while they were still calling themselves "CHRISTIAN MISSIONARIES." These Judaeo-Christian PRIESTS or HOGUMS have forgotten that "CHRISTENDOM" [Roman Catholic, Protestant, and independent], equally TALMUDIC [Rabbinical] JUDAISM, received their fundamental knowledge in "EXORCISM" from indigenous "AFRICAN [Traditional] RELIGIONS" that established the "MYSTERIES SYSTEM OF THE GRAND LODGE OF WA'AT" on the banks of the Nile River in Ta-Merry [Qamt, Mizrain, Egypt, etc.], all of which indigenous "AFRICANS ["Negroes"] SOUTH OF THE SAHARA" created and developed before there was an allegorical story about "ADAM and EVE" and/or "GARDEN OF EDEN" anywhere. But the best example of the rejection of the AFRICAN [Black, Negro, etc.] "EXORCISTS" theology, theosophy and philosophy is to be seen in the following special article:

THE NEW YORK TIMES, MONDAY, DECEMBER 31 1973

Voodoo Colony Home For Harlem Dropouts

By B. DRUMMOND AYRES Jr.
Special to The New York Times

SHELDON, S. C., Dec. 29 —Crooked as a cottonmouth moccasin and mired with dank mud, the road wends forbiddingly into a swampy thicket of stubby myrtle bushes and stunted oaks weighted down with the hanging gray moss that is the flora trademark of the "low country" of coastal South Carolina and Georgia.

At the end, there is a high wooden archway leading to a weedy courtyard encircled by a rude collection of tar-paper huts, each primitively painted with mysterious crosses and circles and animated dancers and spear-carriers.

The residents are black-skinned, their mouths babbling unintelligible words, their cheeks etched with parallel rows of knife-thin scars, their shoulders draped with flowing robes of red and green, blue and brown.

A large sign proclaims:

"Notice: You are leaving the U. S. You are entering Yoruba Kingdom. In the name of His Highness King Efuntola, Peace. Welcome to the Sacred Yoruba Village of Oyo-Tunji, the only village in N. Amerika built by priests of the Orisha-Voodoo cult. As a tribute to our ancestors, the priests preserve the customs, laws and religion of the Afrikan race. Welcome to our land."

And watch your step.

The 35 people who inhabit this 10-acre settlement a few miles north of Savannah—most of them American-born dropouts from the miserable tenements of New York's

The New York Times/Gary Settle

Oba Oseijeman Adefunmi, a chief in the Yoruba village near Sheldon, S.C.,[1] working on a ladder

Harlem—are among the most fanatical devotees of witchcraft in a country increasingly mesmerized by whatever mind-mystifying practice it takes to give reason and meaning to life in the 20th century, be it voodoo, astrology, extrasensory perception, sorcery or satanism.

Ex-Communters Fit

Here in the very heart of the low country, where the black arts have been the poor Negro's fetish since the first African slaves arrived more than three centuries ago, these one-time subway commuters, salesmen, waiters and artists fit in naturally, casting their horrible hexes, exorcising evil spirits, concocting powerful potions.

They founded their "kingdom" four years ago when they became dissatisfied with their spiritual and worldly lives in New York and decided to seek fulfillment by returning to the tribal ways of their African forebears, ways that included polygamy, ancestor worship and voodoo as practiced by the ancient Yorubas of Nigeria.

"We no longer could stand all the negative forces that destroy life's balance in New York," explains King Efuntola, a wiry, goateed pipe-smoker known familiarly as Kabiyesi.

He says he once lived on 115th Street in Harlem and sold African curious in Greenwich Village. But like most members of his tribe, he does not disclose his earlier name, insisting that he now lives in another world.

True, there is a certain amount of old world commercialism in this new world.

The gin that is liberally sloshed over the iron idols during tribal ceremonies can-

1. This expression of African High Culture, if in fact, serious, is worthy of every African support. It is an experiment wherein one of Africa's greatest High Culture is subjected to scrutiny.

not be conjured up without the green power of the almighty dollar. Curious tourists and women's clubs who need a "voodoo lecturer" are asked to kick in to the kingdom's kitty, lest its subjects be forced to live on food stamps or stoop to hard labor in nearby fields.

The local blacks—and poor whites—who seek the assistance of tribal witch doctors usually arrive with cash in hand, comforted by the knowledge that money also works magic. Is $[illegible] too much to ask for a "root"—a shred of colored cloth or a bright stone—that will make an evil enemy fall ill or a wavering woman fall in love?

So much for the spell of the root of all evil.

Still, the unbeliever who would cry "Hokum!" would do well to ponder whether anyone but a true believer would "leave" the United States—even a miserable Harlem tenement—to go native in a crude hovel set in a marshy kingdom that is swarmed by maddening mosquitoes in summer and chilled by gray sea mists in winter.

He Finds Peace

"It's all where you find peace and I happen to find it here in the absolutely simple way we live and in the voodoo," says a former Harlem real estate salesman who now calls himself Chief Afolabi.

Before completing my critical analysis of this article is at end, let my pause bring you to the realization that you have been involved with some of the worse type of anthropological jingoisms. The best example of this is expressed in paragraph six; thus: "...where the black arts have been the poor Negro's fetish since the first African slaves arrived more than three centuries ago,..." etc., etc., etc. In the first place, only in the City of Fete there are "FETISH" items,or "FETISHES." The term, like the word "NEGRO" instead of African, is racist in the same context as this entire article. The so-called "...TRIBAL WAYS..." which the African-Americans returned to according to paragraph seven are very typical to the "TRIBAL WAYS" of the European-American and European Jews about "...the beginning of the world, chosen people, kosher food, hereafter," etc. Yet no one seems to be as much concern about these absurdities. Why? Because too many people are afraid of being called "Anti-Semite" and "Anti-Christ."

Of course the YORUBA Religion and the VOODOO Religion are treated as if they are ONE. The writer seems not even to care about the difference between a "HOGUM" and the comical "HOKUM" of the comic strips we see so much in the various newspapers in the United States of America daily.

The so-called "...PRIMITIVE CUSTOMS..." of the so-called "...DROPOUTS..." from Harlem in their "...VOODOO COLONY HOME...," to me, are no different than the "PRIMITIVE CUSTOMS" surrounding the belief in a "...VIRGIN BIRTH OF JESUS CHRIST, CURSE OF HAM BY NOAH, MOSES RECEIVING THE TEN COMMANDMENTS ON MT. HOREB, THE RED SEA DRIED UP TO LET THE ISRAELITE CHILDREN PASS...," etc., etc., etc. But it is only natural that this "...CULT...," unlike the CHRISTIAN, JEWISH, MOSLEM, JEHOVAH WITNESS, MORMON, CHRISTIAN SCIENTIST and ROMAN CATHOLIC "CULTS," must be also debased for its "...PRIMITIVE CUSTOMS..." which are no different than the cultism we read of on page 392, also in the OLD TESTAMENT, NEW TESTAMENT and HOLY QUR'AN. But, please excuse me, the latter "SACRED SCRIPTURES" were dictated by the one and only WHITE Semitic-Caucasian God named "JEHOVAH, JESUS CHRIST, AL'LAH," etc; not the original AMEN-RA.

The way he lives is a scene straight from Vachel Lindsay, complete with not only authentic African language, dress and idols, but also children underfoot, scrawny dogs slinking off into the bush, open-hearth cooking odors hanging in the air, booming drums, clacking gourds, jangling bells, guttural chants, piercing screams, writhing ebony bodies glistening with sweat, beads, seeds, powders, fire, water, earth and a proud white rooster suddenly gone limp and stained red with the blood of sacrifice.

Sometimes the South Carolina authorities object a bit, particularly to the polygamy and the absence of public schooling for the kingdom's youngsters.

The village leaders counter—successfully, thus far—that no villager has gone through more than one official wedding ceremony. They point out that the settlement's youngsters go to the Royal Yoruba Academy, which in the eyes of the law is but another of those many private scnools that have sprung up all over South Carolina in the wake of desegregation.

The "new Yorubas" purposely cut out their kingdom in the swamps of South Carolina because of the affinity they felt for the ancient, voodoo-practicing slaves—some of them probably Yorubas—who were brought to the low country from Africa back in the sixteen hundreds to provide the bondaged underpinning for the white man's rice and cotton cultures.

Slavery and the rice and cotton have long since disappeared, replaced by weeds and the bondage of some of the most abject poverty in the United States.

But the descendants of the last of those slaves—the great-grandchildren and great - great - grandchildren who were born in the low country and still live here—retain many of their forebears' primitive customs. Many still speak in idiosyncratic "Gullah" language, inverting phrases so that "he goes" often comes out "go he."

There is probably no place in America today where the black arts are taken more seriously than in the low country. What is a hip week-end laugh in Cultise, Calif., is a way of life in Sheldon and surrounding Beaufort County.

Though the most famous of the local witch doctors are dead—men with names like Dr. Buzzard and Dr. Eagle—lesser known practitioners still cast spells and remove hexes. Among them is lanky, bespectacled J. E. McTeer, a 70-year-old white Beaufort Countian who served 37 years as "the high sheriff of the low country" and then wrote three books about all the fun he had.

He contends that the "best" and "truest" witchcraft in America is practiced in the Beaufort area and adds:

"I get a thousand letters a year asking about voodoo. Everybody in the U. S. suddenly seems interested, what with all those factory-made powders and roots that you can now buy.

"But all that stuff is hokum. The real stuff is when a medical doctor from Charleston tells a fellow like me that my voodoo root cured one of his patients who was complaining about constant stomach ailments that not even exploratory surgery could find.

"Get it?"

Some do. Some don't. It depends.

On the coast west of Beaufort, many blacks still coat their window sills with blue paint to ward off evil spirits.

Within Beaufort, black high school students recently put together a booklet, 30 or so pages thick, of low country superstition. A sample:

"If you sing early in the morning, you'll cry before night."

Over on Hilton Head Island, an alarm clock showed up the other day on a grave newly dug in an old Negro graveyard.

All around were modernistic condominiums housing urbane retirees from up North. But somewhere out in the low country, there was a relative of the deceased who believed those stories about the dead arising from the grave to claim favorite worldly possessions left behind.

So much hokum?

The alarm clock is gone.

In otherwords whatever passes as WHITE SEMITIC or WHITE CAUCASIAN that is equally Jewish, Christian [Protestant, Roman Catholic, etc.], and maybe Moslem [not Muslim], every place in the so-called "WESTERN WORLD," particularly in the United States of America,[1] even when totally ridiculous in every respect, must be sanctioned; the complete opposite applies to all religions related to all other ETHNIC, RACIAL and/or COLOR groupings. But, let us stop for one moment and reflect on all that we have gone through so far in this regard. Now let us ask ourselves the following question:

> IS THE "EXORCIST" ARTICLE NOT COMMON TO THE BLACK-WHITE CONFRONTATION IN TALMUDIC JUDAISM vs TORAHDIC JUDAISM, A LA., LILY WHITE CAUCASIAN-SEMITISM?

The Agaw or Kyla [Falashas if you prefer, even "Negro Jews"], Yemenites, Karaites and all other Hebrew [JEWISH] groups throughout the world have as much right to claim

1. See Y. ben-Jochannan's Cultural Genocide In The Black And African Studies Curriculum, 1973.

"AUTHORITY" with regards to their own KOSHER [Jewish] STATUS as do the European, British, European-American and European-Asian JEWS. Torahdic or Talmudic JUDAISM has absolutely nothing whatsoever to do with RACE, COLOR, PHYSICAL CHARACTERISTICS and the ORIGIN OF MANKIND, irrespective of its rabbinical and prophetical claims relating all the way back to the so-called -

"BEGINNING OF THE WORLD" with "ADAM AND EVE."

For in spite of the Biblical Writers, their claim of "Divine Knowledge" died on page 38.

There can be no doubt that the best interest of the AGAW and/or KYLA, as all of the other so-called AFRICAN-NEGRO-COLORED-BLACK, etc. JEWS, is directly tied to the all inclusive PAN-AFRICAN MOVEMENT with their fellow AFRICANS of any and all other religions or none whatsoever. Not with European, British or European-American [WHITE] Jews and their RACIST VERSION of the "Chosen People's" -

LILY-WHITE TALMUDIC [Rabbinical] JUDAISM.

Maybe it will be said that:

'HE IS A BLACK ["Negro"] JEWISH ANTI-SEMITE LIKE
THOSE OF THE CHRISTIAN AND MOSLEM RELIGIONS.

Do you believe it will surprise me?...You! The late historian and ethnologist Joel A. Rogers gave the correct answer when he noted the following, of which I end in concurrence.

> But, as was said, the Negro Jews in Ethiopia are actually Jews. Moreover, it is only in the white men's lands that the Jews are white, this being the result of intermixture with the whites. In the black man's land they are black. If some Romans believed that the Jews were of Ethiopian ancestry, there must certainly have been black Jews in Rome. Negroes were very well known to the Romans.
>
> Moses himself was black. In all likelihood he was the son of Pharaoh's own daughter, which would account for his adoption and rearing for the throne. The story of his finding in the bullrushes is so identical with that told about Sargon, King of Babylon, who preceded him, that to some it seems doubtful."[3] Moreover, this finding a child in the water is an old African tradition.
>
> When Jehovah wished to give Moses a sign, so runs the famous legend, he told him to put his hand into his bosom. The hand came out white, proving that it could not have been white before. The miracle lay in turning a black skin white, and turning it to black again. Hence the perfect logic of the Mohammedan belief that Moses was a Negro.[2]
>
> As Sir T. W. Arnold says: "According to Mohammedan tradition Moses was a black man as may be seen from the following passage in the Koran, 'Now draw thy hand close to thy side; it shall come forth white but unhurt'—another sign (XX, 23). 'Then he drew forth his hand and lo! it was white to the beholders. The nobles of Pharaoh said, "Verily this is an expert enchanter." VII, 105-06).'"[4]

---

1. From J.A. Roger's SEX AND RACE, Volume I, page 92: [3] Jewish Encyclopedia. (See Moses). [4] The Preaching of Islam, p. 358. London, 1913.
2. The word "Negro" does not exist in Arabic, there are others much worse than this.

BIBLICAL QUOTATIONS LISTED CHRONOLOGICALLY ACCORDING TO APPEARANCE IN THE ENTIRE TEXT OF THIS VOLUME

Book	Quote	Page
Exodus 2:1 - 17	Ten Commandments	xl
Genesis 1:26 - 27	Canaan's Curse	2, 332, 338, 381
Songs Of Solomon 1:5	Black, but comely	38
Songs Of Solomon 1:16	I Am Black	38
Job 30:30	My skin is black	38
Psalms 119:83	Battle in smoke	38
Numbers 12:1 - 15	Aaron and Miriam's sin	38, 336
Deutoronomy 18:15, 18, 19; Malachai 3:1; Isaiah 41:2, 3, 4; and Isaiah 9:6, 7	The coming of the Messiah	151
Hosea 13:13, 14; Ezra 37:11, 12; Job 14:5 - 14, 15; 19:26; Isaiah 35:10; Ezekiel 37	Resurrection of the dead	152
Genesis 5:24; 2 Kings 2:11; Hosea 13:13, 14; Psalm 49:6; 9; 118: 17; Proverbs 7:1, 3, 23; 6:23	Heaven	152
Genesis 1:1, 5; Ezekiel 14:6; Isaiah 28:11, 12; Ezekiel 36:26, 28; 14: 26, 31; Jeremiah 31:31; Joel 2:28 - 39; Malachai 1:2	Creation	153
Ezekiel 36:4	The Lord speaks to the mountain	153
	Solomon's wisdom	277, 355
Genesis 1:1 - 15	Making of man	322
Genesis 11:10 - 28	Birth of Abraham	331
Genesis 11:29 - 32	Abraham called	332
Genesis 12:1 - 9	God calls Abraham	332
Genesis 12:10 - 11	Abraham's famine	333
Exodus 2:11 - 20	Moses identified	334
Exodus 7:7	Moses' age	336
Genesis 9:20 - 23	Noah gets drunk with wine	337
Genesis 10:1 - 19	Generation of Noah	338
Exodus 3:14	Tell them I Am sent you	344
Song Of Solomon 1:1-6	Queen of Sheba black?	354
	Don't boil meat in milk	370
	Let dead bury dead	372
Genesis 2:8 - 16	Geography - Garden of Eden	381
	Chosen people	386
XX, 23	Moses' hand turned white	[See Moslem Holy Qur'an or Kor'an]

BIBLIOGRAPHY USED AND CHRONOLOGICALLY LISTED ACCORDING TO APPEARANCE IN THE ENTIRE TEXT OF THIS VOLUME

ben-Jochannan, Y.	NOSOTROS HEBREOS NEGRO, San Juan, Puerto Rico, 1938 [1]
	PENTATEUCH [Five Books Of Moses, Holy Torah, Old Testament]
ben-Jochannan, Y.	THE BLACK MAN'S RELIGION, 3 Vols., New York, 1974
-------------	AFRICA: MOTHER OF WESTERN CIVILIZATION, New York, 1970
Ginsberg, L.	LEGENDS OF THE JEWS, New York, 1938
Nevinson, Henry	A MODERN SLAVERY, New York, 1906
Rapoport, L.	TALES AND MAXIMS FROM THE MIDRASH, New York, 1907
	De la notion de race en anthropolgie [Revue d'Anthrop, 2nd Ser. Vol. 2, Paris, 1879
Freedman and Simon	MIDRASH BABA. SONG OF SONG, New York, 1939
ben-Jochannan, Y.	BLACK MAN OF THE NILE AND HIS FAMILY, New York, 1972
Springer, B.	NATIONALISM AND CULTURE [in: Die Blutmischung als Grundgesetz des Lebens, Berlin, 1937]
Rogers, J.A.	SEX AND RACE, Vol. I., New York, 1947
------	WORLD'S GREAT MENT OF COLOR, Vol. I and II, New York, 1947
------	100 AMAZING FACTS ABOUT THE NEGRO WITH COMPLETE PROOF, New York, 1967
------	NATURE KNOWS NO COLOR LINE, New York, 1952
------	SUPERMAN TO MAN, New York, 1936
Reade, W.	SAVAGE AFRICA, New York, 1864
Parkyn, M.	LIFE IN ABYSSINIA [in: London Quarterly Review, Vol. I and II, 1854]
Froebenius, Leo	AFRICAN GENESIS. ALSO PREHISTORIC ROCK PICTURES IN EUROPE AND AFRICA, Berlin, 1874
Spearing, H.G.	THE CHILDHOOD OF ART, New York, 1912
Jones, H.L. [transl]	GEOGRAPHY, XVI, 2, 34 [vol. 7]
de Las Casas, Bartolome	HISTORIA de las INDIAS, Madrid, 1675
Waitz, I.	INTRODUCTION TO ANTHROPOLOGY, New York, 1863
	MEMOIRES, Vol. 5, New York, 1865
	DESCRIPTION OF GUINEA, New York, London, 1746
	JAMAICA IN 1850, London, 1851
Smith, Homer W.	MAN AND HIS GODS, Boston, 1953
	AMERICA AND EUROPE, New York, 1857
Delacorte, M.	LOS AFRICANOS MOROS y ARABES, Madrid, 1740
Meek, C. K.	A SUDANESE KINGDOM, New York, 1927
Glough, S.B.	THE RISE AND FALL OF CIVILIZATION, New York
Kautsky, Karl	ARE THE JEWS A RACE, New York, 1918
	KEBRA NEGASTE [The Chronicles Of The Kings], Ethiopia, East Africa
Dorese, Jean	ETHIOPIE, New York, 1961
Solomon, M. Debase	THE BETA ISRA'EL, Sudan, 1874
el-Yezdi, Abu Haji	THE KASIDAD [transl. by Sir Richard F. Burton, London, 1878]

1. The original source of this entire project - both volumes enlarged and illustrated for the general public.

[bibliography used continued]

ben-Jochannan, Y.	CULTURAL GENOCIDE IN THE BLACK AND AFRICAN STUDIES CURRICULUM, New York, 1973
Fishberg, M.	THE JEWS, London, 1911
Ullendorf, Edward	THE ETHIOPIANS: AN INTRODUCTION TO COUNTRY AND PEOPLE, London, 1960
Budge, Sir E.A.W.	EGYPTIAN MAGIC, London, 1900
------ [transl. and ed.]	BOOK OF THE DEAD AND PAPYRUS OF ANI, London, 1895
------ "	COFFIN TEXTS
------ "	PYRAMID TEXTS
------ "	OSIRIAN DRAMA
------ "	NEGATIVE CONFESSIONS
------ "	TEACHINGS OF AMEN-EM-EOPE
R. Graves and R. Patai	HEBREW MYTHS: THE BOOK OF GENESIS, New York, 1964[1/]
Churchward, Albert	SIGNS AND SYMBOLS OF PRIMORDIAL MAN, London, 1920
Kendrick, John	ANCIENT EGYPT, Book II
Sandford, Eva B.	THE MEDITERRANEAN WORLD, New York, 1932
DeBono	ANNO XIII
Scott-Keltie, Sir J.	THE PARTITION OF AFRICA, London, 1920
Padmore, George	AFRICA: BRITAIN'S THIRD EMPIRE, New York, 1947
Moon, Parker T.	IMPERIALISM AND WORLD POLITICS, New York, 1936
Lefebure, T.	VOYAGE EN ABSSINE, Paris
Higgins, Sir G.	ANACALYPSIS, London, 1840 [2 vols]
	HISTORY OF MANKIND, Vol. II
Hertslett, Sir E.	THE MAP OF AFRICA BY TREATY, London, 1895 [3 vols]
Skinner, Elliot	HUMAN HISTORY, London, 1934
	NEGRO-CAUCASIAN MIXING IN ALL AGES AND ALL LANDS, New York, 1967
ben-Jochannan, Y.	A CHRONOLOGY OF THE BIBLE: CHALLENGE TO THE STANDARD VERSION, New York, 1973
Marx and Margolis	HISTORY OF THE JEWISH PEOPLE
Pittard, Eugene	RACE AND HISTORY, London, 1926
Prof Dixon	RACIAL HISTORY OF MAN
James, G.G.M.	STOLEN LEGACY, New York, 1954
Leslau, Wolf	FALASHA ANTHOLOGY: THE BLACK JEWS OF ETHIOPIA, New York, 1951
Katz, Shlomo [ed]	NEGRO AND JEW: AN ENCOUNTER IN AMERICA, New York, 1967
G. Saron and L. Hotz	THE JEWS IN SOUTH AFRICA, London, 1955
Garvey, Amy J.[ed]	PHILOSOPHY AND OPINIONS OF MARCUS GARVEY, London, 1924
Mohammad, Elijah	MESSAGE TO THE BLACKMAN IN AMERICA, Chicago, Ill., 1970
Wheless, J.	IS IT GOD'S WORD?, New York, 1926
-------	FOGERY IN CHRISTIANITY, New York, 1930
Y. ben-Jochannan and G.E. Simmonds,	THE BLACK MAN'S NORTH AND EAST AFRICA, New York, 1972
	JEWISH ENCYCLOPEDIA
	THE PREACHING OF ISLAM, London, 1913
	HOLY QUR'AN [Koran]

[bibliography used continued]

PERIODICALS, MAGAZINES, ETC. CHRONOLOGICALLY LISTED ACCORDING TO APPEARANCE IN THE ENTIRE TEXT OF THIS VOLUME

LONDON JEWISH CHRONICLE, April 1973

JEWISH CURRENT EVENTS, February 16 - 28, 1974, Vol. 15 - Number 10, Elmont, New York.

LOS ANGELES TIMES, "Amin-Israel Feud Recalls Facinating Bit Of History," by Stanley Meisler, 1973

LIGHT AND PEACE, 2nd December, 1929

CALENDAR, NATIONAL JEWISH WOMEN'S LEAGUE OF AMERICA, New York, 1972

NEW YORK TIMES, "Panel Of Jewish Scholars Translating The Bible," by E.B. Fisher, Monday, May 21, 1973

EBONY, "America's Black Jews," by Era Bell Thompson, 1972

N.Y. AMSTERDAM NEWS, "Rabbi Matthew, The Organizar," Sat., Dec. 15, 1973 - C9

NEW YORK TIMES, "Church Groups Hit Corporations," by Eleanor Blau, Saturday 26, 1974, L - 45

THE NEW YORK TIMES, "Falasha Jews From Ethiopia In Israel," by Harvey Gilroy, Friday, March 4, 1955

DETROIT FREE PRESS, "Man Tells How Demons Tormented His Family," Monday, January 21, 1974

THE NEW YORK TIMES, "Voodoo Colony Home For Harlem Dropouts," by B. Drummond Ayres Jr., Monday, December 31, 1973

JEWS, CHRISTIANS, MOSLEMS, INDIGENOUS RELIGIOUS BELIEVERS, ET AL., AT MARKET

ADDED BIBLIOGRAPHY USED IN THE PREPARATION OF THE TEXT BUT NOT CITED

Al-Jahis THE MERIT OF THE TURKS.
-------- THE SUPERIORITY OF SPEECH TO SILENCE.
-------- THE PRAISE OF MERCHANTS AND DISPRAISE OF OFFICIALS
-------- THE SUPERIORITY IN THE GLORY OF THE BLACK RACE OVER THE WHITE, CAIRO, EGYPT, 1906.
-------- THE BOOK OF ELOQUENCE AND RHETORIC.
-------- THE BOOK OF ANIMALS, Vol's. I - VII.
Ashe, G. GHANDI New York, 1968.
Apuleius THE GOLDEN ASS.
Allen, W.F.; Ware, Charles P. and Lucey, M. Garrison (eds.) SLAVE SONGS OF THE UNITED STATES, New York, 1867.
Aptheker, H. AMERICAN SLAVE REVOLTS, New York, 1943.
Arnold, Sir T. W. THE PREACHING OF ISLAM, London, 1913.
Achebe, Chinua. THINGS FALL APART, New York, 1959.

Bisland, A. LIFE AND LETTERS OF LAFCADIO HEARN, Vol. I, Boston, 1923.
Blyden, Dr. E.W. CHRISTIANITY, ISLAM, AND THE NEGRO RACE, (1889)
Breasted, J.H. HISTORY OF EGYPT, New York, 1905.
Balfwil, M. THE LIFE OF MOHAMET (n.d.)

Cicero. DE OFFICIIS.
Churchward, Dr. A. ORIGIN AND EVOLUTION OF FREEMASONRY, London, 1920.
---------- ARCANA OF FREEMASONRY, New York , 1915.
---------- ORIGIN AND EVOLUTION OF THE HUMAN RACE, London, 1921.
Collingwood, R.G. ROMAN BRITAIN, Oxford , 1932.
Clavier, A. BIOGRAPHIE UNIVERSELLE, Vol. VIII, PARIS, 1844.
Cronon, E.D. BLACK MOSES, Madison, Milwakee, London, 1968.
Coppin, L. J. UNWRITTEN HISTORY, Philadelphia, 1920.

Darwin, Sir Charles. THE NEXT MILLION YEARS, London, 1952.
Denon, Baron. TRAVELS IN UPPER AND LOWER EGYPT, London, 1789.
Dumond, D. W. ANTISLAVERY, The University, Ann Arbor, Michigan, 1961.
deGraft-Johnson, J.C. AFRICAN GLORY, London, 1954.
Diodorus SICULUS, Book XVII (n.d.).
Digby, Sir Keneln. POWER OF SYMPATHY, London, 1660.
Davidson, THE AFRICAN SLAVE TRADE, New York, 1968.
-------- THE AFRICAN PAST, New York, 1964.
-------- AFRICAN KINGDOM, New York, 1968.

Franklin, J.H. FROM SLAVERY TO FREEDOM, New York, 1964.

Frobenius, Leo AFRICA SPEAKS, 3 Vols., London, 1913 (latest edition, 1969).
Frazier, E.F. THE NEGRO CHURCH IN AMERICA, New York, 1964.

Groves, C.P. THE PLANTING OF CHRISTIANITY IN AFRICA, London, 1948.

Garrucci, R. LA MONETE DEL' HALIA ANTICA, Parte Secunda, LXXV, Roma, 1885.
Gibbs, H.A.R. ARAB LITERATURE, London, 1926.
Garvey, Amy Jacques (ed.), PHILOSOPHY AND OPINIONS OF MARCUS GARVEY, London, 1967.
Gaunt, Mary WHERE THE TWAIN SHALL MEET, London, 1922.

[added bibliography continued]

Hitti, P.K. MAKERS OF ARAB HISTORY, New York, 1940.
Hitti, P.K. HISTORY OF THE ARABS, London, 1927.
Herodotus HISTORIES, Book II (as translated by Aubrey Selencourt), New York. 1954.
Harmack MISSION AND EXPANDSION, Vols. I-IV.
Helibdorus ETHIOPIAN HISTORY UNDERDOWNE, 1857 (London, 1895)
Hertzberg, A. (ed.) JUDAISM, New York, 1962.
Hodgkin, E.C. THE ARABS.
Hugnes SATIRE OF THE SOCIAL PROBLEM OF THE NEGRO IN AMERICA. (n.d.).

Jann, Janheinz MUNTU, New York (translated by Marjorie Greene, New York, 1961).
Johnson, J.W. and Johnson, R. BOOKS OF AMERICAN NEGRO SPIRITUALS. New York, 1940.
Johnson, A.R. THE CULTIC PROPHET IN ANCIENT ISRAEL.

Kenyatta, Jomo FACING MT. KENYA, New York, 1968.

Lincoln, C.E. BLACK MUSLIMS, Boston, 1961.
Liebevitch, L. ANCIENT EGYPT, Cairo, Egypt, 1958.
Leslau, Wolf FALASHA ANTHOLOGY, New Haven, 1951.
Langer, W. L. (ed.) ENCYCLOPEDIA OF WORLD HISTORY, New York, 1952.
Lull, Raymond LULL REPORTS (Haklyut Society, London).
Labourete, H. AFRICA BEFORE THE WHITE MAN, Boston, 1963.
Liciado LIFE OF BARTOLOME DE LAS CASAS, Madrid, 1565.
Lewis and Schacht (eds.) ENCYCLOPEDIA OF ISLAM.

Mendelsohn, Jack GOD, ALLAH AND JU JU, New York, 1962.
Muir, Sir William LIFE OF MOHAMET, London, 1894.
Massey, G.A. BOOK OF THE BEGINNINGS, Vol. II, London.
Meek, T.J. HEBREW ORIGINS, New York, 1960.
Moon, Parker T. IMPERIALISM AND WORLD POLITICS, New York, 1934

Nesfield, J.C. BRIEF VIEW OF THE CAST SYSTEM, India, 1885.
Northcott, W.C. CHRISTIANITY IN AFRICA, Philadelphia, 1963.
Nkeitia, J.H. ART, RITUAL AND MYTHS IN AMERICAN NEGRO STUDIES, Acra, Ghana, 1966.
Nottingham, E.K. METHODISM AND THE FRONTIER, New York, 1941.

Oehler, F. QUINTA SEPTIMU FLORENTIS TERTULLIAN QUAE SUPERSUNT OMNIA, I, Leipzig, 1853.
Oates, W.J. BASIC WRITINGS OF ST. AUGUSTINE, New York, 1948, 2 Vols.
Ovington, M.W. THE WALLS CAME TUMBLING DOWN, New York, 1947.

Robertson, A. ORIGINS OF CHRISTIANITY, New York, 1962.
Ratzel, F. HISTORY OF MANKIND, Vols. I-II, London, 1869.

Smith R. RELIGION OF THE SEMITES.

Soames, Jane COAST OF BARBARY, London.
St. Augustine ON THE BEAUTIFUL AND THE FIT (c370-3?? C.E.).
------------- CONFESSIONS.
------------- ON CHRISTIAN DOCTRINES.

[added bibliography continued]

Stanley, H.M. DARKEST AFRICA, New York, 1890.

Snow, C.P. (Comments in JOHN O'LONDON'S WEEKLY, London, 1952)

Smith, Prof. Elliot HUMAN HISTORY, London, 1934.

Suyuti, S. HISTORY OF THE CALYPHS (translated by H.S. Jarrett, Calcutta, 1881).

Sabine, G.H. A HISTORY OF POLITICAL THEORY, New York, 1961.

Schofield, J.N. HISTORICAL BACKGROUND OF THE BIBLE, London, New York, 1938.

Sabe, A. AL KORAN (1784).

Slade, R. BELGIAN CONGO, Oxford, 1962.

Sonnerson, S. RAPE OF AFRICA.

Syed, Ameer Ali LIFE AND TEACHINGS OF MOHAMMED, London, 1891.

Tanner, B.J. AN APOLOGY FOR AFRICAN METHODISM, Baltimore, 1867.

Temples, Placide BANTU PHILOSOPHY.

Tertullian DE ANIMA.

---------- THE TREATISE AGAINST HERMOGENES.

Volney, Count C.C. RUINS OF EMPIRES, London, 1890.

Wallis-Budge, Sir E.A. BOOK OF THE DEAD, New York, 1960.

------------ OSIRIS, New York, 1954.

Wells, H.G. A SHORT HISTORY OF THE WORLD, New York, 1956.

Wildernissen, D. STANLEY IN AFRICA, Vols. I-II, Germany, 1887.

Weidner, Dr. D. A HISTORY OF AFRICA SOUTH OF THE SAHARA (etc.), New York, 1968.

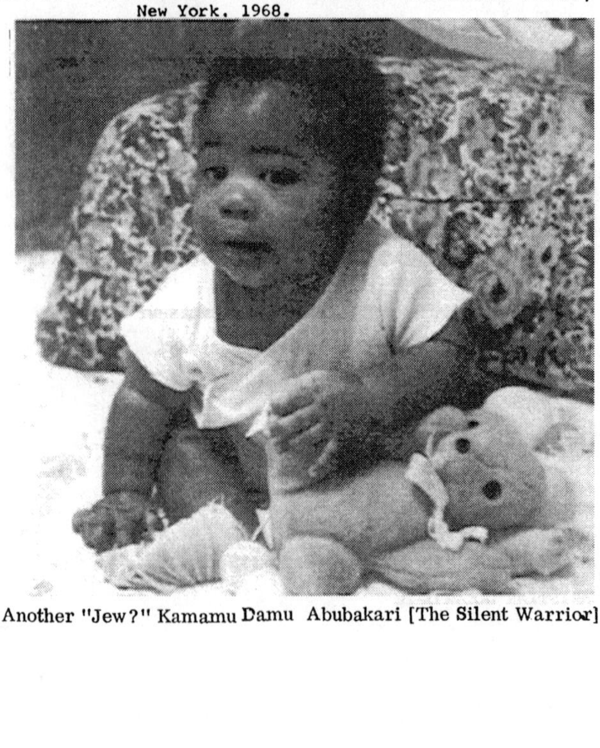

Another "Jew?" Kamamu Damu Abubakari [The Silent Warrior]

MWENEA

He Who Spreads the Word

COALITION NEWSLETTER OF QUEENSBOROUGH COMMUNITY COLLEGE'S THIRD WORLD STUDENTS

March 27, 1974

Dr. ben at QCC

Dr. Yosef ben-Jochannan

Ndugu Gerald Gladney

Dr. Yosef ben-Jochannan is an Afrikan Historian and lecturer. As a lecturer, he is quite unorthodox, in that he makes no claim of being objective and unemotional about what he knows and its relationship to his people.

It is important to understand this in dealing with Dr. ben, for much of the facts he presents are mixed with opinions. So that things that are matters of opinion can be accepted or rejected as you will, but that which is fact is indisputable.

If the author of this work had to give a self-analysis of the information he has presented he probably could not have done as good a job as the student journalist - "Ndugu Gerald Gladney" - did above. Mr Gladney "...PEEPED MY HOLD CARD..." said Doc Ben; "...I must surely use his remarks somewhere in my own work; the brother is entitled to be read by the general Black Community...." Alkebu-lan Books Associates can only add that '...BROTHER DOC BEN DID IT AGAIN....'

A former practicing African/Black/Ethiopian "Jew," ben-Jochannan now considers himself somewhat of an "egnostic." He believes that "all religions are as good and bad as each others."

Certainly it will be said that the author - YOSEF A. A. ben-JOCHANNAN - had to do this book in order to clarify his position to all African people in the struggle for the redemption of African land - all of it. How is this possible if one segment of European can remain safe from any form of criticism in their role as equal slavemasters and slavemistresses of the same African people on their indigenous African continent?

I have taken all precautions to be as fair as was possible. I have left no stone unturned in my search for the truth as seen by an involved African in his own history and heritage; being, however, equally conscious that I have a vested interest in what I am writing about. Thus I make no excuse in saying I have written this work from the point of an African, from an African perspective, and for an African cause.

Again, I repeat.

"AFRICA IS FOR THE AFRICANS, THOSE AT HOME AND THOSE ABROAD"
[From Dr. Edward Wilmot Blyden: "Africa Is For The Africans." From Hon. Marcus Moziah Garvey: "Those At Home And Those Abroad." Blyden in ca. 1881 or 1883 C.E./A.D.; Garvey in ca. 1916 or 1918 C.E./A.D.]